

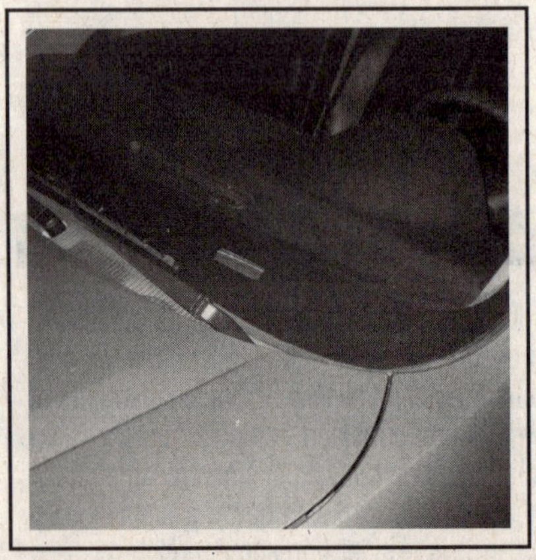

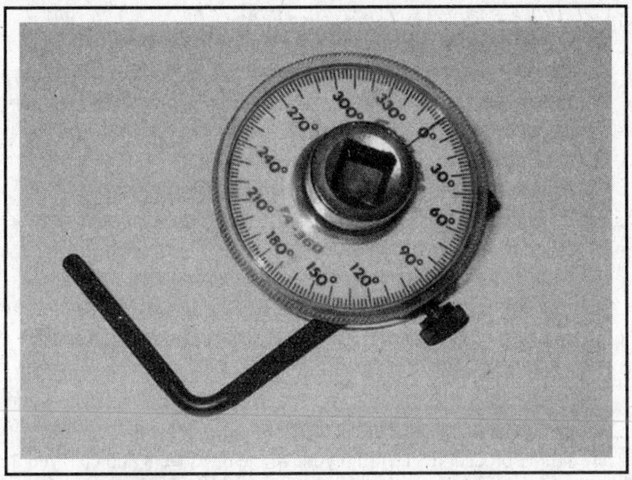

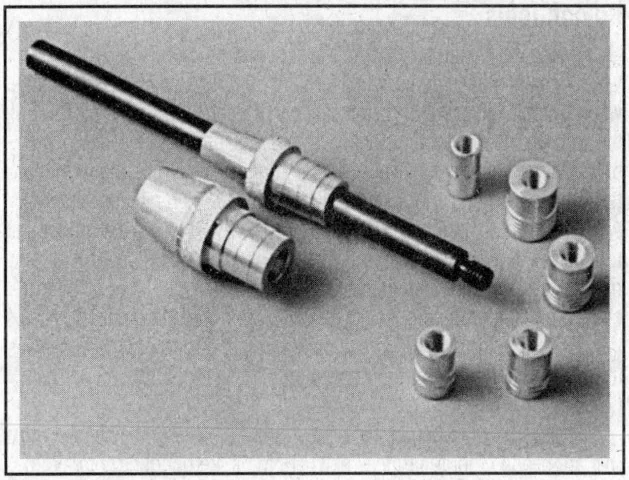

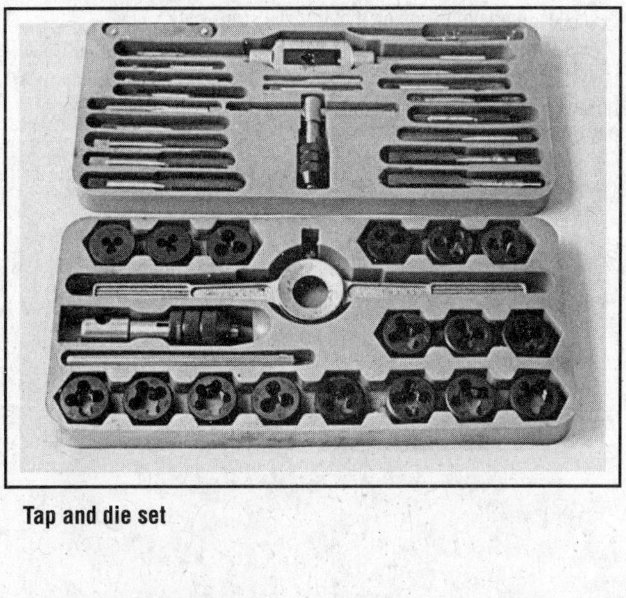

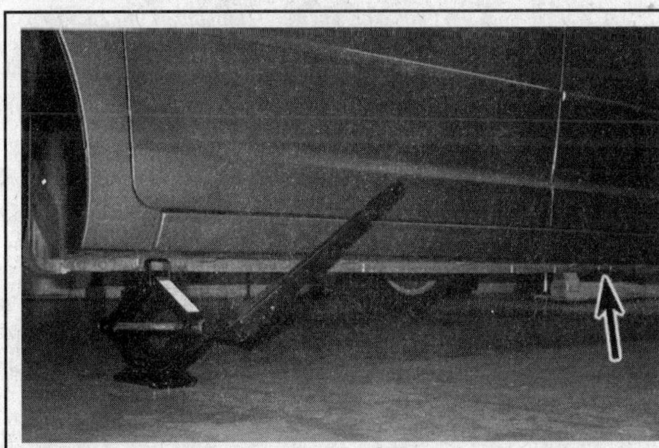

1 TUNE-UP AND ROUTINE MAINTENANCE

Section

FORD

FUSION & MILAN
2006-10 REPAIR MANUAL

CHILTON'S

Covers U.S. and Canadian models of Ford Fusion and Mercury Milan 2006 through 2010

Does not include information specific to hybrid models

by Mike Stubblefield and Jay Storer

CHILTON Automotive Books
PUBLISHED BY **HAYNES NORTH AMERICA, Inc.**

Haynes®

APA AUTOMOTIVE PARTS & ACCESSORIES ASSOCIATION MEMBER

Manufactured in USA

ISBN-13: 978-1-56392-902-1
ISBN-10: 1-56392-902-3
Library of Congress Control Number 2010941800

Haynes Publishing Group
Sparkford Nr Yeovil
Somerset BA22 7JJ England

Haynes North America, Inc
861 Lawrence Drive
Newbury Park
California 91320 USA

ABCDE
FGHIJ
KLMNO
PQRS

Contents

Mechanic and photographer with a 2007 Ford Fusion

ACKNOWLEDGEMENTS

Wiring diagrams provided by Valley Forge Technical Information Services.

About this manual

ITS PURPOSE

The purpose of this manual is to help you get the best value from your vehicle. It can do so in several ways. It can help you decide what work must be done, even if you choose to have it done by a dealer service department or a repair shop; it provides information and procedures for routine maintenance and servicing; and it offers diagnostic and repair procedures to follow when trouble occurs.

We hope you use the manual to tackle the work yourself. For many simpler jobs, doing it yourself may be quicker than arranging an appointment to get the vehicle into a shop and making the trips to leave it and pick it up. More importantly, a lot of money can be saved by avoiding the expense the shop must pass on to you to cover its labor and overhead costs. An added benefit is the sense of satisfaction and accomplishment that you feel after doing the job yourself.

USING THE MANUAL

The manual is divided into Chapters. Each Chapter is divided into numbered Sections. Each Section consists of consecutively numbered paragraphs.

At the beginning of each numbered Section you will be referred to any illustrations which apply to the procedures in that Section. The reference numbers used in illustration captions pinpoint the pertinent Section and the Step within that Section. That is, illustration 3.2 means the illustration refers to Section 3 and Step (or paragraph) 2 within that Section.

Procedures, once described in the text, are not normally repeated. When it's necessary to refer to another Chapter, the reference will be given as Chapter and Section number. Cross references given without use of the word "Chapter" apply to Sections and/or paragraphs in the same Chapter. For example, "see Section 8" means in the same Chapter.

References to the left or right side of the vehicle assume you are sitting in the driver's seat, facing forward.

Even though we have prepared this manual with extreme care, neither the publisher nor the author can accept responsibility for any errors in, or omissions from, the information given.

➡NOTE

A *Note* provides information necessary to properly complete a procedure or information which will make the procedure easier to understand.

⁂ CAUTION

A *Caution* provides a special procedure or special steps which must be taken while completing the procedure where the Caution is found. Not heeding a Caution can result in damage to the assembly being worked on.

⁂ WARNING

A *Warning* provides a special procedure or special steps which must be taken while completing the procedure where the Warning is found. Not heeding a Warning can result in personal injury.

Introduction

This manual covers the Ford Fusion and Mercury Milan. The available engines are: The Duratec 23 (2.3L) in-line four-cylinder engine, Duratec 25 (2.5L) in-line four-cylinder engine and the Duratec 30 (3.0L) V6 engine. On 2010 models, a 3.5L V6 engine was also an option.

The engine drives the front wheels through either a five- or six-speed manual or a six-speed automatic transaxle via independent driveaxles. On All-Wheel Drive (AWD) models, the rear wheels are also propelled via a driveshaft, rear differential, and two rear driveaxles.

Suspension is independent at all four wheels; coil spring/shock absorber assemblies being used at the front with parallel upper and lower control arms, and coil springs and telescopic shock absorbers at the rear with upper and lower control arms and trailing arms. The rack-and-pinion steering unit is mounted on the suspension crossmember.

The brakes are disc at the front and rear, with power assist standard. An Anti-lock Brake System (ABS) is standard on some models.

Vehicle identification numbers

Modifications are a continuing and unpublicized process in vehicle manufacturing. Since spare parts manuals and lists are compiled on a numerical basis, the individual vehicle numbers are essential to correctly identify the component required.

VEHICLE IDENTIFICATION NUMBER (VIN)

This very important identification number is stamped on a plate attached to the dashboard inside the windshield on the driver's side of the vehicle (see illustration). The VIN also appears on the Vehicle Certificate of Title and Registration. It contains information such as where and when the vehicle was manufactured, the model year and the body style.

MANUFACTURER'S CERTIFICATION REGULATION LABEL

The Manufacturer's Certification Regulation label is attached to the driver's side door opening (see illustration). The label contains the name of the manufacturer, the month and year of production, the Gross Vehicle Weight Rating (GVWR), the Gross Axle Weight Rating (GAWR) and the certification statement.

VIN ENGINE CODE

Counting from the left, the engine code letter designation is the 8th character. On all models covered by this manual the engine codes are:

Z .... 2.3L four-cylinder engine
A........................ 2.5L four-cylinder engine
1 .... 3.0L V6 engine (2009 and earlier models)
G........................ 3.0L V6 engine (2010 models)
C........................ 3.5L V6 engine

VIN MODEL YEAR CODE

Counting from the left, the model year code letter designation is the 10th character. On all models covered by this manual the model year codes are:

6 2006
7 2007
8 2008
9 2009
A............................ 2010

ENGINE NUMBER

On four-cylinder models, the engine identification number is stamped into a machined pad on the front side of the engine under the exhaust manifold.

On V6 models, the engine identification number is stamped into a machined pad on the right front end (driver's side) of the engine block (see illustration).

TRANSAXLE IDENTIFICATION

The transaxle identification code is listed at the bottom of the Manufacturer's Certification Regulation label, under the heading "TR." The codes are as follows:

5........................ Mazda G5M, 5-speed manual transaxle
6........................ Mazda 6GM, 6-speed manual transaxle
C........................ Mazda FNR5, 5-speed automatic transaxle
B........................ Aisin AW21, 6-speed automatic transaxle
W....................... 6F35, 6-speed automatic transaxle

The Vehicle Identification Number (VIN) is visible through the driver's side of the windshield

The Manufacturer's Certification Regulation label is located on the driver's door opening

Location of the engine identification number - V6 engine

Recall information

Vehicle recalls are carried out by the manufacturer in the rare event of a possible safety-related defect. The vehicle's registered owner is contacted at the address on file at the Department of Motor Vehicles and given the details of the recall. Remedial work is carried out free of charge at a dealer service department.

If you are the new owner of a used vehicle which was subject to a recall and you want to be sure that the work has been carried out, it's best to contact a dealer service department and ask about your individual vehicle - you'll need to furnish them your Vehicle Identification Number (VIN).

The table below is based on information provided by the National Highway Traffic Safety Administration (NHTSA), the body which oversees vehicle recalls in the United States. The recall database is updated constantly. For the latest information on vehicle recalls, check the NHTSA website at www.nhtsa.gov, www.safercar.gov or call the NHTSA hotline at 1-888-327-4236.

Recall date	Recall campaign number	Model(s) affected	Concern
APR 16, 2010	10V161000	2010 Fusion	Some models manufactured between December 15, 2009 and February 3, 2010 equipped with front seat manual recliners fail to comply with the requirements of Federal Motor Vehicle Safety Standard no. 202, "head restraint." the recliner gear plate teeth may be out of dimension specification which could result in limited pawl-to-gear plate tooth engagement. In the event of a crash, the seatback and head restraint may move rearward, increasing the risk of injury.
MAY 21, 2010	10V222000	2010 Fusion	On some models manufactured from February 27, through March 26, 2010, the park rod guide retention pin may not have been properly installed, which fails to conform to the requirement of Federal Motor Vehicle Safety Standard no. 114, "theft protection and rollaway prevention." A vehicle parked without an engaged park pawl and without an applied parking brake may have unintended movement which may cause a crash.

Buying parts

Replacement parts are available from many sources, which generally fall into one of two categories - authorized dealer parts departments and independent retail auto parts stores. Our advice concerning these parts is as follows:

Retail auto parts stores: Good auto parts stores will stock frequently needed components which wear out relatively fast, such as clutch components, exhaust systems, brake parts, tune-up parts, etc. These stores often supply new or reconditioned parts on an exchange basis, which can save a considerable amount of money. Discount auto parts stores are often very good places to buy materials and parts needed for general vehicle maintenance such as oil, grease, filters, spark plugs, belts, touch-up paint, bulbs, etc. They also usually sell tools and general accessories, have convenient hours, charge lower prices and can often be found not far from home.

Authorized dealer parts department: This is the best source for parts which are unique to the vehicle and not generally available elsewhere (such as major engine parts, transmission parts, trim pieces, etc.).

Warranty information: If the vehicle is still covered under warranty, be sure that any replacement parts purchased - regardless of the source - do not invalidate the warranty!

To be sure of obtaining the correct parts, have engine and chassis numbers available and, if possible, take the old parts along for positive identification.

Maintenance techniques, tools and working facilities

MAINTENANCE TECHNIQUES

There are a number of techniques involved in maintenance and repair that will be referred to throughout this manual. Application of these techniques will enable the home mechanic to be more efficient, better organized and capable of performing the various tasks properly, which will ensure that the repair job is thorough and complete.

Fasteners

Fasteners are nuts, bolts, studs and screws used to hold two or more parts together. There are a few things to keep in mind when working with fasteners. Almost all of them use a locking device of some type, either a lockwasher, locknut, locking tab or thread adhesive. All threaded fasteners should be clean and straight, with undamaged threads and undamaged corners on the hex head where the wrench fits. Develop the habit of replacing all damaged nuts and bolts with new ones. Special locknuts with nylon or fiber inserts can only be used once. If they are removed, they lose their locking ability and must be replaced with new ones.

Rusted nuts and bolts should be treated with a penetrating fluid to ease removal and prevent breakage. Some mechanics use turpentine in a spout-type oil can, which works quite well. After applying the rust penetrant, let it work for a few minutes before trying to loosen the nut or bolt. Badly rusted fasteners may have to be chiseled or sawed off or removed with a special nut breaker, available at tool stores.

If a bolt or stud breaks off in an assembly, it can be drilled and removed with a special tool commonly available for this purpose. Most automotive machine shops can perform this task, as well as other repair procedures, such as the repair of threaded holes that have been stripped out.

Flat washers and lockwashers, when removed from an assembly, should always be replaced exactly as removed. Replace any damaged washers with new ones. Never use a lockwasher on any soft metal surface (such as aluminum), thin sheet metal or plastic.

Fastener sizes

For a number of reasons, automobile manufacturers are making wider and wider use of metric fasteners. Therefore, it is important to be able to tell the difference between standard (sometimes called U.S. or SAE) and metric hardware, since they cannot be interchanged.

All bolts, whether standard or metric, are sized according to diameter, thread pitch and length. For example, a standard 1/2 - 13 x 1 bolt is 1/2 inch in diameter, has 13 threads per inch and is 1 inch long. An M12 - 1.75 x 25 metric bolt is 12 mm in diameter, has a thread pitch of 1.75 mm (the distance between threads) and is 25 mm long. The two bolts are nearly identical, and easily confused, but they are not interchangeable.

In addition to the differences in diameter, thread pitch and length, metric and standard bolts can also be distinguished by examining the bolt heads. To begin with, the distance across the flats on a standard bolt head is measured in inches, while the same dimension on a metric bolt is sized in millimeters (the same is true for nuts). As a result, a standard wrench should not be used on a metric bolt and a metric wrench should not be used on a standard bolt. Also, most standard bolts have slashes radiating out from the center of the head to denote the grade or strength of the bolt, which is an indication of the amount of torque that can be applied to it. The greater the number of slashes, the greater the strength of the bolt. Grades 0 through 5 are commonly used on automobiles. Metric bolts have a property class (grade) number, rather than a slash, molded into their heads to indicate bolt strength. In this case, the higher the number, the stronger the bolt. Property class numbers 8.8, 9.8 and 10.9 are commonly used on automobiles.

Strength markings can also be used to distinguish standard hex nuts from metric hex nuts. Many standard nuts have dots stamped into one side, while metric nuts are marked with a number. The greater the number of dots, or the higher the number, the greater the strength of the nut.

Metric studs are also marked on their ends according to property class (grade). Larger studs are numbered (the same as metric bolts), while smaller studs carry a geometric code to denote grade.

It should be noted that many fasteners, especially Grades 0 through 2, have no distinguishing marks on them. When such is the case, the only way to determine whether it is standard or metric is to measure the thread pitch or compare it to a known fastener of the same size.

Standard fasteners are often referred to as SAE, as opposed to metric. However, it should be noted that SAE technically refers to a non-metric fine thread fastener only. Coarse thread non-metric fasteners are referred to as USS sizes.

Since fasteners of the same size (both standard and metric) may have different strength ratings, be sure to reinstall any bolts, studs or nuts removed from your vehicle in their original locations. Also, when replacing a fastener with a new one, make sure that the new one has a strength rating equal to or greater than the original.

Tightening sequences and procedures

Most threaded fasteners should be tightened to a specific torque value (torque is the twisting force applied to a threaded component such as a nut or bolt). Overtightening the fastener can weaken it and cause it to break, while undertightening can cause it to eventually come loose. Bolts, screws and studs, depending on the material they are made of and their thread diameters, have specific torque values, many of which are noted in the Specifications at the end of each Chapter. Be sure to follow the torque recommendations closely. For fasteners not assigned a specific torque, a general torque value chart is presented here as a guide. These torque values are for dry (unlubricated) fasteners threaded into steel or cast iron (not aluminum). As was previously mentioned, the size and grade of a fastener determine the amount of torque that can safely be applied to it. The figures listed here are approximate for Grade 2 and Grade 3 fasteners. Higher grades can tolerate higher torque values.

Fasteners laid out in a pattern, such as cylinder head bolts, oil pan bolts, differential cover bolts, etc., must be loosened or tightened in sequence to avoid warping the component. This sequence will normally be shown in the appropriate Chapter. If a specific pattern is not given, the following procedures can be used to prevent warping.

Initially, the bolts or nuts should be assembled finger-tight only. Next, they should be tightened one full turn each, in a criss-cross or diagonal pattern. After each one has been tightened one full turn, return to the first one and tighten them all one-half turn, following the same

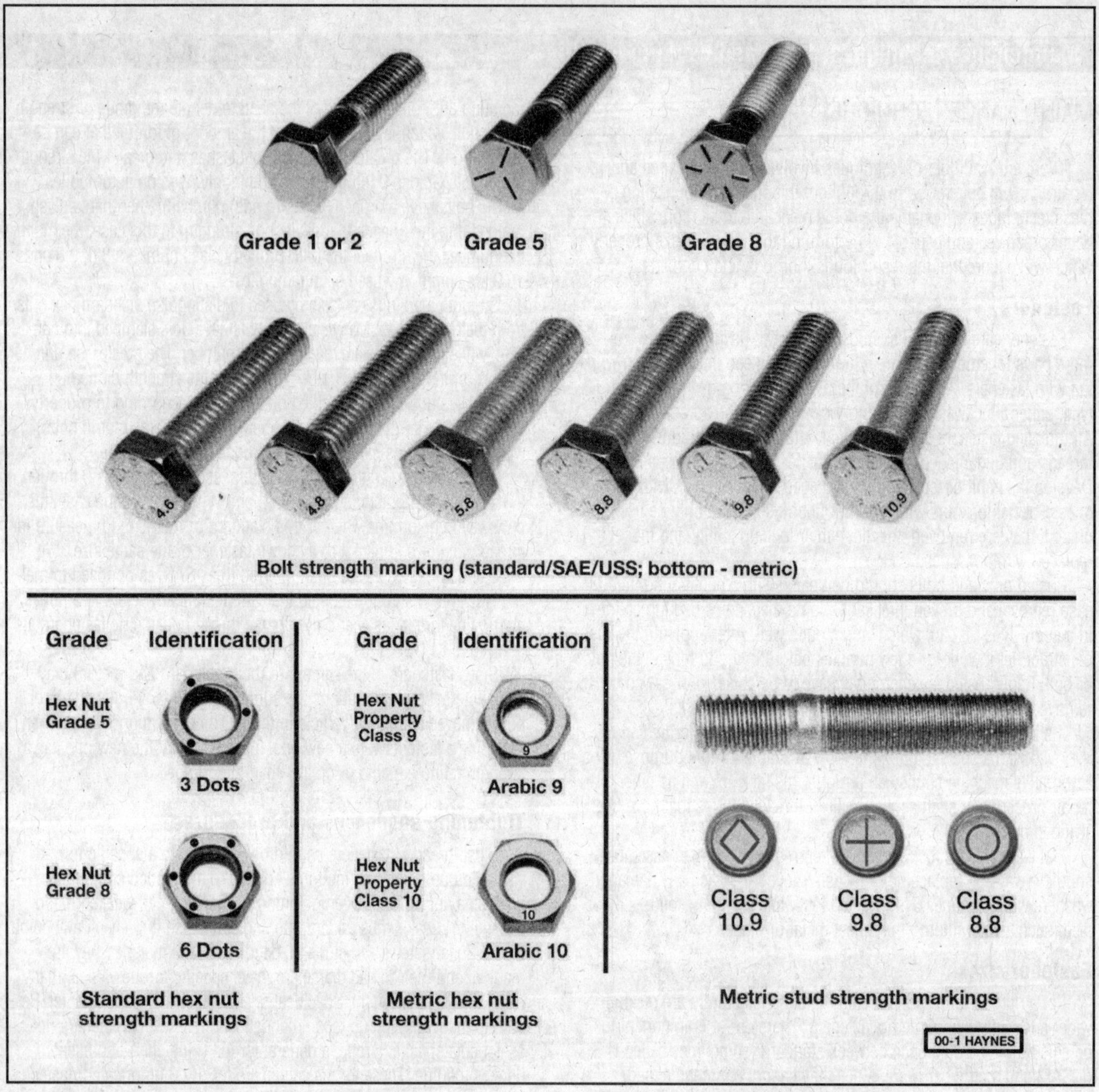

pattern. Finally, tighten each of them one-quarter turn at a time until each fastener has been tightened to the proper torque. To loosen and remove the fasteners, the procedure would be reversed.

Component disassembly

Component disassembly should be done with care and purpose to help ensure that the parts go back together properly. Always keep track of the sequence in which parts are removed. Make note of special characteristics or marks on parts that can be installed more than one way, such as a grooved thrust washer on a shaft. It is a good idea to lay the disassembled parts out on a clean surface in the order that they were removed. It may also be helpful to make sketches or take instant photos of components before removal.

When removing fasteners from a component, keep track of their locations. Sometimes threading a bolt back in a part, or putting the washers and nut back on a stud, can prevent mix-ups later. If nuts and bolts cannot be returned to their original locations, they should be kept in a compartmented box or a series of small boxes. A cupcake or muffin tin is ideal for this purpose, since each cavity can hold the bolts and nuts from a particular area (i.e. oil pan bolts, valve cover bolts, engine

Metric thread sizes	**Ft-lbs**	**Nm**
M-6	6 to 9	9 to 12
M-8	14 to 21	19 to 28
M-10	28 to 40	38 to 54
M-12	50 to 71	68 to 96
M-14	80 to 140	109 to 154
Pipe thread sizes		
1/8	5 to 8	7 to 10
1/4	12 to 18	17 to 24
3/8	22 to 33	30 to 44
1/2	25 to 35	34 to 47
U.S. thread sizes		
1/4 - 20	6 to 9	9 to 12
5/16 - 18	12 to 18	17 to 24
5/16 - 24	14 to 20	19 to 27
3/8 - 16	22 to 32	30 to 43
3/8 - 24	27 to 38	37 to 51
7/16 - 14	40 to 55	55 to 74
7/16 - 20	40 to 60	55 to 81
1/2 - 13	55 to 80	75 to 108

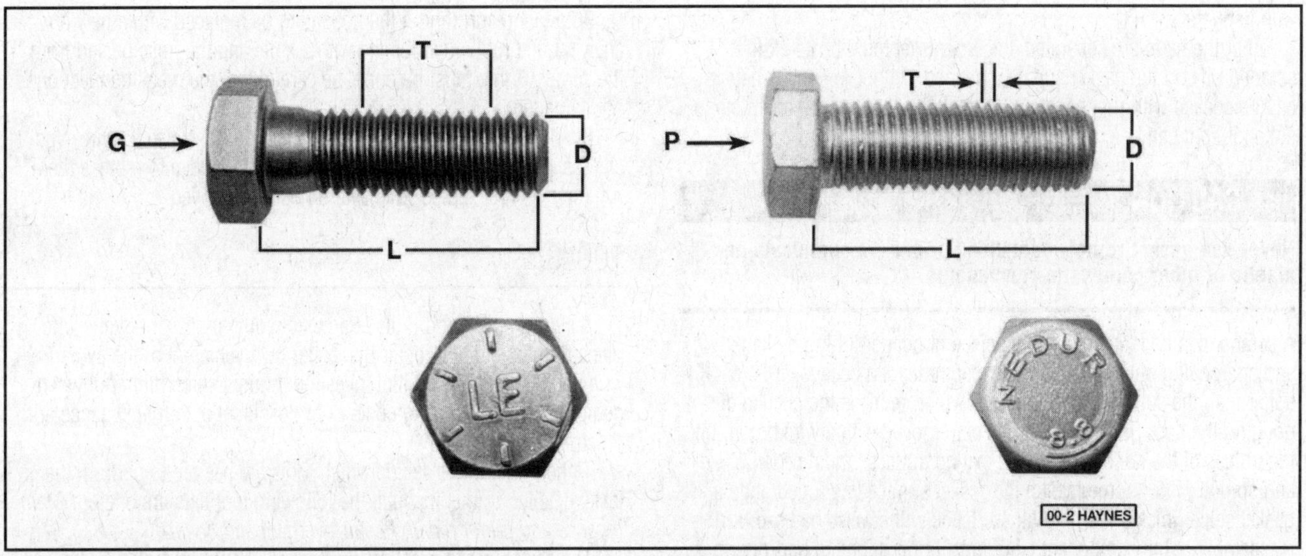

Standard (SAE and USS) bolt dimensions/grade marks

- G *Grade marks (bolt strength)*
- L *Length (in inches)*
- T *Thread pitch (number of threads per inch)*
- D *Nominal diameter (in inches)*

Metric bolt dimensions/grade marks

- P *Property class (bolt strength)*
- L *Length (in millimeters)*
- T *Thread pitch (distance between threads in millimeters)*
- D *Diameter*

mount bolts, etc.). A pan of this type is especially helpful when working on assemblies with very small parts, such as the carburetor, alternator, valve train or interior dash and trim pieces. The cavities can be marked with paint or tape to identify the contents.

Whenever wiring looms, harnesses or connectors are separated, it is a good idea to identify the two halves with numbered pieces of masking tape so they can be easily reconnected.

Gasket sealing surfaces

Throughout any vehicle, gaskets are used to seal the mating surfaces between two parts and keep lubricants, fluids, vacuum or pressure contained in an assembly.

Many times these gaskets are coated with a liquid or paste-type gasket sealing compound before assembly. Age, heat and pressure can sometimes cause the two parts to stick together so tightly that they are very difficult to separate. Often, the assembly can be loosened by striking it with a soft-face hammer near the mating surfaces. A regular hammer can be used if a block of wood is placed between the hammer and the part. Do not hammer on cast parts or parts that could be easily damaged. With any particularly stubborn part, always recheck to make sure that every fastener has been removed.

Avoid using a screwdriver or bar to pry apart an assembly, as they

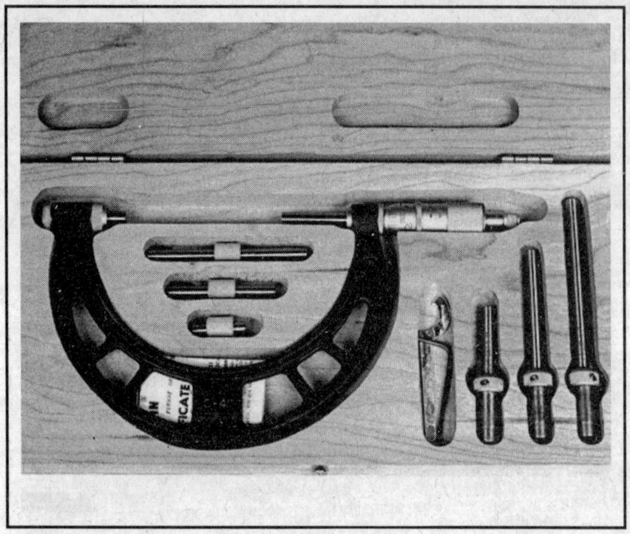

Micrometer set

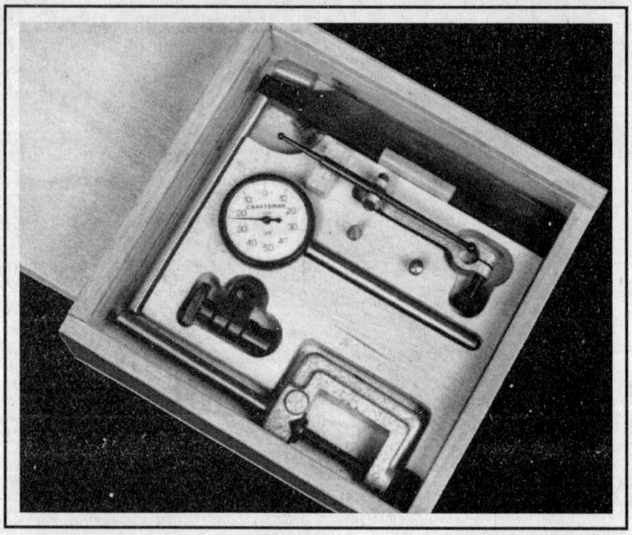

Dial indicator set

can easily mar the gasket sealing surfaces of the parts, which must remain smooth. If prying is absolutely necessary, use an old broom handle, but keep in mind that extra clean up will be necessary if the wood splinters.

After the parts are separated, the old gasket must be carefully scraped off and the gasket surfaces cleaned. Stubborn gasket material can be soaked with rust penetrant or treated with a special chemical to soften it so it can be easily scraped off.

CAUTION:

Never use gasket removal solutions or caustic chemicals on plastic or other composite components.

A scraper can be fashioned from a piece of copper tubing by flattening and sharpening one end. Copper is recommended because it is usually softer than the surfaces to be scraped, which reduces the chance of gouging the part. Some gaskets can be removed with a wire brush, but regardless of the method used, the mating surfaces must be left clean and smooth. If for some reason the gasket surface is gouged, then a gasket sealer thick enough to fill scratches will have to be used during reassembly of the components. For most applications, a non-drying (or semi-drying) gasket sealer should be used.

Hose removal tips

WARNING:

If the vehicle is equipped with air conditioning, do not disconnect any of the A/C hoses without first having the system depressurized by a dealer service department or a service station.

Hose removal precautions closely parallel gasket removal precautions. Avoid scratching or gouging the surface that the hose mates against or the connection may leak. This is especially true for radiator hoses. Because of various chemical reactions, the rubber in hoses can bond itself to the metal spigot that the hose fits over. To remove a hose, first loosen the hose clamps that secure it to the spigot. Then, with slip-joint pliers, grab the hose at the clamp and rotate it around the spigot. Work it back and forth until it is completely free, then pull it off. Silicone or other lubricants will ease removal if they can be applied between the hose and the outside of the spigot. Apply the same lubricant to the inside of the hose and the outside of the spigot to simplify installation.

As a last resort (and if the hose is to be replaced with a new one anyway), the rubber can be slit with a knife and the hose peeled from the spigot. If this must be done, be careful that the metal connection is not damaged.

If a hose clamp is broken or damaged, do not reuse it. Wire-type clamps usually weaken with age, so it is a good idea to replace them with screw-type clamps whenever a hose is removed.

TOOLS

A selection of good tools is a basic requirement for anyone who plans to maintain and repair his or her own vehicle. For the owner who has few tools, the initial investment might seem high, but when compared to the spiraling costs of professional auto maintenance and repair, it is a wise one.

To help the owner decide which tools are needed to perform the tasks detailed in this manual, the following tool lists are offered: *Maintenance and minor repair, Repair/overhaul and Special.*

The newcomer to practical mechanics should start off with the *maintenance and minor repair* tool kit, which is adequate for the simpler jobs performed on a vehicle. Then, as confidence and experience grow, the owner can tackle more difficult tasks, buying additional tools as they are needed. Eventually the basic kit will be expanded into the *repair and overhaul* tool set. Over a period of time, the experienced do-it-yourselfer will assemble a tool set complete enough for most repair and overhaul procedures and will add tools from the special category when it is felt that the expense is justified by the frequency of use.

Maintenance and minor repair tool kit

The tools in this list should be considered the minimum required for performance of routine maintenance, servicing and minor repair work. We recommend the purchase of combination wrenches (box-end and open-end combined in one wrench). While more expensive than open end wrenches, they offer the advantages of both types of wrench.

Combination wrench set (1/4-inch to 1 inch or 6 mm to 19 mm)
Adjustable wrench, 8 inch
Spark plug wrench with rubber insert

Spark plug gap adjusting tool
Feeler gauge set
Brake bleeder wrench
Standard screwdriver (5/16-inch x 6 inch)
Phillips screwdriver (No. 2 x 6 inch)
Combination pliers - 6 inch
Hacksaw and assortment of blades
Tire pressure gauge
Grease gun
Oil can
Fine emery cloth
Wire brush
Battery post and cable cleaning tool
Oil filter wrench
Funnel (medium size)
Safety goggles
Jackstands (2)
Drain pan

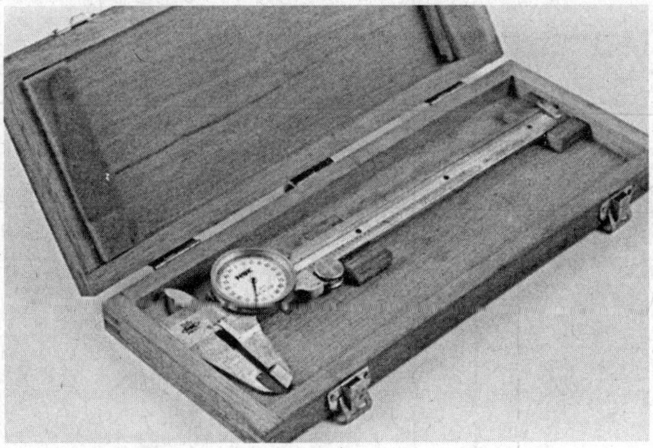

Dial caliper

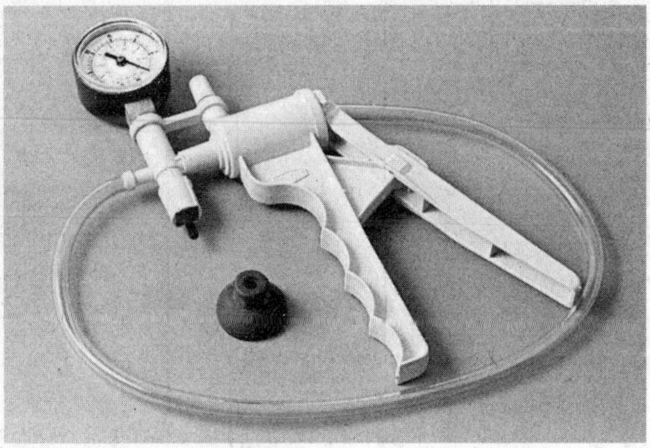

Hand-operated vacuum pump

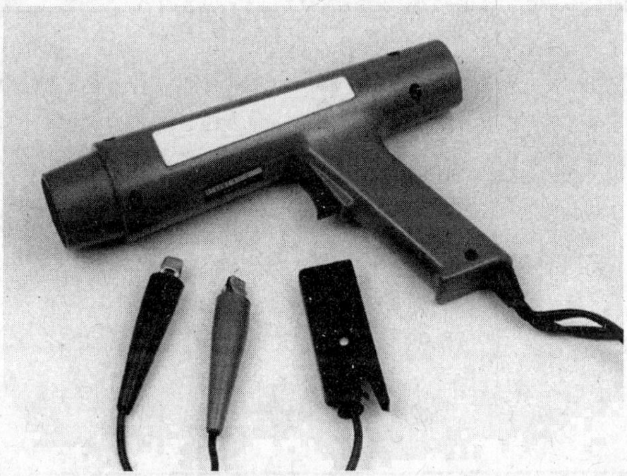

Timing light

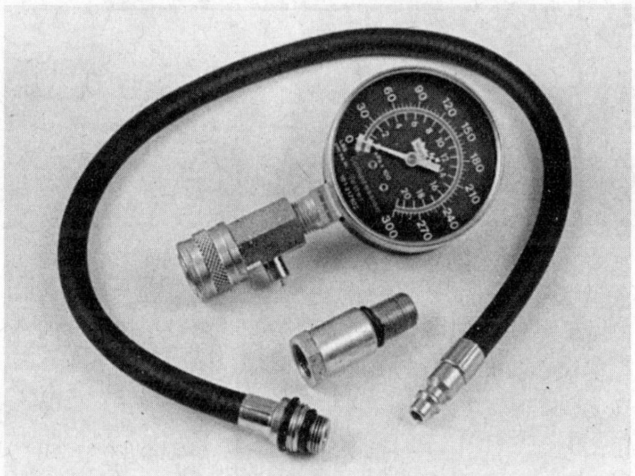

Compression gauge with spark plug hole adapter

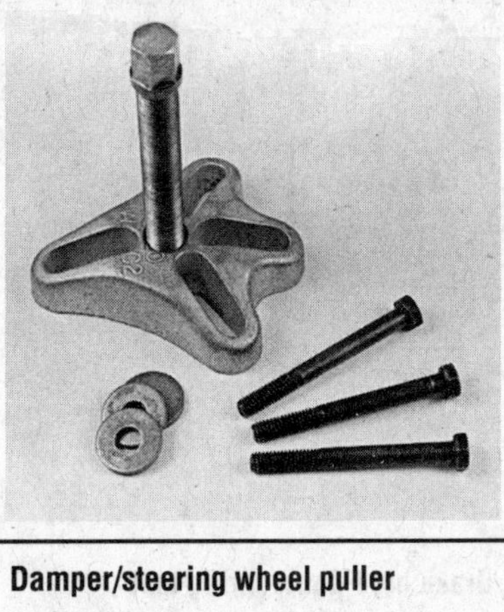

Damper/steering wheel puller

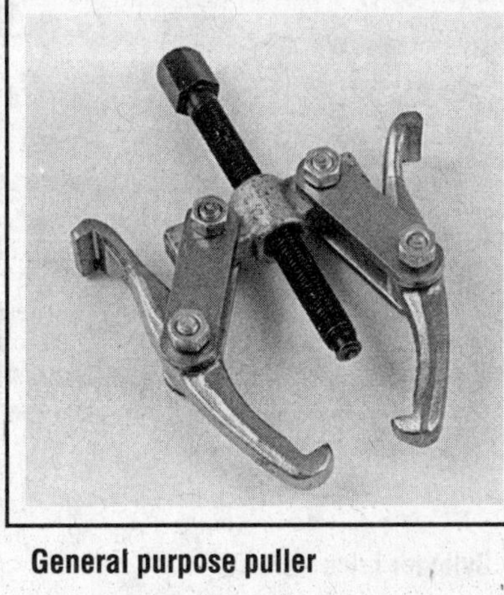

General purpose puller

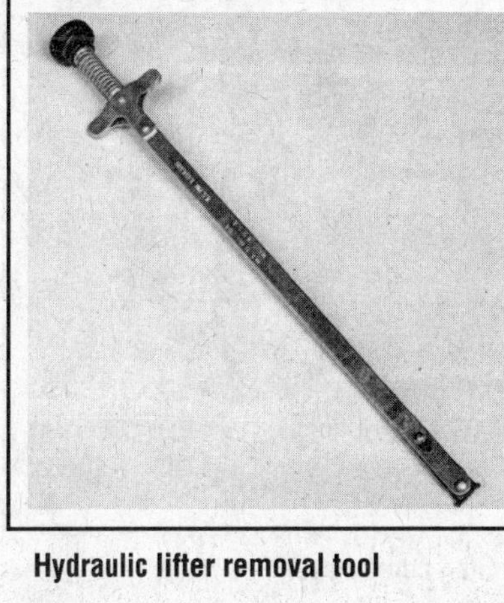

Hydraulic lifter removal tool

➡Note: If basic tune-ups are going to be part of routine maintenance, it will be necessary to purchase a good quality stroboscopic timing light and combination tachometer/dwell meter. Although they are included in the list of special tools, it is mentioned here because they are absolutely necessary for tuning most vehicles properly.

Repair and overhaul tool set

These tools are essential for anyone who plans to perform major repairs and are in addition to those in the maintenance and minor repair tool kit. Included is a comprehensive set of sockets which, though expensive, are invaluable because of their versatility, especially when various extensions and drives are available. We recommend the 1/2-inch drive over the 3/8-inch drive. Although the larger drive is bulky and more expensive, it has the capacity of accepting a very wide range of large sockets. Ideally, however, the mechanic should have a 3/8-inch drive set and a 1/2-inch drive set.

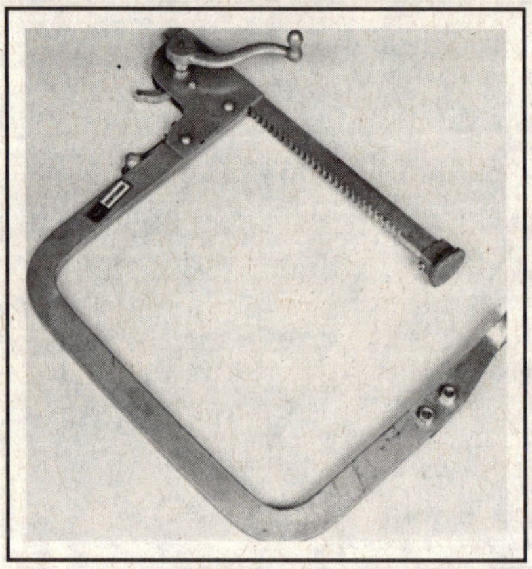

Valve spring compressor

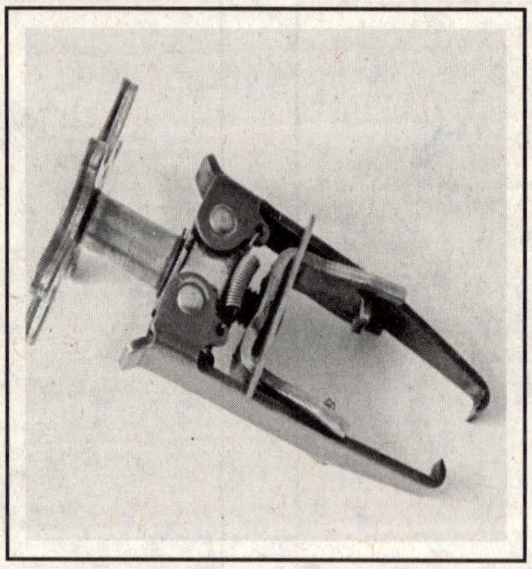

Valve spring compressor

Ridge reamer

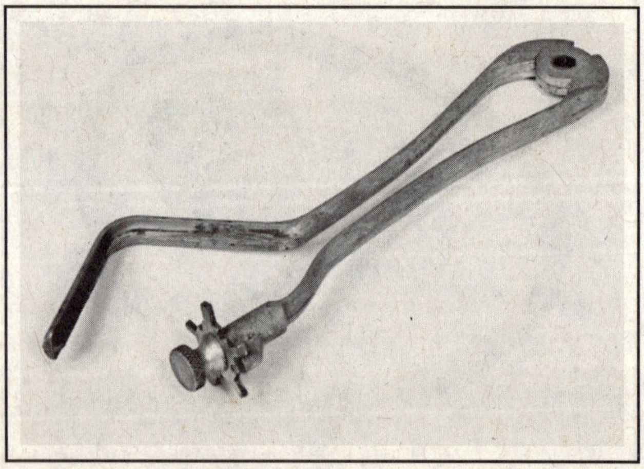

Piston ring groove cleaning tool

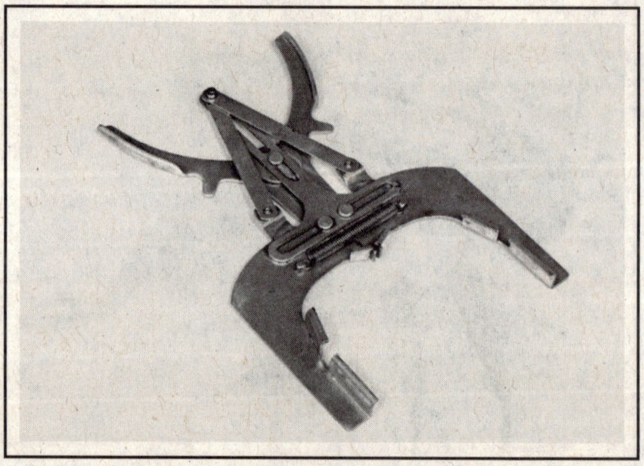

Ring removal/installation tool

Ring compressor

Cylinder hone

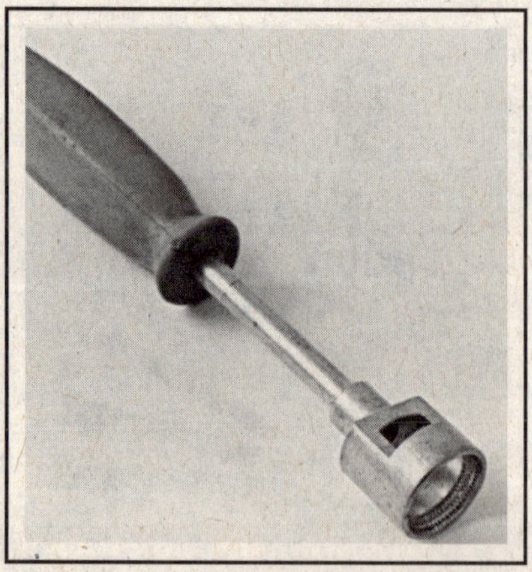

Brake hold-down spring tool

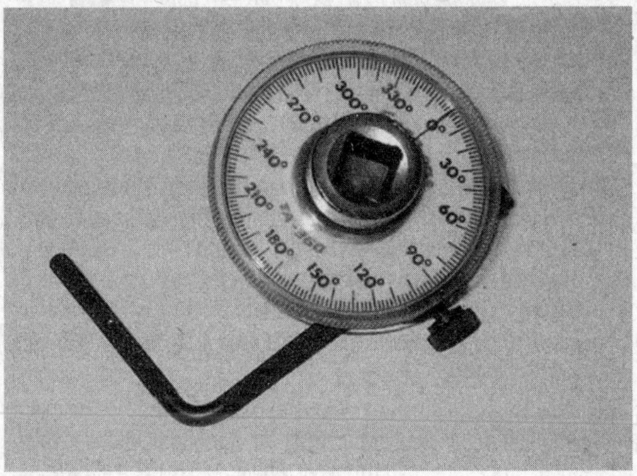

Torque angle gauge

Socket set(s)
Reversible ratchet
Extension - 10 inch
Universal joint
Torque wrench (same size drive as sockets)
Ball peen hammer - 8 ounce
Soft-face hammer (plastic/rubber)
Standard screwdriver (1/4-inch x 6 inch)
Standard screwdriver (stubby - 5/16-inch)
Phillips screwdriver (No. 3 x 8 inch)
Phillips screwdriver (stubby - No. 2)
Pliers - vise grip
Pliers - lineman's
Pliers - needle nose
Pliers - snap-ring (internal and external)
Cold chisel - 1/2-inch
Scribe
Scraper (made from flattened copper tubing)
Centerpunch
Pin punches (1/16, 1/8, 3/16-inch)
Steel rule/straightedge - 12 inch
Allen wrench set (1/8 to 3/8-inch or 4 mm to 10 mm)
A selection of files
Wire brush (large)
Jackstands (second set)
Jack (scissor or hydraulic type)

➡Note: Another tool which is often useful is an electric drill with a chuck capacity of 3/8-inch and a set of good quality drill bits.

Special tools

The tools in this list include those which are not used regularly, are expensive to buy, or which need to be used in accordance with their manufacturer's instructions. Unless these tools will be used frequently, it is not very economical to purchase many of them. A consideration would be to split the cost and use between yourself and a friend or friends. In addition, most of these tools can be obtained from a tool rental shop on a temporary basis.

This list primarily contains only those tools and instruments widely available to the public, and not those special tools produced by the vehicle manufacturer for distribution to dealer service departments. Occasionally, references to the manufacturer's special tools are included in the text of this manual. Generally, an alternative method of doing the job without the special tool is offered. However, sometimes there is no alternative to their use. Where this is the case, and the tool cannot be purchased or borrowed, the work should be turned over to the dealer service department or an automotive repair shop.

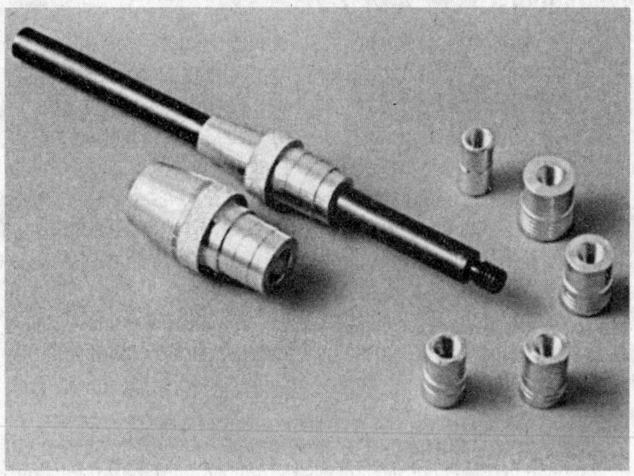

Clutch plate alignment tool

Valve spring compressor
Piston ring groove cleaning tool
Piston ring compressor
Piston ring installation tool
Cylinder compression gauge
Cylinder ridge reamer
Cylinder surfacing hone
Cylinder bore gauge
Micrometers and/or dial calipers
Hydraulic lifter removal tool
Balljoint separator
Universal-type puller
Impact screwdriver
Dial indicator set
Stroboscopic timing light (inductive pick-up)
Hand operated vacuum/pressure pump
Tachometer/dwell meter
Universal electrical multimeter
Cable hoist
Brake spring removal and installation tools
Floor jack

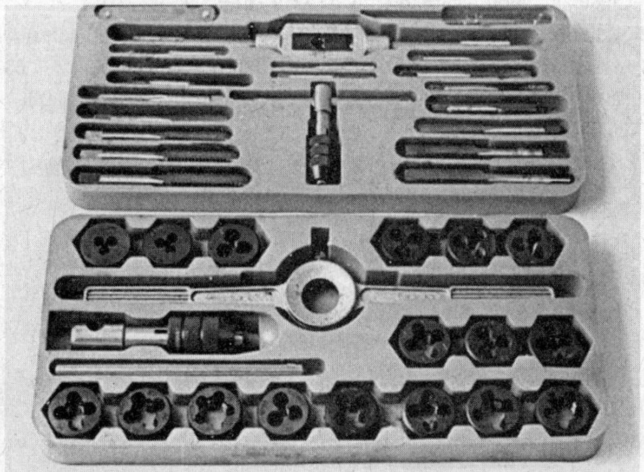

Tap and die set

Buying tools

For the do-it-yourselfer who is just starting to get involved in vehicle maintenance and repair, there are a number of options available when purchasing tools. If maintenance and minor repair is the extent of the work to be done, the purchase of individual tools is satisfactory. If, on the other hand, extensive work is planned, it would be a good idea to purchase a modest tool set from one of the large retail chain stores. A set can usually be bought at a substantial savings over the individual tool prices, and they often come with a tool box. As additional tools are needed, add-on sets, individual tools and a larger tool box can be purchased to expand the tool selection. Building a tool set gradually allows the cost of the tools to be spread over a longer period of time and gives the mechanic the freedom to choose only those tools that will actually be used.

Tool stores will often be the only source of some of the special tools that are needed, but regardless of where tools are bought, try to avoid cheap ones, especially when buying screwdrivers and sockets, because they won't last very long. The expense involved in replacing cheap tools will eventually be greater than the initial cost of quality tools.

Care and maintenance of tools

Good tools are expensive, so it makes sense to treat them with respect. Keep them clean and in usable condition and store them properly when not in use. Always wipe off any dirt, grease or metal chips before putting them away. Never leave tools lying around in the work area. Upon completion of a job, always check closely under the hood for tools that may have been left there so they won't get lost during a test drive.

Some tools, such as screwdrivers, pliers, wrenches and sockets, can be hung on a panel mounted on the garage or workshop wall, while others should be kept in a tool box or tray. Measuring instruments, gauges, meters, etc. must be carefully stored where they cannot be damaged by weather or impact from other tools.

When tools are used with care and stored properly, they will last a very long time. Even with the best of care, though, tools will wear out if used frequently. When a tool is damaged or worn out, replace it. Subsequent jobs will be safer and more enjoyable if you do.

HOW TO REPAIR DAMAGED THREADS

Sometimes, the internal threads of a nut or bolt hole can become stripped, usually from overtightening. Stripping threads is an all-too-common occurrence, especially when working with aluminum parts, because aluminum is so soft that it easily strips out.

Usually, external or internal threads are only partially stripped. After they've been cleaned up with a tap or die, they'll still work. Sometimes, however, threads are badly damaged. When this happens, you've got three choices:

1) *Drill and tap the hole to the next suitable oversize and install a larger diameter bolt, screw or stud.*
2) *Drill and tap the hole to accept a threaded plug, then drill and tap the plug to the original screw size. You can also buy a plug already threaded to the original size. Then you simply drill a hole to the specified size, then run the threaded plug into the hole with a bolt and jam nut. Once the plug is fully seated, remove the jam nut and bolt.*
3) *The third method uses a patented thread repair kit like Heli-Coil or Slimsert. These easy-to-use kits are designed to repair damaged threads in straight-through holes and blind holes. Both are available as kits which can handle a variety of sizes and thread patterns. Drill the hole, then tap it with the special included tap. Install the Heli-Coil and the hole is back to its original diameter and thread pitch.*

Regardless of which method you use, be sure to proceed calmly and carefully. A little impatience or carelessness during one of these relatively simple procedures can ruin your whole day's work and cost you a bundle if you wreck an expensive part.

WORKING FACILITIES

Not to be overlooked when discussing tools is the workshop. If anything more than routine maintenance is to be carried out, some sort of suitable work area is essential.

It is understood, and appreciated, that many home mechanics do not have a good workshop or garage available, and end up removing an engine or doing major repairs outside. It is recommended, however, that the overhaul or repair be completed under the cover of a roof.

A clean, flat workbench or table of comfortable working height is an absolute necessity. The workbench should be equipped with a vise that has a jaw opening of at least four inches.

As mentioned previously, some clean, dry storage space is also required for tools, as well as the lubricants, fluids, cleaning solvents, etc. which soon become necessary.

Sometimes waste oil and fluids, drained from the engine or cooling system during normal maintenance or repairs, present a disposal problem. To avoid pouring them on the ground or into a sewage system, pour the used fluids into large containers, seal them with caps and take them to an authorized disposal site or recycling center. Plastic jugs, such as old antifreeze containers, are ideal for this purpose.

Always keep a supply of old newspapers and clean rags available. Old towels are excellent for mopping up spills. Many mechanics use rolls of paper towels for most work because they are readily available and disposable. To help keep the area under the vehicle clean, a large cardboard box can be cut open and flattened to protect the garage or shop floor.

Whenever working over a painted surface, such as when leaning over a fender to service something under the hood, always cover it with an old blanket or bedspread to protect the finish. Vinyl covered pads, made especially for this purpose, are available at auto parts stores.

Jacking and towing

JACKING

⁂ WARNING:

The jack supplied with the vehicle should only be used for changing a tire or placing jackstands under the frame. Never work under the vehicle or start the engine while this jack is being used as the only means of support.

The vehicle should be on level ground. Place the shift lever in Park, if you have an automatic, or Reverse if you have a manual transaxle. Block the wheel diagonally opposite the wheel being changed. Set the parking brake.

Remove the spare tire and jack from stowage. Remove the wheel cover and trim ring (if so equipped) with the tapered end of the lug nut wrench by inserting and twisting the handle and then prying against the back of the wheel cover. Loosen, but do not remove, the lug nuts (one-half turn is sufficient).

Place the scissors-type jack under the vehicle and adjust the jack height until it engages with the proper jacking point. There is a front and rear jacking point on each side of the vehicle (see illustration).

Turn the jack handle clockwise until the tire clears the ground. Remove the lug nuts and pull the wheel off, then install the spare.

Install the lug nuts with the beveled edges facing in. Tighten them snugly. Don't attempt to tighten them completely until the vehicle is lowered or it could slip off the jack. Turn the jack handle counterclockwise to lower the vehicle. Remove the jack and tighten the lug nuts in a diagonal pattern.

Stow the tire, jack and wrench. Unblock the wheels.

TOWING

Two-wheel drive models can be towed from the front with the front wheels off the ground, using a wheel lift type tow truck. If towed from the rear, the front wheels must be placed on a dolly. All-wheel drive models must be towed with all four wheels off the ground. A sling-type tow truck cannot be used, as body damage will result. The best way to tow the vehicle is with a flat-bed car carrier.

In an emergency the vehicle can be towed a short distance with a cable or chain attached to one of the towing eyelets located under the front or rear bumpers. The driver must remain in the vehicle to operate the steering and brakes (remember that power steering and power brakes will not work with the engine off).

Place the jack between the raised welts on the rocker panel flange

Booster battery (jump) starting

Observe these precautions when using a booster battery to start a vehicle:

a) *Before connecting the booster battery, make sure the ignition switch is in the Off position.*
b) *Turn off the lights, heater and other electrical loads.*
c) *Your eyes should be shielded. Safety goggles are a good idea.*
d) *Make sure the booster battery is the same voltage as the dead one in the vehicle.*
e) *The two vehicles MUST NOT TOUCH each other!*
f) *Make sure the transaxle is in Neutral (manual) or Park (automatic).*
g) *If the booster battery is not a maintenance-free type, remove the vent caps and lay a cloth over the vent holes.*

Connect the red jumper cable to the positive (+) terminals of each battery (see illustration).

Connect one end of the black jumper cable to the negative (-) terminal of the booster battery. The other end of this cable should be connected to a good ground on the vehicle to be started, such as a bolt or bracket on the body.

Start the engine using the booster battery, then, with the engine running at idle speed, disconnect the jumper cables in the reverse order of connection.

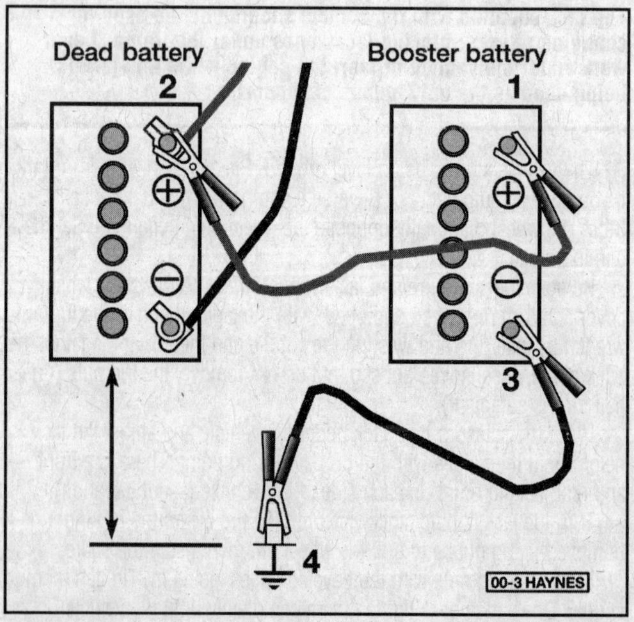

Make the booster battery cable connections in the numerical order shown (note that the negative cable of the booster battery is NOT attached to the negative terminal of the dead battery)

Automotive chemicals and lubricants

A number of automotive chemicals and lubricants are available for use during vehicle maintenance and repair. They include a wide variety of products ranging from cleaning solvents and degreasers to lubricants and protective sprays for rubber, plastic and vinyl.

CLEANERS

Carburetor cleaner and choke cleaner is a strong solvent for gum, varnish and carbon. Most carburetor cleaners leave a dry-type lubricant film which will not harden or gum up. Because of this film it is not recommended for use on electrical components.

Brake system cleaner is used to remove brake dust, grease and brake fluid from the brake system, where clean surfaces are absolutely necessary. It leaves no residue and often eliminates brake squeal caused by contaminants.

Electrical cleaner removes oxidation, corrosion and carbon deposits from electrical contacts, restoring full current flow. It can also be used to clean spark plugs, carburetor jets, voltage regulators and other parts where an oil-free surface is desired.

Demoisturants remove water and moisture from electrical components such as alternators, voltage regulators, electrical connectors and fuse blocks. They are non-conductive and non-corrosive.

Degreasers are heavy-duty solvents used to remove grease from the outside of the engine and from chassis components. They can be sprayed or brushed on and, depending on the type, are rinsed off either with water or solvent.

LUBRICANTS

Motor oil is the lubricant formulated for use in engines. It normally contains a wide variety of additives to prevent corrosion and reduce foaming and wear. Motor oil comes in various weights (viscosity ratings) from 0 to 50. The recommended weight of the oil depends on the season, temperature and the demands on the engine. Light oil is used in cold climates and under light load conditions. Heavy oil is used in hot climates and where high loads are encountered. Multi-viscosity oils are designed to have characteristics of both light and heavy oils and are available in a number of weights from 0W-20 to 20W-50.

Gear oil is designed to be used in differentials, manual transmissions and other areas where high-temperature lubrication is required.

Chassis and wheel bearing grease is a heavy grease used where increased loads and friction are encountered, such as for wheel bearings, balljoints, tie-rod ends and universal joints.

High-temperature wheel bearing grease is designed to withstand the extreme temperatures encountered by wheel bearings in disc brake equipped vehicles. It usually contains molybdenum disulfide (moly), which is a dry-type lubricant.

White grease is a heavy grease for metal-to-metal applications where water is a problem. White grease stays soft under both low and high temperatures (usually from -100 to +190-degrees F), and will not wash off or dilute in the presence of water.

Assembly lube is a special extreme pressure lubricant, usually containing moly, used to lubricate high-load parts (such as main and rod bearings and cam lobes) for initial start-up of a new engine. The assembly lube lubricates the parts without being squeezed out or washed away until the engine oiling system begins to function.

Silicone lubricants are used to protect rubber, plastic, vinyl and nylon parts.

Graphite lubricants are used where oils cannot be used due to contamination problems, such as in locks. The dry graphite will lubricate metal parts while remaining uncontaminated by dirt, water, oil or acids. It is electrically conductive and will not foul electrical contacts in locks such as the ignition switch.

Moly penetrants loosen and lubricate frozen, rusted and corroded fasteners and prevent future rusting or freezing.

Heat-sink grease is a special electrically non-conductive grease that is used for mounting electronic ignition modules where it is essential that heat is transferred away from the module.

SEALANTS

RTV sealant is one of the most widely used gasket compounds. Made from silicone, RTV is air curing, it seals, bonds, waterproofs, fills surface irregularities, remains flexible, doesn't shrink, is relatively easy to remove, and is used as a supplementary sealer with almost all low and medium temperature gaskets.

Anaerobic sealant is much like RTV in that it can be used either to seal gaskets or to form gaskets by itself. It remains flexible, is solvent resistant and fills surface imperfections. The difference between an anaerobic sealant and an RTV-type sealant is in the curing. RTV cures when exposed to air, while an anaerobic sealant cures only in the absence of air. This means that an anaerobic sealant cures only after the assembly of parts, sealing them together.

Thread and pipe sealant is used for sealing hydraulic and pneumatic fittings and vacuum lines. It is usually made from a Teflon compound, and comes in a spray, a paint-on liquid and as a wrap-around tape.

CHEMICALS

Anti-seize compound prevents seizing, galling, cold welding, rust and corrosion in fasteners. High-temperature anti-seize, usually made with copper and graphite lubricants, is used for exhaust system and exhaust manifold bolts.

Anaerobic locking compounds are used to keep fasteners from vibrating or working loose and cure only after installation, in the absence of air. Medium strength locking compound is used for small nuts, bolts and screws that may be removed later. High-strength locking compound is for large nuts, bolts and studs which aren't removed on a regular basis.

Oil additives range from viscosity index improvers to chemical treatments that claim to reduce internal engine friction. It should be noted that most oil manufacturers caution against using additives with their oils.

Gas additives perform several functions, depending on their chemical makeup. They usually contain solvents that help dissolve gum and varnish that build up on carburetor, fuel injection and intake parts. They also serve to break down carbon deposits that form on the inside surfaces of the combustion chambers. Some additives contain upper cylinder lubricants for valves and piston rings, and others contain chemicals to remove condensation from the gas tank.

MISCELLANEOUS

Brake fluid is specially formulated hydraulic fluid that can withstand the heat and pressure encountered in brake systems. Care must be taken so this fluid does not come in contact with painted surfaces or plastics. An opened container should always be resealed to prevent contamination by water or dirt.

Weatherstrip adhesive is used to bond weatherstripping around doors, windows and trunk lids. It is sometimes used to attach trim pieces.

Undercoating is a petroleum-based, tar-like substance that is designed to protect metal surfaces on the underside of the vehicle from corrosion. It also acts as a sound-deadening agent by insulating the bottom of the vehicle.

Waxes and polishes are used to help protect painted and plated surfaces from the weather. Different types of paint may require the use of different types of wax and polish. Some polishes utilize a chemical or abrasive cleaner to help remove the top layer of oxidized (dull) paint on older vehicles. In recent years many non-wax polishes that contain a wide variety of chemicals such as polymers and silicones have been introduced. These non-wax polishes are usually easier to apply and last longer than conventional waxes and polishes.

CONVERSION FACTORS

LENGTH (distance)

Inches (in)	X 25.4	= Millimeters (mm)	X	0.0394	= Inches (in)
Feet (ft)	X 0.305	= Meters (m)	X	3.281	= Feet (ft)
Miles	X 1.609	= Kilometers (km)	X	0.621	= Miles

VOLUME (capacity)

Cubic inches (cu in; in^3)	X 16.387	= Cubic centimeters (cc; cm^3)	X	0.061	= Cubic inches (cu in; in^3)
Imperial pints (Imp pt)	X 0.568	= Liters (l)	X	1.76	= Imperial pints (Imp pt)
Imperial quarts (Imp qt)	X 1.137	= Liters (l)	X	0.88	= Imperial quarts (Imp qt)
Imperial quarts (Imp qt)	X 1.201	= US quarts (US qt)	X	0.833	= Imperial quarts (Imp qt)
US quarts (US qt)	X 0.946	= Liters (l)	X	1.057	= US quarts (US qt)
Imperial gallons (Imp gal)	X 4.546	= Liters (l)	X	0.22	= Imperial gallons (Imp gal)
Imperial gallons (Imp gal)	X 1.201	= US gallons (US gal)	X	0.833	= Imperial gallons (Imp gal)
US gallons (US gal)	X 3.785	= Liters (l)	X	0.264	= US gallons (US gal)

MASS (weight)

Ounces (oz)	X 28.35	= Grams (g)	X	0.035	= Ounces (oz)
Pounds (lb)	X 0.454	= Kilograms (kg)	X	2.205	= Pounds (lb)

FORCE

Ounces-force (ozf; oz)	X 0.278	= Newtons (N)	X	3.6	= Ounces-force (ozf; oz)
Pounds-force (lbf; lb)	X 4.448	= Newtons (N)	X	0.225	= Pounds-force (lbf; lb)
Newtons (N)	X 0.1	= Kilograms-force (kgf; kg)	X	9.81	= Newtons (N)

PRESSURE

Pounds-force per square inch (psi; lbf/in^2; lb/in^2)	X 0.070	= Kilograms-force per square centimeter (kgf/cm^2; kg/cm^2)	X	14.223	= Pounds-force per square inch (psi; lbf/in^2; lb/in^2)
Pounds-force per square inch (psi; lbf/in^2; lb/in^2)	X 0.068	= Atmospheres (atm)	X	14.696	= Pounds-force per square inch (psi; lbf/in^2; lb/in^2)
Pounds-force per square inch (psi; lbf/in^2; lb/in^2)	X 0.069	= Bars	X	14.5	= Pounds-force per square inch (psi; lbf/in^2; lb/in^2)
Pounds-force per square inch (psi; lbf/in^2; lb/in^2)	X 6.895	= Kilopascals (kPa)	X	0.145	= Pounds-force per square inch (psi; lbf/in^2; lb/in^2)
Kilopascals (kPa)	X 0.01	= Kilograms-force per square centimeter (kgf/cm^2; kg/cm^2)	X	98.1	= Kilopascals (kPa)

TORQUE (moment of force)

Pounds-force inches (lbf in; lb in)	X 1.152	= Kilograms-force centimeter (kgf cm; kg cm)	X	0.868	= Pounds-force inches (lbf in; lb in)
Pounds-force inches (lbf in; lb in)	X 0.113	= Newton meters (Nm)	X	8.85	= Pounds-force inches (lbf in; lb in)
Pounds-force inches (lbf in; lb in)	X 0.083	= Pounds-force feet (lbf ft; lb ft)	X	12	= Pounds-force inches (lbf in; lb in)
Pounds-force feet (lbf ft; lb ft)	X 0.138	= Kilograms-force meters (kgf m; kg m)	X	7.233	= Pounds-force feet (lbf ft; lb ft)
Pounds-force feet (lbf ft; lb ft)	X 1.356	= Newton meters (Nm)	X	0.738	= Pounds-force feet (lbf ft; lb ft)
Newton meters (Nm)	X 0.102	= Kilograms-force meters (kgf m; kg m)	X	9.804	= Newton meters (Nm)

VACUUM

Inches mercury (in. Hg)	X 3.377	= Kilopascals (kPa)	X	0.2961	= Inches mercury
Inches mercury (in. Hg)	X 25.4	= Millimeters mercury (mm Hg)	X	0.0394	= Inches mercury

POWER

Horsepower (hp)	X 745.7	= Watts (W)	X	0.0013	= Horsepower (hp)

VELOCITY (speed)

Miles per hour (miles/hr; mph)	X 1.609	= Kilometers per hour (km/hr; kph)	X	0.621	= Miles per hour (miles/hr; mph)

FUEL CONSUMPTION *

Miles per gallon, Imperial (mpg)	X 0.354	= Kilometers per liter (km/l)	X	2.825	= Miles per gallon, Imperial (mpg)
Miles per gallon, US (mpg)	X 0.425	= Kilometers per liter (km/l)	X	2.352	= Miles per gallon, US (mpg)

TEMPERATURE

Degrees Fahrenheit = (°C x 1.8) + 32

Degrees Celsius (Degrees Centigrade; °C) = (°F - 32) x 0.56

******It is common practice to convert from miles per gallon (mpg) to liters/100 kilometers (l/100km), where mpg (Imperial) x l/100 km = 282 and mpg (US) x l/100 km = 235*

FRACTION/DECIMAL/MILLIMETER EQUIVALENTS

DECIMALS TO MILLIMETERS

Decimal	mm
0.001	0.0254
0.002	0.0508
0.003	0.0762
0.004	0.1016
0.005	0.1270
0.006	0.1524
0.007	0.1778
0.008	0.2032
0.009	0.2286
0.010	0.2540
0.020	0.5080
0.030	0.7620
0.040	1.0160
0.050	1.2700
0.060	1.5240
0.070	1.7780
0.080	2.0320
0.090	2.2860
0.100	2.5400
0.110	2.7940
0.120	3.0480
0.130	3.3020
0.140	3.5560
0.150	3.8100
0.160	4.0640
0.170	4.3180
0.180	4.5720
0.190	4.8260
0.200	5.0800
0.210	5.3340
0.220	5.5880
0.230	5.8420
0.240	6.0960
0.250	6.3500
0.260	6.6040
0.270	6.8580
0.280	7.1120
0.290	7.3660
0.300	7.6200
0.310	7.8740
0.320	8.1280
0.330	8.3820
0.340	8.6360
0.350	8.8900
0.360	9.1440
0.370	9.3980
0.380	9.6520
0.390	9.9060
0.400	10.1600
0.410	10.4140
0.420	10.6680
0.430	10.9220
0.440	11.1760
0.450	11.4300
0.460	11.6840
0.470	11.9380
0.480	12.1920
0.490	12.4460

Decimal	mm
0.500	12.7000
0.510	12.9540
0.520	13.2080
0.530	13.4620
0.540	13.7160
0.550	13.9700
0.560	14.2240
0.570	14.4780
0.580	14.7320
0.590	14.9860
0.600	15.2400
0.610	15.4940
0.620	15.7480
0.630	16.0020
0.640	16.2560
0.650	16.5100
0.660	16.7640
0.670	17.0180
0.680	17.2720
0.690	17.5260
0.700	17.7800
0.710	18.0340
0.720	18.2880
0.730	18.5420
0.740	18.7960
0.750	19.0500
0.760	19.3040
0.770	19.5580
0.780	19.8120
0.790	20.0660
0.800	20.3200
0.810	20.5740
0.820	21.8280
0.830	21.0820
0.840	21.3360
0.850	21.5900
0.860	21.8440
0.870	22.0980
0.880	22.3520
0.890	22.6060
0.900	22.8600
0.910	23.1140
0.920	23.3680
0.930	23.6220
0.940	23.8760
0.950	24.1300
0.960	24.3840
0.970	24.6380
0.980	24.8920
0.990	25.1460
1.000	25.4000

FRACTIONS TO DECIMALS TO MILLIMETERS

Fraction	Decimal	mm	Fraction	Decimal	mm
1/64	0.0156	0.3969	33/64	0.5156	13.0969
1/32	0.0312	0.7938	17/32	0.5312	13.4938
3/64	0.0469	1.1906	35/64	0.5469	13.8906
1/16	0.0625	1.5875	9/16	0.5625	14.2875
5/64	0.0781	1.9844	37/64	0.5781	14.6844
3/32	0.0938	2.3812	19/32	0.5938	15.0812
7/64	0.1094	2.7781	39/64	0.6094	15.4781
1/8	0.1250	3.1750	5/8	0.6250	15.8750
9/64	0.1406	3.5719	41/64	0.6406	16.2719
5/32	0.1562	3.9688	21/32	0.6562	16.6688
11/64	0.1719	4.3656	43/64	0.6719	17.0656
3/16	0.1875	4.7625	11/16	0.6875	17.4625
13/64	0.2031	5.1594	45/64	0.7031	17.8594
7/32	0.2188	5.5562	23/32	0.7188	18.2562
15/64	0.2344	5.9531	47/64	0.7344	18.6531
1/4	0.2500	6.3500	3/4	0.7500	19.0500
17/64	0.2656	6.7469	49/64	0.7656	19.4469
9/32	0.2812	7.1438	25/32	0.7812	19.8438
19/64	0.2969	7.5406	51/64	0.7969	20.2406
5/16	0.3125	7.9375	13/16	0.8125	20.6375
21/64	0.3281	8.3344	53/64	0.8281	21.0344
11/32	0.3438	8.7312	27/32	0.8438	21.4312
23/64	0.3594	9.1281	55/64	0.8594	21.8281
3/8	0.3750	9.5250	7/8	0.8750	22.2250
25/64	0.3906	9.9219	57/64	0.8906	22.6219
13/32	0.4062	10.3188	29/32	0.9062	23.0188
27/64	0.4219	10.7156	59/64	0.9219	23.4156
7/16	0.4375	11.1125	15/16	0.9375	23.8125
29/64	0.4531	11.5094	61/64	0.9531	24.2094
15/32	0.4688	11.9062	31/32	0.9688	24.6062
31/64	0.4844	12.3031	63/64	0.9844	25.0031
1/2	0.5000	12.7000	1	1.0000	25.4000

Safety first!

Regardless of how enthusiastic you may be about getting on with the job at hand, take the time to ensure that your safety is not jeopardized. A moment's lack of attention can result in an accident, as can failure to observe certain simple safety precautions. The possibility of an accident will always exist, and the following points should not be considered a comprehensive list of all dangers. Rather, they are intended to make you aware of the risks and to encourage a safety conscious approach to all work you carry out on your vehicle.

ESSENTIAL DOS AND DON'TS

DON'T rely on a jack when working under the vehicle. Always use approved jackstands to support the weight of the vehicle and place them under the recommended lift or support points.
DON'T attempt to loosen extremely tight fasteners (i.e. wheel lug nuts) while the vehicle is on a jack - it may fall.
DON'T start the engine without first making sure that the transmission is in Neutral (or Park where applicable) and the parking brake is set.
DON'T remove the radiator cap from a hot cooling system - let it cool or cover it with a cloth and release the pressure gradually.
DON'T attempt to drain the engine oil until you are sure it has cooled to the point that it will not burn you.
DON'T touch any part of the engine or exhaust system until it has cooled sufficiently to avoid burns.
DON'T siphon toxic liquids such as gasoline, antifreeze and brake fluid by mouth, or allow them to remain on your skin.
DON'T inhale brake lining dust - it is potentially hazardous (see Asbestos below).
DON'T allow spilled oil or grease to remain on the floor - wipe it up before someone slips on it.
DON'T use loose fitting wrenches or other tools which may slip and cause injury.
DON'T push on wrenches when loosening or tightening nuts or bolts. Always try to pull the wrench toward you. If the situation calls for pushing the wrench away, push with an open hand to avoid scraped knuckles if the wrench should slip.
DON'T attempt to lift a heavy component alone - get someone to help you.
DON'T rush or take unsafe shortcuts to finish a job.
DON'T allow children or animals in or around the vehicle while you are working on it.
DO wear eye protection when using power tools such as a drill, sander, bench grinder, etc. and when working under a vehicle.
DO keep loose clothing and long hair well out of the way of moving parts.
DO make sure that any hoist used has a safe working load rating adequate for the job.
DO get someone to check on you periodically when working alone on a vehicle.
DO carry out work in a logical sequence and make sure that everything is correctly assembled and tightened.
DO keep chemicals and fluids tightly capped and out of the reach of children and pets.
DO remember that your vehicle's safety affects that of yourself and others. If in doubt on any point, get professional advice.

STEERING, SUSPENSION AND BRAKES

These systems are essential to driving safety, so make sure you have a qualified shop or individual check your work. Also, compressed suspension springs can cause injury if released suddenly - be sure to use a spring compressor.

AIRBAGS

Airbags are explosive devices that can CAUSE injury if they deploy while you're working on the vehicle. Follow the manufacturer's instructions to disable the airbag whenever you're working in the vicinity of airbag components.

ASBESTOS

Certain friction, insulating, sealing, and other products - such as brake linings, brake bands, clutch linings, torque converters, gaskets, etc. - may contain asbestos or other hazardous friction material. Extreme care must be taken to avoid inhalation of dust from such products, since it is hazardous to health. If in doubt, assume that they do contain asbestos.

FIRE

Remember at all times that gasoline is highly flammable. Never smoke or have any kind of open flame around when working on a vehicle. But the risk does not end there. A spark caused by an electrical short circuit, by two metal surfaces contacting each other, or even by static electricity built up in your body under certain conditions, can ignite gasoline vapors, which in a confined space are highly explosive. Do not, under any circumstances, use gasoline for cleaning parts. Use an approved safety solvent.

Always disconnect the battery ground (-) cable at the battery before working on any part of the fuel system or electrical system. Never risk spilling fuel on a hot engine or exhaust component. It is strongly recommended that a fire extinguisher suitable for use on fuel and electrical fires be kept handy in the garage or workshop at all times. Never try to extinguish a fuel or electrical fire with water.

FUMES

Certain fumes are highly toxic and can quickly cause unconsciousness and even death if inhaled to any extent. Gasoline vapor falls into this category, as do the vapors from some cleaning solvents. Any draining or pouring of such volatile fluids should be done in a well ventilated area.

When using cleaning fluids and solvents, read the instructions on the container carefully. Never use materials from unmarked containers.

Never run the engine in an enclosed space, such as a garage. Exhaust fumes contain carbon monoxide, which is extremely poisonous. If you need to run the engine, always do so in the open air, or at least have the rear of the vehicle outside the work area.

THE BATTERY

Never create a spark or allow a bare light bulb near a battery. They normally give off a certain amount of hydrogen gas, which is highly explosive.

Always disconnect the battery ground (-) cable at the battery before working on the fuel or electrical systems.

If possible, loosen the filler caps or cover when charging the battery from an external source (this does not apply to sealed or maintenance-free batteries). Do not charge at an excessive rate or the battery may burst.

Take care when adding water to a non maintenance-free battery and when carrying a battery. The electrolyte, even when diluted, is very corrosive and should not be allowed to contact clothing or skin.

Always wear eye protection when cleaning the battery to prevent the caustic deposits from entering your eyes.

HOUSEHOLD CURRENT

When using an electric power tool, inspection light, etc., which operates on household current, always make sure that the tool is correctly connected to its plug and that, where necessary, it is properly grounded. Do not use such items in damp conditions and, again, do not create a spark or apply excessive heat in the vicinity of fuel or fuel vapor.

SECONDARY IGNITION SYSTEM VOLTAGE

A severe electric shock can result from touching certain parts of the ignition system (such as the spark plug wires) when the engine is running or being cranked, particularly if components are damp or the insulation is defective. In the case of an electronic ignition system, the secondary system voltage is much higher and could prove fatal.

HYDROFLUORIC ACID

This extremely corrosive acid is formed when certain types of synthetic rubber, found in some O-rings, oil seals, fuel hoses, etc. are exposed to temperatures above 750-degrees F (400-degrees C). The rubber changes into a charred or sticky substance containing the acid. *Once formed, the acid remains dangerous for years. If it gets onto the skin, it may be necessary to amputate the limb concerned.*

When dealing with a vehicle which has suffered a fire, or with components salvaged from such a vehicle, wear protective gloves and discard them after use.

Troubleshooting

CONTENTS

This section provides an easy reference guide to the more common problems which may occur during the operation of your vehicle. These problems and their possible causes are grouped under headings denoting various components or systems, such as Engine, Cooling system, etc. They also refer you to the chapter and/or section which deals with the problem.

Remember that successful troubleshooting is not a mysterious black art practiced only by professional mechanics. It is simply the result of the right knowledge combined with an intelligent, systematic approach to the problem. Always work by a process of elimination, starting with the simplest solution and working through to the most complex - and never overlook the obvious. Anyone can run the gas tank dry or leave the lights on overnight, so don't assume that you are exempt from such oversights.

Finally, always establish a clear idea of why a problem has occurred and take steps to ensure that it doesn't happen again. If the electrical system fails because of a poor connection, check the other connections in the system to make sure that they don't fail as well. If a particular fuse continues to blow, find out why - don't just replace one fuse after another. Remember, failure of a small component can often be indicative of potential failure or incorrect functioning of a more important component or system.

ENGINE

1 Engine will not rotate when attempting to start

1 Battery terminal connections loose or corroded (Chapter 1).
2 Battery discharged or faulty (Chapters 1 and 5).
3 Automatic transaxle not completely engaged in Park (Chapter 7) or clutch pedal not completely depressed (Chapter 6).
4 Broken, loose or disconnected wiring in the starting circuit (Chapters 5 and 12).
5 Starter motor pinion jammed in flywheel ring gear (Chapter 5).
6 Starter solenoid faulty (Chapter 5).
7 Starter motor faulty (Chapter 5).
8 Ignition switch faulty (Chapter 12).
9 Starter pinion or flywheel teeth worn or broken (Chapter 5).

2 Engine rotates but will not start

1 Fuel tank empty.
2 Battery discharged (engine rotates slowly) (Chapter 5).
3 Battery terminal connections loose or corroded (Chapter 1).
4 Leaking fuel injector(s), faulty fuel pump, pressure regulator, etc. (Chapter 4).
5 Broken timing chain (Chapter 2A or 2B).
6 Ignition components damp or damaged (Chapter 5).
7 Worn, faulty or incorrectly-gapped spark plugs (Chapter 1).
8 Broken, loose or disconnected wiring in the starting circuit (Chapter 5).
9 Broken, loose or disconnected wires at the ignition coil or faulty coil (Chapter 5).
10 Defective crankshaft or camshaft sensor (Chapter 6).

3 Engine hard to start when cold

1 Battery discharged or low (Chapter 1).
2 Malfunctioning fuel system (Chapter 4).
3 Faulty coolant temperature sensor or intake air temperature sensor (Chapter 6).
4 Faulty ignition system (Chapter 5).

4 Engine hard to start when hot

1 Air filter clogged (Chapter 1).
2 Fuel not reaching the fuel injection system (Chapter 4).
3 Corroded battery connections (Chapter 1).
4 Faulty coolant temperature sensor or intake air temperature sensor (Chapter 6).

5 Starter motor noisy or excessively rough in engagement

1 Pinion or flywheel gear teeth worn or broken (Chapter 5).
2 Starter motor mounting bolts loose or missing (Chapter 5).

6 Engine starts but stops immediately

1 Insufficient fuel reaching the fuel injector(s) (Chapters 1 and 4).
2 Vacuum leak at the gasket between the intake manifold/plenum and throttle body (Chapter 4).

7 Oil puddle under engine

1 Oil pan gasket and/or oil pan drain bolt washer leaking (Chapter 2).
2 Oil pressure sending unit leaking (Chapter 2).
3 Valve cover leaking (Chapter 2).
4 Engine oil seals leaking (Chapter 2).
5 Oil pump housing leaking (Chapter 2).

8 Engine lopes while idling or idles erratically

1 Vacuum leakage (Chapters 2 and 4).
2 Leaking EGR valve (Chapter 6).
3 Air filter clogged (Chapter 1).
4 Malfunction in the fuel injection or engine control system (Chapters 4 and 6).
5 Leaking head gasket (Chapter 2).
6 Timing chain and/or sprockets worn (Chapter 2).
7 Camshaft lobes worn (Chapter 2).

9 Engine misses at idle speed

1 Spark plugs worn or not gapped properly (Chapter 1).
2 Faulty coil(s) (Chapter 1).
3 Vacuum leaks (Chapter 1).
4 Uneven or low compression (Chapter 2).
5 Problem with the fuel injection system (Chapter 4).

10 Engine misses throughout driving speed range

1 Fuel filter clogged and/or impurities in the fuel system (Chapters 1 and 4).
2 Low fuel pressure (Chapter 4).
3 Faulty or incorrectly gapped spark plugs (Chapter 1).
4 Faulty emission system components (Chapter 6).
5 Low or uneven cylinder compression pressures (Chapter 2).
6 Weak or faulty ignition system (Chapter 5).
7 Vacuum leak in fuel injection system, intake manifold, air control valve or vacuum hoses (Chapters 4 and 6).

11 Engine stumbles on acceleration

1 Spark plugs fouled (Chapter 1).
2 Problem with fuel injection or engine control system (Chapters 4 and 6).
3 Fuel filter clogged (Chapters 1 and 4).
4 Intake manifold air leak (Chapters 2 and 4).
5 Problem with the emissions control system (Chapter 6).

12 Engine surges while holding accelerator steady

1 Intake air leak (Chapter 4).
2 Fuel pump or fuel pressure regulator faulty (Chapter 4).
3 Problem with the fuel injection system (Chapter 4).
4 Problem with the emissions control system (Chapter 6).

13 Engine stalls

1 Idle speed incorrect (Chapter 1).
2 Fuel filter clogged and/or water and impurities in the fuel system (Chapters 1 and 4).
3 Faulty emissions system components (Chapter 6).
4 Faulty or incorrectly-gapped spark plugs (Chapter 1).
5 Vacuum leak in the fuel injection system, intake manifold or vacuum hoses (Chapters 2 and 4).

14 Engine lacks power

1 Obstructed exhaust system (Chapter 4).
2 Faulty or incorrectly-gapped spark plugs (Chapter 1).
3 Problem with the fuel injection system (Chapter 4).
4 Dirty air filter (Chapter 1).
5 Brakes binding (Chapter 9).
6 Automatic transaxle fluid level incorrect (Chapter 1).
7 Clutch slipping (Chapter 8).
8 Fuel filter clogged and/or impurities in the fuel system (Chapters 1 and 4).
9 Emission control system not functioning properly (Chapter 6).
10 Low or uneven cylinder compression pressures (Chapter 2).

15 Engine backfires

1 Emission control system not functioning properly (Chapter 6).
2 Problem with the fuel injection system (Chapter 4).
3 Vacuum leak at fuel injector(s), intake manifold or vacuum hoses (Chapters 2 and 4).
4 Valve clearances incorrectly set (four-cylinder engines) and/or valves sticking (Chapter 2).

16 Pinging or knocking engine sounds during acceleration or uphill

1 Incorrect grade of fuel.
2 Fuel injection system faulty (Chapter 4).
3 Improper or damaged spark plugs or wires (Chapter 1).
4 Knock sensor defective (Chapter 6).
5 EGR valve not functioning (Chapter 6).
6 Vacuum leak (Chapters 2 and 4).

17 Engine runs with oil pressure light on

1 Low oil level (Chapter 1).
2 Idle rpm below specification (Chapter 1).
3 Short in wiring circuit (Chapter 12).
4 Faulty oil pressure sender (Chapter 2).
5 Worn engine bearings and/or oil pump (Chapter 2).

18 Engine continues to run after switching off

Defective ignition switch (Chapter 12).

ENGINE ELECTRICAL SYSTEMS

19 Battery will not hold a charge

1 Drivebelt or tensioner defective (Chapter 1).
2 Battery electrolyte level low (Chapter 1).
3 Battery terminals loose or corroded (Chapter 1).
4 Alternator not charging properly (Chapter 5).
5 Loose, broken or faulty wiring in the charging circuit (Chapter 5).
6 Short in vehicle wiring (Chapter 12).
7 Internally defective battery (Chapters 1 and 5).

20 Alternator light fails to go out

1 Faulty alternator or charging circuit (Chapter 5).
2 Drivebelt or tensioner defective (Chapter 1).

21 Alternator light fails to come on when key is turned on

1 Instrument cluster defective (Chapter 12).
2 Fault in the Smart Junction Box or wiring harness (Chapter 12).

FUEL SYSTEM

22 Excessive fuel consumption

1 Dirty air filter element (Chapter 1).
2 Emissions system not functioning properly (Chapter 6).
3 Fuel injection system not functioning properly (Chapter 4).
4 Low tire pressure or incorrect tire size (Chapter 1).

23 Fuel leakage and/or fuel odor

1 Leaking fuel line (Chapters 1 and 4).
2 Tank overfilled.
3 Evaporative emissions control system problem (Chapters 1 and 6).
4 Problem with the fuel injection system (Chapter 4).

COOLING SYSTEM

24 Overheating

1 Insufficient coolant in system (Chapter 1).
2 Water pump drivebelt defective or out of adjustment (Chapter 1).
3 Radiator core blocked or grille restricted (Chapter 3).
4 Thermostat faulty (Chapter 3).
5 Electric coolant fan inoperative or blades broken (Chapter 3).
6 Expansion tank cap not maintaining proper pressure (Chapter 3).

25 Overcooling

1 Faulty thermostat (Chapter 3).
2 Inaccurate temperature gauge sending unit (Chapter 3).

26 External coolant leakage

1 Deteriorated/damaged hoses; loose clamps (Chapters 1 and 3).
2 Water pump defective (Chapter 3).
3 Leakage from radiator core or coolant reservoir (Chapter 3).
4 Engine drain or water jacket core plugs leaking (Chapter 2).

27 Internal coolant leakage

1 Leaking cylinder head gasket (Chapter 2).
2 Cracked cylinder bore or cylinder head (Chapter 2).

28 Coolant loss

1 Too much coolant in reservoir (Chapter 1).
2 Coolant boiling away because of overheating (Chapter 3).
3 Internal or external leakage (Chapter 3).
4 Faulty radiator cap (Chapter 3).

29 Poor coolant circulation

1 Inoperative water pump (Chapter 3).
2 Restriction in cooling system (Chapters 1 and 3).
3 Drivebelt or tensioner defective (Chapter 1).
4 Thermostat sticking (Chapter 3).

CLUTCH

30 Pedal travels to floor - no pressure or very little resistance

1 Master or release cylinder faulty (Chapter 8).
2 Hose/pipe burst or leaking (Chapter 8).
3 Connections leaking (Chapter 8).
4 No fluid in reservoir (Chapter 8).
5 If fluid level in reservoir rises as pedal is depressed, master cylinder center valve seal is faulty (Chapter 8).
6 If there is fluid on dust seal at master cylinder, piston primary seal is leaking (Chapter 8).
7 Broken release bearing or fork (Chapter 8).
8 Faulty pressure plate diaphragm spring (Chapter 8).

31 Fluid in area of master cylinder dust cover and on pedal

Rear seal failure in master cylinder (Chapter 8).

32 Fluid on release cylinder

Release cylinder plunger seal faulty (Chapter 8).

33 Pedal feels spongy when depressed

Air in system (Chapter 8).

34 Unable to select gears

1 Faulty transaxle (Chapter 7).
2 Faulty clutch disc or pressure plate (Chapter 8).
3 Faulty release lever or release bearing (Chapter 8).
4 Faulty shift lever assembly or control cables (Chapter 8).

35 Clutch slips (engine speed increases with no increase in vehicle speed)

1 Clutch plate worn (Chapter 8).
2 Clutch plate is oil soaked by leaking rear main seal (Chapters 2 and 8).
3 Clutch plate not seated (Chapter 8).
4 Warped pressure plate or flywheel (Chapter 8).
5 Weak diaphragm springs (Chapter 8).
6 Clutch plate overheated. Allow to cool.

36 Grabbing (chattering) as clutch is engaged

1 Oil on clutch plate lining, burned or glazed facings (Chapter 8).
2 Worn or loose engine or transaxle mounts (Chapter 2).
3 Worn splines on clutch plate hub (Chapter 8).
4 Warped pressure plate or flywheel (Chapter 8).
5 Burned or smeared resin on flywheel or pressure plate (Chapter 8).

37 Transaxle rattling (clicking)

1 Release lever loose (Chapter 8).
2 Clutch plate damper spring failure (Chapter 8).

38 Noise in clutch area

1 Fork shaft improperly installed (Chapter 8).
2 Faulty bearing (Chapter 8).

39 Clutch pedal stays on floor

1 Clutch master cylinder piston binding in bore (Chapter 8).
2 Broken release bearing or fork (Chapter 8).

40 High pedal effort

1 Piston binding in bore (Chapter 8).
2 Pressure plate faulty (Chapter 8).
3 Incorrect size master or release cylinder (Chapter 8).

MANUAL TRANSAXLE

41 Knocking noise at low speeds

1 Worn driveaxle constant velocity (CV) joints (Chapter 8).
2 Worn side gear shaft counterbore in differential case (Chapter 7A).*

42 Noise most pronounced when turning

Differential gear noise (Chapter 7A).*

43 Clunk on acceleration or deceleration

1 Loose engine or transaxle mounts (Chapter 2).
2 Worn differential pinion shaft in case.*
3 Worn side gear shaft counterbore in differential case (Chapter 7A).*
4 Worn or damaged driveaxle inboard CV joints (Chapter 8).

44 Clicking noise in turns

Worn or damaged outboard CV joint (Chapter 8).

45 Vibration

1 Rough wheel bearing (Chapter 10).
2 Damaged driveaxle (Chapter 8).
3 Out-of-round tires (Chapter 1).
4 Tire out of balance (Chapters 1 and 10).
5 Worn CV joint (Chapter 8).

46 Noisy in neutral with engine running

1 Damaged input gear bearing (Chapter 7A).*
2 Damaged clutch release bearing (Chapter 8).

47 Noisy in one particular gear

1 Damaged or worn constant mesh gears (Chapter 7A).*
2 Damaged or worn synchronizers (Chapter 7A).*
3 Bent reverse fork (Chapter 7A).*
4 Damaged fourth speed gear or output gear (Chapter 7A).*
5 Worn or damaged reverse idler gear or idler bushing (Chapter 7A).*

48 Noisy in all gears

1 Insufficient lubricant (Chapter 7A).
2 Damaged or worn bearings (Chapter 7A).*
3 Worn or damaged input gear shaft and/or output gear shaft (Chapter 7A).*

49 Slips out of gear

1 Worn or improperly adjusted linkage (Chapter 7A).
2 Shift linkage does not work freely, binds (Chapter 7A).
3 Input gear bearing retainer broken or loose (Chapter 7A).*
4 Worn or bent shift fork (Chapter 7A).*

50 Leaks lubricant

1 Side gear shaft seals worn (Chapter 7).
2 Excessive amount of lubricant in transaxle (Chapters 1 and 7A).
3 Loose or broken input gear shaft bearing retainer (Chapter 7A).*
4 Input gear bearing retainer O-ring and/or lip seal damaged (Chapter 7A).*

51 Locked in gear

Lock pin or interlock pin missing (Chapter 7A).*

** Although the corrective action necessary to remedy the symptoms described is beyond the scope of this manual, the above information should be helpful in isolating the cause of the condition so that the owner can communicate clearly with a professional mechanic.*

AUTOMATIC TRANSAXLE

➡Note: Due to the complexity of the automatic transaxle, it is difficult for the home mechanic to properly diagnose and service this component. For problems other than the following, the vehicle should be taken to a dealer or transmission shop.

52 Fluid leakage

1 Automatic transaxle fluid is a deep red color. Fluid leaks should not be confused with engine oil, which can easily be blown onto the transaxle by air flow.

2 To pinpoint a leak, first remove all built-up dirt and grime from the transaxle housing with degreasing agents and/or steam cleaning. Then drive the vehicle at low speeds so air flow will not blow the leak far from its source. Raise the vehicle and determine where the leak is coming from. Common areas of leakage are:

a) *Dipstick tube (Chapters 1 and 7).*
b) *Transaxle oil lines (Chapter 7).*
c) *Speed sensor (Chapter 6).*
d) *Driveaxle oil seals (Chapter 7).*

53 Transaxle fluid brown or has a burned smell

Transaxle fluid overheated (Chapter 1).

54 General shift mechanism problems

1 Chapter 7, Part B, deals with checking and adjusting the shift linkage on automatic transaxles. Common problems which may be attributed to poorly adjusted linkage are:

a) Engine starting in gears other than Park or Neutral.
b) Indicator on shifter pointing to a gear other than the one actually being used.
c) Vehicle moves when in Park.

2 Refer to Chapter 7B for the shift linkage adjustment procedure.

55 Transaxle slips, shifts roughly, is noisy or has no drive in forward or reverse gears

There are many probable causes for the above problems, but the home mechanic should be concerned with only one possibility - fluid level. Before taking the vehicle to a repair shop, check the level and condition of the fluid as described in Chapter 1. Correct the fluid level as necessary or change the fluid and filter if needed. If the problem persists, have a professional diagnose the cause.

DRIVEAXLES

56 Clicking noise in turns

Worn or damaged outboard CV joint (Chapter 8).

57 Shudder or vibration during acceleration

1 Excessive toe-in (Chapter 10).
2 Worn or damaged inboard or outboard CV joints (Chapter 8).
3 Sticking inboard CV joint assembly (Chapter 8).

58 Vibration at highway speeds

1 Out-of-balance front wheels and/or tires (Chapters 1 and 10).
2 Out-of-round front tires (Chapters 1 and 10).
3 Worn CV joint(s) (Chapter 8).

BRAKES

➡**Note: Before assuming that a brake problem exists, make sure that:**

a) The tires are in good condition and properly inflated (Chapter 1).
b) The front end alignment is correct.
c) The vehicle is not loaded with weight in an unequal manner.

59 Vehicle pulls to one side during braking

1 Incorrect tire pressures (Chapter 1).
2 Front end out of alignment (have the front end aligned).
3 Front, or rear, tire sizes not matched to one another.
4 Restricted brake lines or hoses (Chapter 9).
5 Malfunctioning caliper assembly (Chapter 9).
6 Loose suspension parts (Chapter 10).
7 Excessive wear of pad material or disc on one side (Chapter 9).
8 Contamination (grease or brake fluid) of brake pad material or disc on one side (Chapter 9).

60 Noise (high-pitched squeal when the brakes are applied)

Brake pads worn out. Replace pads with new ones immediately (Chapter 9).

61 Brake roughness or chatter (pedal pulsates)

1 Excessive lateral runout (Chapter 9).
2 Uneven pad wear (Chapter 9).
3 Defective disc (Chapter 9).

62 Excessive brake pedal effort required to stop vehicle

1 Malfunctioning power brake booster (Chapter 9).
2 Partial system failure (Chapter 9).
3 Excessively worn pads (Chapter 9).
4 Piston in caliper stuck or sluggish (Chapter 9).
5 Brake pads contaminated with oil or grease (Chapter 9).
6 Brake disc grooved and/or glazed (Chapter 9).

63 Excessive brake pedal travel

1 Partial brake system failure (Chapter 9).
2 Insufficient fluid in master cylinder (Chapters 1 and 9).
3 Air trapped in system (Chapter 9).

64 Dragging brakes

1 Incorrect adjustment of brake light switch (Chapter 9).
2 Master cylinder pistons not returning correctly (Chapter 9).
3 Caliper piston stuck (Chapter 9).
3 Restricted brakes lines or hoses (Chapter 9).
4 Incorrect parking brake adjustment (Chapter 9).

65 Grabbing or uneven braking action

1 Malfunction of proportioning valve (Chapter 9).
2 Binding brake pedal mechanism (Chapter 9).
3 Contaminated brake linings (Chapter 9).

66 Brake pedal feels spongy when depressed

1 Air in hydraulic lines (Chapter 9).
2 Master cylinder mounting bolts loose (Chapter 9).
3 Master cylinder defective (Chapter 9).

67 Brake pedal travels to the floor with little resistance

1 Little or no fluid in the master cylinder reservoir caused by leaking caliper piston(s) (Chapter 9).
2 Loose, damaged or disconnected brake lines (Chapter 9).

68 Parking brake does not hold

Parking brake improperly adjusted (Chapter 9).

SUSPENSION AND STEERING SYSTEMS

➡Note: Before attempting to diagnose the suspension and steering systems, perform the following preliminary checks:

a) Tires for wrong pressure and uneven wear.
b) Steering universal joints from the column to the rack and pin ion for loose connectors or wear.
c) Front and rear suspension and the rack-and-pinion assembly for loose or damaged parts.
d) Out-of-round or out-of-balance tires, bent rims and loose and/or rough wheel bearings.

69 Vehicle pulls to one side

1 Mismatched or uneven tires (Chapter 10).
2 Broken or sagging springs (Chapter 10).
3 Wheel alignment incorrect. Have the wheels professionally aligned.
4 Front brake dragging (Chapter 9).

70 Abnormal or excessive tire wear

1 Wheel alignment out-of-specification. Have the wheels aligned.
2 Sagging or broken springs (Chapter 10).
3 Tire out-of-balance (Chapter 10).
4 Worn strut damper (Chapter 10).
5 Overloaded vehicle.
6 Tires not rotated regularly.

71 Wheel makes a thumping noise

1 Blister or bump on tire (Chapter 10).
2 Improper strut damper action (Chapter 10).

72 Shimmy, shake or vibration

1 Tire or wheel out-of-balance or out-of-round (Chapter 10).
2 Loose or worn wheel bearings (Chapter 10).
3 Worn tie-rod ends (Chapter 10).
4 Worn balljoints (Chapters 1 and 10).
5 Excessive wheel runout (Chapter 10).
6 Blister or bump on tire (Chapter 10).

73 Hard steering

1 Lack of lubrication at balljoints and/or tie-rod ends (Chapter 10).
2 Wheel alignment out-of-specifications. Have the wheels professionally aligned.
3 Low tire pressure(s) (Chapter 1).
4 Worn steering gear (Chapter 10).

74 Poor returnability of steering to center

1 Worn balljoints or tie-rod ends (Chapter 10).
2 Worn steering gear assembly (Chapter 10).
3 Wheel alignment out-of-specifications. Have the wheels professionally aligned.

75 Abnormal noise at the front end

1 Worn balljoints or tie-rod ends (Chapter 10).
2 Damaged shock absorber mounting (Chapter 10).
3 Worn control arm bushings or tie-rod ends (Chapter 10).
4 Loose stabilizer bar (Chapter 10).
5 Loose wheel nuts (Chapter 1).
6 Loose suspension bolts (Chapter 10).

76 Wander or poor steering stability

1 Mismatched or uneven tires (Chapter 10).
2 Lack of lubrication at balljoints and tie-rod ends (Chapters 1 and 10).
3 Worn shock absorber assemblies (Chapter 10).
4 Loose stabilizer bar (Chapter 10).
5 Broken or sagging springs (Chapter 10).
6 Wheels out of alignment. Have the wheels professionally aligned.

77 Erratic steering when braking

1 Wheel bearings worn (Chapter 10).
2 Broken or sagging springs (Chapter 10).
3 Leaking wheel cylinder or caliper (Chapter 10).
4 Excessive brake disc runout (Chapter 9).

78 Excessive pitching and/or rolling around corners or during braking

1 Loose stabilizer bar (Chapter 10).
2 Worn strut dampers or mountings (Chapter 10).
3 Broken or sagging springs (Chapter 10).
4 Overloaded vehicle.

79 Suspension bottoms

1 Overloaded vehicle.
2 Sagging springs (Chapter 10).

80 Cupped tires

1 Front wheel or rear wheel alignment out-of-specifications. Have the wheels professionally aligned.
2 Worn shock absorbers (Chapter 10).
3 Wheel bearings worn (Chapter 10).
4 Excessive tire or wheel runout (Chapter 10).
5 Worn balljoints (Chapter 10).

81 Excessive tire wear on outside edge

1 Inflation pressures incorrect (Chapter 1).
2 Excessive speed in turns.
3 Wheel alignment incorrect (excessive toe-in). Have professionally aligned.
4 Suspension arm bent or twisted (Chapter 10).

82 Excessive tire wear on inside edge

1 Inflation pressures incorrect (Chapter 1).
2 Wheel alignment incorrect (toe-out). Have professionally aligned.
3 Loose or damaged steering components (Chapter 10).

83 Tire tread worn in one place

1 Tires out-of-balance.
2 Damaged or buckled wheel. Inspect and replace if necessary.
3 Defective tire (Chapter 1).

84 Excessive play or looseness in steering system

1 Wheel bearing(s) worn (Chapter 10).
2 Tie-rod end loose (Chapter 10).
3 Steering gear loose (Chapter 10).
4 Worn or loose steering intermediate shaft U-joint (Chapter 10).

85 Rattling or clicking noise in steering gear

1 Steering gear loose (Chapter 10).
2 Steering gear defective.

1 TUNE-UP AND ROUTINE MAINTENANCE

1 Maintenance schedule

The maintenance intervals in this manual are provided with the assumption that you, not the dealer, will be doing the work. These are the minimum maintenance intervals recommended by the factory for vehicles that are driven daily. If you wish to keep your vehicle in peak condition at all times, you may wish to perform some of these procedures even more often. Because frequent maintenance enhances the efficiency, performance and resale value of your car, we encourage you to do so. If you drive in dusty areas, tow a trailer, idle or drive at low speeds for extended periods or drive for short distances (less than four miles) in below freezing temperatures, shorter intervals are also recommended.

When your vehicle is new, it should be serviced by a factory authorized dealer service department to protect the factory warranty. In many cases, the initial maintenance check is done at no cost to the owner.

EVERY 250 MILES OR WEEKLY, WHICHEVER COMES FIRST

Check the engine oil level (Section 4)
Check the engine coolant level (Section 4)
Check the brake and clutch fluid level (Section 4)
Check the windshield washer fluid level (Section 4)
Check the power steering fluid level (Section 4)
Check the automatic transaxle fluid level (Section 4)
Check the tires and tire pressures (Section 5)

EVERY 3000 MILES OR 3 MONTHS, WHICHEVER COMES FIRST

All items listed above plus:
Change the engine oil and oil filter (Section 6)

EVERY 7500 MILES OR 6 MONTHS, WHICHEVER COMES FIRST

All items listed above plus:
Inspect (and replace, if necessary) the windshield wiper blades (Section 7)
Check and service the battery (Section 8)
Check the cooling system (Section 9)
Rotate the tires (Section 10)
Check the seat belts (Section 11)

EVERY 15,000 MILES OR 12 MONTHS, WHICHEVER COMES FIRST

All items listed above plus:
Check all underhood hoses (Section 12)
Inspect the brake system (Section 13)*
Inspect the suspension, steering and driveaxle boots (Section 14)*
Check the fuel system (Section 15)
Check the manual transaxle lubricant level (Section 16)
Check the transfer case lubricant level (AWD models) (Section 17)
Check (and replace, if necessary) the air filter (Section 18)*
Replace the cabin air filter (Section 19)

EVERY 30,000 MILES OR 24 MONTHS, WHICHEVER COMES FIRST

All items listed above plus:
Check the exhaust system (Section 20)
Service the cooling system (drain, flush and refill) (Section 21)
Change the brake fluid (Section 22)
Check/adjust the engine drivebelts (Section 23)

EVERY 60,000 MILES OR 48 MONTHS, WHICHEVER COMES FIRST

Replace the automatic transaxle fluid (Section 24)**
Replace the manual transaxle lubricant (Section 25)
Replace the rear differential lubricant (AWD) (Section 26)
Check (and replace, if necessary) the spark plugs (conventional, non-platinum or iridium type) (Section 28)

EVERY 100,000 MILES

Replace the spark plugs (platinum-tipped type) (Section 29)

**This item is affected by "severe" operating conditions as described below. If your vehicle is operated under "severe" conditions, perform all maintenance indicated with an asterisk (*) at 3000 mile/3 month intervals. Severe conditions are indicated if you mainly operate your vehicle under one or more of the following conditions:*
Operating in dusty areas
Towing a trailer
Idling for extended periods and/or low speed operation
Operating when outside temperatures remain below freezing and when most trips are less than 4 miles

*** If operated under one or more of the following conditions, change the manual or automatic transaxle fluid and differential lubricant every 30,000 miles:*
Operating in dusty areas
In heavy city traffic where the outside temperature regularly reaches 90-degrees F (32-degrees C) or higher
In hilly or mountainous terrain
On flex-fuel models, using E85 fuel more than 50% of the time

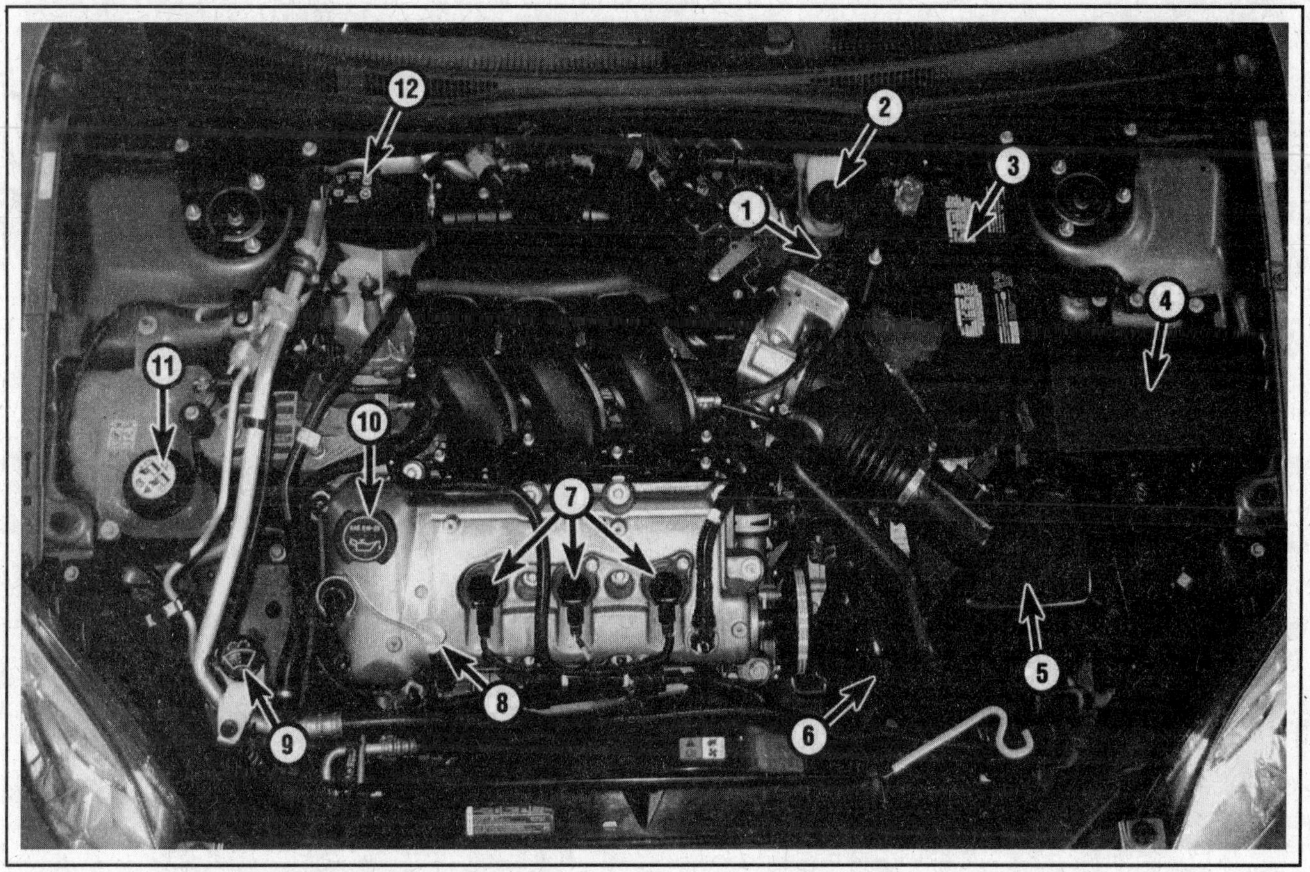

Typical engine compartment components (V6 engine)

1. Automatic transaxle fluid dipstick
2. Brake fluid reservoir
3. Battery
4. Fuse/relay block
5. Air filter housing
6. Radiator hose
7. Front cylinder bank spark plugs (under ignition coils)
8. Engine oil dipstick
9. Windshield washer fluid reservoir
10. Engine oil filler cap
11. Coolant expansion tank
12. Power steering fluid reservoir

Typical engine compartment underside components (V6 engine)

1 *Engine oil filter*
2 *Driveaxle boot*
3 *Front disc brake caliper*
4 *Engine oil drain plug*
5 *Automatic transaxle drain plug*
6 *Exhaust system*

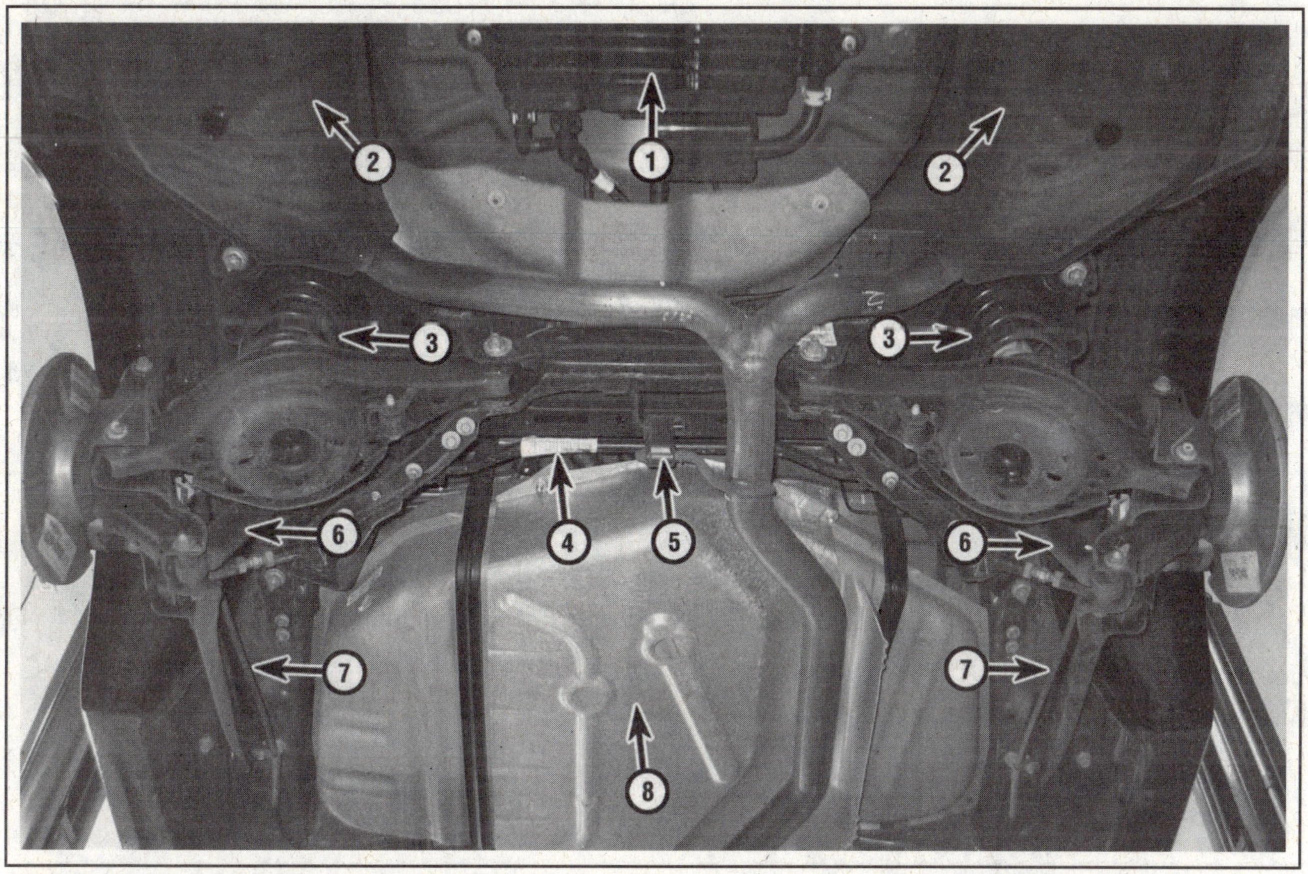

Typical rear underside components (2WD)

1 *EVAP canister*
2 *Mufflers*
3 *Coil springs*
4 *Stabilizer bar*
5 *Exhaust system hanger*
6 *Shock absorbers*
7 *Parking brake cables*
8 *Fuel tank*

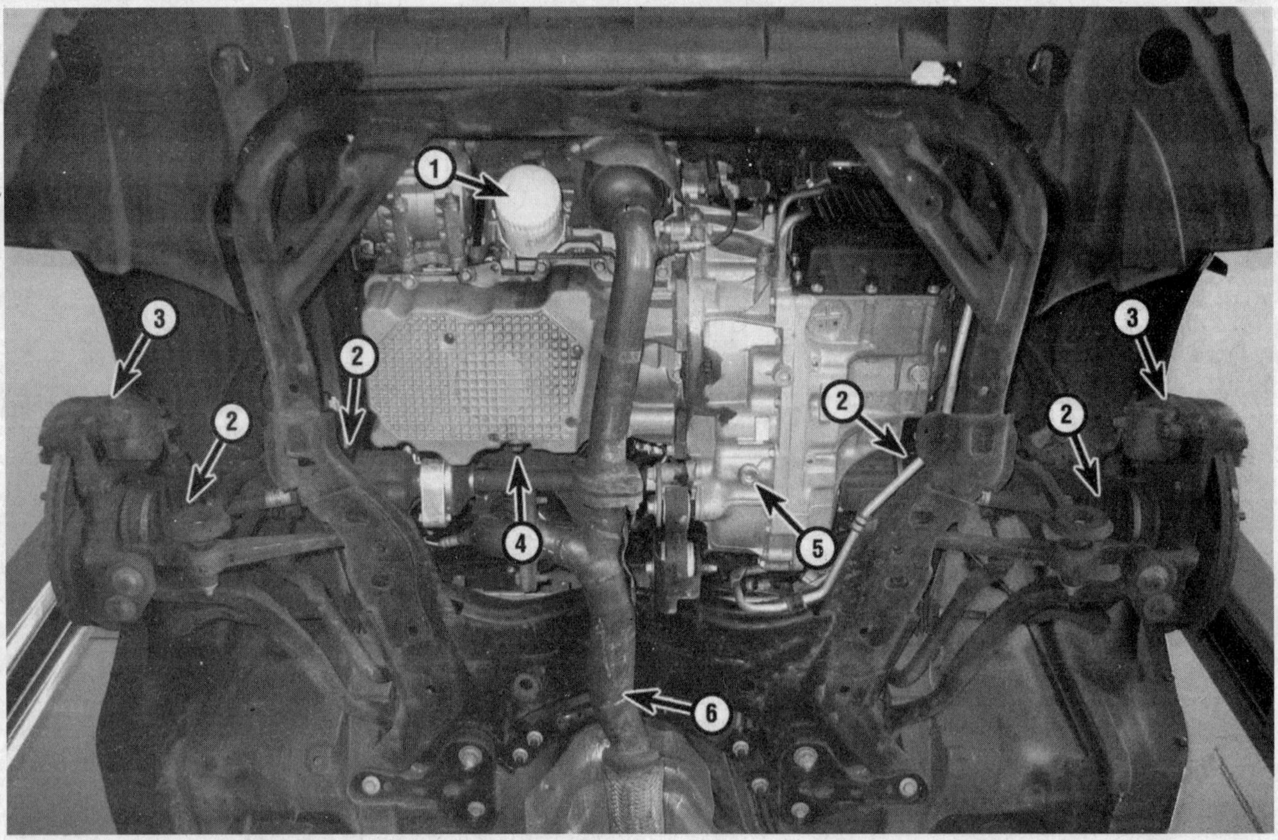

Typical engine compartment components (four-cylinder engine)

1 *Automatic transaxle fluid dipstick*
2 *Brake fluid reservoir*
3 *Battery*
4 *Fuse/relay block*
5 *Air filter housing*
6 *Radiator hose*
7 *Engine oil dipstick*
8 *Drivebelt*
9 *Windshield washer fluid reservoir*
10 *Coolant expansion tank*
11 *Engine oil filler cap*
12 *Spark plugs (under ignition coils)*

2 Introduction

This Chapter is designed to help the home mechanic maintain the Ford Fusion or Mercury Milan with the goals of maximum performance, economy, safety and reliability in mind.

Included is a master maintenance schedule, followed by procedures dealing specifically with each item on the schedule. Visual checks, adjustments, component replacement and other helpful items are included. Refer to the accompanying illustrations of the engine compartment and the underside of the vehicle for the locations of various components.

Servicing the vehicle, in accordance with the mileage/time maintenance schedule and the step-by-step procedures will result in a planned maintenance program that should produce a long and reliable service life. Keep in mind that it is a comprehensive plan, so maintaining some items but not others at the specified intervals will not produce the same results.

As you service the vehicle, you will discover that many of the procedures can - and should - be grouped together because of the nature of the particular procedure you're performing or because of the close proximity of two otherwise unrelated components to one another.

For example, if the vehicle is raised for chassis lubrication, you should inspect the exhaust, suspension, steering and fuel systems while you're under the vehicle. When you're rotating the tires, it makes good sense to check the brakes since the wheels are already removed. Finally, let's suppose you have to borrow or rent a torque wrench. Even if you only need it to tighten the spark plugs, you might as well check the torque of as many critical fasteners as time allows.

The first step in this maintenance program is to prepare yourself before the actual work begins. Read through all the procedures you're planning to do, then gather up all the parts and tools needed. If it looks like you might run into problems during a particular job, seek advice from a mechanic or an experienced do-it-yourselfer.

OWNER'S MANUAL AND VECI LABEL INFORMATION

Your vehicle owner's manual was written for your year and model and contains very specific information on component locations, specifications, fuse ratings, part numbers, etc. The Owner's Manual is an important resource for the do-it-yourselfer to have; if one was not supplied with your vehicle, it can generally be ordered from a dealer parts department.

Among other important information, the Vehicle Emissions Control Information (VECI) label contains specifications and procedures for applicable tune-up adjustments and, in some instances, spark plugs (see Chapter 6 for more information on the VECI label). The information on this label is the exact maintenance data recommended by the manufacturer. This data often varies by intended operating altitude, local emissions regulations, month of manufacture, etc.

This Chapter contains procedural details, safety information and more ambitious maintenance intervals than you might find in manufacturer's literature. However, you may also find procedures or specifications in your Owner's Manual or VECI label that differ with what's printed here. In these cases, the Owner's Manual or VECI label can be considered correct, since it is specific to your particular vehicle.

3 Tune-up general information

The term tune-up is used in this manual to represent a combination of individual operations rather than one specific procedure.

If, from the time the vehicle is new, the routine maintenance schedule is followed closely and frequent checks are made of fluid levels and high wear items, as suggested throughout this manual, the engine will be kept in relatively good running condition and the need for additional work will be minimized.

More likely than not, however, there will be times when the engine is running poorly due to lack of regular maintenance. This is even more likely if a used vehicle, which has not received regular and frequent maintenance checks, is purchased. In such cases, an engine tune-up will be needed outside of the regular routine maintenance intervals.

The first step in any tune-up or diagnostic procedure to help correct a poor running engine is a cylinder compression check. A compression check (see Chapter 2C) will help determine the condition of internal engine components and should be used as a guide for tune-up and repair procedures. If, for instance, a compression check indicates serious internal engine wear, a conventional tune-up will not improve the performance of the engine and would be a waste of time and money. Because of its importance, the compression check should be done by someone with the proper equipment and the knowledge to use it properly.

The following procedures are those most often needed to bring a generally poor running engine back into a proper state of tune.

MINOR TUNE-UP

Check all engine related fluids (Section 4)
Clean, inspect and test the battery (Section 8)
Check the cooling system (Section 9)
Check all underhood hoses (Section 12)
Check the fuel system (Section 15)
Check the air filter (Section 18)
Check the drivebelt (Section 23)

MAJOR TUNE-UP

All items listed under Minor tune-up, plus . . .

Replace the air filter (Section 18)
Replace the PCV valve (Section 28)
Replace the spark plugs (Section 29)

4 Fluid level checks (every 250 miles or weekly)

1 Fluids are an essential part of the lubrication, cooling, brake and windshield washer systems. Because the fluids gradually become depleted and/or contaminated during normal operation of the vehicle, they must be periodically replenished. See *Recommended lubricants and fluids* in this Chapter's Specifications before adding fluid to any of the following components.

➡**Note: The vehicle must be on level ground when fluid levels are checked.**

ENGINE OIL

Refer to illustrations 4.2a, 4.2b and 4.4

2 The oil level is checked with a dipstick, which is attached to the engine block (see illustrations). The dipstick extends through a metal tube down into the oil pan.

3 The oil level should be checked before the vehicle has been driven, or about 5 minutes after the engine has been shut off. If the oil is checked immediately after driving the vehicle, some of the oil will remain in the upper part of the engine, resulting in an inaccurate reading on the dipstick.

4 Pull the dipstick out of the tube and wipe all the oil from the end with a clean rag or paper towel. Insert the clean dipstick all the way back into the tube and pull it out again. Note the oil at the end of the dipstick. At its highest point, the level should be between the MIN and MAX marks on the dipstick (see illustration).

5 It takes one quart of oil to raise the level from the MIN mark to the MAX mark on the dipstick. Do not allow the level to drop below the MIN mark or oil starvation may cause engine damage. Conversely, overfilling the engine (adding oil above the MAX mark) may cause oil fouled spark plugs, oil leaks or oil seal failures. Maintaining the oil level above the MAX mark can cause excessive oil consumption.

6 To add oil, remove the filler cap from the valve cover (see illustration 4.2a). After adding oil, wait a few minutes to allow the level to stabilize, then pull out the dipstick and check the level again. Add more oil if required. Install the filler cap and tighten it by hand only.

7 Checking the oil level is an important preventive maintenance step. A consistently low oil level indicates oil leakage through damaged seals, defective gaskets or past worn rings or valve guides. If the oil looks milky in color or has water droplets in it, the cylinder head gasket(s) may be blown or the head(s) or block may be cracked. The engine should be checked immediately. The condition of the oil should also be checked. Whenever you check the oil level, slide your thumb and index finger up the dipstick before wiping off the oil. If you see small dirt or metal particles clinging to the dipstick, the oil should be changed (see Section 6).

ENGINE COOLANT

Refer to illustrations 4.8 and 4.9

WARNING:

Do not allow antifreeze to come in contact with your skin or painted surfaces of the vehicle. Flush contaminated areas immediately with plenty of water. Don't store new coolant or leave old coolant lying around where it's accessible to children or pets - they're attracted by its sweet smell. Ingestion of even a small amount of coolant can be fatal! Wipe up garage floor and drip pan spills immediately. Keep antifreeze containers covered and repair cooling system leaks as soon as they're noticed.

8 All vehicles covered by this manual are equipped with a pressurized coolant recovery system. A plastic expansion tank located at the right front corner of the engine compartment is connected by hoses to the cooling system (see illustration). As the engine heats up during operation, the expanding coolant fills the tank.

9 The coolant level in the tank should be checked regularly.

WARNING:

Do not remove the expansion tank cap to check the coolant level when the engine is warm!

The level in the tank varies with the temperature of the engine. When the engine is cold, the coolant level should be at the COLD FULL mark on the reservoir. If it isn't, remove the cap from the tank and add a 50/50 mixture of ethylene glycol-based antifreeze and water (see illustration).

4.2a Engine oil dipstick (A) and oil filler cap (B) locations - 3.0L V6

4.2b Engine oil dipstick (A) and oil filler cap (B) locations - 2.5L four-cylinder engine

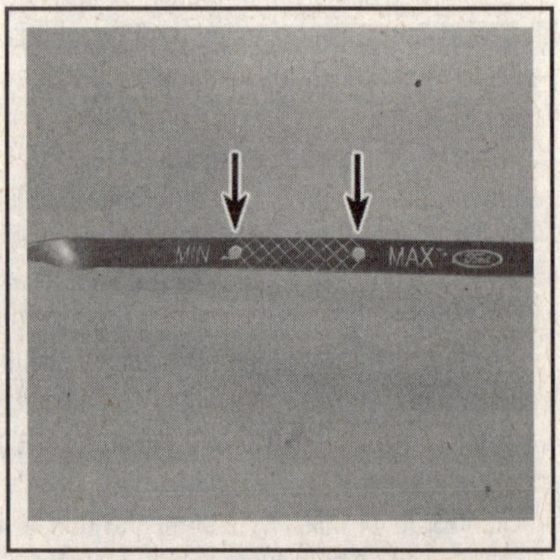

4.4 The oil level should be in the safe range - if it's below the MIN or ADD mark, add enough oil to bring it up to or near the MAX or FULL mark

10 Drive the vehicle, let the engine cool completely then recheck the coolant level. Don't use rust inhibitors or additives. If only a small amount of coolant is required to bring the system up to the proper level, water can be used. However, repeated additions of water will dilute the antifreeze and water solution. In order to maintain the proper ratio of antifreeze and water, always top up the coolant level with the correct mixture. An empty plastic milk jug or bleach bottle makes an excellent container for mixing coolant.

11 If the coolant level drops consistently, there may be a leak in the system. Inspect the radiator, hoses, filler cap, drain plugs and water pump (see Section 9). If no leaks are noted, have the expansion tank cap pressure tested by a service station.

12 If you have to remove the expansion tank cap wait until the engine has cooled completely, then wrap a thick cloth around the cap and unscrew it slowly, stopping if you hear a hissing noise. If coolant or steam escapes, let the engine cool down longer, then remove the cap.

13 Check the condition of the coolant as well. If it's brown or rust colored, the system should be drained, flushed and refilled. Even if the coolant appears to be normal, the corrosion inhibitors wear out, so it must be replaced at the specified intervals.

BRAKE AND CLUTCH FLUID

➧ Refer to illustrations 4.14 and 4.15

14 The brake master cylinder is mounted on the front of the power booster unit in the engine compartment. The hydraulic clutch master cylinder used on manual transaxle vehicles is located next to the brake master cylinder (see illustration).

15 The brake master cylinder and the clutch master cylinder share a common reservoir. To check the fluid level of either system, simply look at the MAX and MIN marks on the brake fluid reservoir (see illustration).

16 If the level is low, wipe the top of the reservoir cover with a clean rag to prevent contamination of the brake system before lifting the cover.

17 Add only the specified brake fluid to the reservoir (refer to *Recommended lubricants and fluids* in this Chapter's Specifications or to your owner's manual). Mixing different types of brake fluid can damage the system. Fill the brake master cylinder reservoir only to the MAX line.

✱✱ WARNING:

Use caution when filling the reservoir - brake fluid can harm your eyes and damage painted surfaces. Do not use brake fluid that is more than one year old or has been left open. Brake fluid absorbs moisture from the air. Excess moisture can cause a dangerous loss of braking.

18 While the reservoir cap is removed, inspect the master cylinder reservoir for contamination. If deposits, dirt particles or water droplets are present, the system should be drained and refilled.

19 After filling the reservoir to the proper level, make sure the lid is properly seated to prevent fluid leakage.

20 The fluid in the brake master cylinder will drop slightly as the brake pads at each wheel wear down during normal operation. If the master cylinder requires repeated replenishing to keep it at the proper

4.8 The cooling system expansion tank is located at the right side of the engine compartment

4.9 When the engine is cold, the coolant level should be in the COLD FILL range

4.14 The clutch master cylinder is located next to the brake master cylinder and the two share a common reservoir

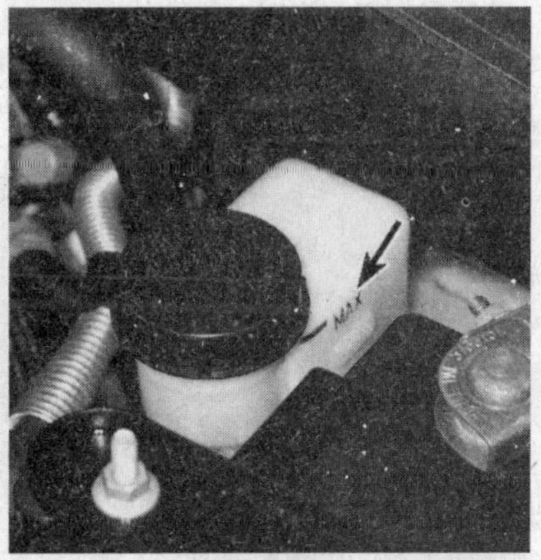

4.15 The brake fluid level should be kept between the MIN and MAX marks on the translucent plastic reservoir; the same reservoir contains the clutch fluid and is connected to the clutch master cylinder by a hose

level, this is an indication of leakage in the brake or clutch system, which should be corrected immediately. If the brake system shows an indication of leakage check all brake lines and connections, along with the calipers and booster (see Section 13 for more information). If the hydraulic clutch system shows an indication of leakage check all clutch lines and connections, along with the clutch release cylinder (see Chapter 8 for more information).

21 If, upon checking the brake or clutch master cylinder fluid level, you discover the reservoir empty or nearly empty, the systems should be bled (see Chapters 8 and 9).

WINDSHIELD WASHER FLUID

Refer to illustration 4.22

22 Fluid for the windshield washer system is stored in a plastic reservoir located at the right front of the engine compartment (see illustration).

23 In milder climates, plain water can be used in the reservoir, but it should be kept no more than 2/3 full to allow for expansion if the water freezes. In colder climates, use windshield washer system antifreeze, available at any auto parts store, to lower the freezing point of the fluid. Mix the antifreeze with water in accordance with the manufacturer's directions on the container.

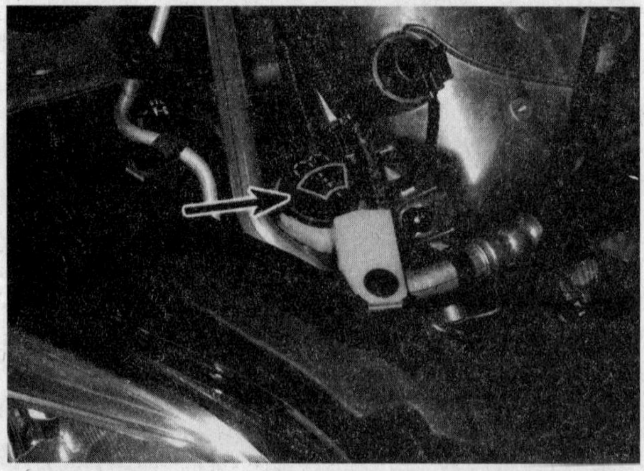

4.22 The windshield/rear window washer fluid reservoir is located in the right front corner of the engine compartment

✱✱ CAUTION:

Do not use cooling system antifreeze - it will damage the vehicle's paint.

POWER STEERING FLUID

➧ **Refer to illustrations 4.25 and 4.28**

24 Check the power steering fluid level periodically to avoid steering system problems, such as damage to the pump.

✱✱ CAUTION:

DO NOT hold the steering wheel against either stop (extreme left or right turn) for more than five seconds. If you do, the power steering pump could be damaged.

25 The power steering reservoir, located at the right side of the engine compartment (see illustration), has MIN and MAX fluid level marks on the side. The fluid level can be seen without removing the reservoir cap.

26 Park the vehicle on level ground and apply the parking brake.

27 Run the engine until it has reached normal operating temperature. With the engine at idle, turn the steering wheel back and forth about 10 times to get any air out of the steering system. Shut the engine off with the wheels in the straight-ahead position.

28 Note the fluid level on the side of the reservoir. It should be between the two marks (see illustration).

29 Add small amounts of fluid until the level is correct.

✱✱ CAUTION:

Do not overfill the reservoir. If too much fluid is added, remove the excess with a clean syringe or suction pump.

30 Check the power steering hoses and connections for leaks and wear.

4.25 The power steering fluid reservoir is located at the right rear corner of the engine compartment

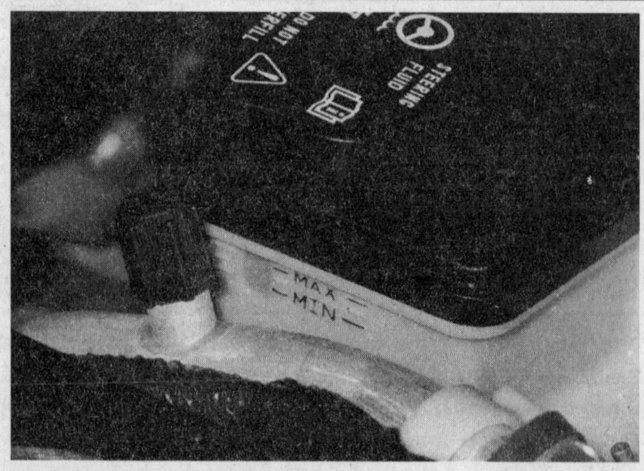

4.28 At normal operating temperature, the power steering fluid level should be between the MAX and MIN marks

4.34a The automatic transaxle dipstick is located at the left rear corner of the engine compartment, near the brake master cylinder

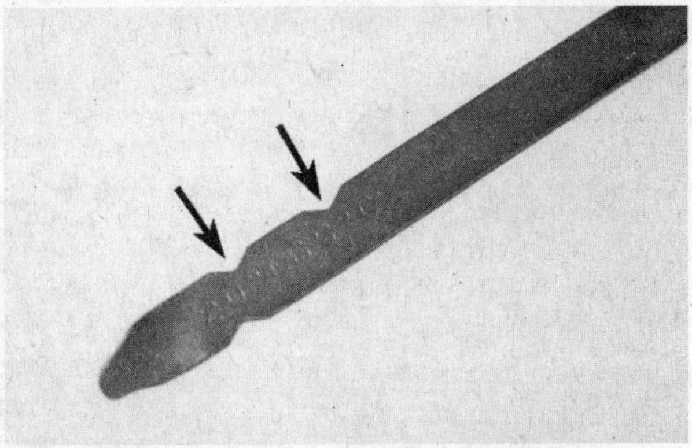

4.34b At operating temperature, the automatic transaxle fluid level should be between the notches, or in the cross-hatched area of the dipstick (depending on transaxle type)

AUTOMATIC TRANSAXLE FLUID

Refer to illustrations 4.34a and 4.34b

31 The level of the automatic transaxle fluid should be carefully maintained. Low fluid level can lead to slipping or loss of drive, while overfilling can cause foaming, loss of fluid and transaxle damage.

32 The transaxle fluid level should only be checked when the transaxle is hot (at its normal operating temperature). If the vehicle has just been driven over 10 miles (15 miles in a frigid climate), and the fluid temperature is 160 to 175-degrees F, the transaxle is hot.

CAUTION:

If the vehicle has just been driven for a long time at high speed or in city traffic in hot weather, or if it has been pulling a trailer, an accurate fluid level reading cannot be obtained. Allow the fluid to cool down for about 30 minutes.

33 If the vehicle has not just been driven, park the vehicle on level ground, set the parking brake and start the engine. While the engine is idling, depress the brake pedal and move the selector lever through all the gear ranges, beginning and ending in Park.

34 With the engine still idling, remove the dipstick from its tube (see illustration). Check the level of the fluid on the dipstick (see illustration) and note its condition.

35 Wipe the fluid from the dipstick with a clean rag and reinsert it back into the filler tube until the cap seats.

36 Pull the dipstick out again and note the fluid level. The fluid level should be in the operating temperature range. If the level is at the low side of either range, add the specified automatic transmission fluid through the dipstick tube with a funnel.

37 Add just enough of the recommended fluid to fill the transaxle to the proper level. It takes about one pint to raise the level from the low mark to the high mark when the fluid is hot, so add the fluid a little at a time and keep checking the level until it is correct.

38 The condition of the fluid should also be checked along with the level. If the fluid at the end of the dipstick is black or a dark reddish brown color, or if it emits a burned smell, the fluid should be changed (see Section 24). If you are in doubt about the condition of the fluid, purchase some new fluid and compare the two for color and smell.

5 Tire and tire pressure checks (every 250 miles or weekly)

Refer to illustrations 5.2, 5.3, 5.4a, 5.4b and 5.8

1 Periodic inspection of the tires may spare you the inconvenience of being stranded with a flat tire. It can also provide you with vital information regarding possible problems in the steering and suspension systems before major damage occurs.

2 The original tires on this vehicle are equipped with 1/2-inch wide bands that will appear when tread depth reaches 1/16-inch, at which point they can be considered worn out. Tread wear can be monitored with a simple, inexpensive device known as a tread depth indicator (see illustration).

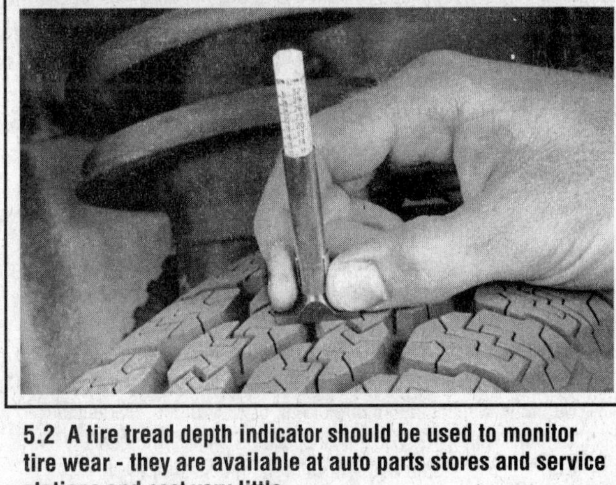

5.2 A tire tread depth indicator should be used to monitor tire wear - they are available at auto parts stores and service stations and cost very little

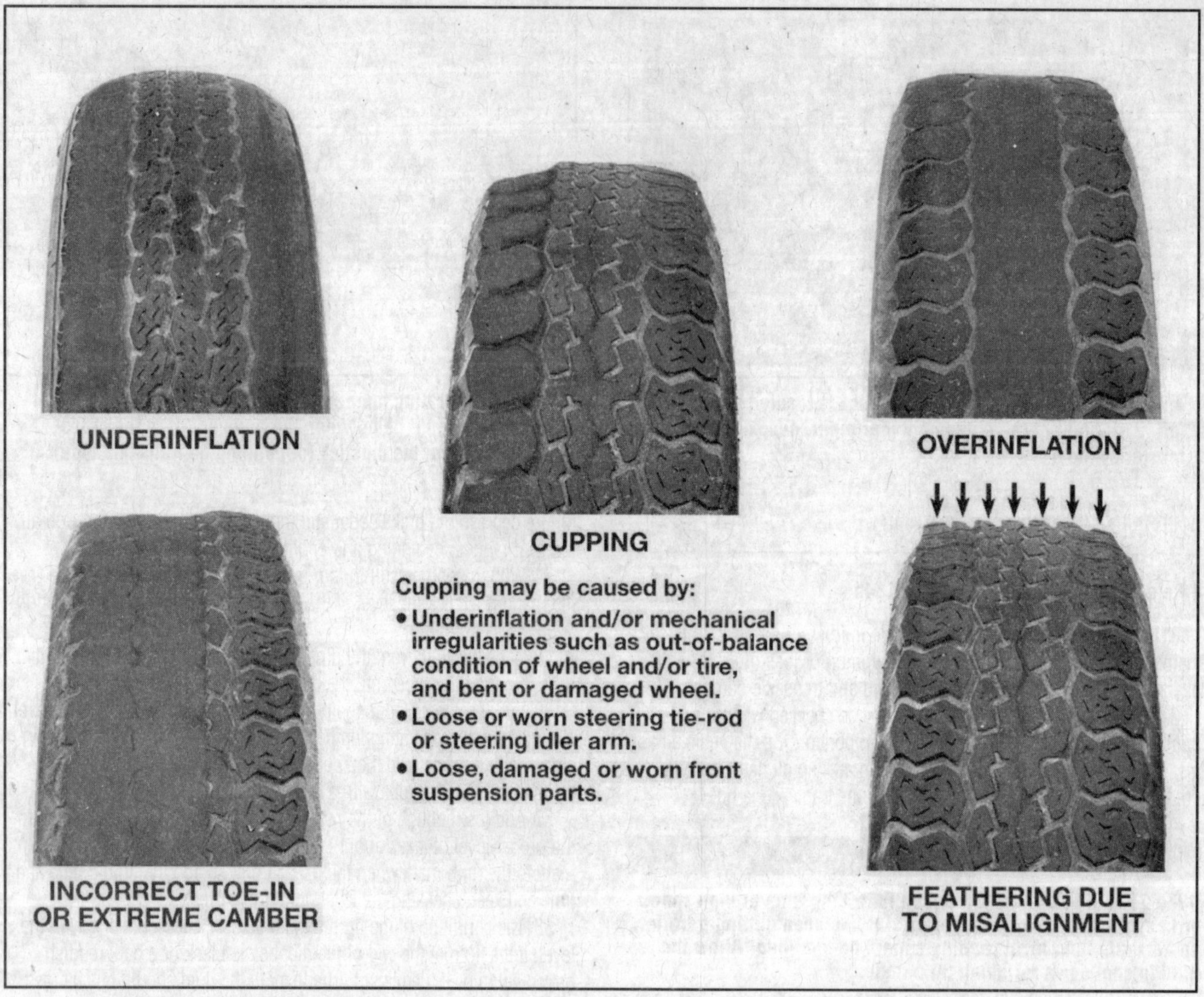

5.3 This chart will help you determine the condition of your tires, the probable cause(s) of abnormal wear and the corrective action necessary

3 Note any abnormal tread wear (see illustration). Tread pattern irregularities such as cupping, flat spots and more wear on one side than the other are indications of front end alignment and/or balance problems. If any of these conditions are noted, take the vehicle to a tire shop or service station to correct the problem.

4 Look closely for cuts, punctures and embedded nails or tacks. Sometimes a tire will hold air pressure for a short time or leak down very slowly after a nail has embedded itself in the tread. If a slow leak persists, check the valve stem core to make sure it is tight (see illustration). Examine the tread for an object that may have embedded itself in the tire or for a plug that may have begun to leak (radial tire punctures are repaired with a plug that is installed in a puncture). If a puncture is suspected, it can be easily verified by spraying a solution of soapy water onto the puncture area (see illustration). The soapy solution will bubble if there is a leak. Unless the puncture is unusually large, a tire shop or service station can usually repair the tire.

5 Carefully inspect the inner sidewall of each tire for evidence of brake fluid leakage. If you see any, inspect the brakes immediately.

6 Correct air pressure adds miles to the life span of the tires, improves mileage and enhances overall ride quality. Tire pressure cannot be accurately estimated by looking at a tire, especially if it's a radial. A tire pressure gauge is essential. Keep an accurate gauge in the glove compartment. The pressure gauges attached to the nozzles of air hoses at gas stations are often inaccurate.

7 Always check tire pressure when the tires are cold. Cold, in this case, means the vehicle has not been driven over a mile in the three hours preceding a tire pressure check. A pressure rise of four to eight pounds is not uncommon once the tires are warm.

8 Unscrew the valve cap protruding from the wheel or hubcap and push the gauge firmly onto the valve stem (see illustration). Note the reading on the gauge and compare the figure to the recommended tire pressure shown on the tire placard on the driver's side door. Be sure to reinstall the valve cap to keep dirt and moisture out of the valve stem mechanism. Check all four tires and, if necessary, add enough air to bring them up to the recommended pressure.

9 Don't forget to keep the spare tire inflated to the specified pressure (refer to the pressure molded into the tire sidewall).

5.4a If a tire loses air on a steady basis, check the valve core first to make sure it's snug (special inexpensive wrenches are commonly available at auto parts stores)

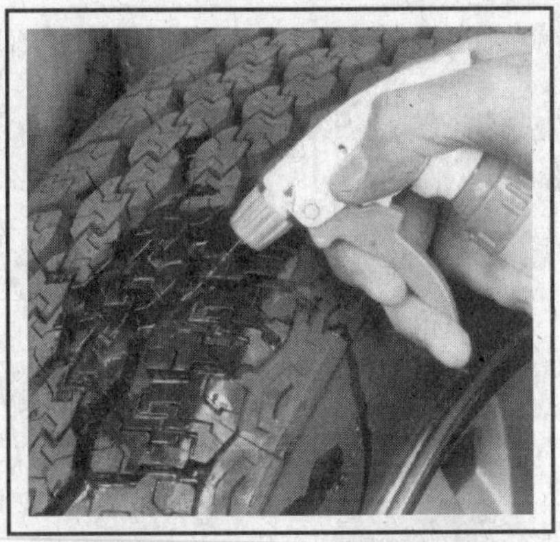

5.4b If the valve core is tight, raise the corner of the vehicle with the low tire and spray a soapy water solution onto the tread as the tire is turned slowly - slow leaks will cause small bubbles to appear

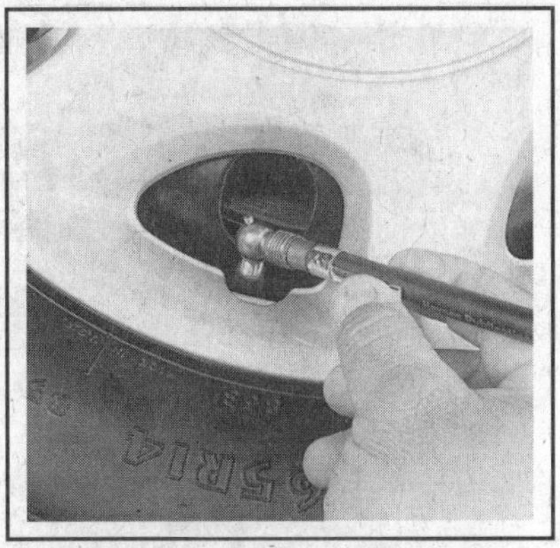

5.8 To extend the life of your tires, check the air pressure at least once a week with an accurate gauge (don't forget the spare!)

6 Engine oil and filter change (every 3000 miles or 3 months)

Refer to illustrations 6.2, 6.7, 6.12 and 6.15

Note: Some models are equipped with an oil life indicator system that illuminates a light or message on the instrument panel when the system deems it necessary to change the oil. A number of factors are taken into consideration to determine when the oil should be considered worn out. Generally, this system will allow the vehicle to accumulate more miles between oil changes than the traditional 3000-mile interval, but we believe that frequent oil changes are cheap insurance and will prolong engine life. If you do decide not to change your oil every 3000 miles and rely on the oil life indicator instead, make sure you don't exceed 7,500 miles before the oil is changed, regardless of what the oil life indicator shows.

1 Frequent oil changes are the most important preventive maintenance procedures that can be done by the home mechanic. As engine oil ages, it becomes diluted and contaminated, which leads to premature engine wear.

2 Make sure that you have all the necessary tools before you begin this procedure (see illustration). You should also have plenty of rags or newspapers handy for mopping up oil spills.

3 Access to the oil drain plug and filter will be improved if the vehicle can be lifted on a hoist, driven onto ramps or supported by jackstands.

WARNING:

Do not work under a vehicle supported only by a jack - always use jackstands!

4 If you haven't changed the oil on this vehicle before, get under it and locate the oil drain plug and the oil filter. The exhaust components will be warm as you work, so note how they are routed to avoid touching them when you are under the vehicle.

5 Start the engine and allow it to reach normal operating temperature - oil and sludge will flow out more easily when warm. If new oil, a filter or tools are needed, use the vehicle to go get them and warm up the engine/oil at the same time. Park on a level surface and shut off the

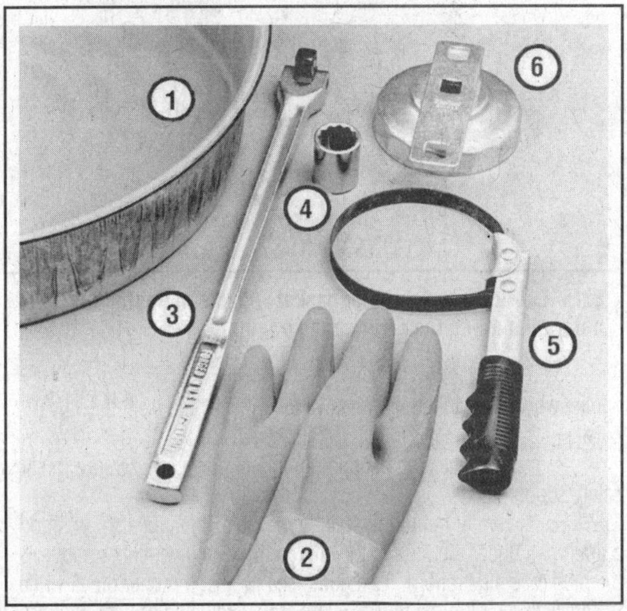

6.2 These tools are required when changing the engine oil and filter

1 ***Drain pan*** *- It should be fairly shallow in depth, but wide in order to prevent spills*
2 ***Rubber gloves*** *- When removing the drain plug and filter, it is inevitable that you will get oil on your hands (the gloves will prevent burns)*
3 ***Breaker bar*** *- Sometimes the oil drain plug is pretty tight and a long breaker bar is needed to loosen it*
4 ***Socket*** *- To be used with the breaker bar or a ratchet (must be the correct size to fit the drain plug)*
5 ***Filter wrench*** *- This is a metal band-type wrench, which requires clearance around the filter to be effective*
6 ***Filter wrench*** *- This type fits on the bottom of the filter and can be turned with a ratchet or breaker bar (different size wrenches are available for different types of filters)*

6.7 Use a proper size box-end wrench or socket to remove the oil drain plug and avoid rounding it off

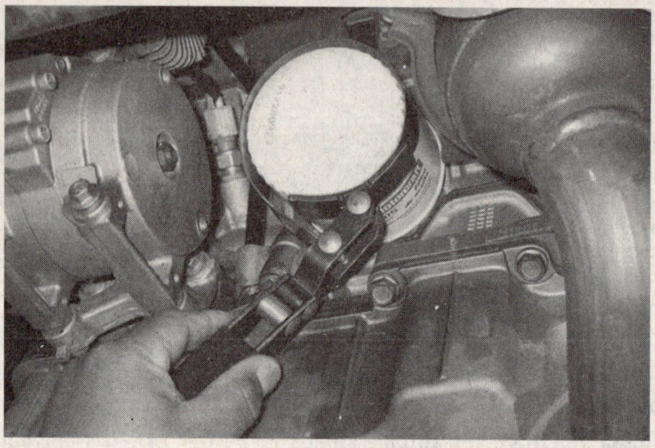

6.12 Use an oil filter wrench to remove the filter (V6 engine shown)

6.15 Lubricate the oil filter gasket with clean engine oil before installing the filter on the engine

engine when it's warmed up. Remove the oil filler cap from the valve cover.

6 Raise the vehicle and support it on jackstands. Make sure it is safely supported!

7 Being careful not to touch the hot exhaust components, position a drain pan under the plug in the bottom of the engine, then remove the plug (see illustration). It's a good idea to wear a rubber glove while unscrewing the plug the final few turns to avoid being scalded by hot oil.

8 It may be necessary to move the drain pan slightly as oil flow slows to a trickle. Inspect the old oil for the presence of metal particles.

9 After all the oil has drained, wipe off the drain plug with a clean rag. Any small metal particles clinging to the plug would immediately contaminate the new oil.

10 Clean the area around the drain plug opening, reinstall the plug and tighten it to the torque listed in this Chapter's Specifications.

11 Move the drain pan into position under the oil filter.

12 Loosen the oil filter by turning it counterclockwise with a filter wrench (see illustration). Any standard filter wrench will work.

13 Once the filter is loose, use your hands to unscrew it from the block. Just as the filter is detached from the block, immediately tilt the open end up to prevent the oil inside the filter from spilling out.

14 Using a clean rag, wipe off the mounting surface on the block. Also, make sure that none of the old gasket remains stuck to the mounting surface. It can be removed with a scraper if necessary.

15 Compare the old filter with the new one to make sure they are the same type. Smear some engine oil on the rubber gasket of the new filter and screw it into place (see illustration). Overtightening the filter will damage the gasket, so don't use a filter wrench. Most filter manufacturers recommend tightening the filter by hand only. Normally they should be tightened 3/4-turn after the gasket contacts the block, but be sure to follow the directions on the filter or container.

16 Remove all tools and materials from under the vehicle, being careful not to spill the oil in the drain pan, then lower the vehicle.

17 Add new oil to the engine through the oil filler cap. Use a funnel to prevent oil from spilling onto the top of the engine. Pour four quarts of fresh oil into the engine. Wait a few minutes to allow the oil to drain into the pan, then check the level on the dipstick (see Section 4 if necessary). If the oil level is in the OK range, install the filler cap.

18 Start the engine and run it for about a minute. While the engine is running, look under the vehicle and check for leaks at the oil pan drain plug and around the oil filter. If either one is leaking, stop the engine and tighten the plug or filter slightly.

19 Wait a few minutes, then recheck the level on the dipstick. Add oil as necessary to bring the level into the OK range.

20 During the first few trips after an oil change, make it a point to check frequently for leaks and proper oil level.

21 The old oil drained from the engine cannot be reused in its present state and should be disposed of. Check with your local auto parts store, disposal facility or environmental agency to see if they will accept the oil for recycling. After the oil has cooled it can be drained into a container (capped plastic jugs, topped bottles, milk cartons, etc.) for transport to one of these disposal sites. Don't dispose of the oil by pouring it on the ground or down a drain!

OIL LIFE MONITOR RESETTING

➡Note: Not all models are equipped with an oil life monitor.

22 Press the SETUP button to display "OIL LIFE XXX% HOLD RESET=NEW."

23 Press and hold the RESET button for two seconds, then release it. The indicator should now read "OIL LIFE SET TO 100%," which is approximately a 7,500-mile interval. This interval can be shortened by pressing and releasing the RESET button; each push of the button reduces the interval by 10-percent.

7 Windshield wiper blade inspection and replacement (every 7500 miles or 6 months)

Refer to illustrations 7.4a and 7.4b

1 The windshield wiper and blade assembly should be inspected periodically for damage, loose components and cracked or worn blade elements.

2 Road film can build up on the wiper blades and affect their efficiency, so they should be washed regularly with a mild detergent solution.

3 If the wiper blade elements are cracked, worn or warped, or no longer clean adequately, they should be replaced with new ones.

4 Lift the arm assembly away from the glass for clearance, press on the release lever, then slide the wiper blade assembly out of the hook in the end of the arm (see illustrations).

5 Attach the new wiper to the arm. Connection can be confirmed by an audible click.

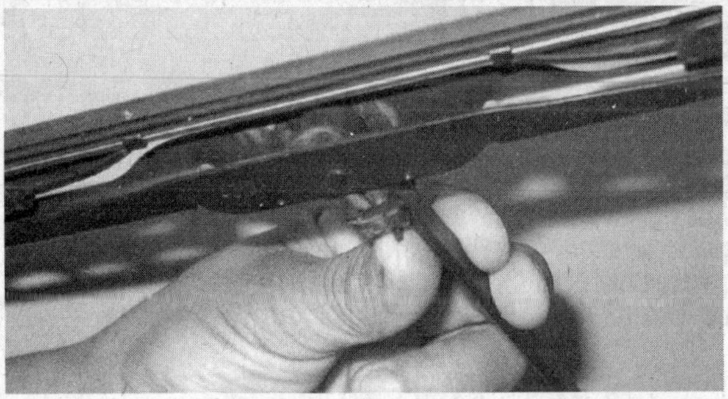

7.4a To release the blade holder, push the release pin . . .

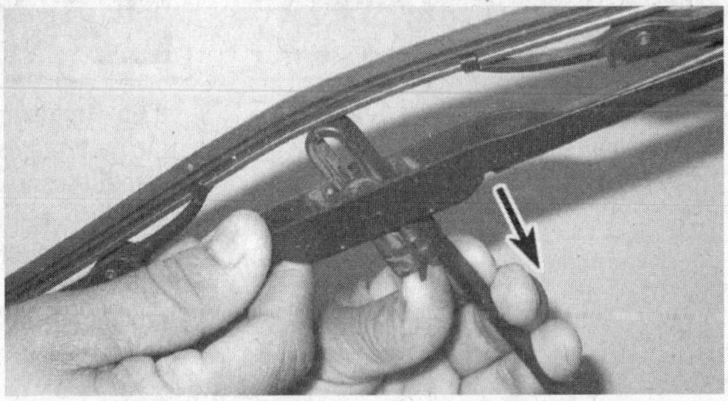

7.4b . . . and pull the wiper blade in the direction of the arrow to separate it from the arm

8 Battery check, maintenance and charging (every 7500 miles or 6 months)

Refer to illustrations 8.1, 8.6a, 8.6b, 8.7a, 8.7b and 8.8

WARNING:

Certain precautions must be followed when checking and servicing the battery. Hydrogen gas, which is highly flammable, is always present in the battery cells, so keep lighted tobacco and all other open flames and sparks away from the battery. The electrolyte inside the battery is actually diluted sulfuric acid, which will cause injury if splashed on your skin or in your eyes. It will also ruin clothes and painted surfaces. When removing the battery cables, always detach the negative cable first and hook it up last!

1 A routine preventive maintenance program for the battery in your vehicle is the only way to ensure quick and reliable starts. But before performing any battery maintenance, make sure that you have the proper equipment necessary to work safely around the battery (see illustration).

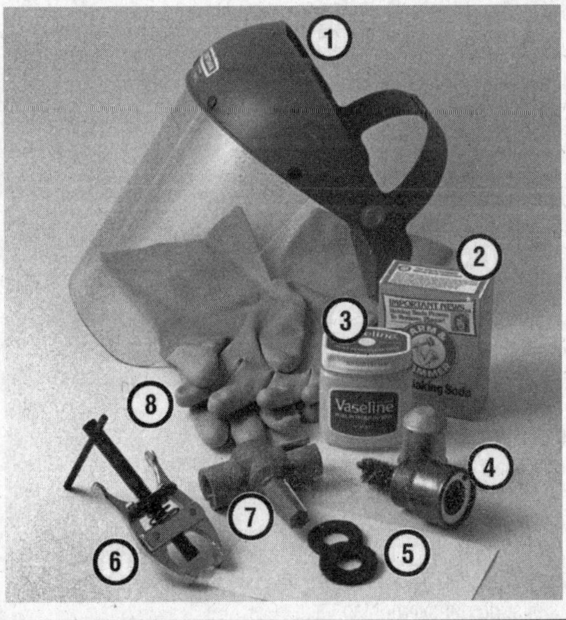

8.1 Tools and materials required for battery maintenance

1 ***Face shield/safety goggles*** - *When removing corrosion with a brush, the acidic particles can easily fly up into your eyes*
2 ***Baking soda*** - *A solution of baking soda and water can be used to neutralize corrosion*
3 ***Petroleum jelly*** - *A layer of this on the battery posts will help prevent corrosion*
4 ***Battery post/cable cleaner*** - *This wire brush cleaning tool will remove all traces of corrosion from the battery posts and cable clamps*
5 ***Treated felt washers*** - *Placing one of these on each post, directly under the cable clamps, will help prevent corrosion*
6 ***Puller*** - *Sometimes the cable clamps are very difficult to pull off the posts, even after the nut/bolt has been completely loosened. This tool pulls the clamp straight up and off the post without damage*
7 ***Battery post/cable cleaner*** - *Here is another cleaning tool which is a slightly different version of number 4 above, but it does the same thing*
8 ***Rubber gloves*** - *Another safety item to consider when servicing the battery; remember that's acid inside the battery*

8.6a Battery terminal corrosion usually appears as light, fluffy powder

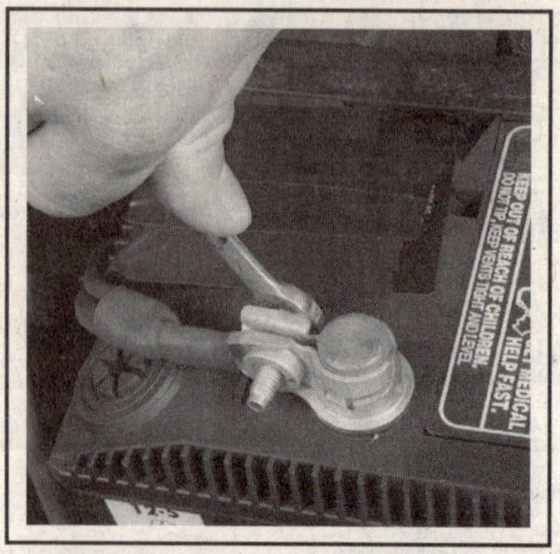

8.6b Removing a cable from the battery post with a wrench - sometimes a pair of special battery pliers are required for this procedure if corrosion has caused deterioration of the nut hex. Always remove the ground (-) cable first and hook it up last!

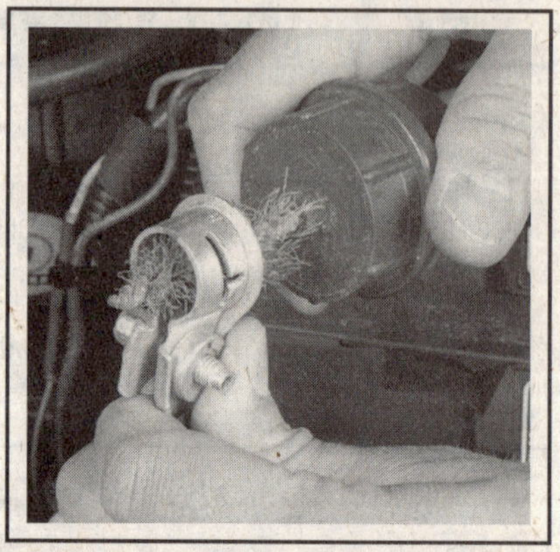

8.7a When cleaning the cable clamps, all corrosion must be removed (the inside of the clamp is tapered to match the taper on the post, so don't remove too much material)

8.7b Regardless of the type of tool used to clean the battery posts, a clean, shiny surface should be the result

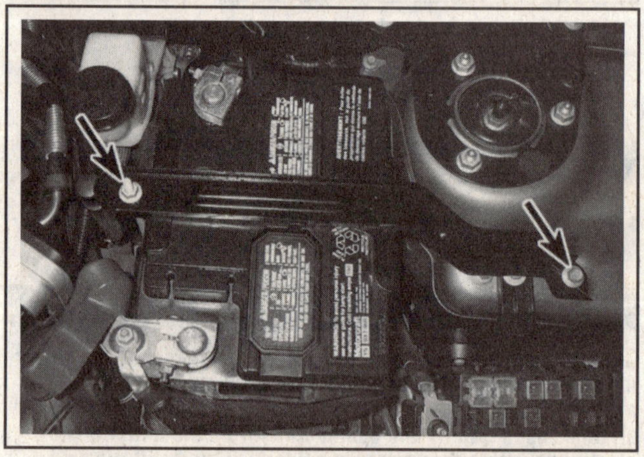

8.8 Make sure the battery hold-down fasteners are tight

2 There are also several precautions that should be taken whenever battery maintenance is performed. Before servicing the battery, always turn the engine and all accessories off and disconnect the cables from the negative terminal of the battery (see Chapter 5).

3 The battery produces hydrogen gas, which is both flammable and explosive. Never create a spark, smoke or light a match around the battery. Always charge the battery in a ventilated area.

4 Electrolyte contains poisonous and corrosive sulfuric acid. Do not allow it to get in your eyes, on your skin on your clothes. Never ingest it. Wear protective safety glasses when working near the battery. Keep children away from the battery.

5 Note the external condition of the battery. If the positive terminal and cable clamp on your vehicle's battery is equipped with a rubber protector, make sure that it's not torn or damaged. It should completely cover the terminal. Look for any corroded or loose connections, cracks in the case or cover or loose hold-down clamps. Also check the entire length of each cable for cracks and frayed conductors.

6 If corrosion, which looks like white, fluffy deposits (see illustration) is evident, particularly around the terminals, the battery should be removed for cleaning. Loosen the cable clamp bolts with a wrench, being careful to remove the ground cable first, and slide them off the terminals (see illustration). Then disconnect the hold-down clamp bolt and nut, remove the clamp and lift the battery from the engine compartment.

7 Clean the cable clamps thoroughly with a battery brush or a terminal cleaner and a solution of warm water and baking soda (see illustration). Wash the terminals and the top of the battery case with the same solution but make sure that the solution doesn't get into the battery. When cleaning the cables, terminals and battery top, wear safety goggles and rubber gloves to prevent any solution from coming in contact with your eyes or hands. Wear old clothes too - even diluted, sulfuric acid splashed onto clothes will burn holes in them. If the terminals have been extensively corroded, clean them up with a terminal cleaner (see illustration). Thoroughly wash all cleaned areas with plain water.

8 Make sure that the battery tray is in good condition and the hold-down clamp fasteners are tight (see illustration). If the battery is removed from the tray, make sure no parts remain in the bottom of the tray when the battery is reinstalled. When reinstalling the hold-down clamp bolts, do not overtighten them.

9 Information on removing and installing the battery can be found in Chapter 5. If you disconnected the cable(s) from the negative and/or positive battery terminals, the powertrain control module (PCM) must relearn its idle and fuel trim strategy for optimum driveability and performance (see Chapter 5 for this procedure). Information on jump starting can be found at the front of this manual.

CLEANING

10 Corrosion on the hold-down components, battery case and surrounding areas can be removed with a solution of water and baking soda. Thoroughly rinse all cleaned areas with plain water.

11 Any metal parts of the vehicle damaged by corrosion should be covered with a zinc-based primer, then painted.

CHARGING

**** WARNING:**

When batteries are being charged, hydrogen gas, which is very explosive and flammable, is produced. Do not smoke or allow open flames near a charging or a recently charged battery. Wear eye protection when near the battery during charging. Also, make sure the charger is unplugged before connecting or disconnecting the battery from the charger.

12 Slow-rate charging is the best way to restore a battery that's discharged to the point where it will not start the engine. It's also a good way to maintain the battery charge in a vehicle that's only driven a few miles between starts. Maintaining the battery charge is particularly important in the winter when the battery must work harder to start the engine and electrical accessories that drain the battery are in greater use.

13 It's best to use a one or two-amp battery charger (sometimes called a "trickle" charger). They are the safest and put the least strain on the battery. They are also the least expensive. For a faster charge, you can use a higher amperage charger, but don't use one rated more than 1/10th the amp/hour rating of the battery. Rapid boost charges that claim to restore the power of the battery in one to two hours are hardest on the battery and can damage batteries not in good condition. This type of charging should only be used in emergency situations.

14 The average time necessary to charge a battery should be listed in the instructions that come with the charger. As a general rule, a trickle charger will charge a battery in 12 to 16 hours.

9 Cooling system check (every 7,500 miles or 6 months)

Refer to illustration 9.4

1 Many major engine failures can be caused by a faulty cooling system.

2 The engine must be cold for the cooling system check, so perform the following procedure before the vehicle is driven for the day or after it has been shut off for at least three hours.

3 Remove the pressure-relief cap from the expansion tank at the right side of the engine compartment. Clean the cap thoroughly, inside and out, with clean water. The presence of rust or corrosion in the expansion tank means the coolant should be changed (see Section 21). The coolant inside the expansion tank should be relatively clean and transparent. If it's rust colored, drain the system and refill it with new coolant.

4 Carefully check the radiator hoses and the smaller diameter heater hoses (see illustrations in Chapter 3). Inspect each coolant hose along its entire length, replacing any hose which is cracked, swollen or deteriorated (see illustration). Cracks will show up better if the hose is squeezed. Pay close attention to hose clamps that secure the hoses to cooling system components. Hose clamps can pinch and puncture hoses, resulting in coolant leaks.

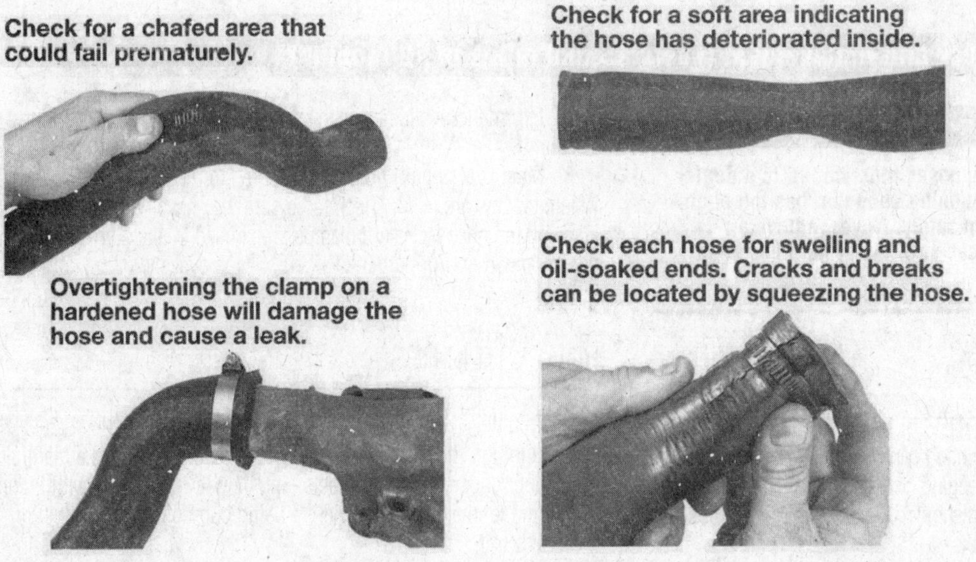

9.4 Hoses, like drivebelts, have a habit of failing at the worst possible time - to prevent the inconvenience of a blown radiator or heater hose, inspect them carefully as shown here

5 Make sure that all hose connections are tight. A leak in the cooling system will usually show up as white or rust colored deposits on the area adjoining the leak. If wire-type clamps are used on the hoses, it may be a good idea to replace them with screw-type clamps.

6 Clean the front of the radiator and air conditioning condenser with compressed air, if available, or a soft brush. Remove all bugs, leaves, etc. embedded in the radiator fins. Be extremely careful not to damage the cooling fins or cut your fingers on them.

7 If the coolant level has been dropping consistently and no leaks are detectable, have the expansion tank cap and cooling system pressure checked at a service station.

10 Tire rotation (every 7,500 miles or 6 months)

Refer to illustration 10.2

1 The tires should be rotated at the specified intervals and whenever uneven wear is noticed. Since the vehicle will be raised and the tires removed anyway, check the brakes also (see Section 13).

2 Radial tires must be rotated in a specific pattern (see illustration). Don't include the spare tire in the rotation pattern.

3 Refer to the information in *Jacking and towing* at the front of this manual for the proper procedure to follow when raising the vehicle and changing a tire. If the brakes must be checked, don't apply the parking brake as stated.

4 The vehicle must be raised on a hoist or supported on jackstands to get all four wheels off the ground. Make sure the vehicle is safely supported!

5 After the rotation procedure is finished, check and adjust the tire pressures as necessary and be sure to check the lug nut tightness.

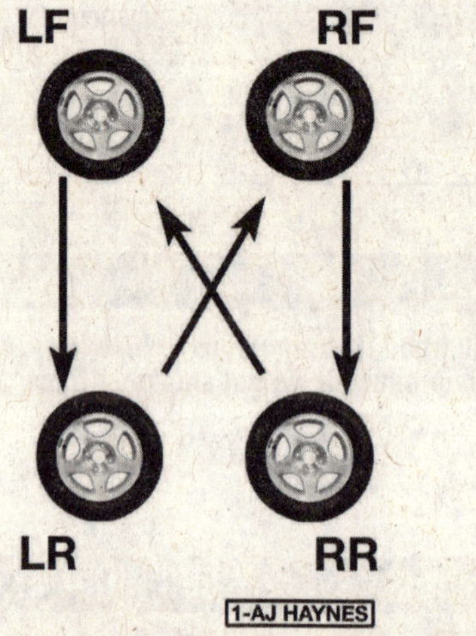

10.2 The recommended tire rotation pattern for these vehicles (FWD and AWD)

11 Seat belt check (every 7,500 miles or 6 months)

1 Check seat belts, buckles, latch plates and guide loops for obvious damage and signs of wear.

2 See if the seat belt reminder light comes on when the key is turned to the Run or Start position. A chime should also sound.

3 The seat belts are designed to lock up during a sudden stop or impact, yet allow free movement during normal driving. Make sure the retractors return the belt against your chest while driving and rewind the belt fully when the buckle is unlatched.

4 If any of the above checks reveal problems with the seat belt system, replace parts as necessary.

12 Underhood hose check and replacement (every 15,000 miles or 12 months)

WARNING:

Replacement of air conditioning hoses must be left to a dealer service department or air conditioning shop that has the equipment to depressurize the system safely. Never remove air conditioning components or hoses until the system has been depressurized.

GENERAL

1 High temperatures under the hood can cause deterioration of the rubber and plastic hoses used for engine, accessory and emission systems operation. Periodic inspection should be made for cracks, loose clamps, material hardening and leaks.

2 Information specific to the cooling system hoses can be found in Section 9.

3 Most (but not all) hoses are secured to the fittings with clamps. Where clamps are used, check to be sure they haven't lost their tension, allowing the hose to leak. If clamps aren't used, make sure the hose has not expanded and/or hardened where it slips over the fitting, allowing it to leak.

PCV SYSTEM HOSE

4 To reduce hydrocarbon emissions, crankcase blow-by gas is vented through the PCV valve in the valve cover to the intake manifold via a rubber hose on most models. The blow-by gases mix with incoming air in the intake manifold before being burned in the combustion chambers.

5 Check the PCV hose for cracks, leaks and other damage. Disconnect it from the valve cover and the intake manifold and check the inside for obstructions. If it's clogged, clean it out with solvent.

VACUUM HOSES

6 It's quite common for vacuum hoses, especially those in the emissions system, to be color coded or identified by colored stripes molded into them. Various systems require hoses with different wall thickness, collapse resistance and temperature resistance. When replacing hoses, be sure the new ones are made of the same material.

7 Often the only effective way to check a hose is to remove it completely from the vehicle. If more than one hose is removed, be sure to label the hoses and fittings to ensure correct installation.

8 When checking vacuum hoses, be sure to include any plastic T-fittings in the check. Inspect the fittings for cracks and the hose where it fits over each fitting for distortion, which could cause leakage.

9 A small piece of vacuum hose (1/4-inch inside diameter) can be used as a stethoscope to detect vacuum leaks. Hold one end of the hose to your ear and probe around vacuum hoses and fittings, listening for the hissing sound characteristic of a vacuum leak.

WARNING:

When probing with the vacuum hose stethoscope, be careful not to come into contact with moving engine components such as drivebelts, the cooling fan, etc.

FUEL HOSE

WARNING:

Gasoline is flammable, so take extra precautions when you work on any part of the fuel system. Don't smoke or allow open flames or bare light bulbs near the work area, and don't work in a garage where a gas-type appliance (such as a water heater or clothes dryer) is present. Since fuel is carcinogenic, wear fuel-resistant gloves when there's a possibility of being exposed to fuel, and, if you spill any fuel on your skin, rinse it off immediately with soap and water. Mop up any spills immediately and do not store fuel-soaked rags where they could ignite. The fuel system is under constant pressure, so, if any fuel lines are to be disconnected, the fuel pressure in the system must be relieved first (see Chapter 4 for more information). When you perform any kind of work on the fuel system, wear safety glasses and have a Class B type fire extinguisher on hand.

10 The fuel lines are usually under pressure, so if any fuel lines are to be disconnected be prepared to catch spilled fuel.

WARNING:

Your vehicle is equipped with fuel injection and you must relieve the fuel system pressure before servicing the fuel lines. Refer to Chapter 4 for the fuel system pressure relief procedure.

11 Check all flexible fuel lines for deterioration and chafing. Check especially for cracks in areas where the hose bends and just before fittings, such as where the fuel line attaches to the fuel rail.

12 When replacing a hose, use only hose that is specifically designed for your fuel injection system.

13 Some fuel lines use quick-connect fittings, which require a special tool to disconnect. See Chapter 4 for more information on these types of fittings.

METAL LINES

14 Sections of metal line are often used for fuel line that runs underneath the vehicle. Check carefully to make sure the line isn't bent, crimped or cracked.

15 If a section of metal fuel line must be replaced, use seamless steel tubing only, since copper and aluminum tubing do not have the strength necessary to withstand vibration caused by the engine.

16 Check the metal brake lines where they enter the master cylinder and brake proportioning unit (if used) for cracks in the lines and loose fittings. Any sign of brake fluid leakage calls for an immediate thorough inspection of the brake system.

13 Brake check (every 15,000 miles or 12 months)

WARNING:

Dust created by the brake system is harmful to your health. Never blow it out with compressed air and don't inhale any of it. An approved filtering mask should be worn when working on brakes. Do not, under any circumstances, use petroleum-based solvents to clean brake parts. Use brake system cleaner only!

1 The brakes should be inspected every time the wheels are removed or whenever a defect is suspected. Indications of a potential brake system problem include the vehicle pulling to one side when the brake pedal is depressed, noises coming from the brakes when they are applied, excessive brake pedal travel, a pulsating pedal and leakage of fluid, usually seen on the inside of the tire or wheel.

Note: It is normal for a vehicle equipped with an Anti-lock Brake System (ABS) to exhibit brake pedal pulsations during severe braking conditions.

DISC BRAKES

Refer to illustrations 13.5a and 13.5b

2 Disc brakes can be visually checked without removing any parts except the wheels. Remove the hub caps (if applicable) and loosen the wheel lug nuts a quarter turn each.

13.5a You will find an inspection hole like this in each caliper through which you can view the thickness of remaining friction material for the inner pad

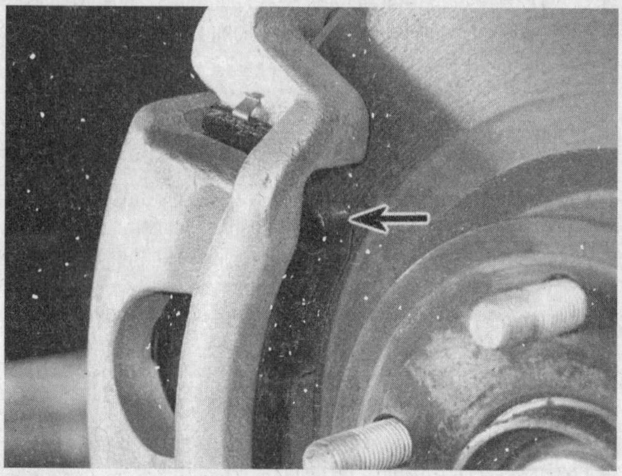

13.5b Be sure to check the thickness of the outer pad material, too

3 Raise the vehicle and place it securely on jackstands.

WARNING:

Never work under a vehicle that is supported only by a jack!

4 Remove the wheels. Now visible is the disc brake caliper which contains the pads. There is an outer brake pad and an inner pad. Both must be checked for wear.

Note: Usually the inner pad wears faster than the outer pad.

5 Measure the thickness of the outer pad at each end of the caliper and the inner pad through the inspection hole in the caliper body (see illustrations). Compare the measurement with the limit given in this Chapter's Specifications; if any brake pad thickness is less than specified, then all brake pads must be replaced (see Chapter 9).

6 If you're in doubt as to the exact pad thickness or quality, remove them for measurement and further inspection (see Chapter 9).

7 Check the disc for score marks, wear and burned spots. If any of these conditions exist, the disc should be removed for servicing or replacement (see Chapter 9).

8 Before installing the wheels, check all the brake lines and hoses for damage, wear, deformation, cracks, corrosion, leakage, bends and twists, particularly in the vicinity of the rubber hoses and calipers.

9 Install the wheels, lower the vehicle and tighten the wheel lug nuts to the torque given in this Chapter's Specifications.

PARKING BRAKE

10 Slowly pull up on the parking brake and count the number of clicks you hear until the handle is up as far as it will go. The adjustment is correct if you hear the specified number of clicks (see this Chapter's Specifications). If you hear more or fewer clicks, it's time to adjust the parking brake (see Chapter 9).

11 An alternative method of checking the parking brake is to park the vehicle on a steep hill with the engine running (so you can apply the brakes if necessary) with the parking brake set and the transaxle in Neutral. If the parking brake cannot prevent the vehicle from rolling, it needs adjustment (see Chapter 9).

14 Steering, suspension and driveaxle boot check (every 15,000 miles or 12 months)

Note: For detailed illustrations of the steering and suspension components, refer to Chapter 10.

SHOCK ABSORBER CHECK

Refer to illustration 14.6

1 Park the vehicle on level ground, turn the engine off and set the parking brake. Check the tire pressures.

2 Push down at one corner of the vehicle, then release it while noting the movement of the body. It should stop moving and come to rest in a level position within one or two bounces.

3 If the vehicle continues to move up-and-down or if it fails to return to its original position, a worn or weak shock absorber is probably the reason.

4 Repeat the above check at each of the three remaining corners of the vehicle.

5 Raise the vehicle and support it securely on jackstands.

14.6 Check the shocks for leakage at the indicated area

14.11 To check a balljoint for wear, try to pry the control arm up and down to make sure there is no play in the balljoint (if there is, replace it)

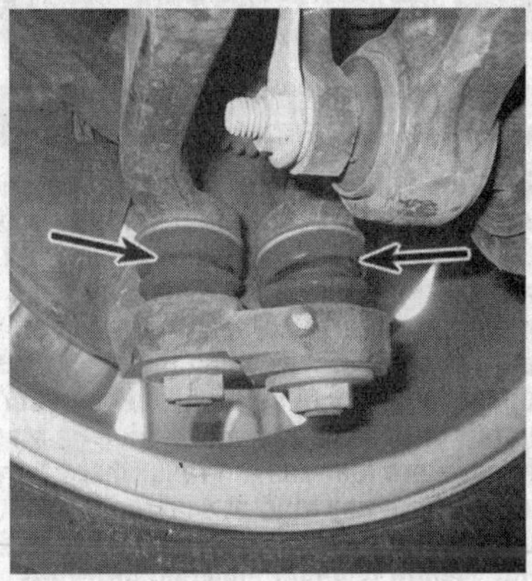

14.12 Check the balljoint boots for damage

6 Check the shock absorbers for evidence of fluid leakage (see illustration). A light film of fluid is no cause for concern. Make sure that any fluid noted is from the shocks and not from some other source. If leakage is noted, replace the shocks as a set.

7 Check the shocks to be sure that they are securely mounted and undamaged. Check the upper mounts for damage and wear. If damage or wear is noted, replace the shocks as a set (front or rear).

8 If the shocks must be replaced, refer to Chapter 10 for the procedure.

STEERING AND SUSPENSION CHECK

➧ Refer to illustrations 14.11 and 14.12

9 Check the tires for irregular wear patterns and proper inflation. See Section 5 in this Chapter for information regarding tire wear and Chapter 10 for information on wheel bearing replacement.

10 Inspect the universal joint between the steering shaft and the steering gear housing. Check the steering gear housing for lubricant leakage. Make sure that the dust boots are not damaged and that the boot clamps are not loose. Check the tie-rod ends for excessive play. Look for loose bolts, broken or disconnected parts and deteriorated rubber bushings on all suspension and steering components. While an assistant turns the steering wheel from side to side, check the steering components for free movement, chafing and binding. If the steering components do not seem to be reacting with the movement of the steering wheel, try to determine where the slack is located.

11 Check the balljoints for wear by trying to move each control arm up and down with a prybar (see illustration) to ensure that its balljoint has no play. If any balljoint does have play, it's worn out. See Chapter 10 for the control arm replacement procedure (the balljoints aren't replaceable separately).

12 Inspect the balljoint boots for damage and leaking grease (see illustration).

13 At the rear of the vehicle, inspect the suspension arm bushings for deterioration. Additional information on suspension components can be found in Chapter 10.

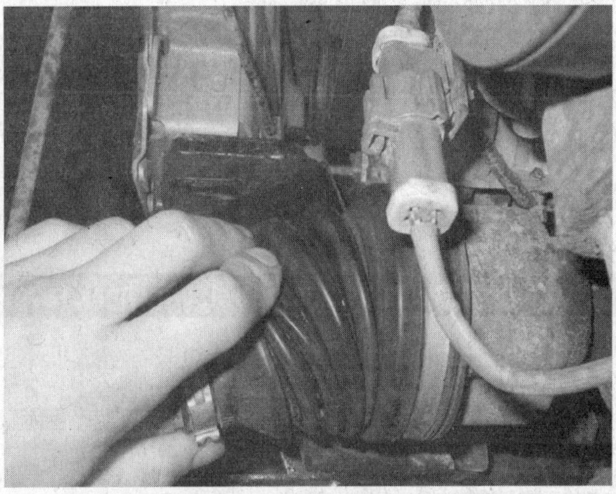

14.15 Flex the driveaxle boots by hand to check for cracks and/or leaking grease

DRIVEAXLE BOOT CHECK

➧ Refer to illustration 14.15

14 The driveaxle boots are very important because they prevent dirt, water and foreign material from entering and damaging the constant velocity (CV) joints. Oil and grease can cause the boot material to deteriorate prematurely, so it's a good idea to wash the boots with soap and water. Because it constantly pivots back and forth following the steering action of the front hub, the outer CV boot wears out sooner and should be inspected regularly.

15 Inspect the boots for tears and cracks as well as loose clamps (see illustration). If there is any evidence of cracks or leaking lubricant, they must be replaced as described in Chapter 8.

15 Fuel system check (every 15,000 miles or 12 months)

WARNING:

Gasoline is flammable, so take extra precautions when you work on any part of the fuel system. Don't smoke or allow open flames or bare light bulbs near the work area, and don't work in a garage where a gas-type appliance (such as a water heater or clothes dryer) is present. Since fuel is carcinogenic, wear fuel-resistant gloves when there's a possibility of being exposed to fuel, and, if you spill any fuel on your skin, rinse it off immediately with soap and water. Mop up any spills immediately and do not store fuel-soaked rags where they could ignite. When you perform any kind of work on the fuel system, wear safety glasses and have a Class B type fire extinguisher on hand. The fuel system is under constant pressure, so, before any lines are disconnected, the fuel system pressure must be relieved (see Chapter 4).

1 If you smell gasoline while driving or after the vehicle has been sitting in the sun, inspect the fuel system immediately.

2 Remove the fuel filler cap and inspect if for damage and corrosion. The gasket should have an unbroken sealing imprint. If the gasket is damaged or corroded, install a new cap.

3 Inspect the fuel feed line for cracks. Make sure that the connections between the fuel lines and the fuel injection system and between the fuel lines and the fuel tank (inspect from below) are tight and dry.

WARNING:

Your vehicle is fuel injected, so you must relieve the fuel system pressure before servicing fuel system components. The fuel system pressure relief procedure is outlined in Chapter 4.

4 Since some components of the fuel system - the fuel tank and part of the fuel feed line, for example - are underneath the vehicle, they can be inspected more easily with the vehicle raised on a hoist. If that's not possible, raise the vehicle and support it on jackstands.

5 With the vehicle raised and safely supported, inspect the gas tank and filler neck for punctures, cracks and other damage. The connection between the filler neck and the tank is particularly critical. Sometimes a rubber filler neck will leak because of loose clamps or deteriorated rubber. Inspect all fuel tank mounting brackets and straps to be sure that the tank is securely attached to the vehicle.

WARNING:

Do not, under any circumstances, try to repair a fuel tank (except rubber components). A welding torch or any open flame can easily cause fuel vapors inside the tank to explode.

6 Carefully check all rubber hoses and metal lines leading away from the fuel tank. Check for loose connections, deteriorated hoses, crimped lines and other damage. Repair or replace damaged sections as necessary (see Chapter 4).

16 Manual transaxle lubricant level check (every 15,000 miles or 12 months)

1 The manual transaxle does not have a dipstick. To check the fluid level, raise the vehicle and support it securely on jackstands. On the front side of the transaxle housing you will a fill plug about half-way up on the transaxle case; it's the larger of the two hex-head bolts.

CAUTION:

Do not remove the smaller hex-head bolt above the back-up light switch.

Remove the plug; if the lubricant level is correct, it should be up to the lower edge of the hole.

2 If the transaxle needs more lubricant (if the level is not up to the hole), use a syringe or a gear oil pump to add more. Stop filling the transaxle when the lubricant begins to run out of the hole.

3 Install the plug and tighten it to the torque listed in this Chapter's Specifications. Drive the vehicle a short distance, then check for leaks.

17 Transfer case lubricant level check (AWD models) (every 15,000 miles or 12 months)

Refer to illustrations 17.2 and 17.3

1 Raise the vehicle and support it securely on jackstands.

2 Using a ratchet or breaker bar, unscrew the check/fill plug from the transfer case (see illustration).

3 On 2007 models with a high-mounted check plug, make a lubricant level check tool from a plastic tie-strap. Make a mark on the strap 1-3/4 inches from the tip and bend the strap in a 90-degree angle at that point, then make another mark a quarter-inch from the tip (see illustration). Insert the marked portion of the strap into the hole with the tip down. Remove the strap. The lubricant level should be at the mark closest to the tip. Add lubricant if needed, but be careful not to overfill the transfer case.

4 On 2008 and later models, use your little finger to reach inside the housing to feel the lubricant level. The level should be at or near the bottom of the plug hole. If it isn't, add the recommended lubricant through the plug hole with a syringe or squeeze bottle.

5 Install and tighten the plug. On 2008 and later models, the manufacturer recommends that a new fill/check plug be installed. On 2007 models, wrap the threads of the plug with Teflon tape prior to installation. Check for leaks after the first few miles of driving.

Note: The manufacturer states that if the transfer case is ever submerged in water, the entire unit must be replaced (see Chapter 7C). However, it may be worth trying to drain the lubricant and refill the unit with fresh lubricant to try to gain more service life from the unit (see Section 27).

17.2 Transfer case check/fill plug

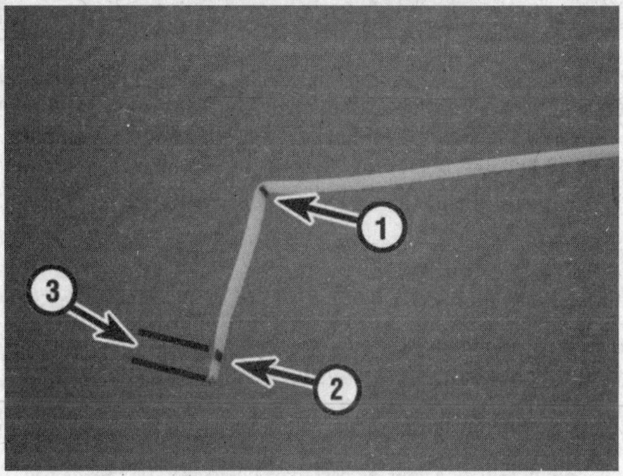

17.3 On 2007 models, make a dipstick from a plastic tie strap to check the lubricant level

1 90-degree bend, 1-3/4 inch from the tip
2 Mark 1/4-inch from the tip
3 Lubricant level should be within this range

18 Air filter check and replacement (every 15,000 miles or 12 months)

Refer to illustrations 18.1a and 18.1b

1 The air filter is located inside a housing at the left (driver's) side of the engine compartment. To remove the air filter, release the clamps that secure the two halves of the air cleaner housing together, then separate the cover halves and remove the air filter element (see illustrations).

2 Inspect the outer surface of the filter element. If it is dirty, replace it. If it is only moderately dusty, it can be reused by blowing it clean from the back to the front surface with compressed air. Because it is a pleated paper type filter, it cannot be washed or oiled. If it cannot be cleaned satisfactorily with compressed air, discard and replace it. While the cover is off, be careful not to drop anything down into the housing.

CAUTION:

Never drive the vehicle with the air cleaner removed. Excessive engine wear could result and backfiring could even cause a fire under the hood.

3 Wipe out the inside of the air cleaner housing.

4 Place the new filter into the air cleaner housing, making sure it seats properly.

5 Make sure the top half of the housing is seated properly, then secure it with the clamps.

18.1a Unlatch these clips . . .

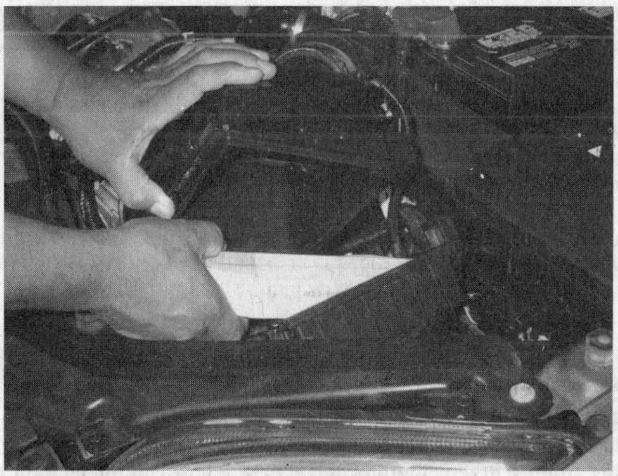

18.1b . . . pull the cover out of the way and lift the element out

19 Cabin air filter replacement (every 15,000 miles or 12 months)

➡Note: 2009 and earlier models are not equipped from the factory with a cabin air filter. Check with your local auto parts store or dealer parts department to see if a retrofit filter is available for these models.

1 Remove the glove box (see Chapter 11, Section 22).

2 Remove the access door, then pull the filter from the housing.

➡Note: The flap on the right side of the filter must be bent downward so it doesn't contact the glove box damper.

3 Installation is the reverse of removal.

20 Exhaust system check (every 30,000 miles or 24 months)

➧ Refer to illustration 20.2

1 With the engine cold (at least three hours after the vehicle has been driven), check the complete exhaust system from the engine to the end of the tailpipe. Ideally, the inspection should be done with the vehicle on a hoist to permit unrestricted access. If a hoist isn't available, raise the vehicle and support it securely on jackstands.

2 Check the exhaust pipes and connections for evidence of leaks, severe corrosion and damage. Make sure that all brackets and hangers are in good condition and tight (see illustration).

3 At the same time, inspect the underside of the body for holes, corrosion, open seams, etc. which may allow exhaust gases to enter the passenger compartment. Seal all body openings with silicone or body putty.

4 Rattles and other noises can often be traced to the exhaust system, especially the mounts and hangers. Try to move the pipes, muffler and catalytic converter. If the components can come in contact with the body or suspension parts, secure the exhaust system with new mounts.

5 Check the running condition of the engine by inspecting inside the end of the tailpipe. The exhaust deposits here are an indication of engine state-of-tune. If the pipe is black and sooty or coated with white deposits, the engine may need a tune-up, including a thorough fuel system inspection and adjustment.

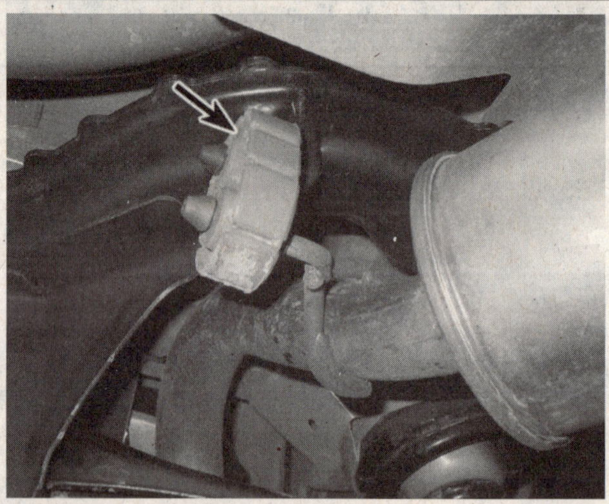

20.2 Be sure to check each exhaust system rubber hanger for damage

21 Cooling system servicing (draining, flushing and refilling) (every 30,000 miles or 24 months)

⁂ WARNING:

Do not allow antifreeze to come in contact with your skin or painted surfaces of the vehicle. Rinse off spills immediately with plenty of water. Antifreeze is highly toxic if ingested. Never leave antifreeze lying around in an open container or in puddles on the floor; children and pets are attracted by its sweet smell and may drink it. Check with local authorities about disposing of used antifreeze. Many communities have collection centers which will see that antifreeze is disposed of safely. Never dump used antifreeze on the ground or pour it into drains.

⁂ CAUTION:

Do not mix coolants of different colors. Doing so might damage the cooling system and/or the engine. The manufacturer specifies either a green colored coolant or a yellow colored coolant to be used in these systems. Read the warning label in the engine compartment for additional information.

➡Note: Non-toxic antifreeze is now manufactured and available at local auto parts stores, but even this type must be disposed of properly.

1 Periodically, the cooling system should be drained, flushed and refilled to replenish the antifreeze mixture and prevent formation of rust and corrosion, which can impair the performance of the cooling system and cause engine damage. When the cooling system is serviced, all hoses and the expansion tank cap should be checked and replaced if necessary.

DRAINING

➧ Refer to illustrations 21.4a, 21.4b and 21.5

2 Apply the parking brake and block the wheels. If the vehicle has just been driven, wait several hours to allow the engine to cool down before beginning this procedure.

21.4a Location of the cooling system bleed screw on a four-cylinder engine

21.4b Location of the cooling system bleed screw on 2006 through 2009 3.0L V6 models

21.5 The radiator drain fitting is located at the lower left corner of the radiator - before opening the valve, push a short length of rubber hose onto the plastic fitting to prevent the coolant from splashing

3 Once the engine is completely cool, remove the expansion tank cap.

4 On four-cylinder and 3.0L V6 engines, loosen the cooling system bleed screw:

a) Four-cylinder engines - The bleed screw is located in a small hose attached to the water outlet at the left end (driver's side) of the cylinder head (see illustration).

b) 2006 through 2009 3.0L V6 engine - The bleed screw is located in a plastic fitting in the upper radiator hose.

c) 2010 3.0L V6 engine - The bleed screw (hex plug) is located on top of the water pump housing.

➡Note: On models with a plastic bleed screw, it's only necessary to turn the screw counterclockwise about 1/4-turn.

5 Move a large container under the radiator drain to catch the coolant. Attach a length of hose to the drain fitting to direct the coolant into the container, then open the drain fitting (a pair of pliers may be required to turn it) (see illustration).

6 While the coolant is draining, check the condition of the radiator hoses, heater hoses and clamps (refer to Section 9 if necessary). Replace any damaged clamps or hoses.

FLUSHING

7 Fill the cooling system with clean water, following the Refilling procedure (see Step 13).

8 Start the engine and allow it to reach normal operating temperature, then rev up the engine a few times.

9 Turn the engine off and allow it to cool completely, then drain the system as described earlier.

10 Repeat Steps 7 through 9 until the water being drained is free of contaminants.

11 In severe cases of contamination or clogging of the radiator, remove the radiator (see Chapter 3) and have a radiator repair facility clean and repair it if necessary.

12 Many deposits can be removed by the chemical action of a cleaner available at auto parts stores. Follow the procedure outlined in the manufacturer's instructions.

➡Note: When the coolant is regularly drained and the system refilled with the correct antifreeze/water mixture, there should be no need to use chemical cleaners or descalers.

REFILLING

13 Close and tighten the radiator drain.

14 Place the heater temperature control in the maximum heat position.

15 If you're working on a model with a four-cylinder or 3.0L V6 engine, slowly add new coolant (a 50/50 mixture of water and antifreeze) until coolant flows from the bleed screw, then tighten the bleed screw and continue to fill the expansion tank to the MAX fill mark. If you're working on a model with a 3.5L V6 engine, add coolant to the expansion tank until the level is at the MAX fill mark on the expansion tank.

16 Install the expansion tank cap and run the engine at 2500 rpm for ten minutes.

⁂ CAUTION:

If at any time the engine begins to overheat, or the coolant level falls below the MIN fill line on the expansion tank, turn off the engine, allow it to cool completely, then add coolant to the expansion tank to the MAX fill line.

17 Turn the engine off and let it cool. Add more coolant mixture to bring the level to the MAX fill mark on the expansion tank.

18 Repeat Steps 16 and 17 if necessary.

19 Start the engine, allow it to reach normal operating temperature and check for leaks. Also, set the heater and blower controls to the maximum setting and check to see that the heater output from the air ducts is warm. This is a good indication that all air has been purged from the cooling system.

22 Brake fluid change (every 30,000 miles or 24 months)

WARNING:

Brake fluid can harm your eyes and damage painted surfaces, so use extreme caution when handling or pouring it. Do not use brake fluid that has been standing open or is more than one year old. Brake fluid absorbs moisture from the air. Excess moisture can cause a dangerous loss of braking effectiveness.

1 At the specified intervals, the brake fluid should be drained and replaced. Since the brake fluid may drip or splash when pouring it, place plenty of rags around the master cylinder to protect any surrounding painted surfaces.

2 Before beginning work, purchase the specified brake fluid (see *Recommended lubricants and fluids* in this Chapter's Specifications).

3 Remove the cap from the master cylinder reservoir.

4 Using a hand suction pump or similar device, withdraw the fluid from the master cylinder reservoir.

5 Add new fluid to the master cylinder until it rises to the base of the filler neck.

6 Bleed the brake system as described in Chapter 9 at all four brakes until new and uncontaminated fluid is expelled from the bleeder screw. Be sure to maintain the fluid level in the master cylinder as you perform the bleeding process. If you allow the master cylinder to run dry, air will enter the system.

7 Refill the master cylinder with fluid and check the operation of the brakes. The pedal should feel solid when depressed, with no sponginess.

WARNING:

Do not operate the vehicle if you are in doubt about the effectiveness of the brake system.

23 Drivebelt check and replacement (every 30,000 miles or 24 months)

ACCESSORY DRIVEBELT

1 A single serpentine drivebelt is located at the front of the engine and plays an important role in the overall operation of the engine and its components. Due to its function and material make up, the belt is prone to wear and should be periodically inspected. The serpentine belt drives the alternator, power steering pump, water pump (four-cylinder models) and air conditioning compressor. Although the belt should be inspected at the recommended intervals, replacement may not be necessary for more than 100,000 miles.

Check

Refer to illustrations 23.2 and 23.4

2 Since the drivebelt is located very close to the right-hand side of the engine compartment, it is possible to gain better access by raising the front of the vehicle and removing the right-hand wheel, then removing the splash shield in the right fenderwell (see illustration). Be sure to support the front of the vehicle securely on jackstands.

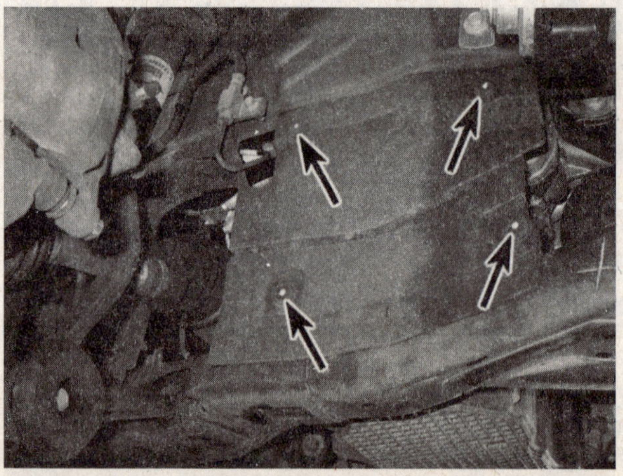

23.2 Remove screws from the front of the inner fender liner and pull it back for access (see Chapter 11), then remove this splash shield from the right fenderwell to gain access to the drivebelt tensioner (two rear pushpins not visible in this photo)

3 With the engine stopped, inspect the full length of the drivebelt for cracks and separation of the belt plies. It will be necessary to turn the engine (using a wrench or socket and bar on the crankshaft pulley bolt, working clockwise only) in order to move the belt from the pulleys so that the belt can be inspected thoroughly. Twist the belt between the pulleys so that both sides can be viewed. Also check for fraying, and glazing which gives the belt a shiny appearance. Check the pulleys for nicks, cracks, distortion and corrosion.

4 Note that it is not unusual for a ribbed belt to exhibit small cracks in the edges of the belt ribs, and unless these are extensive or very deep, belt replacement is not essential (see illustration).

Replacement

Refer to illustration 23.6

5 Disconnect the cable from the negative terminal of the battery (see Chapter 5). Loosen the right front wheel lug nuts, then raise the front of the vehicle and support it on jackstands. Remove the right front wheel and the splash shield (see illustration 23.2).

6 Note how the drivebelt is routed, then remove the belt from the pulleys. If you're working on a four-cylinder engine, use a wrench on the hex cast into the tensioner and turn the tensioner to release the drivebelt tension. If you're working on a V6 engine, insert a 3/8-inch drive ratchet or breaker bar into the tensioner hole and pull the handle to release the drivebelt tension (see illustration). Once tension has been released, remove the belt from the pulleys.

7 Fit the new drivebelt onto the crankshaft, alternator, power steering pump, and air conditioning compressor pulleys, as applicable, then

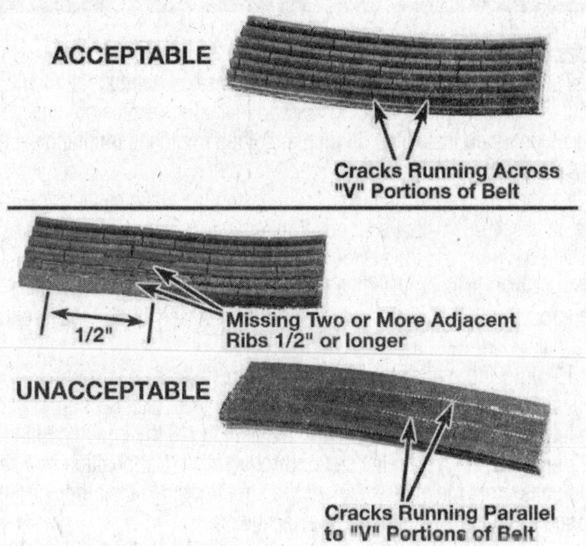

23.4 Small cracks in the underside of a V-ribbed belt are acceptable - lengthwise cracks, or missing pieces that cause the belt to make noise, are cause for replacement

23.6 To remove the drivebelt on a V6 model, insert a 3/8-inch drive ratchet or breaker bar into the square hole (A) and rotate the tensioner arm to relieve belt tension. (B) is the tensioner mounting bolt (2009 and earlier V6 models)

turn the tensioner back and locate the drivebelt on the pulley. Make sure that the drivebelt is correctly seated in all of the pulley grooves, then release the tensioner.

8 Install the splash shield and wheel, then lower the car to the ground. Tighten the lug nuts to the torque listed in this Chapter's Specifications.

WATER PUMP DRIVEBELT (3.0L V6 ENGINE)

Replacement

➧ Refer to illustration 23.10

9 The water pump drivebelt is located at the left end of the engine and is driven by a pulley attached to the end of the front cylinder bank exhaust camshaft. The belt and pulley are protected by a cover. The belt is of a unique design, called a "stretchy belt," which provides tension without the use of a mechanical tensioner.

10 Disconnect the cable from the negative terminal of the battery (see Chapter 5). Remove the cover from over the pulley. Insert a length of flexible material such as a leather or plastic strap under the belt at the pulley at the end of the camshaft, then have an assistant rotate the engine (clockwise) by using a socket and breaker bar on the crankshaft pulley bolt, while you feed the remover strap between the belt and the pulley (see illustration). Pull the strap quickly to force the belt from the pulley on the camshaft.

✻✻ CAUTION:

Do not use hard plastic or metal tools to pry the belt off; it can be easily damaged.

➡Note: If the belt is not going to be re-used, you can simply cut it off.

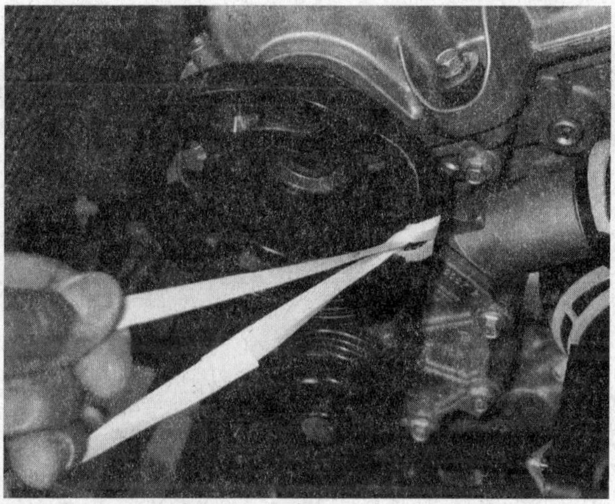

23.10 Removing the water pump belt on a 3.0L V6 engine. Warning: While doing this, rotate the engine by hand only (do not use the starter)

11 Route the new belt under the water pump pulley, then over the pulley on the camshaft, and have your assistant rotate the engine again; the belt should "pop" over the pulley on the camshaft. Make sure the belt is positioned properly on both pulleys.

12 Reinstall the cover and tighten the fasteners securely.

ACCESSORY DRIVEBELT TENSIONER

13 On four-cylinder models, remove the two bolts securing the tensioner to the engine block. On V6 models, remove the bolt (2009 and earlier models) or three bolts (2010 models) securing the tensioner to the timing chain cover, then detach the tensioner from the cover (see illustration 23.6).

14 Installation is the reverse of removal. Be sure to tighten the tensioners bolt(s) to the torque listed in this Chapter's Specifications.

24 Automatic transaxle fluid change (every 60,000 miles or 48 months)

➡**Note: For transmission identification, refer to the Vehicle Identification Numbers information at the front of this manual.**

1 The automatic transaxle fluid should be changed at the recommended intervals.

2 Before beginning work, purchase the specified transmission fluid (see *Recommended lubricants and fluids* in this Chapter's Specifications).

3 Other tools necessary for this job include jackstands to support the vehicle in a raised position, wrenches, a drain pan, newspapers and clean rags.

4 The fluid should be drained immediately after the vehicle has been driven. Hot fluid is more effective than cold fluid at removing built-up sediment.

✻✻ WARNING:

Fluid temperature can exceed 350-degrees F in a hot transaxle. Wear protective gloves.

5 After the vehicle has been driven to warm up the fluid, raise the front of the vehicle and support it securely on jackstands.

✻✻ WARNING:

Never work under a vehicle that is supported only by a jack!

AISIN AW21 TRANSAXLE

➧ **Refer to illustrations 24.6 and 24.7**

6 Place the drain pan under the drain plug in the transaxle pan and remove the drain plug (see illustration). Once the fluid has drained, reinstall the drain plug and tighten it to the torque listed in this Chapter's Specifications.

7 Lower the vehicle and remove the fill plug from the top of the transaxle (see illustration).

8 Add five quarts of new fluid to the transaxle through the fill plug hole (see *Recommended lubricants and fluids* for the recommended fluid type), then install the fill plug and tighten it to the torque listed in this Chapter's Specifications.

9 Start the engine and, while depressing the brake pedal, cycle the shifter through each gear position and return it to Park. With the engine running, add fluid through the dipstick tube, 1/2-pint at a time as necessary (cycling the shifter through each gear position between additions) until the level is up the COLD notch (the lowest notch) on the dipstick.

10 Drive the vehicle a few miles until the fluid is up to normal operating temperature, then recheck the fluid level (see Section 4); it should be in the range indicated in illustration 4.34b. If not, add fluid a little at a time (cycling the shifter through each gear position between additions) until the level is correct. Be sure to tighten the fill plug to the torque listed in this Chapter's Specifications.

11 If you wish to flush the torque converter of old fluid, repeat Steps 6 through 10 one or two more times.

6F35 TRANSAXLE

12 Place the drain pan under the drain plug in the transaxle pan and remove the drain plug. Once the fluid has drained, reinstall the drain plug and tighten it to the torque listed in this Chapter's Specifications.

13 Lower the vehicle.

14 Measure the amount of fluid drained and record this figure for reference when refilling.

15 With the engine off, add new fluid to the transaxle through the dipstick tube (see *Recommended lubricants and fluids* for the recommended fluid type). Begin the refill procedure by initially adding 1/3 of the amount drained. Then, with the engine running, add 1/2-pint at a time (cycling the shifter through each gear position between additions) until the level is correct on the dipstick.

16 Repeat Steps 12 through 15 two more times to flush any contaminated fluid from the torque converter.

17 Drive the vehicle a few miles until the fluid is up to normal oper-

24.6 Location of the transaxle drain plug (AW21 transaxle)

24.7 The fluid fill plug on the AW21 transaxle is located on the left side of the transaxle (air filter housing removed for clarity)

ating temperature, then recheck the fluid level (see Section 4); it should be in the cross-hatched range (or in the range between the hot operation lines). If not, add fluid a little at a time (cycling the shifter through each gear position between additions) until the level is correct.

FNR5 TRANSAXLE

18 Position a drain pan under the transaxle, then disconnect the transmission fluid cooler return line from the transaxle; it's the cooler line closest to the left (driver's) side of the transaxle. Direct the end of the hose into the drain pan.

19 Start the engine and let it run at idle speed until three quarts of fluid has been pumped out of the hose into the drain pan, then turn the engine Off.

20 Remove the transaxle fluid dipstick and add three quarts of new fluid of the correct type to the transaxle (see *Recommended lubricants and fluids* for the recommended fluid type).

21 Repeat Steps 19 and 20 two more times, then reconnect the cooler line to the transaxle. Lower the vehicle and check the fluid level (see Section 4), adding a little at a time (cycling the shifter through each gear position between additions) until the level is up to the lower notch on the dipstick.

22 Drive the vehicle a few miles until the fluid is up to normal operating temperature, then recheck the fluid level (see Section 4); it should be between the two notches. If not, add fluid a little at a time (cycling the shifter through each gear position between additions) until the level is correct.

FLUID DISPOSAL

23 The old fluid drained from the transaxle cannot be reused in its present state and should be disposed of. Check with your local auto parts store, disposal facility or environmental agency to see if they will accept the fluid for recycling. After the fluid has cooled it can be drained into a container (capped plastic jugs, topped bottles, milk cartons, etc.) for transport to one of these disposal sites. Don't dispose of the fluid by pouring it on the ground or down a drain!

25 Manual transaxle lubricant change (every 60,000 miles or 48 months)

1 This procedure should be performed after the vehicle has been driven so the lubricant will be warm and therefore flow out of the transaxle more easily.

2 Raise the vehicle and support it securely on jackstands. Position a drain pan under the transaxle. Remove the transaxle fill plug on the front of the case; it's about half-way up on the transaxle case and is the larger of the two hex-head bolts.

⁂ CAUTION:

Do not remove the smaller hex-head bolt above the back-up light switch. Remove the drain plug at the bottom of the case and allow the lubricant to drain into the pan.

3 After the lubricant has drained completely, reinstall the drain plug and tighten it securely.

4 Using a hand pump, syringe or funnel, fill the transaxle with the specified lubricant until it is level with the lower edge of the filler hole. Using a new sealing washer, reinstall the fill plug and tighten it to the torque listed in this Chapter's Specifications.

5 Lower the vehicle.

6 Drive the vehicle for a short distance, then check the drain and fill plugs for leakage.

7 The old lubricant drained from the transaxle cannot be reused in its present state and should be disposed of. Check with your local auto parts store, disposal facility or environmental agency to see if they will accept the lubricant for recycling. After the lubricant has cooled it can be drained into a container (capped plastic jugs, topped bottles, milk cartons, etc.) for transport to one of these disposal sites. Don't dispose of the lubricant by pouring it on the ground or down a drain!

26 Differential lubricant change (AWD models) (every 60,000 miles or 48 months)

DRAIN

1 This procedure should be performed after the vehicle has been driven so the lubricant will be warm and therefore flow out of the differential more easily.

2 Raise the vehicle and support it securely on jackstands.

3 The easiest way to drain the differential is to remove the lubricant through the filler plug hole with a suction pump. If the differential cover gasket is leaking, it will be necessary to remove the cover to drain the lubricant (which will also allow you to inspect the differential).

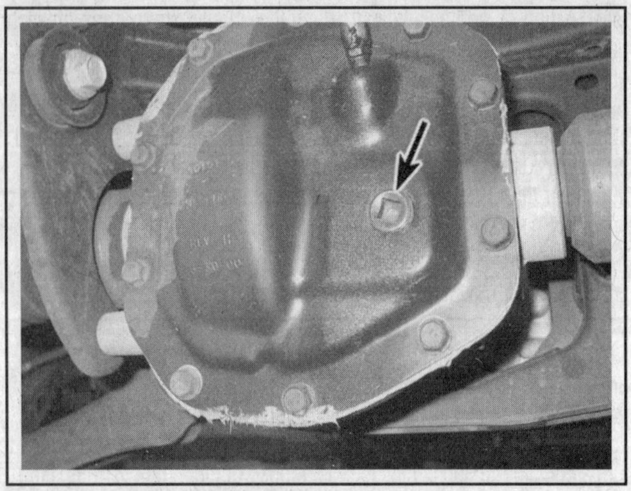

26.4 Rear differential check/fill plug

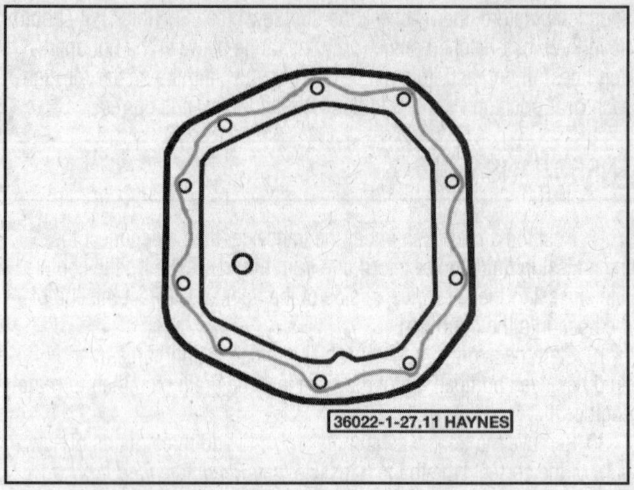

26.11 Apply a continuous bead of RTV sealant to the cover

Changing the lubricant with a suction pump

➧ Refer to illustration 26.4

4 Remove the filler plug from the differential (see illustration).

5 Insert the flexible hose.

6 Work the hose down to the bottom of the differential housing and pump the lubricant out.

Changing the lubricant by removing the cover

➧ Refer to illustration 26.11

7 Move a drain pan, rags, newspapers and wrenches under the vehicle.

8 Remove the bolts on the lower half of the cover. Loosen the bolts on the upper half and use them to loosely retain the cover. Allow the oil to drain into the pan, then completely remove the cover.

9 Using a lint-free rag, clean the inside of the cover and the accessible areas of the differential housing. As this is done, check for chipped gears and metal particles in the lubricant, indicating that the differential should be more thoroughly inspected and/or repaired.

10 Thoroughly clean the gasket mating surfaces of the differential housing and the cover plate. Use a gasket scraper or putty knife to remove all traces of the old gasket.

11 Apply a bead of RTV sealant to the cover flange (see illustration). Make sure the bolt holes align properly, then install the cover and tighten the fasteners to the torque listed in this Chapter's Specifications.

REFILL

12 Use a hand pump, syringe or funnel to fill the differential housing with the specified lubricant until it's within 1/8 to 3/16-inch (3 to 5 mm) from the bottom of the filler plug hole.

13 Install the fill plug and tighten it to the torque listed in this Chapter's Specifications.

14 The old lubricant drained from the differential cannot be reused in its present state and should be disposed of. Check with your local auto parts store, disposal facility or environmental agency to see if they will accept the lubricant for recycling. After the lubricant has cooled it can be drained into a container (capped plastic jugs, topped bottles, milk cartons, etc.) for transport to one of these disposal sites. Don't dispose of the lubricant by pouring it on the ground or down a drain!

27 Transfer case lubricant change (AWD models)

➡ **Note: Technically, the transfer case is filled for life; routine fluid changes aren't necessary unless the fluid somehow becomes contaminated.**

These transfer cases are not equipped with drain plugs. The manufacturer states that the transfer case must be removed from the vehicle in order to drain it; the removal procedure is included in Chapter 7C. If you wish to attempt to drain the fluid using the same method as described in Section 26, Steps 4 through 6, that may be a viable alternative.

28 Spark plug check and replacement (see Maintenance schedule for service intervals)

Refer to illustrations 28.2, 28.5a, 28.5b, 28.6a, 28.6b, 28.8, 28.9, 28.10a and 28.10b

1 On these vehicles the spark plugs are located in the center of the valve cover(s). Access to the rear cylinder bank spark plugs on V6 models requires removal of the upper intake manifold (see Chapter 2B).

2 In most cases, the tools necessary for spark plug replacement include a spark plug socket which fits onto a ratchet (spark plug sockets are padded inside to prevent damage to the porcelain insulators on the new plugs), various extensions and a gap gauge to check and adjust the gaps on the new plugs (see illustration). A torque wrench should be used to tighten the new plugs.

3 The best approach when replacing the spark plugs is to purchase the new ones in advance, adjust them to the proper gap and replace the plugs one at a time. When buying the new spark plugs, be sure to obtain the correct plug type for your particular engine. This information can be found in this Chapter's Specifications or in the factory owner's manual.

4 Allow the engine to cool completely before attempting to remove any of the plugs. These engines are equipped with aluminum cylinder heads, which can be damaged if the spark plugs are removed when the engine is hot. While you are waiting for the engine to cool, check the new plugs for defects and adjust the gaps.

5 The gap is checked by inserting the proper-thickness gauge between the electrodes at the tip of the plug (see illustration). The gap between the electrodes should be the same as the one specified on the Emissions Control Information label or in this Chapter's Specifications. The gauge should just slide between the electrodes with a slight amount of drag. If the gap is incorrect, use the adjuster on the gauge body to bend the curved side electrode slightly until the proper gap is obtained (see illustration). If the side electrode is not exactly over the center electrode, bend it with the adjuster until it is. Check for cracks in the porcelain insulator (if any are found, the plug should not be used).

Note: We recommend using a tapered thickness gauge when checking platinum- or iridium-type spark plugs. Other types of gauges may scrape the thin coating from the electrodes, thus dramatically shortening the life of the plugs. However, if dual-electrode spark plugs are used, a wire-type gauge will have to be used.

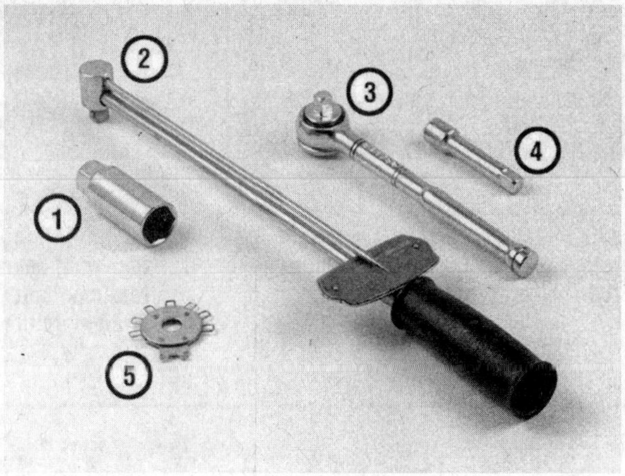

28.2 Tools required for changing spark plugs

1 ***Spark plug socket*** - *This will have special padding inside to protect the spark plug porcelain insulator*
2 ***Torque wrench*** - *Although not mandatory, use of this tool is the best way to ensure that the plugs are tightened properly*
3 ***Ratchet*** - *Standard hand tool to fit the plug socket*
4 ***Extension*** - *Depending on model and accessories, you may need special extensions and universal joints to reach one or more of the plugs*
5 ***Spark plug gap gauge*** - *This gauge for checking the gap comes in a variety of styles. Make sure the gap for your engine is included*

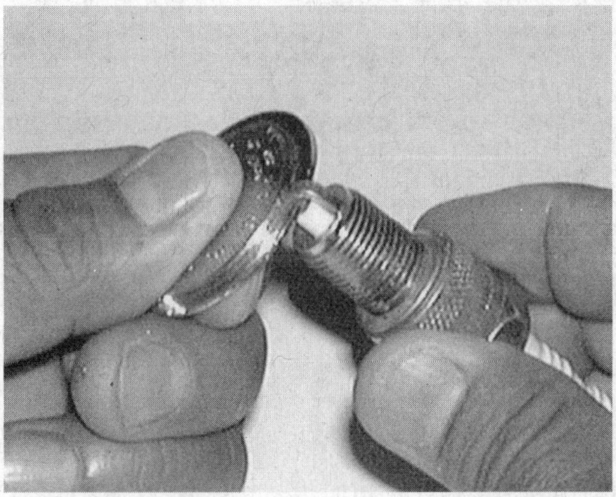

28.5a Using a tapered thickness gauge to check the spark plug gap - slide the thin side into the gap and turn it until the gauge just fills the gap, then read the thickness on the gauge - do not force the tool into the gap or use the tapered portion to widen a gap

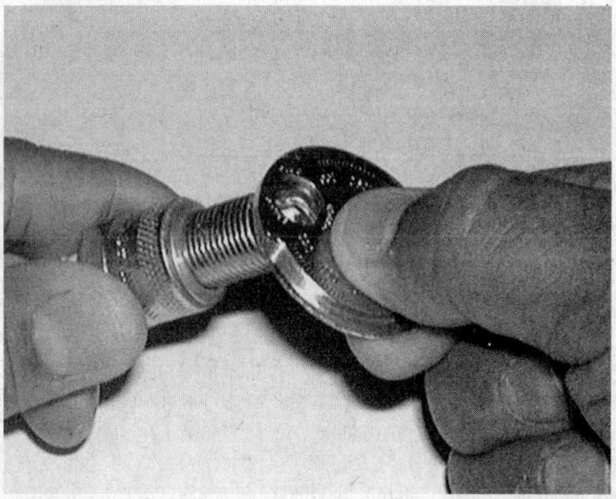

28.5b To change the gap, bend the side electrode only, using the adjuster hole in the tool, and be very careful not to crack or chip the porcelain insulator surrounding the center electrode

28.6a All models are equipped with individual coils which must be removed to access the spark plugs (V6 shown, front bank)

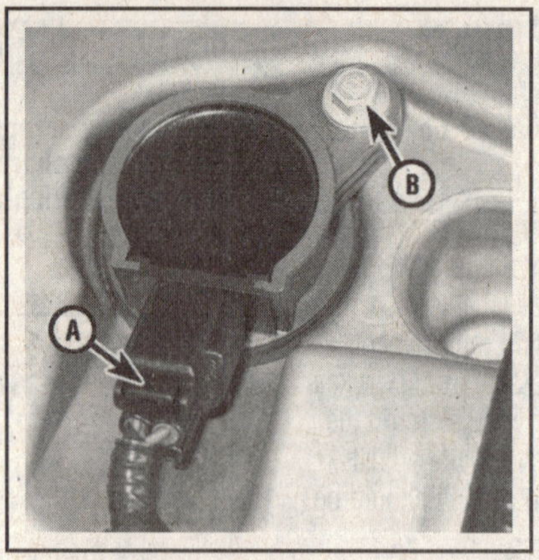

28.6b To remove the coils, depress the tab (A) and disconnect the electrical connector, remove the coil retaining bolt (B), then pull the coil straight up to remove it

28.8 Use a ratchet and extension to remove the spark plugs

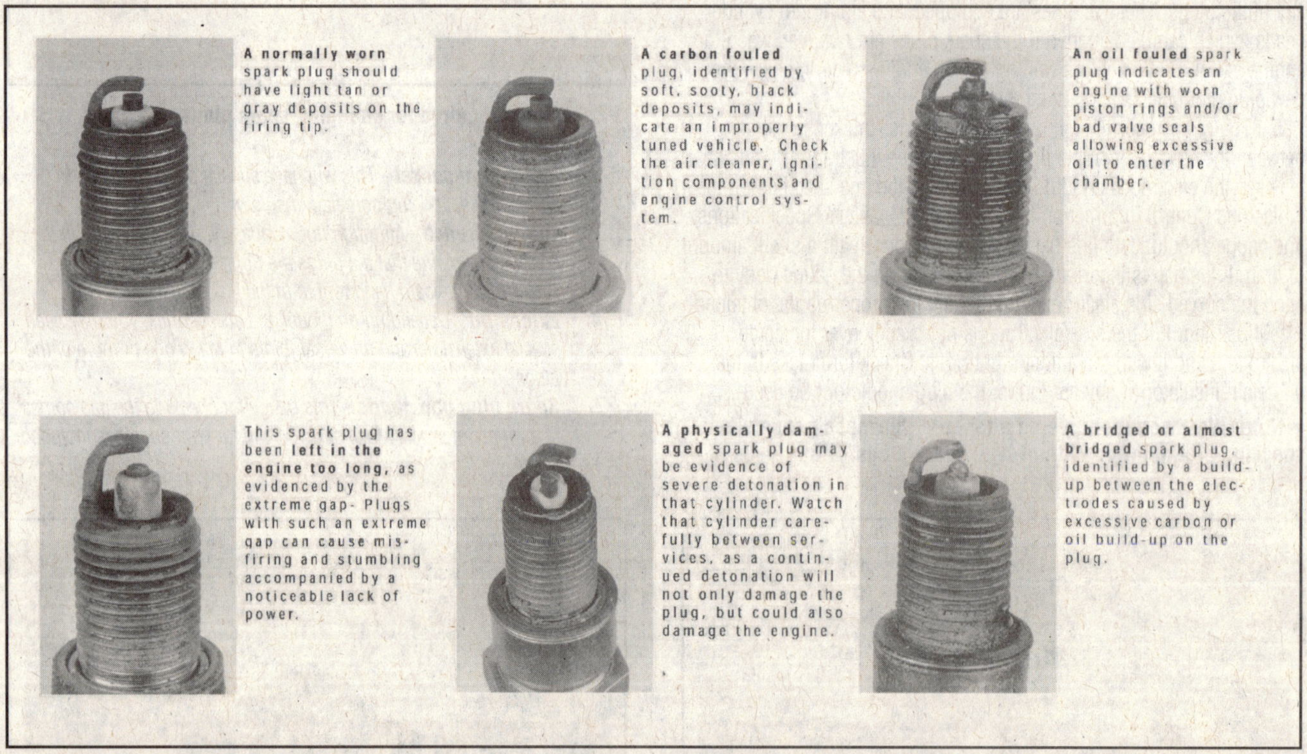

28.9 Inspect the spark plug to determine engine running conditions

6 All models are equipped with individual ignition coils which must be removed first to access the spark plugs (see illustrations).

7 If compressed air is available, use it to blow any dirt or foreign material away from the spark plug hole. The idea here is to eliminate the possibility of debris falling into the cylinder as the spark plug is removed.

8 Place the spark plug socket over the plug and remove it from the engine by turning it in a counterclockwise direction (see illustration).

9 Compare the spark plug with this chart (see illustration) to get an ation of the overall running condition of the engine.

10 Apply a small amount of anti-seize compound to the spark plug threads (see illustration). Install one of the new plugs into the hole until you can no longer turn it with your fingers, then tighten it with a torque wrench (if available) or the ratchet. It is a good idea to slip a short length of rubber hose over the end of the plug to use as a tool to thread it into place (see illustration). The hose will grip the plug well enough to turn it, but will start to slip if the plug begins to cross-thread in the hole - this will prevent damaged threads and the accompanying repair costs.

11 Repeat the procedure for the remaining spark plugs.

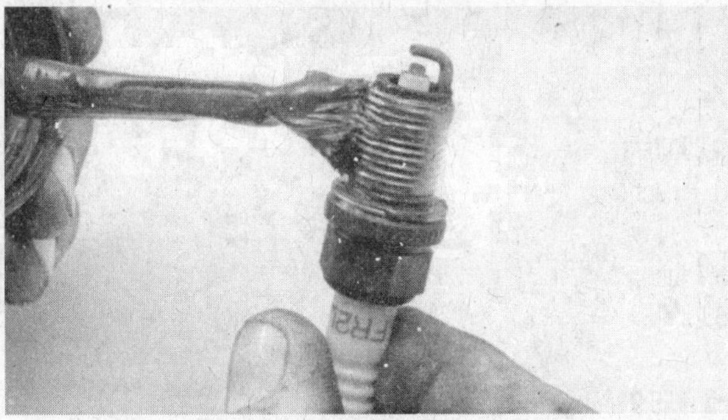

28.10a Apply a thin coat of anti-seize compound to the spark plug threads

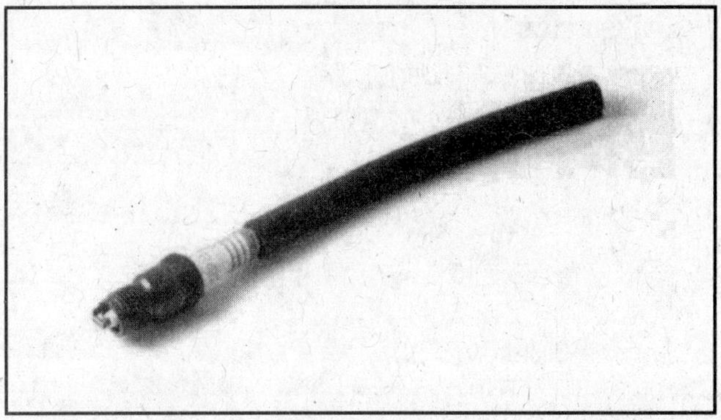

28.10b A length of snug-fitting rubber hose will save time and prevent damaged threads when installing the spark plugs

Specifications

Recommended lubricants and fluids

➡Note: Listed here are manufacturer recommendations at the time this manual was written. Manufacturers occasionally upgrade their fluid and lubricant specifications, so check with your local auto parts store for current recommendations.

Engine oil	
Type	API "certified for gasoline engines"
Viscosity	SAE 5W-20
Fuel	Unleaded gasoline, 87 octane
Automatic transaxle fluid*	
5-speed	Motorcraft FNR5 Automatic Transmission Fluid
6-speed	
2006 through 2009 models	Motorcraft Premium Automatic Transmission Fluid
2010 models	
Aisin AW21 transaxle	Motorcraft Premium Automatic Transmission Fluid
6F35 transaxle	MERCON LV Automatic Transmission Fluid

CAUTION:

Do not use MERCON® V or dual usage MERCON®/MERCON® V automatic transmission fluid.

Manual transaxle lubricant	SAE 75W-90 gear oil
Transfer case (AWD models)	SAE 75W-140
Rear differential lubricant (AWD models)	SAE 80W-90 Premium Rear Axle Lubricant
Brake fluid	DOT 3 brake fluid
Clutch fluid	DOT 3 brake fluid
Engine coolant	50/50 mixture of Motorcraft Premium Engine Coolant (green col ored) or Motorcraft Premium Gold Engine Coolant (yellow colored) and distilled water

CAUTION:

Do not mix coolants of different colors. Doing so might damage the cooling system and/or the engine. The manufacturer specifies either a green colored coolant or a yellow colored coolant to be used in these systems, depending on what was originally installed in the vehicle.

Power steering system	
2006 and 2007 models	MERCON automatic transmission fluid
2008 and later models	MERCON V automatic transmissiofluid

** For automatic transaxle identification, refer to the "Vehicle Identification Numbers" Section at the front of this manual.*

Capacities*

Engine oil (including filter)	
Four-cylinder engines	
2.3L	4.5 quarts (4.25 liters)
2.5L	5.3 quarts (5.0 liters
V6 engines	
3.0L	6.0 quarts (5.7 liters)
3.5L	5.5 quarts (5.2 liters)
Coolant	
Four-cylinder engines	Up to 8.6 quarts (8.2 liters)
V6 engines	
3.0L	
2009 and earlier models	Up to 10 quarts (9.5 liters)
2010 models	Up to 10.6 quarts (10.0 liters)
3.5L	Up to 11.1 quarts (10.5 liters)
Automatic transaxle (dry fill)	Up to 9.0 quarts (8.5 liters)

➡Note: Since this is a dry-fill specification, the amount required during a routine fluid change will be substantially less. The best way to determine the amount of fluid to add during a routine fluid change is to measure the amount drained. Begin the refill procedure by initially adding 1/3 of the amount drained. Then, with the engine running, add 1/2-pint at a time (cycling the shifter through each gear position between additions) until the level is correct on the dipstick. It is important to not overfill the transaxle. You will, however, need to purchase a few extra quarts, since the fluid replacement procedure involves flushing the torque converter (see Section 24).

Manual transaxle	Up to 3.0 quarts (2.87 liters)
Transfer case (AWD models)	Up to 12 ounces (0.35 liters)
Rear differential (AWD models)	Up to 1.2 quarts (1.1 liters)

**All capacities approximate. Add as necessary to bring up to appropriate level.*

Ignition system

Spark plug type and gap	
Type	
Four-cylinder engines	
2.3L	Motorcraft AZFS-32F or equivalent
2.5L	Motorcraft AZFS-32FE or equivalent
V6 engines	
3.0L	Motorcraft AWSF-32F or equivalent
3.5L	Motorcraft AYSF-22FM or equivalent
Gap	
2.0L four-cylinder engine	0.048 to 0.052 inch (1.22 to 1.32 mm)
2.3L four-cylinder engine	0.054 inch (1.37 mm)
V6 engines	0.052 to 0.056 inch (1.3 to 1.4 mm)
Engine firing order	
Four-cylinder engines	1-3-4-2
V6 engines	1-4-2-5-3-6

Cylinder location - four-cylinder engines

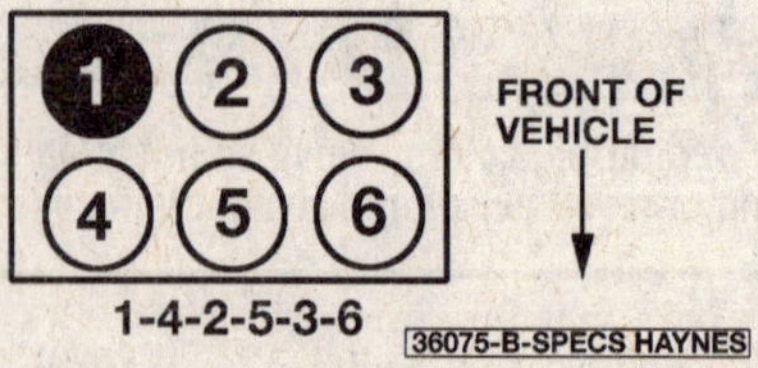

Cylinder location - V6 engines

Valve clearances (engine cold)

Four-cylinder engines	
Intake valve	0.008 to 0.011 inch (0.22 to 0.28 mm)
Exhaust valve	0.010 to 0.013 inch (0.25 to 0.33 mm)
3.0L V6 engine	Not adjustable (hydraulic lash adjusters)
3.5L V6 engine	
Intake	0.006 to 0.010 inch (0.15 to 0.25 mm)
Exhaust	0.014 to 0.018 inch (0.36 to 0.46 mm)

Clutch pedal

Freeplay	0.20 to 0.51 inch (5 to 13 mm)
Height	8.27 to 8.50 inches (210 to 216 mm)

Brakes

Disc brake pad lining thickness (minimum)	1/8 inch (3 mm)
Drum brake shoe lining thickness (minimum)	1/16 inch (1.5 mm)
Parking brake adjustment	3 to 5 clicks

Torque specifications	Ft-lbs (unless otherwise indicated)	Nm

➡Note: One foot-pound (ft-lb) of torque is equivalent to 12 inch-pounds (in-lbs) of torque. Torque values below approximately 15 foot-pounds are expressed in inch-pounds, because most foot-pound torque wrenches are not accurate at these smaller values.

Engine oil drain plug		
Four-cylinder engines		
2006 models	19	26
2007 and later models	21	28
V6 engines	19	26
Automatic transaxle drain plug*		
Aisin AW21	35	47
Mazda FNR5	21	29
6F35	106 in-lbs	12
Automatic transaxle fill plug (Aisin AW21)*	29	39
Manual transaxle drain and fill plugs	36	49
Rear differential cover bolts (AWD)	17	23
Rear differential check/fill plug (AWD)	21	28
Transfer case check/fill plug	15	20
Spark plugs		
Four-cylinder engines	106 in-lbs	12
V6 engines	132 in-lbs	15
Drivebelt tensioner bolts		
Four-cylinder engines	18	25
3.0L V6 engine		
2009 and earlier models	33	45
2010 models	18	25
3.5L V6 engine	97 in-lbs	11
Wheel lug nuts	98	133

** For automatic transaxle identification, refer to the "Vehicle Identification Numbers" Section at the front of this manual.*

Notes

2A

FOUR-CYLINDER ENGINES

Reference to other Chapters

Drivebelt check and replacement - See Chapter 1
Engine oil and filter change - See Chapter 1
Engine/transaxle - removal and installation - See Chapter 2C

1 General information

HOW TO USE THIS CHAPTER

This Part of Chapter 2 is devoted to repair procedures possible while the engine is still installed in the vehicle. Since these procedures are based on the assumption that the engine is installed in the vehicle, if the engine has been removed from the vehicle and mounted on a stand, some of the preliminary dismantling steps outlined will not apply.

Information concerning engine/transaxle removal and replacement and engine overhaul, can be found in Part C of this Chapter.

ENGINE DESCRIPTION

These engines are sixteen-valve, double overhead camshaft (DOHC), four-cylinder, in-line type, mounted transversely at the front of the vehicle, with the transmission on the left-hand end. They incorporate an aluminum cylinder head and an aluminum cylinder block.

The two camshafts are driven by a timing chain, each operating eight valves via conventional lifters. Each camshaft rotates in five bearings that are line-bored directly in the cylinder head and the (bolted-on) bearing caps. This means that the bearing caps are not available separately from the cylinder head, and must not be interchanged with caps from another engine.

These engines incorporate an aluminum timing chain cover and oil pan, and the crankshaft main caps are part of a one-piece lower block support. When working on these engines, note that Torx-type (both male and female heads) and hexagon socket (Allen head) fasteners are widely used. A good selection of sockets, with the necessary adapters, will be required, so that these can be unscrewed without damage and, on reassembly, tightened to the torque wrench settings specified.

LUBRICATION SYSTEM

The oil pump is driven via a chain from the front of the crankshaft, using the same sprocket that drives the timing chain. The pump forces oil through an externally mounted full-flow cartridge-type filter. From the filter, the oil is pumped into a main gallery in the cylinder block/crankcase, from where it is distributed to the crankshaft (main bearings) and cylinder head.

The connecting rod bearings are supplied with oil via internal drillings in the crankshaft. Each piston crown and connecting rod is cooled by a spray of oil.

The cylinder head is provided with two oil galleries, one on the intake side and one on the exhaust, to ensure constant oil supply to the camshaft bearings and lifters. A retaining valve (inserted into the cylinder head's top surface, in the middle, on the intake side) prevents these galleries from being drained when the engine is switched off. The valve incorporates a ventilation hole in its upper end, to allow air bubbles to escape from the system when the engine is restarted.

2 Repair operations possible with the engine in the vehicle

Many major repair operations can be accomplished without removing the engine from the vehicle.

Clean the engine compartment and the exterior of the engine with some type of degreaser before any work is done. It will make the job easier and help keep dirt out of the internal areas of the engine.

Depending on the components involved, it may be helpful to remove the hood to improve access to the engine as repairs are performed (refer to Chapter 11 if necessary). Cover the fenders to prevent damage to the paint. Special pads are available, but an old bedspread or blanket will also work.

If vacuum, exhaust, oil or coolant leaks develop, indicating a need for gasket or seal replacement, the repairs can generally be made with the engine in the vehicle. The intake and exhaust manifold gaskets, oil pan gasket, crankshaft oil seals and cylinder head gasket are all accessible with the engine in place.

Exterior engine components, such as the intake and exhaust manifolds, the oil pan, the oil pump, the water pump, the starter motor, the alternator and the fuel system components can be removed for repair with the engine in place.

Since the camshaft(s) and cylinder head can be removed without pulling the engine, valve component servicing can also be accomplished with the engine in the vehicle. Replacement of the timing chain and sprockets is also possible with the engine in the vehicle.

In extreme cases caused by a lack of necessary equipment, repair or replacement of piston rings, pistons, connecting rods and rod bearings is possible with the engine in the vehicle. However, this practice is not recommended because of the cleaning and preparation work that must be done to the components involved.

3 Top Dead Center (TDC) for number 1 piston - locating

Refer to illustrations 3.4, 3.5, 3.7a and 3.7b

Note: You will need two special tools for this procedure: the camshaft positioning tool (303-465, or equivalent) and the timing pin (303-507).

1 Disconnect the battery negative cable (see Chapter 5).

2 Remove the valve cover (see Section 4).

3 Using a wrench or socket on the crankshaft pulley bolt, rotate the crankshaft clockwise until the intake valves for no. 1 cylinder have opened and just closed again. The threaded hole in the crankshaft pulley should be near the corresponding hole in the timing chain cover (see illustration 8.10).

3.4 Remove the timing hole plug . . .

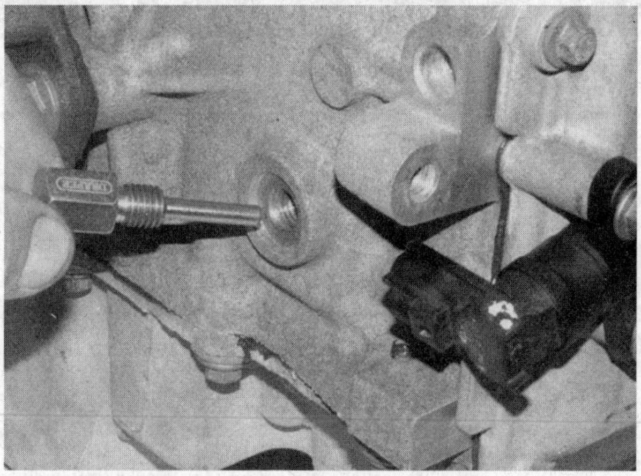

3.5 . . . and insert the timing pin tool

3.7a Turn the engine so that the camshaft end slots are aligned . . .

3.7b . . . then insert the metal strip into the slots to locate and set the shafts to TDC

4 A TDC timing hole is located near the lower right front corner of the engine block (on the firewall side) to provide a means of accurately positioning the no. 1 cylinder at TDC. When you locate this hole, remove the timing pin plug (see illustration).

5 Screw in the timing pin (see illustration).

**** CAUTION:**

We don't recommend trying to fabricate a timing pin with a bolt because while you would be able to determine the correct bolt diameter and thread pitch, it is impossible to determine what the length of the bolt should be. These pins come in several lengths, depending on the engine family. There is no way to determine the correct pin length without comparing it to a factory or aftermarket tool designed to be used with this engine. Using a bolt of the wrong length could damage the engine. Also, never use the timing pin as a means to stop the engine from rotating - tool breakage and/or engine damage can result.

6 Turn the crankshaft slowly clockwise until the crankshaft counterweight comes into contact with the timing pin - in this position, the engine is set to TDC on no. 1 cylinder.

7 The camshafts each have a machined slot at the transaxle end of the engine. Both slots will be completely horizontal, and at the same height as the cylinder head machined surface, when the engine is at TDC on the Number 1 cylinder. Manufacturer service tool 303-465 is used to check this position, and to positively locate the camshafts in position. Fortunately, a substitute tool can be made from a strip of metal 5 mm thick. While the strip's thickness is critical, its length and width are not, but should be approximately 180 to 230 mm long by 20 to 30 mm wide (see illustrations).

**** CAUTION:**

Never use the camshaft alignment tool as a means to stop the engine from rotating - engine damage can result.

8 Before rotating the crankshaft again, make sure that the tools are removed. Do not forget to install the blanking plug and tighten it securely.

9 Once no. 1 cylinder has been positioned at TDC on the compression stroke, TDC for any of the other cylinders can then be located by rotating the crankshaft clockwise 180-degrees at a time and following the firing order (see this Chapter's Specifications).

4 Valve cover - removal and installation

REMOVAL

1 Disconnect the cable from the negative battery terminal (see Chapter 5).

2 Remove the individual ignition coil assemblies from the spark plugs (see Chapter 5).

3 Disconnect the electrical connectors for the variable camshaft timing, cylinder head temperature sensor and the camshaft position sensor.

4 Remove the bracket for the wiring harness on the valve cover stud, then set the harness aside.

5 Remove the engine oil dipstick.

6 Working progressively, unscrew the valve cover retaining fasteners, noting the (captive) spacer sleeve and rubber seal, then withdraw the cover.

7 Discard the cover gasket. This must be replaced whenever it is disturbed. Check that the sealing faces are undamaged and that the rubber seal at each bolt hole is serviceable. Replace any worn or damaged seals.

INSTALLATION

8 On installation, clean the cover and cylinder head gasket faces carefully, then install a new gasket onto the valve cover, ensuring that it is located correctly by the rubber seals and spacer sleeves.

9 At the top of the timing chain cover, apply a small bead of RTV sealant to the joints where the valve cover and timing cover meet the engine.

10 Install the cover to the cylinder head, ensuring as the cover is tightened that the gasket remains seated.

11 Working in a diagonal sequence from the center outwards, first tighten the cover bolts by hand only. Once all the bolts are hand-tight, go around once more in sequence, and tighten the bolts to the torque listed in this Chapter Specifications.

12 Reconnect the battery.

13 Run the engine and check for signs of oil leakage.

5 Valve clearances - checking and adjustment

➧ Refer to illustration 5.4

1 Disconnect the battery cable from the negative battery terminal (see Chapter 5).

2 Remove all the spark plugs as described in Chapter 1, then remove the valve cover as described in Section 4.

3 Loosen the right front wheel lug nuts, raise the front of the vehicle and support it securely on jackstands, then remove the wheel. Remove the fender splash shield.

4 Using a wrench or socket on the crankshaft pulley bolt, rotate the crankshaft clockwise and check each lifter when its camshaft lobe is straight up, ensuring that the measurement is between the base circle of the camshaft lobe and the top of the lifter. Use feeler gauges to measure the clearances (see illustration).

5 The clearance must be checked between each camshaft lobe and the lifter it operates. Keep careful notes of the measurements recorded for each lifter.

6 If some measurements fall outside the recommended clearances in this Chapter's Specifications, the camshafts must be removed and the out-of-spec lifters removed (see Section 11). New lifters are available with various thicknesses to correct the valve clearances. Each lifter is marked with a thickness number. Only refer to the numbers after the decimal point. A "0.650" marking refers to an actual thickness of 3.650 mm.

7 To arrive at the desired thickness for new lifters: add the thickness of the original lifter (such as 0.650 mm) to the clearance you measured. Subtract the midrange figure for ideal clearance (see the Specifications) from that number and you have the proper lifter thickness to order. Every thickness is not available, so choose the closest to your requirement.

5.4 Check the valve clearances with a feeler gauge of the specified thickness. If the clearance is correct, you should feel a slight drag as the feeler gauge is slid between the lifter and the camshaft

8 Refer to Section 11 for installation of the camshafts. Once the camshafts and timing chain have been installed, recheck the valve clearances.

9 The remainder of installation is the reverse of removal. Run the engine and check for oil leaks.

6 Intake manifold - removal and installation

REMOVAL

1 Relieve the fuel system pressure (see Chapter 4)

2 Disconnect the cable from the negative battery terminal (see Chapter 5).

3 Remove the air cleaner outlet hose (see Chapter 4).

4 On 2.3L engines, remove the alternator air intake duct (see Chapter 5).

5 Disconnect the electrical connectors for the swirl control, throttle body, MAP sensor, and oil pressure sender. Remove the air intake duct from the throttle body.

➡Note: If you're simply removing the intake manifold plenum to remove or service the cylinder head, it's not necessary to remove the throttle body from the intake manifold.

6 Release the brake booster vacuum hose from the intake manifold by depressing the lock spring and pulling the hose upward at the same time.

7 If equipped with AIR injection, disconnect the AIR pump connector and remove the AIR pump (see Chapter 6).

8 Release the harness clips and set aside the wiring harness at the top of the intake manifold.

9 Remove the fuel rail heat shield (see Chapter 4).

10 The intake manifold is secured with 8 bolts, one below and seven along the top.

➡Note: There are two sizes of bolts; make note of where the bolts were originally installed.

Remove the bolts and pull the intake manifold away from the engine enough to access and disconnect the EGR pipe (if equipped) and the crankcase vent hose from the oil separator. Squeeze the two clips on the vent hose to release it.

INSTALLATION

11 There are individual gaskets for each of the four ports of the intake manifold. Using new manifold gaskets, install the intake manifold. Tighten the bolts and nuts in several stages, working from the center out, to the torque listed in this Chapter's Specifications.

12 Installation is otherwise the reverse of removal.

7 Exhaust manifold - removal and installation

⁂ WARNING:

Allow the engine to cool completely before beginning this procedure.

➡Note: On some models, the catalytic converter is integral with the exhaust manifold, and they must be replaced as a unit (see Chapter 6).

REMOVAL

1 Raise the vehicle and place it securely on jackstands.

2 When the engine has cooled, it will be helpful to soak the manifold heat-shield retaining nuts with penetrating oil to loosen any rust. Remove the heat shield. Apply penetrating oil to the exhaust manifold mounting bolts.

3 Disconnect the exhaust pipe from the exhaust manifold (see Chapter 4). Remove and discard the old flange gasket.

4 Unplug the electrical connector for the oxygen sensor and remove the oxygen sensor from the exhaust manifold (see Chapter 6).

5 Remove the exhaust manifold mounting nuts, then remove the exhaust manifold and the old manifold gasket.

6 Use a stud removal tool or two nuts tightened against each other to remove the old studs from the cylinder head.

INSPECTION

7 Inspect the exhaust manifold for cracks and any other obvious damage. If the manifold is cracked or damaged in any way, replace it.

8 Using a scraper, remove all traces of gasket material from the mating surfaces and inspect them for wear and cracks.

⁂ CAUTION:

When removing gasket material from any surface, especially aluminum, be very careful not to scratch or gouge the gasket surface. Any damage to the surface may cause an exhaust leak. Gasket removal solvents are available from auto parts stores and may prove helpful.

9 Using a straightedge and feeler gauge, inspect the exhaust manifold mating surface for warpage. Also check the exhaust manifold surface on the cylinder head. If the warpage on any surface exceeds the limits listed in this Chapter's Specifications, the exhaust manifold and/or cylinder head must be replaced or resurfaced at an automotive machine shop.

INSTALLATION

10 Install new exhaust studs in the cylinder head and install the manifold with a new gasket and new self-locking nuts.

➡Note: Coat the threads of the exhaust manifold studs with an anti-seize compound. Tighten the nuts in several stages, working from the center out, to the torque listed in this Chapter's Specifications.

11 The remainder of installation is the reverse of removal. Run the engine and check for exhaust leaks.

8 Crankshaft pulley - removal and installation

REMOVAL

➧ Refer to illustration 8.4

CAUTION:

Once the crankshaft pulley is loosened, the crankshaft (timing) sprocket will be loosened as well. The engine is considered out-of-time at this point. The installation procedure in this Section must be followed exactly to re-time the engine properly. Severe engine damage may occur otherwise.

1 Remove the drivebelt (see Chapter 1).

2 On 2.3L engines with an automatic transaxle, remove the two bolts from the right driveaxle intermediate shaft bracket and slide the intermediate shaft out of the transmission 1/2-inch.

3 Set the engine to TDC using the camshaft and crankshaft locking tools (see Section 3).

4 The crankshaft must be held to prevent its rotation while the pulley bolt is unscrewed. A special tool to hold the crankshaft pulley is needed for this. The tool for 2.3L engines is available at most auto supply stores or equipment rental locations, but a suitable equivalent can be fabricated from a length of strap steel, bolts, washers and nuts (see illustration). The 2.5L engine uses a different tool that engages with the hub; it's manufacturer tool no. 303-1416.

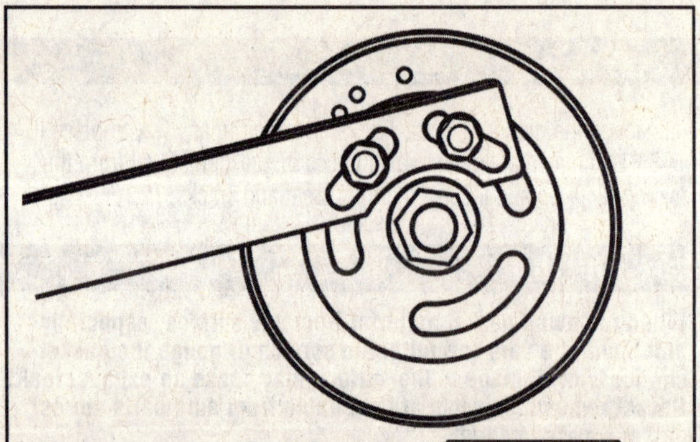

8.4 The crankshaft pulley holding tool installed

8.10 Install the M6 bolt to verify TDC

CAUTION:

Use of a pry bar or similar tool can damage the crankshaft pulley.

5 Insert the holding tool into the spaces in the front face of the pulley to hold it in place while turning the crankshaft pulley bolt with a large wrench or socket/breaker-bar combination.

CAUTION:

Failure to hold the crankshaft pulley securely while removing the pulley bolt could result in engine damage. NEVER use the timing pin or the camshaft alignment tool as a means of locking the crankshaft - they are designed for calibration only. Engine damage could occur by using these tools for anything other than their intended purpose.

6 Unscrew the pulley bolt and the holding tool.

7 Remove the pulley and, if you're working on a 2.5L engine, the "diamond" washer behind it. Obtain a new pulley bolt and washer and, if you're working on a 2.5L engine, a new diamond washer.

INSTALLATION

➧ Refer to illustrations 8.10 and 8.19

8 If you're working on a 2.5L engine, install a new diamond washer onto the nose of the crankshaft.

9 Lightly coat the crankshaft front seal with clean engine oil, then install the crankshaft pulley.

➡Note: If the seal shows signs of leakage, you may want to replace it before installing the crankshaft pulley (see Section 10).

Install a new crankshaft pulley bolt and washer and hand tighten only. Attempt to closely align the hole in the pulley with the threaded hole in the timing chain cover.

10 Install a crankshaft pulley alignment bolt (M6 x 18 mm) through the pulley and into the front engine cover (hand-tight only) (see illustration). Rotate the pulley as necessary to do this.

➡Note: This correctly aligns the pulley with the crankshaft.

11 Insert the holding tool into the pulley and tighten the crankshaft pulley bolt to the torque listed in this Chapter's Specifications.

12 Remove the crankshaft pulley holding tool and the threaded crankshaft alignment bolt from the pulley and front engine cover.

13 Remove the timing pin from the cylinder block.

14 Remove the camshaft alignment tool.

15 Remove the spark plugs and rotate the engine clockwise two complete revolutions by turning the crankshaft pulley bolt with a wrench or large socket.

CAUTION:

If you feel resistance at any point, stop and find out why. If the valve timing is incorrect, the valves may be contacting the pistons.

16 Rotate the engine again to achieve TDC (see Section 3).

Note: Rotate the engine in the clockwise direction only.

17 Install the timing pin into the cylinder block.

18 Install the crankshaft pulley alignment bolt (M6 x 18 mm). If it cannot be installed, the crankshaft pulley must be removed and aligned. Repeat Steps 8 through 18 until crankshaft pulley alignment is correct.

19 With the crankshaft pulley alignment bolt (M6 x 18 mm) installed, install the camshaft alignment tool and check the position of the camshafts (see illustration). If the tool cannot be installed, the engine timing must be corrected by repeating Steps 8 through 18.

20 The correct engine timing is achieved when the camshaft alignment tool, timing pin and the crankshaft pulley alignment bolt tool can be placed simultaneously.

21 Once correct engine timing is achieved, remove all the alignment tools and bolts and install the timing pin plug.

22 Reinstall all components removed previously.

8.19 The camshaft alignment tool installed

9 Timing chain cover, timing chain and tensioner - removal and installation

TIMING CHAIN COVER

Removal

1 Disconnect the negative battery cable (see Chapter 5).

2 Loosen the water pump pulley bolts, then remove the drivebelt and drivebelt idler pulley (see Chapter 1) and the water pump pulley (see Chapter 3).

3 Remove the crankshaft pulley (see Section 8). After this Step, the engine must remain at TDC with the valve cover removed.

4 Disconnect the Crankshaft Position (CKP) sensor electrical connector, then remove the sensor (see Chapter 6).

Note: Unfortunately with this engine, anytime this sensor is removed, a new sensor must be installed. The new sensor is packaged with a special sensor alignment tool that is critical for installation.

5 Support the engine from above with a support fixture (see Chapter 2C). Raise the engine enough to remove the right engine mount (see Section 17).

6 Disconnect the electrical connector to the power steering pressure switch. The switch is located on a high-pressure hose within the power steering system. Unbolt and set aside the power steering pump without disconnecting the hoses (see Chapter 10).

7 Remove the crankshaft front oil seal (see Section 10).

8 Remove the bolts and the timing cover.

Installation

Refer to illustration 9.9

9 Installation is the reverse of removal noting the following:

a) Clean the mating surfaces of all sealant.

Note: Be careful not to gouge or use any abrasives on the mating surfaces.

b) Install the engine cover within four minutes of applying a 2.5 mm bead of RTV sealant.

c) Tighten the bolts a little at a time, in sequence, to the torque listed in this Chapter's Specifications (see illustration).

d) Install a new crankshaft front oil seal.

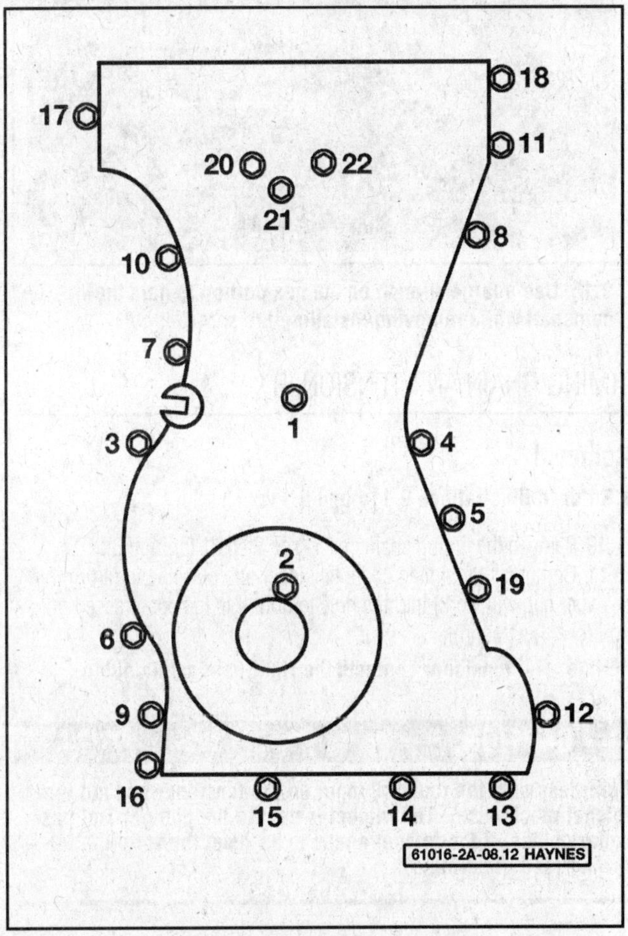

9.9 Timing chain cover bolt tightening sequence

e) Be sure to re-time the engine as described in Section 8 and also use a new crankshaft position sensor which includes the necessary alignment tool (see Chapter 6). Do not tighten the sensor mounting bolts until the installation tool is in place.

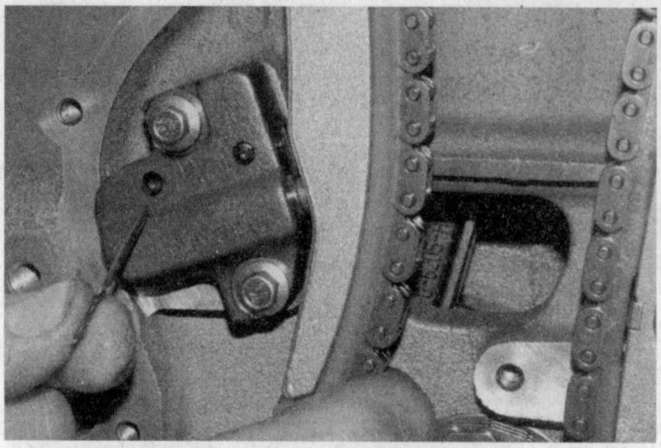

9.11a Compress the tensioner and insert the lock pin

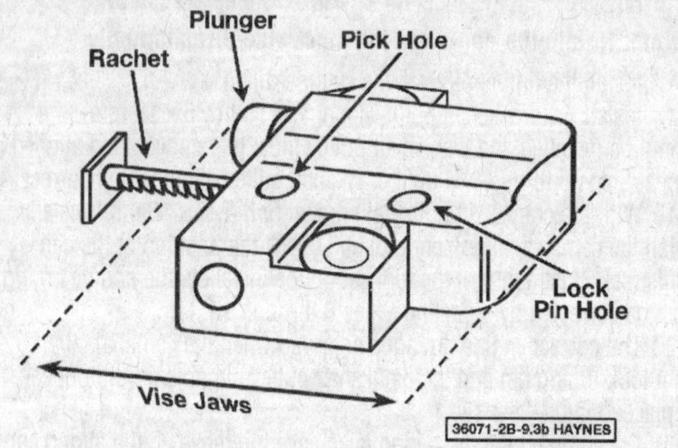

9.11b Timing chain tensioner details

9.16 Use a large wrench on the hex portion to hold the camshaft while removing/installing the sprocket bolt

9.20 Compress the tensioner to release the lock pin

TIMING CHAIN AND TENSIONER

Removal

➧ **Refer to illustrations 9.11a and 9.11b**

10 Remove the timing chain cover (see Steps 1 through 8).

11 Compress the timing chain tensioner and place a pin (a drill bit or paper clip will work) into the hole to hold it in the compressed position (see illustration).

➡**Note: The tensioner contacts the right-hand chain guide.**

CAUTION:

Compress only the round plunger on the tensioner and not the ratchet mechanism. The ratchet is next to the plunger and has square sides. If the ratchet needs to be reset, perform the following (see illustration):

a) *Remove the tensioner and place it lightly in a vise using the plunger and tensioner housing.*
b) *Place a pick-type tool in the hole closest to the ratchet to relieve the tension on the ratchet mechanism.*
c) *While holding the pick tool in place, move the ratchet back into the tensioner, then install a pin into the other hole to keep the plunger and ratchet compressed.*
d) *Remove the tensioner from the vise.*

12 Remove the two tensioner mounting bolts, then remove the tensioner.

13 Remove the loose timing chain guide (right). Remove the timing chain.

14 The left chain guide and camshaft sprockets can now be removed if necessary.

Installation

➧ **Refer to illustrations 9.16 and 9.20**

15 Remove the camshaft alignment tool (if installed).

16 Loosen both camshaft sprocket bolts but don't remove them. Use a wrench on the hexagonal area of the camshaft to hold it while turning the camshaft sprocket bolt (see illustration).

CAUTION:

Damage to the valves or pistons may occur if the camshafts are rotated during this procedure.

17 Install the left chain guide (if removed).

18 Install the timing chain.

19 Install the right chain guide.

20 Install the timing chain tensioner and tighten the fasteners to the torque listed in this Chapter's Specifications. Remove the pin to release the tensioner to engage the chain guide (see illustration).

21 Install the camshaft alignment tool.

22 Tighten the camshaft sprocket bolts to the torque listed in this Chapter's Specifications while holding the camshafts in place with a wrench.

CAUTION:

Do not rely on the camshaft alignment tool to hold the camshafts while tightening the camshaft sprocket bolts. Tool and engine damage may occur.

23 The timing chain cover can now be installed (see Step 9).

10 Crankshaft front oil seal - replacement

Refer to illustrations 10.5 and 10.6

1 Remove the crankshaft pulley (see Section 8).

2 Use a screwdriver or hook tool to carefully pry out the seal.

Note: Be careful not to damage the timing chain cover bore where the seal is seated or the nose and sealing surface of the crankshaft.

3 Another procedure for removing the seal is to drill a small hole on each side of the seal and place a self-tapping screw in each hole. Use these screws as a means of pulling the seal out without having to pry on it.

4 Wipe the sealing surfaces in the engine cover and on the crankshaft. Clean and coat them with clean engine oil.

5 Start installing the new seal by pressing it into the timing chain cover (see illustration).

6 Once started, use a seal driver or a suitable socket of the correct size to carefully drive the seal squarely into place (see illustration).

7 The seal should be flush with the engine cover and remain square when installed.

8 Coat the lip of the seal (where it contacts the crankshaft) with clean engine oil.

9 Install the crankshaft pulley (see Section 8).

10.5 Make certain that the oil seal is kept square as it is placed in the bore

10.6 A socket of the correct size can be used to install the new seal

11 Camshafts and lifters - removal, inspection and installation

Note: Whenever the camshafts are to be removed for a procedure, it's a good idea to check the valve clearances before disassembly (see Section 5), so any required new lifters can be ordered from a dealership.

REMOVAL

Refer to illustrations 11.3 and 11.4

1 Remove the timing chain as described in Section 9.

Note: Before removing the timing chain, note the positions of the no. 1 cylinder cam lobes and the slots in the ends of the camshafts (for the alignment tool). When installing the camshafts, the lobes and the slots in the ends of the camshafts must be in the same positions.

2 Remove the camshaft sprockets.

Note: The camshaft phaser/sprocket on the intake camshaft should be marked with indelible ink so that it can be reinstalled on the intake camshaft in the same position.

When loosening the camshaft sprocket bolts, place a wrench on the hexagonal area of the camshaft to prevent it from turning (see illustration 9.16)

11.3 **Location of the camshaft bearing designations**

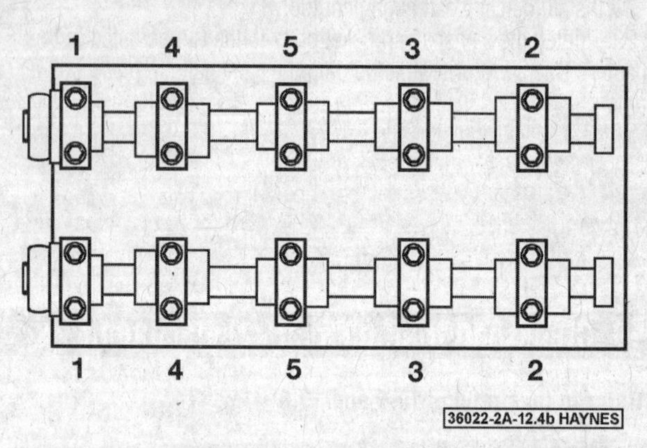

11.4 Camshaft bearing cap loosening sequence - loosen each pair of bolts on the designated bearing cap in sequence

3 All the camshaft bearing caps have a single-digit identifying number etched on them. The exhaust camshaft's bearing caps are numbered in sequence from 0 (right-hand cap) to 4 (left-hand cap); the intake's are numbered from 5 (right-hand cap) to 9 (left-hand cap). Each cap is to be fitted so that its numbered side faces the same direction (see illustration). If no marks are present, or they are hard to see, make your own - the bearing caps must be reinstalled in their original positions.

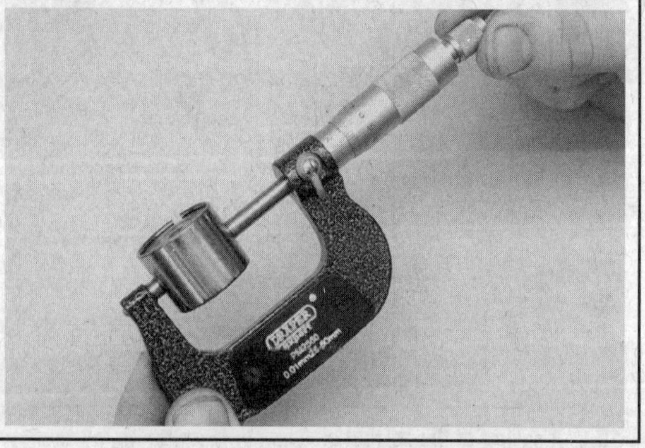

11.8 Measure the lifter outside diameter at several points

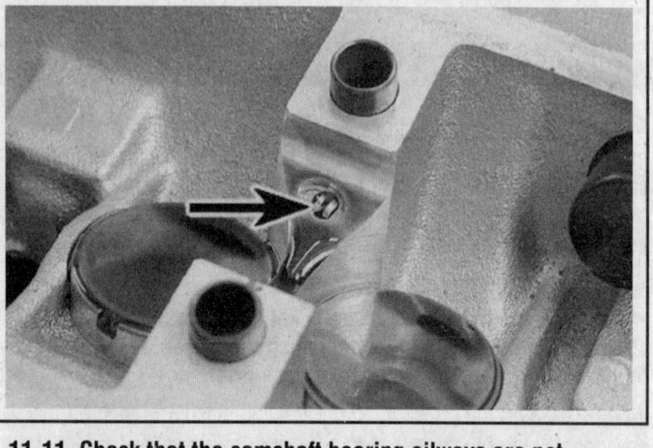

11.11 Check that the camshaft bearing oilways are not blocked with debris

4 Working in the sequence shown, loosen the camshaft bearing cap bolts progressively by half a turn at a time (see illustration). Work only as described, to release gradually and evenly the pressure of the valve springs on the caps.

5 Withdraw the caps, noting their markings and the presence of the locating dowels, then remove the camshafts. The intake camshaft can be identified by the reference lobe for the camshaft position sensor; therefore, there is no need to mark the camshafts.

6 Obtain sixteen small, clean containers, and number them 1 to 16. Using a rubber suction tool (such as a valve-lapping tool), withdraw each lifter in turn and place them in the containers. Do not interchange the lifters.

INSPECTION

➧ Refer to illustrations 11.8 and 11.11

7 With the camshafts and lifters removed, check each for signs of obvious wear (scoring, pitting, etc) and for roundness and replace if necessary.

8 Measure the outside diameter of each lifter - take measurements at the top and bottom of each lifter, then a second set at right-angles to the first; if any measurement is significantly different from the others, the lifter is tapered or oval (as applicable) and must be replaced (see illustration). If the necessary equipment is available, measure the inside diameter of the corresponding cylinder head bore. No manufacturer's specifications were available at the time of writing; if the lifters or the cylinder head bores are excessively worn, new lifters and/or a new cylinder head may be required.

9 If the engine's valve components have sounded noisy, it may be just that the valve clearances need adjusting. Although this is part of the routine maintenance schedule in Chapter 1, the extended checking interval and the need for dismantling or special tools may result in the task being overlooked.

10 Visually examine the camshaft lobes for score marks, pitting, galling (wear due to rubbing) and evidence of overheating (blue, discolored areas). Look for flaking away of the hardened surface layer of each lobe. If any such signs are evident, replace the component concerned.

11 Examine the camshaft bearing journals and the cylinder head bearing surfaces for signs of obvious wear or pitting. If any such signs are evident, consult an automotive machine shop for advice. Also check that the bearing oilways in the cylinder head are clear (see illustration).

12 Using a micrometer, measure the diameter of each journal at several points. If the diameter of any one journal is less than the specified value, replace the camshaft.

13 To check the bearing journal running clearance, remove the lifters, use a suitable solvent and a clean lint-free rag to carefully clean all bearing surfaces, then install the camshafts and bearing caps with a strand of Plastigage across each journal. Tighten the bearing cap bolts in the proper sequence (see illustration 11.23) to the specified torque setting (do not rotate the camshafts), then remove the bearing caps and use the scale provided to measure the width of the compressed strands. Scrape off the Plastigage with your fingernail or the edge of a credit card - don't scratch or nick the journals or bearing caps.

14 If the running clearance of any bearing is found to be worn to beyond the specified service limits, install a new camshaft and repeat the check; if the clearance is still excessive, the cylinder head must be replaced.

15 To check camshaft endplay, remove the lifters, clean the bearing surfaces carefully and install the camshafts and bearing caps. Tighten the bearing cap bolts to the specified torque wrench setting, then measure the endplay using a dial indicator mounted on the cylinder head so that its tip bears on the camshaft right-hand end.

16 Tap the camshaft fully towards the gauge, zero the gauge, then tap the camshaft fully away from the gauge and note the gauge reading. If the endplay measured is found to be at or beyond the specified service limit, install a new camshaft and repeat the check; if the clearance is still excessive, the cylinder head must be replaced.

INSTALLATION

➧ **Refer to illustration 11.23**

17 Confirm that the crankshaft is still positioned at TDC and that the timing pin is in place.

18 Liberally oil the cylinder head lifter bores and the lifters. Carefully install the lifters to the cylinder head, ensuring that each lifter is replaced to its original bore.

19 Liberally oil the camshaft bearing surfaces in the cylinder head, taking care not to get any on the camshaft cap mating surface.

20 Ensuring that each camshaft is in its original location, install the camshafts, locating each so that lobes for cylinder no. 1 are in the same position as noted in Step 1 and the slot in its left-hand end is parallel to, and just above, the cylinder head mating surface. Check that, as each camshaft is laid in position, the TDC setting tool will fit into the slot.

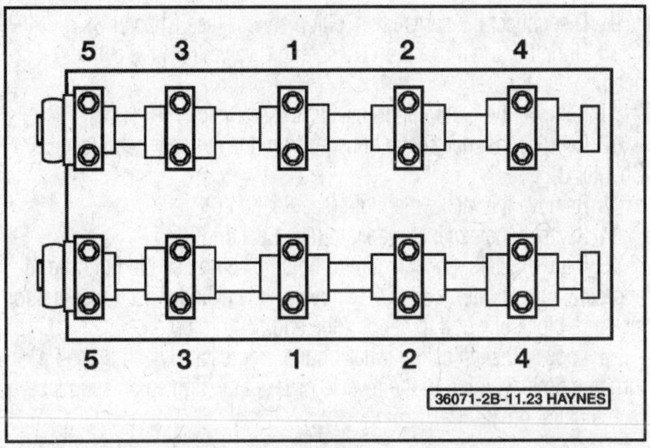

11.23 Camshaft bearing cap tightening sequence

⁂ CAUTION:

When the camshaft bearing caps are tightened, it is imperative that the camshafts do not rotate from their TDC positions.

21 Ensure that the locating dowels are pressed firmly into their recesses and check that all mating surfaces are completely clean, unmarked and free from oil.

22 Apply a little oil to the camshaft journals and lobes, then install each of the camshaft bearing caps to its previously-noted position, so that its numbered side faces outwards, to the front (exhaust) or to the rear (intake).

23 Ensuring that each cap is kept square to the cylinder head as it is tightened down and working in the sequence shown, tighten the camshaft bearing cap bolts slowly and by one turn at a time, until each cap touches the cylinder head (see illustration). This is the Step 1 torque.

24 Next, using the same sequence, tighten the bearing cap bolts to the Step 2 torque listed in this Chapter's Specifications.

25 Tighten the bearing cap bolts to the Step 3 torque listed in this Chapter's Specifications.

26 Install the sprockets to the camshafts, tightening the retaining bolts loosely.

27 The remainder of the reassembly procedure, including replacement of the timing chain and setting the valve timing, is as described in Section 9.

28 Before installing the valve cover, check the valve clearances (see Section 5).

12 Cylinder head - removal and installation

⁂ WARNING:

Wait until the engine is completely cool before beginning this procedure.

REMOVAL

1 Relieve the fuel pressure (see Chapter 4).

2 Disconnect the cable from the negative battery terminal (see Chapter 5).

3 Remove the intake duct from the air filter housing (see Chapter 4).

4 Remove the alternator and its air duct, if equipped (see Chapter 5).

5 Drain the cooling system (see Chapter 1).

6 Remove the coolant recovery tank (see Chapter 3).

7 Remove the timing chain (see Section 9).

8 Remove the camshafts (see Section 11).

➡**Note: Whenever the camshafts are to be removed for a procedure, it's a good idea to check the valve clearances before disassembly, so any required new lifters can be ordered from a dealership.**

9 Disconnect the camshaft position sensor (see Chapter 6).

10 Unbolt and remove the VCT solenoid valve from the cylinder head.

11 Remove the fuel rail and injectors (see Chapter 4).

12 Remove the thermostat housing from the cylinder head (see Chapter 3).

13 Remove the intake manifold (see Section 6).

14 Remove the exhaust manifold (see Section 7).

15 If an engine support fixture or hoist is being used to hold the engine up and it interferes with removal of the cylinder head, use a floor jack and block of wood to support the engine from below.

16 Loosen the ten cylinder head bolts progressively and by half a turn at a time, working in the reverse order of the tightening sequence (see illustration 12.30a).

CAUTION:

The head bolts are torque-to-yield bolts that must be replaced with new ones on installation.

17 Lift the cylinder head from the engine compartment (see illustration).

18 If the head is stuck, be careful how you choose to free it. Remember that the cylinder head is made of aluminum alloy, which is easily damaged. Striking the head with tools carries the risk of damage, and the head is located on two dowels, so its movement will be limited. Do not, under any circumstances, pry the head between the mating surfaces, as this will certainly damage the sealing surfaces for the gasket, leading to leaks. Try rocking the head free, to break the seal, taking care not to damage any of the surrounding components.

19 Once the head has been removed, remove and discard the gasket. Check for the presence of locating dowels in the cylinder block and cylinder head. If dowels are present, make sure they are returned to their original locations after cleaning the components.

INSPECTION

20 The mating faces of the cylinder head and cylinder block must be perfectly clean before replacing the head. Use spray-on gasket remover and a hard plastic or wood scraper to remove all traces of gasket and carbon.

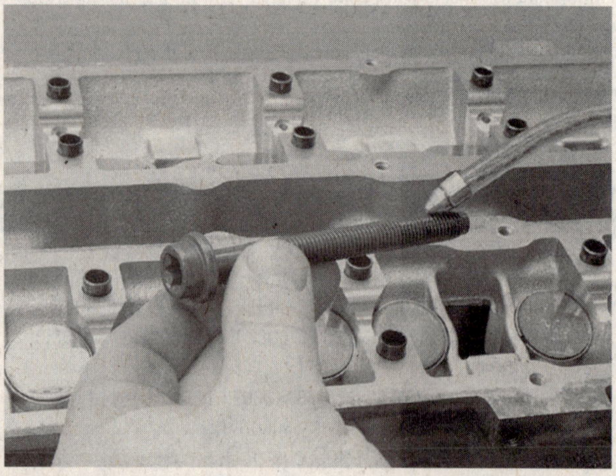

12.29 Apply a light coat of oil to the cylinder head bolt threads

21 Take particular care during the cleaning operations, as aluminum alloy is easily damaged. Also, make sure that the carbon is not allowed to enter the oil and water passages - this is particularly important for the lubrication system, as carbon could block the oil supply to the engine's components.

22 To prevent carbon entering the gap between the pistons and bores, smear a little grease in the gap. After cleaning each piston, use a small brush to remove all traces of grease and carbon from the gap, then wipe away the remainder with a clean rag.

23 Check the mating surfaces of the cylinder block and the cylinder head for nicks, deep scratches and other damage. Also check the cylinder head gasket surface and the cylinder block gasket surface with a precision straight-edge and feeler gauges. If either surface exceeds the warpage limit listed in this Chapter's Specifications, the manufacturer states that the component out of specification must be replaced. If the gasket mating surface of your cylinder head or block is out of specification or is severely nicked or scratched, you may want to consult with an automotive machine shop for advice.

INSTALLATION

Refer to illustrations 12.29, 12.30a and 12.30b

24 Wipe clean the mating surfaces of the cylinder head and cylinder block. If equipped, install the alignment dowels into their original locations.

25 The cylinder head bolt holes must be free from oil or water. This is most important, because a hydraulic lock in a cylinder head bolt hole can cause a fracture of the block casting when the bolt is tightened. Note the location of the cylinder head alignment dowels in the block.

26 Position a new gasket on the cylinder block surface, so that the "TOP" mark is facing up.

27 As the cylinder head is such a heavy and awkward assembly to install, it is helpful to make up a pair of guide studs from two 10 mm (thread size) studs approximately 90 mm long, with a screwdriver slot cut in one end - you can use two of the old cylinder head bolts with their heads cut off. Screw these guide studs, screwdriver slot upwards to permit removal, into the bolt holes at diagonally-opposite corners of the cylinder block surface; ensure that approximately 70 mm of stud protrudes above the gasket.

28 Install the cylinder head, sliding it down the guide studs (if used) and locating it on the dowels. Unscrew the guide studs (if used) when the head is in place.

29 Coat the threads with engine oil - do not apply more than a light film of oil (see illustration). Install the new cylinder head bolts and screw them in by hand only until finger-tight.

Note: New cylinder head bolts must be used.

30 Working progressively and in the sequence shown, first tighten all the bolts to the specified Step 1 torque setting listed in this Chapter's Specifications (see illustration). On these engines there are five tightening stages, the final two using the angle torque method (see illustration).

31 Replacement of the other components removed is a reversal of removal.

32 Change the engine oil and filter and refill the cooling system (see Chapter 1).

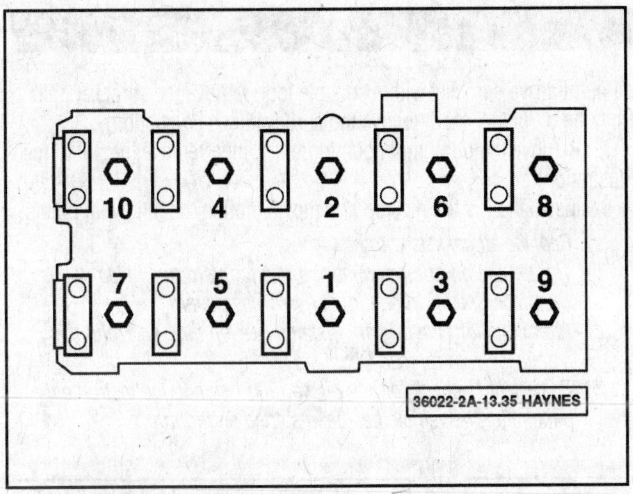

12.30a Cylinder head bolt tightening sequence

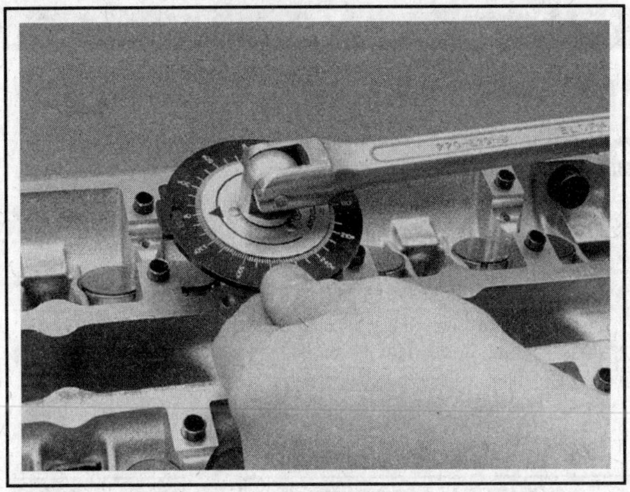

12.30b You can use a torque angle gauge, or you can carefully note the starting and stopping points of the wrench handle

13 Oil pan - removal and installation

REMOVAL

1 Raise the vehicle and support it securely on jackstands (see *Jacking and Towing* at the front of this manual).

2 Drain the engine oil (see Chapter 1), then clean and install the engine oil drain plug, tightening it to the torque listed in the Chapter 1 Specifications. Remove and discard the oil filter, so that it can be replaced with the oil.

3 Remove the engine lower splash shield.

4 Remove the air filter housing (see Chapter 1).

5 On models with an automatic transaxle, remove the battery and battery tray (see Chapter 5).

6 The transaxle must be moved slightly back from the engine. Support the engine from above with an engine support fixture (connected to the left end of the engine, near the transaxle), and support the transaxle with a floor jack. Loosen the upper engine-to-transaxle mounting bolts and back them off about 0.20-inch (5 mm), loosen the left-side engine-to-bellhousing bolts, then loosen the right-side bolts.

7 Remove the two oil pan-to-bellhousing bolts, and the one bellhousing-to-pan bolt. Also remove the timing chain cover-to-oil pan fasteners.

8 Use a screwdriver to pry between the engine and transaxle until the bellhousing has moved away from the block to the limit of the loosened bolts (about 0.20-inch [5 mm]).

9 Progressively unscrew the oil pan retaining bolts in the reverse of the tightening sequence (see illustration 13.12). Use a rubber mallet to loosen the oil pan seal, then lower the oil pan, turning it as necessary to clear the exhaust system. Unfortunately, the use of sealant can make removal of the oil pan more difficult. Be careful when prying between the mating surfaces, otherwise they will be damaged, resulting in leaks when finished. With care, a putty knife can be used to cut through the sealant.

INSTALLATION

10 Thoroughly clean and degrease the mating surfaces of the lower engine block/crankcase and oil pan, removing all traces of sealant, then use a clean rag to wipe out the oil pan.

11 Apply a 1/8-inch wide bead of sealant to the oil pan flange so that the bead is approximately 3/16-inch from the outside edge of the flange. Make sure the bead is around the inside edge of the bolt holes. Also apply sealant to the front flange of the oil pan where it meets the timing chain cover.

➡**Note: The oil pan must be installed within 4 minutes of applying the sealant.**

12 Install the oil pan bolts, only tightening them finger tight at this time.

13 Install the timing chain cover-to-oil pan fasteners and tighten them to the torque listed in this Chapter's Specifications.

14 Tighten the oil pan-to engine block bolts, a little at a time, working from the center outwards in a criss-cross pattern, to the torque listed in this Chapter's Specifications.

15 Tighten the oil pan-to-bellhousing bolts and the transaxle to engine bolts, a little at a time to draw them together evenly, to the torque listed in this Chapter's Specifications.

16 Lower the vehicle to the ground. Before refilling the engine with oil, wait at least 1 hour for the sealant to cure, or whatever time is indicated by the sealant manufacturer. Trim off the excess sealant with a sharp knife. Install a new oil filter (see Chapter 1).

14 Oil pump - removal and installation

Refer to illustrations 14.4, 14.6 and 14.7

Note: The oil pump is serviced as a complete unit without any sub-assembly or internal inspection.

1 Drain the engine oil and remove the oil filter (see Chapter 1).
2 Remove the timing chain cover (see Section 9).
3 Remove the oil pan (see Section 13).
4 Remove the oil pick-up tube (see illustration).
5 Use a screwdriver to pry the end of the oil pump drive chain tensioner's spring from under the shouldered bolt. Remove the two bolts and the tensioner.
6 Remove the chain from the oil pump sprocket. While holding the oil pump drive sprocket with a suitable tool, remove the sprocket bolt from the oil pump, then remove the sprocket (see illustration).
7 Remove the oil pump mounting bolts, then remove the pump (see illustration).
8 Installation is the reverse of removal, noting the following points:

a) *Replace all gaskets with new ones.*
b) *Tighten the oil pump mounting bolts to the torque listed in this Chapter's Specifications in a criss-cross pattern.*
c) *After installing the oil pan, install a new oil filter and refill the crankcase with oil (see Chapter 1).*
d) *Be certain to check for any oil warning lights in the instrument panel after the vehicle has been started and idling.*

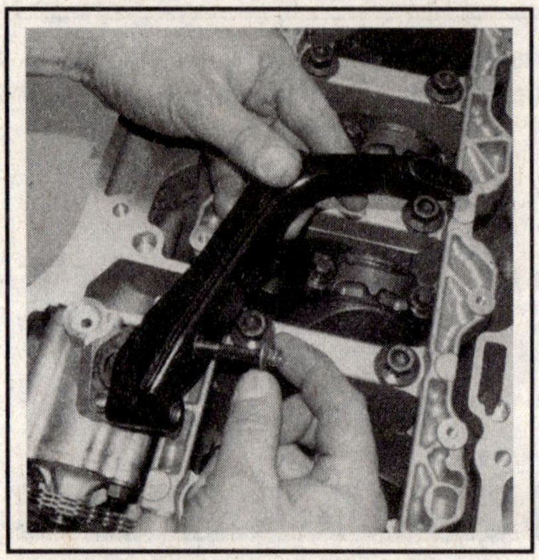

14.4 The oil pump pick-up tube is held by two mounting bolts (typical)

14.6 Using a holding tool on the oil pump drive sprocket to remove the retaining bolt

14.7 Remove the four mounting bolts for the oil pump

15 Flywheel/driveplate - removal, inspection and installation

REMOVAL

1 Remove the transaxle as described in Chapter 7A or 7B. Now is a good time to check components such as oil seals and replace them if necessary.
2 On manual transaxle models, remove the clutch as described in Chapter 8. Now is a good time to check or replace the clutch components and release bearing.
3 Use a center-punch or paint to make alignment marks on the flywheel and crankshaft to make replacement easier - the bolt holes are slightly offset, and will only line up one way, but making a mark eliminates the guesswork (and the flywheel is heavy).
4 Hold the flywheel/driveplate stationary and unscrew the bolts. To prevent the flywheel/driveplate from turning, insert one of the transaxle mounting bolts into the cylinder block and have an assistant engage a wide-bladed screwdriver with the starter ring gear teeth while the flywheel or driveplate bolts are loosened.
5 Loosen and remove each bolt in turn and ensure that new replacements are obtained for reassembly. These bolts are subjected to severe stresses and so must be replaced, regardless of their apparent condition, whenever they are removed.
6 Remove the flywheel, remembering that it is very heavy - do not drop it. The driveplate used with automatic transaxles is much lighter.

INSPECTION

7 Clean the flywheel to remove grease and oil. Inspect the surface for cracks, rivet grooves, burned areas and score marks. Light scoring can be removed with emery cloth. Check for cracked and broken ring gear teeth. Lay the flywheel on a flat surface and use a straight-edge to check for warpage.
8 Clean and inspect the mating surfaces of the flywheel and the crankshaft. If the oil seal is leaking, replace it (see Section 16) before replacing the flywheel. If the engine has high mileage, it may be worth installing a new seal as a matter of course, given the amount of work needed to access it.

9 While the flywheel is removed, carefully clean its inboard face, particularly the recesses that serve as the reference points for the crankshaft speed/position sensor. Clean the sensor's tip and check that the sensor is securely fastened.

INSTALLATION

10 On installation, ensure that the engine/transaxle adapter plate is in place (where necessary), then install the flywheel/driveplate on the crankshaft so that all bolt holes align - it will fit only one way - check this using the marks made on removal. Install the new bolts, tightening them by hand.

11 Lock the flywheel by the method used on disassembly. Working in a diagonal sequence to tighten them evenly and increasing to the final amount in two or three stages, tighten the new bolts to the torque listed in this Chapter's Specifications.

12 The remainder of reassembly is the reverse of the removal procedure

16 Rear main oil seal - replacement

Refer to illustration 16.9

1 The one piece rear main oil seal is pressed into the rear main oil seal carrier mounted at the rear of the block. Remove the transaxle (see Chapter 7A or 7B) and the flywheel/driveplate (see Section 15).

2 Remove the oil pan (see Section 13).

3 Unbolt the oil seal and carrier.

4 Clean the mating surface for the oil seal carrier on the cylinder block and the crankshaft. Carefully remove and polish any burrs or raised edges on the crankshaft that may have caused the seal to fail.

5 Lightly coat the inside lip of the new seal with clean engine oil. Use a thin (but durable) two-inch wide plastic strip (or a two-liter plastic beverage bottle cut to size) around the inside circumference of the seal to act as a liner for installation. A manufacturer tool (#303-328) for this purpose also works well.

6 With the plastic seal liner or tool in place, carefully move the new carrier (with seal factory-installed) into position by sliding it onto the contact surface of the crankshaft.

7 Install the oil seal carrier bolts and finger tighten them while holding the carrier in place. Align the bottom of the seal carrier precisely with the bottom edge of the engine block to ensure that the surfaces are flush before tightening the carrier mounting bolts.

CAUTION:

The oil pan may leak if the two surfaces are not perfectly flush.

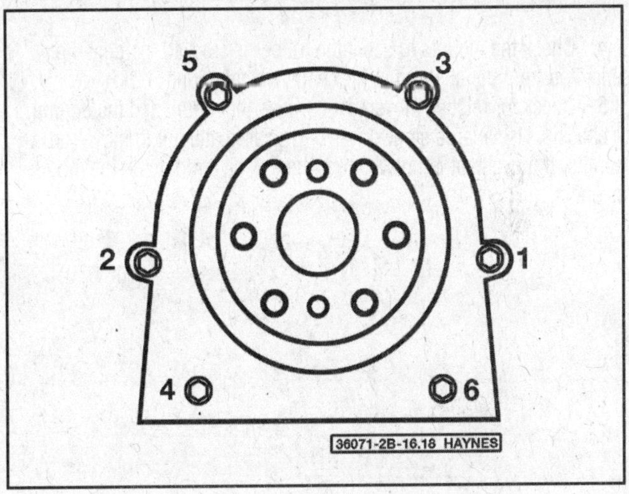

16.9 Rear oil seal carrier tightening sequence

8 Carefully remove the plastic liner or tool so that the new seal contacts the crankshaft mating surface correctly.

9 Tighten the oil seal carrier to the torque listed in this Chapter's Specifications using the proper sequence (see illustration).

10 The remainder of installation is the reverse of removal.

17 Engine mounts - check and replacement

1 Engine mounts seldom require attention, but broken or deteriorated mounts should be replaced immediately or the added strain placed on the driveline components may cause damage or wear.

CHECK

2 During the check, the engine must be raised slightly to remove the weight from the mounts.

3 Raise the vehicle and support it securely on jackstands, then position a jack under the engine oil pan. Place a large wood block between the jack head and the oil pan to prevent oil pan damage, then carefully raise the engine just enough to take the weight off the mounts.

WARNING:

DO NOT place any part of your body under the engine when it's supported only by a jack!

17.8 Remove the fasteners and lift the engine mount upper bracket off the engine mount

4 Check the mounts to see if the rubber is cracked, hardened or separated from the bushing in the center of the mount.

5 Check for relative movement between the mount and the engine or chassis. Use a large screwdriver or prybar to attempt to move the mounts. If movement is noted, lower the engine and tighten the mount fasteners.

REPLACEMENT

Refer to illustration 17.8

Note: Refer to Chapter 7 for information on the transaxle mounts.

6 Disconnect the cable from the negative terminal of the battery (see Chapter 5), then raise the vehicle and support it securely on jackstands (if not already done).

7 Place a floor jack under the engine with a wood block between the jack head and oil pan and raise the engine slightly to relieve the weight from the mounts.

8 Remove the fasteners and detach the mount from the frame and engine (see illustration).

CAUTION:

Do not disconnect more than one mount at a time, except during engine removal.

9 Installation is the reverse of removal. Use thread-locking compound on the mount bolts and be sure to tighten them securely.

Specifications

General

2.3L engine	
Engine type	Four cylinder, in-line DOHC
Displacement	140 cubic inches (2261 cc)
Engine VIN code	Z
Firing order	1-3-4-2
Bore	3.44 inches (87.5 mm)
Stroke	3.70 inches (94.0 mm)
Compression ratio	9.7: 1
Compression pressure	See Chapter 2C
Oil pressure	See Chapter 2C
2.5L engine	
Engine type	Four-cylinder, in-line, DOHC
Displacement	153 cubic inches (2507 cc)
Engine VIN code	A
Firing order	1-3-4-2
Bore	3.503 inches (89.0 mm)
Stroke	3.940 inches (100.0 mm)
Compression ratio	9.7:1
Compression pressure	See Chapter 2C
Oil pressure	See Chapter 2C

Cylinder locations

Camshafts

2.3L engine	
Lobe height	
Intake	0.324 inch (8.25 mm)
Exhaust	0.307 inch (7.8 mm)
Bearing journal diameter	0.982 inch (24.94 mm)
Endplay	0.003 to 0.009 inches (0.08 to 0.23 mm)
2.5L engine	
Lobe height	
Intake	0.324 inch (8.25 mm)
Exhaust	0.307 inch (7.8 mm)
Bearing journal diameter	0.984 to 0.985 inch (24.99 to 25.02 mm)
Endplay	0.003 to 0.009 inch (0.08 to 0.23 mm)

Valve clearances (cold)

Intake	0.008 to 0.011 inches (0.20 to 0.28 mm)
Exhaust	0.011 to 0.013 inches (0.28 to 0.33 mm)

Warpage limits

Cylinder head gasket surfaces (head and block)	0.002 inch (0.05 mm)
Exhaust manifold	0.030 inch (0.76 mm)

Torque specifications	Ft-lbs (unless otherwise indicated)	Nm

➡Note: One foot-pound (ft-lb) of torque is equivalent to 12 inch-pounds (in-lbs) of torque. Torque values below approximately 15 foot-pounds are expressed in inch-pounds, because most foot-pound torque wrenches are not accurate at these smaller values.

Torque specifications	Ft-lbs (unless otherwise indicated)	Nm
Camshaft bearing cap bolts (in sequence - see illustration 11.23)		
2.3L engine		
Step 1	Hand tighten all bolts	
Step 2	62 in-lbs	7
Step 3	144 in-lbs	16
2.5L engine		
Step 1	Hand tighten all bolts	
Step 2	62 in-lbs	7
Step 3	144 in-lbs	16
Camshaft sprocket bolts	50	68
Crankshaft pulley bolt	85	115
Cylinder head bolts (in sequence - see illustration 12.30a)		
Step 1	62 in-lbs	7
Step 2	132 in-lbs	15
Step 3	33	45
Step 4	Tighten an additional 90-degrees	
Step 5	Tighten an additional 90-degrees	
Variable Camshaft Timing (VCT) solenoid bolt	89 in-lbs	10
Valve cover bolts	89 in-lbs	10
Exhaust manifold/catalytic converter nuts (2.3L engine)		
Step 1	41	56
Step 2	41	56
Exhaust manifold nuts (2.5L engine)	35	47
Flywheel/driveplate bolts		
Step 1	37	50
Step 2	59	80
Step 3	83	112
Intake manifold nuts and bolts	156 in-lbs	17.5
Crankshaft rear oil seal and retainer	89 in-lbs	10
Oil pan-to-bellhousing bolts	35	48
Timing chain cover-to-oil pan bolts	89 in-lbs	10
Oil pan-to-engine block bolts	177 in-lbs	20
Oil pick-up pipe bolts	89 in-lbs	10
Oil pump-to-cylinder block bolts		
Step 1	89 in-lbs	10
Step 2	15	20
Sprocket bolt	18	24
Oil pump chain tensioner and guide bolts	89 in-lbs	10
Timing chain cover		
8 mm bolts	71 in-lbs	8
13 mm bolts	35	47
Timing chain guide bolts	89 in-lbs	10
Timing chain tensioner bolts	89 in-lbs	10
Transaxle-to-engine bolts	35	48

2B

V6 ENGINES

Section

1 General information

This Part of Chapter 2 covers in-vehicle repairs for the 3.0L and 3.5L Double Overhead Camshaft (DOHC) V6 Duratec engines. These engines feature aluminum engine blocks and aluminum cylinder heads with dual overhead camshafts and four valves per cylinder.

All information on engine removal and installation, as well as general overhaul procedures, is in Part C of Chapter 2.

The following repair procedures are based on the assumption that the engine is installed in the vehicle. If the engine has been removed and mounted on a stand, many of the Steps in this Part of Chapter 2 will not apply. Some procedures on the 3.5L engine do, however, require engine removal.

In this Chapter, "left" and "right" are used to describe locations on the vehicle. These directions are in relation to the vehicle overall from the position of sitting in the driver's seat. However, for simplicity in describing the cylinder banks of the V6 engine, they are termed "front" (closest to the radiator) and "rear" (closest to the firewall).

2 Repair operations possible with the engine in the vehicle

Many major repairs can be done without removing the engine from the vehicle. Clean the engine compartment and the exterior of the engine with a pressure washer or degreaser solvent before doing any work. Cleaning the engine and engine compartment will make repairs easier and help to keep dirt out of the engine.

It may help to remove the hood for better access to the engine. Refer to Chapter 11, if necessary.

If the engine has vacuum, exhaust, oil, or coolant leaks that indicate the need for gasket replacement, repairs to the 3.0L engine can usually be done with the engine in the vehicle. The intake and exhaust manifold gaskets, the timing chain cover gasket, the oil pan gasket, crankshaft oil seals, and cylinder head gaskets are all accessible with the engine in the vehicle.

Exterior engine components, such as the intake and exhaust manifolds, the oil pan (3.0L V6), the water pump, the starter motor, the alternator, and many fuel system components also can be serviced with the engine installed. On 3.5L engines, the oil pan, timing chain cover, timing chain, camshaft and cylinder head procedures must be performed with the engine removed from the vehicle.

On the 3.0L V6 engine, the timing chain and sprockets also can be replaced without removing the engine, although clearance is very limited.

3 Top Dead Center (TDC) for number one piston - locating

1 Top Dead Center (TDC) is the highest point in the cylinder that each piston reaches as it travels upward when the crankshaft turns. Each piston reaches TDC on the compression stroke and on the exhaust stroke, but TDC usually refers to piston position on the compression stroke.

2 Positioning one or more pistons at TDC is an essential part of several procedures such as rocker arm removal, valve adjustment, and timing chain replacement. These engines do not have TDC marks on the crankshaft pulley or front cover. The timing chain procedure in Section 9 describes setting the engine at TDC for cylinder Number 1.

3 After the number one piston is at TDC on the compression stroke, TDC for any of the remaining cylinders can be located by turning the crankshaft and following the firing order (refer to the Specifications). Divide the crankshaft pulley into three equal sections with chalk marks at three points, each indicating 120-degrees of crankshaft rotation, and a corresponding mark on the timing chain cover, next to the TDC mark for cylinder number 1. For example, rotating the engine 120-degrees past TDC for number 1 piston will place the engine at TDC for cylinder number 4. Refer to the firing order for the remaining cylinder numbers.

4 Valve covers - removal and installation

➡Note: The number and location of stud-bolts and standard bolts used to secure the valve covers may vary, depending on the year and build date of the vehicle. Keep track of the stud locations for reassembly.

1 Remove the engine access cover, if equipped.

FRONT VALVE COVER

➧ Refer to illustrations 4.2, 4.7a, 4.7b, 4.9, 4.10a, 4.10b, 4.14a, 4.14b and 4.14c

2 Disconnect the crankcase ventilation tube (see illustration).

3 Remove the ignition coils (see Chapter 5). Remove the air cleaner housing and duct (see Chapter 4).

4 Disconnect the wiring harness from the valve cover and position it off to the side. On 3.5L engines, remove the engine oil dipstick and tube.

5 Disconnect the VCT electrical connector and oxygen sensor connector.

6 Loosen the valve cover bolts/nuts gradually and evenly until all are loose. Follow the reverse of the tightening sequence (see illustration 4.14a, 4.14b or 4.14c). Remove the valve cover fasteners and lift the valve cover off the engine.

7 Remove and discard the valve cover gaskets and spark plug tube

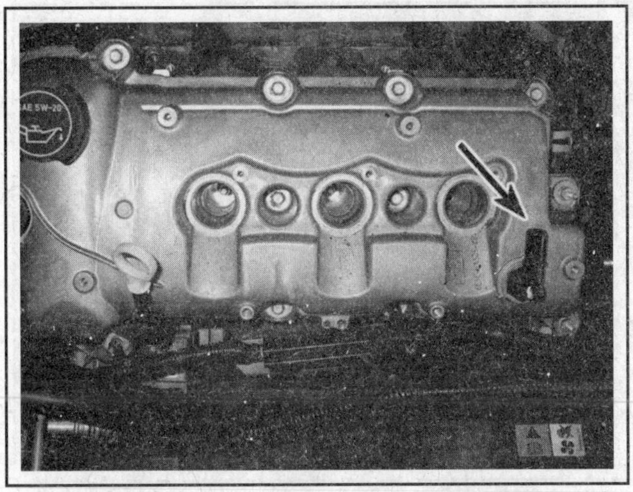

4.2 Disconnect the crankcase ventilation tube from the front valve cover

4.7a Remove and discard the old valve cover gasket - it must be replaced during assembly to prevent leakage

4.7b Remove and discard the spark plug tube seals from the valve cover (3.0L engine)

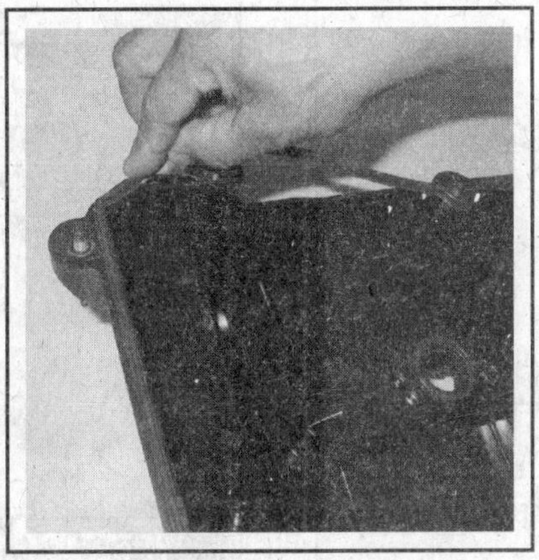

4.9 Press the new gasket into the groove in the valve cover, making sure it isn't twisted

4.10a Apply a 5/16-inch bead of RTV sealant to the seams of the timing chain cover/cylinder head . . .

seals (see illustrations). Install new gaskets and seals during reassembly.

➡Note: The spark plug tube seals can be re-used if they are in good condition and were not leaking.

8 Inspect the valve cover and cylinder head sealing surfaces for nicks or other damage. Clean the sealing surfaces with brake system cleaner.

9 Install a new valve cover gasket, making sure the gasket is properly seated in the groove (see illustration). Press the corner sections of the gasket in first, then the areas around the bolt holes, and finally the sections in between. If there is evidence of damage to the spark plug tube seals, replace these and the seal that surrounds the VCT solenoid.

10 Apply a 5/16-inch bead of RTV sealant at the locations shown (see illustrations).

11 Lower the valve cover into position, making sure that the gaskets stay in place. Install the cover fasteners and tighten them gradually and evenly to the torque listed in this Chapter's Specifications.

12 Reconnect the wiring harness to the bracket studs.

13 Reconnect the crankcase ventilation tube to the valve cover.

4.10b . . . and, on 3.0L engines, the camshaft seal retainer/cylinder head

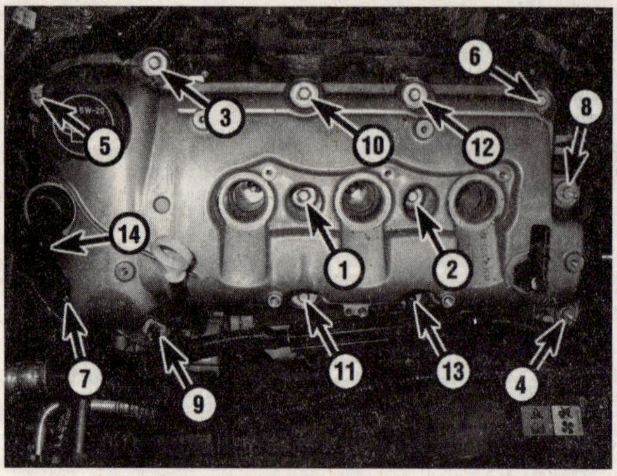

4.14a Valve cover bolt tightening sequence for the left valve cover (front) - 3.0L V6 engine

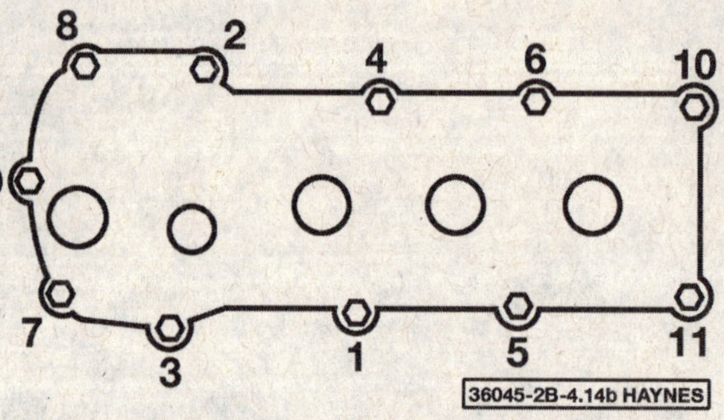

4.14b Valve cover bolt tightening sequence for the left valve cover (front) - 3.5L V6 engine, early production (11 bolts)

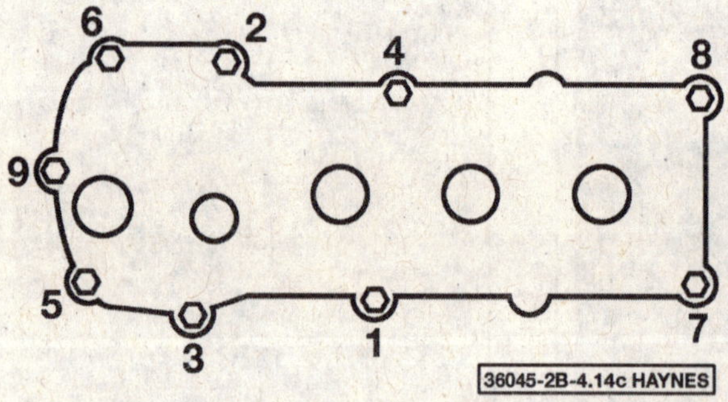

4.14c Valve cover bolt tightening sequence for the left valve cover (front) - 3.5L V6 engine, late production (9 bolts)

4.22a Remove the bolts and studs from the rear valve cover

14 Tighten the valve cover bolts to the torque listed in this Chapter's Specifications. Follow the correct torque sequence (see illustration).

15 The remaining installation is the reverse of removal.

REAR VALVE COVER

➧ Refer to illustrations 4.22a, 4.22b, 4.27a, 4.27b and 4.27c

16 Remove the power steering fluid reservoir (see Chapter 10), the lower cowl cover (see Chapter 11), and the windshield washer fluid reservoir (see Chapter 1).

17 Remove the upper intake manifold (see Section 5), then remove the ignition coils from the top of the valve cover (see Chapter 5).

18 Disconnect the oxygen sensor connector and position the wiring harness off to the side.

19 Remove the radio/ignition interference capacitor from the stud on the valve cover (not on all models).

20 Disconnect the crankcase ventilation tube.

21 On 3.5L engines, remove the bolts securing the air conditioning refrigerant pipe and move the pipe aside to clear the valve cover.

⁂ WARNING:

Do not disconnect the refrigerant line/hose connections.

22 Loosen the valve cover fasteners gradually and evenly, until all fasteners are loose (see illustrations). Follow the reverse of the tightening sequence (see illustration 4.27). Then, unscrew and remove the fasteners. Keep track of the stud locations for reassembly. Lift the valve cover off the cylinder head.

23 Remove and discard the valve cover gasket and inspect the spark plug tube seals (see illustrations 4.7a, 4.7b and 4.9). Install new gaskets and seals during reassembly.

➡Note: The spark plug tube seals can be re-used if they are in good condition and were not leaking.

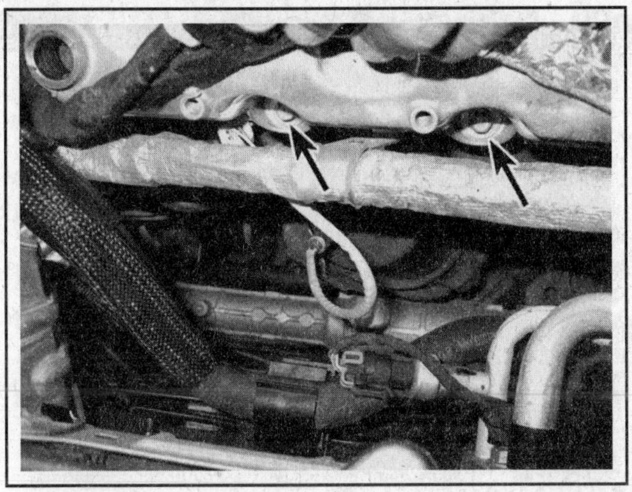

4.22b Raise the wiring harness at the rear of the rear cover to access the rear bolts

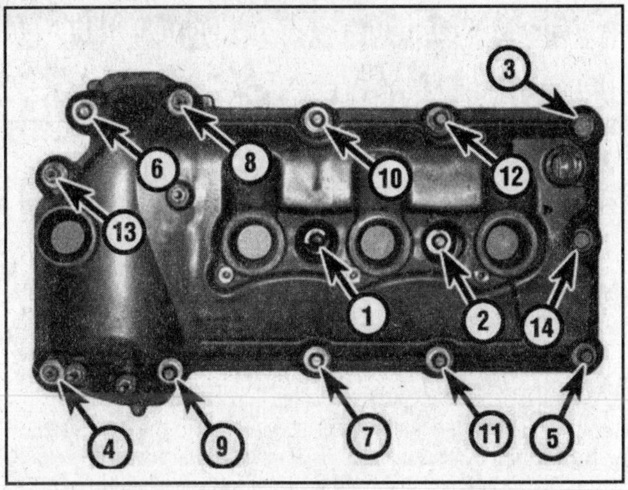

4.27a Valve cover bolt tightening sequence for the right valve cover (rear) - 3.0L V6 engine

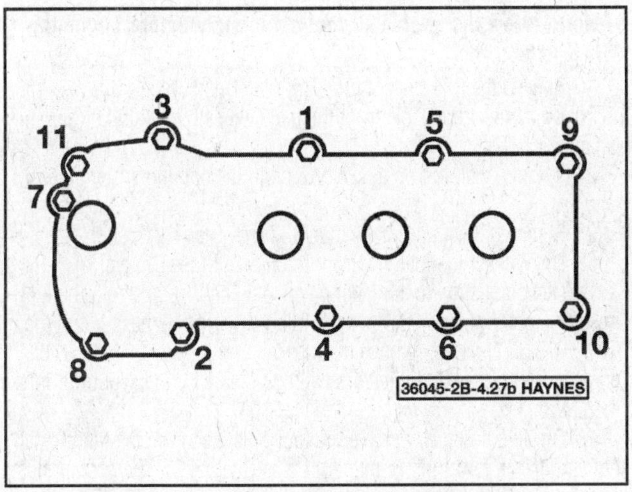

4.27b Valve cover bolt tightening sequence for the right valve cover (rear) - 3.5L V6 engine, early production (11 bolts)

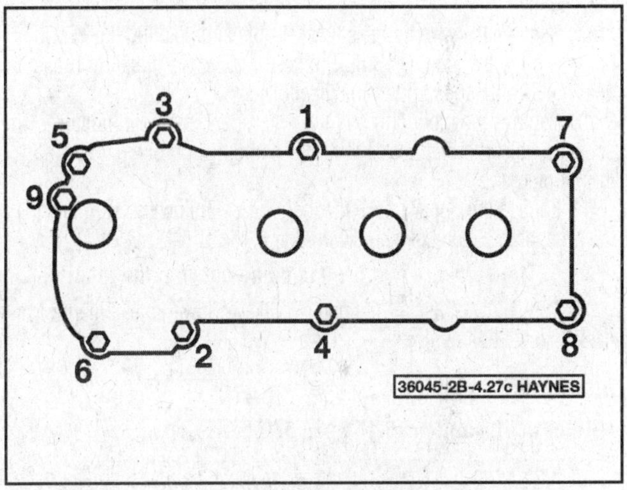

4.27c Valve cover bolt tightening sequence for the right valve cover (rear) - 3.5L V6 engine, late production (9 bolts)

24 Inspect the valve cover and cylinder head sealing surfaces for nicks or other damage. Clean the sealing surfaces with brake system cleaner.

25 Install a new valve cover gasket, making sure the gasket is properly seated in the groove (see Steps 7 through 10). Press the corner sections of the gasket in first, then the areas around the bolt holes, and finally the sections in between. If there is evidence of damage to the spark plug tube seals, replace these and the seal that surrounds the VCT solenoid.

26 Apply a 5/16-inch bead of RTV sealant to the head-to-front cover joints and the cam seal retainer (see illustrations 4.10a and 4.10b).

27 Install the valve cover fasteners and tighten them gradually and evenly to the torque listed in this Chapter's Specifications. Follow the correct torque sequence (see illustrations).

28 Reinstall all wiring harnesses and brackets.

29 Reinstall the ignition coils (see Chapter 5).

30 Install the upper intake manifold (see Section 5).

31 The remaining installation is the reverse of removal.

5 Intake manifold - removal and installation

UPPER INTAKE MANIFOLD

Removal

➧ Refer to illustrations 5.5 and 5.12

1 Disconnect the cable from the negative battery terminal (see Chapter 5).

2 Remove the air filter housing and the intake duct (see Chapter 4).

3 Remove the engine cover, if equipped.

4 Disconnect the connector at the electronic throttle body, and any coolant hoses or other connectors at the throttle body.

5 On 3.0L engines, disconnect the MAP sensor connector, the EGR valve electrical connector and the EGR pipe (see illustration).

6 Disconnect the EVAP hose, brake booster vacuum hose and PCV hose.

7 On 3.5L engines, disconnect the heated PCV valve connector.

8 Disconnect the vacuum lines and electrical connectors from the upper intake manifold. Be sure to mark them with tape to insure correct reassembly.

9 Remove the wire harness bracket nuts and position the wiring harness off to the side. On 3.5L engines, remove the manifold brace, near the throttle body end of the manifold.

10 Remove the mounting bolt from the upper manifold brace(s). On some models, there is both a long brace and a short brace (near the throttle body).

11 Loosen the upper intake manifold bolts. Follow the opposite of the tightening sequence (see illustration 5.15a or 5.15b).

➡Note: The bolts are captive and come out with the manifold.

12 Remove and discard the upper intake-to-lower intake manifold gaskets (see illustration).

Installation

➧ Refer to illustrations 5.15a and 5.15b

13 If the gasket was leaking, check the mating surfaces for warpage. Check carefully around the mounting points of components such as the EGR pipe. Replace the manifold if it is cracked or badly warped.

14 Install new gaskets. If the mating surfaces are clean and flat, new gaskets will ensure the joint is sealed. Don't use any kind of sealant on any part of the fuel system or intake manifold.

15 Locate the upper manifold on the lower manifold and install the fasteners. Tighten the fasteners in three or four steps, in the sequence shown (see illustrations), to the torque listed in this Chapter's Specifications.

16 Install the remaining parts in the reverse order of removal.

17 Reconnect the battery. After you're done, the Powertrain Control Module (PCM) must relearn its idle and fuel trim strategy for optimum driveability and performance (see Chapter 5).

18 When the engine is fully warm, check for fuel and vacuum leaks. Road test the vehicle and check for proper operation of all components.

LOWER INTAKE MANIFOLD

Removal

➡Note: Allow the engine to cool completely before beginning this procedure.

19 Relieve the fuel system pressure (see Chapter 4).

20 Disconnect the cable from the negative battery terminal (see Chapter 5).

21 If you're working on a 3.5L V6, drain the cooling system (see Chapter 1).

22 Remove the upper intake manifold (see Steps 1 through 12).

23 Disconnect the fuel line from the fuel rail (see Chapter 4).

24 Disconnect the fuel injection electrical connectors from the fuel injectors (see Chapter 4). Move the injector wiring harness out of the way. On 3.5L engines, remove the fuel rail and injectors (on the 3.0L engine, the fuel rail and injectors will come off with the two lower intake manifolds).

25 On 3.5L engines, remove the four bolts securing the thermostat housing to the lower intake manifold (see Chapter 3). The coolant hoses can remain on the thermostat housing.

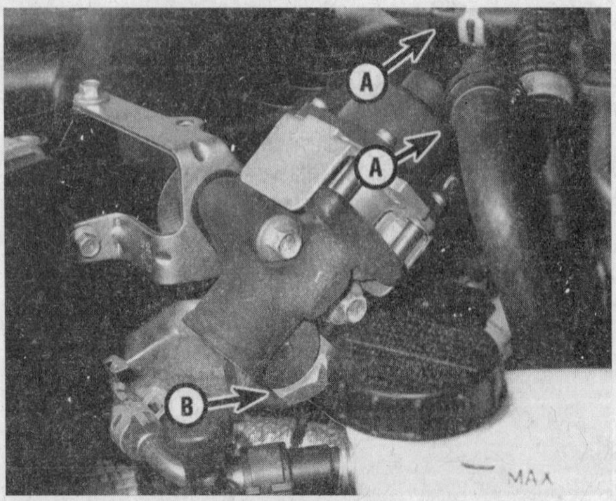

5.5 At the left end of the manifold, disconnect the hoses (A) and the EGR pipe (B)

5.12 Remove the gaskets from the upper intake manifold

26 Loosen the lower manifold bolts gradually and evenly in the reverse of the tightening sequence until all are loose (see illustrations 5.31a and 5.31b), then remove the bolts.

27 Lift the lower intake manifold(s) from the engine. Remove and discard the manifold gaskets.

28 Carefully clean all gasket material from the manifold and cylinder head mating surfaces. Don't nick, scratch or gouge the sealing surfaces.

CAUTION:

Be very careful when scraping on aluminum engine parts. Aluminum is soft and gouges easily. Severely gouged parts may require replacement. Inspect all parts for cracks or other damage. If the manifold gaskets were leaking, check the mating surfaces for warpage.

Installation

Refer to illustrations 5.31a and 5.31b

29 Install new lower intake manifold gaskets on the cylinder heads.

30 Place the lower manifold(s) into position on the cylinder heads. Make sure the gaskets are not dislodged.

Note: If you're working on a 3.0L V6, assemble the fuel rail to the manifolds, installing the fuel rail bolts loosely. After the intake manifold bolts have been tightened in the next Step, tighten the fuel rail bolts.

31 Install the lower manifold bolts. Tighten the bolts gradually and evenly, in the sequence shown (see illustrations), to the torque listed in this Chapter's Specifications.

32 The remainder of installation is the reverse of the removal procedure. Tighten the fasteners to the torque listed in this Chapter's Specifications.

33 If you're working on a 3.5L V6, change the engine oil and filter, then refill and bleed the cooling system (see Chapter 1).

5.15a Upper intake manifold bolt TIGHTENING sequence - 3.0L V6

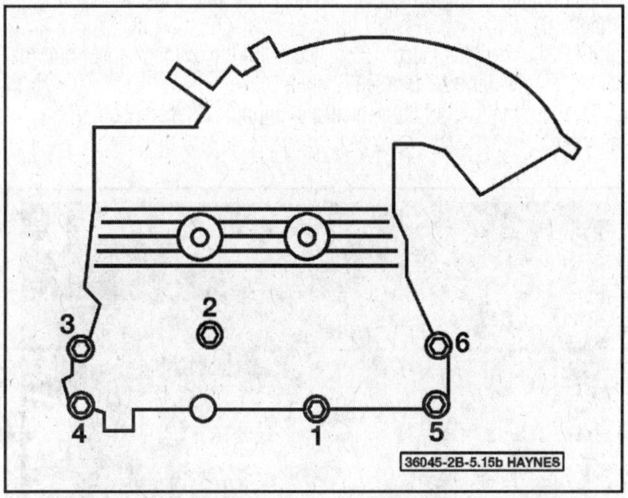

5.15b Upper intake manifold bolt TIGHTENING sequence - 3.5L V6

5.31a Lower intake manifold bolt TIGHTENING sequence - 3.0L V6

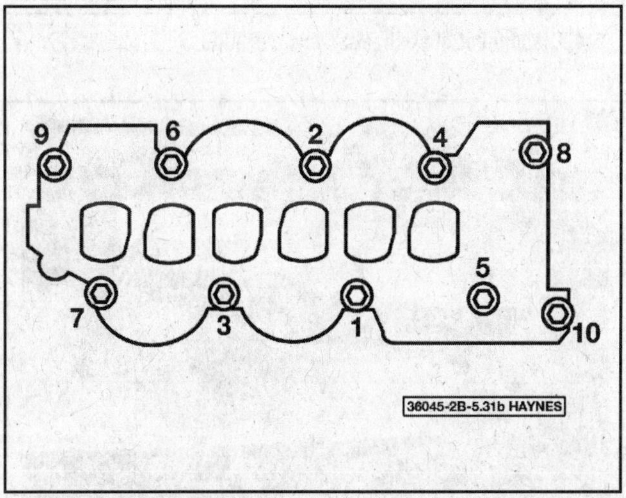

5.31b Lower intake manifold bolt TIGHTENING sequence - 3.5L V6

6 Exhaust manifolds - removal and installation

➡Note: Before beginning this procedure, allow the engine to cool completely, and apply penetrating oil to the manifold and converter fasteners.

➡Note: Most models have a catalytic converter that is an integral part of the exhaust manifold.

FRONT EXHAUST MANIFOLD

➧ Refer to illustrations 6.4, 6.5 and 6.6

⁂ WARNING:

The engine and exhaust system must be completely cool before performing this procedure.

1 Disconnect the cable from the negative battery terminal (see Chapter 5).

2 Disconnect the electrical connector for the oxygen sensor and the catalytic converter monitor (see Chapter 6).

3 Raise the front of the vehicle and support it securely on jackstands.

6.4 Disconnect the exhaust crossover pipe

4 From below, disconnect the crossover pipe (see illustration).

5 Remove the heat shield over the front exhaust manifold (see illustration).

6 Remove the six nuts securing the exhaust manifold (see illustration). Remove and discard the manifold gasket and the six nuts.

7 Remove the exhaust manifold.

8 Using a stud holding tool (available at auto parts stores) or a pair of nuts tightened together over a stud, extract the exhaust manifold studs and discard them.

9 Using a scraper, remove all old gasket material and carbon deposits from the manifold and cylinder head mating surfaces.

⁂ CAUTION:

Be very careful when scraping on aluminum engine parts such as the cylinder heads. Aluminum is soft and gouges easily. Severely gouged parts may require replacement. If the gasket was leaking, check the manifold for warpage and have it resurfaced if necessary.

10 Install new exhaust manifold studs with light oil on the threads, then install a new manifold gasket over the studs. Install the manifold and new self-locking nuts.

11 Tighten the nuts, starting with the center fasteners and working towards the ends, to the torque listed in this Chapter's Specifications.

12 The remainder of installation is the reverse of the removal procedure.

REAR EXHAUST MANIFOLD

➧ Refer to illustration 6.18

⁂ WARNING:

The engine and exhaust system must be completely cool before performing this procedure.

13 Disconnect the cable from the negative battery terminal (see Chapter 5).

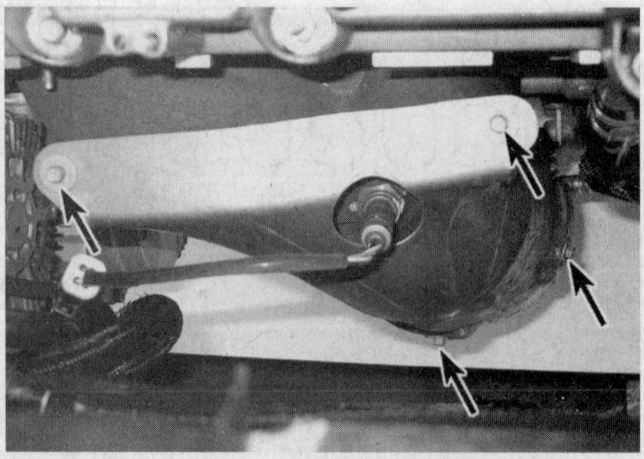

6.5 Front exhaust heat shield bolts

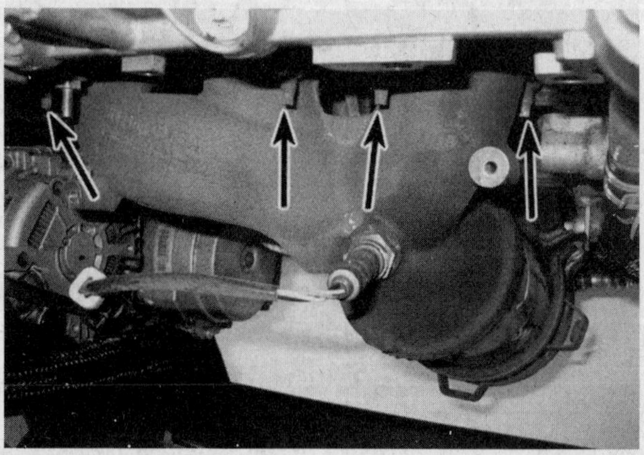

6.6 Remove the front exhaust mounting nuts from the studs (four of six shown)

14 On 3.0L engines, remove the EGR pipe from the exhaust manifold (see Chapter 6).

15 Disconnect the connector to the rear bank oxygen sensor.

16 On 3.5L engines, remove the rear-bank catalytic converter (see Chapter 6).

➡Note: The converter heat shield on AWD models with 3.0L engines cannot be removed from the vehicle without first removing the heat shield over the steering gear. Remove the two bolts and the steering gear heat shield.

17 Remove the nuts from the exhaust manifold flange and separate the crossover pipe from the manifold (see Chapter 4).

18 Remove the six exhaust manifold mounting nuts and remove the manifold from the engine (see illustration). Remove and discard the manifold gasket.

19 Using a stud holding tool (available at auto parts stores) or a pair of new nuts tightened together over a stud, extract the exhaust manifold studs and discard them.

20 Using a scraper, remove all gasket material and carbon deposits from the exhaust manifold and cylinder head mating surfaces.

CAUTION:

Be very careful when scraping on aluminum engine parts. Aluminum is soft and gouges easily. Severely gouged parts may require replacement. If the gasket was leaking, check the manifold for warpage and have it resurfaced if necessary.

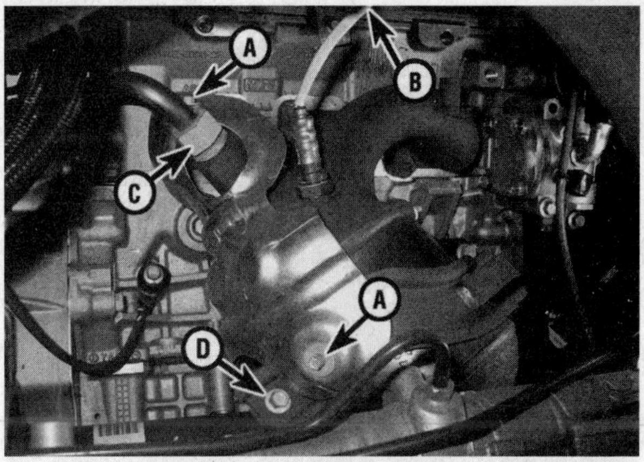

6.18 Remove the rear exhaust heat shield bolts (A), then disconnect the oxygen sensor connector (B) and the EGR pipe (C). Remove the catalytic converter brace bolt (D) - 3.0L V6 engine

21 Install new exhaust manifold studs with light oil on the threads, then install a new manifold gasket over the studs. Install the manifold and new self-locking nuts.

22 Tighten the nuts, starting with the center fasteners and working towards the ends, to the torque listed in this Chapter's Specifications.

23 Complete the installation by reversing the removal procedure.

7 Crankshaft pulley and front oil seal - removal and installation

REMOVAL

➧ Refer to illustrations 7.5 and 7.6

1 Disconnect the cable from the negative battery terminal (see Chapter 5).

2 Loosen the right front wheel lug nuts. Raise the front of the vehicle and support it securely on jackstands, then remove the wheel.

3 Remove the fender splash shield.

4 Remove the drivebelt (see Chapter 1).

5 Use a two-pin spanner to hold the crankshaft pulley while removing the crankshaft pulley retaining bolt (see illustration).

6 Using a three-jaw puller, remove the crankshaft pulley (see illustration).

CAUTION:

Be sure to use the proper adapter on the end of the crankshaft to prevent damage to the threads or end of the crankshaft. Also, the jaws of the puller must grasp the hub of the pulley, not the outer diameter.

7.5 Use a two-pin spanner to hold the pulley while removing the bolt

7.6 Remove the crankshaft pulley with a three-jaw puller

7.10 **Using a pulley installation tool, rotate the nut to drive the pulley onto the nose of the crankshaft**

7 Using a seal puller, remove the seal from the timing chain cover. Note the depth at which the seal fits in the front cover and the orientation of the sealing lip so that the new seal will be installed in the same direction and to the same depth.

INSTALLATION

Refer to illustration 7.10

8 Inspect the front cover and the pulley seal surface for nicks, burrs, or other roughness that could damage the new seal. Correct as necessary.

9 Lubricate the new seal with clean engine oil and install it in the engine timing chain cover with a suitable seal driver which draws the seal in slowly. Be sure that the lip of the seal faces inward. If a seal driver is unavailable, carefully tap the seal into place with a large socket and hammer until it's flush with the timing chain cover surface.

10 On 3.0L engines, apply RTV sealant to the keyway and inner bore of the pulley and lubricate the outer sealing surface of the pulley with clean engine oil. The pulley should be installed and tightened within four minutes of applying the sealant. Align the pulley keyway with the crankshaft key and install the pulley with a suitable pulley installation tool available at auto parts stores (see illustration). Install and tighten the pulley bolt to the torque listed in this Chapter's Specifications.

Note: The manufacturer suggests that a new pulley bolt be installed.

11 Reinstall the remaining parts in the reverse order of removal. Tighten the wheel lug nuts to the torque listed in the Chapter 1 Specifications.

12 Reconnect the battery, then start the engine and check for oil leaks.

8 Timing chain cover - removal and installation

WARNING:

Wait until the engine is completely cool before beginning this procedure.

Note: On 3.0L engines, the timing chain cover can be removed with the engine in the vehicle. On 3.5L engines, the engine must be removed to perform this procedure (see Chapter 2C); ignore the steps here which don't apply.

REMOVAL

Refer to illustrations 8.10, 8.11, 8.13a, 8.13b, 8.13c and 8.14

1 Relieve the fuel system pressure (see Chapter 4).

2 Disconnect the cable from the negative battery terminal (see Chapter 5).

3 Loosen the right front wheel lug nuts. Raise the front of the vehicle and support it securely on jackstands, then remove the wheel.

4 Remove the drivebelt (see Chapter 1).

5 Remove the drivebelt tensioner and two idler pulleys from the front cover.

6 Remove the valve covers (see Section 4).

7 Remove the alternator and alternator mounting bracket (see Chapter 5).

Remove the crankshaft pulley (see Section 7).

9 Remove the power steering pump (see Chapter 10).

10 Disconnect the crankshaft position sensor. Remove the camshaft position sensors in front of each cylinder head (see illustration).

11 Support the engine from above with a hoist or engine support fixture, using chains fastened to the engine lift brackets (see illustration).

12 Disconnect the electrical connectors at the air conditioning compressor, then loosen the compressor mounting bolts and move the compressor aside as required for access to the engine cover. Remove

8.10 Disconnect the camshaft position sensor connector (A) and the sensor mounting bolt (B)

8.11 The engine must be supported from above with a support fixture and chains

8.13b Front cover fasteners (seen from above)

the compressor bracket from the front cover.

WARNING:

The air conditioning system is under high pressure. Do not disconnect the hoses from the compressor.

Remove or disconnect any remaining wires, hoses, clamps, or brackets that will interfere with engine cover removal.

13 3.0L engine: Loosen the timing chain cover fasteners gradually and evenly, then remove the fasteners. Start with the oil pan-to-cover bolts, then the other bolts and studs (see illustrations). Remove the timing chain cover.

Note: Take a digital photo or draw a sketch of the timing chain cover and fasteners. Identify the location of all stud bolts for installation in their original locations.

14 3.5L engine: Remove the cover bolts (see illustration 8.22), take six of them and install them into the threaded holes in the cover (see illustration). Tightening the bolts evenly a few turns will push the cover from the engine without damage.

CAUTION:

Make sure all of the timing chain cover bolts are removed before attempting to remove the cover.

15 Remove and discard the cover-to-cylinder block gaskets.

8.13a Remove the cover fasteners - note the locations of all studs and bolts for installation reference

8.13c Front cover fasteners (seen from below)

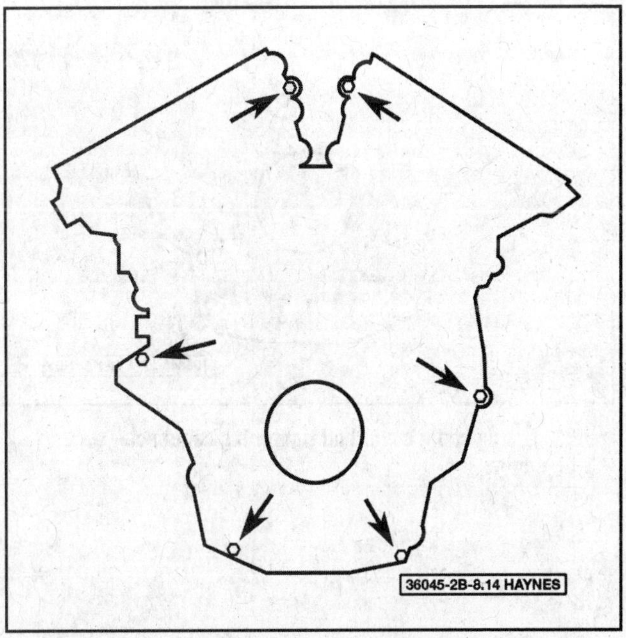

8.14 Location for inserting six bolts to push front cover off (3.5L engine only)

8.18 Apply a bead of RTV sealant at the locations shown

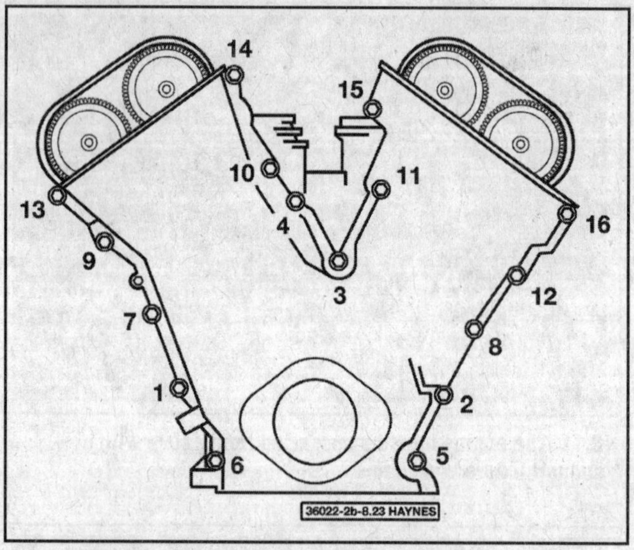

8.21 Timing chain cover bolt tightening sequence - 3.0L engine

INSTALLATION

➧ **Refer to illustrations 8.18, 8.21 and 8.22**

16 Inspect and clean all sealing surfaces of the timing chain cover and the block.

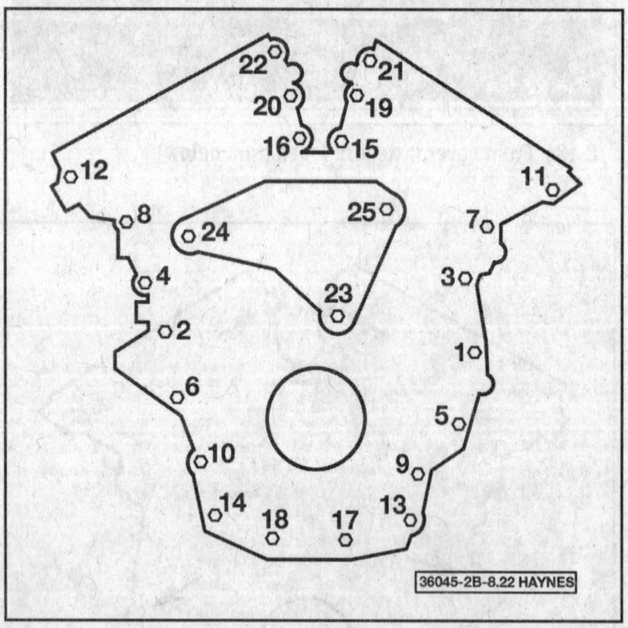

8.22 Timing chain cover bolt tightening sequence - 3.5L engine

✻✻ CAUTION:

Be very careful when scraping on aluminum engine parts. Aluminum is soft and gouges easily. Severely gouged parts may require replacement.

17 Replace the crankshaft seal in the front cover (see Section 7).

18 Apply a bead of RTV sealant approximately 1/8-inch wide at the locations shown (see illustration).

19 Install new front cover gaskets into the grooves on the cover. On 3.5L engines, install two dowel pins (bolts with heads cut off) into holes 21 and 22 in the engine block (see illustration 8.22).

20 Install the timing chain cover and cover fasteners. Make sure the fasteners are in their original locations. Tighten the fasteners by hand until the cover is contacting the block and cylinder heads around its entire periphery.

21 3.0L engine: Following the correct sequence (see illustration), tighten the bolts to the torque listed in this Chapter's Specifications.

22 3.5L engine: Install bolts 17 through 20 and remove the locating pins (see illustration). Install the rest of the bolts and tighten in sequence to the torque steps listed in this Chapter's Specifications. Install the engine mount.

23 Install the drivebelt and tensioner. Tighten the tensioner pulley to the torque listed in this Chapter's Specifications.

24 Install the crankshaft pulley (see Section 7).

25 Connect the wiring harness connectors to the camshaft and crankshaft position sensors.

26 Install the power steering pump and hoses (see Chapter 10).

27 Reinstall the remaining parts in the reverse order of removal.

28 Reconnect the battery, then start the engine and check for leaks.

9 Timing chains, tensioners, and chain guides - removal, inspection, and installation

➡Note: On 3.5L engines, the procedure can only be done with the engine removed (see Chapter 2C); ignore the steps here which don't apply.

REMOVAL

3.0L engines

➧ Refer to illustrations 9.1, 9.3a, 9.3b, 9.3c, 9.3d, 9.4a, 9.4b, 9.5, 9.10 and 9.11

⁂ CAUTION:

The timing system is complex. Severe engine damage will occur if you make any mistakes. Do not attempt this procedure unless you are highly experienced with this type of repair. If you are at all unsure of your abilities, consult an expert. Double-check all your work and be sure everything is correct before you attempt to start the engine.

1 Remove the timing chain cover (see Section 8). Slide the crankshaft position sensor trigger wheel off the crankshaft.

⁂ CAUTION:

The pulse (trigger) wheel has slots for more than one engine. Note the exact position of the pulse wheel to insure correct reassembly. On 3.0L engines the slot marked in orange and stamped "30 RFF" must align over the crankshaft/pulley key (see illustration).

2 Remove the spark plugs (see Chapter 1). 3.0L engines have two timing chains, the front most chain drives the camshaft sprockets on the rear cylinder head, while the chain closest to the block drives the camshafts for the front cylinder head.

3 Install the crankshaft pulley retaining bolt, then use a wrench on the bolt to turn the crankshaft clockwise and place the crankshaft keyway at the 11 o'clock position. TDC number 1 is the starting position and the ending position for this procedure. Verify TDC by observing the index marks on the front of the camshaft sprockets (see illustrations). If not properly aligned, turn the crankshaft exactly one full turn and again position the crankshaft keyway at 11 o'clock.

⁂ CAUTION:

Turning the crankshaft counterclockwise can cause the timing chains to bind and damage the chains, sprockets and tensioners. Turn the crankshaft only clockwise.

9.1 The trigger wheel must be installed in the original orientation - on 3.0L engines, align this slot with the keyway

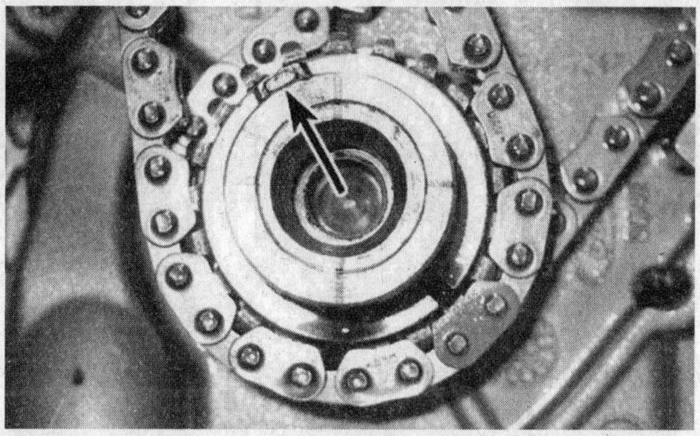

9.3a Position the crankshaft keyway at 11 o'clock; if the engine is at TDC for the number one piston . . .

9.3b . . . the rear bank exhaust camshaft sprocket timing marks will be positioned like this . . .

9.3c . . . the rear bank intake camshaft sprocket timing marks will be positioned like this . . .

9.3d . . . and the front bank camshaft sprocket timing marks will be positioned like this - intake at left, exhaust at right (3.0L engine)

9.4a Crankshaft keyway positioned at 3 o'clock for Neutral position of rear bank camshafts - 3.0L engine

9.4b Position of rear bank camshaft timing marks and colored links for Neutral position - 3.0L engine

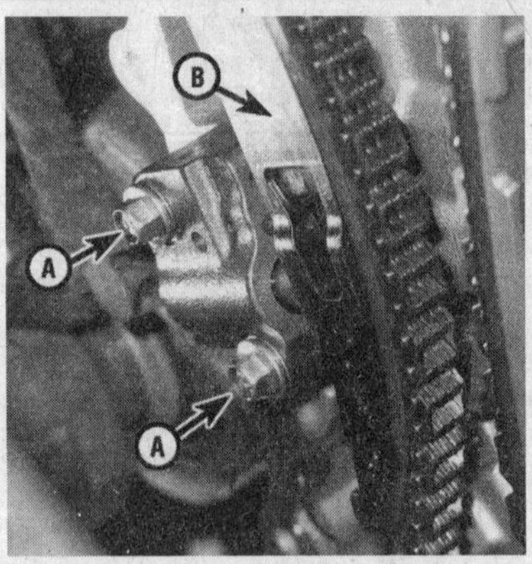

9.5 Remove the bolts (A) securing the rear timing chain tensioner and remove the tensioner, then slide the tensioner arm (B) off its pivot - 3.0L engine

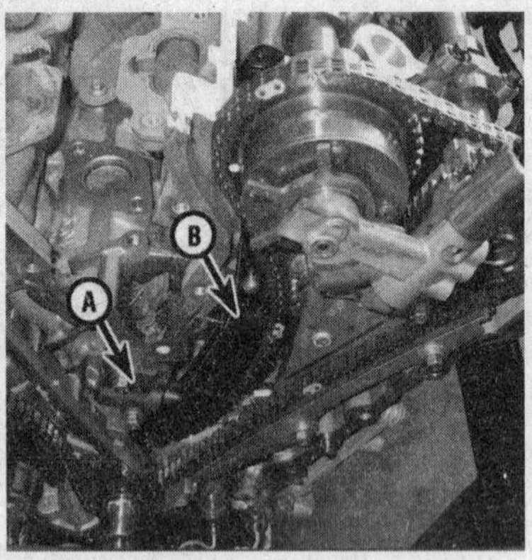

9.10 Remove the front timing chain tensioner (A) and the tensioner arm (B)

9.11 Remove the these bolts to remove the VCT assembly (front shown, rear similar) - 2009 and earlier 3.0L engines

4 Recheck the marks on the sprockets. If there are no marks on the chain links, mark the links directly above the camshaft sprocket marks. Continue to turn the crankshaft clockwise until the keyway is at the 3 o'clock position, which will set the camshafts on the rear cylinder head in their neutral position (see illustrations). This ensures that the valves in the rear cylinder head will not contact the pistons. Remove the mounting bolts for the VCT assembly on the rear cylinder head.

5 Remove the two bolts securing the timing chain tensioner for the rear chain. Remove the tensioner, then remove the tensioner arm (see illustration). Mark all parts that will be reused so they can be reinstalled in their original locations.

6 Lift the rear timing chain from the cam sprockets and remove the chain.

7 Remove the mounting bolts for the chain guide/VCT assembly on the rear cylinder head.

8 Slide the sprocket for the rear timing chain off the crankshaft.

9 Rotate the crankshaft 600-degrees (1-2/3 turns) clockwise, until the keyway is in the 11 o'clock position, setting the camshafts in the front cylinder head in their neutral position (see illustration 9.3d).

10 Remove the front timing chain tensioner mounting bolts. Remove the tensioner and tensioner arm (see illustration).

11 Lift the front timing chain off the sprockets and remove the chain. On 2009 and earlier models, remove the VCT assembly from the front cylinder head (see illustration).

12 If necessary, slide the crankshaft sprocket for the front timing chain off the crankshaft. If you are removing the intake phaser/sprocket(s), insert a 3/8-inch-drive ratchet and extension in the hole at the back of the camshaft while loosening the phaser bolt(s).

3.5L engine

Refer to illustration 9.13

Note: Two special camshaft holding tools (manufacturer tool no. 303-1248) are required for this procedure.

Note: Since the water pump on this engine is located behind the timing chain and components, it makes sense to replace the water pump while it is easily accessed during a timing chain replacement procedure.

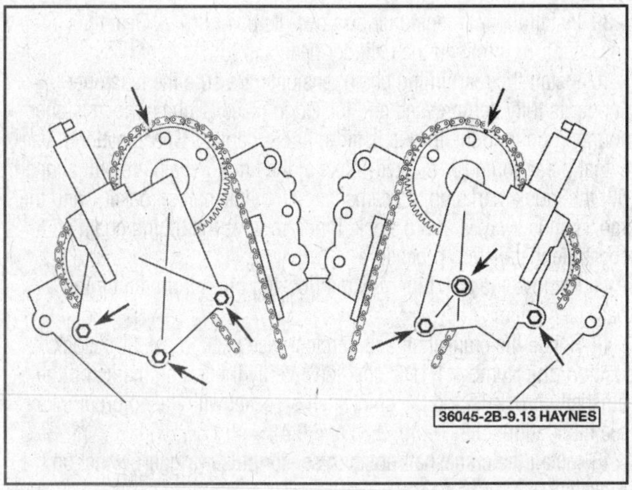

9.13 The position of the intake cam sprocket marks when the engine is set to TDC compression for cylinder no. 1 (upper arrows) on 3.5L engines - lower arrows indicate the VCT assembly mounting bolts

13 Remove the timing chain cover (see Section 8). Reinstall the crankshaft sprocket bolt and set the engine to TDC for cylinder number 1 (see illustration).

➡**Note: At this point the TDC position will be approximate; when the special tools are installed in Step 15, the TDC position will be exact.**

14 3.5L engines have three timing chains: The long primary chain drives the intake cam VCT sprocket on each intake camshaft and the water pump, while a smaller chain on each head drives the exhaust camshafts.

15 Install the special camshaft holding tools (manufacturer tool no. 303-1248) on each cylinder head to lock the camshafts in the TDC position.

16 Remove the VCT assembly mounting bolts from the rear cylinder head, then the front cylinder head (see illustration 9.13).

17 Remove the bolts and the primary timing chain tensioner and tensioner arm. Remove the lower chain guide from the front cylinder bank. Mark the chain links opposite the timing marks on the camshafts (if not already marked), and remove the primary timing chain.

18 Remove the upper chain guide from the front cylinder bank. If necessary, remove the crankshaft sprocket.

19 If the secondary timing chains and camshaft sprockets are to be removed for inspection or another procedure, compress the tensioner(s) and insert a pin into the hole in the tensioner to hold the tensioner in the retracted position. Unscrew the bolts for the intake (VCT) and exhaust camshaft sprockets, then remove both sprockets and the chain as an assembly.

⁂ CAUTION:

Make sure the camshaft holding tool is in place and prevents the camshafts from turning while unscrewing the bolts. Also, new bolts must be used for reassembly.

20 Remove the bolts and the secondary chain tensioners.

➡**Note: The camshaft holding tool must be loosened and tilted (toward the flywheel end of the engine) to access the rearmost bolt of the tensioner.**

INSPECTION

➡**Note: Do not mix parts from the front and rear timing chains and tensioners, and on 3.5L engines, keep the primary and secondary tensioners separate.**

21 Clean all parts with clean solvent. Dry with compressed air, if available.

22 Inspect the chain tensioners and tensioner arms for excessive wear or other damage.

23 Inspect the timing chain guides for deep grooves, excessive wear, or other damage.

24 Inspect the timing chain for excessive wear or damage.

25 Inspect the camshaft and crankshaft sprockets for chipped or broken teeth, excessive wear, or damage.

26 Replace any component that is in questionable condition.

INSTALLATION

⁂ CAUTION:

Before starting the engine, carefully rotate the crankshaft by hand through at least two full revolutions (use a socket and breaker bar on the crankshaft pulley center bolt). If you feel any resistance, STOP! There is something wrong - most likely, valves are contacting the pistons. You must find the problem before proceeding. Check your work and see if any updated repair information is available.

➡**Note: The installation procedure is very much the reverse of the removal procedure, but refer to both the Removal and Installation Steps to ensure that you understand.**

3.0L engine

27 The timing chain tensioners must be fully compressed and locked in place before chain installation. To prepare the chain tensioners for installation:

a) *Insert a small pick into the hole in the tensioner and release the pawl mechanism.*
b) *Using a soft-jawed vise, compress the plunger into the tensioner housing until the plunger is bottomed in its bore.*
c) *Insert a 1/16-inch drill bit or a straightened paper clip into the small hole above the pawl mechanism to hold the plunger in place.*
d) *Repeat this procedure for the other tensioner.*

28 If removed, install the crankshaft sprocket for the front timing chain. Make sure the crankshaft keyway is still at 11 o'clock.

29 Look at the index marks on the sprockets of the front bank intake and exhaust camshafts. The marks should be at 9 o'clock (intake) and at 12 o'clock (exhaust) in relation to the top of the cylinder head (see illustration 9.3d).

⁂ CAUTION:

The timing chains have three links that are a different color than the rest of the links. When installed, the colored links on the chain must be aligned with the index marks on the camshaft and crankshaft sprockets.

➡Note: If you are installing new timing chains and the colored links are not visible, mark the chain as follows:

- a) *Lay the chain on a flat surface in a circular shape. Select any link and mark it with a permanent marker.*
- b) *Count 29 links counterclockwise and mark that link.*
- c) *Continue counting (counterclockwise) and mark the 42nd link.*

30 Install the front timing chain guide/VCT assembly. Tighten the mounting bolts to the torque listed in this Chapter's Specifications.

31 Install the front timing chain around the camshaft and crankshaft sprockets. Make sure the index marks on the sprockets are aligned with the colored (or marked) links of the chain.

32 Install the front tensioner arm over its pivot dowel. Seat the tensioner arm firmly on the cylinder head and block.

33 Install the front timing chain tensioner. Be sure the tensioner plunger is fully compressed and locked in place. Tighten the tensioner mounting bolts to the torque listed in this Chapter's Specifications. Verify that the colored (or marked) links of the timing chain are still aligned with the index marks on the camshaft and crankshaft sprockets, and the crankshaft keyway is at 11 o'clock. If not, remove the timing chain and repeat the installation procedure.

34 Install the crankshaft sprocket for the rear timing chain on the crankshaft.

35 Rotate the crankshaft clockwise until the crankshaft keyway is in the 3 o'clock position. This will correctly position the pistons for installation of the rear timing chain.

36 Install the rear timing chain guide/VCT assembly. Tighten the mounting bolts to the torque listed in this Chapter's Specifications.

37 Double-check the position of the rear camshafts so the index marks on the sprockets are at (approximately) 3 o'clock (intake) and at 12 o'clock (exhaust) in relation to the top of the cylinder head (see illustration 9.4b).

⁂ CAUTION:

The timing chains have three links that are a different color than the rest of the links. When installed, the colored (or marked) links on the chain must be aligned with the index marks on the camshaft and crankshaft sprockets.

38 Install the rear timing chain around the camshaft and crankshaft sprockets. Make sure the colored (or marked) links of the chain are aligned with the index marks on the front of the camshaft and crankshaft sprockets.

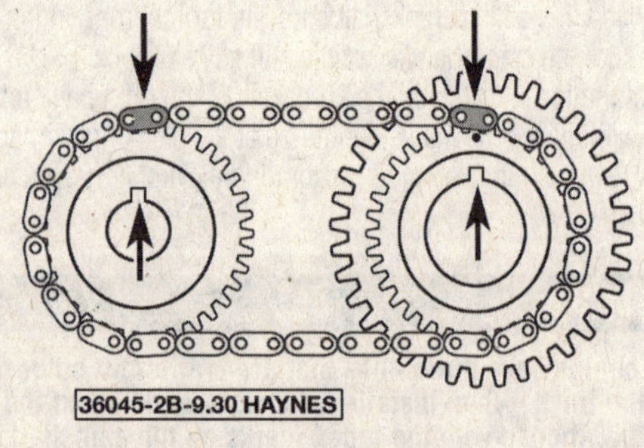

9.51 Align the secondary timing chain colored links with the keyways of the sprockets - 3.5L engine

39 Install the rear tensioner arm over its pivot dowel. Seat the tensioner arm firmly on the cylinder head and block.

40 Install the rear timing chain tensioner. Be sure the tensioner plunger is fully compressed and locked in place. Tighten the tensioner mounting bolts to the torque listed in this Chapter's Specifications. Verify that the colored (or marked) links of the timing chain are still aligned with the index marks on the camshaft and crankshaft sprockets, and the crankshaft keyway is at 3 o'clock. If not, remove the timing chain and repeat the installation procedure.

41 Remove the drill bits or wires (locking pins) from the timing chain tensioners.

42 Rotate the crankshaft counterclockwise back to the 11 o'clock position (the Number 1 TDC position). Verify the timing marks on the camshaft sprockets and the crankshaft sprocket with the colored links (see illustrations 9.3a, 9.3b, 9.3c and 9.4).

43 Install the crankshaft position sensor pulse (trigger) wheel on the crankshaft.

⁂ CAUTION:

Make sure the pulse wheel is installed with the crankshaft key in the slot marked "30 RFF" (see illustration 9.1).

44 Rotate the engine by hand at least two revolutions and verify that there is no binding.

⁂ CAUTION:

If any resistance is felt, STOP; double-check your work and find out why.

45 Install the timing chain cover (see Section 8).

46 Reinstall the remaining parts in the reverse order of removal.

47 Fill the crankcase with the recommended oil (see Chapter 1).

48 Reconnect the battery (see Chapter 5, Section 1), then start the engine and check for leaks.

3.5L engine

➧ Refer to illustration 9.51

49 Install the primary timing chain guide for the rear (right) cylinder bank and tighten the bolts to the torque listed in this Chapter's Specifications.

50 Tilt the rear (right) cylinder bank camshaft holding tool to the rear and install the secondary timing chain tensioner, tightening the bolts to the torque listed in this Chapter's Specifications. Don't remove the lock pin from the tensioner yet.

51 Install the secondary timing chains onto the camshaft sprockets. The colored links on the chain must align with the marks/camshaft keyway slots in the sprockets (see illustration).

52 Install the sprockets/VCT actuator (phaser)/secondary timing chain onto the rear camshafts. When installing the camshaft sprocket bolts, NEW bolts must be used. Tighten the bolts to the torque listed in this Chapter's Specifications.

53 Tilt the front (left) cylinder bank camshaft holding tool to the rear and install the secondary timing chain tensioner, tightening the bolts to the torque listed in this Chapter's Specifications. Don't remove the lock pin from the tensioner yet.

54 Install the sprockets/VCT actuator (phaser)/secondary timing chain (with the marks aligned as shown in illustration 9.51) onto the front camshafts. When installing the camshaft sprocket bolts, NEW bolts

must be used. Tighten the bolts to the torque listed in this Chapter's Specifications. Remove the lock pin from the tensioner.

55 Install the crankshaft sprocket.

56 Install the primary timing chain onto the crankshaft sprocket and the VCT sprockets, making sure the colored links (or marks) on the chain align with the marks on the sprockets.

➡Note: At TDC compression for cylinder no. 1, the crankshaft sprocket keyway will be in approximately the 11 o'clock position and the timing mark on the crankshaft sprocket will be in approximately the 4 o'clock position.

57 Install the upper chain guide on the front (left) cylinder bank, tightening the bolts to the torque listed in this Chapter's Specifications.

58 Install the lower chain guide for the front cylinder bank, tightening the bolts to the torque listed in this Chapter's Specifications.

59 Install the primary timing chain tensioner arm to the rear cylinder bank.

60 Place the timing chain tensioner in a soft-jawed vise, with the jaws bearing on the tensioner body and the plunger. Swing the lever on the tensioner counterclockwise, then tighten the vise until the tensioner plunger has been retracted. Swing the lever clockwise, aligning the hole in the lever with the hole in the tensioner body, then install a lock pin made of heavy wire or a drill bit or small Allen wrench. Remove the tensioner from the vise.

61 Install the primary timing chain tensioner, tightening the bolts to the torque listed in this Chapter's Specifications.

➡Note: It might be necessary to rotate the crankshaft slightly to create a little slack in the chain to enable the tensioner to be installed. Remove the lock pin from the tensioner.

62 Recheck the timing marks to make sure they are all in proper alignment.

63 Check the seals on the VCT housing, replacing them if necessary.

64 Install the VCT housings, making sure the dowels engage completely with their corresponding holes in the cylinder head, then install the bolts and tighten them a little at a time to the torque listed in this Chapter's Specifications.

65 Remove the camshaft holding tools, then rotate the engine by hand at least two revolutions and verify that there is no binding.

⁂ CAUTION:

If any resistance is felt, STOP; double-check your work and find out why.

66 Install the timing chain cover (see Section 8).

67 Reinstall the engine/transaxle. Refill the engine with oil (install a new filter) and coolant (see Chapter 1).

10 Camshafts and valvetrain - removal inspection, and installation

3.0L V6 ENGINE

Removal

Rear bank cylinder head

➧ Refer to illustration 10.6

1 Remove the timing chain for the rear cylinder bank (see Section 9).

2 Note the location of each camshaft cap. Use a marker on each cap or notes on paper or cardboard if they're not marked. Do not mix any of the camshaft caps.

3 Working in the order opposite that of the tightening sequence (see illustrations 10.31a and 10.31b), gradually loosen the bolts that secure the camshaft bearing caps to the cylinder head, then remove the camshaft caps. It may be necessary to tap the caps lightly with a soft-faced mallet to loosen them from the locating dowels.

⁂ CAUTION:

The camshaft bearing caps and cylinder heads are numbered to identify the locations of the caps. The caps must be installed in their original locations. Keep all parts from each camshaft together; never mix parts from one camshaft with those for another.

4 Mark the intake and exhaust camshafts to prevent reinstalling them in the wrong locations, then lift the camshafts straight up and out of the cylinder head.

5 Mark the positions of the rocker arms so they can be reinstalled in their original locations, then remove the rocker arms.

6 Place the rocker arms in a suitable container so they can be separated and identified (see illustration).

7 Lift the hydraulic lash adjusters from their bores in the cylinder head. Identify and separate the adjusters so they can be reinstalled in their original locations.

Front bank cylinder head

8 To place the front bank camshafts in the neutral position turn the crankshaft 1-2/3 turns (clockwise) until the crankshaft keyway is at 11 o'clock (see illustration 9.3a).

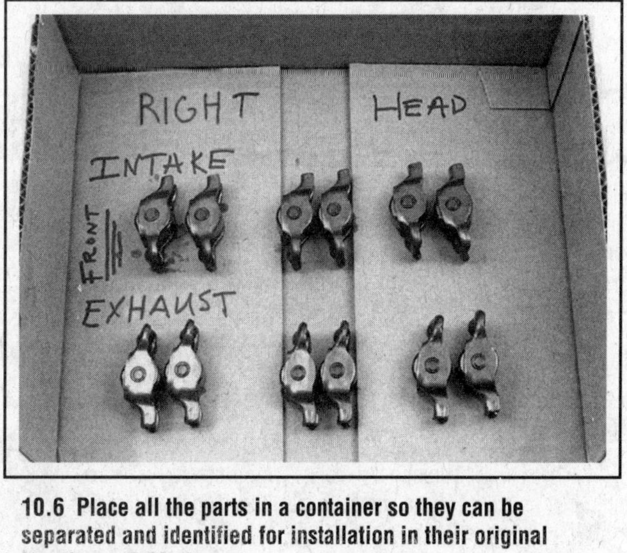

10.6 Place all the parts in a container so they can be separated and identified for installation in their original locations - 3.0L shown

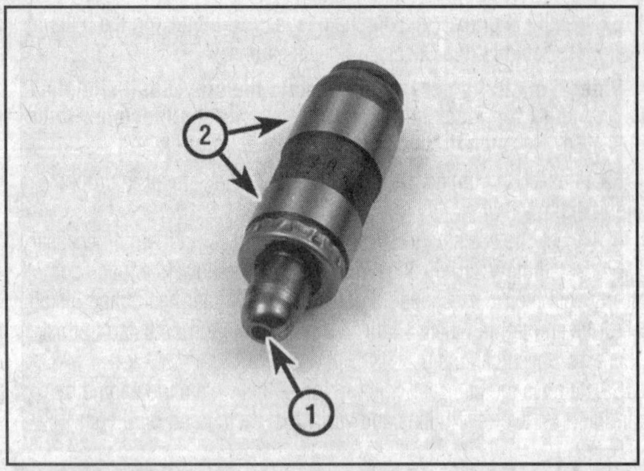

10.11 Inspect the lash adjusters for signs of excessive wear or damage, such as pitting, scoring or signs of overheating (bluing or discoloration), where the tip contacts the rocker arm (1) and the side surfaces that contact the bore in the cylinder head (2) - 3.0L models

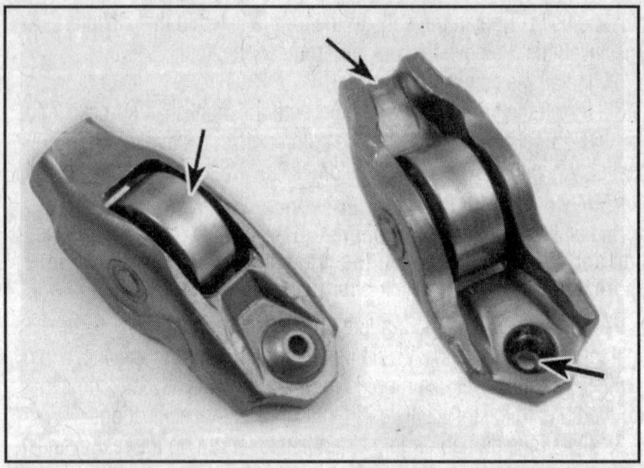

10.13 Check the roller surface (left arrow) of the rocker arm and the areas where the valve stem and lash adjuster contact the rocker arm (right arrows) - 3.0L models

10.14 Check the cam lobes for pitting, excessive wear, and scoring. If scoring is excessive, as shown here, replace the camshaft

9 Remove the timing chain for the front cylinder bank (see Section 9). Also remove the water pump pulley and oil seal retainer from the rear of the exhaust camshaft.

➡Note: Refer to Chapter 3, Section 8 for the pulley removal procedure.

10 Repeat Steps 3 to 7 to remove the front (left side) camshafts, rocker arms and lash adjusters. Be sure to loosen the bearing caps on the front camshafts in the order opposite that of the tightening sequence (see illustrations 10.25a and 10.25b).

Inspection

➧ Refer to illustrations 10.11, 10.13, 10.14, 10.15a, 10.15b, 10.16, 10.17 and 10.18

11 Check each hydraulic lash adjuster for excessive wear, scoring, pitting, or an out-of-round condition (see illustration). Replace as necessary.

12 Measure the outside diameter of each adjuster at the top and bottom of the adjuster. Then take a second set of measurements at a right angle to the first. If any measurement is significantly different from the others, the adjuster is tapered or out of round and must be replaced. If the necessary equipment is available, measure the diameter of the lash adjuster and the inside diameter of the corresponding cylinder head bore. Subtract the diameter of the lash adjuster from the bore diameter to obtain the oil clearance. Compare the measurements obtained to those given in this Chapter's Specifications. If the adjusters or the cylinder head bores are excessively worn, new adjusters or a new cylinder head, or both, may be required. If the valve train is noisy, particularly if the noise persists after a cold start, you can suspect a faulty hydraulic adjuster.

13 Inspect the rocker arms for signs of wear or damage. The areas of wear are the tip that contacts the valve stem, the socket that contacts the lash adjuster and the roller that contacts the camshaft (see illustration).

14 Examine the camshaft lobes for scoring, pitting, galling (wear due to rubbing), and evidence of overheating (blue, discolored areas). Look for flaking of the hardened surface layer of each lobe (see illustration). If any such wear is evident, replace the camshaft.

15 Calculate the camshaft lobe lift by measuring the lobe height and the diameter of the base circle of the lobe (see illustrations). Subtract the base circle measurement from the lobe height to determine the lobe lift. If the lobe lift is less than that listed in this Chapter's Specifications the camshaft lobe is worn and should be replaced.

16 Inspect the camshaft bearing journals and the cylinder head bearing surfaces for pitting or excessive wear. If any such wear is evident, replace the component concerned. Using a micrometer, measure the diameter of each camshaft bearing journal at several points (see illustration). If the diameter of any journal is less than specified, replace the camshaft.

17 To check the bearing journal oil clearance, remove the rocker arms and hydraulic lash adjusters (if not already done), use a suitable solvent and a clean lint-free rag to clean all bearing surfaces, then install the camshafts and bearing caps with a piece of Plastigage across each journal (see illustration). Tighten the bearing cap bolts to the specified torque. Don't rotate the camshafts.

18 Remove the bearing caps and meas

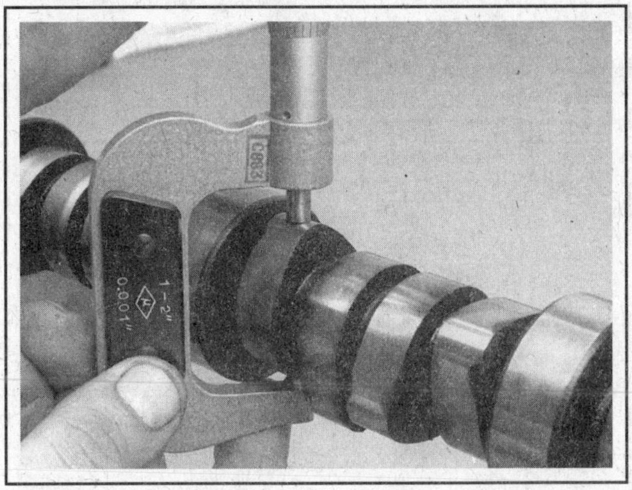

10.15a Measure the camshaft lobe height (greatest dimension) . . .

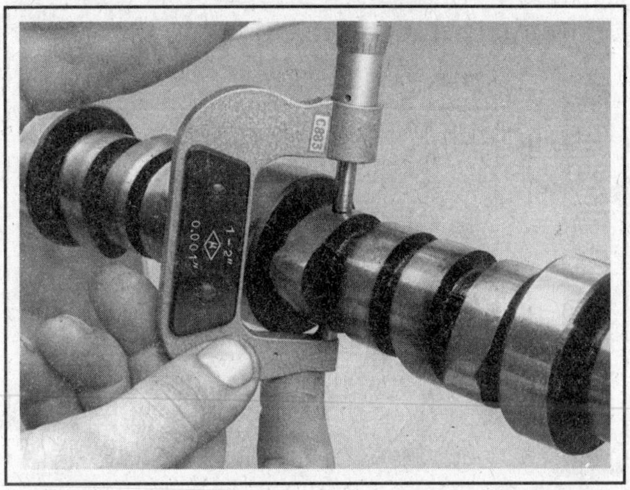

10.15b . . . and subtract the camshaft lobe base circle diameter (smallest dimension) to obtain the lobe lift specification

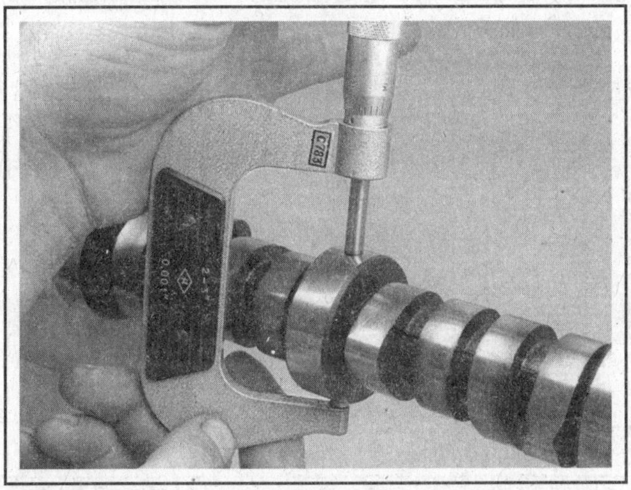

10.16 Measure each journal diameter with a micrometer. If any journal is less than the specified minimum, replace the camshaft

10.17 Lay a strip of Plastigage on each camshaft journal, in line with the camshaft

tened Plastigage with the Plastigage scale (see illustration). Scrape off the Plastigage with your fingernail or the edge of a credit card. Don't scratch or nick the journals or bearing caps.

19 If the oil clearance of any bearing is worn beyond the specified service limit, install a new camshaft and repeat the check. If the clearance is still excessive, replace the cylinder head.

20 To check camshaft endplay, clean the bearing surfaces and install the camshafts (without the lash adjusters or rocker arms) and bearing caps. Tighten the bearing cap bolts to the specified torque, then measure the endplay using a dial indicator mounted on the cylinder head so that its tip bears on the camshaft end.

21 Lightly but firmly tap the camshaft fully toward the gauge, zero the gauge, then tap the camshaft fully away from the gauge and note the gauge reading. If the measured endplay is at or beyond the specified service limit, install a new camshaft thrust cap and repeat the check. If the clearance is still excessive, the camshaft or the cylinder head must be replaced.

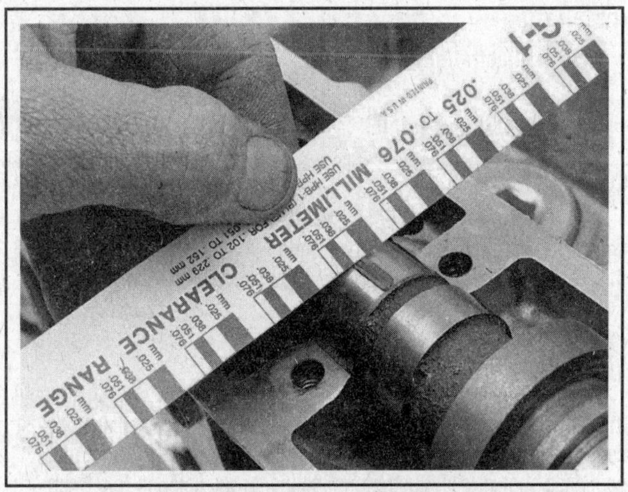

10.18 Compare the width of the crushed Plastigage to the scale on the package to determine the journal oil clearance

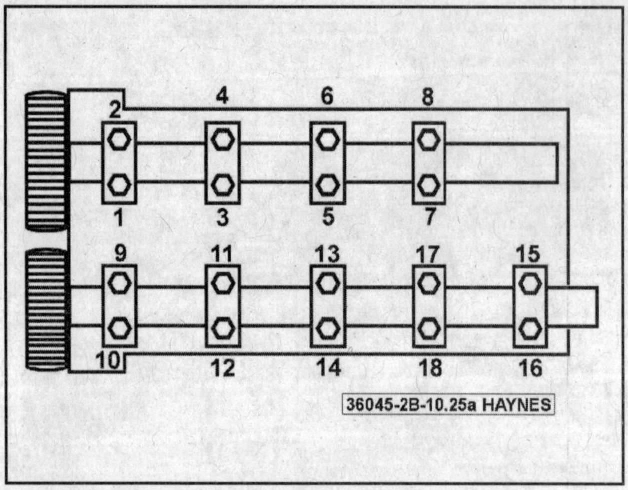

10.25a Front bank camshaft bearing cap tightening sequence - 2008 and earlier 3.0L models

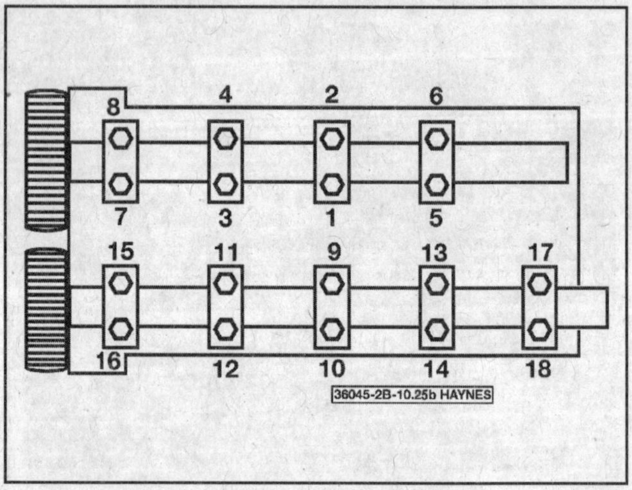

10.25b Front bank camshaft bearing cap tightening sequence - 2009 and later 3.0L models

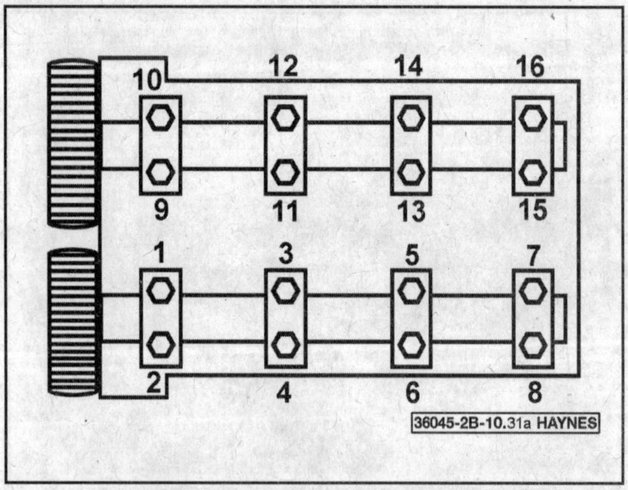

10.31a Rear bank camshaft bearing cap tightening sequence - 2008 and earlier 3.0L models

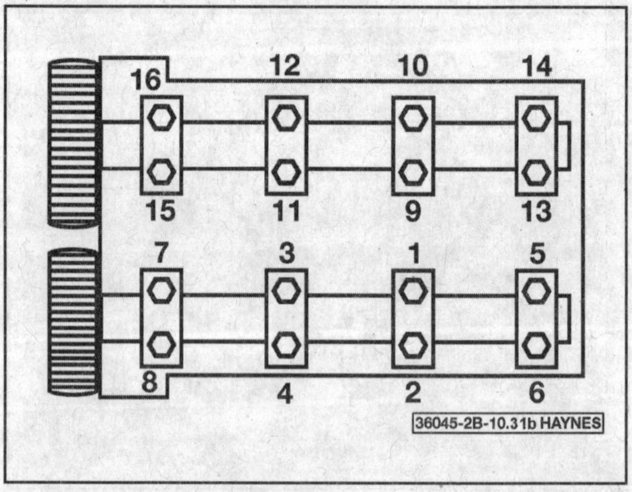

10.31b Rear bank camshaft bearing cap tightening sequence - 2009 and later 3.0L models

Installation

➧ **Refer to illustrations 10.25a, 10.25b, 10.31a and 10.31b**

Front bank cylinder head

22 Make sure the crankshaft keyway is at the 11 o'clock position (see illustration 9.2).

23 Lubricate the rocker arms and hydraulic lash adjusters with engine assembly lubricant or fresh engine oil. Install the adjusters into their original bores, then install the rocker arms in their correct locations.

24 Similarly lubricate the camshafts and install them in their correct locations.

25 Install the camshaft bearing caps in their correct locations. Install the cap bolts and tighten by hand until snug. Install the camshaft thrust caps and bolts. Tighten the bolts in four to five steps, following the sequence shown (see illustrations), to the torque listed in this Chapter's Specifications.

26 Install the seal retainer with a new seal over the left end of the exhaust camshaft. Tighten the bolts to the torque listed in this Chapter's Specifications.

27 Install the front timing chain sprocket on the crankshaft. Install the front timing chain (see Section 9). Install the water pump pulley onto the left end of the exhaust camshaft.

➡**Note: Refer to Chapter 3, Section 8 for the pulley installation procedure.**

Rear bank cylinder head

28 Turn the crankshaft clockwise and position the crankshaft keyway at the 3 o'clock position.

29 Lubricate the rocker arms and hydraulic lash adjusters with engine assembly lubricant or fresh engine oil. Install the adjusters into their original bores, then install the rocker arms in their correct locations.

30 Similarly lubricate the camshafts and install them in their correct locations.

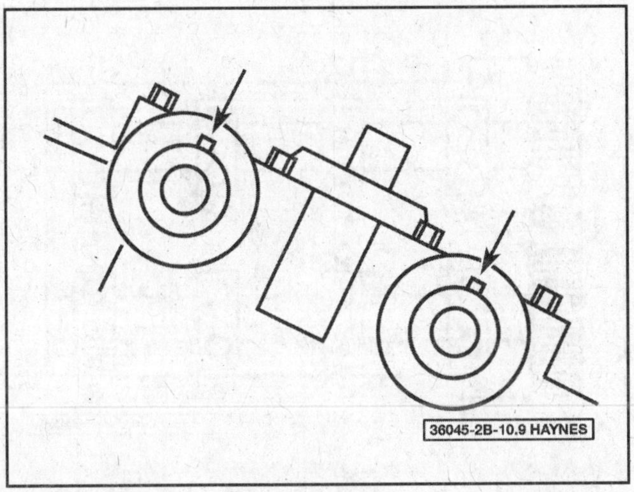

10.37 Front (left) bank camshaft timing marks (keyways) in the neutral position - 3.5L engine

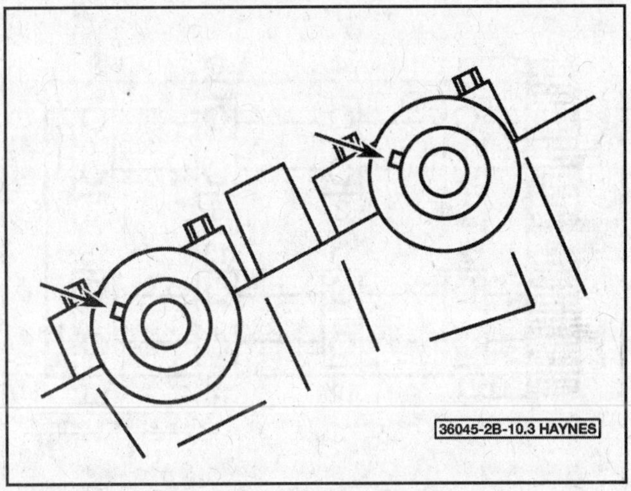

10.40 Rear (right) bank camshaft timing marks (keyways) in the neutral position - 3.5L engine

31 Install the camshaft bearing caps in their correct locations. Install the cap bolts and tighten by hand until snug, then install the camshaft thrust caps and bolts. Tighten the bolts in four to five steps, following the sequence shown (see illustrations) to the torque listed in this Chapter's Specifications.

32 Install the rear timing chain (see Section 9).

33 Install the timing chain cover (see Section 8).

34 Reinstall the remaining parts in the reverse order of removal.

35 Refer to Chapter 1 and fill the crankcase with the recommended oil; fill the power steering reservoir with the correct fluid and refill the cooling system.

36 Reconnect the battery, then start the engine and check for leaks.

3.5L V6 ENGINE

➡Note: This procedure can only be done with the engine removed (see Chapter 2C).

➡Note: Two special camshaft holding tools (manufacturer tool no. 303-1248) are required for this procedure.

➡Note: Before removing the camshafts, check the valve clearances as described in Chapter 2A, Section 5 (but refer to this Chapter's Specifications).

Removal

➧ Refer to illustrations 10.37 and 10.40

37 Remove the primary timing chain and the front (left) cylinder bank VCT assembly/camshaft sprockets/secondary timing chain (see Section 9), then remove the camshaft holding tool from the front (left) cylinder bank camshafts. Confirm that the camshafts are in the neutral positions after the holding tool has been removed (see illustration).

38 Note the location of each camshaft cap. Use a marker on each cap or notes on paper or cardboard if they're not marked.

39 Working in the order opposite that of the tightening sequence (see illustration 10.49), remove the camshaft bearing cap bolts. Remove the caps, then lift the camshafts from the cylinder head. Lay all of the parts out in order to prevent mixing them up.

40 Remove the primary timing chain and the rear (right) cylinder bank VCT assembly/camshaft sprockets/secondary timing chain (see Section 9), then remove the camshaft holding tool from the rear (right) cylinder bank camshafts. Confirm that the camshafts are in the neutral positions after the holding tool has been removed (see illustration).

41 Note the location of each camshaft cap. Use a marker on each cap or notes on paper or cardboard if they're not marked.

42 Working in the order opposite that of the tightening sequence (see illustration 10.51), remove the camshaft bearing cap bolts. Remove the caps, then lift the camshafts from the cylinder head. Lay all of the parts out in order to prevent mixing them up.

43 Remove the lifters from their bores and lay them out in order. A magnet or suction cup can be used.

Inspection

Lifters

44 Inspect the contact and sliding surfaces of each lifter for wear and scratches.

➡Note: If the lifter face is worn, be sure to check the corresponding camshaft lobe carefully.

45 Verify that each lifter moves up and down freely in its bore.

Camshafts

46 Inspect the camshafts as described in Steps 14 through 21.

Installation

➧ Refer to illustrations 10.49 and 10.51

47 Turn the crankshaft counterclockwise to place the keyway in the 9 o'clock position.

⁂ CAUTION:

The crankshaft must remain in this position until the camshafts are installed and the valve clearances are checked and, if necessary, adjusted.

48 Lubricate the camshafts and bearing saddles in the cylinder head for the front (left) cylinder bank with clean engine oil or camshaft installation lube. Set the camshafts in the cylinder head, making sure they are in their neutral positions (see illustration 10.37).

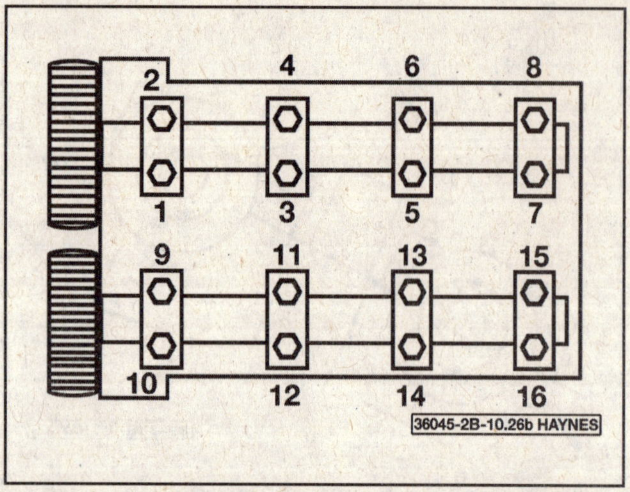

10.49 Front (left) bank camshaft bearing cap tightening sequence - 3.5L engine

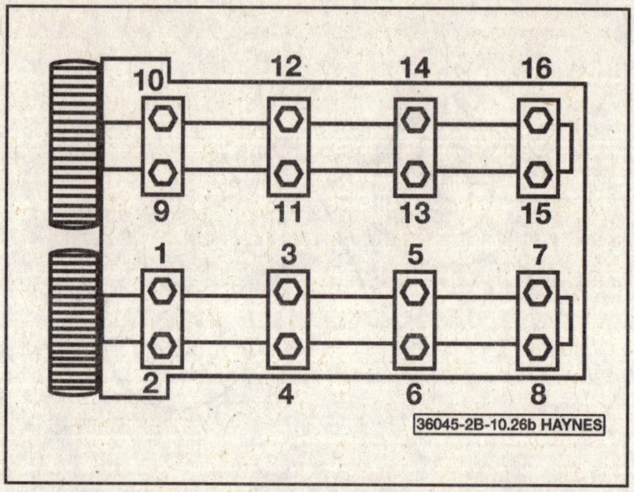

10.51 Rear (right) bank camshaft bearing cap tightening sequence - 3.5L engine

49 Lubricate the friction surfaces of the camshaft bearing caps with clean engine oil or camshaft installation lube and install them in their proper positions. Install the bolts and tighten them, in the proper sequence (see illustration), to the torque listed in this Chapter's Specifications.

50 Lubricate the camshafts and bearing saddles in the cylinder head for the rear (right) cylinder bank with clean engine oil or camshaft installation lube. Set the camshafts in the cylinder head, making sure they are in their neutral positions (see illustration 10.40).

51 Lubricate the friction surfaces of the camshaft bearing caps with clean engine oil or camshaft installation lube and install them in their proper positions. Install the bolts and tighten them, in the proper sequence (see illustration), to the torque listed in this Chapter's Specifications.

52 Check and if necessary, adjust the valve clearances as described in Chapter 2A, Section 5.

➡**Note: Since the crankshaft is in its neutral position, the camshafts can be turned without the danger of the valves contacting the pistons. Insert a bolt into the front of the camshaft to turn it.**

53 Return the camshafts to their positions shown in illustrations 10.37 and 10.40, then install the camshaft holding tools.

54 Install the secondary timing chains, VCT actuator and camshaft sprockets as described in Section 9.

55 Turn the crankshaft clockwise 60-degrees until the keyway is in the 11 o'clock position.

56 Install the primary timing chain and timing chain cover (see Section 9).

11 Cylinder heads - removal and installation

⁂ WARNING:

Wait until the engine is completely cool before beginning this procedure.

➡**Note: On 3.5L V6 engines, this procedure can only be done with the engine removed (see Chapter 2C). Ignore the steps which don't apply.**

REMOVAL

1 Relieve the fuel system pressure (see Chapter 4), then disconnect the cable from the negative battery terminal (see Chapter 5).

2 Drain the cooling system (see Chapter 1).

3 Remove the upper and lower intake manifolds (see Section 5).

4 With the vehicle raised and supported properly, disconnect the front oxygen sensors and the catalytic converters (see Chapter 4).

5 Disconnect the CHT sensor, catalytic converter monitor sensor, and camshaft position sensors (see Chapter 6).

6 Remove the camshafts from the cylinder head to be removed (see Section 10).

7 Where applicable, disconnect bolts or clips that secure wiring harnesses or ground straps to the cylinder heads.

8 Remove the exhaust manifold(s) (see Section 6).

9 Remove any additional components that might interfere with cylinder head removal, referring to the appropriate Chapters of this manual.

10 Remove the hoses and any electrical connectors from the coolant bypass tube. Remove the two fasteners securing the coolant bypass tube, then remove the tube.

11 Loosen each cylinder head bolt, one turn at a time, following the reverse order of the tightening sequence (see illustrations 11.20a or 11.20b and 11.20c). When all cylinder head bolts are loose, remove and discard the bolts. New torque-to-yield cylinder head bolts must be used during installation.

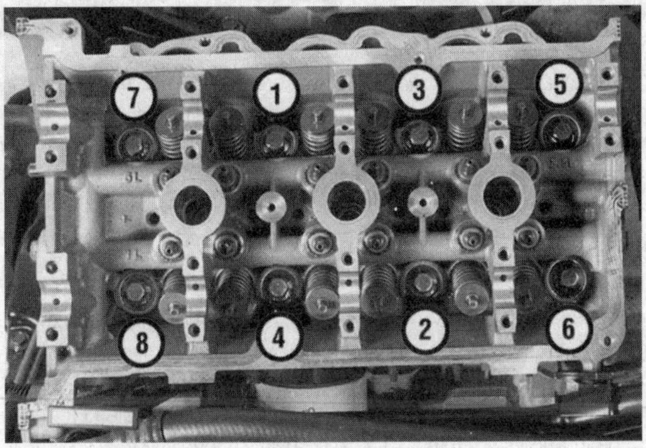

11.20a Cylinder head bolt TIGHTENING sequence - 3.0L engines

11.20b Cylinder head bolt TIGHTENING sequence - 3.5L engines

12 Remove the cylinder head from the engine block and place it on a workbench.

⁂ CAUTION:

If the cylinder head sticks to the block, pry only on a casting protrusion to prevent damaging the mating surfaces.

Remove and discard the cylinder head gasket.

INSTALLATION

➧ Refer to illustrations 11.20a, 11.20b and 11.20c

13 The mating surfaces of the cylinder head and the block must be perfectly clean before installing the cylinder head. Clean the surfaces with a scraper, but be careful not to gouge the aluminum.

⁂ CAUTION:

Be very careful when scraping on aluminum engine parts. Aluminum is soft and gouges easily. Severely gouged parts may require replacement.

14 Check the mating surfaces of the block and the cylinder head for nicks, deep scratches, and other damage. If slight, they can be removed carefully with a file; if excessive, machining may be the only alternative to replacement.

15 If you suspect warpage of the cylinder head gasket surface, use a straightedge to check it for distortion. If the gasket mating surface of your cylinder head or block is out of specification or is severely nicked or scratched, consult an automotive machine shop for advice.

16 Clean the mating surfaces of the cylinder head and block with a clean shop towel and brake system cleaner

17 Ensure that the two locating dowels are in position in the cylinder block and that all cylinder head bolt holes are free of oil, corrosion, or other contamination.

18 Install new cylinder head gaskets on the block, over the locating dowels.

19 Carefully install the cylinder heads. Use caution when lowering the cylinder heads onto the cylinder block to prevent damage to the cylinder heads or block. Make sure the cylinder heads fit properly over the locating dowels in the block.

11.20c An angle gauge takes the guesswork out of tightening the torque-to-yield cylinder head bolts

20 Install new cylinder head bolts and turn down by hand until snug.

⁂ CAUTION:

The cylinder head bolts are the torque-to-yield type and are stretched during tightening. Therefore, the original bolts must be discarded and new bolts installed during assembly.

Tighten the cylinder head bolts in the sequence shown to the torque and angle of rotation listed in this Chapter's Specifications (see illustrations).

➡Note: The method used for the cylinder head bolt tightening procedure is referred to as the "torque angle" or "torque-to-yield" method; follow the procedure exactly. Tighten the bolts using a torque wrench, then use a breaker bar and a special torque angle adapter (available at auto parts stores) to tighten the bolts the required angle.

21 Install the rest of the parts in the reverse order of removal. Tighten fasteners to the torque values listed in this Chapter's Specifications.

22 Refer to Chapter 1 and change the engine oil and filter, then fill and bleed the cooling system.

23 Start the engine and check for leaks.

12 Oil pan - removal and installation

➡Note: On 3.5L engines, the procedure can only be done with the engine removed. In the Steps below, it is assumed that the 3.5L engine has been removed; ignore the steps which don't apply.

REMOVAL

➧ Refer to illustrations 12.8 and 12.10

1 Disconnect the cable from the negative battery terminal (see Chapter 5).

2 Raise the vehicle and support it securely on jackstands.

3 Drain the engine oil (see Chapter 1). Reinstall the oil drain plug and tighten it to the torque listed in the Chapter 1 Specifications, using a new sealing washer.

4 Remove the oil filter (see Chapter 1).

5 Disconnect the oxygen sensor connector(s) (see Chapter 6).

6 Remove the crossover and flexible exhaust pipe and converter assembly from the vehicle (see Chapter 4).

7 Remove the driveplate access cover. On 3.5L engines, remove the nut and stud from the alternator.

8 Remove the bolts that secure the oil pan to the transaxle (see illustration).

9 On 3.5L engines, remove the timing chain cover (see Section 8), the flywheel (see Section 15), and the timing ring for the crankshaft position sensor. Mount the engine to an engine stand.

➡Note: Bolt only at the bellhousing flange, not the oil pan.

10 Remove the oil pan fasteners and remove the oil pan (see illustration). Note the location of any stud bolts. On 3.5L engines, install two of the original oil pan bolts in the two threaded holes at the front and rear of the pan. Tighten the bolts to push the pan evenly away from the block.

11 Remove and discard the oil pan gasket. If necessary, remove the fasteners that secure the oil screen and pick-up tube and remove the screen and tube assembly.

12 Thoroughly clean the oil pan and cylinder block mating surfaces using lacquer thinner or acetone. The surfaces must be free of any residue that will keep the sealant from adhering properly. Clean the oil pan inside and out with solvent and dry with compressed air. Use RTV sealant remover rather than scraping the pan or block surfaces.

INSTALLATION

13 If removed, install a new O-ring seal onto the oil pick-up tube. Install the tube and screen assembly and tighten the retaining fasteners to the torque listed in this Chapter's Specifications. Use a new self-locking nut to secure the pick-up tube support bracket. Tighten the nut to the torque listed in this Chapter's Specifications.

14 On 3.0L engines, install a new gasket on the oil pan. Apply a 1/8-inch bead of RTV sealant to the oil pan gasket in the area of the timing chain cover-to-cylinder block parting line.

15 On 3.0L engines, install the pan bolts and tighten by hand. Be sure to install any stud bolts in the locations noted during removal. Install the oil pan-to-transaxle bolts. Firmly push the oil pan against the transaxle and tighten the pan-to-transaxle bolts snugly, then, tighten the oil pan bolts gradually and evenly, to the torque listed in this Chapter's Specifications.

16 On 3.5L engines, apply a 1/8-inch bead of RTV to the oil pan flange and install the pan with only the four corner bolts hand-tight. Align the pan to the boss under the alternator and hold a straightedge to align the pan flush to the rear face of the block. Work quickly to install the rest of the bolts and tighten them a little at a time, in a criss-cross pattern, to the specified torque in this Chapter's Specifications.

17 The remainder of installation is the reverse of removal, noting the following items:

a) *Tighten all fasteners to the torque values listed in this Chapter's Specifications.*
b) *Always replace any self-locking nuts disturbed on removal.*
c) *Refer to Chapter 1 and fill the engine with fresh engine oil. Install a new oil filter.*
d) *Start the engine and check for leaks.*

12.8 Remove these bolts that secure the oil pan to the transaxle

12.10 Oil pan bolts on the rear side of the pan (not all seen here)

13 Oil pump - removal, inspection and installation

➡Note: On 3.5L engines, the procedure can only be done with the engine removed. In the Steps below, it is assumed that the 3.5L engine has been removed; ignore the steps which don't apply.

REMOVAL

1 Remove the oil pan and oil screen and pick-up tube assembly (see Section 12).

2 Remove the timing chain cover (see Section 8), timing chains and crankshaft sprockets (see Section 9).

3 Loosen each of the four oil pump mounting bolts one turn (three bolts on 3.5L engines), then gradually and evenly loosen each bolt in several steps. When all bolts are loose, remove the bolts and oil pump. On 3.5L engines, rotate the oil pump housing clockwise to separate it from the oil pickup tube.

INSPECTION

4 Remove the oil pump cover from the oil pump body.

5 Note any identification marks on the rotors and withdraw the rotors from the pump body.

6 Thoroughly clean and dry the components.

7 Inspect the rotors for obvious wear or damage. If either rotor, the pump body or the cover is scored or damaged, the complete oil pump assembly must be replaced.

8 If the oil pump components are in acceptable condition, dip the rotors in clean engine oil and install them into the pump body with any identification marks positioned as noted during disassembly.

9 Install the cover and tighten the screws securely.

INSTALLATION

10 Rotate the oil pump inner rotor so it aligns with the flats on the crankshaft. Install the oil pump over the crankshaft and fit it firmly against the cylinder block. On 3.5L engines, rotate the pump assembly counterclockwise to seat it against the oil pickup tube's O-ring.

11 Install the oil pump bolts and tighten by hand until snug. Tighten the bolts gradually and evenly, in a criss-cross pattern, to the torque listed in this Chapter's Specifications.

12 Install the remainder of the components in the reverse order of removal.

13 Refer to Chapter 1 and fill the engine with fresh engine oil. Install a new oil filter.

14 Start the engine and check for leaks.

14 Rear main oil seal - replacement

1 The one-piece rear main oil seal is pressed into a rear main oil seal carrier mounted at the rear of the block. On 3.0L models, remove the transaxle (see Chapter 7).

➡Note: On 3.5L engines, the engine must be out of the vehicle and supported on an engine crane.

2 Remove the oil pan (see Section 12).

3 On 3.0L engines, use a seal-removal tool to remove the rear seal.

4 On 3.5L engines, remove the CKP sensor (see Chapter 6), and remove the 8 bolts securing the oil seal carrier to the block. Remove the two oil pan-to carrier bolts and insert them into the two threaded holes in the carrier. Tighten them evenly (a few turns should do it) until the carrier is forced off the engine.

5 Clean the mating surface for the oil seal carrier on the cylinder block and the crankshaft. Carefully remove and polish any burrs or raised edges on the crankshaft that may have caused the seal to fail.

6 Lightly coat the inside lip of the new seal with clean engine oil. Then, use a thin (but durable) two-inch wide plastic strip (or a two-liter plastic beverage bottle cut to size) around the inside circumference of the seal to act as a liner for installation.

7 With the plastic seal liner in place, carefully move the new seal into position by sliding it onto the contact surface of the crankshaft. A special seal installer can be used (manufacturer tool #303-178) which uses two studs threaded into the crankshaft and two nuts (which when tightened on the studs will force the seal evenly into place), or a large socket or piece of pipe the correct size can be used with a small hammer to tap the seal in place on the block.

8 On 3.5L engines, install the oil seal carrier bolts and finger tighten them while holding the carrier in place. Align the bottom of the seal carrier precisely with the bottom edge of the engine block to ensure that the surfaces are flush before tightening the carrier mounting bolts.

⁂ CAUTION:

The oil pan may leak if the two surfaces are not perfectly flush.

9 Carefully remove the plastic liner or tool so that the new seal contacts the crankshaft mating surface correctly.

10 Tighten the oil seal carrier bolts to the torque listed in this Chapter's Specifications, alternating from left to right evenly.

11 Be sure to check for signs of oil leakage when the engine is operable.

15 Driveplate - removal and installation

This procedure is essentially the same as the flywheel/driveplate removal procedure for the four-cylinder engine. Refer to Chapter 2, Part A and follow the procedure outlined there. However, use the bolt torque listed in this Chapter's Specifications.

➡Note: On 3.5L engines, the bolt pattern of the driveplate will only align one way with the crankshaft flange.

16 Engine mounts - inspection and replacement

Refer to illustrations 16.1a and 16.1b

This procedure is essentially the same as for the four cylinder engine. The engine must be fully supported when removing/installing engine mounts. Refer to Chapter 2, Part A and follow the procedure outlined there but refer to the illustrations for this Section.

16.1a Remove the two bolts (A) and the roll restrictor (B) from the frame bracket

16.1b Remove the engine mount bracket nuts (A) and the bracket-to-mount bolt (B)

Specifications

General

3.0L V6 engine	
Engine type	Double overhead cam (DOHC) V6
Displacement	182 cubic inches
Engine VIN code	1
Bore	3.50 inches (89.0 mm)
Stroke	3.12 inches (79.5 mm)
Compression ratio	10.3:1
Compression pressure	See Chapter 2C
Firing order	1-4-2-5-3-6
Oil pressure	See Chapter 2C
3.5L V6 engine	
Engine type	Double overhead cam (DOHC) V6
Displacement	214 cubic inches
Engine VIN code	C
Bore	3.64 inches (92.5 mm)
Stroke	3.41 inches (86.7 mm)
Compression ratio	10.3:1
Compression pressure	See Chapter 2C
Firing order	1-4-2-5-3-6
Oil pressure	See Chapter 2C

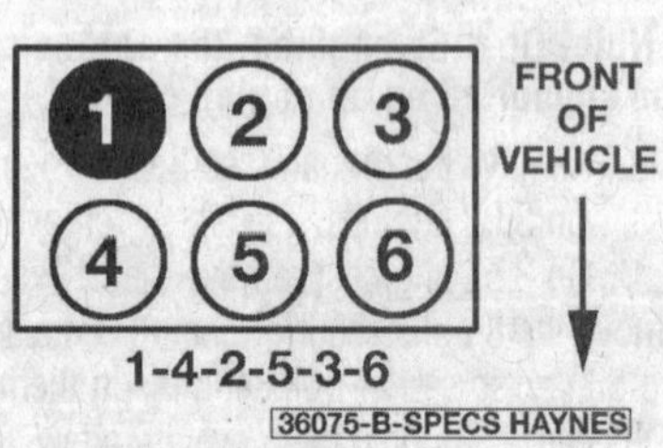

Cylinder location diagram

Camshafts

- 3.0L V6 engine
  - Lobe lift (intake and exhaust)
    - 2009 and earlier models: 0.188 inch (4.79 mm)
    - 2010 models: 0.020 inch (5.08 mm)
  - Journal diameter: 1.060 to 1.061 inches (26.936 to 26.962 mm)
  - Bearing inside diameter: 1.062 to 1.063 inches (26.987 to 27.012 mm)
  - Journal-to-bearing oil clearance
    - Standard: 0.001 to 0.003 inch (0.025 to 0.076 mm)
    - Service limit
      - 2009 and earlier models: 0.0047 inch (0.121 mm)
      - 2010 models: 0.007 inch (0.190 mm)
  - Endplay
    - Standard: 0.001 to 0.0064 inch (0.025 to 0.165 mm)
    - Service limit: 0.0075 inch (0.190 mm)
- 3.5L V6 engine
  - Lobe lift (intake and exhaust): 0.030 inch (9.68 mm)
  - Journal diameter
    - First journal: 1.2202 to 1.2209 inches (30.993 to 31.013 mm)
    - Others: 1.021 to 1.022 inches (25.937 to 25.963 mm)
  - Bearing inside diameter
    - First journal: 1.221 to 1.222 inches (31.0375 to 31.0625 mm)
    - Others: 1.023 to 1.024 inches (25.987 to 26.012 mm)
  - Journal-to-bearing oil clearance (maximum)
    - First journal: 0.0027 inch (0.070 mm)
    - Others: 0.0030 inch (0.075 mm)
  - Endplay
    - Standard: 0.001 to 0.0066 inch (0.025 to 0.170 mm)
    - Service limit: 0.0075 inch (0.190 mm)

Hydraulic lash adjuster (3.0L V6 only)

- Diameter: 0.6290 to 0.6294 inch (15.988 to 16.000 mm)
- Lash adjuster-to-bore clearance
  - Standard: 0.0007 to 0.0027 inch (0.018 to 0.069 mm)
  - Minimum: 0.0006 inch (0.016 mm)

Valve clearances (3.5L V6 engine only) - engine cold

- Intake: 0.006 to 0.010 inch (0.15 to 0.25 mm)
- Exhaust: 0.014 to 0.018 inch (0.36 to 0.46 mm)

Warpage limits

- Head gasket surface warpage limit
  - 3.0L V6
    - End-to-end: 0.005 inch (0.127 mm)
    - Side-to-side: 0.002 inch (0.050 mm)
  - 3.5L V6
    - End-to-end: 0.003 inch (0.076 mm)
    - Side-to-side: 0.002 inch (0.050 mm)

Torque specifications*	Ft-lbs (unless otherwise indicated)	Nm
➡Note: One foot-pound (ft-lb) of torque is equivalent to 12 inch-pounds (in-lbs) of torque. Torque values below approximately 15 foot-pounds are expressed in inch-pounds, because most foot-pound torque wrenches are not accurate at these smaller values.		
Camshaft bearing cap bolts	89 in-lbs	10
Camshaft oil seal retainer bolts (3.0L V6 engine)	89 in-lbs	10
Camshaft sprocket bolt		
3.0L V6 engine		
2009 and earlier models		
Step 1	30	40
Step 2	Tighten an additional 90-degrees	
2010 models	159 in-lbs	18
3.5L V6 engine		
Step 1	30	40
Step 2	Loosen one turn	
Step 3	89 in-lbs	10
Step 4	Tighten an additional 90-degrees	
Crankshaft pulley bolt		
Step 1	89	121
Step 2	Loosen one full turn (360-degrees)	
Step 3	37	50
Step 4	Tighten an additional 90-degrees	
Cylinder head bolts		
3.0L engine (in sequence - see illustration 11.23a)		
Step 1	30	40
Step 2	Tighten an additional 90-degrees	
Step 3	Loosen one full turn (360-degrees)	
Step 4	30	40
Step 5	Tighten an additional 90-degrees	
Step 6	Tighten an additional 90-degrees	
3.5L engine		
Main bolts (in sequence - see illustration 11.23b)		
Step 1	177 in-lbs	20
Stcp 2	26	35
Step 3	Tighten an additional 90-degrees	
Step 4	Tighten an additional 90-degrees	
Step 5	Tighten an additional 90-degrees	
M6 bolt (at front of cylinder head)	89 in-lbs	10
Drivebelt tensioner bolt	18	24
Driveplate-to-crankshaft bolts	59	80
Exhaust manifold/catalytic converter nuts		
3.0L V6	15	20
3.5L V6		
Step 1	15	20
Step 2	18	25
Intake manifold assembly (in sequence - see illustrations in Section 5)		
Upper intake manifold bolts	89 in-lbs	10
Lower intake manifold bolts	89 in-lbs	10

** Refer to Chapter 2, Part C for additional torque specifications*

Torque specifications* (continued)	Ft-lbs (unless otherwise indicated)	Nm

➡Note: One foot-pound (ft-lb) of torque is equivalent to 12 inch-pounds (in-lbs) of torque. Torque values below approximately 15 foot-pounds are expressed in inch-pounds, because most foot-pound torque wrenches are not accurate at these smaller values.

Oil pan bolts (in sequence - see illustrations in Section 12)		
3.0L V6 engine		
To engine block	18	24
To transaxle	35	47
3.5L V6 engine		
Step 1, bolts 10 ,11, 13, 14	27 in-lbs	3
Step 2	Loosen 1/2-turn	
Step 3	Align oil pan with rear of cylinder block	
Step 4, bolts 10 ,11, 13, 14	27 in-lbs	3
Step 5, bolts 1 through 14	18	24
Step 6, bolts 15 and 16	89 in-lbs	10
Oil pump screen cover and tube bolts	89 in-lbs	10
Oil pump-to-engine block bolts	89 in-lbs	10
Oil pan baffle bolts		
Step 1		
Smaller nuts	44 in-lbs	5
Larger nuts	132 in-lbs	15
Step 2	Tighten all 8 nuts an additional 45-degrees	
Timing chain cover bolts		
3.0L engines (in sequence - see illustration 8.21)	18	24
3.5L engines (in sequence - see illustration 8.22)		
Step 1, bolts 17 through 20	27 in-lbs	3
Step 2, bolts 1 through 22	89 in-lbs	10
Step 3, bolts 23 through 25	133 in-lbs	15
Step 4, bolts 1 through 22	18	24
Step 5, bolts 23 through 25	55	75
Timing chain guides		
3.0L V6 engine	18	24
3.5L V6 engine	89 in-lbs	10
Timing chain tensioner arm bolts		
3.0L V6 engine	18	24
3.5L V6 engine	89 in-lbs	10
Timing chain tensioner bolts		
3.0L V6 engine	18	24
3.5L V6 engine	89 in-lbs	10
Valve cover bolts (in sequence - see illustrations in Section 4)	89 in-lbs	10
Variable Camshaft Timing (VCT)		
3.0L V6 engine		
Actuator bolt		
2009 and earlier models		
Step 1	30	40
Step 2	Tighten an additional 90-degrees	
2010 models	159 in-lbs	18

** Refer to Chapter 2, Part C for additional torque specifications*

Torque specifications* (continued)	Ft-lbs (unless otherwise indicated)	Nm

➡Note: One foot-pound (ft-lb) of torque is equivalent to 12 inch-pounds (in-lbs) of torque. Torque values below approximately 15 foot-pounds are expressed in inch-pounds, because most foot-pound torque wrenches are not accurate at these smaller values.

Variable Camshaft Timing (VCT) (continued)		
3.0L V6 engine		
Assembly (housing)	18	24
Solenoid	89 in-lbs	10
3.5L V6 engine		
Actuator bolt		
Step 1	30	40
Step 2	Loosen one turn	
Step 3	89 in-lbs	10
Step 4	Tighten an additional 90-degrees	
Assembly (housing)	89 in-lbs	10
Solenoid	89 in-lbs	10

** Refer to Chapter 2, Part C for additional torque specifications*

2C

GENERAL ENGINE OVERHAUL PROCEDURES

Section

Reference to other Chapters

CHECK ENGINE light on - See Chapter 6

1 General information - engine overhaul

Refer to illustrations 1.1, 1.2, 1.3, 1.4, 1.5 and 1.6

Included in this portion of Chapter 2 are general information and diagnostic testing procedures for determining the overall mechanical condition of your engine.

The information ranges from advice concerning preparation for an overhaul and the purchase of replacement parts and/or components to detailed, step-by-step procedures covering removal and installation.

The following Sections have been written to help you determine whether your engine needs to be overhauled and how to remove and install it once you've determined it needs to be rebuilt. For information concerning in-vehicle engine repair, see Chapter 2A or 2B.

It's not always easy to determine when, or if, an engine should be completely overhauled, because a number of factors must be considered.

High mileage is not necessarily an indication that an overhaul is needed, while low mileage doesn't preclude the need for an overhaul. Frequency of servicing is probably the most important consideration. An engine that's had regular and frequent oil and filter changes, as well as other required maintenance, will most likely give many thousands of miles of reliable service. Conversely, a neglected engine may require an overhaul very early in its service life.

Excessive oil consumption is an indication that piston rings, valve seals and/or valve guides are in need of attention. Make sure that oil leaks aren't responsible before deciding that the rings and/or guides are bad. Perform a cylinder compression check to determine the extent of the work required (see Section 3). Also check the vacuum readings under various conditions (see Section 4).

Check the oil pressure with a gauge installed in place of the oil pressure sending unit and compare it to this Chapter's Specifications (see Section 2). If it's extremely low, the bearings and/or oil pump are probably worn out.

Loss of power, rough running, knocking or metallic engine noises, excessive valve train noise and high fuel consumption rates may also point to the need for an overhaul, especially if they're all present at the same time. If a complete tune-up doesn't remedy the situation, major mechanical work is the only solution.

An engine overhaul involves restoring the internal parts to the specifications of a new engine. During an overhaul, the piston rings are replaced and the cylinder walls are reconditioned (rebored and/or honed) (see illustrations 1.1 and 1.2). If a rebore is done by an automotive machine shop, new oversize pistons will also be installed. The main

1.1 An engine block being bored - an engine rebuilder will use special machinery to recondition the cylinder bores

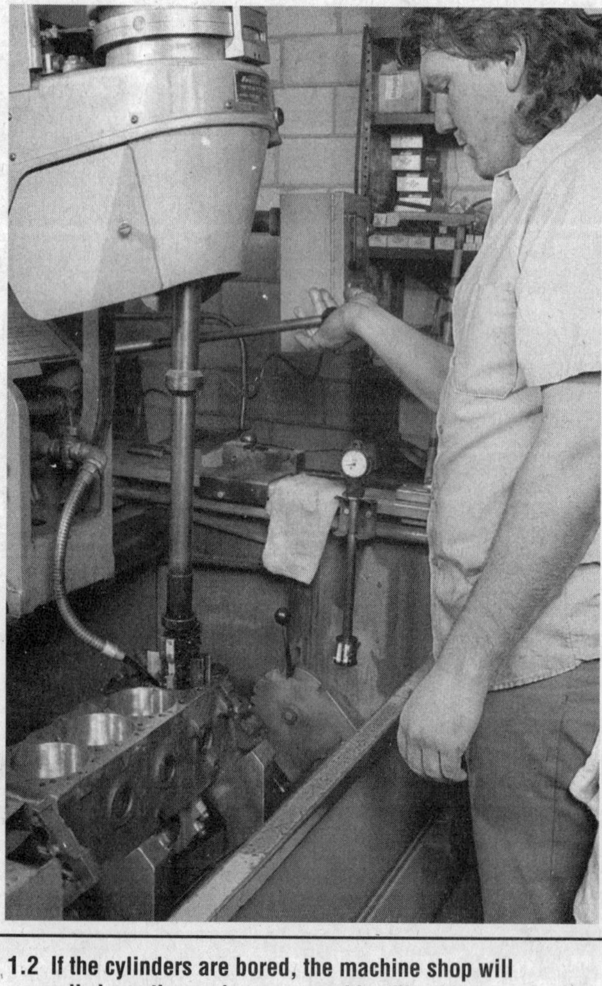

1.2 If the cylinders are bored, the machine shop will normally hone the engine on a machine like this

1.3 A crankshaft having a main bearing journal ground

1.4 A machinist checks for a bent connecting rod, using specialized equipment

1.5 A bore gauge being used to check the main bearing bore

1.6 Uneven piston wear like this indicates a bent connecting rod

bearings and connecting rod bearings are generally replaced with new ones and, if necessary, the crankshaft may be reground to restore the journals (see illustration 1.3). Generally, the valves are serviced as well, since they're usually in less-than-perfect condition at this point. While the engine is being overhauled, other components, such as the starter and alternator, can be rebuilt as well. The end result should be a like-new engine that will give many trouble-free miles.

➡Note: Critical cooling system components such as the hoses, drivebelts, thermostat and water pump should be replaced with new parts when an engine is overhauled. The radiator should be checked carefully to ensure that it isn't clogged or leaking (see Chapter 3). If you purchase a rebuilt engine or short block, some rebuilders will not warranty their engines unless the radiator has been professionally flushed. Also, we don't recommend overhauling the oil pump - always install a new one when an engine is rebuilt.

Overhauling the internal components on today's engines is a difficult and time-consuming task that requires a significant amount of specialty tools and is best left to a professional engine rebuilder (see illustrations 1.4, 1.5 and 1.6). A competent engine rebuilder will handle the inspection of your old parts and offer advice concerning the reconditioning or replacement of the original engine. Never purchase parts or have machine work done on other components until the block has been thoroughly inspected by a professional machine shop. As a general rule, time is the primary cost of an overhaul, especially since the vehicle may be tied up for a minimum of two weeks or more. Be aware that some engine builders only have the capability to rebuild the engine you bring them while other rebuilders have a large inventory of rebuilt exchange engines in stock. Also be aware that many machine shops could take as much as two weeks time to completely rebuild your engine depending on shop workload. Sometimes it makes more sense to simply exchange your engine for another engine that's already rebuilt to save time.

2 Oil pressure check

Refer to illustrations 2.2 and 2.3

1 Low engine oil pressure can be a sign of an engine in need of rebuilding. A low oil pressure indicator (often called an "idiot light") is not a test of the oiling system. Such indicators only come on when the oil pressure is dangerously low. Even a factory oil pressure gauge in the instrument panel is only a relative indication, although much better for driver information than a warning light. A better test is with a mechanical (not electrical) oil pressure gauge.

2 Locate the oil pressure sending unit on the engine block:

a) *On four-cylinder engines, the oil pressure sending unit is located on the front of the engine block, threaded into the oil filter adapter.*

b) *On V6 engines, the sending unit is located near the oil filter housing behind the air conditioning compressor, on the front side of the block (see illustration).*

3 Unscrew the oil pressure sending unit and screw in the hose for your oil pressure gauge (see illustration). If necessary, install an adapter fitting. Use Teflon tape or thread sealant on the threads of the adapter and/or the fitting on the end of your gauge's hose.

4 Connect an accurate tachometer to the engine, according to the tachometer manufacturer's instructions.

5 Check the oil pressure with the engine running (normal operating temperature) at the specified engine speed, and compare it to this Chapter's Specifications. If it's extremely low, the bearings and/or oil pump are probably worn out.

2.2 On V6 engines the oil pressure sending unit is located on the front of the engine block behind the air conditioning compressor (3.0L V6 shown)

2.3 The oil pressure can be checked by removing the sending unit and installing a pressure gauge in its place

3 Cylinder compression check

Refer to illustration 3.6

1 A compression check will tell you what mechanical condition the upper end of your engine (pistons, rings, valves, head gaskets) is in. Specifically, it can tell you if the compression is down due to leakage caused by worn piston rings, defective valves and seats or a blown head gasket.

Note: The engine must be at normal operating temperature and the battery must be fully charged for this check.

2 Begin by cleaning the area around the ignition coils before you remove them (compressed air should be used, if available). The idea is to prevent dirt from getting into the cylinders as the compression check is being done.

3 Remove all of the spark plugs from the engine (see Chapter 1).

4 Remove the air intake duct from the throttle body, then block the throttle wide open.

5 Remove the fuel pump relay (see Chapter 4, Section 2).

6 Install a compression gauge in the spark plug hole (see illustration).

7 Crank the engine over at least seven compression strokes and

watch the gauge. The compression should build up quickly in a healthy engine. Low compression on the first stroke, followed by gradually increasing pressure on successive strokes, indicates worn piston rings. A low compression reading on the first stroke, which doesn't build up during successive strokes, indicates leaking valves or a blown head gasket (a cracked head could also be the cause). Deposits on the undersides of the valve heads can also cause low compression. Record the highest gauge reading obtained.

8 Repeat the procedure for the remaining cylinders and compare the results to this Chapter's Specifications.

9 Add some engine oil (about three squirts from a plunger-type oil can) to each cylinder, through the spark plug hole, and repeat the test.

10 If the compression increases after the oil is added, the piston rings are definitely worn. If the compression doesn't increase significantly, the leakage is occurring at the valves or head gasket. Leakage past the valves may be caused by burned valve seats and/or faces or warped, cracked or bent valves.

11 If two adjacent cylinders have equally low compression, there's a strong possibility that the head gasket between them is blown. The appearance of coolant in the combustion chambers or the crankcase would verify this condition.

12 If one cylinder is slightly lower than the others, and the engine has a slightly rough idle, a worn lobe on the camshaft could be the cause.

13 If the compression is unusually high, the combustion chambers are probably coated with carbon deposits. If that's the case, the cylinder head(s) should be removed and decarbonized.

3.6 Use a compression gauge with a threaded fitting for the spark plug hole, not the type that requires hand pressure to maintain the seal

14 If compression is way down or varies greatly between cylinders, it would be a good idea to have a leak-down test performed by an automotive repair shop. This test will pinpoint exactly where the leakage is occurring and how severe it is.

15 After performing the test, don't forget to unblock the throttle plate.

4 Vacuum gauge diagnostic checks

➧ Refer to illustrations 4.4 and 4.6

1 A vacuum gauge provides inexpensive but valuable information about what is going on in the engine. You can check for worn rings or cylinder walls, leaking head or intake manifold gaskets, restricted exhaust, stuck or burned valves, weak valve springs, improper ignition or valve timing and ignition problems.

2 Unfortunately, vacuum gauge readings are easy to misinterpret, so they should be used in conjunction with other tests to confirm the diagnosis.

3 Both the absolute readings and the rate of needle movement are important for accurate interpretation. Most gauges measure vacuum in inches of mercury (in-Hg). The following references to vacuum assume the diagnosis is being performed at sea level. As elevation increases (or atmospheric pressure decreases), the reading will decrease. For every 1,000-foot increase in elevation above approximately 2000 feet, the gauge readings will decrease about one inch of mercury.

4 Connect the vacuum gauge directly to the intake manifold vacuum, not to ported (throttle body) vacuum (see illustration). Be sure no hoses are left disconnected during the test or false readings will result.

5 Before you begin the test, allow the engine to warm up completely. Block the wheels and set the parking brake. With the transmission in Park, start the engine and allow it to run at normal idle speed.

4.4 A simple vacuum gauge can be handy in diagnosing engine condition and performance. Connect it to an intake manifold vacuum source, not a ported (throttle body) source

WARNING:

Keep your hands and the vacuum gauge clear of the fans and drivebelts.

6 Read the vacuum gauge; an average, healthy engine should normally produce about 17 to 22 in-Hg with a fairly steady needle (see illustration). Refer to the following vacuum gauge readings and what they indicate about the engine's condition:

7 A low steady reading usually indicates a leaking gasket between the intake manifold and cylinder head(s) or throttle body, a leaky vacuum hose, late ignition timing or incorrect camshaft timing. Check ignition timing with a timing light and eliminate all other possible causes, utilizing the tests provided in this Chapter before you remove the timing belt cover to check the timing marks.

8 If the reading is three to eight inches below normal and it fluctuates at that low reading, suspect an intake manifold gasket leak at an intake port or a faulty fuel injector.

9 If the needle has regular drops of about two-to-four inches at a steady rate, the valves are probably leaking. Perform a compression check or leak-down test to confirm this.

10 An irregular drop or down-flick of the needle can be caused by a sticking valve or an ignition misfire. Perform a compression check or leak-down test and read the spark plugs.

11 A rapid vibration of about four in-Hg variation at idle combined with exhaust smoke indicates worn valve guides. Perform a leak-down test to confirm this. If the rapid vibration occurs with an increase in engine speed, check for a leaking intake manifold gasket or head gasket, weak valve springs, burned valves or ignition misfire.

12 A slight fluctuation, say one inch up and down, may mean ignition problems. Check all the usual tune-up items and, if necessary, run the engine on an ignition analyzer.

13 If there is a large fluctuation, perform a compression or leak-down test to look for a weak or dead cylinder or a blown head gasket.

14 If the needle moves slowly through a wide range, check for a clogged PCV system, incorrect idle fuel mixture, throttle body or intake manifold gasket leaks.

15 Check for a slow return after revving the engine by quickly snapping the throttle open until the engine reaches about 2,500 rpm and let it shut. Normally the reading should drop to near zero, rise above normal idle reading (about 5 in-Hg over) and then return to the previous idle reading. If the vacuum returns slowly and doesn't peak when the throttle is snapped shut, the rings may be worn. If there is a long delay, look for a restricted exhaust system (often the muffler or catalytic converter). An easy way to check this is to temporarily disconnect the exhaust ahead of the suspected part and redo the test.

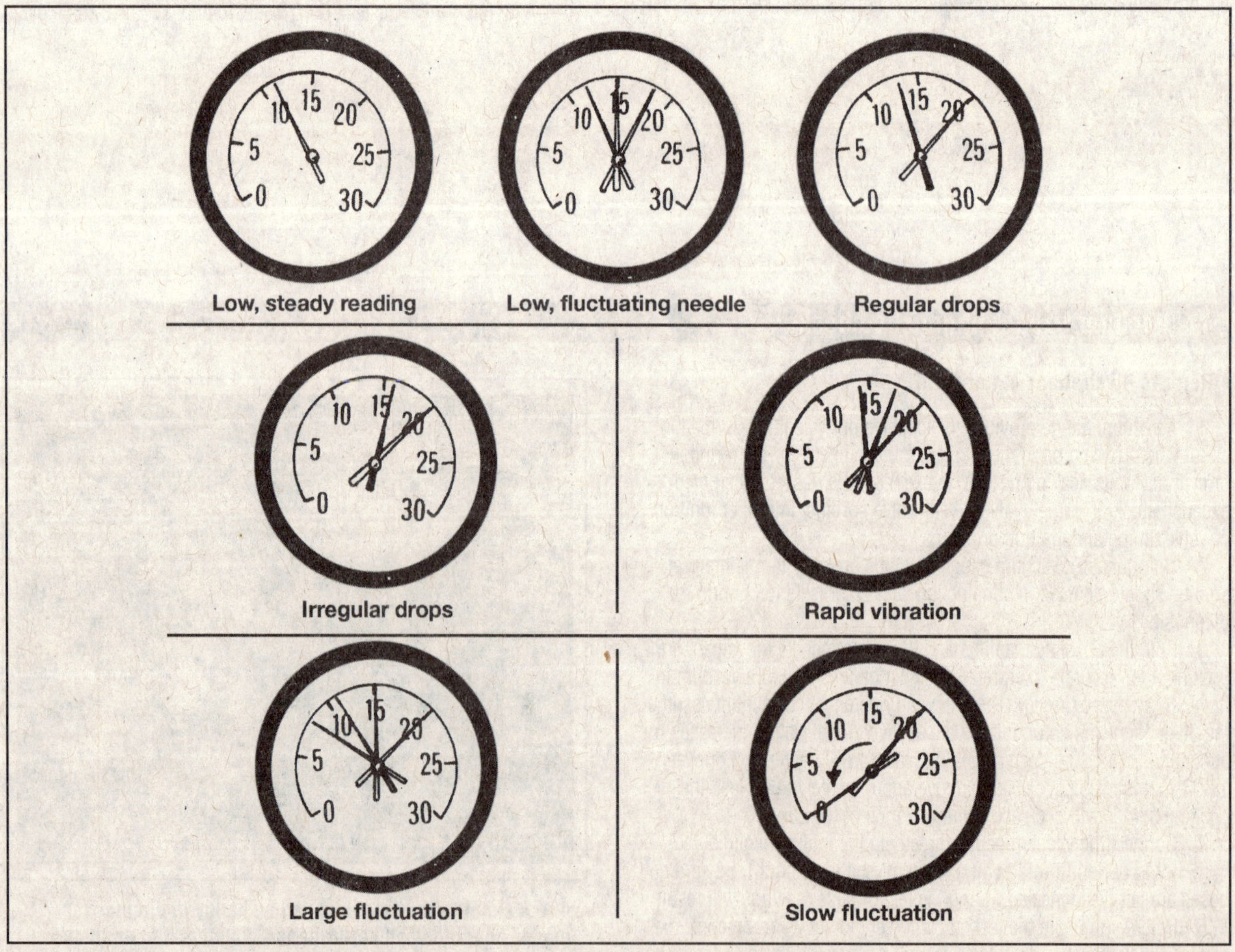

4.6 Typical vacuum gauge readings

5 Engine rebuilding alternatives

The do-it-yourselfer is faced with a number of options when purchasing a rebuilt engine. The major considerations are cost, warranty, parts availability and the time required for the rebuilder to complete the project. The decision to replace the engine block, piston/connecting rod assemblies and crankshaft depends on the final inspection results of your engine. Only then can you make a cost effective decision whether to have your engine overhauled or simply purchase an exchange engine for your vehicle.

Some of the rebuilding alternatives include:

Individual parts - If the inspection procedures reveal that the engine block and most engine components are in reusable condition, purchasing individual parts and having a rebuilder rebuild your engine may be the most economical alternative. The block, crankshaft and piston/connecting rod assemblies should all be inspected carefully by a machine shop first.

Short block - A short block consists of an engine block with a crankshaft and piston/connecting rod assemblies already installed. All new bearings are incorporated and all clearances will be correct. The existing camshafts, valve train components, cylinder head and external parts can be bolted to the short block with little or no machine shop work necessary.

Long block - A long block consists of a short block plus an oil pump, oil pan, cylinder head, valve cover, camshaft and valve train components, timing sprockets and belt or gears and timing cover. All components are installed with new bearings, seals and gaskets incorporated throughout. The installation of manifolds and external parts is all that's necessary.

Low mileage used engines - Some companies now offer low mileage used engines that are a very cost effective way to get your vehicle up and running again. These engines often come from vehicles that have been in totaled in accidents or come from other countries that have a higher vehicle turn over rate. A low mileage used engine also usually has a similar warranty like the newly remanufactured engines.

Give careful thought to which alternative is best for you and discuss the situation with local automotive machine shops, auto parts dealers and experienced rebuilders before ordering or purchasing replacement parts.

6 Engine removal - methods and precautions

Refer to illustrations 6.1, 6.2, 6.3 and 6.4

If you've decided that an engine must be removed for overhaul or major repair work, several preliminary steps should be taken. Read all removal and installation procedures carefully prior to committing to this job. These engines are removed by lowering the engine to the floor, along with the transmission, and then raising the vehicle sufficiently to slide the assembly out; this will require a vehicle hoist as well as an engine hoist. Make sure the engine hoist is rated in excess of the combined weight of the engine and transmission. A transmission jack is also very helpful. Safety is of primary importance, considering the potential hazards involved in removing the engine from the vehicle.

Locating a suitable place to work is extremely important. Adequate work space, along with storage space for the vehicle, will be needed. If a shop or garage isn't available, at the very least a flat, level, clean work surface made of concrete or asphalt is required.

Cleaning the engine compartment and engine before beginning the removal procedure will help keep tools clean and organized (see illustrations 6.1 and 6.2).

If you're a novice at engine removal, get at least one helper. One person cannot easily do all the things you need to do to remove a big heavy engine and transmission assembly from the engine compartment.

6.1 After tightly wrapping water-vulnerable components, use a spray cleaner on everything, with particular concentration on the greasiest areas, usually around the valve cover and lower edges of the block. If one section dries out, apply more cleaner

6.2 Depending on how dirty the engine is, let the cleaner soak in according to the directions and then hose off the grime and cleaner. Get the rinse water down into every area you can get at; then dry important components with a hair dryer or paper towels

Also helpful is to seek advice and assistance from someone who's experienced in engine removal.

Plan the operation ahead of time. Arrange for or obtain all of the tools and equipment you'll need prior to beginning the job (see illustrations 6.3 and 6.4). Some of the equipment necessary to perform engine removal and installation safely and with relative ease are (in addition to a vehicle hoist and an engine hoist) a heavy duty floor jack (preferably fitted with a transmission jack head adapter), complete sets of wrenches and sockets as described in the front of this manual, wooden blocks, plenty of rags and cleaning solvent for mopping up spilled oil, coolant and gasoline.

Plan for the vehicle to be out of use for quite a while. A machine shop can do the work that is beyond the scope of the home mechanic. Machine shops often have a busy schedule, so before removing the engine, consult the shop for an estimate of how long it will take to rebuild or repair the components that may need work.

6.3 Get an engine stand sturdy enough to firmly support the engine while you're working on it. Stay away from three-wheeled models: they have a tendency to tip over more easily, so get a four-wheeled unit

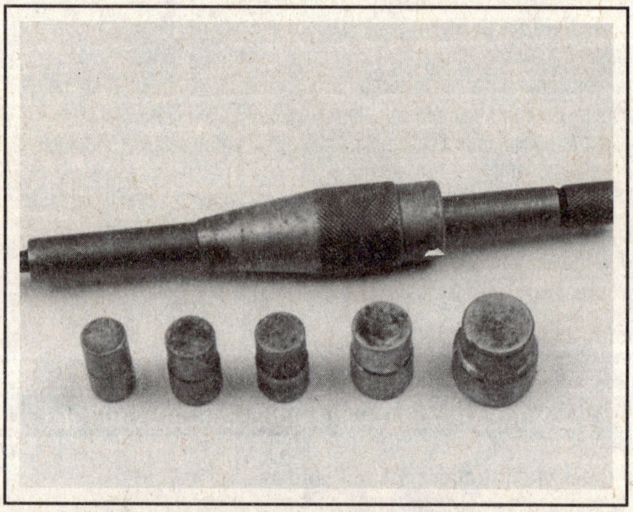

6.4 A clutch alignment tool is necessary if you plan to install a rebuilt engine mated to a manual transaxle

7 Engine - removal and installation

⁂ WARNING:

The models covered by this manual are equipped with Supplemental Restraint systems (SRS), more commonly known as airbags. Always disable the airbag system before working in the vicinity of airbag system components to avoid the possibility of accidental deployment of the airbag, which could cause personal injury (see Chapter 12).

⁂ WARNING:

Gasoline is extremely flammable, so take extra precautions when you work on any part of the fuel system. Don't smoke or allow open flames or bare light bulbs near the work area, and don't work in a garage where a gas-type appliance (such as a water heater or clothes dryer) is present. Since gasoline is carcinogenic, wear fuel-resistant gloves when there's a possibility of being exposed to fuel, and, if you spill any fuel on your skin, rinse it off immediately with soap and water. Mop up any spills immediately and do not store fuel-soaked rags where they could ignite. The fuel system is under constant pressure, so, if any fuel lines are to be disconnected, the fuel pressure in the system must be relieved first (see Chapter 4 for more information). When you perform any kind of work on the fuel system, wear safety glasses and have a Class B type fire extinguisher on hand.

⁂ WARNING:

The engine must be completely cool before beginning this procedure.

➡Note: Engine removal on these models is a difficult job, especially for the do-it-yourself mechanic working at home. Because of the vehicle's design, the manufacturer states that the engine and transaxle have to be removed as a unit from the bottom of the vehicle, not the top. With a floor jack and jackstands the vehicle can't be raised high enough and supported safely enough for the engine/transaxle assembly to slide out from underneath. The manufacturer recommends that removal of the engine/transaxle assembly only be performed on a vehicle hoist.

REMOVAL

1 Have the air conditioning system discharged by an automotive air conditioning technician.

2 Park the vehicle on a frame-contact type vehicle hoist. The pads of the hoist arms must contact the body welt along each side of the vehicle.

3 Relieve the fuel system pressure (see Chapter 4), then disconnect the negative cable from the battery.

4 Place protective covers on the fenders and cowl and remove the hood (see Chapter 11).

5 Remove the air filter housing (see Chapter 4).

6 Remove the cowl panels (see Chapter 11).

7 Remove the battery and battery tray (see Chapter 5).

8 Loosen the front wheel lug nuts and the driveaxle/hub nuts, then raise the vehicle on the hoist. Drain the cooling system and engine oil and remove the drivebelt (see Chapter 1).

9 Clearly label, then disconnect all vacuum lines, coolant and emissions hoses, wiring harness connectors, ground straps and fuel lines. Masking tape and/or a touch up paint applicator work well for marking items (see illustration). Take instant photos or sketch the locations of components and brackets.

10 On V6 models, remove the upper intake manifold (see Chapter 2B).

11 Remove the alternator and the starter (see Chapter 5).

12 Remove the power steering pump (see Chapter 10).

13 Remove the engine cooling fan and radiator (see Chapter 3).

➡Note: This step is not absolutely necessary, but it will help avoid damage to the cooling fans and radiator as the engine is lowered out of the vehicle. If the radiator is not taken out it will still be necessary to detach the transaxle oil cooler lines from the bottom of the radiator on automatic transaxle equipped vehicles.

14 Disconnect the shift cable(s) from the transaxle (see Chapter 7A or 7B). Also disconnect any wiring harness connectors from the transaxle.

15 Remove the air conditioning compressor (see Chapter 3).

16 Detach the steering column shaft from the steering gear (see Chapter 10).

17 If equipped with a manual transaxle, disconnect the clutch release cylinder from the transaxle (see Chapter 8).

18 Detach the exhaust pipe(s) from the exhaust manifold(s) (see Chapter 4).

19 Detach all wiring harnesses and hoses from between the engine/transaxle and the chassis. Be sure to mark all connectors to facilitate reassembly.

20 Remove the driveaxles (see Chapter 8). On AWD vehicles, remove the rear driveshaft.

21 Detach the stabilizer bar links from the bar, separate the lower control arms from the steering knuckles and detach the shock absorber damper forks from the front lower control arms. Also detach the tie-rod ends from the steering knuckles (see Chapter 10).

22 On automatic transaxle models, mark the relationship of the torque converter to the driveplate, then remove the torque converter-to-driveplate nuts (see Chapter 7B).

23 Remove the roll restrictor between the lower rear part of the engine and the subframe.

24 Attach a lifting sling or chain to the engine. Position an engine hoist and connect the sling to it. If no lifting hooks or brackets are present, you'll have to fasten the chains or slings to some substantial part of the engine - ones that are strong enough to take the weight, but in locations that will provide good balance. Take up the slack until there is slight tension on the sling or chain. Position the chain on the hoist so it balances the engine and the transaxle level with the vehicle.

25 Mark the position of each corner of the subframe to the chassis. Support the subframe with two floor jacks, then remove the fasteners and lower the subframe. Remove it from underneath the vehicle.

26 Remove the transaxle mount and the engine mount.

27 Recheck to be sure nothing except the mounts are still connecting the engine to the vehicle or to the transaxle. Disconnect and label anything still remaining.

28 Slowly lower the engine/transaxle from the vehicle.

➡Note: Placing a sheet of hardboard or paneling between the engine and the floor makes moving the powertrain easier.

29 Once the powertrain is on the floor, disconnect the engine lifting hoist and raise the vehicle hoist until the powertrain can be slid out from underneath.

➡Note: A helper will be needed to move the powertrain.

30 Reconnect the chain or sling and raise the engine/transaxle with the hoist. Support the transmission with a jack (preferably one with a transmission jack head adapter). Separate the engine from the transaxle (see Chapter 7).

31 Remove the driveplate/flywheel and mount the engine on a stand.

INSTALLATION

➡Note: The manufacturer recommends replacing all subframe and suspension fasteners with new ones whenever they are loosened or removed.

32 Installation is the reverse of removal, noting the following points:

a) Check the engine/transaxle mounts. If they're worn or damaged, replace them.

b) Attach the transaxle to the engine following the procedure described in Chapter 7.

c) Add coolant, oil, power steering and transmission fluids as needed (see Chapter 1).

d) Align the subframe reference marks before tightening the bolts.

e) Tighten the subframe mounting fasteners to the torque listed in the Chapter 10 Specifications.

f) Reconnect the negative battery cable. Refer to Chapter 5, Section 1.

g) Run the engine and check for proper operation and leaks. Shut off the engine and recheck fluid levels.

h) Have the air conditioning system re-charged and leak tested by the shop that discharged it.

8 Engine overhaul - disassembly sequence

1 It's much easier to disassemble the engine if it's mounted on a portable engine stand. A stand can often be rented quite cheaply from an equipment rental yard. Before the engine is mounted on a stand, the driveplate should be removed from the engine.

2 If a stand isn't available, it's possible to remove the external engine components with it blocked up on the floor. Be extra careful not to tip or drop the engine when working without a stand.

3 If you're going to obtain a rebuilt engine, all external components must come off first, to be transferred to the replacement engine. These components include:

Driveplate
Ignition system components
Emissions-related components
Engine mounts and mount brackets
Fuel injection components
Intake/exhaust manifolds
Oil filter
Thermostat and housing assembly
Water pump

Note: When removing the external components from the engine, pay close attention to details that may be helpful or important during installation. Note the installed position of gaskets, seals, spacers, pins, brackets, washers, bolts and other small items.

4 If you're going to obtain a short block (assembled engine block, crankshaft, pistons and connecting rods), then you should remove the timing belt, cylinder head, oil pan, oil pump pick-up tube, oil pump and water pump from your engine so that you can turn in your old short block to the rebuilder as a core. See *Engine rebuilding alternatives* for additional information regarding the different possibilities to be considered.

9 Pistons and connecting rods - removal and installation

REMOVAL

Refer to illustrations 9.1, 9.3 and 9.4

Note: Prior to removing the piston/connecting rod assemblies, remove the cylinder head and oil pan (see Chapter 2A).

1 Use your fingernail to feel if a ridge has formed at the upper limit of ring travel (about 1/4-inch down from the top of each cylinder). If carbon deposits or cylinder wear have produced ridges, they must be completely removed with a special tool (see illustration). Follow the manufacturer's instructions provided with the tool. Failure to remove the ridges before attempting to remove the piston/connecting rod assemblies may result in piston breakage.

2 After the cylinder ridges have been removed, turn the engine so the crankshaft is facing up. On four-cylinder engines, remove the balance shaft assembly (see Section 13). On 3.5L V6 engines remove the main bearing cap support brace.

3 Before the main bearing caps or main-bearing support bridge and connecting rods are removed, check the connecting rod endplay with feeler gauges. Slide them between the first connecting rod and the crankshaft throw until the play is removed (see illustration). Repeat this procedure for each connecting rod. The endplay is equal to the thickness of the feeler gauge(s). Check with an automotive machine shop for the endplay service limit (a typical end play limit should measure between 0.005 to 0.015 inch [0.127 to 0.381 mm]). If the play exceeds the service limit, new connecting rods will be required. If new rods (or a new crankshaft) are installed, the endplay may fall under the minimum allowable. If it does, the rods will have to be machined to restore it. If necessary, consult an automotive machine shop for advice.

9.1 Before you try to remove the pistons, use a ridge reamer to remove the raised material (ridge) from the top of the cylinders

9.3 Checking the connecting rod endplay (side clearance)

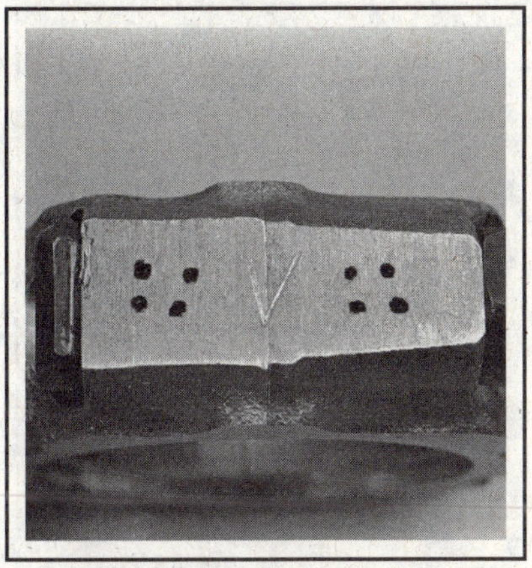

9.4 If the connecting rods and caps are not marked, use permanent ink or paint to mark the caps to the rods by cylinder number (for example, this would be the No. 4 connecting rod)

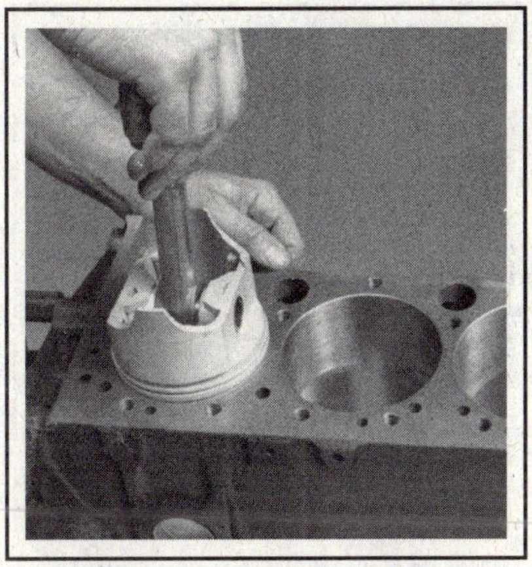

9.13 Install the piston ring into the cylinder then push it down into position using a piston so the ring will be square in the cylinder

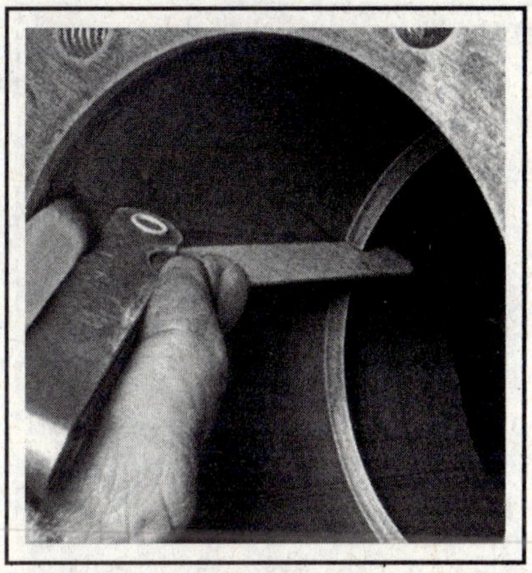

9.14 With the ring square in the cylinder, measure the ring end gap with a feeler gauge

4 Check the connecting rods and caps for identification marks. If they aren't plainly marked, use paint or marker to clearly identify each rod and cap (1, 2, 3, etc., depending on the cylinder they're associated with) (see illustration).

5 Loosen each of the connecting rod cap bolts 1/2-turn at a time until they can be removed by hand.

➡Note: New connecting rod cap bolts must be used when reassembling the engine, but save the old bolts for use when checking the connecting rod bearing oil clearance.

6 Remove the number one connecting rod cap and bearing insert. Don't drop the bearing insert out of the cap.

7 Remove the bearing insert and push the connecting rod/piston assembly out through the top of the engine. Use a wooden or plastic hammer handle to push on the upper bearing surface in the connecting rod. If resistance is felt, double-check to make sure that all of the ridge was removed from the cylinder.

8 Repeat the procedure for the remaining cylinders.

9 After removal, reassemble the connecting rod caps and bearing inserts in their respective connecting rods and install the cap bolts finger tight. Leaving the old bearing inserts in place until reassembly will help prevent the connecting rod bearing surfaces from being accidentally nicked or gouged.

10 The pistons and connecting rods are now ready for inspection and overhaul at an automotive machine shop.

PISTON RING INSTALLATION

➧ Refer to illustrations 9.13, 9.14, 9.15, 9.19a, 9.19b and 9.22

11 Before installing the new piston rings, the ring end gaps must be checked. It's assumed that the piston ring side clearance has been checked and verified correct.

12 Lay out the piston/connecting rod assemblies and the new ring sets so the ring sets will be matched with the same piston and cylinder during the end gap measurement and engine assembly.

13 Insert the top (number one) ring into the first cylinder and square it up with the cylinder walls by pushing it in with the top of the piston (see illustration). The ring should be near the bottom of the cylinder, at the lower limit of ring travel.

14 To measure the end gap, slip feeler gauges between the ends of the ring until a gauge equal to the gap width is found (see illustration). The feeler gauge should slide between the ring ends with a slight amount of drag. A typical ring gap should fall between 0.010 and 0.020 inch (0.25 to 0.50 mm) for compression rings and up to 0.030 inch (0.76 mm) for the oil ring steel rails. If the gap is larger or smaller than specified, double-check to make sure you have the correct rings before proceeding.

15 If the gap is too small, it must be enlarged or the ring ends may come in contact with each other during engine operation, which can cause serious damage to the engine. If necessary, increase the end gaps by filing the ring ends very carefully with a fine file. Mount the file in a vise equipped with soft jaws, slip the ring over the file with the ends contacting the file face and slowly move the ring to remove material from the ends. When performing this operation, file only by pushing the ring from the outside end of the file towards the vise (see illustration).

16 Excess end gap isn't critical unless it's greater than 0.040 inch (1.01 mm). Again, double-check to make sure you have the correct ring type.

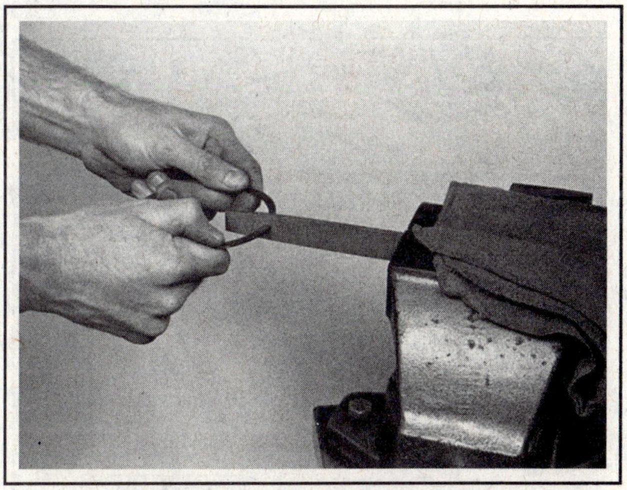

9.15 If the ring end gap is too small, clamp a file in a vise as shown and file the piston ring ends - be sure to remove all raised material

9.19a Installing the spacer/expander in the oil ring groove

9.19b DO NOT use a piston ring installation tool when installing the oil control side rails

9.22 Use a piston ring installation tool to install the number 2 and the number 1 (top) rings - be sure the directional mark on the piston ring(s) is facing toward the top of the piston

17 Repeat the procedure for each ring that will be installed in the first cylinder and for each ring in the remaining cylinders. Remember to keep rings, pistons and cylinders matched up.

18 Once the ring end gaps have been checked/corrected, the rings can be installed on the pistons.

19 The oil control ring (lowest one on the piston) is usually installed first. It's composed of three separate components. Slip the spacer/expander into the groove (see illustration). If an anti-rotation tang is used, make sure it's inserted into the drilled hole in the ring groove. Next, install the upper side rail in the same manner (see illustration). Don't use a piston ring installation tool on the oil ring side rails, as they may be damaged. Instead, place one end of the side rail into the groove between the spacer/expander and the ring land, hold it firmly in place and slide a finger around the piston while pushing the rail into the groove. Finally, install the lower side rail.

20 After the three oil ring components have been installed, check to make sure that both the upper and lower side rails can be rotated smoothly inside the ring grooves.

21 The number two (middle) ring is installed next. It's usually stamped with a mark which must face up, toward the top of the piston.

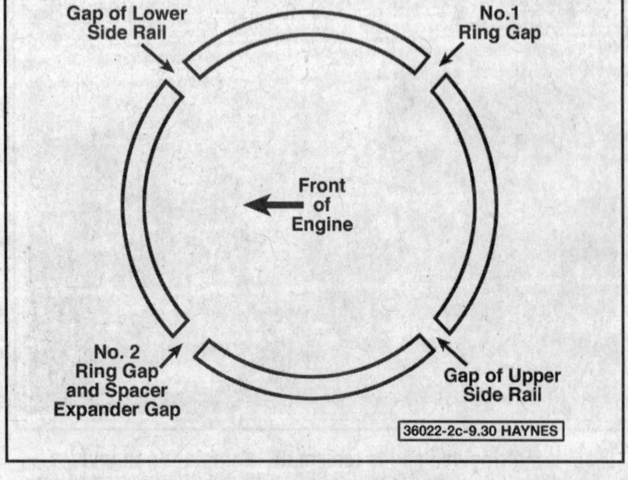

9.30 Position the piston ring end gaps as shown

Do not mix up the top and middle rings, as they have different cross-sections.

➡Note: Always follow the instructions printed on the ring package or box - different manufacturers may require different approaches.

22 Use a piston ring installation tool and make sure the identification mark is facing the top of the piston, then slip the ring into the middle groove on the piston (see illustration). Don't expand the ring any more than necessary to slide it over the piston.

23 Install the number one (top) ring in the same manner. Make sure the mark is facing up. Be careful not to confuse the number one and number two rings.

24 Repeat the procedure for the remaining pistons and rings.

INSTALLATION

25 Before installing the piston/connecting rod assemblies, the cylinder walls must be perfectly clean, the top edge of each cylinder bore must be chamfered, and the crankshaft must be in place.

26 Remove the cap from the end of the number one connecting rod (refer to the marks made during removal). Remove the original bearing inserts and wipe the bearing surfaces of the connecting rod and cap with a clean, lint-free cloth. They must be kept spotlessly clean.

Connecting rod bearing oil clearance check

➧ Refer to illustrations 9.30, 9.35, 9.37 and 9.41

27 Clean the back side of the new upper bearing insert, then lay it in place in the connecting rod.

28 Make sure the tab on the bearing fits into the recess in the rod. Don't hammer the bearing insert into place and be very careful not to nick or gouge the bearing face. Don't lubricate the bearing at this time.

29 Clean the back side of the other bearing insert and install it in the rod cap. Again, make sure the tab on the bearing fits into the recess in the cap, and don't apply any lubricant. It's critically important that the mating surfaces of the bearing and connecting rod are perfectly clean and oil free when they're assembled.

30 Position the piston ring gaps at 90-degree intervals around the piston as shown (see illustration).

31 Lubricate the piston and rings with clean engine oil and attach a piston ring compressor to the piston. Leave the skirt protruding about 1/4-inch to guide the piston into the cylinder. The rings must be compressed until they're flush with the piston.

32 Rotate the crankshaft until the number one connecting rod journal is at BDC (bottom dead center) and apply a liberal coat of engine oil to the cylinder walls.

33 With the mark on top of the piston facing the front (timing belt or chain end) of the engine, gently insert the piston/connecting rod assembly into the number one cylinder bore and rest the bottom edge of the ring compressor on the engine block.

34 Tap the top edge of the ring compressor to make sure it's contacting the block around its entire circumference.

35 Gently tap on the top of the piston with the end of a wooden or plastic hammer handle (see illustration) while guiding the end of the connecting rod into place on the crankshaft journal. The piston rings may try to pop out of the ring compressor just before entering the cylinder bore, so keep some downward pressure on the ring compressor. Work slowly, and if any resistance is felt as the piston enters the cylinder, stop immediately. Find out what's hanging up and fix it before proceeding. Do not, for any reason, force the piston into the cylinder - you might break a ring and/or the piston.

36 Once the piston/connecting rod assembly is installed, the connecting rod bearing oil clearance must be checked before the rod cap is permanently installed.

37 Cut a piece of the appropriate size Plastigage slightly shorter than the width of the connecting rod bearing and lay it in place on the number one connecting rod journal, parallel with the journal axis (see illustration).

38 Clean the connecting rod cap bearing face and install the rod cap. Make sure the mating mark on the cap is on the same side as the mark on the connecting rod (see illustration 9.4).

39 Install the old rod bolts, at this time, and tighten them to the torque listed in this Chapter's Specifications.

➡Note: Use a thin-wall socket to avoid erroneous torque readings that can result if the socket is wedged between the rod cap and the bolt head. If the socket tends to wedge itself between the fastener and the cap, lift up on it slightly until it no longer contacts the cap. DO NOT rotate the crankshaft at any time during this operation.

40 Remove the fasteners and detach the rod cap, being very careful not to disturb the Plastigage.

41 Compare the width of the crushed Plastigage to the scale printed on the Plastigage envelope to obtain the oil clearance (see illustration). The connecting rod oil clearance is usually about 0.001 to 0.002 inch (0.025 to 0.05 mm). Consult an automotive machine shop for the clearance specified for the rod bearings on your engine. One the covered vehicles, code numbers on the block and crankshaft are used to select the proper bearings, using a chart at a dealership service/parts department.

42 If the clearance is not as specified, the bearing inserts may be the wrong size (which means different ones will be required). Before deciding that different inserts are needed, make sure that no dirt or oil was between the bearing inserts and the connecting rod or cap when the clearance was measured. Also, recheck the journal diameter. If the Plastigage was wider at one end than the other, the journal may be tapered. If the clearance still exceeds the limit specified, the bearing will have to be replaced with an undersize bearing.

⁂ CAUTION:

When installing a new crankshaft always use a standard size bearing.

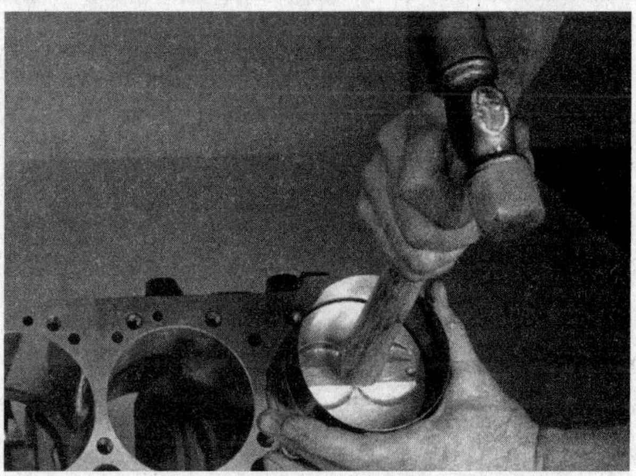

9.35 Use a plastic or wooden hammer handle to push the piston into the cylinder

9.37 Place Plastigage on each connecting rod bearing journal parallel to the crankshaft centerline

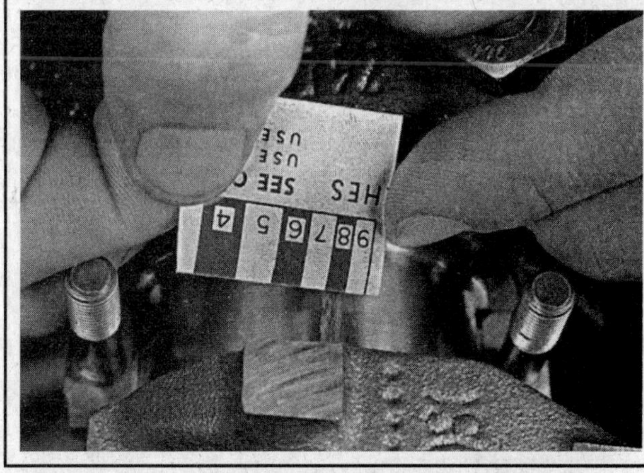

9.41 Use the scale on the Plastigage package to determine the bearing oil clearance - be sure to measure the widest part of the Plastigage and use the correct scale; it comes with both standard and metric scales

ENGINE BEARING ANALYSIS

Debris

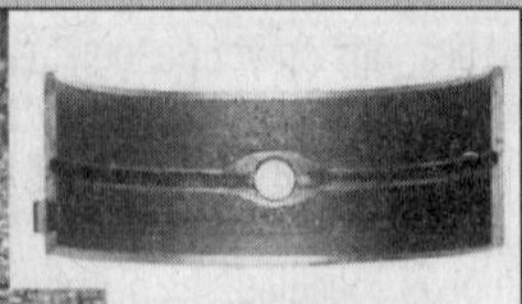

Babbitt bearing embedded with debris from machinings

Microscopic detail of debris

Microscopic detail of gouges

Overplated copper alloy bearing gouged by cast iron debris

Aluminum bearing embedded with glass beads

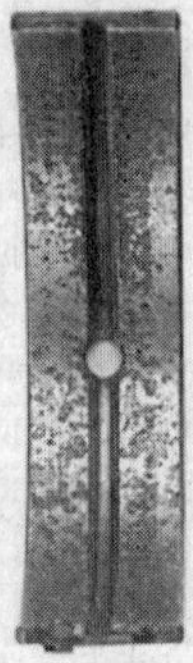

Microscopic detail of glass beads

Damaged lining caused by dirt left on the bearing back

Misassembly

Result of a lower half assembled as an upper - blocking the oil flow

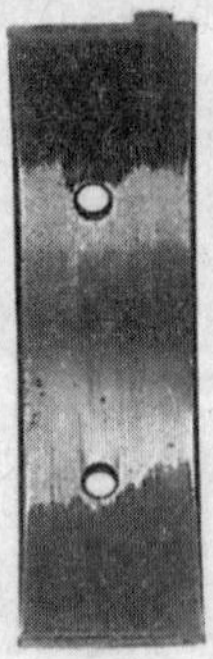

Excessive oil clearance is indicated by a short contact arc

Polished and oil-stained backs are a result of a poor fit in the housing bore

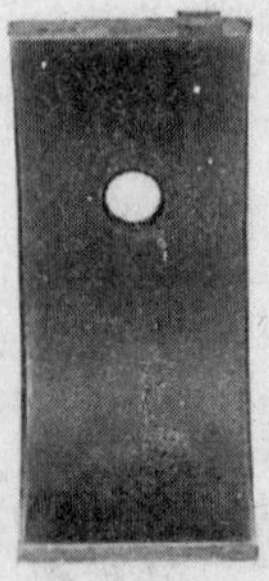

Result of a wrong, reversed, or shifted cap

Overloading

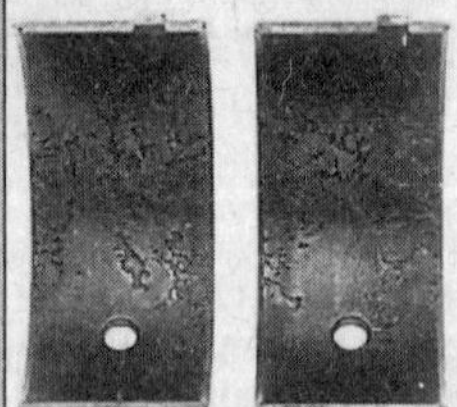

Damage from excessive idling which resulted in an oil film unable to support the load imposed

Damaged upper connecting rod bearings caused by engine lugging; the lower main bearings (not shown) were similarly affected

The damage shown in these upper and lower connecting rod bearings was caused by engine operation at a higher-than-rated speed under load

Misalignment

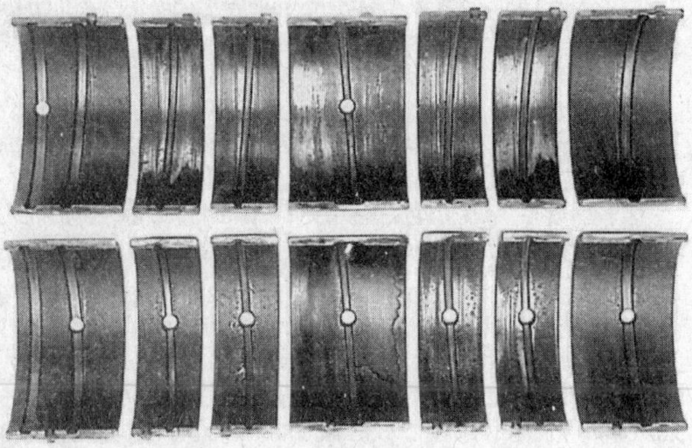

A warped crankshaft caused this pattern of severe wear in the center, diminishing toward the ends

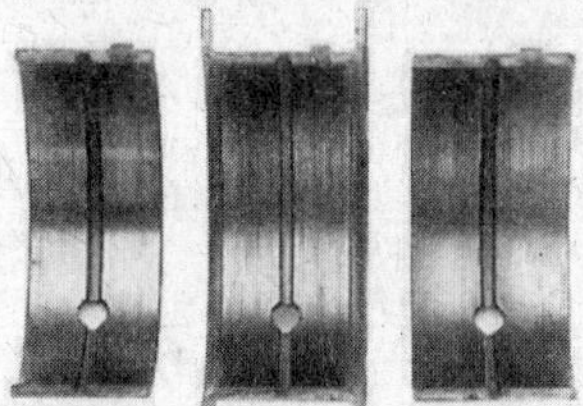

A poorly finished crankshaft caused the equally spaced scoring shown

A tapered housing bore caused the damage along one edge of this pair

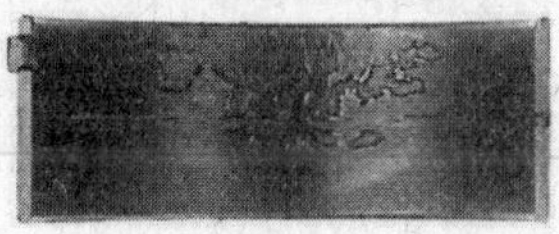

A bent connecting rod led to the damage in the "V" pattern

Lubrication

Result of dry start: The bearings on the left, farthest from the oil pump, show more damage

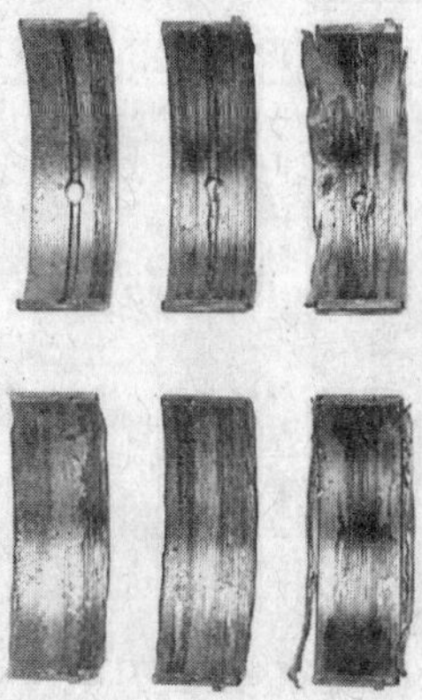

Result of a low oil supply or oil starvation

Severe wear as a result of inadequate oil clearance

Corrosion

Microscopic detail of corrosion

Corrosion is an acid attack on the bearing lining generally caused by inadequate maintenance, extremely hot or cold operation, or inferior oils or fuels

Microscopic detail of cavitation

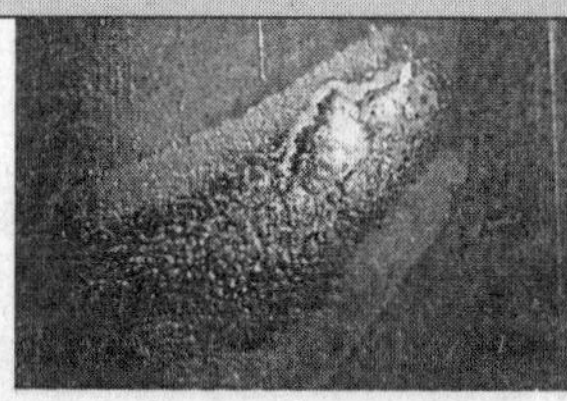

Example of cavitation - a surface erosion caused by pressure changes in the oil film

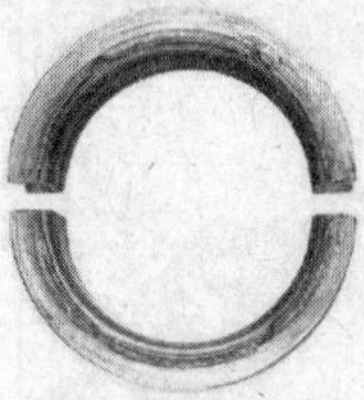

Damage from excessive thrust or insufficient axial clearance

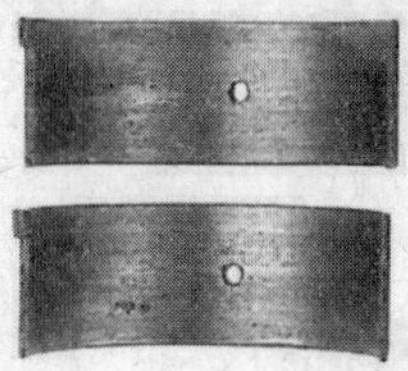

Bearing affected by oil dilution caused by excessive blow-by or a rich mixture

Final installation

43 Carefully scrape all traces of the Plastigage material off the rod journal and/or bearing face. Be very careful not to scratch the bearing - use your fingernail or the edge of a plastic card.

44 Make sure the bearing faces are perfectly clean, then apply a uniform layer of clean moly-base grease or engine assembly lube to both of them. You'll have to push the piston into the cylinder to expose the face of the bearing insert in the connecting rod.

45 Slide the connecting rod back into place on the journal, install the rod cap, install the new bolts and tighten them to the torque listed in this Chapter's Specifications.

CAUTION:

Install new connecting rod cap bolts. Do NOT reuse old bolts - they have stretched and cannot be reused. Again, work up to the torque in three steps.

46 Repeat the entire procedure for the remaining pistons/connecting rods.

47 The important points to remember are:

a) Keep the back sides of the bearing inserts and the insides of the connecting rods and caps perfectly clean when assembling them.
b) Make sure you have the correct piston/rod assembly for each cylinder.
c) The mark on the piston must face the front (timing belt end [four-cylinder engine] or timing chain [V6 engine] end) of the engine.
d) Lubricate the cylinder walls liberally with clean oil.
e) Lubricate the bearing faces when installing the rod caps after the oil clearance has been checked.

48 After all the piston/connecting rod assemblies have been correctly installed, rotate the crankshaft a number of times by hand to check for any obvious binding.

49 As a final step, check the connecting rod endplay, as described in Step 3. If it was correct before disassembly and the original crankshaft and rods were reinstalled, it should still be correct. If new rods or a new crankshaft were installed, the endplay may be inadequate. If so, the rods will have to be removed and taken to an automotive machine shop for resizing.

10 Crankshaft - removal and installation

REMOVAL

Refer to illustrations 10.1 and 10.3

Note: The crankshaft can be removed only after the engine has been removed from the vehicle. It's assumed that the flywheel or driveplate, crankshaft pulley, timing belt, oil pan, oil pump body, oil filter and piston/connecting rod assemblies have already been removed. The rear main oil seal retainer must be unbolted and separated from the block before proceeding with crankshaft removal.

1 Before the crankshaft is removed, measure the endplay. Mount a dial indicator with the indicator in line with the crankshaft and just touching the end of the crankshaft as shown (see illustration).

2 Pry the crankshaft all the way to the rear and zero the dial indicator. Next, pry the crankshaft to the front as far as possible and check the reading on the dial indicator. The distance traveled is the endplay. A typical crankshaft endplay will fall between 0.003 to 0.010 inch (0.076 to 0.254 mm). If it is greater than that, check the crankshaft thrust surfaces for wear after it's removed. If no wear is evident, new main bearings should correct the endplay.

3 If a dial indicator isn't available, feeler gauges can be used. Gently pry the crankshaft all the way to the front of the engine. Slip feeler gauges between the crankshaft and the front face of the thrust bearing or washer to determine the clearance (see illustration).

4 Loosen the main bearing cap beam bolts (four-cylinder engines), lower cylinder block bolts (3.0L V6 engine) or main bearing cap support brace and main bearing cap bolts (3.5L V6 engine) 1/4-turn at a time each, until they can be removed by hand. Loosen the bolts in the reverse of the tightening sequence (see illustrations 10.19a, 10.19b or 10.19c and 10.19d).

5 If you're working on a four-cylinder engine, remove the main

10.1 Checking crankshaft endplay with a dial indicator

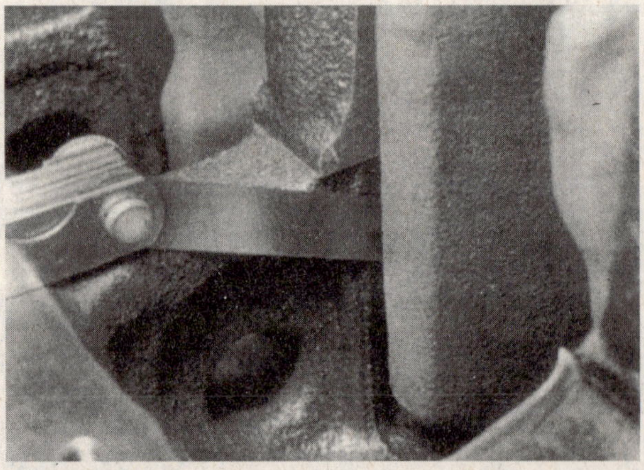

10.3 Checking the crankshaft endplay with feeler gauges at the thrust bearing journal

bearing cap support beam. If you're working on a 3.0L V6 engine, gently tap the lower cylinder block with a soft-face hammer around its perimeter and pull the lower cylinder block straight up and off the cylinder block. If you're working on a 3.5L V6 engine, remove the main bearing caps. Try not to drop the bearing inserts if they come out with the assembly.

6 Carefully lift the crankshaft out of the engine. It may be a good idea to have an assistant available, since the crankshaft is quite heavy and awkward to handle. With the bearing inserts in place inside the engine block and main bearing caps or lower cylinder block, reinstall the main bearing caps or lower cylinder block onto the engine block and tighten the bolts finger tight.

INSTALLATION

7 Crankshaft installation is the first step in engine reassembly. It's assumed at this point that the engine block and crankshaft have been cleaned, inspected and repaired or reconditioned.

8 Position the engine block with the bottom facing up.

9 Remove the bolts and lift off the support beam, main bearing caps or lower cylinder block, as applicable.

10 If they're still in place, remove the original bearing inserts. Wipe the bearing surfaces of the block and main bearing cap assembly with a clean, lint-free cloth. They must be kept spotlessly clean. This is critical for determining the correct bearing oil clearance.

Main bearing oil clearance check

Refer to illustrations 10.17, 10.19a, 10.19b, 10.19c, 10.19d and 10.21

11 Without mixing them up, clean the back sides of the new upper main bearing inserts (with grooves and oil holes) and lay one in each main bearing saddle in the engine block. Each upper bearing (engine block) has an oil groove and oil hole in it.

CAUTION:

The oil holes in the block must line up with the oil holes in the upper bearing inserts.

Note: The thrust bearing on the four-cylinder engine is located on the engine block number 3 (center) journal. The flanged thrust bearing on the 3.0L V6 engine is located on the 4th journal on the lower cylinder block, and a thrust washer at the rear of the rear (number four) main saddle on the cylinder block. The thrust washers on the 3.5L V6 engine are located on the 4th journal (two upper on each side of the main saddle, one lower on the rear of the main bearing cap). The grooves on shim-type thrust washers must face the crankshaft (not the main bearing saddle).

Clean the back sides of the lower main bearing inserts and lay them in the corresponding location in the main bearing caps or the lower cylinder block. Make sure the tab on the bearing insert fits into its corresponding recess.

CAUTION:

Do not hammer the bearing insert into place and don't nick or gouge the bearing faces. DO NOT apply any lubrication at this time.

12 Clean the faces of the bearing inserts in the block and the crankshaft main bearing journals with a clean, lint-free cloth.

13 Check or clean the oil holes in the crankshaft, as any dirt here can go only one way - straight through the new bearings.

14 Once you're certain the crankshaft is clean, carefully lay it in position in the cylinder block.

15 Before the crankshaft can be permanently installed, the main bearing oil clearance must be checked.

16 Cut several strips of the appropriate size of Plastigage. They must be slightly shorter than the width of the main bearing journal.

17 Place one piece on each crankshaft main bearing journal, parallel with the journal axis as shown (see illustration).

18 Clean the faces of the bearing inserts in the main bearing caps or the lower cylinder block. Hold the bearing inserts in place and install the caps or the lower cylinder block onto the crankshaft and cylinder block. DO NOT disturb the Plastigage.

19 Apply clean engine oil to all bolt threads prior to installation, then install all bolts finger-tight. Tighten the bolts in the sequence shown (see illustrations) progressing in steps, to the torque listed in this Chapter's Specifications. DO NOT rotate the crankshaft at any time during this operation.

10.17 Place the Plastigage onto the crankshaft bearing journal as shown

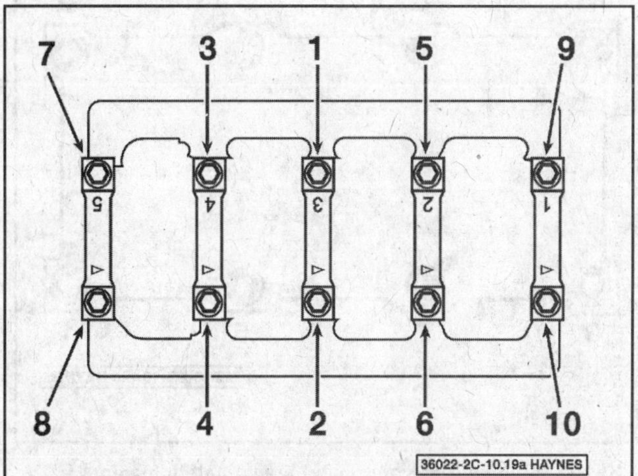

10.19a Main bearing cap beam bolt tightening sequence - four-cylinder engines

20 Remove the bolts in the reverse order of the tightening sequence and carefully lift the caps or the lower cylinder block straight up and off the block. Do not disturb the Plastigage or rotate the crankshaft.

21 Compare the width of the crushed Plastigage on each journal to the scale printed on the Plastigage envelope to determine the main bearing oil clearance (see illustration). Check with an automotive machine shop for the oil clearance for your engine.

22 If the clearance is not as specified, the bearing inserts may be the wrong size (which means different ones will be required). Before deciding if different inserts are needed, make sure that no dirt or oil was between the bearing inserts and the cap assembly or block when the clearance was measured. If the Plastigage was wider at one end than the other, the crankshaft journal may be tapered. If the clearance still exceeds the limit specified, the bearing insert(s) will have to be replaced with an undersize bearing insert(s).

CAUTION:

When installing a new crankshaft always install a standard bearing insert set.

23 Carefully scrape all traces of the Plastigage material off the main bearing journals and/or the bearing insert faces. Be sure to remove all residue from the oil holes. Use your fingernail or the edge of a plastic card - don't nick or scratch the bearing faces.

Final installation

Refer to illustration 10.28

24 Carefully lift the crankshaft out of the cylinder block.

25 Clean the bearing insert faces in the cylinder block, then apply

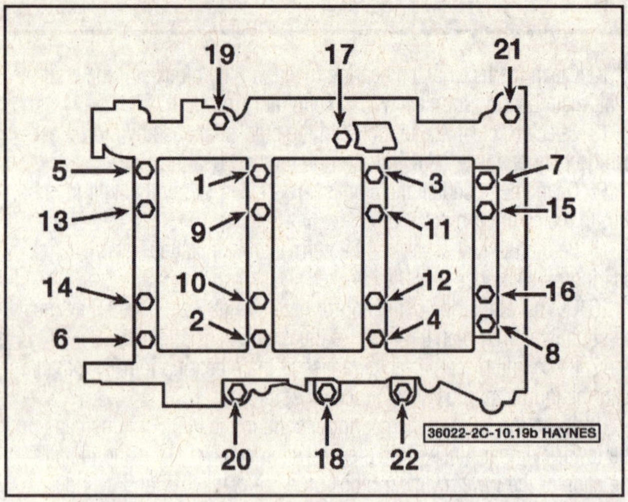

10.19b Lower cylinder block bolt tightening sequence - 3.0L V6 engines

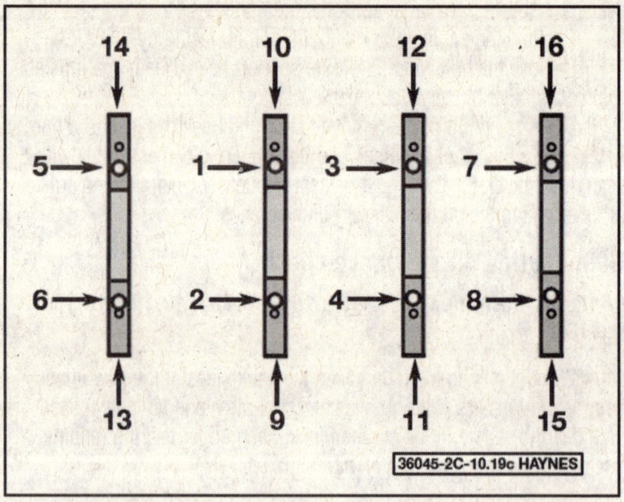

10.19c Main bearing cap bolt tightening sequence - 3.5L V6

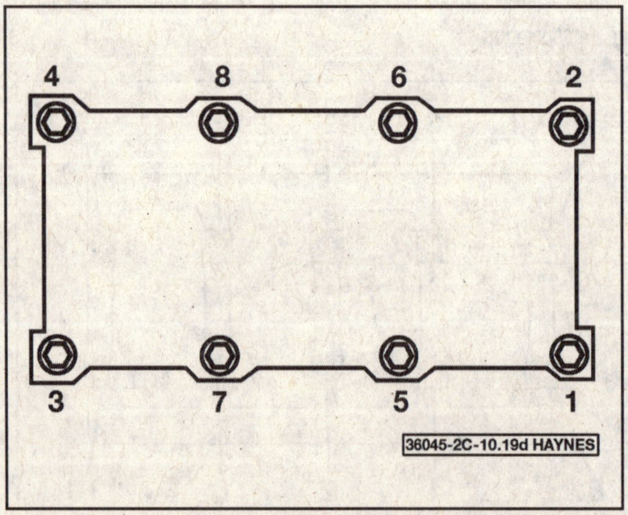

10.19d Main bearing cap support brace, bolt tightening sequence - 3.5L V6

10.21 Use the scale on the Plastigage package to determine the bearing oil clearance - be sure to measure the widest part of the Plastigage and use the correct scale; it comes with both standard and metric scales

a thin, uniform layer of moly-base grease or engine assembly lube to each of the bearing surfaces. Be sure to coat the thrust faces as well as the journal face of the thrust bearing.

26 Make sure the crankshaft journals are clean, then lay the crankshaft back in place in the cylinder block.

27 Clean the bearing insert faces and apply the same lubricant to them. Clean the engine block and the bearing caps/lower cylinder block thoroughly. The surfaces must be free of oil residue.

28 On 3.0L V6 engines, apply a bead of RTV to the engine block before installing the lower cylinder block. Be sure the bead is the correct thickness (see illustration).

**** CAUTION:**

You have only four minutes to install the lower block mounting bolts and studs. If it takes longer the lower block will have to be removed, cleaned of all sealant, and the installation procedure repeated.

29 On V6 engines, install the lower cylinder block onto the crankshaft and cylinder block. If you're working on a four-cylinder engine, install the main bearing caps in their proper locations, with the arrows on the caps facing the front of the engine.

30 Prior to installation, apply clean engine oil to all bolt threads wiping off any excess, then install all bolts finger-tight.

31 Tighten the lower cylinder block (3.0L V6 engines), support beam (four-cylinder engine) or caps (3.5L V6 engine), following the correct torque sequence (see illustrations 10.19a, 10.19b or 10.19c). Torque the bolts to the Specifications listed in this Chapter. On 3.5L V6 engines, install the main bearing cap support brace, tightening the bolts to the torque listed in this Chapter's Specifications in the proper sequence (see illustration 10.19d).

32 Recheck the crankshaft endplay with a feeler gauge or a dial indicator. The endplay should be correct if the crankshaft thrust faces aren't worn or damaged and if new bearings have been installed.

33 Rotate the crankshaft a number of times by hand to check for any obvious binding. It should rotate with a running torque of 50 in-lbs or less. If the running torque is too high, correct the problem at this time.

34 Install a new rear main oil seal (see Chapter 2A or 2B).

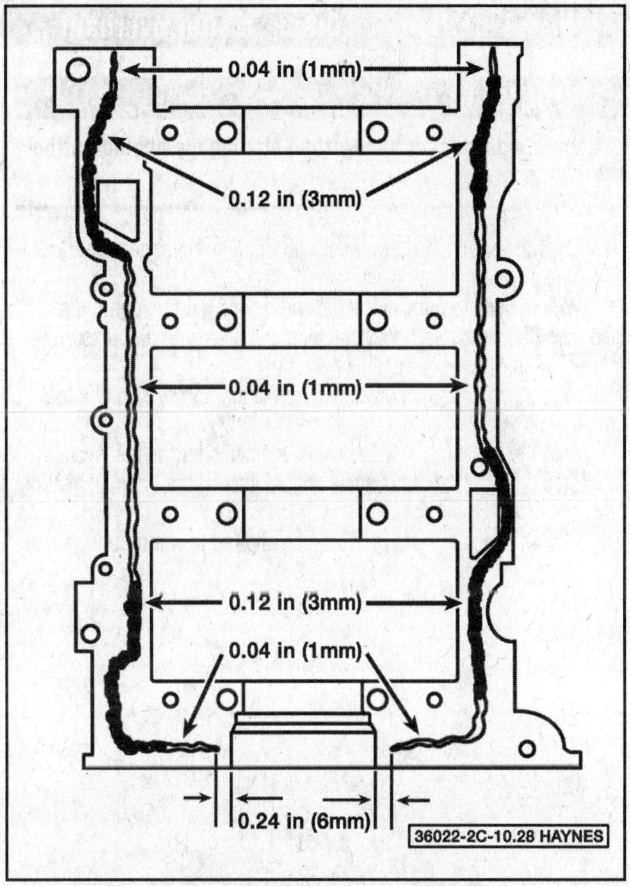

10.28 3.0L V6 engine: Apply RTV sealant to the cylinder block mating surface - make sure the bead of sealant is the correct diameter

11 Engine overhaul - reassembly sequence

1 Before beginning engine reassembly, make sure you have all the necessary new parts, gaskets and seals as well as the following items on hand:

Common hand tools
A 1/2-inch drive torque wrench
New engine oil
Gasket sealant
Thread locking compound

2 If you obtained a short block it will be necessary to install the cylinder head, the oil pump and pick-up tube, the oil pan, the water pump, the timing belt and timing cover, and the valve cover (see Chapter 2A or 2B). In order to save time and avoid problems, the external components must be installed in the following general order:

Thermostat and housing cover
Water pump
Intake and exhaust manifolds
Fuel injection components
Emission control components
Spark plugs
Ignition coils
Oil filter
Engine mounts and mount brackets
Clutch and flywheel (manual transaxle)
Driveplate (automatic transaxle)

12 Initial start-up and break-in after overhaul

**** WARNING:**

Have a fire extinguisher handy when starting the engine for the first time.

1 Once the engine has been installed in the vehicle, double-check the engine oil and coolant levels.

2 With the spark plugs out of the engine and the fuel pump disabled (see Chapter 4, Section 3), crank the engine until oil pressure registers on the gauge or the light goes out.

3 Install the spark plugs, and restore the ignition system and fuel pump functions.

4 Start the engine. It may take a few moments for the fuel system to build up pressure, but the engine should start without a great deal of effort.

5 After the engine starts, it should be allowed to warm up to normal operating temperature. While the engine is warming up, make a thorough check for fuel, oil and coolant leaks.

6 Shut the engine off and recheck the engine oil and coolant levels.

7 Drive the vehicle to an area with minimum traffic, accelerate from 30 to 50 mph, then allow the vehicle to slow to 30 mph with the throttle closed. Repeat the procedure 10 or 12 times. This will load the piston rings and cause them to seat properly against the cylinder walls. Check again for oil and coolant leaks.

8 Drive the vehicle gently for the first 500 miles (no sustained high speeds) and keep a constant check on the oil level. It is not unusual for an engine to use oil during the break-in period.

9 At approximately 500 to 600 miles, change the oil and filter.

10 For the next few hundred miles, drive the vehicle normally. Do not pamper it or abuse it.

11 After 2,000 miles, change the oil and filter again and consider the engine broken in.

13 Balance shaft assembly (four-cylinder engines) - removal and installation

1 The balance shaft assembly is bolted to the crankshaft main bearing support beam. A gear on the crankshaft meshes with a gear on the balance shaft assembly. When the engine is operating, the assembly smoothes engine vibrations.

2 The balancer is a precision-machined assembly, there are no serviceable parts inside and it should not be disassembled. If the backlash is out of Specification (see Steps 5 through 8), the assembly must be replaced as a complete unit.

REMOVAL

3 Position the crankshaft at TDC (see Chapter 2A). Remove the four mounting bolts.

4 With the engine turned crankshaft side up on the engine stand, lift the assembly straight up from the engine.

INSPECTION

Refer to illustration 13.6

5 When the balance shaft assembly is in place, the backlash between the drive gear (on the crankshaft) and the driven gear on the assembly can be checked. Remove the timing peg.

6 Attach a 5 mm Allen wrench to the top of the driveshaft with the long end of the wrench pointing straight up. Secure a dial-indicator fixture to the engine so that the tip of the indicator is against the top of the wrench (see illustration).

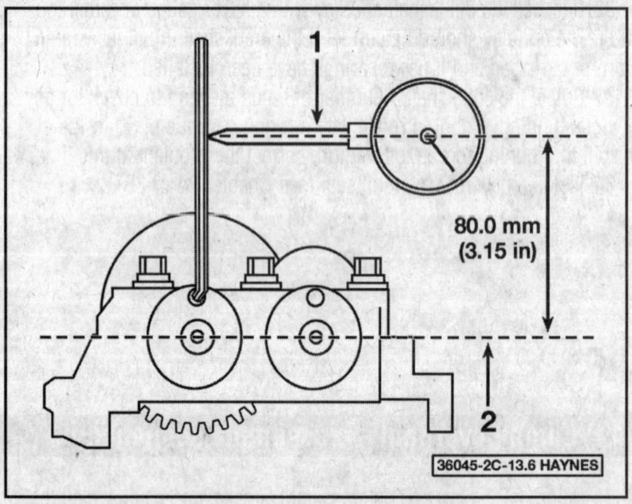

13.6 Method of checking the backlash in the balancer assembly

7 Use a pry tool against the crankshaft front counterweight to apply thrust pressure, while turning the crankshaft back-and-forth. Record the measurements of the dial-indicator. Measurements should be taken at the following degrees of engine rotation: 10, 30, 100, 190 and 210 degrees. Compare your results with the allowable range of backlash given in this Chapter's Specifications.

8 If the backlash is out of range, the

INSTALLATION

Refer to illustration 13.9

9 When installing the balance shaft assembly, the engine must set to TDC for cylinder number 1. Before installing the assembly, rotate the assembly to align the timing marks on both shafts of the assembly (see illustration). Bolt the assembly to the engine and recheck that the timing marks are still aligned and that the crankshaft has not moved. Tighten the bolts in a criss-cross pattern to the torque listed in this Chapter's Specifications.

10 The crankshaft timing peg should remain installed to keep the engine at TDC until installation of the timing chain and sprockets is completed.

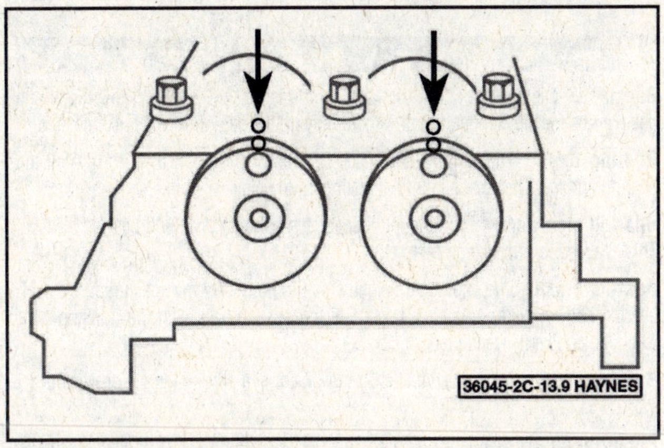

13.9 Remove/install the balance shaft assembly bolts only when the crank is at TDC and these balancer dots align

GLOSSARY

B

Backlash - The amount of play between two parts. Usually refers to how much one gear can be moved back and forth without moving the gear with which it's meshed.

Bearing Caps - The caps held in place by nuts or bolts which, in turn, hold the bearing surface. This space is for lubricating oil to enter.

Bearing clearance - The amount of space left between shaft and bearing surface. This space is for lubricating oil to enter.

Bearing crush - The additional height which is purposely manufactured into each bearing half to ensure complete contact of the bearing back with the housing bore when the engine is assembled.

Bearing knock - The noise created by movement of a part in a loose or worn bearing.

Blueprinting - Dismantling an engine and reassembling it to EXACT specifications.

Bore - An engine cylinder, or any cylindrical hole; also used to describe the process of enlarging or accurately refinishing a hole with a cutting tool, as to bore an engine cylinder. The bore size is the diameter of the hole.

Boring - Renewing the cylinders by cutting them out to a specified size. A boring bar is used to make the cut.

Bottom end - A term which refers collectively to the engine block, crankshaft, main bearings and the big ends of the connecting rods.

Break-in - The period of operation between installation of new or rebuilt parts and time in which parts are worn to the correct fit. Driving at reduced and varying speed for a specified mileage to permit parts to wear to the correct fit.

Bushing - A one-piece sleeve placed in a bore to serve as a bearing surface for shaft, piston pin, etc. Usually replaceable.

C

Camshaft - The shaft in the engine, on which a series of lobes are located for operating the valve mechanisms. The camshaft is driven by gears or sprockets and a timing chain. Usually referred to simply as the cam.

Carbon - Hard, or soft, black deposits found in combustion chamber, on plugs, under rings, on and under valve heads.

Cast iron - An alloy of iron and more than two percent carbon, used for engine blocks and heads because it's relatively inexpensive and easy to mold into complex shapes.

Chamfer - To bevel across (or a bevel on) the sharp edge of an object.

Chase - To repair damaged threads with a tap or die.

Combustion chamber - The space between the piston and the cylinder head, with the piston at top dead center, in which air-fuel mixture is burned.

Compression ratio - The relationship between cylinder volume (clearance volume) when the piston is at top dead center and cylinder volume when the piston is at bottom dead center.

Connecting rod - The rod that connects the crank on the crankshaft with the piston. Sometimes called a con rod.

Connecting rod cap - The part of the connecting rod assembly that attaches the rod to the crankpin.

Core plug - Soft metal plug used to plug the casting holes for the coolant passages in the block.

Crankcase - The lower part of the engine in which the crankshaft rotates; includes the lower section of the cylinder block and the oil pan.

Crank kit - A reground or reconditioned crankshaft and new main and connecting rod bearings.

Crankpin - The part of a crankshaft to which a connecting rod is attached.

Crankshaft - The main rotating member, or shaft, running the length of the crankcase, with offset throws to which the connecting rods are attached; changes the reciprocating motion of the pistons into rotating motion.

Cylinder sleeve - A replaceable sleeve, or liner, pressed into the cylinder block to form the cylinder bore.

D

Deburring - Removing the burrs (rough edges or areas) from a bearing.

Deglazer - A tool, rotated by an electric motor, used to remove glaze from cylinder walls so a new set of rings will seat.

E

Endplay - The amount of lengthwise movement between two parts. As applied to a crankshaft, the distance that the crankshaft can move forward and back in the cylinder block.

F

Face - A machinist's term that refers to removing metal from the end of a shaft or the face of a larger part, such as a flywheel.

Fatigue - A breakdown of material through a large number of loading and unloading cycles. The first signs are cracks followed shortly by breaks.

Feeler gauge - A thin strip of hardened steel, ground to an exact thickness, used to check clearances between parts.

Free height - The unloaded length or height of a spring.

Freeplay - The looseness in a linkage, or an assembly of parts, between the initial application of force and actual movement. Usually perceived as slop or slight delay.

Freeze plug - See Core plug.

G

Gallery - A large passage in the block that forms a reservoir for engine oil pressure.

Glaze - The very smooth, glassy finish that develops on cylinder walls while an engine is in service.

H

Heli-Coil - A rethreading device used when threads are worn or damaged. The device is installed in a retapped hole to reduce the thread size to the original size.

I

Installed height - The spring's measured length or height, as installed on the cylinder head. Installed height is measured from the spring seat to the underside of the spring retainer.

J

Journal - The surface of a rotating shaft which turns in a bearing.

K

Keeper - The split lock that holds the valve spring retainer in position on the valve stem.

Key - A small piece of metal inserted into matching grooves machined into two parts fitted together - such as a gear pressed onto a shaft - which prevents slippage between the two parts.

Knock - The heavy metallic engine sound, produced in the combustion chamber as a result of abnormal combustion - usually detonation. Knock is usually caused by a loose or worn bearing. Also referred to as detonation, pinging and spark knock. Connecting rod or main bearing knocks are created by too much oil clearance or insufficient lubrication.

L

Lands - The portions of metal between the piston ring grooves.

Lapping the valves - Grinding a valve face and its seat together with lapping compound.

Lash - The amount of free motion in a gear train, between gears, or in a mechanical assembly, that occurs before movement can begin. Usually refers to the lash in a valve train.

Lifter - The part that rides against the cam to transfer motion to the rest of the valve train.

M

Machining - The process of using a machine to remove metal from a metal part.

Main bearings - The plain, or babbitt, bearings that support the crankshaft.

Main bearing caps - The cast iron caps, bolted to the bottom of the block, that support the main bearings.

O

O.D. - Outside diameter.

Oil gallery - A pipe or drilled passageway in the engine used to carry engine oil from one area to another.

Oil ring - The lower ring, or rings, of a piston; designed to prevent excessive amounts of oil from working up the cylinder walls and into the combustion chamber. Also called an oil-control ring.

Oil seal - A seal which keeps oil from leaking out of a compartment. Usually refers to a dynamic seal around a rotating shaft or other moving part.

O-ring - A type of sealing ring made of a special rubberlike material; in use, the O-ring is compressed into a groove to provide the sealing action.

Overhaul - To completely disassemble a unit, clean and inspect all parts, reassemble it with the original or new parts and make all adjustments necessary for proper operation.

P

Pilot bearing - A small bearing installed in the center of the flywheel (or the rear end of the crankshaft) to support the front end of the input shaft of the transmission.

Pip mark - A little dot or indentation which indicates the top side of a compression ring.

Piston - The cylindrical part, attached to the connecting rod, that moves up and down in the cylinder as the crankshaft rotates. When the fuel charge is fired, the piston transfers the force of the explosion to the connecting rod, then to the crankshaft.

Piston pin (or wrist pin) - The cylindrical and usually hollow steel pin that passes through the piston. The piston pin fastens the piston to the upper end of the connecting rod.

Piston ring - The split ring fitted to the groove in a piston. The ring contacts the sides of the ring groove and also rubs against the cylinder wall, thus sealing space between piston and wall. There are two types of rings: Compression rings seal the compression pressure in the combustion chamber; oil rings scrape excessive oil off the cylinder wall.

Piston ring groove - The slots or grooves cut in piston heads to hold piston rings in position.

Piston skirt - The portion of the piston below the rings and the piston pin hole.

Plastigage - A thin strip of plastic thread, available in different sizes, used for measuring clearances. For example, a strip of plastigage is laid across a bearing journal and mashed as parts are assembled. Then parts are disassembled and the width of the strip is measured to determine clearance between journal and bearing. Commonly used to measure crankshaft main-bearing and connecting rod bearing clearances.

Press-fit - A tight fit between two parts that requires pressure to force the parts together. Also referred to as drive, or force, fit.

Prussian blue - A blue pigment; in solution, useful in determining the area of contact between two surfaces. Prussian blue is commonly used to determine the width and location of the contact area between the valve face and the valve seat.

R

Race (bearing) - The inner or outer ring that provides a contact surface for balls or rollers in bearing.

Ream - To size, enlarge or smooth a hole by using a round cutting tool with fluted edges.

Ring job - The process of reconditioning the cylinders and installing new rings.

Runout - Wobble. The amount a shaft rotates out-of-true.

S

Saddle - The upper main bearing seat.

Scored - Scratched or grooved, as a cylinder wall may be scored by abrasive particles moved up and down by the piston rings.

Scuffing - A type of wear in which there's a transfer of material between parts moving against each other; shows up as pits or grooves in the mating surfaces.

Seat - The surface upon which another part rests or seats. For example, the valve seat is the matched surface upon which the valve face rests. Also used to refer to wearing into a good fit; for example, piston rings seat after a few miles of driving.

Short block - An engine block complete with crankshaft and piston and, usually, camshaft assemblies.

Static balance - The balance of an object while it's stationary.

Step - The wear on the lower portion of a ring land caused by excessive side and back-clearance. The height of the step indicates the ring's extra side clearance and the length of the step projecting from the back wall of the groove represents the ring's back clearance.

Stroke - The distance the piston moves when traveling from top dead center to bottom dead center, or from bottom dead center to top dead center.

Stud - A metal rod with threads on both ends.

T

Tang - A lip on the end of a plain bearing used to align the bearing during assembly.

Tap - To cut threads in a hole. Also refers to the fluted tool used to cut threads.

Taper - A gradual reduction in the width of a shaft or hole; in an engine cylinder, taper usually takes the form of uneven wear, more pronounced at the top than at the bottom.

Throws - The offset portions of the crankshaft to which the connecting rods are affixed.

Thrust bearing - The main bearing that has thrust faces to prevent excessive endplay, or forward and backward movement of the crankshaft.

Thrust washer - A bronze or hardened steel washer placed between two moving parts. The washer prevents longitudinal movement and provides a bearing surface for thrust surfaces of parts.

Tolerance - The amount of variation permitted from an exact size of measurement. Actual amount from smallest acceptable dimension to largest acceptable dimension.

U

Umbrella - An oil deflector placed near the valve tip to throw oil from the valve stem area.

Undercut - A machined groove below the normal surface.

Undersize bearings - Smaller diameter bearings used with re-ground crankshaft journals.

V

Valve grinding - Refacing a valve in a valve-refacing machine.

Valve train - The valve-operating mechanism of an engine; includes all components from the camshaft to the valve.

Vibration damper - A cylindrical weight attached to the front of the crankshaft to minimize torsional vibration (the twist-untwist actions of the crankshaft caused by the cylinder firing impulses). Also called a harmonic balancer.

W

Water jacket - The spaces around the cylinders, between the inner and outer shells of the cylinder block or head, through which coolant circulates.

Web - A supporting structure across a cavity.

Woodruff key - A key with a radiused backside (viewed from the side).

Specifications

General

Cylinder compression	Lowest cylinder must be within 75% of the highest cylinder
Oil pressure	
Four-cylinder engines, warm, at 2000 rpm	29 to 39 psi (200 to 268 kPa)
3.0L V6 engine, warm, at 1500 rpm	
2006 through 2008 models	11 psi (76 kPa)
2009 models	20 psi (138 kPa)
2010 models	25 psi (172 kPa)
3.5L V6 engine	30 psi (206 kPa)
Balance shaft assembly backlash 2.3L/2.50L	0.00019 to 0.0039 inch (0.005 to 0.101 mm)

Torque specifications	Ft-lbs (unless otherwise indicated)	Nm

➡Note: One foot-pound (ft-lb) of torque is equivalent to 12 inch-pounds (in-lbs) of torque. Torque values below approximately 15 foot-pounds are expressed in inch-pounds, because most foot-pound torque wrenches are not accurate at these smaller values.

Torque specifications	Ft-lbs (unless otherwise indicated)	Nm
Balance shaft assembly mounting bolts (four-cylinder engines)		
Step 1	18	24
Step 2	37	50
Connecting rod bolts		
Four-cylinder engines		
Step 1	21	28
Step 2	Tighten an additional 90 degrees	
3.0L V6 engine		
Step 1	17	23
Step 2	32	43
3.5L V6 engine		
Step 1	17	23
Step 2	32	43
Step 3	Tighten an additional 90 degrees	
Main bearing bolts		
Four-cylinder engines		
Step 1	44 in-lbs	5
Step 2	18	24
Step 3	Tighten an additional 90 degrees	
3.0L V6 engine (lower block)		
Step 1, bolts 1 through 8	18	24
Step 2, bolts 9 through 16	30	40
Step 3, bolts 1 through 16	Tighten an additional 90 degrees	
Step 4, bolts 17 through 22 (side bolts)	18	24
3.5L V6 engine		
Step 1, bolts 1 through 8	44	60
Step 2, bolts 1 through 8	Tighten an additional 90 degrees	
Step 3, side bolts 1 through 8	33	45
Step 4, side bolts 1 through 8	Tighten an additional 90 degrees	
Main bearing cap support brace (3.5L V6 engine)		
Step 1	177 in-lbs	20
Step 2	Tighten an additional 90-degrees	

3 COOLING, HEATING AND AIR CONDITIONING SYSTEMS

Reference to other Chapters

Coolant level check - See Chapter 1
Cooling system check - See Chapter 1
Cooling system servicing (draining, flushing and refilling) - See Chapter 1
Drivebelt check, adjustment and replacement - See Chapter 1
Underhood hose check and replacement - See Chapter 1

1 General information

WARNING:

Do not allow antifreeze to come in contact with your skin or painted surfaces of the vehicle. Rinse off spills immediately with plenty of water. Antifreeze is highly toxic if ingested. Never leave antifreeze lying around in an open container or in puddles on the floor; children and pets are attracted by it's sweet smell and may drink it. Check with local authorities about disposing of used antifreeze. Many communities have collection centers which will see that antifreeze is disposed of safely. Never dump used antifreeze on the ground or pour it into drains.

ENGINE COOLING SYSTEM

All modern vehicles employ a pressurized engine cooling system with thermostatically controlled coolant circulation. The cooling system consists of a radiator, an expansion tank or coolant reservoir, a pressure cap (located on the expansion tank or radiator), a thermostat, a cooling fan, and a water pump.

The water pump circulates coolant through the engine. The coolant flows around each cylinder and around the intake and exhaust ports, near the spark plug areas and in close proximity to the exhaust valve guides.

A thermostat controls engine coolant temperature. During warm up, the closed thermostat prevents coolant from circulating through the radiator. As the engine nears normal operating temperature, the thermostat opens and allows hot coolant to travel through the radiator, where it's cooled before returning to the engine.

HEATING SYSTEM

The heating system consists of a blower fan and heater core located in a housing under the dash, the hoses connecting the heater core to the engine cooling system and the heater/air conditioning control head on the dashboard. Hot engine coolant is circulated through the heater core. When the heater mode is activated, a flap door in the housing opens to expose the heater core to the passenger compartment through air ducts. A fan switch on the control head activates the blower motor, which forces air through the core, heating the air.

AIR CONDITIONING SYSTEM

The air conditioning system consists of a condenser mounted in front of the radiator, an evaporator mounted adjacent to the heater core, a compressor mounted on the engine, a receiver-drier or accumulator and the plumbing connecting all of the above components.

A blower fan forces the warmer air of the passenger compartment through the evaporator core (sort of a radiator-in-reverse), transferring the heat from the air to the refrigerant. The liquid refrigerant boils off into low pressure vapor, taking the heat with it when it leaves the evaporator.

2 Troubleshooting

COOLANT LEAKS

Refer to illustration 2.2

1 A coolant leak can develop anywhere in the cooling system, but the most common causes are:

a) A loose or weak hose clamp
b) A defective hose
c) A faulty pressure cap
d) A damaged radiator
e) A bad heater core
f) A faulty water pump
g) A leaking gasket at any joint that carries coolant

2 Coolant leaks aren't always easy to find. Sometimes they can only be detected when the cooling system is under pressure. Here's where a cooling system pressure tester comes in handy. After the engine has cooled completely, the tester is attached in place of the pressure cap, then pumped up to the pressure value equal to that of the pressure cap rating (see illustration). Now, leaks that only exist when the engine is fully warmed up will become apparent. The tester can be left connected to locate a nagging slow leak.

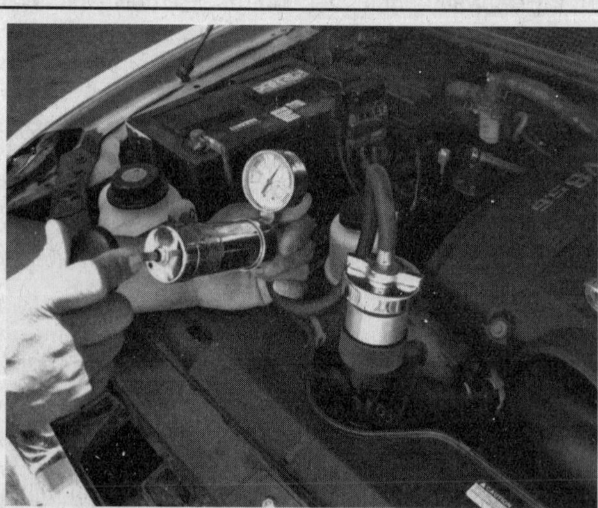

2.2 The cooling system pressure tester is connected in place of the pressure cap, then pumped up to pressurize the system

2.5a The combustion leak detector consists of a bulb, syringe and test fluid

2.5b Place the tester over the cooling system filler neck and use the bulb to draw a sample into the tester

COOLANT LEVEL DROPS, BUT NO EXTERNAL LEAKS

Refer to illustrations 2.5a and 2.5b

3 If you find it necessary to keep adding coolant, but there are no external leaks, the probable causes include:

a) *A blown head gasket*
b) *A leaking intake manifold gasket (only on engines that have coolant passages in the manifold)*
c) *A cracked cylinder head or cylinder block*

4 Any of the above problems will also usually result in contamination of the engine oil, which will cause it to take on a milkshake-like appearance. A bad head gasket or cracked head or block can also result in engine oil contaminating the cooling system.

5 Combustion leak detectors (also known as block testers) are available at most auto parts stores. These work by detecting exhaust gases in the cooling system, which indicates a compression leak from a cylinder into the coolant. The tester consists of a large bulb-type syringe and bottle of test fluid (see illustration). A measured amount of the fluid is added to the syringe. The syringe is placed over the cooling system filler neck and, with the engine running, the bulb is squeezed and a sample of the gases present in the cooling system are drawn up through the test fluid (see illustration). If any combustion gases are present in the sample taken, the test fluid will change color.

6 If the test indicates combustion gas is present in the cooling system, you can be sure that the engine has a blown head gasket or a crack in the cylinder head or block, and will require disassembly to repair.

PRESSURE CAP

Refer to illustration 2.8

WARNING:

Wait until the engine is completely cool before beginning this check.

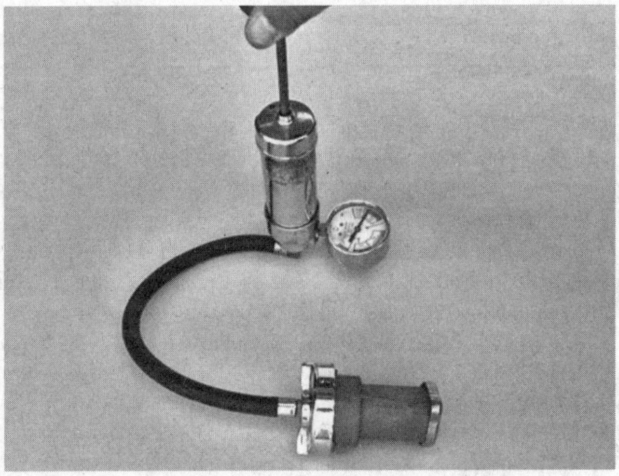

2.8 Checking the cooling system pressure cap with a cooling system pressure tester

7 The cooling system is sealed by a spring-loaded cap, which raises the boiling point of the coolant. If the cap's seal or spring are worn out, the coolant can boil and escape past the cap. With the engine completely cool, remove the cap and check the seal; if it's cracked, hardened or deteriorated in any way, replace it with a new one.

8 Even if the seal is good, the spring might not be; this can be checked with a cooling system pressure tester (see illustration). If the cap can't hold a pressure within approximately 1-1/2 lbs of its rated pressure (which is marked on the cap), replace it with a new one.

9 The cap is also equipped with a vacuum relief spring. When the engine cools off, a vacuum is created in the cooling system. The vacuum relief spring allows air back into the system, which will equalize the pressure and prevent damage to the radiator (the radiator tanks could collapse if the vacuum is great enough). If, after turning the engine off and allowing it to cool down you notice any of the cooling system hoses collapsing, replace the pressure cap with a new one.

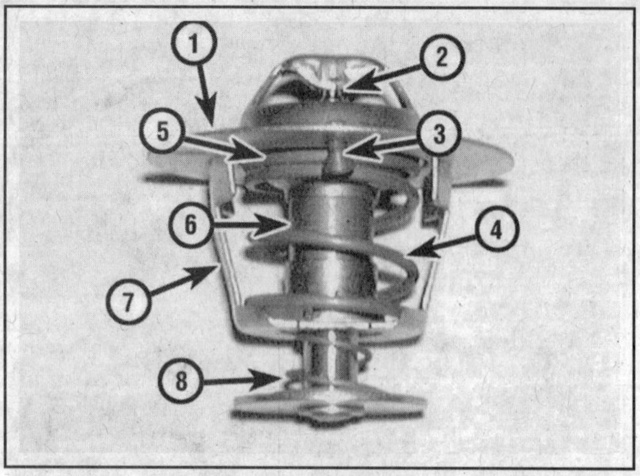

2.10 Typical thermostat:

1	*Flange*	5	*Valve seat*
2	*Piston*	6	*Valve*
3	*Jiggle valve*	7	*Frame*
4	*Main coil spring*	8	*Secondary coil spring*

THERMOSTAT

➧ Refer to illustration 2.10

10 Before assuming the thermostat (see illustration) is responsible for a cooling system problem, check the coolant level (see Chapter 1), drivebelt tension (see Chapter 1) and temperature gauge (or light) operation.

11 If the engine takes a long time to warm up (as indicated by the temperature gauge or heater operation), the thermostat is probably stuck open. Replace the thermostat with a new one.

12 If the engine runs hot or overheats, a thorough test of the thermostat should be performed.

13 Definitive testing of the thermostat can only be made when it is removed from the vehicle. If the thermostat is stuck in the open position at room temperature, it is faulty and must be replaced.

**** CAUTION:**

Do not drive the vehicle without a thermostat. The computer may stay in open loop and emissions and fuel economy will suffer.

14 To test a thermostat, suspend the (closed) thermostat on a length of string or wire in a pot of cold water.

15 Heat the water on a stove while observing thermostat. The thermostat should fully open before the water boils.

16 If the thermostat doesn't open and close as specified, or sticks in any position, replace it.

COOLING FAN

Electric cooling fan

17 If the engine is overheating and the cooling fan is not coming on when the engine temperature rises to an excessive level, unplug the fan motor electrical connector(s) and connect the motor directly to the battery with fused jumper wires. If the fan motor doesn't come on, replace the motor.

2.28 The water pump weep hole is generally located on the underside of the pump

18 If the radiator fan motor is okay, but it isn't coming on when the engine gets hot, the fan relay might be defective. A relay is used to control a circuit by turning it on and off in response to a control decision by the Powertrain Control Module (PCM). These control circuits are fairly complex, and checking them should be left to a qualified automotive technician. Sometimes, the control system can be fixed by simply identifying and replacing a bad relay.

19 Locate the fan relays in the engine compartment fuse/relay box.

20 Test the relay (see Chapter 12).

21 If the relay is okay, check all wiring and connections to the fan motor. Refer to the wiring diagrams at the end of Chapter 12. If no obvious problems are found, the problem could be the Engine Coolant Temperature (ECT) sensor or the Powertrain Control Module (PCM). Have the cooling fan system and circuit diagnosed by a dealer service department or repair shop with the proper diagnostic equipment.

Belt-driven cooling fan

22 Disconnect the cable from the negative terminal of the battery and rock the fan back and forth by hand to check for excessive bearing play.

23 With the engine cold (and not running), turn the fan blades by hand. The fan should turn freely.

24 Visually inspect for substantial fluid leakage from the clutch assembly. If problems are noted, replace the clutch assembly.

25 With the engine completely warmed up, turn off the ignition switch and disconnect the negative battery cable from the battery. Turn the fan by hand. Some drag should be evident. If the fan turns easily, replace the fan clutch.

WATER PUMP

26 A failure in the water pump can cause serious engine damage due to overheating.

Drivebelt-driven water pump

➧ Refer to illustration 2.28

27 There are two ways to check the operation of the water pump while it's installed on the engine. If the pump is found to be defective, it should be replaced with a new or rebuilt unit.

28 Water pumps are equipped with weep (or vent) holes (see illustration). If a failure occurs in the pump seal, coolant will leak from the hole.

29 If the water pump shaft bearings fail, there may be a howling sound at the pump while it's running. Shaft wear can be felt with the drivebelt removed if the water pump pulley is rocked up and down (with the engine off). Don't mistake drivebelt slippage, which causes a squealing sound, for water pump bearing failure.

Timing chain or timing belt-driven water pump

30 Water pumps driven by the timing chain or timing belt are located underneath the timing chain or timing belt cover.

31 Checking the water pump is limited because of where it is located. However, some basic checks can be made before deciding to remove the water pump. If the pump is found to be defective, it should be replaced with a new or rebuilt unit.

32 One sign that the water pump may be failing is that the heater (climate control) may not work well. Warm the engine to normal operating temperature, confirm that the coolant level is correct, then run the heater and check for hot air coming from the ducts.

33 Check for noises coming from the water pump area. If the water pump impeller shaft or bearings are failing, there may be a howling sound at the pump while the engine is running.

➡Note: Be careful not to mistake drivebelt noise (squealing) for water pump bearing or shaft failure.

34 It you suspect water pump failure due to noise, wear can be confirmed by feeling for play at the pump shaft. This can be done by rocking the drive sprocket on the pump shaft up and down. To do this you will need to remove the tension on the timing chain or belt as well as access the water pump.

All water pumps

35 In rare cases or on high-mileage vehicles, another sign of water pump failure may be the presence of coolant in the engine oil. This condition will adversely affect the engine in varying degrees.

➡Note: Finding coolant in the engine oil could indicate other serious issues besides a failed water pump, such as a blown head gasket or a cracked cylinder head or block.

36 Even a pump that exhibits no outward signs of a problem, such as noise or leakage, can still be due for replacement. Removal for close examination is the only sure way to tell. Sometimes the fins on the back of the impeller can corrode to the point that cooling efficiency is diminished significantly.

HEATER SYSTEM

37 Little can go wrong with a heater. If the fan motor will run at all speeds, the electrical part of the system is okay. The three basic heater problems fall into the following general categories:

a) *Not enough heat*
b) *Heat all the time*
c) *No heat*

38 If there's not enough heat, the control valve or door is stuck in a partially open position, the coolant coming from the engine isn't hot enough, or the heater core is restricted. If the coolant isn't hot enough, the thermostat in the engine cooling system is stuck open, allowing coolant to pass through the engine so rapidly that it doesn't heat up quickly enough. If the vehicle is equipped with a temperature gauge instead of a warning light, watch to see if the engine temperature rises to the normal operating range after driving for a reasonable distance.

39 If there's heat all the time, the control valve or the door is stuck wide open.

40 If there's no heat, coolant is probably not reaching the heater core, or the heater core is plugged. The likely cause is a collapsed or plugged hose, core, or a frozen heater control valve. If the heater is the type that flows coolant all the time, the cause is a stuck door or a broken or kinked control cable.

AIR CONDITIONING SYSTEM

41 If the cool air output is inadequate:

a) *Inspect the condenser coils and fins to make sure they're clear*
b) *Check the compressor clutch for slippage.*
c) *Check the blower motor for proper operation.*
d) *Inspect the blower discharge passage for obstructions.*
e) *Check the system air intake filter for clogging.*

42 If the system provides intermittent cooling air:

a) *Check the circuit breaker, blower switch and blower motor for a malfunction.*
b) *Make sure the compressor clutch isn't slipping.*
c) *Inspect the plenum door to make sure it's operating properly.*
d) *Inspect the evaporator to make sure it isn't clogged.*
e) *If the unit is icing up, it may be caused by excessive moisture in the system, incorrect super heat switch adjustment or low thermostat adjustment.*

43 If the system provides no cooling air:

a) *Inspect the compressor drivebelt. Make sure It's not loose or broken.*
b) *Make sure the compressor clutch engages. If it doesn't, check for a blown fuse.*
c) *Inspect the wire harness for broken or disconnected wires.*
d) *If the compressor clutch doesn't engage, bridge the terminals of the A/C pressure switch(es) with a jumper wire; if the clutch now engages, and the system is properly charged, the pressure switch is bad.*
e) *Make sure the blower motor is not disconnected or burned out.*
f) *Make sure the compressor isn't partially or completely seized.*
g) *Inspect the refrigerant lines for leaks.*
h) *Check the components for leaks.*
i) *Inspect the receiver-drier/accumulator or expansion valve/tube for clogged screens.*

44 If the system is noisy:

a) *Look for loose panels in the passenger compartment.*
b) *Inspect the compressor drivebelt. It may be loose or worn.*
c) *Check the compressor mounting bolts. They should be tight.*
d) *Listen carefully to the compressor. It may be worn out.*
e) *Listen to the idler pulley and bearing and the clutch. Either may be defective.*
f) *The winding in the compressor clutch coil or solenoid may be defective.*
g) *The compressor oil level may be low.*
h) *The blower motor fan bushing or the motor itself may be worn out.*
i) *If there is an excessive charge in the system, you'll hear a rumbling noise in the high pressure line, a thumping noise in the compressor, or see bubbles or cloudiness in the sight glass.*
j) *If there's a low charge in the system, you might hear hissing in the evaporator case at the expansion valve, or see bubbles or cloudiness in the sight glass.*

3 Air conditioning and heating system - check and maintenance

AIR CONDITIONING SYSTEM

➧ Refer to illustration 3.1

WARNING:

The air conditioning system is under high pressure. Do not loosen any hose fittings or remove any components until after the system has been discharged. Air conditioning refrigerant should be properly discharged into an EPA-approved recovery/recycling unit at a dealer service department or an automotive air conditioning repair facility. Always wear eye protection when disconnecting air conditioning system fittings.

CAUTION:

All models covered by this manual use environmentally friendly R-134a. This refrigerant (and its appropriate refrigerant oils) are not compatible with R-12 refrigerant system components and must never be mixed or the components will be damaged.

CAUTION:

When replacing entire components, additional refrigerant oil should be added equal to the amount that is removed with the component being replaced. Be sure to read the can before adding any oil to the system, to make sure it is compatible with the R-134a system.

1 The following maintenance checks should be performed on a regular basis to ensure that the air conditioning continues to operate at peak efficiency.

a) *Inspect the condition of the compressor drivebelt. If it is worn or deteriorated, replace it (see Chapter 1).*
b) *Check the drivebelt tension (see Chapter 1).*
c) *Inspect the system hoses. Look for cracks, bubbles, hardening and deterioration. Inspect the hoses and all fittings for oil bubbles or seepage. If there is any evidence of wear, damage or leakage, replace the hose(s).*
d) *Inspect the condenser fins for leaves, bugs and any other foreign material that may have embedded itself in the fins. Use a fin comb or compressed air to remove debris from the condenser.*
e) *Make sure the system has the correct refrigerant charge.*
f) *If you hear water sloshing around in the dash area or have water dripping on the carpet, check the evaporator housing drain tube (see illustration) and insert a piece of wire into the opening to check for blockage.*

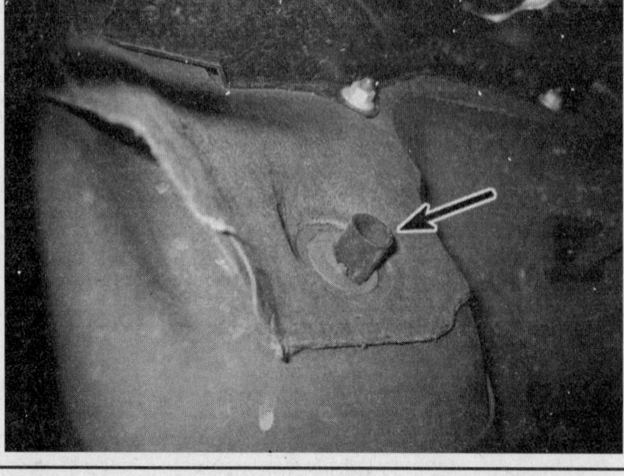

3.1 The evaporator drain hose is located on the passenger's side of the firewall

2 It's a good idea to operate the system for about ten minutes at least once a month. This is particularly important during the winter months because long term non-use can cause hardening, and subsequent failure, of the seals. Note that using the Defrost function operates the compressor.

3 If the air conditioning system is not working properly, proceed to Step 6 and perform the general checks outlined below.

4 Because of the complexity of the air conditioning system and the special equipment necessary to service it, in-depth troubleshooting and repairs beyond checking the refrigerant charge and the compressor clutch operation are not included in this manual. However, simple checks and component replacement procedures are provided in this Chapter.

5 The most common cause of poor cooling is simply a low system refrigerant charge. If a noticeable drop in system cooling ability occurs, one of the following quick checks will help you determine if the refrigerant level is low.

Checking the refrigerant charge

➧ Refer to illustration 3.9

6 Warm the engine up to normal operating temperature.

7 Place the air conditioning temperature selector at the coldest setting and put the blower at the highest setting.

8 After the system reaches operating temperature, feel the larger pipe exiting the evaporator at the firewall. The outlet pipe should be cold (the tubing that leads back to the compressor). If the evaporator outlet pipe is warm, the system probably needs a charge.

9 Insert a thermometer in the center air distribution duct (see illustration) while operating the air conditioning system at its maximum setting - the temperature of the output air should be 35 to 40 degrees F below the ambient air temperature (down to approximately 40 degrees F). If the ambient (outside) air temperature is very high, say 110 degrees F, the duct air temperature may be as high as 60 degrees F, but generally the air conditioning is 35 to 40 degrees F cooler than the ambient air.

10 Further inspection or testing of the system requires special tools and techniques and is beyond the scope of the home mechanic.

Adding refrigerant

➧ Refer to illustrations 3.11 and 3.13

CAUTION:

Make sure any refrigerant, refrigerant oil or replacement component you purchase is designated as compatible with R-134a systems.

3.9 Insert a thermometer in the center vent, turn on the air conditioning system and wait for it to cool down; depending on the humidity, the output air should be 30 to 40 degrees cooler than the ambient air temperature

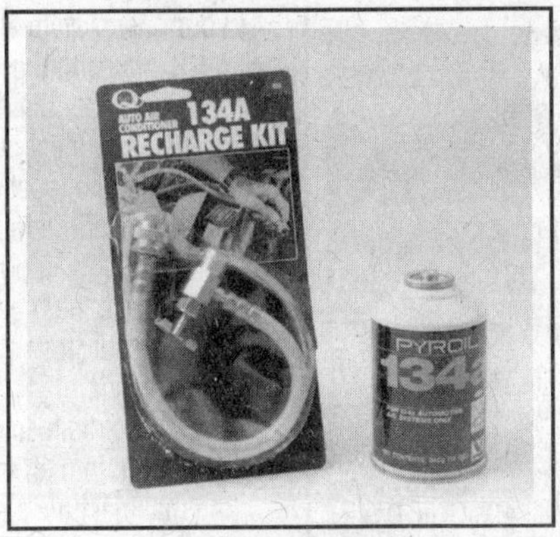

3.11 R-134a automotive air conditioning charging kit

3.13 Location of the low-side charging port

11 Purchase an R-134a automotive charging kit at an auto parts store (see illustration). A charging kit includes a can of refrigerant, a tap valve and a short section of hose that can be attached between the tap valve and the system low side service valve.

✳✳ CAUTION:

Never add more than one can of refrigerant to the system. If more refrigerant than that is required, the system should be evacuated and leak tested.

12 Back off the valve handle on the charging kit and screw the kit onto the refrigerant can, making sure first that the O-ring or rubber seal inside the threaded portion of the kit is in place.

✳✳ WARNING:

Wear protective eyewear when dealing with pressurized refrigerant cans.

13 Remove the dust cap from the low-side charging port and attach the hose's quick-connect fitting to the port (see illustration).

✳✳ WARNING:

DO NOT hook the charging kit hose to the system high side! The fittings on the charging kit are designed to fit only on the low side of the system.

14 Warm up the engine and turn On the air conditioning. Keep the charging kit hose away from the fan and other moving parts.

➡Note: The charging process requires the compressor to be running. If the clutch cycles off, you can put the air conditioning switch on High and leave the car doors open to keep the clutch on and compressor working. The compressor can be kept on during the charging by removing the connector from the pressure switch and bridging it with a paper clip or jumper wire during the procedure.

15 Turn the valve handle on the kit until the stem pierces the can, then back the handle out to release the refrigerant. You should be able to hear the rush of gas. Keep the can upright at all times, but shake it occasionally. Allow stabilization time between each addition.

➡Note: The charging process will go faster if you wrap the can with a hot-water-soaked rag to keep the can from freezing up.

16 If you have an accurate thermometer, you can place it in the center air conditioning duct inside the vehicle and keep track of the output air temperature. A charged system that is working properly should cool down to approximately 40 degrees F. If the ambient (outside) air temperature is very high, say 110 degrees F, the duct air temperature may be as high as 60 degrees F, but generally the air conditioning is 35 to 40 degrees F cooler than the ambient air.

17 When the can is empty, turn the valve handle to the closed position and release the connection from the low-side port. Reinstall the dust cap.

18 Remove the charging kit from the can and store the kit for future use with the piercing valve in the UP position, to prevent inadvertently piercing the can on the next use.

HEATING SYSTEMS

19 If the carpet under the heater core is damp, or if antifreeze vapor or steam is coming through the vents, the heater core is leaking. Remove it (see Section 12) and install a new unit (most radiator shops will not repair a leaking heater core).

20 If the air coming out of the heater vents isn't hot, the problem could stem from any of the following causes:

a) *The thermostat is stuck open, preventing the engine coolant from warming up enough to carry heat to the heater core. Replace the thermostat (see Section 4).*
b) *There is a blockage in the system, preventing the flow of coolant through the heater core. Feel both heater hoses at the firewall. They should be hot. If one of them is cold, there is an obstruction in one of the hoses or in the heater core, or the heater control valve is shut. Detach the hoses and back flush the heater core with a water hose. If the heater core is clear but circulation is impeded, remove the two hoses and flush them out with a water hose.*
c) *If flushing fails to remove the blockage from the heater core, the core must be replaced (see Section 12).*

3.24 Insert the nozzle of the disinfectant can into the return-air intake behind the glove box

ELIMINATING AIR CONDITIONING ODORS

Refer to illustration 3.24

21 Unpleasant odors that often develop in air conditioning systems are caused by the growth of a fungus, usually on the surface of the evaporator core. The warm, humid environment there is a perfect breeding ground for mildew to develop.

22 The evaporator core on most vehicles is difficult to access, and factory dealerships have a lengthy, expensive process for eliminating the fungus by opening up the evaporator case and using a powerful disinfectant and rinse on the core until the fungus is gone. You can service your own system at home, but it takes something much stronger than basic household germ-killers or deodorizers.

23 Aerosol disinfectants for automotive air conditioning systems are available in most auto parts stores, but remember when shopping for them that the most effective treatments are also the most expensive. The basic procedure for using these sprays is to start by running the system in the RECIRC mode for ten minutes with the blower on its highest speed. Use the highest heat mode to dry out the system and keep the compressor from engaging by disconnecting the wiring connector at the compressor.

24 The disinfectant can usually comes with a long spray hose. Insert the nozzle into an intake port inside the cabin, and spray according to the manufacturer's recommendations (see illustration). Try to cover the whole surface of the evaporator core, by aiming the spray up, down and sideways. Follow the manufacturer's recommendations for the length of spray and waiting time between applications.

25 Once the evaporator has been cleaned, the best way to prevent the mildew from coming back again is to make sure your evaporator housing drain tube is clear (see illustration 3.1).

AUTOMATIC HEATING AND AIR CONDITIONING SYSTEMS

26 Some vehicles are equipped with an optional automatic climate control system. This system has its own computer that receives inputs from various sensors in the heating and air conditioning system. This computer, like the PCM, has self-diagnostic capabilities to help pinpoint problems or faults within the system. Vehicles equipped with automatic heating and air conditioning systems are very complex and considered beyond the scope of the home mechanic. Vehicles equipped with automatic heating and air conditioning systems should be taken to dealer service department or other qualified facility for repair.

4 Thermostat - replacement

✲✲ WARNING:

Wait until the engine is completely cool before performing this procedure.

REMOVAL

➧ Refer to illustrations 4.4a and 4.4b

➡Note: The thermostat and thermostat housing on four-cylinder models are replaced as an assembly.

1 Disconnect the cable from the negative battery terminal (see Chapter 5).

2 Drain the cooling system (see Chapter 1). If the coolant is relatively new and still in good condition, save it and reuse it.

3 Follow the lower radiator hose to the engine to locate the thermostat housing.

4 Loosen the hose clamp, then detach the hose from the fitting (see illustrations). If it's stuck, grasp it near the end with a pair of adjustable pliers and twist it to break the seal, then pull it off. If the hose is old or if it has deteriorated, cut it off and install a new one.

5 If the outer surface of the thermostat housing cover, which mates with the hose, is already corroded, pitted, or otherwise deteriorated, it might be damaged even more by hose removal. If it is, replace the thermostat housing cover.

Four-cylinder models

6 Disconnect the electrical connector from the knock sensor, then remove the heater hose from the thermostat housing.

7 Remove the thermostat housing bolts, then detach the housing and remove the radiator hose from the housing.

V6 models

➧ Refer to illustrations 4.9 and 4.10

8 On 3.5L V6 engines, remove the filter housing and duct (see Chapter 4).

9 Remove the fasteners and detach the thermostat housing cover (see illustration). If the cover is stuck, tap it with a soft-face hammer to jar it loose. Be prepared for some coolant to spill as the gasket seal is broken.

10 Note how it's installed, which end is facing up, or out, then remove the thermostat (see illustration).

4.4a Remove the spring clamp from the radiator hose at the thermostat housing cover - V6 engine shown

4.4b Disconnect the radiator hose from the thermostat housing cover - four-cylinder engine shown

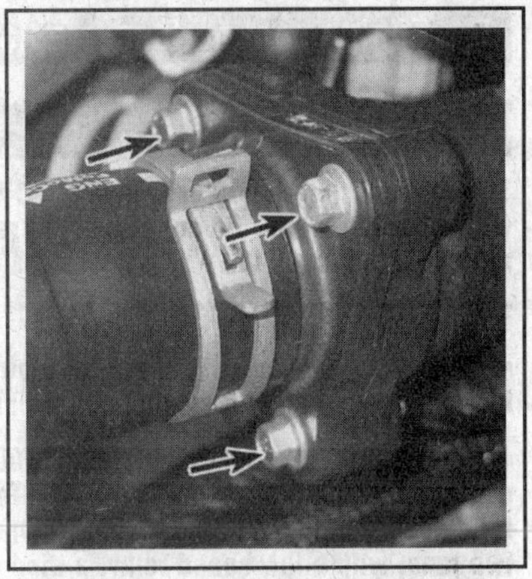

4.9 Remove the thermostat housing cover to access the thermostat

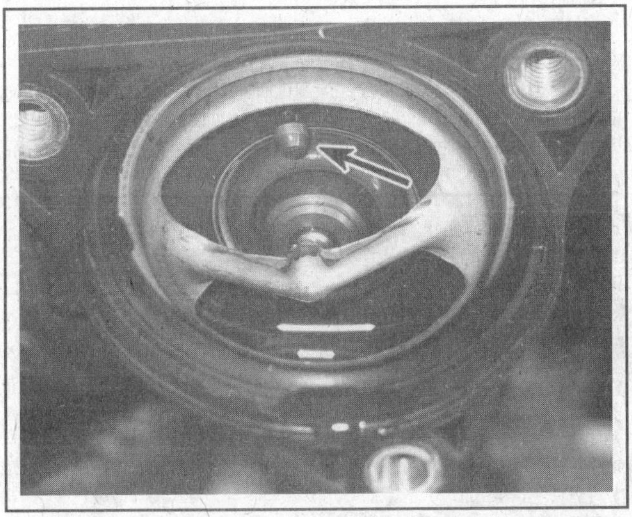

4.10 Remove the thermostat from the housing, but note that the jiggle valve on the thermostat is located in the 12 o'clock position

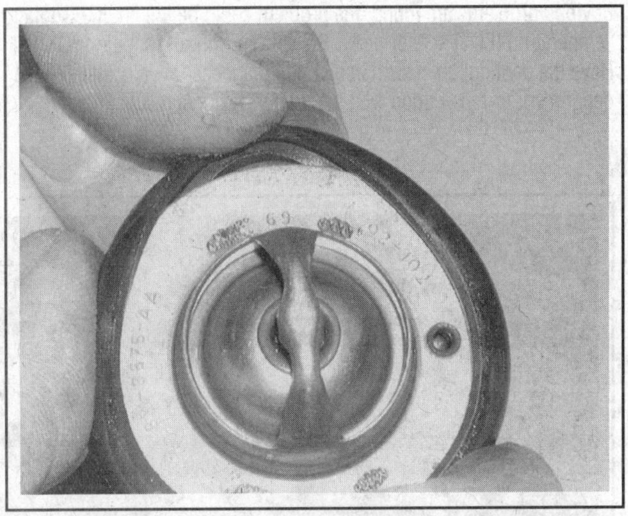

4.13 Install a new rubber seal around the perimeter of the thermostat

INSTALLATION

Refer to illustration 4.13

11 Clean the sealing surfaces. Also inspect the hoses, replacing them as necessary.

Four-cylinder models

12 Install the thermostat housing, using a new gasket. Reconnect the radiator hose, then install the housing and tighten the bolts to the torque listed in this Chapter's Specifications. Reconnect the heater hose.

V6 models

13 Install a new rubber gasket or O-ring on the thermostat (see illustration), then install the thermostat in the housing, spring-end first. Make sure that you install the thermostat with the jiggle valve at 12 o'clock (see illustration 4.10).

14 Install the thermostat housing cover and bolts, then tighten the bolts to the torque listed in this Chapter's Specifications.

15 Reattach the lower radiator hose to the thermostat housing cover. Make sure that the hose clamp is still tight. If it isn't, replace it.

All models

16 Refill the cooling system and bleed the air from the system (see Chapter 1).

17 Start the engine and allow it to reach normal operating temperature, then check for leaks and proper thermostat operation.

5 Engine cooling fans - replacement

WARNING:

To avoid possible injury or damage, DO NOT operate the engine with a damaged fan. Do not attempt to repair fan blades - replace a damaged fan with a new one.

Note: Always be sure to check for blown fuses before attempting to diagnose an electrical circuit problem.

Note: 2.3L, 2.5L four-cylinder and 3.0L V6 models are equipped with a high, a medium and a low speed cooling fan relay, controlling one fan. 3.5L V6 engines are equipped with two fans, with a low speed relay, a medium speed relay and two high speed fan relays that are controlled by the PCM.

1 If the engine is overheating and the cooling fan is not coming on when the engine temperature rises to an excessive level, see Section 2. Check the fan relays in the underhood fuse/relay box.

2 If the relays are okay, check all wiring and connections to the fan motor. Refer to the wiring diagrams at the end of Chapter 12. If no obvious problems are found, the problem could be the Engine Coolant Temperature (ECT) sensor or the Powertrain Control Module (PCM). Have the cooling fan system and circuit diagnosed by a dealer service department or repair shop with the proper diagnostic equipment.

REPLACEMENT

Refer to illustrations 5.5, 5.7, 5.11, 5.12 and 5.13

WARNING:

Wait until the engine is completely cool before performing this procedure.

WARNING:

These models have an airbag sensor mounted near the radiator support bracket. It will be necessary to disarm the system prior to performing any work around the radiator, fans or other components in this area (see Chapter 12).

3 Disconnect the cable from the negative battery terminal (see Chapter 5).

4 Disconnect the fan motor electrical connector(s). On 2.3L engines, remove the alternator air duct.

5 Raise the vehicle and secure it on jackstands. On V6 models, remove the air filter housing and inlet air resonator (see Chapter 4). On all models, remove the lower splash apron under the radiator (see illustration).

5.5 Remove the splash shield below the radiator

5.7 Release the transmission fluid cooler lines from the clips

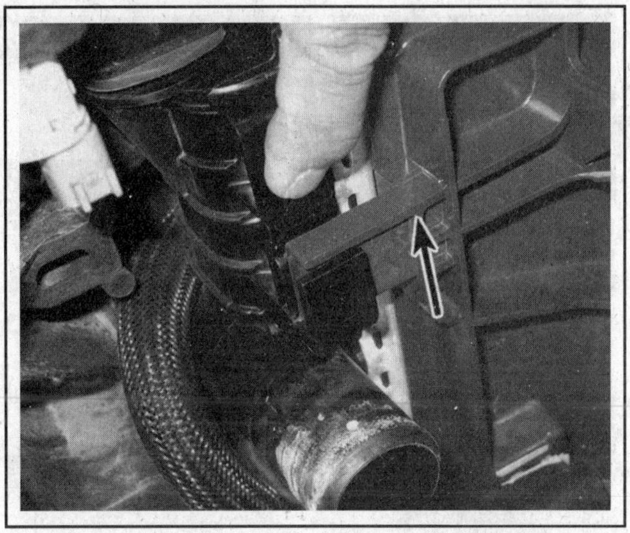

5.11 Release the clip on each side and pull the fan/shroud up and out

5.12 Use a flat-bladed screwdriver and drive the locking washer off the fan motor shaft

5.13 Remove the fan motor mounting bolts

6 Drain the cooling system (see Chapter 1). If the coolant is relatively new and still in good condition, save it and reuse it. Detach the upper radiator hose from the radiator and position it aside.

7 On automatic transaxle-equipped vehicles, disconnect the clips securing the transmission cooling lines to the fan shroud (see illustration).

8 Disconnect the electrical connectors to the fan-control electronic module.

9 Detach the wire harness clips from the fan shroud and move the harness away from the shroud.

10 On 3.5L V6 engines, remove the five pushpins securing the shroud.

11 Release the two large clips at the top of the fan shroud and lift the fan/shroud assembly from the vehicle (see illustration).

12 To detach the fan blade from the motor, remove the nut or retaining clip from the motor shaft (see illustration). Remove the fan blade from the motor.

13 To detach the motor from the shroud, remove the retaining bolts (see illustration).

14 Installation is the reverse of removal.

➡Note: When reinstalling the fan assembly, make sure the rubber air shields around the shroud are still in place - without them, the cooling system may not work efficiently.

15 Reconnect the battery, refill the cooling system and bleed the air from the system (see Chapter 1).

16 Start the engine and allow it to reach normal operating temperature, then check for leaks and proper operation.

6 Coolant expansion tank - removal and installation

➧ **Refer to illustration 6.3**

WARNING:

Wait until the engine is completely cool before beginning this procedure.

1 Drain the cooling system (see Chapter 1).
2 Remove the fasteners securing the expansion tank to the fender.
3 Lift the tank up enough to disconnect the hoses (see illustration).
4 Clean out the tank with soapy water and a brush to remove any deposits inside. Inspect the reservoir carefully for cracks. If you find a crack, replace the reservoir.
5 Installation is the reverse of removal.

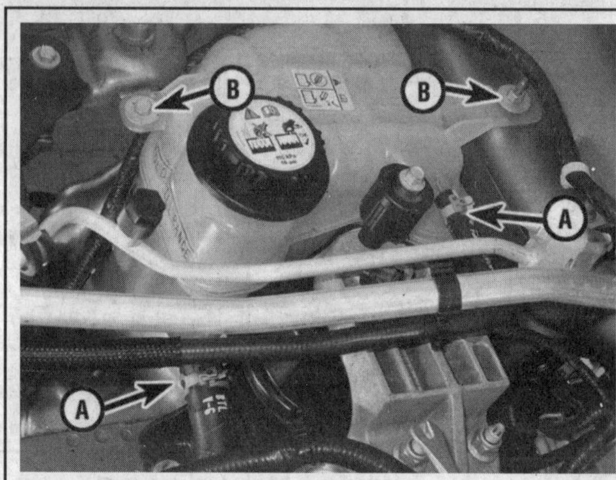

6.3 Disconnect the expansion tank hoses (A), then remove the mounting fasteners (B)

7 Radiator - removal and installation

WARNING:

Wait until the engine is completely cool before beginning this procedure.

WARNING:

These models have a an airbag sensor mounted near the radiator support. It will be necessary to disarm the airbag system prior to performing any work around the radiator, fans or other components in this area (see Chapter 12)

REMOVAL

➧ **Refer to illustration 7.6a and 7.6b**

1 Disconnect the cable from the negative battery terminal (see Chapter 5).
2 Raise the vehicle and place it securely on jackstands. Remove the lower splash shield.
3 Drain the cooling system (see Chapter 1). If the coolant is relatively new and in good condition, save it and reuse it. Detach the radiator hose from the bottom of the radiator.
4 Remove the cooling fan/shroud assembly from the radiator (see Section 5).
5 Remove any pushpins securing the radiator to the condenser.
6 Remove the upper radiator support, then squeeze the large plastic tabs to release the condenser from the radiator (see illustrations).
7 If you're working on a vehicle equipped with an automatic transaxle, disconnect the transaxle cooler lines from the radiator. Use a drip pan to catch spilled fluid and plug the lines and fittings.
8 Carefully lift out the radiator. Don't spill coolant on the vehicle or scratch the paint. Make sure the rubber radiator insulators that fit on the bottom of the radiator and into the sockets in the body remain in place in the body for proper reinstallation of the radiator.
9 Remove bugs and dirt from the radiator with compressed air and a soft brush. Don't bend the cooling fins. Inspect the radiator for leaks and damage. If it needs repair, have a radiator shop or a dealer service department do the work.

INSTALLATION

10 Inspect the rubber insulators in the lower crossmember for cracks and deterioration. Make sure that they're free of dirt and gravel. When installing the radiator, make sure that it's correctly seated on the insulators before fastening the top brackets.
11 Installation is otherwise the reverse of the removal procedure. After installation, fill the cooling system with the correct mixture of antifreeze and water, then bleed the air from the system (see Chapter 1).
12 Start the engine and check for leaks. Allow the engine to reach normal operating temperature, indicated by the upper radiator hose becoming hot. Recheck the coolant level and add more if required.
13 If you're working on an automatic transaxle-equipped vehicle, check and add fluid as needed.

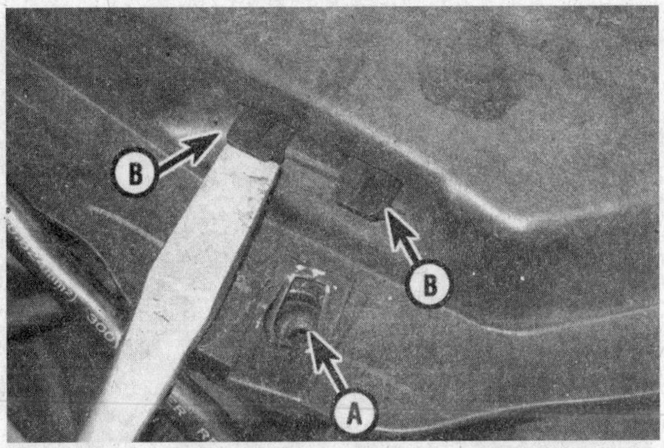

7.6a Remove the bolts (A, one per side) and pry the clips (B) to remove the upper radiator support

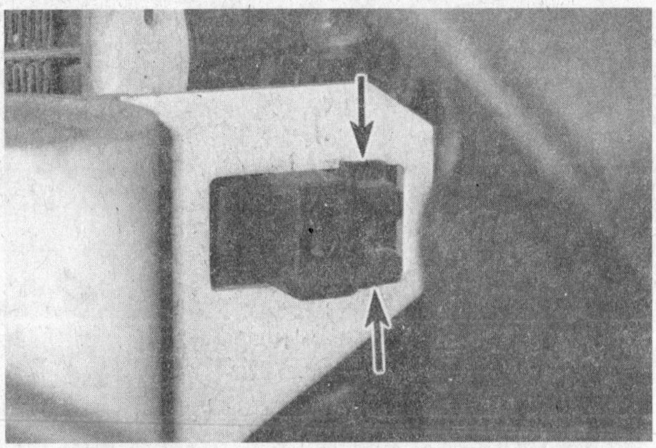

7.6b Release the clips at each side securing the condenser to the radiator

8 Water pump - replacement

WARNING:

Wait until the engine is completely cool before beginning this procedure.

REMOVAL

1 Disconnect the cable from the negative battery terminal (see Chapter 5).

2 Drain the cooling system (see Chapter 1).

3 Loosen the water pump pulley bolts on four-cylinder engines, then remove the drivebelt.

4 On 3.0L V6 models, remove the water pump drivebelt (see Chapter 1).

Four-cylinder models

Refer to illustration 8.7, 8.8 and 8.9

5 Loosen the right front wheel lug nuts. Raise the vehicle and secure it on jackstands.

6 Remove the right front wheel and the fender splash shield (see Chapter 11).

7 Remove the water pump pulley (see illustration).

8 Remove the bolts attaching the water pump to the engine block and remove the pump from the engine (see illustration). If the water pump is stuck, gently tap it with a soft-faced hammer to break the seal.

8.7 Remove the bolts and separate the water pump pulley from the pump

8.8 Remove the water pump bolts

8.9 Clean the water pump bolt threads, the threaded holes in the housing and the pump mating surface of the housing

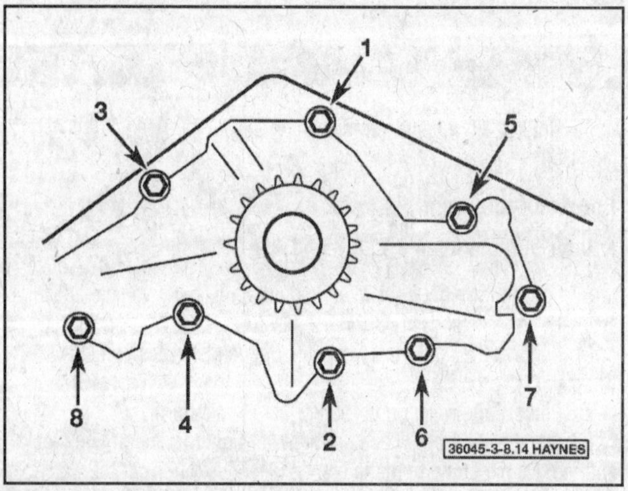

8.14 Water pump bolt locations and tightening sequence - 3.5L V6

9 Clean the bolt threads and the threaded holes in the engine (see illustration) and remove all corrosion and sealant. Remove all traces of old gasket material from the sealing surfaces.

3.0L V6 models

➧ **Refer to illustrations 8.12 and 8.14**

10 Remove the water pump drivebelt (see Chapter 1).

11 To access all the water pump bolts on 3.0L engines, several special tools are required to remove the pulley from the camshaft (manufacturer tool numbers: #303-456, #303-457, and #303-009).

12 Leave the water pump-to-thermostat housing hose connected to the pump, but disconnect it from the thermostat housing. Disconnect

8.12 Two water pump bolts (not visible in this photo) are accessible only after the drive pulley is removed from the end of the exhaust camshaft with special tools - 3.0L V6

the other water pump hoses, then remove the water pump mounting bolts (see illustration).

13 Clean all the gasket and O-ring surfaces on the pump and the housing.

3.5L V6 models

14 On 3.5L V6 engines, the water pump is mounted to the front of the block but is driven by the timing chain and thus not accessible without removing the timing chain (see Chapter 2B). Remove the pump mounting bolts (see illustration).

INSTALLATION

15 Compare the new pump to the old one to make sure that they're identical.

16 Apply a thin film of RTV sealant to hold the new gasket in place during installation. O-rings should be coated with clean coolant.

⁂ CAUTION:

Make sure that the gasket is correctly positioned on the water pump and the mating surfaces are clean and free of old gasket material.

Carefully mate the pump to the water pump housing.

17 Install the water pump bolts and tighten them to the torque listed in this Chapter's Specifications.

18 The remainder of installation is the reverse of removal. Refill and bleed the cooling system when you're done (see Chapter 1).

19 On 3.0L V6 engines, two special tools (manufacturer tool numbers: #303-459 and #303-458) are required to reinstall the water pump pulley to the camshaft.

20 Operate the engine to check for leaks.

9 Coolant temperature sending unit - check and replacement

WARNING:

Wait until the engine is completely cool before beginning this procedure.

➡**Note: Four-cylinder engines and 3.5L V6 engines are equipped with a cylinder head temperature sensor instead of a coolant temperature sensor (as on 3.0L V6 engines). Refer to Chapter 6 for additional information.**

The coolant temperature indicator system consists of a warning light or a temperature gauge on the dash and a coolant temperature sending unit mounted on the engine. On the models covered by this manual, the Cylinder Head Temperature (CHT) sensor (four cylinder and 3.5L V6) or Engine Coolant Temperature (ECT) sensor (3.0L V6 models) is an information sensor for the Powertrain Control Module (PCM) and also functions as the coolant temperature sending unit for the temperature gauge. Information on the CHT and ECT sensors can be found in Chapter 6.

10 Blower motor resistor and blower motor - replacement

WARNING:

The models covered by this manual are equipped with Supplemental Restraint Systems (SRS), more commonly known as airbags. Always disable the airbag system before working in the vicinity of any airbag system component to avoid the possibility of accidental deployment of the airbag, which could cause personal injury (see Chapter 12).

BLOWER MOTOR RESISTOR

Refer to illustration 10.2

1 Remove the lower trim panel from below the glovebox (see Chapter 11).

2 Disconnect the electrical connector from the blower motor resistor (see illustration).

3 Remove the blower motor resistor mounting screws and remove the resistor from the evaporator housing.

4 Installation is the reverse of removal.

BLOWER MOTOR

Refer to illustration 10.6

5 Remove the lower trim panel from below the glovebox (see Chapter 11).

6 Disconnect the blower motor electrical connector (see illustration).

7 Remove the blower motor mounting screws and remove the blower motor.

8 Installation is the reverse of removal.

10.2 Unplug the blower motor resistor connector, then remove the mounting screws

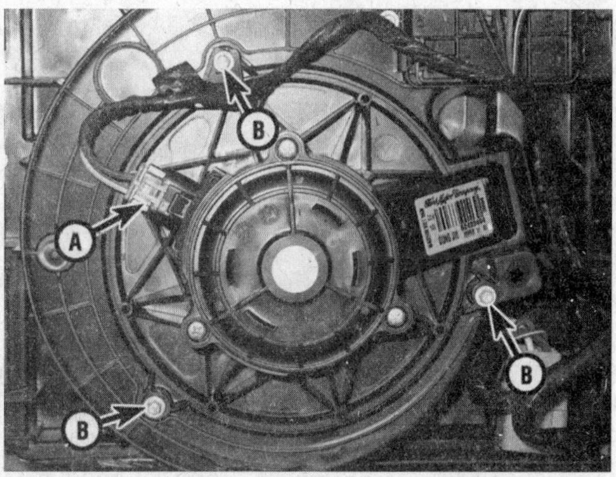

10.6 Location of the blower motor electrical connector (A) and the blower motor mounting screws (B)

11 Heater/air conditioner control assembly - removal and installation

➧ **Refer to illustrations 11.2 and 11.4**

⁂ WARNING:

The models covered by this manual are equipped with Supplemental Restraint Systems (SRS), more commonly known as airbags. Always disable the airbag system before working in the vicinity of any airbag system component to avoid the possibility of accidental deployment of the airbag, which could cause personal injury (see Chapter 12).

1 Disconnect the cable from the negative battery terminal (see Chapter 5).

2 Use a plastic trim tool to pry the lower trim panel/control assembly from its retaining clips (see illustration).

3 Disconnect the electrical connectors at the module.

4 Remove the heater/air conditioner control assembly retaining screws on the back of the panel (see illustration).

5 Installation is the reverse of removal.

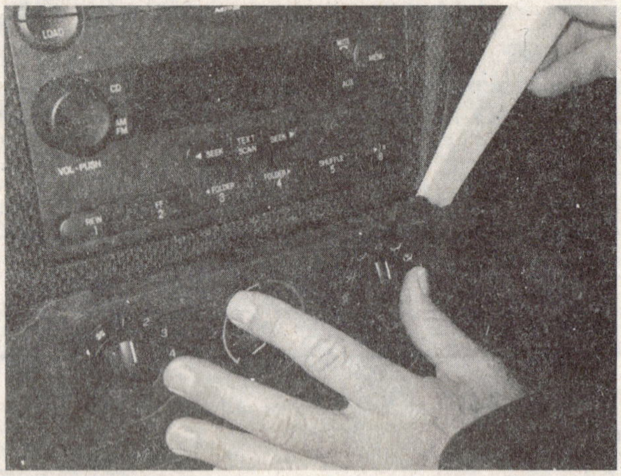

11.2 Pry out the center lower dash panel

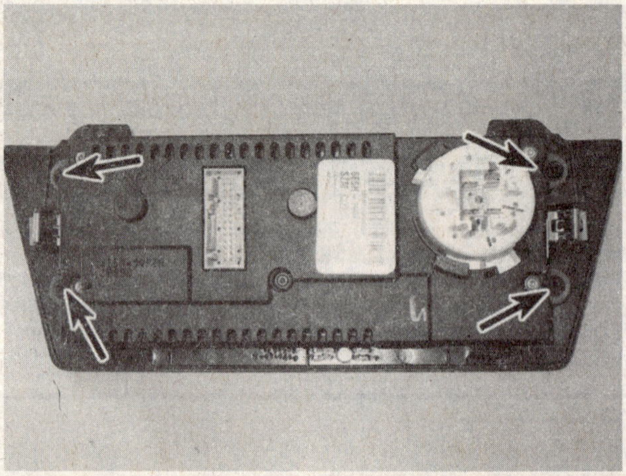

11.4 Location of the heater/air conditioner control assembly mounting screws

12 Heater core - replacement

➧ **Refer to illustrations 12.3 and 12.5**

⁂ WARNING:

The models covered by this manual are equipped with Supplemental Restraint Systems (SRS), more commonly known as airbags. Always disarm the airbag system before working in the vicinity of any airbag system component to avoid the possibility of accidental deployment of the airbag, which could cause personal injury (see Chapter 12).

⁂ WARNING:

Wait until the engine is completely cool before beginning this procedure.

➡ **Note: This is a difficult procedure for the home mechanic, involving numerous hard-to-find fasteners, clips and electrical connectors.**

1 Have the air conditioning refrigerant recovered at a dealer service department or air conditioning shop.

2 Disconnect the cable from the negative battery terminal (see Chapter 5).

3 Drain the cooling system (see Chapter 1). Disconnect the heater hoses from the heater core inlet and outlet pipes at the firewall and disconnect the thermal expansion valve and the two refrigerant pipes (see illustration).

4 Remove the instrument panel (see Chapter 11). On V6 models, remove the lower cowl grille panel to access some HVAC unit fasteners.

5 Tag and disconnect the cables (if equipped) and electrical connectors from the HVAC unit. Remove the mounting fasteners (see illustration).

6 The heater core is in the right half of the HVAC unit, above the blower motor housing. Remove the heater core cover screws and pull the heater core out of the housing.

7 Installation is the reverse of removal. Don't forget to reconnect the heater core inlet and outlet hoses at the firewall. Use a new gasket where the two air conditioning pipes meet the expansion valve at the firewall.

8 Refill and bleed the cooling system when you're done (see Chapter 1). Have the refrigerant recharged.

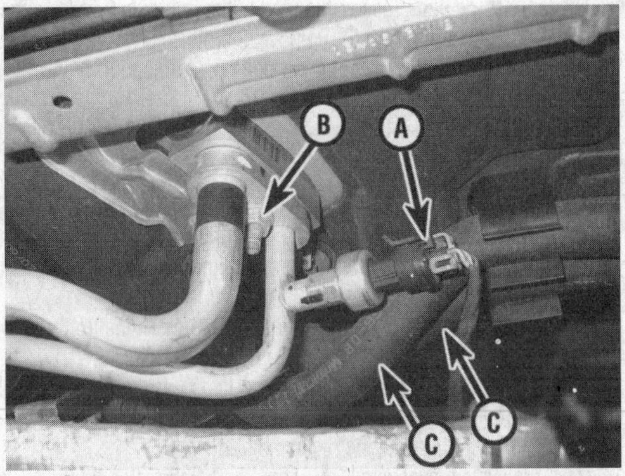

12.3 Disconnect the AC pressure switch (A), remove the nut securing the expansion valve and two pipes to the firewall (B), then remove the two heater core hoses (C)

12.5 Remove the fasteners securing the HVAC housing from the firewall (not all fasteners visible here)

13 Air conditioning compressor - removal and installation

⁂ WARNING:

The air conditioning system is under high pressure. DO NOT loosen any fittings or remove any components until after the system has been discharged. Air conditioning refrigerant must be properly discharged into an EPA-approved container at a dealer service department or an automotive air conditioning repair facility. Always wear eye protection when disconnecting air conditioning system fittings.

⁂ CAUTION:

If the compressor is being replaced due to failure, the rest of the system should be flushed by a technician to remove particles or contaminants.

REMOVAL

Refer to illustrations 13.5 and 13.9

1 Have the air conditioning system recovered by a dealer service department or by an automotive air conditioning shop before proceeding (see **Warning** above).

2 Loosen the right front wheel lug nuts. Raise the vehicle and secure it on jackstands. Remove the right front wheel.

3 Remove the right front fender splash shield and the splash shield under the radiator.

4 Remove the drivebelt (see Chapter 1).

5 Disconnect the electrical connector from the compressor clutch field coil (see illustration).

6 Disconnect the compressor inlet and outlet line manifold from the compressor. Remove and discard the old O-rings.

7 On four-cylinder engines, remove the mounting bolts for the AIR pump and tie the AIR pump aside (see Chapter 6).

13.5 Disconnect the electrical connector (A) and remove the bolt (B) securing the refrigerant pipes to the compressor

13.9 Compressor mounting bolts (upper bolt not visible here)

8 Disconnect the compressor inlet and outlet line manifold from the compressor (see illustration 13.5). Remove and discard the old O-rings.

9 Remove the compressor mounting bolts (see illustration) and remove the compressor.

INSTALLATION

10 If a new compressor is being installed, follow the directions that came with the compressor regarding the draining of excess oil prior to installation.

11 The clutch may have to be transferred from the original to the new compressor.

12 Before reconnecting the inlet and outlet lines to the compressor, replace all manifold O-rings and lubricate them with refrigerant oil.

13 Installation is otherwise the reverse of removal.

14 Have the system evacuated, recharged and leak-tested by the shop that discharged it.

14 Air conditioning condenser - removal and installation

➧ **Refer to illustration 14.6**

⁂ WARNING:

The air conditioning system is under high pressure. DO NOT loosen any fittings or remove any components until after the system has been discharged. Air conditioning refrigerant must be properly discharged into an EPA-approved container at a dealer service department or an automotive air conditioning repair facility. Always wear eye protection when disconnecting air conditioning system fittings.

14.6 Remove the radiator brackets on each side

1 Have the air conditioning system discharged by a dealer service department or an automotive air conditioning shop before proceeding (see **Warning** above).

2 The condenser is combined with a power steering cooler, with the upper passages used for the power steering fluid cooling. At the bottom left of the condenser, there is a replaceable receiver/drier cartridge inside the condenser that is accessible by removing a threaded plug on the bottom of the condenser on the left end.

3 Disconnect the refrigerant inlet and outlet pipes from the condenser. Remove the bolt or nut securing the pipes to the block that is part of the condenser. Cap the lines to prevent contamination. The refrigerant pipe block is retained by a bolt and a rivet that must be drilled out.

4 Remove the power steering cooler hoses from the top of the condenser and position them off to the side.

5 Release the clips securing the condenser to the radiator (see illustrations 7.6a and 7.6b).

6 Remove the left and right radiator support brackets (see illustration).

7 Remove the condenser. If you're going to reinstall the same condenser, store it with the line fittings facing up to prevent oil from draining out.

8 If you're going to install a new condenser, pour one ounce of refrigerant oil of the correct type into it prior to installation.

9 Before reconnecting the refrigerant lines to the condenser, be sure to coat a pair of new O-rings with refrigerant oil, install them in the refrigerant line fittings and tighten the condenser inlet and outlet nuts to the torque listed in this Chapter's Specifications.

10 Installation is otherwise the reverse of removal.

11 Have the system evacuated, recharged and leak tested by the shop that discharged it.

15 Air conditioning pressure cycling switch - replacement

WARNING:

The air conditioning system is under high pressure. DO NOT loosen any fittings or remove any components until after the system has been discharged. Air conditioning refrigerant must be properly discharged into an EPA-approved container at a dealer service department or an automotive air conditioning repair facility. Always wear eye protection when disconnecting air conditioning system fittings.

1 The pressure cycling switch is located on top of the hard line from the condenser to the air conditioning thermostatic expansion valve (TXV). The pressure cycling switch detects low refrigerant line pressure, switches the A/C system off, then back on again to provide higher pressure. If the pressure increases too high, the pressure cut-off switch, located in the high pressure side of the system, shuts the system off.

2 Have the air conditioning system recovered by a dealer service department or by an automotive air conditioning shop before proceeding (see **Warning** above).

3 Unplug the electrical connector from the pressure cycling switch (see illustration 12.3).

4 Unscrew the pressure cycling switch.

5 Lubricate the switch O-ring with clean refrigerant oil of the correct type.

6 Screw the new switch into place until hand tight, then tighten it securely.

7 Reconnect the electrical connector.

16 Air conditioning thermostatic expansion valve (TXV) - general information

WARNING:

The air conditioning system is under high pressure. DO NOT loosen any hose fittings or remove any components until the system has been discharged. Air conditioning refrigerant must be properly discharged into an EPA-approved recovery/recycling unit by a dealer service department or an automotive air conditioning repair facility. Always wear eye protection when disconnecting air conditioning system fittings.

There are several ways that air conditioning systems convert the high-pressure liquid refrigerant from the compressor to lower-pressure vapor. The conversion takes place at the air conditioning evaporator; the evaporator is chilled as the refrigerant passes through, cooling the airflow through the evaporator for delivery to the vents. The conversion is usually accomplished by a sudden change in the tubing size. Many vehicles have a removable controlled orifice in one of the AC pipes at the firewall.

The models covered by this manual use a thermostatic expansion valve or TXV that accomplishes the same purpose as a controlled orifice. To remove the TXV, have the air conditioning system discharged by a licensed air conditioning technician, then disconnect the refrigerant lines from the TXV at the firewall, remove the two bolts securing the valve, then remove the valve.

Specifications

General

Expansion tank cap pressure rating	13 to 18 psi (90 to 123 kPa)
Cooling system capacity	See Chapter 1
Refrigerant type	R-134a
Refrigerant capacity	Refer to HVAC specification tag

Torque specifications

➡Note: One foot-pound (ft-lb) of torque is equivalent to 12 inch-pounds (in-lbs) of torque. Torque values below approximately 15 foot-pounds are expressed in inch-pounds, because most foot-pound torque wrenches are not accurate at these smaller values.

Torque specifications	Ft-lbs (unless otherwise indicated)	Nm
Condenser inlet and outlet nuts	71 in-lbs	8
Coolant inlet pipe bolts	89 in-lbs	10
Thermostat housing cover bolts	89 in-lbs	10
Water pump fasteners		
Four-cylinder and 3.0L V6 engines	89 in-lbs	10
3.5L V6		
Step 1	89 in-lbs	10
Step 2	Tighten an additional 45 degrees	
Water pump housing fasteners (3.0L V6)	89 in-lbs	10
Water pump pulley bolts	177 in-lbs	20

4

FUEL AND EXHAUST SYSTEMS

Section

1 General information

FUEL SYSTEM WARNINGS

Gasoline is extremely flammable and repairing fuel system components can be dangerous. Consider your automotive repair knowledge and experience before attempting repairs which may be better suited for a professional mechanic.

- *Don't smoke or allow open flames or bare light bulbs near the work area*
- *Don't work in a garage with a gas-type appliance (water heater, clothes dryer)*
- *Use fuel-resistant gloves. If any fuel spills on your skin, wash it off immediately with soap and water*
- *Clean up spills immediately*
- *Do not store fuel-soaked rags where they could ignite*
- *Prior to disconnecting any fuel line, you must relieve the fuel pressure (see Section 3)*
- *Wear safety glasses*
- *Have a proper fire extinguisher on hand*

FUEL SYSTEM

The fuel system consists of the fuel tank, electric fuel pump/fuel level sending unit (located in the fuel tank), fuel rail and fuel injectors. The fuel injection system is a multi-port system; multi-port fuel injection uses timed impulses to inject the fuel directly into the intake port of each cylinder. The Powertrain Control Module (PCM) controls the injectors. The PCM monitors various engine parameters and delivers the exact amount of fuel required into the intake ports.

Fuel is circulated from the fuel pump to the fuel rail through fuel lines running along the underside of the vehicle. Various sections of the fuel line are either rigid metal or nylon, or flexible fuel hose. The various sections of the fuel hose are connected either by quick-connect fittings or threaded metal fittings.

EXHAUST SYSTEM

The exhaust system consists of the exhaust manifold(s), catalytic converter(s), muffler(s), tailpipe and all connecting pipes, flanges and clamps. The catalytic converters are an emission control device added to the exhaust system to reduce pollutants.

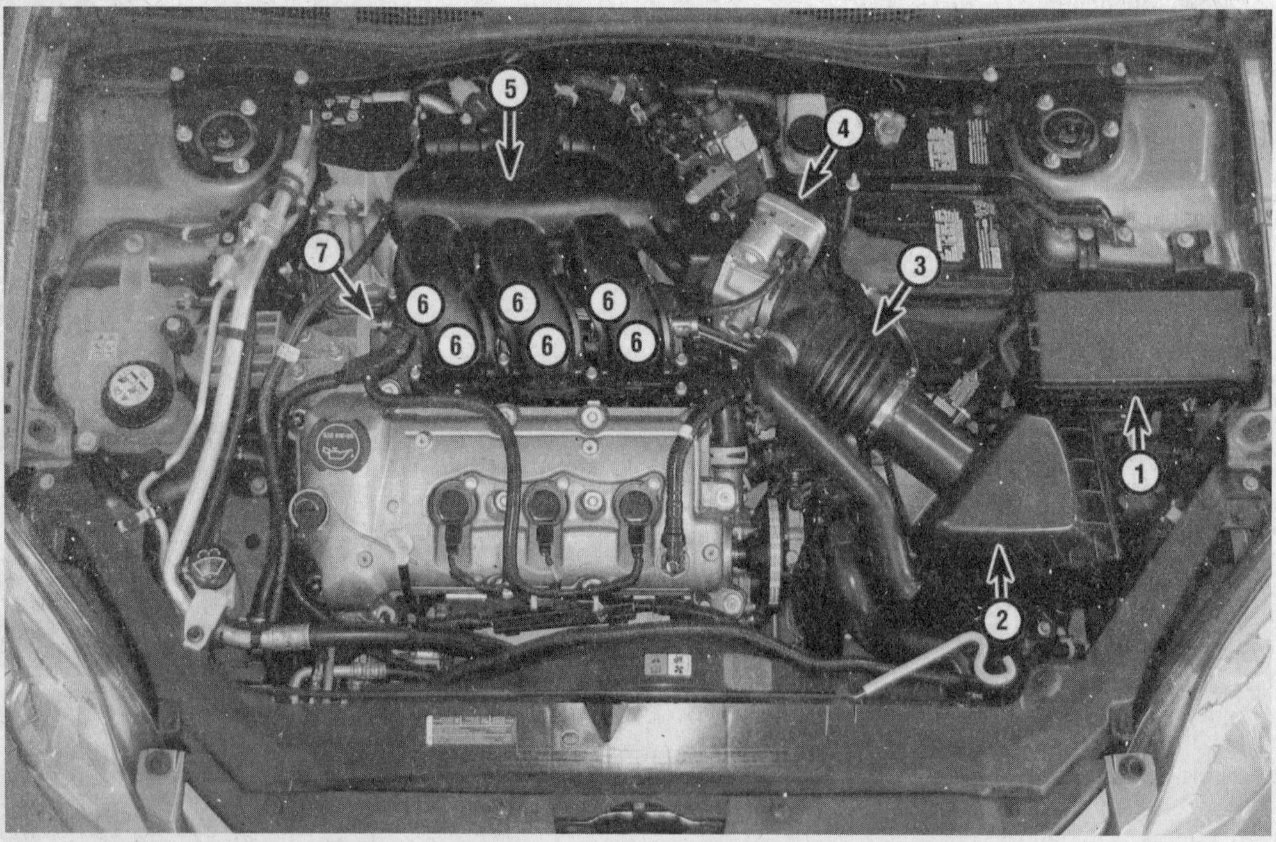

Fuel system components (3.0L V6 engine)

1. *Engine compartment fuse and relay box (fuel pump fuse and fuel pump relay)*
2. *Air filter housing*
3. *Air intake duct*
4. *Throttle body*
5. *Upper intake manifold*
6. *Fuel injectors (under upper intake manifold)*
7. *Fuel pressure test port*

2 Troubleshooting

FUEL PUMP

➧ **Refer to illustrations 2.2a and 2.2b**

1 The fuel pump is located inside the fuel tank. Sit inside the vehicle with the windows closed, turn the ignition key to ON (not START) and listen for the sound of the fuel pump as it's briefly activated. You will only hear the sound for a second or two, but that sound tells you that the pump is working. Alternatively, have an assistant listen at the fuel filler cap.

2 If the pump does not come on, make sure that the inertia switch (see illustration) has not opened the fuel pump circuit. The inertia switch is a resettable circuit breaker that automatically opens the fuel pump circuit in the event of an accident. To access it, remove the right front door opening weather strip/sill panel/kick panel (see illustration 24.3 in Chapter 11). If the inertia switch was not the problem, check the fuel pump fuse and relay (see illustration). If the fuse and relay are okay, check the wiring back to the fuel pump. If the fuse, relay, wiring and inertia switch are okay, the fuel pump is probably defective. If the pump runs continuously with the ignition key in the ON position, the Powertrain Control Module (PCM) is probably defective. Have the PCM checked by a professional mechanic.

FUEL INJECTION SYSTEM

➧ **Refer to illustration 2.9**

➡**Note: The following procedure is based on the assumption that the fuel pump is working and the fuel pressure is adequate (see Section 4).**

3 Check all electrical connectors that are related to the system. Check the ground wire connections for tightness.

4 Verify that the battery is fully charged (see Chapter 5).

5 Inspect the air filter element (see Chapter 1).

6 Check all fuses related to the fuel system (see Chapter 12).

7 Check the air induction system between the throttle body and the intake manifold for air leaks. Also inspect the condition of all vacuum hoses connected to the intake manifold and to the throttle body.

8 Remove the air intake duct from the throttle body and look for dirt, carbon, varnish, or other residue in the throttle body, particularly around the throttle plate. If it's dirty, clean it with carb cleaner, a toothbrush and a clean shop towel.

9 With the engine running, place an automotive stethoscope against each injector, one at a time, and listen for a clicking sound that indicates operation (see illustration).

⁂ WARNING:

Stay clear of the drivebelt and any rotating or hot components.

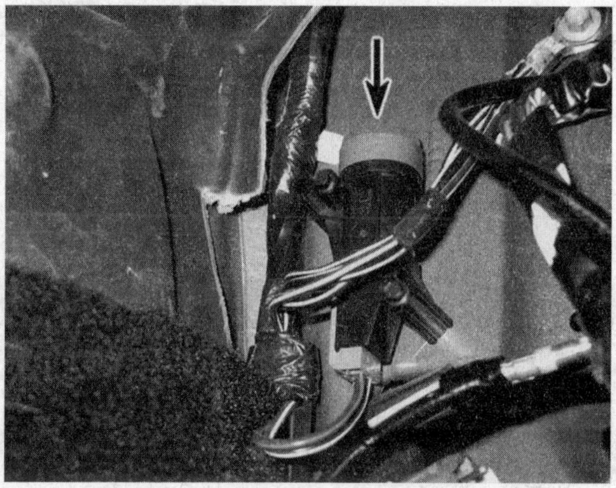

2.2a The fuel pump inertia switch is located behind the right kick panel. To reset it, push the button on top

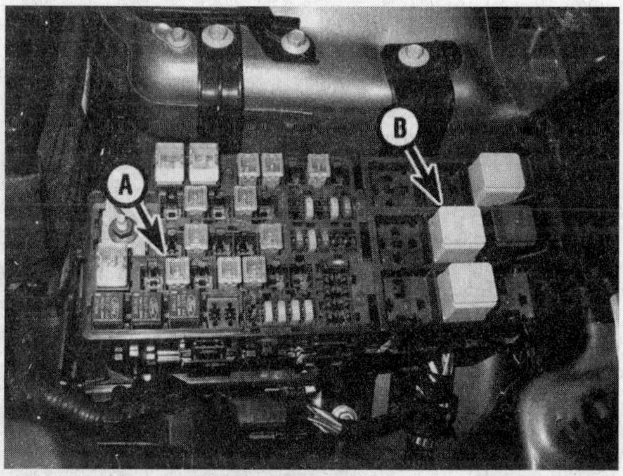

2.2b The fuel pump fuse (A) is located in the engine compartment fuse box; (B) is the fuel pump relay (the location of the fuse and relay may vary with model and year - refer to the guide on the underside of the fuse box cover and the guide in your owner's manual)

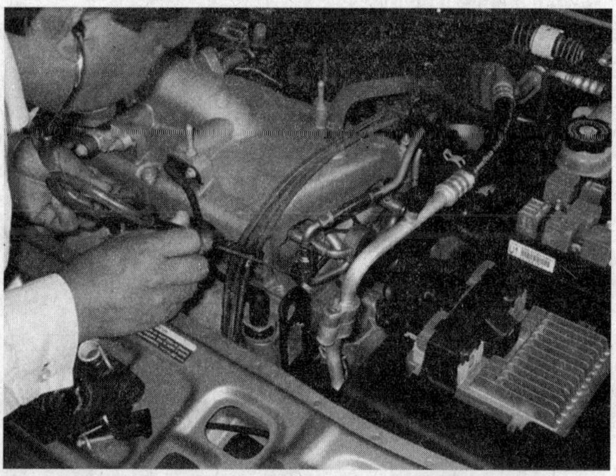

2.9 An automotive stethoscope is used to listen to the fuel injectors in operation

10 If you can hear the injectors operating, but the engine is misfiring, the electrical circuits are functioning correctly, but the injectors might be dirty or clogged. Try a commercial injector cleaning product (available at auto parts stores). If cleaning the injectors doesn't help, replace the injectors.

11 If an injector is not operating (it makes no sound), disconnect the injector electrical connector and measure the resistance across the injector terminals with an ohmmeter. Compare this measurement to the other injectors. If the resistance of the non-operational injector is quite different from the other injectors, replace it.

12 If the injector is not operating, but the resistance reading is within the range of resistance of the other injectors, the PCM or the circuit between the PCM and the injector might be faulty.

3 Fuel pressure relief procedure

⁂ WARNING:

Gasoline is extremely flammable. See Fuel system warnings in Section 1.

1 Remove the fuel filler cap to relieve any pressure built-up in the fuel tank.

2 Remove the fuel pump relay from the underhood fuse/relay box (see illustration 2.2b).

3 Attempt to start the engine; it should immediately stall. Crank the engine several more times to ensure the fuel system has been completely relieved. Disconnect the cable from the negative terminal of the battery before working on the fuel system.

4 It's a good idea to cover any fuel connection to be disassembled with rags to absorb the residual fuel that may leak out. Properly dispose of the rags.

4 Fuel pressure - check

Refer to illustrations 4.1a and 4.1b

⁂ WARNING:

Gasoline is extremely flammable. See Fuel system warnings in Section 1.

Note: The following procedure assumes that the fuel pump is receiving voltage and runs.

MODELS WITH A TEST PORT ON THE FUEL RAIL

1 Locate the fuel pressure test port on the fuel rail, unscrew the cap and connect a fuel pressure gauge (see illustrations).

2 Start the engine and allow it to idle. Note the gauge reading as soon as the pressure stabilizes, and compare it with the pressure listed in this Chapter's Specifications.

3 If the fuel pressure is not within specifications, check the following:

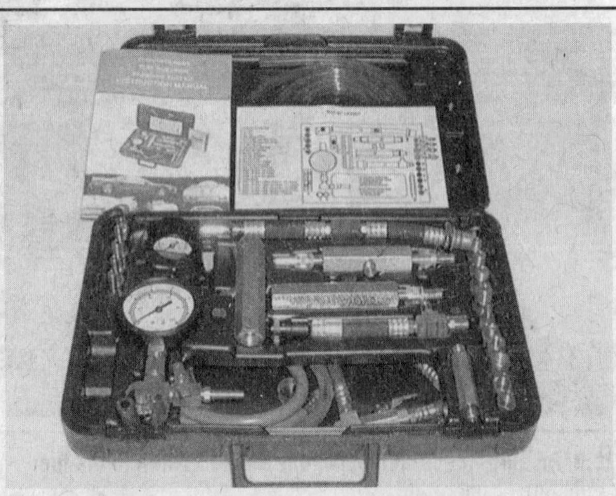

4.1a This fuel pressure testing kit contains all the necessary fittings and adapters, along with the fuel pressure gauge, to test most automotive systems

4.1b The fuel pressure test port is located on the fuel rail

a) *Check for a restriction in the fuel system (kinked fuel line, plugged fuel pump inlet strainer or clogged fuel filter). If no restrictions are found, replace the fuel pump module (see Section 7).*
b) *If the fuel pressure is higher than specified, replace the fuel pump module (see Section 7).*

4 Turn off the engine. Fuel pressure should not fall more than 8 psi over five minutes. If it does, the problem could be a leaky fuel injector, fuel line leak, or faulty fuel pump module.

5 Disconnect the fuel pressure gauge. Wipe up any spilled gasoline.

MODELS WITHOUT A TEST PORT ON THE FUEL RAIL

6 Disconnect the fuel supply line at the fuel rail (see *Disconnecting Fuel Line Fittings* on page 4-6), then use an adapter to connect the fuel pressure gauge between the fuel line and the fuel rail.

7 Refer to Steps 2 through 4 for the fuel pressure check.

8 Relieve the fuel system pressure (see Section 3), then disconnect the fuel pressure gauge.

9 Reconnect the fuel line to the fuel rail.

10 Reconnect the battery (see Chapter 5). Turn the ignition key to the On position and check for fuel leaks.

5 Fuel lines and fittings - general information and disconnection

**** WARNING:**

Gasoline is extremely flammable. See Fuel system warnings in Section 1.

1 Relieve the fuel pressure before servicing fuel lines or fittings (see Section 3), then disconnect the cable from the negative battery terminal (see Chapter 5) before proceeding.

2 The fuel supply line connects the fuel pump in the fuel tank to the fuel rail on the engine. The Evaporative Emission (EVAP) system lines connect the fuel tank to the EVAP canister and connect the canister to the intake manifold.

3 Whenever you're working under the vehicle, be sure to inspect all fuel and evaporative emission lines for leaks, kinks, dents and other damage. Always replace a damaged fuel or EVAP line immediately.

4 If you find signs of dirt in the lines during disassembly, disconnect all lines and blow them out with compressed air. Inspect the fuel strainer on the fuel pump pick-up unit for damage and deterioration.

STEEL TUBING

5 It is critical that the fuel lines be replaced with lines of equivalent type and specification.

6 Some steel fuel lines have threaded fittings. When loosening these fittings, hold the stationary fitting with a wrench while turning the tube nut.

PLASTIC TUBING

7 When replacing fuel system plastic tubing, use only original equipment replacement plastic tubing.

**** CAUTION:**

When removing or installing plastic fuel line tubing, be careful not to bend or twist it too much, which can damage it. Also, plastic fuel tubing is NOT heat resistant, so keep it away from excessive heat.

FLEXIBLE HOSES

8 When replacing fuel system flexible hoses, use only original equipment replacements.

9 Don't route fuel hoses (or metal lines) within four inches of the exhaust system or within ten inches of the catalytic converter. Make sure that no rubber hoses are installed directly against the vehicle, particularly in places where there is any vibration. If allowed to touch some vibrating part of the vehicle, a hose can easily become chafed and it might start leaking. A good rule of thumb is to maintain a minimum of 1/4-inch clearance around a hose (or metal line) to prevent contact with the vehicle underbody.

Disconnecting Fuel Line Fittings

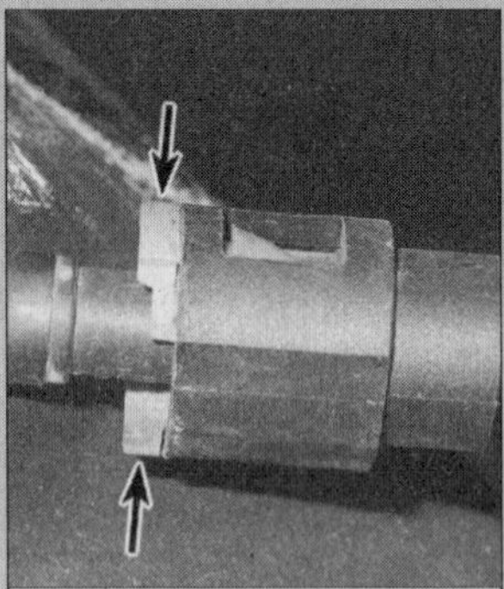

Two-tab type fitting; depress both tabs with your fingers, then pull the fuel line and the fitting apart

On this type of fitting, depress the two buttons on opposite sides of the fitting, then pull it off the fuel line

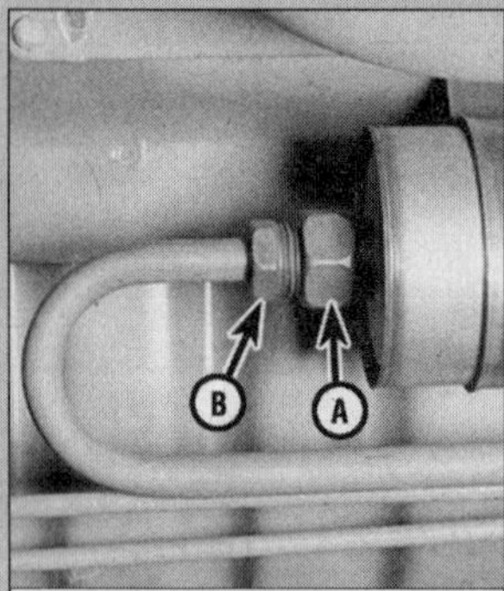

Threaded fuel line fitting; hold the stationary portion of the line or component (A) while loosening the tube nut (B) with a flare-nut wrench

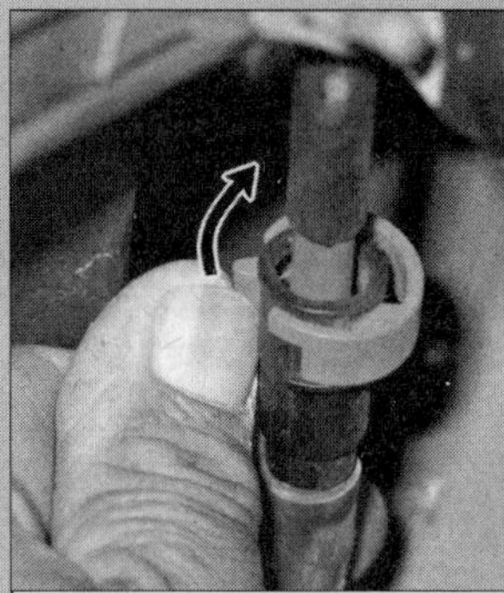

Plastic collar-type fitting; rotate the outer part of the fitting

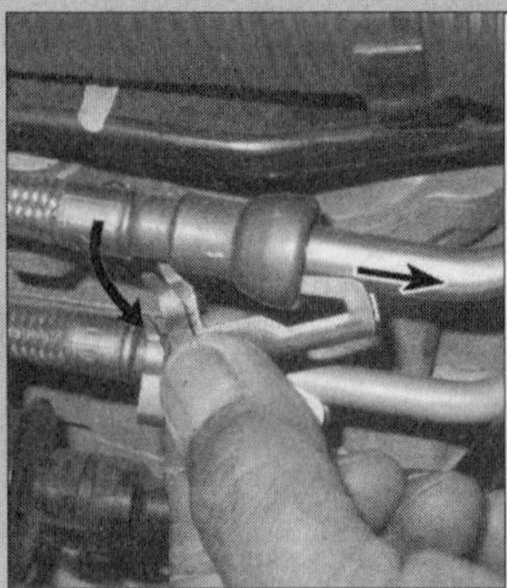

Metal collar quick-connect fitting; pull the end of the retainer off the fuel line, and disengage the other end from the female side of the fitting . . .

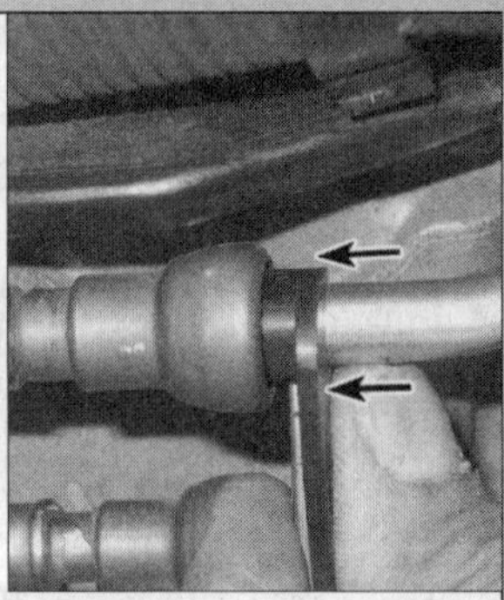

. . . insert a fuel line separator tool into the female side of the fitting, push it into the fitting until it releases the locking tabs inside the fitting, and pull the two halves of the fitting apart

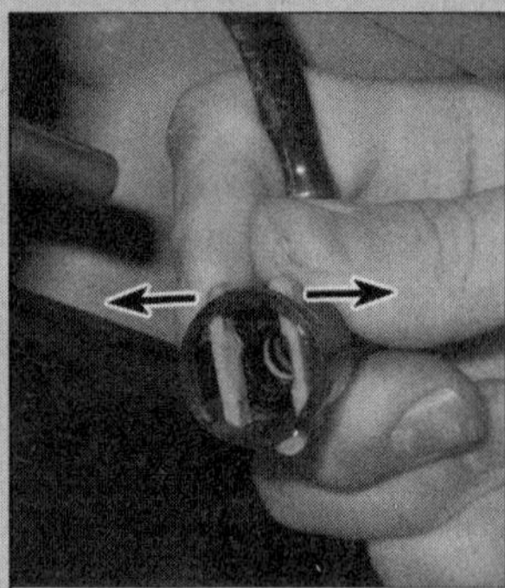

Hairpin-type clip; spread the two legs of the clip apart . . .

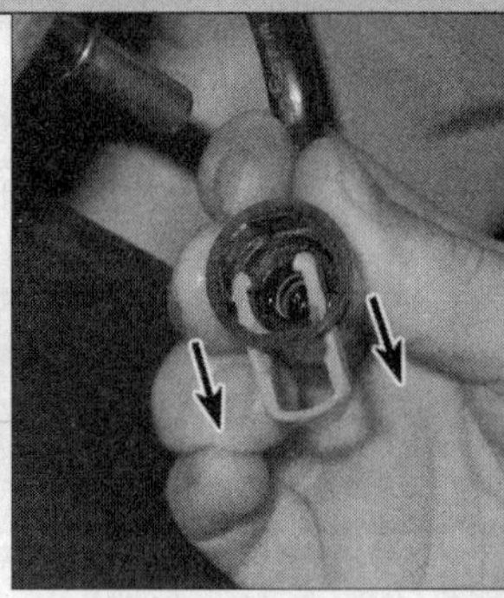

. . . pull the clip out and detach the coupling from the component (fitting detached for clarity)

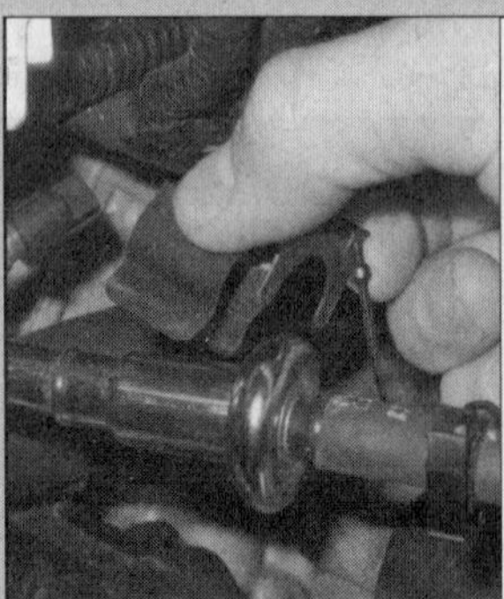

Spring-lock coupling; remove the safety cover . . .

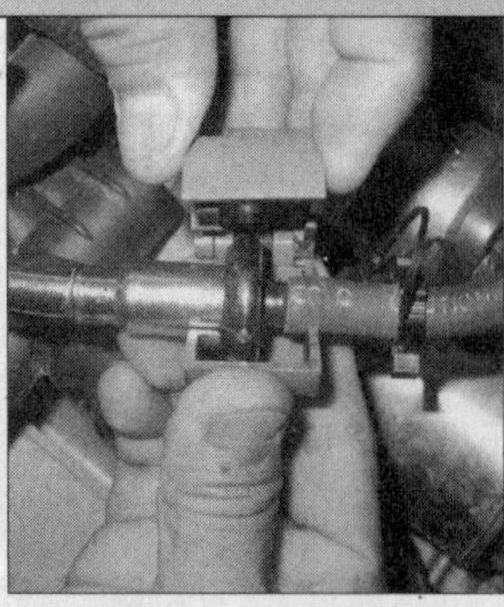

. . . install a coupling release tool and close the clamshell halves of the tool around the coupling . . .

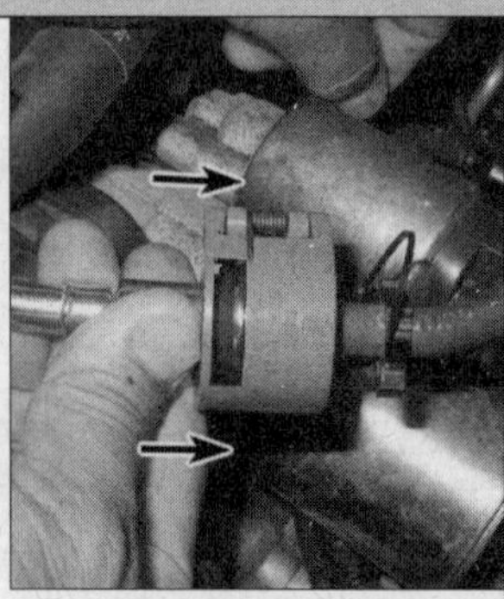

. . . push the tool into the fitting, then pull the two lines apart

6 Exhaust system servicing - general information

➧ **Refer to illustration 6.1**

✱✱ WARNING:

Allow exhaust system components to cool before inspection or repair. Also, when working under the vehicle, make sure it is securely supported on jackstands.

1 The exhaust system consists of the exhaust manifolds, catalytic converter, muffler, tailpipe and all connecting pipes, flanges and clamps. The exhaust system is isolated from the vehicle body and from chassis components by a series of rubber hangers (see illustration). Periodically inspect these hangers for cracks or other signs of deterioration, replacing them as necessary.

2 Conduct regular inspections of the exhaust system to keep it safe and quiet. Look for any damaged or bent parts, open seams, holes, loose connections, excessive corrosion or other defects which could allow exhaust fumes to enter the vehicle. Do not repair deteriorated exhaust system components; replace them with new parts.

3 If the exhaust system components are extremely corroded, or rusted together, a cutting torch is the most convenient tool for removal. Consult a properly-equipped repair shop. If a cutting torch is not available, you can use a hacksaw, or if you have compressed air, there are special pneumatic cutting chisels that can also be used. Wear safety goggles to protect your eyes from metal chips and wear work gloves to protect your hands.

4 Here are some simple guidelines to follow when repairing the exhaust system:

a) Work from the back to the front when removing exhaust system components.

6.1 A typical exhaust system hanger. Inspect regularly and replace at the first sign of damage or deterioration

b) Apply penetrating oil to the exhaust system component fasteners to make them easier to remove.
c) Use new gaskets, hangers and clamps.
d) Apply anti-seize compound to the threads of all exhaust system fasteners during reassembly.
e) Be sure to allow sufficient clearance between newly installed parts and all points on the underbody to avoid overheating the floor pan and possibly damaging the interior carpet and insulation. Pay particularly close attention to the catalytic converter and heat shield.

7 Fuel pump module - removal and installation

FUEL PUMP MODULE

➧ **Refer to illustrations 7.3, 7.4 and 7.5**

✱✱ WARNING:

Gasoline is extremely flammable. See Fuel system warnings in Section 1.

➡**Note: The fuel pump module includes the fuel pump, the fuel level sending unit, a fuel filter and, on mechanical returnless pumps, a fuel pressure regulator. On electronic returnless pumps there is no regulator; fuel pressure is regulated by a Fuel Pump Control Module (FPCM). None of these components is separately serviceable**

1 Disconnect the cable from the negative battery terminal (see Chapter 5). Relieve the fuel system pressure (see Section 3).

2 Remove the rear seat cushion (see Chapter 11).

3 Remove the fuel pump access cover screws (see illustration).

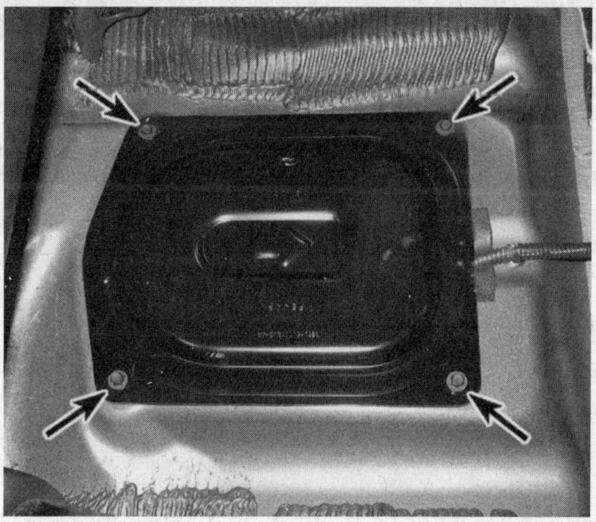

7.3 Fuel pump module access cover screws

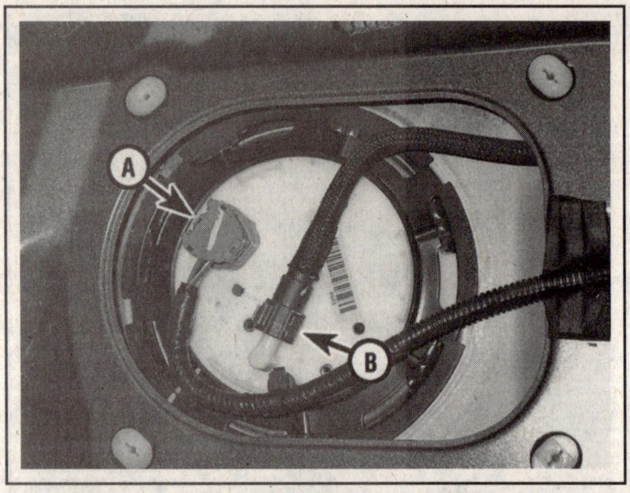

7.4 Fuel pump module electrical connector (A) and fuel supply line quick-connect fitting (B)

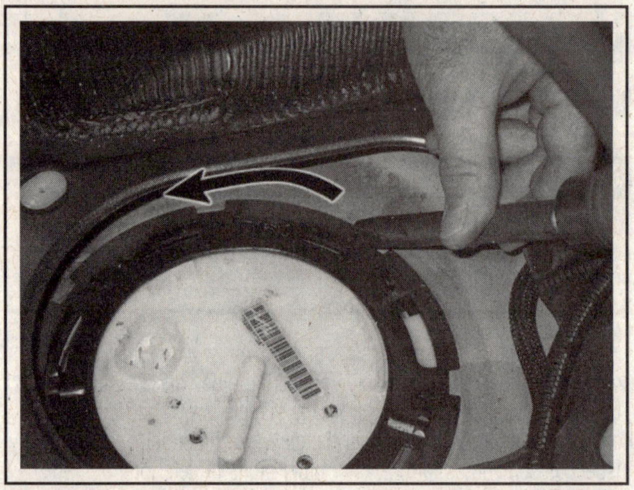

7.5 Use a brass punch and a hammer to loosen and unscrew the fuel pump module lock ring

4 Disconnect the electrical connector and the fuel supply line quick-connect fitting from the fuel pump module (see illustration).

5 Tap the fuel tank module lock ring counterclockwise with a hammer and brass punch (to avoid sparks) (see illustration).

6 Carefully pull the fuel pump module out of the tank. Angle it as necessary to protect the fuel level sensor float arm.

7 Inspect the O-ring and replace it if it shows any sign of deterioration.

8 Installation is the reverse of removal.

FUEL PUMP CONTROL MODULE (FPCM)

➡Note: On vehicles equipped with an electronic returnless fuel system, the fuel pump module speed, and therefore the output and pressure, is controlled by the FPCM, which is located in the left rear part of the trunk.

9 Remove the carpet trim from the left rear part of the trunk.

10 Disconnect the electrical connector from the FPCM.

11 Remove the pin-type retainers and remove the FPCM.

12 Installation is the reverse of removal.

8 Fuel tank - removal and installation

➧ Refer to illustrations 8.6, 8.9a and 8.9b

⁂ WARNING:

Gasoline is extremely flammable. See Fuel system warnings in Section 1.

⁂ WARNING:

The following procedure is much easier to perform if the fuel tank is empty.

1 Remove the fuel tank filler cap to relieve fuel tank pressure.

2 Relieve the fuel system pressure (see Section 3).

3 Disconnect the cable from the negative battery terminal (see Chapter 5).

4 Disconnect the electrical connector and fuel supply line quick-connect fitting from the fuel pump module (see Section 7).

5 Raise the rear of the vehicle and support it securely on jackstands.

6 Loosen the hose clamps and disconnect the fuel filler neck hose

8.6 EVAP vapor hose quick-connect fitting (A) and fuel tank filler neck hose clamp (B)

7 Remove the exhaust pipe (see Section

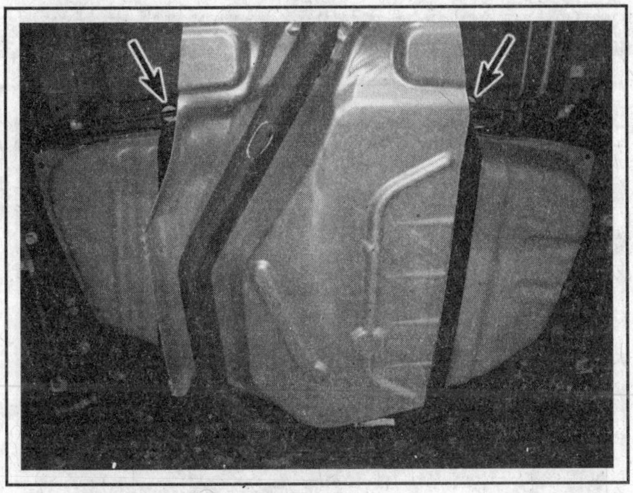

8.9a Front fuel tank strap bolts

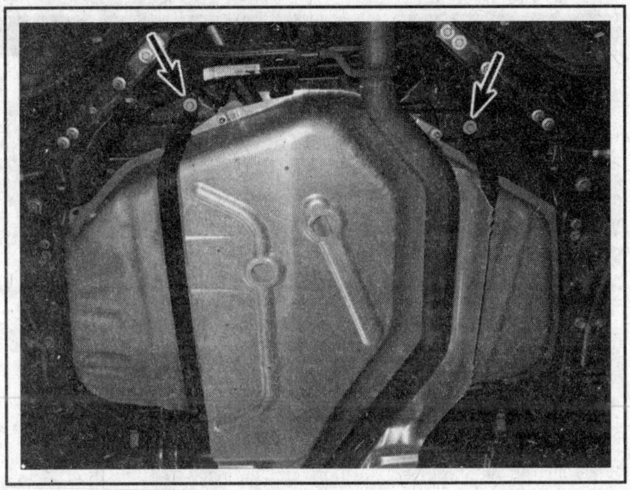

8.9b Rear fuel tank strap bolts

9 Support the fuel tank securely, then remove the fuel tank retaining strap bolts (see illustrations). Remove the straps and carefully lower the fuel tank.

10 Installation is the reverse of removal. Be sure to tighten the fuel tank strap bolts securely.

11 Reconnect the cable to the negative battery terminal (see Chapter 5), then start the engine and check for fuel leaks.

9 Air filter housing - removal and installation

AIR INTAKE DUCT

Refer to illustration 9.1

1 Disconnect the PCV fresh air hose from the air intake duct (see illustration). On Partial Zero Emissions Vehicle (PZEV) models, also disconnect the secondary air injection hose from the intake duct.

2 Loosen the clamps at the air filter housing and the throttle body and remove the air intake duct.

3 Installation is the reverse of removal.

AIR FILTER HOUSING

4 Remove the air intake duct.

5 Disconnect the electrical connector from the MAF sensor (see Chapter 6).

6 Remove the air filter housing.

7 Inspect the condition of the filter housing mounting grommets. If they're cracked, torn or deteriorated, replace them.

8 Installation is the reverse of removal.

9.1 Air intake duct details (3.0L V6 shown, other models similar)

1 PCV fresh air hose
2 Hose clamps

10 Throttle body - removal and installation

➧ **Refer to illustration 10.3**

⁂ WARNING:

Wait until the engine is completely cool before beginning this procedure.

1 Disconnect the cable from the negative battery terminal (see Chapter 5).

2 Remove the air intake duct (see Section 9).

3 Disconnect the electrical connector from the throttle body (see illustration).

4 Clamp-off and disconnect the coolant hoses from the throttle body.

5 Remove the throttle body mounting fasteners and detach the throttle body from the intake manifold. Discard the gasket; it should be replaced with a new one. Cover the intake manifold opening with a clean shop towel.

6 Installation is the reverse of removal. Be sure to use a new gasket and tighten the throttle body fasteners to the torque listed in this Chapter's Specifications.

10.3 Throttle body details (3.0L V6 engine shown)

1 Electrical connector (pull out the locking tab [A] to release)
2 Coolant hoses
3 Throttle body mounting fasteners

11 Fuel rail and injectors - removal and installation

⁂ WARNING:

Gasoline is extremely flammable. See Fuel system warnings in Section 1.

1 Relieve the fuel system pressure (see Section 3).

2 Disconnect the cable from the negative battery terminal (see Chapter 5).

FOUR-CYLINDER MODELS

3 On 2.3L models, remove the alternator inlet duct (see *Alternator - removal and installation* in Chapter 5).

4 Disconnect the fuel supply line quick-connect fitting from the fuel rail (see *Disconnecting Fuel Line Fittings* on page 4-6).

5 Disconnect the two wiring harness retainers from the fuel rail and remove the fuel rail insulator.

6 Disconnect the electrical connectors for all wiring that shares the harness with the fuel injectors, then disconnect the four fuel injector electrical connectors. Using a trim removal tool, disengage the two pin-type retainers that secure the wiring harness and harness insulator from the fuel rail, then push the harness aside.

7 On 2.5L models, remove the nut that secures the radio capacitor to one of the fuel rail mounting studs and remove the capacitor.

8 Remove the fuel rail mounting fasteners, then remove both fuel rails and their injectors as an assembly.

9 Remove each fuel injector retaining clip with a pair of needle-nose pliers and remove the injector from its bore in the fuel rail. Remove and discard the upper and lower injector O-rings. Repeat this procedure for each injector.

➡**Note: Even if you only removed the fuel rail assembly to replace a single injector or a leaking O-ring, it's a good idea to remove all of the injectors from the fuel rail and replace all of the O-rings at the same time.**

10 Coat the new upper O-rings with clean engine oil and slide them into place on each of the fuel injectors. Coat the new lower O-rings with clean engine oil and install them on the lower ends of the injectors.

11 Coat the outside surface of each upper O-ring with clean engine oil, then insert each injector into its bore in the fuel rail. Install the isolators with new seals on the injectors, if equipped.

12 Install the injectors and fuel rail assembly on the intake manifold. Tighten the fuel rail mounting fasteners securely.

13 The remainder of installation is the reverse of removal.

14 Reconnect the cable to the negative battery terminal (see Chapter 5).

15 Turn the ignition switch to ON (but don't operate the starter). This activates the fuel pump for about two seconds, which builds up fuel pressure in the fuel lines and the fuel rail. Repeat this step two or three times, then check the fuel lines, fuel rails and injectors for fuel leaks.

11.19 Disconnect the injector electrical connectors (A, three not visible in this photo), then detach the harness retainers (B) from the fuel rail (3.0L model shown; 3.5L model similar)

11.21 Lower intake manifold bolt tightening sequence and fuel rail mounting bolts (3.0L models)

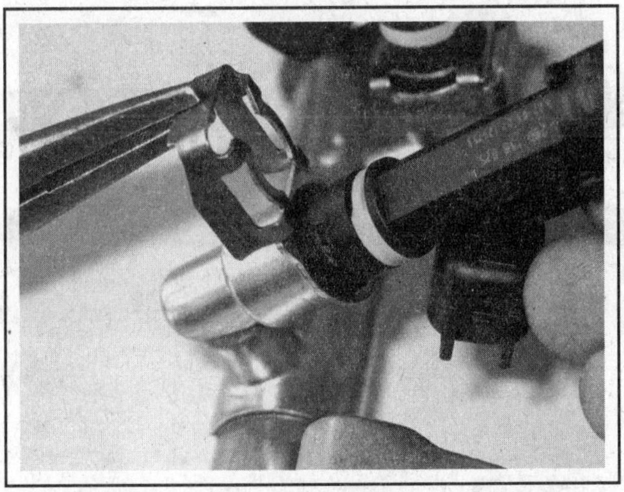

11.23 Before removing the injector retaining clips, note how they're installed to ensure that they're correctly reinstalled

11.24 Injector O-rings

V6 MODELS

➧ **Refer to illustrations 11.19, 11.21, 11.23, 11.24 and 11.27**

16 Remove the upper intake manifold (see Chapter 2B).

17 Disconnect the fuel supply line at the fuel rail (see *Disconnecting Fuel Line Fittings* on page 4-6).

18 On 3.0L models, use a trim removal tool to detach the two engine harness retainers from the left valve cover studs.

19 Disconnect the electrical connector from each fuel injector (see illustration).

20 Detach the three pin-type retainers from the fuel rail, push the wiring harness aside and remove the other three injector electrical connectors.

21 On 3.0L models, remove the eight lower intake manifold bolts in the reverse of the tightening sequence (see illustration), then remove the two lower intake manifolds and the fuel rail and injectors as a single assembly. Remove the fuel rail mounting bolts and pull the two lower intake manifolds off the injectors.

22 On 3.5L models, remove the four fuel rail mounting bolts, then remove the fuel rail and injectors as a single assembly.

23 Release the fuel injector retaining clip (see illustration) and remove each injector from its bore in the fuel rail.

24 Remove the upper and lower injector O-rings (see illustration) from each injector and discard them.

➡**Note: Even if you only removed the fuel rail assembly to replace a single injector or a leaking O-ring, it's a good idea to remove all of the injectors from the fuel rail and replace all of the O-rings at the same time.**

25 Coat the new upper O-rings with clean engine oil and slide them into place on each of the fuel injectors. Coat the new lower O-rings with clean engine oil and install them on the lower ends of the injectors.

26 Coat the outside surface of each upper O-ring with clean engine oil, then insert each injector into its bore in the fuel rail. Secure the

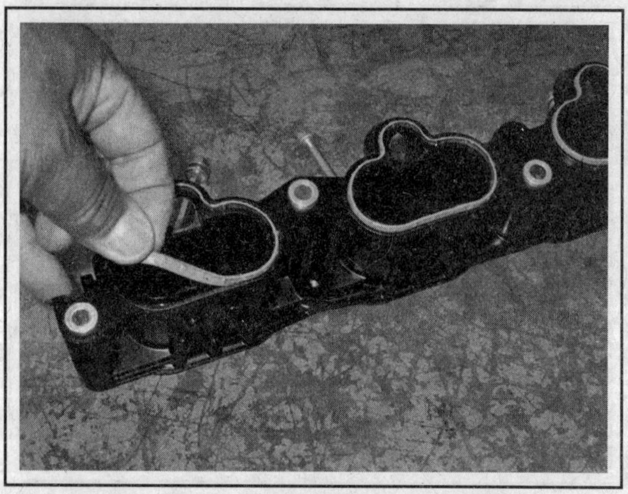

11.27 Remove and inspect the intake manifold gaskets

injectors to the fuel rail with the injector retaining clips.

27 On 3.0L models, remove the intake manifold gaskets and install new ones (see illustration).

28 On 3.0L models, install the intake manifolds on the injectors, then attach the fuel rail assembly to the intake manifolds, tightening the bolts by hand. Install the fuel rail and intake manifolds as a single assembly. Be sure to tighten the intake manifold bolts in the correct sequence (see illustration 11.21) to the torque listed in this Chapter's Specifications.

29 On all models, be sure to tighten the fuel rail bolts securely. The remainder of installation is the reverse of removal.

30 Reconnect the cable to the negative battery terminal (see Chapter 5). Then turn the ignition switch to ON (but don't operate the starter).This activates the fuel pump for about two seconds, which builds up fuel pressure in the fuel lines and the fuel rail. Repeat this step two or three times, then check the fuel lines, fuel rails and injectors for fuel leaks.

Specifications

Fuel system pressure (approximate)	56 to 62 psi (384 to 425 kPa)

Torque specifications

➡Note: One foot-pound (ft-lb) of torque is equivalent to 12 inch-pounds (in-lbs) of torque. Torque values below approximately 15 ft-lbs are expressed in inch-pounds, since most foot-pound torque wrenches are not accurate at these smaller values.

Throttle body mounting fasteners	89 in-lbs	10 Nm
Intake manifold bolts (3.0L V6 models)	89 in-lbs	10 Nm

5

ENGINE ELECTRICAL SYSTEMS

Section

1 General information and precautions

GENERAL INFORMATION

Ignition system

The electronic ignition system consists of the Crankshaft Position (CKP) sensor, the Camshaft Position (CMP) sensor, the Knock Sensor (KS), the Powertrain Control Module (PCM), the ignition switch, the battery, the individual ignition coils or a coil pack, and the spark plugs. For more information on the CKP, CMP and KS sensors, as well as the PCM, refer to Chapter 6.

Charging system

The charging system includes the alternator (with an integral voltage regulator), the Powertrain Control Module (PCM), the Body Control Module (BCM), a charge indicator light on the dash, the battery, a fuse or fusible link and the wiring connecting all of these components. The charging system supplies electrical power for the ignition system, the lights, the radio, etc. The alternator is driven by a drivebelt.

Starting system

The starting system consists of the battery, the ignition switch, the starter relay, the Powertrain Control Module (PCM), the Body Control Module (BCM), the Transmission Range (TR) switch, the starter motor and solenoid assembly, and the wiring connecting all of the components.

PRECAUTIONS

Always observe the following precautions when working on the electrical system:

a) *Be extremely careful when servicing engine electrical components. They are easily damaged if checked, connected or handled improperly.*
b) *Never leave the ignition switched on for long periods of time when the engine is not running.*
c) *Never disconnect the battery cables while the engine is running.*
d) *Maintain correct polarity when connecting battery cables from another vehicle during jump starting - see the "Booster battery (jump) starting" Section at the front of this manual.*
e) *Always disconnect the cable from the negative battery terminal before working on the electrical system, but read the battery disconnection procedure first (see Section 3).*

It's also a good idea to review the safety-related information regarding the engine electrical systems located in the *Safety first!* Section at the front of this manual before beginning any operation included in this Chapter.

2 Troubleshooting

IGNITION SYSTEM

1 If a malfunction occurs in the ignition system, do not immediately assume that any particular part is causing the problem. First, check the following items:

a) *Make sure that the cable clamps at the battery terminals are clean and tight.*
b) *Test the condition of the battery (see Steps 21 through 24). If it doesn't pass all the tests, replace it.*
c) *Check the ignition coil or coil pack connections.*
d) *Check any relevant fuses in the engine compartment fuse and relay box (see Chapter 12). If they're burned, determine the cause and repair the circuit.*

Check

Refer to illustration 2.3

WARNING:

Because of the high voltage generated by the ignition system, use extreme care when performing a procedure involving ignition components.

Note: The ignition system components on these vehicles are difficult to diagnose. In the event of ignition system failure that you can't diagnose, have the vehicle tested at a dealer service department or other qualified auto repair facility.

Note: You'll need a spark tester for the following test. Spark testers are available at most auto supply stores.

2 If the engine turns over but won't start, verify that there is sufficient ignition voltage to fire the spark plugs as follows.

3 On models with a coil-over-plug type ignition system, remove a coil and install the tester between the boot at the lower end of the coil and the spark plug (see illustration). On models with spark plug wires, disconnect a spark plug wire from a spark plug and install the tester between the spark plug wire boot and the spark plug.

4 Crank the engine and note whether or not the tester flashes.

CAUTION:

Do NOT crank the engine or allow it to run for more than five seconds; running the engine for more than five seconds may set a Diagnostic Trouble Code (DTC) for a cylinder misfire.

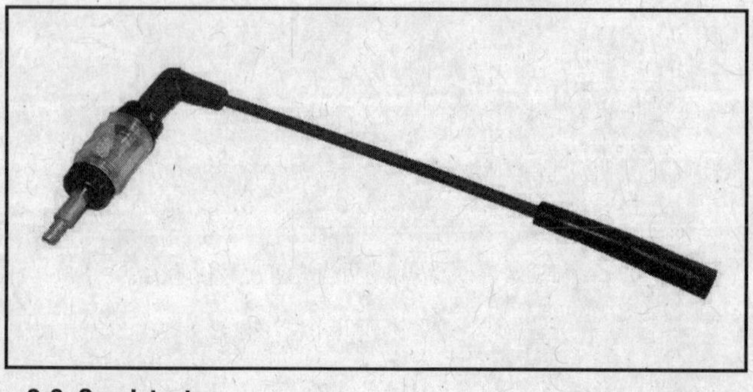

2.3 Spark tester

Models with a coil-over-plug type ignition system

5 If the tester flashes during cranking, the coil is delivering sufficient voltage to the spark plug to fire it. Repeat this test for each cylinder to verify that the other coils are OK.

6 If the tester doesn't flash, remove a coil from another cylinder and swap it for the one being tested. If the tester now flashes, you know that the original coil is bad. If the tester still doesn't flash, the PCM or wiring harness is probably defective. Have the PCM checked out by a dealer service department or other qualified repair shop (testing the PCM is beyond the scope of the do-it-yourselfer because it requires expensive special tools).

7 If the tester flashes during cranking but a misfire code (related to the cylinder being tested) has been stored, the spark plug could be fouled or defective.

Models with spark plug wires

8 If the tester flashes during cranking, sufficient voltage is reaching the spark plug to fire it.

9 Repeat this test on the remaining cylinders.

10 Proceed on this basis until you have verified that there's a good spark from each spark plug wire. If there is, then you have verified that the coils in the coil pack are functioning correctly and that the spark plug wires are OK.

11 If there is no spark from a spark plug wire, then either the coil is bad, the plug wire is bad or a connection at one end of the plug wire is loose. Assuming that you're using new plug wires or known good wires, then the coil is probably defective. Also inspect the coil pack electrical connector. Make sure that it's clean, tight and in good condition.

12 If all the coils are firing correctly, but the engine misfires, then one or more of the plugs might be fouled. Remove and check the spark plugs or install new ones (see Chapter 1).

13 No further testing of the ignition system is possible without special tools. If the problem persists, have the ignition system tested by a dealer service department or other qualified repair shop.

CHARGING SYSTEM

14 If a malfunction occurs in the charging system, do not automatically assume the alternator is causing the problem. First check the following items:

a) *Check the drivebelt tension and condition, as described in Chapter 1. Replace it if it's worn or deteriorated.*
b) *Make sure the alternator mounting bolts are tight.*
c) *Inspect the alternator wiring harness and the connectors at the alternator and voltage regulator. They must be in good condition, tight and have no corrosion.*
d) *Check the fusible link (if equipped) or main fuse in the underhood fuse/relay box. If it is burned, determine the cause, repair the circuit and replace the link or fuse (the vehicle will not start and/or the accessories will not work if the fusible link or main fuse is blown).*
e) *Start the engine and check the alternator for abnormal noises (a shrieking or squealing sound indicates a bad bearing).*
f) *Check the battery. Make sure it's fully charged and in good condition (one bad cell in a battery can cause overcharging by the alternator).*
g) *Disconnect the battery cables (negative first, then positive). Inspect the battery posts and the cable clamps for corrosion. Clean them thoroughly if necessary (see Chapter 1). Reconnect the cables (positive first, negative last).*

Alternator - check

15 Use a voltmeter to check the battery voltage with the engine off. It should be at least 12.6 volts (see illustration 2.21).

16 Start the engine and check the battery voltage again. It should now be approximately 13.5 to 15 volts.

17 If the voltage reading is more or less than the specified charging voltage, the voltage regulator is probably defective, which will require replacement of the alternator (the voltage regulator is not replaceable separately). Remove the alternator and have it bench tested (most auto parts stores will do this for you).

18 The charging system (battery) light on the instrument cluster lights up when the ignition key is turned to ON, but it should go out when the engine starts.

19 If the charging system light stays on after the engine has been started, there is a problem with the charging system. Before replacing the alternator, check the battery condition, alternator belt tension and electrical cable connections.

20 If replacing the alternator doesn't restore voltage to the specified range, have the charging system tested by a dealer service department or other qualified repair shop.

Battery - check

Refer to illustrations 2.21 and 2.23

21 Check the battery state of charge. Visually inspect the indicator eye on the top of the battery (if equipped with one); if the indicator eye is black in color, charge the battery as described in Chapter 1. Next perform an open circuit voltage test using a digital voltmeter.

Note: The battery's surface charge must be removed before accurate voltage measurements can be made. Turn on the high beams for ten seconds, then turn them off and let the vehicle stand for two minutes.

With the engine and all accessories Off, touch the negative probe of the voltmeter to the negative terminal of the battery and the positive probe to the positive terminal of the battery (see illustration). The battery voltage should be 12.6 volts or slightly above. If the battery is less than the specified voltage, charge the battery before proceeding to the next test. Do not proceed with the battery load test unless the battery charge is correct.

2.21 To test the open circuit voltage of the battery, touch the black probe of the voltmeter to the negative terminal and the red probe to the positive terminal of the battery; a fully charged battery should be at least 12.6 volts

2.23 Connect a battery load tester to the battery and check the battery condition under load following the tool manufacturer's instructions

22 Disconnect the negative battery cable, then the positive cable from the battery.

23 Perform a battery load test. An accurate check of the battery condition can only be performed with a load tester (see illustration). This test evaluates the ability of the battery to operate the starter and other accessories during periods of high current draw. Connect the load tester to the battery terminals. Load test the battery according to the tool manufacturer's instructions. This tool increases the load demand (current draw) on the battery.

24 Maintain the load on the battery for 15 seconds and observe that the battery voltage does not drop below 9.6 volts. If the battery condition is weak or defective, the tool will indicate this condition immediately.

➡**Note: Cold temperatures will cause the minimum voltage reading to drop slightly. Follow the chart given in the manufacturer's instructions to compensate for cold climates. Minimum load voltage for freezing temperatures (32 degrees F) should be approximately 9.1 volts.**

STARTING SYSTEM

The starter rotates, but the engine doesn't

25 Remove the starter (see Section 8). Check the overrunning clutch and bench test the starter to make sure the drive mechanism extends fully for proper engagement with the flywheel ring gear. If it doesn't, replace the starter.

26 Check the flywheel ring gear for missing teeth and other damage. With the ignition turned off, rotate the flywheel so you can check the entire ring gear.

The starter is noisy

27 If the solenoid is making a chattering noise, first check the battery (see Steps 21 through 24). If the battery is okay, check the cables and connections.

28 If you hear a grinding, crashing metallic sound when you turn the key to Start, check for loose starter mounting bolts. If they're tight, remove the starter and inspect the teeth on the starter pinion gear and flywheel ring gear. Look for missing or damaged teeth.

29 If the starter sounds fine when you first turn the key to Start, but then stops rotating the engine and emits a zinging sound, the problem is probably a defective starter drive that's not staying engaged with the ring gear. Replace the starter.

The starter rotates slowly

30 Check the battery (see Steps 21 through 24).

31 If the battery is okay, verify all connections (at the battery, the starter solenoid and motor) are clean, corrosion-free and tight. Make sure the cables aren't frayed or damaged.

32 Check that the starter mounting bolts are tight so it grounds properly. Also check the pinion gear and flywheel ring gear for evidence of a mechanical bind (galling, deformed gear teeth or other damage).

The starter does not rotate at all

33 Check the battery (see Steps 21 through 24).

34 If the battery is okay, verify all connections (at the battery, the starter solenoid and motor) are clean, corrosion-free and tight. Make sure the cables aren't frayed or damaged.

35 Check all of the fuses in the underhood fuse/relay box.

36 Check that the starter mounting bolts are tight so it grounds properly.

37 Check for voltage at the starter solenoid "S" terminal when the ignition key is turned to the start position. If voltage is present, replace the starter/solenoid assembly. If no voltage is present, the problem could be the starter relay, the Transmission Range (TR) switch (see Chapter 6) or clutch start switch (see Chapter 8), or with an electrical connector somewhere in the circuit (see the wiring diagrams at the end of Chapter 12). Also, on many modern vehicles, the Powertrain Control Module (PCM) and the Body Control Module (BCM) control the voltage signal to the starter solenoid; on such vehicles a special scan tool is required for diagnosis.

3 Battery - disconnection

✻✻ CAUTION:

Always disconnect the cable from the negative battery terminal FIRST and hook it up LAST or the battery may be shorted by the tool being used to loosen the cable clamps.

Some systems on the vehicle require battery power to be available at all times, either to maintain continuous operation (alarm system, power door locks, etc.), or to maintain control unit memory (radio station presets, Powertrain Control Module and other control units). When the battery is disconnected, the power that maintains these systems is cut. So, before you disconnect the battery, please note that on a vehicle with power door locks, it's a wise precaution to remove the key from the ignition and to keep it with you, so that it does not get locked inside if the power door locks should engage accidentally when the battery is reconnected!

Devices known as "memory-savers" can be used to avoid some of these problems. Precise details vary according to the device used. The typical memory saver is plugged into the cigarette lighter and is connected to a spare battery. Then the vehicle battery can be disconnected from the electrical system. The memory saver will provide sufficient current to maintain audio unit security codes, PCM memory, etc. and will provide power to always hot circuits such as the clock and radio memory circuits.

WARNING 1:

Some memory savers deliver a considerable amount of current in order to keep vehicle systems operational after the main battery is disconnected. If you're using a memory saver, make sure that the circuit concerned is actually open before servicing it.

WARNING 2:

If you're going to work near any of the airbag system components, the battery MUST be disconnected and a memory saver must NOT be used. If a memory saver is used, power will be supplied to the airbag, which means that it could accidentally deploy and cause serious personal injury.

To disconnect the battery for service procedures requiring power to be cut from the vehicle, loosen the cable end bolt and disconnect the cable from the negative battery terminal. Isolate the cable end to prevent it from coming into accidental contact with the battery terminal.

4 Battery - removal and installation

Refer to illustrations 4.1a and 4.1b

1 Disconnect the cable from the negative battery terminal first, then disconnect the cable from the positive battery terminal (see illustrations).

2 Remove the battery hold-down clamp.

3 Lift out the battery. Be careful - it's heavy.

Note: Battery straps and handlers are available at most auto parts stores for reasonable prices. They make it easier to remove and carry the battery.

4 If you are replacing the battery, make sure you get one that's identical, with the same dimensions, amperage rating, cold cranking rating, etc. Also, be sure to remove the heat shield from the old battery and install it on the new battery.

5 Installation is the reverse of removal. Be sure to connect the positive cable first and the negative cable last.

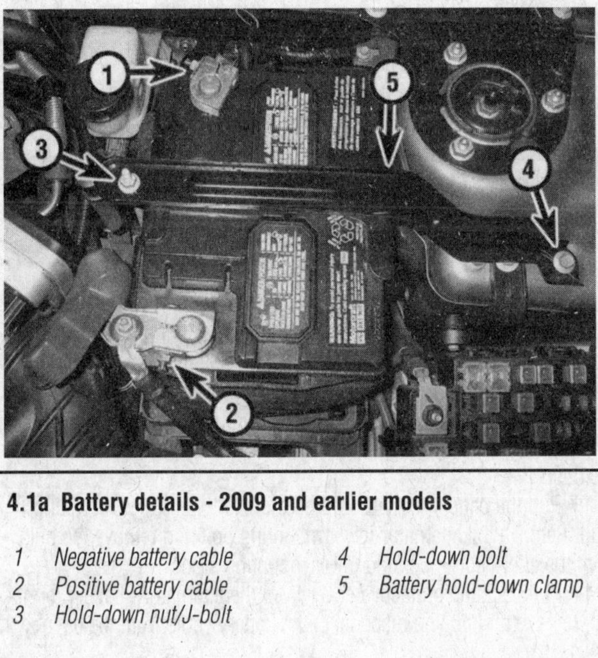

4.1a Battery details - 2009 and earlier models

1 Negative battery cable
2 Positive battery cable
3 Hold-down nut/J-bolt
4 Hold-down bolt
5 Battery hold-down clamp

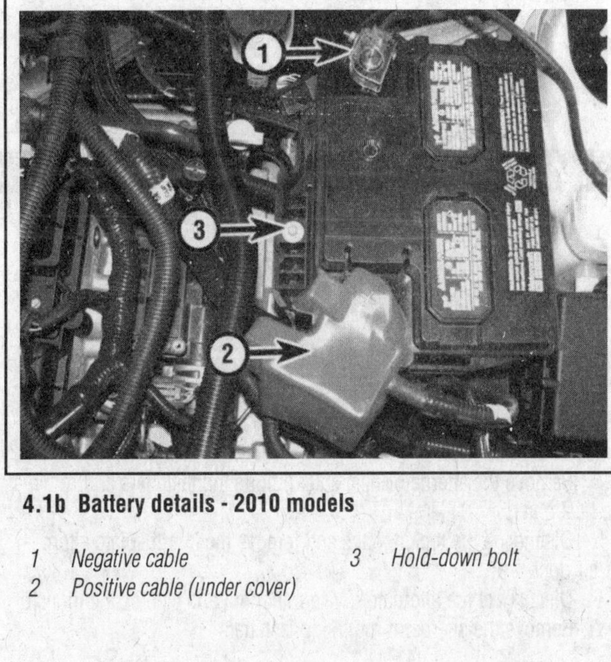

4.1b Battery details - 2010 models

1 Negative cable
2 Positive cable (under cover)
3 Hold-down bolt

5 Battery cables - replacement

1 When removing the cables, always disconnect the cable from the negative battery terminal first and hook it up last, or you might accidentally short out the battery with the tool you're using to loosen the cable clamps. Even if you're only replacing the cable for the positive terminal, be sure to disconnect the negative cable from the battery first.

2 Disconnect the old cables from the battery, then trace each of them to their opposite ends and disconnect them. Be sure to note the routing of each cable before disconnecting it to ensure correct installation.

3 If you are replacing any of the old cables, take them with you when buying new cables. It is vitally important that you replace the cables with identical parts.

4 Clean the threads of the solenoid or ground connection with a wire brush to remove rust and corrosion. Apply a light coat of battery terminal corrosion inhibitor or petroleum jelly to the threads to prevent future corrosion.

5 Attach the cable to the solenoid or ground connection and tighten the mounting nut/bolt securely.

6 Before connecting a new cable to the battery, make sure that it reaches the battery post without having to be stretched.

7 Connect the cable to the positive battery terminal first, then connect the ground cable to the negative battery terminal.

6 Ignition coils - replacement

Refer to illustration 6.2

1 Disconnect the cable from the negative battery terminal (see Section 3).

2 Disconnect the electrical connector from the ignition coil (see illustration).

3 Remove the mounting fastener from the ignition coil.

4 Grasp the coil firmly and pull it off the spark plug.

5 Installation is the reverse of removal.

6.2 Ignition coil details (3.0L V6 engine shown, other engines similar)

1 Electrical connector
2 Mounting fastener

7 Alternator - removal and installation

1 Disconnect the cable from the negative battery terminal (see Section 3).

2 Remove the drivebelt (see Chapter 1).

2.3L FOUR-CYLINDER MODELS

3 Remove the alternator upper air duct mounting bolt and nuts and remove the upper duct.

4 Remove the alternator heat shield mounting fasteners and remove the heat shield.

5 Disengage the locking tabs and remove the intermediate alternator air duct.

6 Disconnect the alternator B+ terminal nut and electrical connector.

7 Remove the alternator mounting fasteners.

2.5L FOUR-CYLINDER MODELS

8 Loosen the right front wheel lug nuts. Raise the front of the vehicle and place it securely on jackstands. Remove the right front wheel.

9 Remove the splash shield screws and pushpins and remove the splash shield (see *Front fender - removal and installation* in Chapter 11).

10 Working from above in the engine compartment, depress the locking tab to disengage the alternator lower cooling duct and remove the duct.

11 Pull the battery harness clip off the alternator lower mounting stud. Remove the alternator lower mounting bolt and remove the nuts from the alternator upper and lower mounting studs.

12 Pull back the protective cover from the alternator's battery terminal, remove the nut and disconnect the battery cable from the alternator.

7.16 Alternator battery terminal (A) and electrical connector (B)

7.17 Alternator upper mounting bolt (3.0L V6 models)

Set the battery cable aside. Disconnect the electrical connector from the alternator.

13 Remove the two alternator mounting studs and remove the alternator.

14 Remove the three upper cooling duct screws and remove the duct from the alternator.

3.0L V6 MODELS

➧ Refer to illustrations 7.16, 7.17 and 7.18

15 Remove the air conditioning compressor (see Chapter 3).

16 Push back the protective cover from the alternator's battery terminal, remove the nut and disconnect the battery cable from the alternator (see illustration). Disconnect the electrical connector from the alternator.

17 Remove the upper alternator mounting bolt (see illustration).

18 Pull the harness clip off the stud on the alternator lower mounting bolt, then remove the lower mounting bolts (see illustration) and remove the alternator.

3.5L V6 MODELS

19 Drain the engine oil and remove the oil filter (see Chapter 1).

20 Remove the air conditioning compressor (see Chapter 3).

21 Push back the protective cover from the alternator's battery terminal, remove the nut and disconnect the battery cable from the alternator (see illustration 7.16). Disconnect the electrical connector from the alternator.

22 Remove the alternator upper mounting stud nut.

23 Remove the alternator lower mounting bolt and remove the alternator.

ALL MODELS

24 If you're replacing the alternator, take the old one with you when purchasing the replacement unit. Make sure that the new/rebuilt unit

7.18 Alternator lower mounting bolts (3.0L V6 models)

looks identical to the old alternator. Look at the electrical terminals on the backside of the alternator. They should be the same in number, size and location as the terminals on the old alternator. Finally, look at the identification numbers. They will be stamped into the housing or printed on a tag attached to the housing. Make sure that the ID numbers are the same on both alternators.

25 Many new/rebuilt alternators DO NOT have a pulley installed, so you might have to swap the pulley from the old unit to the new/rebuilt one. When buying an alternator, find out the store's policy regarding pulley swaps. Some stores perform this service free of charge. If your local auto parts store doesn't offer this service, you'll have to purchase a puller for removing the pulley and do it yourself.

26 Installation is the reverse of removal. Be sure to tighten the alternator mounting bolts securely.

27 Reconnect the cable to the negative terminal of the battery. Check the charging voltage (see Section 2) to verify that the alternator is operating correctly.

8 Starter motor - removal and installation

FOUR-CYLINDER MODELS

1 Detach the cable from the negative terminal of the battery (see Section 3).

2 Raise the vehicle and support it securely on jackstands. Remove the underbody cover.

3 Disconnect the starter motor solenoid wire nut and the starter motor battery cable nut and disconnect both wires from the starter.

4 On 2.3L models, pull the wire harness clip off the starter mounting stud, then remove the mounting stud and mounting bolt and remove the starter. On 2.5L models, remove the nut that secures the ground wire to the starter mounting stud and disconnect the ground wire from the stud, then remove the mounting stud and mounting bolt and remove the starter.

5 Installation is the reverse of removal. Be sure to tighten the starter mounting stud and bolt securely.

V6 MODELS

➧ Refer to illustrations 8.7 and 8.8

6 Remove the battery (see Section 4) and the battery tray.

7 Remove the starter motor solenoid wire nut and the starter motor battery cable nut, then disconnect both wires from the starter motor (see illustration).

8 Remove the starter motor mounting fasteners (see illustration) and remove the starter motor.

9 Installation is the reverse of removal.

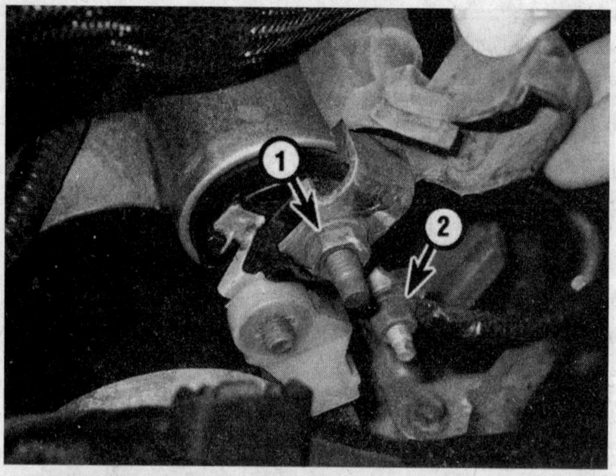

8.7 Starter motor details (3.0L V6 model shown, 3.5L V6 similar)

1 Starter motor battery terminal
2 Starter solenoid terminal

8.8 Starter motor mounting bolt (other bolt not visible) (3.0L V6 model shown, 3.5L V6 similar)

6

EMISSIONS AND ENGINE CONTROL SYSTEMS

Section

1 General information

To prevent pollution of the atmosphere from incompletely burned and evaporating gases, and to maintain good driveability and fuel economy, a number of emission control systems are incorporated. They include the:

CATALYTIC CONVERTER

A catalytic converter is an emission control device in the exhaust system that reduces certain pollutants in the exhaust gas stream. There are two types of converters: oxidation converters and reduction converters.

Oxidation converters contain a monolithic substrate (a ceramic honeycomb) coated with the semi-precious metals platinum and palladium. An oxidation catalyst reduces unburned hydrocarbons (HC) and carbon monoxide (CO) by adding oxygen to the exhaust stream as it passes through the substrate, which, in the presence of high temperature and the catalyst materials, converts the HC and CO to water vapor ($H2O$) and carbon dioxide ($CO2$).

Reduction converters contain a monolithic substrate coated with platinum and rhodium. A reduction catalyst reduces oxides of nitrogen (NOx) by removing oxygen, which in the presence of high temperature and the catalyst material produces nitrogen (N) and carbon dioxide ($CO2$).

Catalytic converters that combine both types of catalysts in one assembly are known as "three-way catalysts" or TWCs. A TWC can reduce all three pollutants.

EVAPORATIVE EMISSIONS CONTROL (EVAP) SYSTEM

The Evaporative Emissions Control (EVAP) system prevents fuel system vapors (which contain unburned hydrocarbons) from escaping into the atmosphere. On warm days, vapors trapped inside the fuel tank expand until the pressure reaches a certain threshold. Then the fuel vapors are routed from the fuel tank through the fuel vapor vent valve and the fuel vapor control valve to the EVAP canister, where they're stored temporarily until the next time the vehicle is operated. When the conditions are right (engine warmed up, vehicle up to speed, moderate or heavy load on the engine, etc.) the PCM opens the canister purge valve, which allows fuel vapors to be drawn from the canister into the intake manifold. Once in the intake manifold, the fuel vapors mix with incoming air before being drawn through the intake ports into the combustion chambers where they're burned up with the rest of the air/fuel mixture. The EVAP system is complex and virtually impossible to troubleshoot without the right tools and training.

EXHAUST GAS RECIRCULATION (EGR) SYSTEM

The EGR system reduces oxides of nitrogen by recirculating exhaust gases from the exhaust manifold, through the EGR valve and intake manifold, then back to the combustion chambers, where it mixes with the incoming air/fuel mixture before being consumed. These recirculated exhaust gases dilute the incoming air/fuel mixture, which cools the combustion chambers, thereby reducing NOx emissions.

The EGR system consists of the Powertrain Control Module (PCM), the EGR valve, the EGR valve position sensor and various other information sensors that the PCM uses to determine when to open the EGR valve. The degree to which the EGR valve is opened is referred to as "EGR valve lift." The PCM is programmed to produce the ideal EGR valve lift for varying operating conditions. The EGR valve position sensor, which is an integral part of the EGR valve, detects the amount of EGR valve lift and sends this information to the PCM. The PCM then compares it with the appropriate EGR valve lift for the operating conditions. The PCM increases current flow to the EGR valve to increase valve lift and reduces the current to reduce the amount of lift. If EGR flow is inappropriate to the operating conditions (idle, cold engine, etc.) the PCM simply cuts the current to the EGR valve and the valve closes.

SECONDARY AIR INJECTION (AIR) SYSTEM

Some models are equipped with a secondary air injection (AIR) system. The secondary air injection system is used to reduce tailpipe emissions on initial engine start-up. The system uses an electric motor/pump assembly, relay, vacuum valve/solenoid, air shut-off valve, check valves and tubing to inject fresh air directly into the exhaust manifolds. The fresh air (oxygen) reacts with the exhaust gas in the catalytic converter to reduce HC and CO levels. The air pump and solenoid are controlled by the PCM through the AIR relay. During initial start-up, the PCM energizes the AIR relay, the relay supplies battery voltage to the air pump and the vacuum valve/solenoid, engine vacuum is applied to the air shut-off valve which opens and allows air to flow through the tubing into the exhaust manifolds. The PCM will operate the air pump until closed loop operation is reached (approximately four minutes). During normal operation, the check valves prevent exhaust backflow into the system.

POWERTRAIN CONTROL MODULE (PCM)

The Powertrain Control Module (PCM) is the brain of the engine management system. It also controls a wide variety of other vehicle systems. In order to program the new PCM, the dealer needs the vehicle as well as the new PCM. If you're planning to replace the PCM with a new one, there is no point in trying to do so at home because you won't be able to program it yourself.

POSITIVE CRANKCASE VENTILATION (PCV) SYSTEM

The Positive Crankcase Ventilation (PCV) system reduces hydrocarbon emissions by scavenging crankcase vapors, which are rich in unburned hydrocarbons. A PCV valve or orifice regulates the flow of gases into the intake manifold in proportion to the amount of intake vacuum available.

The PCV system generally consists of the fresh air inlet hose, the PCV valve or orifice and the crankcase ventilation hose (or PCV hose). The fresh air inlet hose connects the air intake duct to a pipe on the valve cover. The crankcase ventilation hose (or PCV hose) connects the PCV valve or orifice in the valve cover to the intake manifold.

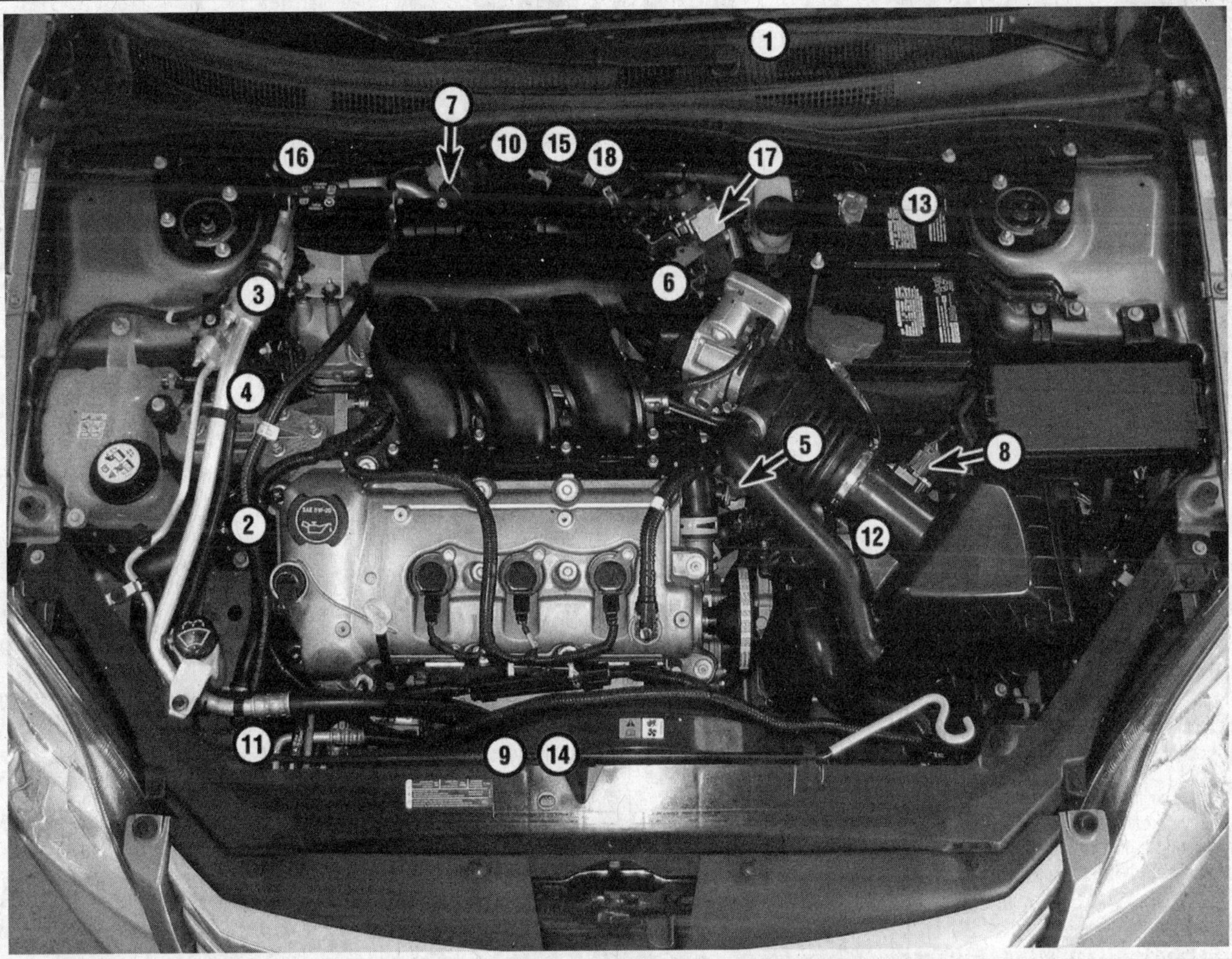

Emissions and engine control components (3.0L V6 engine shown):

1 *Accelerator Pedal Position (APP) sensor (at the top of accelerator pedal assembly)*
2 *Camshaft Position (CMP) sensor (front cylinder head, at right end of head, near intake camshaft)*
3 *Camshaft Position (CMP) sensor (rear cylinder head, at right end of head, near intake camshaft)*
4 *Crankshaft Position (CKP) sensor (lower right rear corner of block, near crankshaft pulley)*
5 *Engine Coolant Temperature (ECT) sensor (on coolant passage at left end of engine, behind water pump)*
6 *Knock sensor (on lower left rear side of engine block)*
7 *Manifold Absolute Pressure (MAP) sensor*
8 *Mass Air Flow/Intake Air Temperature (MAF/IAT) sensor*
9 *Upstream and downstream oxygen sensor, front cylinder head (exhaust manifold/catalyst and exhaust pipe)*
10 *Upstream and downstream oxygen sensor, rear cylinder head (exhaust manifold/catalyst)*
11 *Power Steering Pressure (PSP) switch (on underside of power steering pump)*
12 *Transmission Control Module (TCM) with integral TR sensor, 6-speed automatic (on top of transaxle, at selector shaft)*
13 *Powertrain Control Module (PCM) (behind and below the battery box)*
14 *Front catalytic converter (integral component of front exhaust manifold)*
15 *Rear catalytic converter (integral component of rear exhaust manifold)*
16 *EVAP canister purge solenoid valve (lower right rear corner of engine compartment, below lower cowl cover)*
17 *Exhaust Gas Recirculation (EGR) valve*
18 *Positive Crankcase Ventilation (PCV) valve (on left end of rear valve cover)*

Information Sensors

Accelerator Pedal Position (APP) sensor - as you press the accelerator pedal, the APP sensor alters its voltage signal to the PCM in proportion to the angle of the pedal, and the PCM commands a motor inside the throttle body to open or close the throttle plate accordingly

Camshaft Position (CMP) sensor - produces a signal that the PCM uses to identify the number 1 cylinder and to time the firing sequence of the fuel injectors

Crankshaft Position (CKP) sensor - produces a signal that the PCM uses to calculate engine speed and crankshaft position, which enables it to synchronize ignition timing with fuel injector timing, and to detect misfires

Engine Coolant Temperature (ECT) sensor - a thermistor (temperature-sensitive variable resistor) that sends a voltage signal to the PCM, which uses this data to determine the temperature of the engine coolant

Fuel tank pressure sensor - measures the fuel tank pressure and controls fuel tank pressure by signaling the EVAP system to purge the fuel tank vapors when the pressure becomes excessive

Intake Air Temperature (IAT) sensor - monitors the temperature of the air entering the engine and sends a signal to the PCM to determine injector pulse-width (the duration of each injector's on-time) and to adjust spark timing (to prevent spark knock)

Knock sensor - a piezoelectric crystal that oscillates in proportion to engine vibration which produces a voltage output that is monitored by the PCM. This retards the ignition timing when the oscillation exceeds a certain threshold

Manifold Absolute Pressure (MAP) sensor - monitors the pressure or vacuum inside the intake manifold. The PCM uses this data to determine engine load so that it can alter the ignition advance and fuel enrichment

Mass Air Flow (MAF) sensor - measures the amount of intake air drawn into the engine. It uses a hot-wire sensing element to measure the amount of air entering the engine

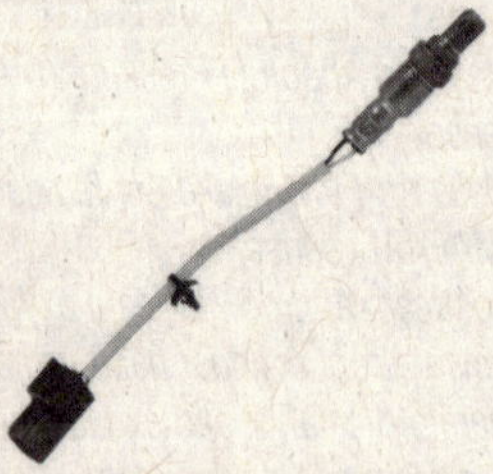

Oxygen sensors - generates a small variable voltage signal in proportion to the difference between the oxygen content in the exhaust stream and the oxygen content in the ambient air. The PCM uses this information to maintain the proper air/fuel ratio. A second oxygen sensor monitors the efficiency of the catalytic converter

Throttle Position (TP) sensor - a potentiometer that generates a voltage signal that varies in relation to the opening angle of the throttle plate inside the throttle body. Works with the PCM and other sensors to calculate injector pulse width (the duration of each injector's on-time)

Photos courtesy of Wells Manufacturing, except APP and MAF sensors.

2 On Board Diagnosis (OBD) system

GENERAL DESCRIPTION

1 All models are equipped with the second generation OBD-II system. This system consists of an on-board computer known as the Powertrain Control Module (PCM), and information sensors, which monitor various functions of the engine and send data to the PCM. This system incorporates a series of diagnostic monitors that detect and identify fuel injection and emissions control system faults and store the information in the computer memory. This system also tests sensors and output actuators, diagnoses drive cycles, freezes data and clears codes.

2 The PCM is the brain of the electronically controlled fuel and emissions system. It receives data from a number of sensors and other electronic components (switches, relays, etc.). Based on the information it receives, the PCM generates output signals to control various relays, solenoids (fuel injectors) and other actuators. The PCM is specifically calibrated to optimize the emissions, fuel economy and driveability of the vehicle.

3 It isn't a good idea to attempt diagnosis or replacement of the PCM or emission control components at home while the vehicle is under warranty. Because of a federally-mandated warranty which covers the emissions system components and because any owner-induced damage to the PCM, the sensors and/or the control devices may void this warranty, take the vehicle to a dealer service department if the PCM or a system component malfunctions.

SCAN TOOL INFORMATION

Refer to illustrations 2.4a and 2.4b

4 Because extracting the Diagnostic Trouble Codes (DTCs) from an engine management system is now the first step in troubleshooting many computer-controlled systems and components, a code reader, at the very least, will be required (see illustration). More powerful scan tools can also perform many of the diagnostics once associated with expensive factory scan tools (see illustration). If you're planning to obtain a generic scan tool for your vehicle, make sure that it's compatible with OBD-II systems. If you don't plan to purchase a code reader or scan tool and don't have access to one, you can have the codes extracted by a dealer service department or an independent repair shop.

Note: Some auto parts stores even provide this service.

2.4a Simple code readers are an economical way to extract trouble codes when the CHECK ENGINE light comes on

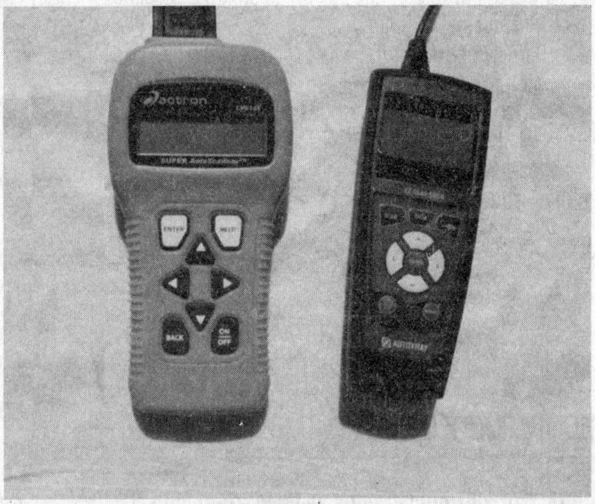

2.4b Hand-held scan tools like these can extract computer codes and also perform diagnostics

3 Obtaining and clearing Diagnostic Trouble Codes (DTCs)

All models covered by this manual are equipped with on-board diagnostics. When the PCM recognizes a malfunction in a monitored emission or engine control system, component or circuit, it turns on the Malfunction Indicator Light (MIL) on the dash. The PCM will continue to display the MIL until the problem is fixed and the Diagnostic Trouble Code (DTC) is cleared from the PCM's memory. You'll need a scan tool to access any DTCs stored in the PCM.

Before outputting any DTCs stored in the PCM, thoroughly inspect ALL electrical connectors and hoses. Make sure that all electrical connections are tight, clean and free of corrosion. And make sure that all hoses are correctly connected, fit tightly and are in good condition (no cracks or tears).

ACCESSING THE DTCS

➧ Refer to illustration 3.1

1 The Diagnostic Trouble Codes (DTCs) can only be accessed with a code reader or scan tool. Professional scan tools are expensive, but relatively inexpensive generic code readers or scan tools (see illustrations 2.4a and 2.4b) are available at most auto parts stores. Simply plug the connector of the scan tool into the diagnostic connector (see illustration). Then follow the instructions included with the scan tool to extract the DTCs.

2 Once you have outputted all of the stored DTCs, look them up on the accompanying DTC chart.

3 After troubleshooting the source of each DTC, make any necessary repairs or replace the defective component(s).

Clearing the DTCs

4 Clear the DTCs with the code reader or scan tool in accordance with the instructions provided by the tool's manufacturer.

DIAGNOSTIC TROUBLE CODES

5 The accompanying tables are a list of the Diagnostic Trouble Codes (DTCs) that can be accessed by a do-it-yourselfer working at home (there are many, many more DTCs available to professional mechanics with proprietary scan tools and software, but those codes cannot be accessed by a generic scan tool). If, after you have checked and repaired the connectors, wire harness and vacuum hoses (if applicable) for an emission-related system, component or circuit, the problem persists, have the vehicle checked by a dealer service department or other qualified repair shop.

3.1 The Data Link Connector (DLC) is located under the lower edge of the dash, to the left of the steering column

OBD-II TROUBLE CODES

➡Note: Not all trouble codes apply to all models.

Code	Probable cause
P0010	Intake camshaft position actuator, open circuit (Bank 1)
P0011	Intake camshaft position timing over-advanced (Bank 1)
P0012	Intake camshaft position timing, over-retarded (Bank 1)
P013A	Oxygen sensor slow response, rich to lean (Bank 1, Sensor 2)
P013C	Oxygen sensor slow response, rich to lean (Bank 2, Sensor 2)
P013E	Oxygen sensor delayed response, rich to lean (Bank 1, Sensor 2)
P014A	Oxygen sensor delayed response, rich to lean (Bank 2, Sensor 2)

Code	Probable cause
P0016	Crankshaft position-to-camshaft position correlation (Bank 1)
P0018	Crankshaft position-to-camshaft position correlation (Bank 2)
P0020	Intake camshaft position actuator, open circuit (Bank 2)
P0201	Injector open circuit, cylinder 1
P0202	Injector open circuit, cylinder 2
P0203	Injector open circuit, cylinder 3
P0204	Injector open circuit, cylinder 4
P0205	Injector open circuit, cylinder 5
P0206	Injector open circuit, cylinder 6
P0021	Intake camshaft position timing over-advanced (Bank 2)
P0022	Intake camshaft position timing over-retarded (Bank 2)
P025A	Fuel pump module control circuit open
P025B	Fuel pump module control circuit range or performance problem
P0030	Oxygen sensor heater control circuit (Bank 1, Sensor 1)
P0301	Cylinder 1 misfire
P0302	Cylinder 2 misfire
P0303	Cylinder 3 misfire
P0304	Cylinder 4 misfire
P0305	Cylinder 5 misfire
P0306	Cylinder 6 misfire
P0040	Oxygen sensor signals swapped (Bank 1, Sensor 1/Bank 2, Sensor 1)
P0041	Oxygen sensor signals swapped (Bank 1, Sensor 2/Bank 2, Sensor 2)
P0050	Oxygen sensor heater control circuit (Bank 2, Sensor 1)
P050A	Cold start idle air control performance
P050B	Cold start ignition timing performance
P050E	Cold start engine exhaust temperature out of range
P052A	Cold start camshaft position timing over-advanced (Bank 1)
P052B	Cold start camshaft position timing over-retarded (Bank 1)
P052C	Cold start camshaft position timing over-advanced (Bank 2)
P052D	Cold start camshaft position timing over-retarded (Bank 2)

OBD-II TROUBLE CODES (CONTINUED)

➡**Note: Not all trouble codes apply to all models.**

Code	Probable cause
P0053	Oxygen sensor heater resistance (Bank 1, Sensor 1)
P053A	Positive Crankcase Ventilation (PCV) heater control circuit open
P0054	Oxygen sensor heater resistance (Bank 1, Sensor 2)
P0055	Oxygen sensor heater resistance (Bank 1, Sensor 3)
P0059	Oxygen sensor heater resistance (Bank 2, Sensor 1)
P0060	Oxygen sensor heater resistance (Bank 2, Sensor 2)
P060A	Internal control module monitoring processor performance
P060B	Internal control module analog/digital processing performance
P060C	Internal control module main processor performance
P060D	Internal control module accelerator pedal position performance
P061B	Internal control module torque calculation performance
P061C	Internal control module engine rpm performance
P061D	Internal control module engine air mass performance
P061F	Internal control module throttle actuator controller performance
P062C	Internal control module vehicle speed performance
P064D	Internal control module oxygen sensor processor performance (Bank 1)
P064E	Internal control module oxygen sensor processor performance (Bank 2)
P065B	Alternator control circuit range or performance problem
P0068	Manifold Absolute Pressure (MAP) sensor/Mass Air Flow (MAF) sensor-to-throttle position correlation
P0097	Intake Air Temperature (IAT) sensor 2 circuit, low voltage
P0098	Intake Air Temperature (IAT) sensor 2 circuit, high voltage
P0102	Mass or volume air flow A circuit, low voltage
P0103	Mass or volume air flow A circuit, high voltage
P0104	Mass Air Flow (MAF) sensor A circuit, intermittent or erratic signal
P0106	Manifold Absolute Pressure (MAP) sensor circuit, range or performance problem
P0107	Manifold Absolute Pressure (MAP) sensor circuit, low voltage
P0108	Manifold Absolute Pressure (MAP) sensor circuit, high voltage

Code	Probable cause
P0109	Manifold Absolute Pressure (MAP) sensor circuit, intermittent signal
P0111	Intake Air Temperature (IAT) sensor circuit, range or performance problem
P0112	Intake Air Temperature (IAT) sensor circuit, low voltage
P0113	Intake Air Temperature (IAT) sensor circuit, high voltage
P0114	Intake Air Temperature (IAT) sensor circuit, intermittent or erratic signal
P0116	Engine Coolant Temperature (ECT) sensor circuit, range or performance problem
P0117	Engine Coolant Temperature (ECT) sensor circuit, low voltage
P0118	Engine Coolant Temperature (ECT) sensor circuit, high voltage
P0119	Engine Coolant Temperature (ECT) sensor circuit, intermittent or erratic signal
P0121	Throttle Position (TP) sensor A circuit, range or performance problem
P0122	Throttle Position (TP) sensor A circuit, low voltage
P0123	Throttle Position (TP) sensor A circuit, high voltage
P0125	Insufficient coolant temperature for closed loop fuel control
P0128	Coolant temperature below coolant thermostat's regulating temperature
P0130	Oxygen sensor circuit malfunction (Bank 1, Sensor 1)
P0132	Oxygen sensor circuit, high voltage (Bank 1, Sensor 1)
P0133	Oxygen sensor circuit, slow response (Bank 1, Sensor 1)
P0134	Oxygen sensor circuit, no activity detected (Bank 1, Sensor 1)
P0135	Oxygen sensor heater circuit malfunction (Bank 1, Sensor 1)
P0138	Oxygen sensor circuit, high voltage (Bank 1, Sensor 2)
P0139	Oxygen sensor circuit, slow response (Bank 1, Sensor 2)
P0144	Oxygen sensor circuit, high voltage (Bank 1, Sensor 3)
P0147	Oxygen sensor heater circuit malfunction (Bank 1, Sensor 3)
P0148	Fuel delivery error
P0150	Oxygen sensor circuit malfunction (Bank 2, Sensor 1)
P0152	Oxygen sensor circuit, high voltage (Bank 2, Sensor 1)
P0153	Oxygen sensor circuit, slow response (Bank 2, Sensor 1)
P0154	Oxygen sensor circuit, no activity detected (Bank 2, Sensor 1)
P0155	Oxygen sensor heater circuit malfunction (Bank 2, Sensor 1)
P0158	O[illegible] high voltage (Bank 2, Sensor 2)

OBD-II TROUBLE CODES (CONTINUED)

➡Note: Not all trouble codes apply to all models.

Code	Probable cause
P0159	Oxygen sensor circuit, slow response (Bank 2, Sensor 2)
P0161	Oxygen sensor heater circuit malfunction (Bank 2, Sensor 2)
P0171	System too lean (Bank 1)
P0172	System too rich (Bank 1)
P0174	System too lean (Bank 2)
P0175	System too rich (Bank 2)
P0180	Fuel temperature sensor circuit malfunction
P0181	Fuel temperature sensor circuit, range or performance problem
P0182	Fuel temperature sensor circuit, low voltage
P0183	Fuel temperature sensor circuit, high voltage
P0191	Fuel rail pressure sensor circuit, range or performance problem
P0192	Fuel rail pressure sensor circuit, low voltage
P0193	Fuel rail pressure sensor circuit, high voltage
P0196	Engine Oil Temperature (EOT) sensor circuit, range or performance problem
P0197	Engine Oil Temperature (EOT) sensor circuit, low voltage
P0198	Engine Oil Temperature (EOT) sensor circuit, high voltage
P0217	Engine coolant over-temperature condition
P0218	Transaxle fluid temperature over-temperature condition
P0219	Engine over-speed condition
P0221	Throttle Position (TP) sensor circuit, range or performance problem
P0222	Throttle Position (TP) sensor circuit, low voltage
P0223	Throttle Position (TP) sensor circuit, high voltage
P0230	Fuel pump primary circuit malfunction
P0231	Fuel pump secondary circuit, low voltage
P0232	Fuel pump secondary circuit, high voltage
P0297	Vehicle over-speed condition
P0298	Engine oil over-temperature condition

Code	Probable cause
P0300	Random misfire detected
P0315	Crankshaft position system variation not learned
P0316	Misfire detected on start-up (first 1000 revolutions)
P0320	Ignition/distributor engine speed input circuit
P0325	Knock sensor 1 circuit malfunction (Bank 1)
P0326	Knock sensor 1 circuit, range or performance problem (Bank 1)
P0330	Knock sensor 2 circuit malfunction (Bank 2)
P0331	Knock sensor 2 circuit, range or performance problem (Bank 2)
P0340	Camshaft Position (CMP) sensor circuit malfunction (Bank 1 or single sensor)
P0341	Camshaft Position (CMP) sensor circuit, range or performance problem (Bank 1 or single sensor)
P0344	Camshaft Position (CMP) sensor circuit, intermittent signal (Bank 1 or single sensor)
P0345	Camshaft Position (CMP) sensor circuit malfunction (Bank 2)
P0346	Camshaft Position (CMP) sensor circuit, range or performance problem (Bank 2)
P0349	Camshaft Position (CMP) sensor circuit, intermittent signal (Bank 2)
P0350	Ignition coil primary/secondary circuit malfunction
P0351	Ignition coil A primary/secondary circuit malfunction
P0352	Ignition coil B primary/secondary circuit malfunction
P0353	Ignition coil C primary/secondary circuit malfunction
P0354	Ignition coil D primary/secondary circuit malfunction
P0355	Ignition coil E primary/secondary circuit malfunction
P0356	Ignition coil F primary/secondary circuit malfunction
P0400	Exhaust Gas Recirculation (EGR) system flow
P0401	Exhaust Gas Recirculation (EGR) system, insufficient flow detected
P0402	Exhaust Gas Recirculation (EGR) system, excessive flow detected
P0403	Exhaust Gas Recirculation (EGR) system control circuit malfunction
P0405	Exhaust Gas Recirculation (EGR) system, differential pressure feedback sensor circuit, low voltage
P0406	Exhaust Gas Recirculation (EGR) system, differential pressure feedback sensor circuit, high voltage
P0410	Secondary Air Injection (AIR) system
P0412	Secondary Air Injection (AIR) system, switching valve circuit malfunction
P0420	Catalyst system efficiency below threshold (Bank 1)

OBD-II TROUBLE CODES (CONTINUED)

➡**Note: Not all trouble codes apply to all models.**

Code	Probable cause
P0430	Catalyst system efficiency below threshold (Bank 2)
P0442	Evaporative Emission (EVAP) system, small leak detected
P0443	Evaporative Emission (EVAP) system, purge control valve circuit malfunction
P0446	Evaporative Emission (EVAP) system, vent control circuit malfunction
P0451	Evaporative Emission (EVAP) system, pressure sensor range or performance problem
P0452	Evaporative Emission (EVAP) system, pressure sensor, low voltage
P0453	Evaporative Emission (EVAP) system, pressure sensor, high voltage
P0454	Evaporative Emission (EVAP) system, pressure sensor, intermittent signal
P0455	Evaporative Emission (EVAP) system, gross leak detected/no flow
P0456	Evaporative Emission (EVAP) system, very small leak detected
P0457	Evaporative Emission (EVAP) system, leak detected (fuel cap loose or off)
P0460	Fuel level sensor circuit malfunction
P0461	Fuel level sensor circuit, range or performance problem
P0462	Fuel level sensor circuit, low voltage
P0463	Fuel level sensor circuit, high voltage
P0480	Fan 1 control circuit malfunction
P0481	Fan 2 control circuit malfunction
P0483	Fan performance
P0491	Secondary Air Injection (AIR) system, insufficient flow (Bank 1)
P0500	Vehicle Speed Sensor (VSS)
P0503	Vehicle Speed Sensor (VSS), intermittent, erratic or high signal
P0505	Idle Air Control (IAC) system
P0506	Idle Air Control (IAC) system, rpm lower than expected
P0507	Idle Air Control (IAC) system, rpm higher than expected
P0511	Idle Air Control (IAC) system circuit malfunction
P0512	Starter request circuit malfunction
P0528	Fan speed sensor circuit, no signal

Code	Probable cause
P0532	Air conditioning refrigerant pressure sensor circuit, low voltage
P0533	Air conditioning refrigerant pressure sensor circuit, high voltage
P0534	Air conditioning refrigerant charge loss
P0537	Air conditioning evaporator temperature sensor circuit, low voltage
P0538	A/C evaporator temperature sensor circuit, high voltage
P0552	Power Steering Pressure (PSP) sensor circuit, low voltage
P0553	Power Steering Pressure (PSP) sensor circuit, high voltage
P0562	System voltage low
P0563	System voltage high
P0571	Brake switch circuit malfunction
P0572	Brake switch circuit, low voltage
P0573	Brake switch circuit, high voltage
P0579	Cruise control multifunction input circuit, ranger or performance problem
P0581	Cruise control multifunction input circuit, high voltage
P0600	Serial communication link
P0601	Powertrain Control Module (PCM), memory checksum error
P0602	Powertrain Control Module (PCM) programming error
P0603	Powertrain Control Module (PCM), Keep Alive Memory (KAM) error
P0604	Powertrain Control Module (PCM), Random Access Memory (RAM) error
P0605	Powertrain Control Module (PCM), Read Only Memory (ROM) error
P0606	Powertrain Control Module (PCM) processor
P0607	Powertrain Control Module (PCM) performance
P0610	Powertrain Control Module (PCM) options error
P0620	Alternator control circuit malfunction
P0622	Alternator field terminal, circuit malfunction
P0625	Alternator field terminal, low circuit voltage
P0626	Alternator field terminal, high circuit voltage
P0627	Fuel pump, open control circuit
P062F	Internal control module EEPROM error
P0642	Sensor reference voltage (VREF) circuit below VREF minimum voltage

OBD-II TROUBLE CODES (CONTINUED)

➡Note: Not all trouble codes apply to all models.

Code	Probable cause
P0643	Sensor reference voltage (VREF) circuit, high voltage
P0645	Air conditioning clutch relay control circuit malfunction
P0657	Actuator supply voltage, open circuit
P065B	Alternator control circuit range or performance problem
P0660	Intake Manifold Tuning Valve (IMTV) control circuit, open circuit (Bank 1)
P0663	Intake Manifold Tuning Valve (IMTV) control circuit, open circuit (Bank 2)
P0685	Powertrain Control Module (PCM) power relay control circuit open
P0689	Powertrain Control Module (PCM) power relay sense circuit, low voltage
P0690	Powertrain Control Module (PCM) power relay sense circuit, high voltage
P0703	Brake switch input circuit malfunction
P0704	Clutch switch input circuit malfunction
P0705	Transmission Range (TR) sensor circuit (PRNDL) input problem
P0706	Transmission Range (TR) sensor circuit, range or performance problem
P0707	Transmission Range (TR) sensor circuit, low voltage
P0708	Transmission range sensor circuit, high voltage
P0711	Transmission fluid temperature sensor circuit, range or performance problem
P0712	Transmission fluid temperature sensor circuit, low input
P0713	Transmission fluid temperature sensor circuit, high input
P0715	Input/turbine speed sensor circuit malfunction
P0716	Input/turbine speed sensor circuit, range or performance problem
P0717	Input/turbine speed sensor circuit, no signal
P0720	Output Shaft Speed (OSS) sensor circuit malfunction
P0721	Output Shaft Speed (OSS) sensor circuit, range or performance problem
P0722	No signal from Output Shaft Speed (OSS) sensor
P0723	Output Shaft Speed (OSS) sensor circuit, intermittent signal
P06B8	Internal control module Non-volatile random access memory (NVRAM) error
P0729	Gear 6 incorrect ratio

Code	Probable cause
P0730	Incorrect gear ratio
P0731	Incorrect gear ratio, first gear
P0732	Incorrect gear ratio, second gear
P0733	Incorrect gear ratio, third gear
P0734	Incorrect gear ratio, fourth gear
P0735	Incorrect gear ratio, fifth gear
P0736	Incorrect gear ratio, reverse gear
P0741	Torque converter clutch, circuit performance problem or stuck in Off position
P0742	Torque converter clutch circuit, stuck in On position
P0744	Torque converter clutch circuit, intermittent
P0745	Pressure control solenoid malfunction
P0751	Shift solenoid A, performance problem or stuck in Off position
P0752	Shift solenoid A, stuck in On position
P0753	Shift solenoid A, electrical problem
P0756	Shift solenoid B, performance problem or stuck in Off position
P0757	Shift solenoid B, stuck in On position
P0758	Shift solenoid B, electrical problem
P0761	Shift solenoid C, performance problem or stuck in Off position
P0762	Shift solenoid C, stuck in On position
P0763	Shift solenoid C, electrical problem
P0766	Shift solenoid D, performance problem or stuck in Off position
P0767	Shift solenoid D, stuck in On position
P0768	Shift solenoid D, electrical problem
P0771	Shift solenoid E, performance problem or stuck in Off position
P0772	Shift solenoid E, stuck in On position
P0773	Shift solenoid E, electrical problem
P0777	Pressure control solenoid "B" stuck On
P0778	Pressure control solenoid "B" electrical
P0780	Shift malfunction
P0791	Intermediate shaft speed sensor circuit malfunction

OBD-II TROUBLE CODES (CONTINUED)

➡Note: Not all trouble codes apply to all models.

Code	Probable cause
P0812	Reverse input circuit malfunction
P0815	Upshift switch circuit malfunction
P0817	Starter disable circuit malfunction
P0830	Clutch pedal switch circuit malfunction
P0840	Transmission fluid pressure sensor circuit malfunction
P0841	Transmission fluid pressure sensor/switch "A" circuit range/performance problem
P0882	Transmission control module (TCM) power input signal low
P0894	Transmission component slipping
P0961	Pressure control (PC) solenoid A - control circuit range/performance problem
P0962	Pressure control (PC) solenoid A - control circuit low
P0963	Pressure control (PC) solenoid A - control circuit high
P0973	Shift solenoid (SS) A - control circuit low
P0974	Shift solenoid (SS) A - control circuit high
P0976	Shift solenoid (SS) B - control circuit low
P0977	Shift solenoid (SS) B - control circuit high
P0978	Shift solenoid (SS) C - control circuit range/performance problem
P0979	Shift solenoid (SS) C - control circuit low
P0980	Shift solenoid (SS) C - control circuit high
P0981	Shift solenoid (SS) D - control circuit range/performance problem
P0982	Shift solenoid (SS) D - control circuit low
P0983	Shift solenoid (SS) D - control circuit high
P0984	Shift solenoid (SS) E - control circuit range/performance problem
P0985	Shift solenoid (SS) E - control circuit low
P0986	Shift solenoid (SS) E - control circuit high
P0997	Shift solenoid (SS) F - control circuit range/performance problem
P0998	Shift solenoid (SS) F - control circuit low
P0999	Shift solenoid (SS) F - control circuit high

4 Accelerator Pedal Position (APP) sensor - replacement

➧ Refer to illustration 4.2

➡Note: Replacing the APP sensor is difficult. The APP sensor is located at the upper end of the accelerator pedal assembly, between the brake pedal assembly and the housing for the heater core and air conditioning evaporator.

1 Remove the knee bolster trim panel and the knee bolster (see *Dashboard trim panels - removal and installation* in Chapter 11).

2 Using a flashlight and mirror, disconnect the electrical connector from the upper end of the APP sensor assembly (see illustration).

3 Remove the accelerator pedal/APP sensor assembly mounting nuts and remove the assembly.

4 Installation is the reverse of removal.

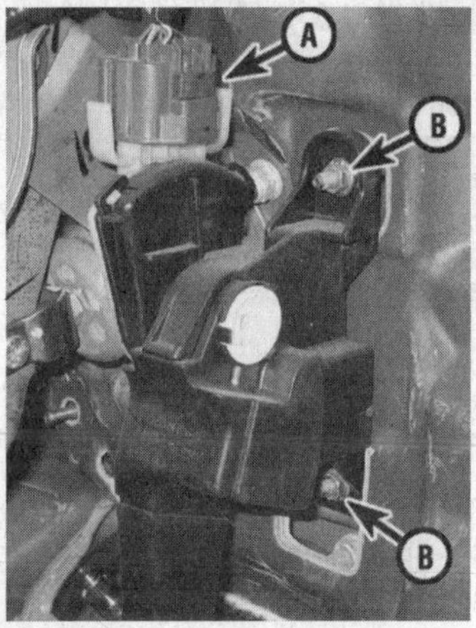

4.2 APP sensor electrical connector (A) and mounting nuts (B) (instrument panel and heater core/air conditioning evaporator housing removed for clarity)

5 Camshaft Position (CMP) sensor - replacement

1 Disconnect the cable from the negative battery terminal (see Chapter 5).

FOUR-CYLINDER MODELS

➡Note: The CMP sensor is located at the left front corner of the valve cover, above the left end of the exhaust camshaft.

2 Disconnect the CMP sensor electrical connector.

3 Remove the CMP sensor mounting bolt and remove the CMP sensor.

4 Inspect the condition of the CMP sensor O-ring. If it's cracked, torn or deteriorated, replace it.

5 Installation is the reverse of removal.

V6 MODELS

➧ Refer to illustrations 5.8a and 5.8b

➡Note: On 3.5L engines, there are two CMP sensors, one on the left end of each cylinder head. On 3.0L engines, see illustrations 5.8a and 5.8b.

6 If you're removing the CMP sensor from the front cylinder head on a 3.0L engine, detach the wiring harness clip from the valve cover stud and set it aside. If you're removing the CMP sensor from the rear cylinder head on a 3.0L engine, remove the radio frequency interference capacitor from the valve cover stud and set it aside.

7 If you're removing either CMP sensor on a 3.5L engine, remove the air intake duct (see *Air filter housing - removal and installation* in Chapter 4.

8 Disconnect the CMP sensor electrical connector (see illustrations).

9 Remove the CMP sensor mounting bolt and remove the CMP sensor.

10 Remove the CMP sensor O-ring and inspect its condition. If it's cracked, torn or otherwise deteriorated, replace it.

11 Be sure to lubricate the sensor O-ring with clean engine oil. Installation is otherwise the reverse of removal.

5.8a The CMP sensor for the front cylinder head is located on the right end of the head (3.0L V6 engine)

5.8b The CMP sensor for the rear cylinder head is located on the right end of the head (3.0L V6 engine)

6 Crankshaft Position (CKP) sensor - replacement

➧ Refer to illustrations 6.2a and 6.2b

1 Disconnect the cable from the negative battery terminal (see Chapter 5).

2 On all models except 3.5L V6 models, loosen the right front wheel lug nuts. On all models, raise the front of the vehicle and place it securely on jackstands. On all models except 3.5L V6 models, remove the right front wheel, then remove the smaller access panel below the larger fender splash shield (see illustrations). On 3.5L V6 models, remove the engine under-cover.

FOUR-CYLINDER MODELS

Removal

➧ Refer to illustration 6.4

➡Note: The CKP sensor is located at the lower rear corner of the timing chain cover, behind the crankshaft pulley.

3 Put the No. 1 cylinder at Top Dead Center (TDC) (see Chapter 2A).

4 Disconnect the electrical connector from the CKP sensor (see illustration).

5 Unscrew the CKP sensor mounting bolts and remove the sensor.

Installation

➧ Refer to illustrations 6.6 and 6.9

➡Note: If you're installing a new CKP sensor, the new sensor comes with a special alignment jig that, according to the manufacturer, is available only with a new sensor. You might, however, be able to find an aftermarket tool that does the same thing. If, on the other hand, you removed the CKP sensor simply to access some other component, like the timing chain, use the alternate method of aligning the CKP sensor included here.

6 Install a 6 mm x 18 mm (0.23 x 0.7 inch) bolt in the threaded hole provided in the crankshaft pulley (see illustration) and screw it into the timing chain cover.

7 Install the CKP sensor but don't tighten the sensor mounting bolts.

8 If you're installing a new CKP sensor, align the sensor with the special alignment jig (included with the new sensor) in accordance with the manufacturer's instructions. With the alignment jig in place, tighten the CKP sensor bolts securely, then remove the alignment jig.

9 If you're installing the old CKP sensor, look at the sensor trigger wheel, or timing plate, that's mounted on the backside of the crankshaft pulley. Note the small "teeth" that stick out from the circumference of the timing plate. At about ten o'clock there is a blank spot on the edge of the timing plate, where there are no teeth. From this blank area, count

6.2a CKP sensor access panel retainers (front)

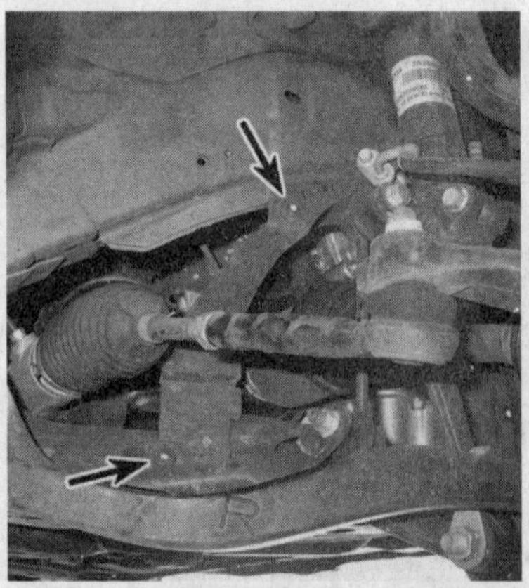

6.2b CKP sensor access panel retainers (rear) (four-cylinder and 3.0L V6 models)

6.4 CKP sensor details (fourcylinder models):

1 *Electrical connector*
2 *Mounting bolts*
3 *CKP sensor*

6.6 Insert the correct size bolt into the threaded hole in the pulley and timing chain cover

five teeth in a counterclockwise direction, then, using a straightedge, draw a straight line from the center of this fifth tooth through the center of the crankshaft pulley (see illustration). Position the centerline of the CKP sensor with the line that you made, then tighten the sensor bolts securely.

10 Remove the crankshaft pulley bolt that you installed in Step 6, then remove the special timing tool and install the cylinder block plug (see Chapter 2A). Installation is otherwise the reverse of removal.

➡Note: On 2010 models, replacing the CKP sensor might set a Diagnostic Trouble Code (DTC). If it does, and if you have a generic scan tool that can clear codes, erase the code and see if it reappears. If it does, have a dealer service department perform a Misfire Monitor Neutral Profile Correction procedure with a factory scan tool.

V6 MODELS

3.0L engine

➧ Refer to illustration 6.12

11 Loosen the right front wheel lug nuts, then raise the front of the vehicle and place it securely on jackstands. Remove the right front wheel. Remove the smaller access panel below the larger fender splash shield (see illustrations 6.2a and 6.2b).

12 Disconnect the electrical connector from the CKP sensor (see illustration).

13 Unscrew the CKP sensor mounting bolt and remove the CKP sensor.

14 Remove and inspect the sensor O-ring. If it's cut, torn or otherwise deteriorated, replace it.

15 Lubricate the sensor O-ring with clean engine oil. Installation is otherwise the reverse of removal.

➡Note: Replacing the CKP sensor might set a Diagnostic Trouble Code (DTC). If it does, and if you have a generic scan tool that can clear codes, erase the code and see if it reappears. If it does, drive the vehicle to a dealer service department and have it perform a Misfire Monitor Neutral Profile Correction procedure with a factory scan tool.

3.5L engine

➡Note: The CKP sensor is located on the left front side of the engine block, near the transaxle.

16 Remove the upstream and downstream oxygen sensors from the catalytic converter for the front cylinder head (see Section 12), then remove the catalyst for the front cylinder head (see Section 18).

17 Remove the CKP sensor heat shield mounting bolt and nut and remove the heat shield.

18 Remove the rubber grommet cover.

19 Disconnect the CKP sensor electrical connector.

20 Remove the CKP sensor mounting bolt and remove the sensor.

21 Installation is otherwise the reverse of removal.

➡Note: Replacing the CKP sensor might set a Diagnostic Trouble Code (DTC). If it does, and if you have a generic scan tool that can clear codes, erase the code and see if it reappears. If it does, drive the vehicle to a dealer service department and have it perform a Misfire Monitor Neutral Profile Correction procedure with a factory scan tool.

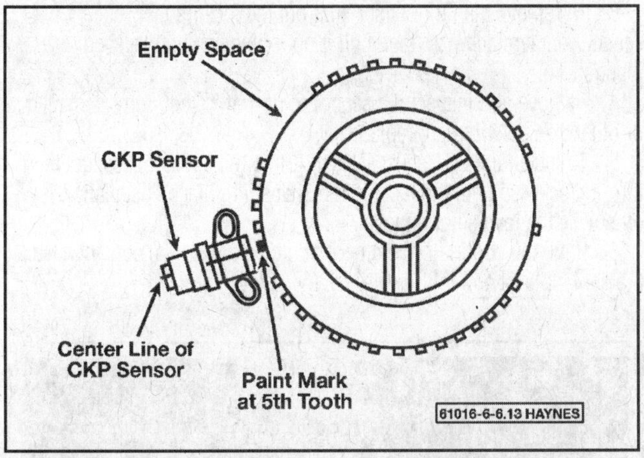

6.9 CKP sensor alignment details (four-cylinder models)

6.12 On 3.0L V6 models, the CKP sensor is located at the lower rear edge of the timing chain cover, behind the crankshaft pulley

7 Cylinder Head Temperature (CHT) sensor - replacement

FOUR-CYLINDER MODELS

⁂ WARNING:

Wait until the engine has cooled completely before beginning this procedure.

➡Note: All four-cylinder models are equipped with a CHT sensor, which is screwed into the cylinder head. Don't confuse this sensor, which monitors the temperature of the metal cylinder head itself, with an Engine Coolant Temperature (ECT) sensor, which monitors the temperature of the engine coolant.

1 Disconnect the cable from the negative battery terminal (see Chapter 5).

2 On 2.3L models, remove the alternator air inlet duct (see *Alternator - removal and installation* in Chapter 5).

3 Pull back the rubber weather cover from the CHT sensor electrical connector and disconnect the connector.

4 Unscrew the CHT sensor from the cylinder head.

5 When installing the CHT sensor, be sure to tighten it to the torque listed in this Chapter's Specifications. Installation is the reverse of removal.

V6 MODELS

⁂ WARNING:

Wait until the engine has cooled completely before beginning this procedure.

➡Note: Only 2010 V6 models are equipped with a CHT sensor. On 3.0L engines, the CHT sensor is screwed into the left end of the rear cylinder head; on 3.5L engines, it's located in the valley below the lower intake manifold, and is screwed into the rear cylinder head.

6 Disconnect the cable from the negative battery terminal (see Chapter 5).

7 On 3.0L models, remove the battery and the battery tray (see Chapter 5). On 3.5L models, remove the lower intake manifold (see Chapter 2B).

8 Disconnect the CHT sensor electrical connector.

9 Unscrew and remove the CHT sensor.

10 When installing the CHT sensor, be sure to tighten it to the torque listed in this Chapter's Specifications. Installation is otherwise the reverse of removal.

8 Engine Coolant Temperature (ECT) sensor - replacement

➧ Refer to illustrations 8.2 and 8.3

⁂ WARNING:

Wait until the engine has cooled completely before beginning this procedure.

➡Note: The ECT sensor is used on 2006 through 2009 3.0L V6 engines.

1 Drain the engine coolant (see Chapter 1).

2 Disconnect the electrical connector from the ECT sensor (see illustration).

3 To remove the ECT sensor, pull out the locking tab, rotate the sensor counterclockwise, then pull it out of the coolant passage (see illustration).

4 Remove and inspect the sensor O-ring. If it's cut, torn, damaged or otherwise deteriorated, replace it.

5 To install the ECT sensor, insert it into the coolant passage, then turn it clockwise until the locking tab snaps into place. Installation is otherwise the reverse of removal.

6 Refill the cooling system or, if you didn't drain the coolant, check the coolant level and refill as necessary (see Chapter 1).

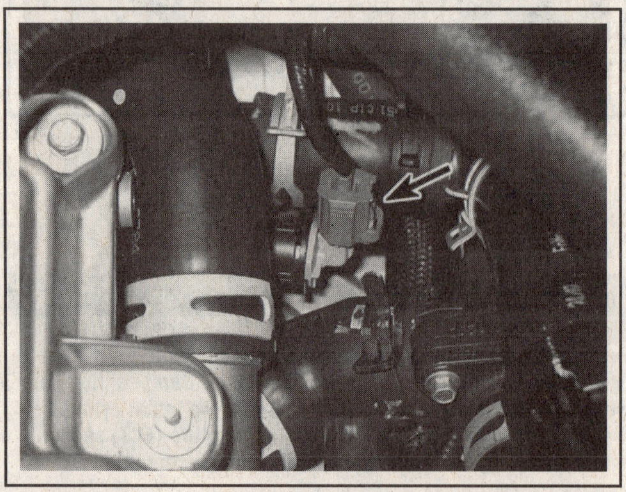

8.2 The ECT sensor is located at the left end of the engine (3.0L V6 engine)

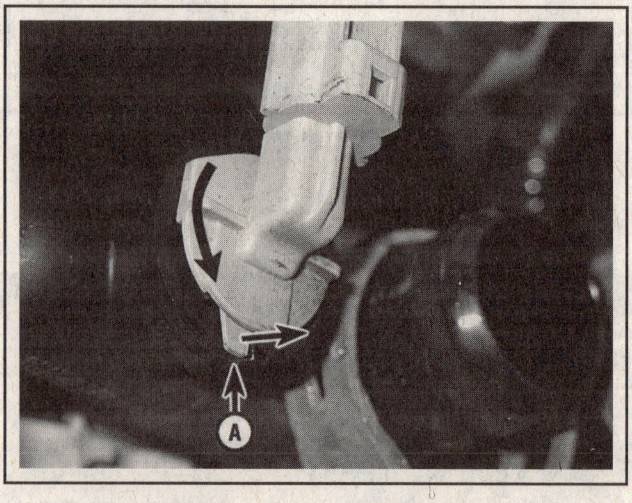

8.3 Pull out the locking tab (A), rotate the sensor counterclockwise, then pull it out of the coolant passage

9 Knock sensor - replacement

FOUR-CYLINDER MODELS

Note: The knock sensor is located on the front side of the block, behind the intake manifold runners.

1 Disconnect the cable from the negative battery terminal (see Chapter 5).

2 Remove the intake manifold (see Chapter 2A).

3 Disconnect the electrical connector from the knock sensor.

4 Remove the knock sensor bolt and remove the knock sensor.

5 Installation is the reverse of removal. Be sure to tighten the knock sensor bolt to the torque listed in this Chapter's Specifications.

V6 MODELS

2006 through 2009 3.0L V6 models

Refer to illustration 9.8

6 Disconnect the cable from the negative battery terminal (see Chapter 5).

7 Raise the vehicle and place it securely on jackstands. Remove the engine compartment under-cover.

8 Disconnect the knock sensor electrical connector (see illustration).

9 Remove the knock sensor retaining bolt and remove the knock sensor.

10 Installation is the reverse of removal. Be sure to tighten the knock sensor bolt to the torque listed in this Chapter's Specifications.

2010 models

Note: On 3.0L engines, the knock sensor is located in the valley between the cylinder heads. On 3.5L engines, there are two knock sensors, both of which are located in the valley between the cylinder heads.

11 Remove the upper intake manifold (see Chapter 2B).

12 Remove the lower intake manifold (3.0L engines, see *Fuel rail and injectors - removal and installation* in Chapter 4; 3.5L engines, see Chapter 2B).

13 Disconnect the knock sensor electrical connector(s).

14 Remove the knock sensor bolt(s) and remove the knock sensor(s).

15 Installation is the reverse of removal.

9.8 The knock sensor is located on the left rear side of the engine block (2006 through 2009 3.0L V6 engines)

10 Manifold Absolute Pressure (MAP) sensor - replacement

FOUR-CYLINDER MODELS

Note: The MAP sensor is located on the front left side of the block, to the left of the lower end of the intake manifold, above the starter motor (2.3L engine) or above the oil filter adapter (2.5L engine).

1 Disconnect the cable from the negative battery terminal (see Chapter 5).

2 Disconnect the electrical connector from the MAP sensor.

3 Remove the MAP sensor retaining bolt and remove the sensor.

4 Installation is the reverse of removal.

V6 MODELS

Refer to illustration 10.6

5 Disconnect the cable from the negative battery terminal (see Chapter 5).

6 Disconnect the electrical connector from the MAP sensor (see illustration).

10.6 The MAP sensor is located on top of the intake manifold (3.0L V6 engine shown, 3.5L engine similar)

7 Remove the MAP sensor retaining bolt and remove the sensor.

8 Installation is the reverse of removal.

11 Mass Air Flow (MAF)/Intake Air Temperature (IAT) sensor - replacement

Refer to illustration 11.2

1 Remove the air intake duct (see *Air filter housing - removal and installation* in Chapter 4).

2 Disconnect the electrical connector from the MAF/IAT sensor (see illustration).

3 Remove the MAF/IAT sensor mounting fasteners and remove the sensor from the air filter housing.

4 Installation is the reverse of removal.

11.2 The MAF/IAT sensor is located on the air filter housing cover (3.0L V6 engine shown, other engines similar)

12 Oxygen sensors - replacement

Note: Because it is installed in the exhaust manifold or pipe, both of which contract when cool, an oxygen sensor might be very difficult to loosen when the engine is cold. Rather than risk damage to the sensor or its mounting threads, start and run the engine for a minute or two, then shut it off. Be careful not to burn yourself during the following procedure.

1 Be particularly careful when servicing an oxygen sensor:

a) *Oxygen sensors have a permanently attached pigtail and an electrical connector that cannot be removed. Damaging or removing the pigtail or electrical connector will render the sensor useless.*

b) *Keep grease, dirt and other contaminants away from the electrical connector and the louvered end of the sensor.*

c) *Do not use cleaning solvents of any kind on an oxygen sensor.*

d) *Oxygen sensors are extremely delicate. Do not drop a sensor or handle it roughly.*

e) *Make sure that the silicone boot on the sensor is installed in the correct position. Otherwise, the boot might melt and it might prevent the sensor from operating correctly.*

REPLACEMENT

2 Disconnect the cable from the negative battery terminal (see Chapter 5).

3 To access downstream sensors on all models, and the upstream sensor on the exhaust manifold for the rear cylinder head on V6 models, raise the front of the vehicle and place it securely on jackstands. Remove the engine under-cover.

Upstream oxygen sensor

Refer to illustrations 12.4a and 12.4b

Note: The upstream sensor is installed in the upper part of the integral exhaust manifold/catalytic converter assembly. There is an upstream sensor in each exhaust manifold on V6 models.

4 Locate the upstream oxygen sensor (see illustrations), then trace the sensor's electrical lead to its electrical connector and disconnect the connector. Disengage any harness clips.

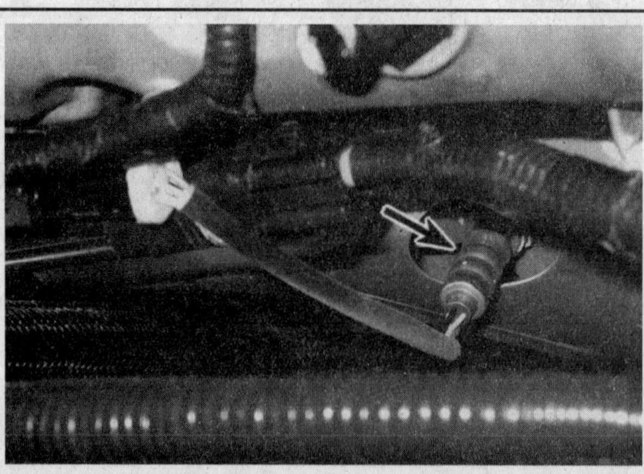

12.4a Upstream oxygen sensor location on the front cylinder head exhaust manifold (3.0L V6 engine shown, other engines similar)

12.4b Upstream and downstream oxygen sensor locations on the rear cylinder head exhaust manifold (3.0L V6 engine shown, 3.5L V6 similar)

5 Using a wrench or an oxygen sensor socket, unscrew the upstream oxygen sensor.

6 If you're going to install the old sensor, apply anti-seize compound to the threads of the sensor to facilitate future removal. If you're going to install a new oxygen sensor, it's not necessary to apply anti-seize compound to the threads; the threads on new sensors already have anti-seize compound on them.

7 Installation is the reverse of removal. Be sure to tighten the oxygen sensor to the torque listed in this Chapter's Specifications.

Downstream oxygen sensor

Refer to illustration 12.8

➡Note: The downstream oxygen sensor is located in the lower end of the exhaust manifold/catalytic converter assembly or on the short section of exhaust pipe, just below the catalyst. There is a downstream oxygen sensor in each exhaust pipe on V6 models.

8 Locate the downstream oxygen sensor (front cylinder head on a V6 engine, see illustration; rear cylinder on a V6, see illustration 12.4b), then trace the lead up to the electrical connector and disconnect the connector. Disengage any harness clips.

9 Using a wrench or an oxygen sensor socket, unscrew the downstream oxygen sensor.

10 If you're going to install the old sensor, apply anti-seize compound to the threads of the sensor to facilitate future removal. If you're going to install a new oxygen sensor, it's not necessary to apply anti-seize compound to the threads. The threads on new sensors already have anti-seize compound on them.

12.8 Downstream oxygen sensor location on the front cylinder head exhaust (3.0L V6 engine shown, other engines similar)

11 Installation is the reverse of removal. Be sure to tighten the oxygen sensor securely.

13 Power Steering Pressure (PSP) switch - replacement

➧ Refer to illustration 13.3

➡Note: The PSP switch is located on top of the power steering pump on 2.3L four-cylinder and 3.5L V6 models. On 3.0L V6 models, see illustration 13.3.

1 If you're replacing the PSP switch on a 3.0L V6 model, raise the front of the vehicle and place it securely on jackstands. Remove the engine under-cover.

2 If you're replacing the PSP switch on a 3.0L V6 model, siphon the power steering fluid from the power steering reservoir, or be prepared to catch spilled power steering fluid when you unscrew the PSP switch.

3 Disconnect the electrical connector from the PSP switch (see illustration).

4 Using a deep socket, unscrew the PSP switch.

5 Installation is the reverse of removal. On 3.0L V6 models, refill the power steering system as necessary (see Chapter 1).

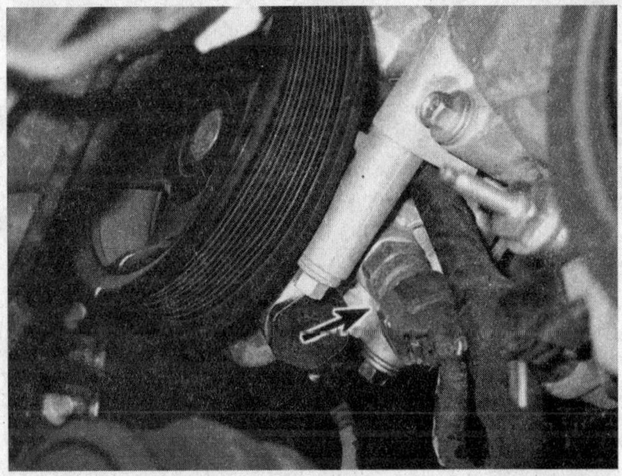

13.3 On 3.0L V6 engines, the Power Steering Pressure (PSP) switch is located on the underside of the pump

14 Throttle Position (TP) sensor - replacement

The TP sensor is an integral component of the electronic throttle body, and is not separately serviceable. If you need to replace the TP sensor you must replace the throttle body (see Chapter 4).

15 Transmission Range (TR) sensor - removal and installation

FNR5 (5-SPEED) TRANSAXLE

➡Note: Before beginning this procedure, you'll need to acquire a special alignment tool (SST #307-571) to align the TR sensor during installation.

➡Note: The TR sensor is located on the lower left front side of the transaxle.

Removal

1 Place the shift lever in NEUTRAL, raise the vehicle and support it securely on jackstands. Remove the underbody cover.

2 Disconnect the electrical connector from the TR sensor.

3 Pry the end of the shift cable off the ball stud on the manual control lever.

4 Remove the manual control lever nut and lock washer and remove the manual control lever.

⁂ CAUTION:

To protect the internal shift mechanism from damage, use an appropriate tool to immobilize the manual control lever to prevent it from turning while loosening the nut.

5 Remove the TR sensor mounting bolts and remove the sensor.

Installation

6 Install the TR sensor and loosely install the sensor mounting bolts. Before tightening the mounting bolts, install the special alignment tool (SST #307-571) to align the sensor, then tighten the mounting bolts.

7 Install the manual lever, lock washer and nut and tighten it securely.

⁂ CAUTION:

To protect the internal shift mechanism from damage, use an appropriate tool to immobilize the manual lever to prevent it from turning while tightening the nut.

8 Before reconnecting the shift cable to the manual control lever, verify that the manual lever is in the DRIVE position. When the manual lever is in the DRIVE position, the marks on the manual control lever will line up with the marks on the TR sensor.

9 Reconnect the electrical connector to the TR sensor.

10 The remainder of installation is the reverse of removal. After lowering the vehicle, verify that the engine will only start in PARK or NEUTRAL.

6-SPEED TRANSAXLE

Removal

➧ Refer to illustration 15.12

➡Note: On this transaxle, the TR sensor is an integral component of the Transaxle Control Module (TCM) and is not separately serviceable. If you need to replace the TR sensor, you must replace the TCM. The TCM cannot be replaced at home, because the replacement unit must be programmed with a factory scan tool before it will operate properly. The following procedure assumes that you are simply removing the current TCM unit from the old transaxle and installing it on a replacement transaxle.

➡Note: The TCM is located on top of the transaxle.

11 Place the shift lever in NEUTRAL, then remove the air filter housing (see Chapter 4).

12 Disconnect the electrical connector from the TCM (see illustration).

13 Using a trim removal tool or a screwdriver, carefully pry the end of the shift cable off the ball stud on the manual control lever.

14 Remove the manual control lever nut and remove the lever.

15 Remove the TCM mounting bolts and remove the TCM.

Installation

➧ Refer to illustration 15.16

16 Before installing the TCM, verify that the manual control lever is in the NEUTRAL position by aligning the mark on the control lever with the stationary mark on the TCM (see illustration).

15.12 Transaxle Control Module (TCM) details (sixspeed transaxle):

1 *Electrical connector*
2 *Shift cable*
3 *Manual control lever nut*
4 *Manual control lever*
5 *TR sensor bolts*

15.16 TCM manual control lever NEUTRAL position alignment marks (6-speed transaxle)

17 Install the TCM and tighten the TCM mounting bolts securely.

18 Install the manual control lever, install the lever nut and tighten it securely.

19 Reconnect the electrical connector to the TCM.

20 Reconnect the shift cable to the ball stud on the manual control lever.

21 The remainder of installation is the reverse of removal. Verify that the engine will only start in PARK or NEUTRAL.

16 Vehicle Speed Sensor (VSS) - replacement

MANUAL TRANSAXLE

➡Note: The VSS is located on the right rear corner of the transaxle, above the inner CV joint for the right driveaxle.

1 Raise the vehicle and place it securely on jackstands. Remove the engine under-cover.

2 Disconnect the electrical connector from the VSS.

3 Remove the VSS mounting bolt and remove the VSS.

4 Remove and discard the old VSS O-ring.

5 When installing the VSS, be sure to use a new O-ring. Installation is otherwise the reverse of removal.

AUTOMATIC TRANSAXLE

FNR5 (5-speed) transaxle

➡Note: There are three speed sensors: the Intermediate Shaft Speed (ISS) sensor, the Turbine Shaft Speed (TSS) sensor and the Output Shaft Speed (OSS) sensor. The ISS and TSS sensors are located on top of the transaxle. The TSS sensor is the forward unit; the ISS sensor is the rear unit. The OSS sensor is located near the lower left rear corner of the transaxle. The following procedure applies to all three sensors.

6 If you're replacing the OSS sensor, raise the vehicle and place it securely on jackstands. Remove the engine under-cover.

7 Disconnect the electrical connector from the sensor.

8 Remove the sensor mounting bolt and remove the sensor.

9 Remove and discard the old sensor O-ring.

10 When installing the sensor, be sure to use a new O-ring. Installation is otherwise the reverse of removal.

6-speed transaxle

11 The speed sensors on the 6-speed automatic transaxle are all integral components of the transaxle assembly and cannot be replaced at home.

17 Powertrain Control Module (PCM) - removal and installation

➧ Refer to illustration 17.2

⁂ CAUTION:

To avoid electrostatic discharge damage to the PCM, handle the PCM only by its case. Do not touch the electrical terminals during removal and installation. If available, ground yourself to the vehicle with an anti-static ground strap, available at computer supply stores.

➡Note: This procedure applies only to disconnecting, removing and installing the PCM that is already installed in your vehicle. If the PCM is defective and has to be replaced, it must be programmed with new software and calibrations. This procedure requires the use of GM's TECH-2 scan tool and GM's latest PCM-programming software, so you WILL NOT BE ABLE TO REPLACE THE PCM AT HOME.

1 Remove the battery and the battery tray (see Chapter 5).

2 Disconnect the electrical connectors from the PCM (see illustration).

3 Remove the PCM mounting bolts and remove the PCM.

4 Installation is the reverse of removal.

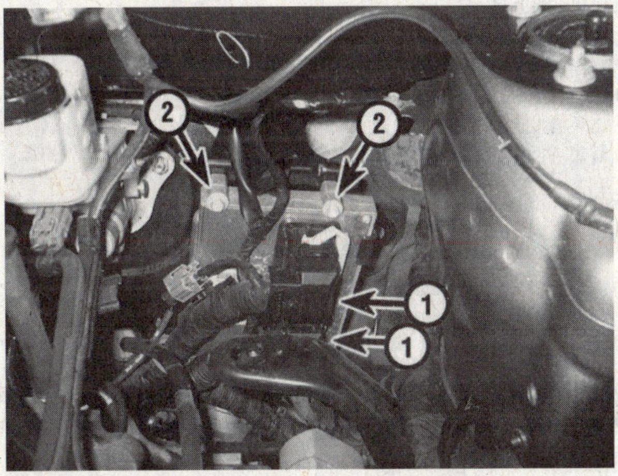

17.2 Powertrain Control Module (PCM) details:

1 Electrical connectors
2 PCM mounting bolts (lower bolts not visible)

18 Catalytic converter - replacement

ALL 2006 THROUGH 2009 MODELS

1 On all 2003 through 2006 engines, the catalytic converters are integral components of the exhaust manifolds and cannot be serviced separately. To replace the catalyst on a 2.3L four-cylinder model, refer to *Exhaust manifold - removal and installation* in Chapter 2A. To replace either of the catalysts on a 3.0L V6 model, refer to *Exhaust manifold - removal and installation* in Chapter 2B.

2010 MODELS

2.5L four-cylinder engine

Non-Partial Zero Emissions (PZEV) vehicles

WARNING:

Wait until the engine has cooled completely before beginning this procedure.

➡Note: On these vehicles, the catalyst is located under the vehicle.

2 Raise the vehicle and place it securely on jackstands.

3 Locate the downstream oxygen sensor on the upper central part of the catalyst, trace the sensor to its electrical connector and disconnect it. Unscrew and remove the downstream oxygen sensor from the catalyst (see Section 12).

4 Remove the nuts and bolts that secure the flange at the front end of the catalyst to the exhaust down pipe. If the threads are severely damaged or rusted, apply some penetrant to the threads and wait awhile before loosening them.

5 Loosen the fasteners on the clamp that secures the rear end of the catalyst to the exhaust system. If the threads are severely damaged or rusted, apply some penetrant to the threads and wait awhile before loosening them.

6 Remove the catalytic converter.

7 Remove and discard the old gasket between the exhaust down pipe and the catalyst mounting flange.

8 Installation is the reverse of removal. Be sure to use a new gasket and, if necessary, new fasteners.

Partial Zero Emissions (PZEV) vehicles

9 The catalytic converter is an integral component of the exhaust manifold and cannot be serviced separately. To replace it, refer to *Exhaust manifold - removal and installation* in Chapter 2A.

V6 engines

Front cylinder head (3.0L engine)

10 The catalyst for the front cylinder head is an integral component of the exhaust manifold. To replace it, refer to *Exhaust manifold - removal and installation* in Chapter 2B.

Rear cylinder head (3.0L engine) and front or rear cylinder head (3.5L engine)

WARNING:

Wait until the engine has cooled completely before beginning this procedure.

11 Raise the front of the vehicle and place it securely on jackstands. Remove the engine under-cover.

12 Locate the upstream and downstream oxygen sensors, trace their electrical leads to their respective connectors and disconnect them. Remove both oxygen sensors (see Section 12).

13 If the catalyst and/or exhaust manifold is equipped with a heat shield, remove the heat shield bolts and remove the heat shield from the exhaust manifold. On 3.5L models, there is another heat shield protecting the steering gear assembly. If necessary, remove this heat shield as well.

14 Remove the fasteners that secure the heat shield mounting bracket and remove the bracket.

15 Remove the fasteners that secure the catalyst's upper mounting flange to the exhaust manifold. If the threads are severely damaged or rusted, apply some penetrant to the threads and wait awhile before loosening them.

16 Remove the fasteners that secure the lower mounting flange to the exhaust pipe. If the threads are severely damaged or rusted, apply some penetrant to the threads and wait awhile before loosening them.

17 Pull the exhaust pipe down far enough to clear the lower end of the catalyst.

18 Remove the catalyst from the exhaust manifold.

19 Remove and discard the old gaskets between the exhaust manifold flange and the upper catalyst flange and, if equipped, between the lower catalyst flange and the exhaust pipe flange.

20 Installation is the reverse of removal. Be sure to use new flange gaskets.

19 Evaporative Emissions Control (EVAP) system - component replacement

EVAP CANISTER PURGE VALVE

Refer to illustration 19.3

1 Disconnect the cable from the negative battery terminal (see Chapter 5).

2 On V6 models, remove the lower cowl trim panel (see Chapter 11).

3 Disconnect the electrical connector from the canister purge valve (see illustration).

4 Disconnect the EVAP line quick-connect fittings (see Chapter 4 for information on quick-connect fittings).

5 Remove the purge valve and mounting bracket as a single assembly, then depress the lock tab and slide the purge valve off the mounting bracket.

19.3 The EVAP canister purge valve is located in the right rear corner of the engine compartment, at the right shock tower

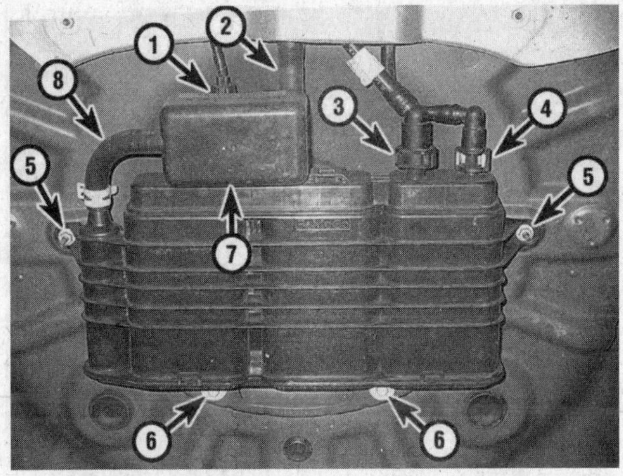

19.9 Typical EVAP canister details:

1. *EVAP canister vent solenoid and dust separator electrical connector*
2. *Fuel vapor hose*
3. *Fuel vapor hose quick-connect fitting*
4. *Fuel vapor hose quick-connect fitting*
5. *EVAP canister mounting nuts*
6. *EVAP canister mounting bolts*
7. *Heat shield for EVAP canister vent solenoid and dust separator*
8. *Fuel vapor hose*

6 Installation is the reverse of removal.

EVAP CANISTER

Refer to illustration 19.9

Note: The EVAP canister is located under the vehicle, on the underside of the spare tire well.

7 Disconnect the cable from the negative battery terminal (see Chapter 5).

8 Raise the vehicle and support it securely on jackstands.

9 Disconnect the electrical connector and the vapor hose quick-connect fitting from the EVAP canister vent solenoid (see illustration).

10 Disconnect the two EVAP line quick-connect fittings from the EVAP canister (see Chapter 4 for information on quick-connect fittings).

11 Remove the mounting fasteners that secure the canister and remove the canister.

12 Installation is the reverse of removal.

EVAP CANISTER VENT SOLENOID AND DUST SEPARATOR ASSEMBLY

Note: The EVAP canister vent solenoid is mounted on the EVAP canister.

13 Remove the EVAP canister (see Steps 7 through 11).

14 Release the two lock tabs and remove the EVAP canister vent solenoid heat shield from the canister by pushing it straight down.

15 Loosen the hose clamp and disconnect the fuel vapor hose from the vent solenoid.

16 Release the lock tab and detach the vent solenoid and dust separator assembly from the EVAP canister.

17 Installation is the reverse of removal.

20 Exhaust Gas Recirculation (EGR) valve - replacement

FOUR-CYLINDER MODELS

Note: The EGR valve is located at the left end of the cylinder head, behind the throttle body.

1 Disconnect the cable from the negative battery terminal (see Chapter 5).

2 Drain the cooling system (see Chapter 1).

3 Remove the air intake duct (see *Air filter housing - removal and installation* in Chapter 4).

4 Disconnect the electrical connector from the EGR valve.

5 On 2.3L engines, release the coolant hose clamp and disconnect the upper radiator hose from the coolant outlet passage.

6 Release the clamp and disconnect the coolant hose from the EGR valve.

7 Remove the two EGR valve mounting bolts and remove the EGR valve.

8 Remove and discard the EGR valve gasket, then clean the gasket mating surfaces of the cylinder head and the EGR valve.

9 Installation is the reverse of removal. Be sure to use a new EGR valve gasket, and tighten the EGR valve mounting bolts.

10 Refill the coolant system (see Chapter 1).

20.12 EGR valve electrical connector (3.0L V6 models)

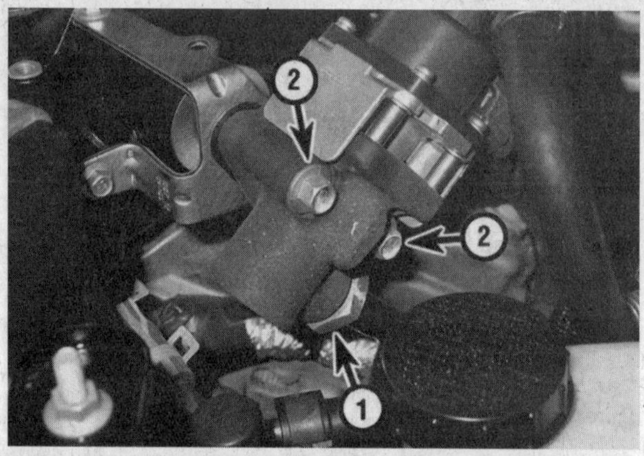

20.13 EGR valve mounting details (3.0L V6 models):

1 EGR tube nut fitting *2 EGR valve mounting bolts*

3.0L V6 MODELS

Refer to illustrations 20.12 and 20.13

Note: The EGR valve is located at the left end of the intake manifold, behind the throttle body.

11 Disconnect the cable from the negative battery terminal (see Chapter 5).

12 Disconnect the electrical connector from the EGR valve (see illustration).

13 Unscrew the tube nut fitting (see illustration) and disconnect the EGR pipe from the EGR valve.

14 Remove the EGR valve mounting bolts and remove the EGR valve.

15 Remove and discard the EGR valve gasket, then clean the gasket mating surfaces of the intake manifold and the EGR valve.

16 Installation is the reverse of removal. Be sure to use a new EGR valve gasket, and tighten the EGR valve mounting nuts securely.

21 Positive Crankcase Ventilation (PCV) valve - replacement

FOUR-CYLINDER MODELS

Note: The PCV valve is located on the crankcase vent oil separator, which is located on the front side of the engine block, under the intake manifold.

1 Remove the intake manifold (see Chapter 2A).

2 Loosen the hose clamp and disconnect the PCV hose from the PCV valve.

3 Pull the PCV valve out of the crankcase vent oil separator.

4 Installation is the reverse of removal.

V6 MODELS

Refer to illustration 21.6

Note: On 3.5L engines, the PCV valve is located on the rear valve cover. On 3.0L engines, see illustration 21.6. According to the manufacturer, the PCV valve must be replaced if it's removed.

5 Disconnect the cable from the negative battery terminal (see Chapter 5).

6 Disconnect the electrical connector from the PCV valve (see illustration).

7 Turn the PCV valve counterclockwise and remove it from the valve cover.

8 You must discard the PCV valve every time that you remove it and replace it with a new unit because the locking mechanism of the PCV valve is damaged by removal.

9 When installing the new PCV valve, make sure that the new valve is oriented correctly before screwing it into place, so that the terminal faces toward the wiring harness. If you install the new PCV valve so that it's facing in the wrong direction, you will have to unscrew it and once you do that, you must replace it again.

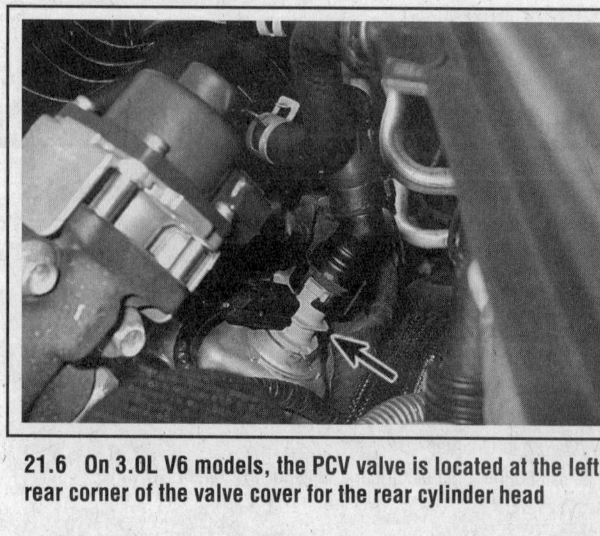

21.6 On 3.0L V6 models, the PCV valve is located at the left rear corner of the valve cover for the rear cylinder head

22 Secondary air injection system - component replacement

➡Note: The secondary air injection system is used only on 2.3L four-cylinder models.

1 Disconnect the cable from the negative battery terminal (see Chapter 5).

SECONDARY AIR INJECTION PUMP

➡Note: The secondary air injection pump is located at the lower front part of the engine compartment.

2 Raise the vehicle and place it securely on jackstands. Remove the underbody cover.

3 Disconnect the electrical connector from the secondary air injection pump.

4 Disengage the three wire harness clips/retainers from the secondary air injection pump air hoses.

5 Loosen the hose clamp and disconnect the inlet air hose from the air intake duct.

6 Loosen the hose clamp and disconnect the air hose from the secondary air diverter valve.

7 Remove the secondary air injection pump mounting bolts and remove the pump and hoses as a single assembly.

➡Note: Crimp style clamps are used to secure the hoses to the secondary air injection pump, so it's much easier to remove the pump and hoses as a single assembly, then cut off the clamps afterwards.

8 Be sure to use the same crimp style hose clamps to secure the inlet and outlet hoses to the air injection pump before installing the pump. Installation is otherwise the reverse of removal.

SECONDARY AIR VALVE

➡Note: The secondary air valve is located at the left rear corner of the engine, behind the left rear corner of the valve cover.

9 Disconnect the vacuum hose and the outlet and inlet hoses from the secondary air valve.

10 Remove the secondary air valve mounting bolts and remove the air valve.

11 Installation is the reverse of removal.

23 Variable Valve Timing (VVT) system - description

1 The VVT system controls intake valve timing to increase engine torque in the low and mid-speed range and to increase horsepower in the high-speed range.

2 The VVT system consists of the PCM-controlled Oil Control Valve (OCV), which is mounted on top of the cylinder head, and the VVT actuator, which is mounted on the front end of the intake camshaft.

3 The PCM-controlled OCV varies the oil pressure in the VVT actuator, which continually varies the timing of the intake cam in relation to the fixed timing of the exhaust cam.

4 Refer to Chapter 2 for component replacement procedures for the OCV and VVT actuator.

Torque specifications	Ft-lbs (unless otherwise indicated)	Nm

➡Note: One foot-pound (ft-lb) of torque is equivalent to 12 inch-pounds (in-lbs) of torque. Torque values below approximately 15 ft-lbs are expressed in inch-pounds, since most foot-pound torque wrenches are not accurate at these smaller values.

Torque specifications	Ft-lbs (unless otherwise indicated)	Nm
Cylinder Heat Temperature (CHT) sensor		
Four-cylinder engines	106 in-lbs	12
3.0L V6 engine	97 in-lbs	11
3.5L V6 engine	89 in-lbs	10
Knock sensor mounting bolt	15	20
Oxygen sensor	35	47

7A

MANUAL TRANSAXLE

Section

1 General information

The vehicles covered by this manual are equipped with either a 5-speed manual or a 5- or 6-speed automatic transaxle. This Part of Chapter 7 contains information on the manual transaxle. Service procedures for the automatic transaxle are contained in Part B. Information on the transfer case used on AWD models can be found in Part C.

The transaxle is contained in a cast-aluminum alloy casing bolted to the engine's left-hand end, and consists of the gearbox and final drive differential. The transaxle unit type is stamped on a plate attached to the transaxle.

TRANSAXLE OVERHAUL

Because of the complexity of the assembly, possible unavailability of replacement parts and special tools necessary, internal repair procedures for the transaxle are not recommended for the home mechanic. The bulk of the information in this Chapter is devoted to removal and installation procedures.

2 Shift lever - removal and installation

1 Apply the parking brake. Place the shift lever in Neutral. Remove the shift lever knob.

2 Remove the center console (see Chapter 11).

3 Working through the openings in the shifter housing, use a small screwdriver to release the Selector cable from the ball-stud on the shift assembly.

4 Remove the nut securing the Shift cable to the shift assembly.

5 Remove the four nuts securing the shift lever and remove the shifter.

6 Installation is the reverse of removal.

3 Shift cables - adjustment and replacement

**** WARNING:**

These models are equipped with a Supplemental Restraint System (SRS), more commonly known as airbags. Always disable the airbag system before working in the vicinity of any airbag system component to avoid the possibility of accidental deployment of the airbag(s), which could cause personal injury (see Chapter 12). Do not use a memory saving device to preserve the PCM or radio memory when working on or near airbag system components.

**** WARNING:**

The air conditioning system is under high pressure. DO NOT loosen any fittings or remove any components until after the system has been discharged. Air conditioning refrigerant must be properly discharged into an EPA-approved container at a dealer service department or an automotive air conditioning repair facility. Always wear eye protection when disconnecting air conditioning system fittings.

➡Note: This is a difficult procedure for the home mechanic, since replacement of the cables requires removal of the instrument panel and the HVAC module under the instrument panel.

REPLACEMENT

1 Have the air conditioning refrigerant discharged at a dealer service department or air conditioning shop.

2 If the vehicle has just been driven, wait several hours to allow the engine to cool down before beginning this procedure. Disconnect both the negative and positive cables from the battery (see Chapter 5). Wait at least two minutes before proceeding.

3 Remove the battery and battery tray (see Chapter 5).

4 Remove the center console (see Chapter 11)

5 Remove the heater core/evaporator core housing (see Chapter 3).

6 Remove the shift lever and disconnect the shift cables from the shift lever (see Section 2).

7 Remove the clips securing the shift linkage cables to the shift lever arms at the transaxle. Do not damage the spring clips.

➡Note: The spring clips can be rotated for easier removal if the cable end is lifted to take pressure from the clips.

8 Release the cable housing ends at the transaxle from the transaxle support bracket, taking care not to damage the plastic flanges of the cable housing.

9 Disconnect and remove the airbag module ahead of the console area of the floor, then remove the insulation pad (see Chapter 12). Release the two clips securing the airbag module harness and push the harness forward.

10 Remove the fasteners securing the transmission cable plate/grommet where the cable goes through the floor.

11 Pull the shift cables through the floor from the inside.

➡Note: The grommet is integral to the cable assembly.

12 Installation is the reverse of removal. Be sure to adjust the new cable after installation (see Steps 14 through 20).

13 Refill and bleed the cooling system when you're done (see Chapter 1). Have the refrigerant recharged.

ADJUSTMENT

14 With the parking brake set, remove the gearshift knob and center console trim panel (see Chapter 11).

15 Slide the safety lock away from the shifter ball stud.

16 Slide the cable lock away from the shift cable end fitting.

17 Place the shift lever in the center position. The lever and the transaxle should now be in the Neutral position.

18 Push the cable lock onto the cable.

19 Slide the safety lock over the primary shift cable lock.

20 Install the center console trim panel and the gearshift knob.

4 Driveaxle oil seals - replacement

1 Oil leaks frequently occur due to wear of the driveaxle oil seals. Replacement of these seals is relatively easy, since the repair can be performed without removing the transaxle from the vehicle.

2 Driveaxle oil seals are located at the sides of the transaxle, where the driveaxles are attached. If leakage at the seal is suspected, raise the vehicle and support it securely on jackstands. If the seal is leaking, lubricant will be found on the sides of the transaxle, below the seals.

3 Refer to Chapter 8 and remove the driveaxles.

4 Use a screwdriver or prybar to carefully pry the oil seal out of the transaxle bore.

5 If the oil seal cannot be removed with a screwdriver or prybar, a special oil seal removal tool (available at auto parts stores) will be required.

6 Using a large section of pipe or a large deep socket (slightly smaller than the outside diameter of the seal) as a drift, install the new oil seal. Drive it into the bore squarely and make sure it's completely seated. Coat the seal lip with transaxle lubricant.

7 Install the driveaxle(s). Be careful not to damage the lip of the new seal with the inboard splines of the driveaxle.

5 Manual transaxle - removal and installation

➡Note: This is a difficult procedure, requiring the use of a vehicle hoist, an engine support fixture, a powertrain platform jack large enough to support removing the vehicle front subframe, and a transmission jack.

REMOVAL

1 Disconnect the cables from the battery and remove the battery and battery tray (see Chapter 5).

2 Remove the air filter housing and duct (see Chapter 4).

3 Disconnect the electrical connectors for the back-up light switch.

4 Disconnect the shift cables from the transaxle shift arms (see Section 3).

5 Remove the transaxle front and rear wire harness brackets from the transaxle.

6 Disconnect the electrical connector for the vehicle speed sensor (see Chapter 6).

7 Attach an engine support fixture to the lifting hook at the transaxle end of the engine. If no hook is provided, use a bolt of the proper size and thread pitch to attach the support fixture chain to a hole at the end of the cylinder head.

➡Note: Engine support fixtures can be obtained at most equipment rental yards and some auto parts stores.

8 Remove the three upper engine-to-transmission mounting bolts.

9 Loosen the driveaxle/hub nuts and the wheel lug nuts, raise the front of the vehicle and support it securely on jackstands. Remove the wheels.

10 Disconnect the clutch release cylinder and line from the transaxle and remove the clutch cable mounting bracket bolts (see Chapter 8).

11 Remove the left and right front transaxle mounts and brackets.

12 Remove the rear transaxle mount through-bolt.

13 Remove the starter (see Chapter 5).

14 On AWD models, remove the rear driveshaft and wire it aside

15 Remove the driveaxles (see Chapter 8).

16 Drain the transaxle lubricant (see Chapter 1).

17 Remove the three bolts securing the transaxle support insulator bracket, then remove the bracket.

18 Remove the suspension subframe (see Chapter 2C, Section 7).

19 Remove the longitudinal crossmember and the engine roll restrictor (see Chapter 2A or 2B).

20 Remove the upper and lower left-side splash shields.

21 If you're working on an AWD model, remove the transfer case (see Chapter 7C).

22 Support the transaxle with a jack - preferably a transmission jack made for this purpose (available at most tool rental yards). Safety chains will help steady the transaxle on the jack.

23 Remove the remaining bolts securing the transaxle to the engine.

24 Move the transaxle away from the engine to disengage it from the engine block dowel pins. Carefully lower the transmission jack to the floor and remove the transaxle.

INSTALLATION

25 Lubricate the input shaft with a light coat of high-temperature grease. With the transaxle secured to the jack, raise it into position behind the engine and carefully slide it forward, engaging the input shaft with the clutch. Do not use excessive force to install the transaxle - If the input shaft won't slide into place, readjust the angle of the transaxle or turn the input shaft so the splines engage properly with the clutch.

26 Once the transaxle is flush with the engine, install the transaxle-to-engine bolts. Tighten the bolts to the torque listed in this Chapter's Specifications.

⁂ CAUTION:

Don't use the bolts to force the transaxle and engine together.

27 The remainder of installation is the reverse of removal, noting the following points:

a) *Tighten the suspension crossmember mounting bolts to the torque values listed in this Chapter's Specifications.*
b) *Tighten the driveaxle/hub nuts to the torque value listed in the Chapter 8 Specifications.*
c) *Tighten the starter mounting bolts to the torque value listed in the Chapter 5 Specifications.*
d) *If installing the transfer case, refer to Chapter 7C.*
e) *Tighten the wheel lug nuts to the torque listed in the Chapter 1 Specifications.*
f) *Fill the transaxle with the correct type and amount of transaxle fluid as described in Chapter 1.*

6 Manual transaxle overhaul - general information

1 Overhauling a manual transaxle is a difficult job for the do-it-yourselfer. It involves the disassembly and reassembly of many small parts. Numerous clearances must be precisely measured and, if necessary, changed with select-fit spacers and snap-rings. As a result, if transaxle problems arise, it can be removed and installed by a competent do-it-yourselfer, but overhaul should be left to a transmission repair shop. Rebuilt transaxles may be available - check with your dealer parts department and auto parts stores. At any rate, the time and money involved in an overhaul is almost sure to exceed the cost of a rebuilt unit.

2 Nevertheless, it's not impossible for an inexperienced mechanic to rebuild a transaxle if the special tools are available and the job is done in a deliberate step-by-step manner so nothing is overlooked.

3 The tools necessary for an overhaul include internal and external snap-ring pliers, a bearing puller, a slide hammer, a set of pin punches, a dial indicator and possibly a hydraulic press. In addition, a large, sturdy workbench and a vise or transaxle stand will be required.

4 During disassembly of the transaxle, make careful notes of how each piece comes off, where it fits in relation to other pieces and what holds it in place.

5 Before taking the transaxle apart for repair, it will help if you have some idea what area of the transaxle is malfunctioning. Certain problems can be closely tied to specific areas in the transaxle, which can make component examination and replacement easier. Refer to the *Troubleshooting* Section at the front of this manual for information regarding possible sources of trouble.

7 Transaxle mount - replacement

1 Insert a large screwdriver or prybar between the mount and the transaxle and pry up.

2 The transaxle should not move excessively away from the mount. If it does, replace the mount.

3 Remove the battery and batter tray (see Chapter 5).

4 Remove the air filter housing (see Chapter 4)

5 Unbolt and set aside the underhood fuse/relay box (see Chapter 12).

6 Supporting the transaxle with a floorjack, remove the nuts and bolts and remove the mount. It may be necessary to raise the transaxle slightly to provide enough clearance to remove the mount.

7 Disconnect the two clips securing the clutch hydraulic hose (one metal U-clip, one plastic clip on the transmission mount).

8 Remove the remaining mount bolts.

9 Installation is the reverse of removal.

➡**Note: Install all of the mount fasteners before tightening any of them.**

Specifications

General

Transaxle oil type	See Chapter 1
Transaxle oil capacity	See Chapter 1

Torque specifications

➡**Note: One foot-pound (ft-lb) of torque is equivalent to 12 inch-pounds (in-lbs) of torque. Torque values below approximately 15 foot-pounds are expressed in inch-pounds, because most foot-pound torque wrenches are not accurate at these smaller values.**

Torque specifications	Ft-lbs (unless otherwise indicated)	Nm
Transaxle-to-engine mounting bolts	35	47
Oil pan-to-transaxle bolts	35	47
Transaxle-to-oil pan bolts	35	47
Transaxle drain plug	36	49
Crossmember-to-subframe bolts	85	115
Left transaxle mount bolts/nuts	46	62
Engine roll restrictor mounting bolts/nuts	66	89
Shifter assembly mounting bolts	16	22
Clutch slave cylinder mounting bolts	177 in-lbs	20

7B

AUTOMATIC TRANSAXLE

Section

Reference to other Chapters

Driveaxle oil seals - replacement - See Chapter 7A
Transaxle mount - replacement - See Chapter 7A

1 General information

All information on the automatic transaxles is included in this Part of Chapter 7. Information for the manual transaxle can be found in Part A of this Chapter.

Because of the complexity of the automatic transaxles and the specialized equipment necessary to perform most service operations, this Chapter contains only those procedures related to general diagnosis, routine maintenance, adjustment and removal and installation.

If the transaxle requires major repair work, it should be left to a dealer service department or an automotive or transmission repair shop. Once properly diagnosed you can, however, remove and install the transaxle yourself and save the expense, even if the repair work is done by a transmission shop.

2 Diagnosis - general

1 Automatic transaxle malfunctions may be caused by five general conditions:

a) Poor engine performance
b) Improper adjustments
c) Hydraulic malfunctions
d) Mechanical malfunctions
e) Malfunctions in the computer or its signal network

2 Diagnosis of these problems should always begin with a check of the easily repaired items: fluid level and condition (see Chapter 1), shift cable adjustment and shift lever installation. Next, perform a road test to determine if the problem has been corrected or if more diagnosis is necessary. If the problem persists after the preliminary tests and corrections are completed, additional diagnosis should be performed by a dealer service department or other qualified transmission repair shop. On modern electronically-controlled automatic transaxles, a scan tool is helpful in retrieving trouble codes relating to the transaxle. Refer to the *Troubleshooting* Section at the front of this manual for information on symptoms of transaxle problems.

PRELIMINARY CHECKS

3 Drive the vehicle to warm the transaxle to normal operating temperature.

4 Check the fluid level as described in Chapter 1:

a) If the fluid level is unusually low, add enough fluid to bring the level within the designated area of the dipstick, then check for external leaks (see following).
b) If the fluid level is abnormally high, drain off the excess, then check the drained fluid for contamination by coolant. The presence of engine coolant in the automatic transmission fluid indicates that a failure has occurred in the internal radiator oil cooler walls that separate the coolant from the transmission fluid (see Chapter 3).
c) If the fluid is foaming, drain it and refill the transaxle, then check for coolant in the fluid, or a high fluid level.

5 Check the engine idle speed.

➡Note: If the engine is malfunctioning, do not proceed with the preliminary checks until it has been repaired and runs normally.

6 Check and adjust the shift cable, if necessary (see Section 4).

7 If hard shifting is experienced, inspect the shift cable under the steering column and at the manual lever on the transaxle (see Section 4).

FLUID LEAK DIAGNOSIS

8 Most fluid leaks are easy to locate visually. Repair usually consists of replacing a seal or gasket. If a leak is difficult to find, the following procedure may help.

9 Identify the fluid. Make sure it's transmission fluid and not engine oil or brake fluid (automatic transmission fluid is a deep red color).

10 Try to pinpoint the source of the leak. Drive the vehicle several miles, then park it over a large sheet of cardboard. After a minute or two, you should be able to locate the leak by determining the source of the fluid dripping onto the cardboard.

11 Make a careful visual inspection of the suspected component and the area immediately around it. Pay particular attention to gasket mating surfaces. A mirror is often helpful for finding leaks in areas that are hard to see.

12 If the leak still cannot be found, clean the suspected area thoroughly with a degreaser or solvent, then dry it thoroughly.

13 Drive the vehicle for several miles at normal operating temperature and varying speeds. After driving the vehicle, visually inspect the suspected component again.

14 Once the leak has been located, the cause must be determined before it can be properly repaired. If a gasket is replaced but the sealing flange is bent, the new gasket will not stop the leak. The bent flange must be straightened.

15 Before attempting to repair a leak, check to make sure that the following conditions are corrected or they may cause another leak.

➡Note: Some of the following conditions cannot be fixed without highly specialized tools and expertise. Such problems must be referred to a qualified transmission shop or a dealer service department.

Gasket leaks

16 Check the pan periodically. Make sure the bolts are tight, no bolts are missing, the gasket is in good condition and the pan is flat (dents in the pan may indicate damage to the valve body inside).

17 If the pan gasket is leaking, the fluid level or the fluid pressure may be too high, the vent may be plugged, the pan bolts may be too tight, the pan sealing flange may be warped, the sealing surface of the transaxle housing may be damaged, the gasket may be damaged or the transaxle casting may be cracked or porous. If sealant instead of gasket material has been used to form a seal between the pan and the transaxle housing, it may be the wrong type of sealant.

Seal leaks

18 If a transaxle seal is leaking, the fluid level or pressure may be too high, the vent may be plugged, the seal bore may be damaged, the seal itself may be damaged or improperly installed, the surface of the shaft protruding through the seal may be damaged or a loose bearing may be causing excessive shaft movement.

19 Make sure the dipstick tube seal is in good condition and the tube is properly seated. Periodically check the area around the sensors for leakage. If transmission fluid is evident, check the seals for damage.

Case leaks

20 If the case itself appears to be leaking, the casting is porous and will have to be repaired or replaced.

21 Make sure the oil cooler hose fittings are tight and in good condition.

Fluid comes out vent pipe or fill tube

22 If this condition occurs the possible causes are: the transaxle is overfilled; there is coolant in the fluid; the case is porous; the dipstick is incorrect; the vent is plugged or the drain-back holes are plugged.

3 Shift lever - replacement

⁂ WARNING:

These models are equipped with a Supplemental Restraint System (SRS), more commonly known as airbags. Always disable the airbag system before working in the vicinity of any airbag system component to avoid the possibility of accidental deployment of the airbag(s), which could cause personal injury (see Chapter 12).

⁂ WARNING:

Do not use a memory saving device to preserve the PCM or radio memory when working on or near airbag system components.

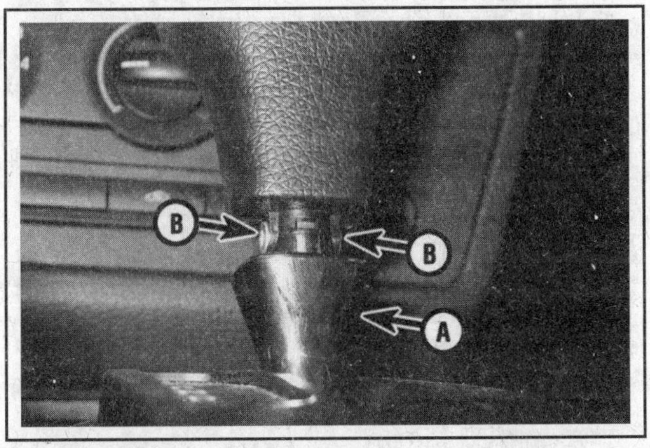

3.3 Pull the shift knob bezel down (A), then remove the two screws (B)

SHIFT KNOB

➧ Refer to illustration 3.3

1 Remove the upper bezel of the floor console around the shifter (see Chapter 11).

2 On models with 2.5L engines, disconnect the TCS switch electrical connector at the shifter.

3 Pull the shift knob bezel down, then remove the two screws in the knob assembly and remove the knob (see illustration).

4 Installation is the reverse of the removal procedure.

SHIFT LEVER ASSEMBLY

➧ Refer to illustrations 3.7, 3.8 and 3.10

5 Disconnect the cable from the negative battery terminal (see Chapter 5). Wait at least two minutes before proceeding.

6 Remove the floor console (see Chapter 11).

7 Use a trim tool to pry the cable eye from the ballstud on the shifter (see illustration).

8 Pull back on the clip securing the cable to the cable bracket on the shift assembly (see illustration).

9 Disconnect any electrical connectors at the shift assembly.

10 Remove the four mounting nuts and remove the shift assembly from the floor (see illustration).

11 Installation is the reverse of removal. The shift cable should be adjusted anytime it has been disconnected (see Section 4).

3.7 Pry the cable end from the ballstud on the shifter

3.8 Twist the cable housing end to release it from the serrated bracket

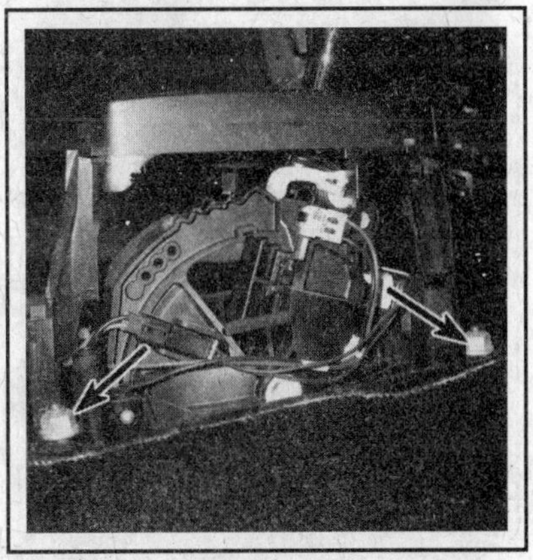

3.10 To remove the shifter assembly, remove the four mounting nuts (two seen here)

4 Shift cable - replacement and adjustment

✱✱ WARNING:

The models covered by this manual are equipped with Supplemental Restraint Systems (SRS), more commonly known as airbags. Always disarm the airbag system before working in the vicinity of any airbag system component to avoid the possibility of accidental deployment of the airbag, which could cause personal injury (see Chapter 12). Do not use a memory saving device to preserve the PCM or radio memory when working on or near airbag system components.

✱✱ WARNING:

The air conditioning system is under high pressure. DO NOT loosen any fittings or remove any components until after the system has been discharged. Air conditioning refrigerant must be properly discharged into an EPA-approved container at a dealer service department or an automotive air conditioning repair facility. Always wear eye protection when disconnecting air conditioning system fittings.

➡Note: This is a difficult procedure for the home mechanic, since replacement of the cables requires removal of the instrument panel and the HVAC housing under the instrument panel.

REPLACEMENT

➧ Refer to illustrations 4.9 and 4.10

1 Have the air conditioning refrigerant discharged at a dealer service department or air conditioning shop.

2 If the vehicle has just been driven, wait several hours to allow the engine to cool down before beginning this procedure. Disconnect both the negative and positive cables from the battery (see Chapter 5). Wait at least two minutes before proceeding.

3 Remove the battery and battery tray (see Chapter 5).

4 Remove the center console (see Chapter 11)

5 Remove the heater core/evaporator core housing (see Chapter 3).

6 Disconnect and remove the airbag module ahead of the console area of the floor, then remove the insulation pad (see Chapter 12). Release the two clips securing the airbag module harness and push the harness forward.

7 Disconnect the cable from the shift assembly on the floor and release the clips securing the cable housing end (see Section 3).

8 Remove the insulation from the floor area under the center of the instrument panel to access the fasteners securing the cable grommet to the floorpan. Remove the fasteners securing the transaxle cable plate/grommet.

9 To disconnect the shift cable at the transaxle control arm, lift the cable end to release pressure on the spring clip, then rotate the clip for removal. On some models, the cable end is released by squeezing two clips and pulling the cable from the ball-stud (see illustration).

✱✱ CAUTION:

Take care not to damage the spring clip.

10 Release the clips to remove the cable housing end from the mounting bracket on the transaxle, without damaging the plastic groove that holds the cable end (see illustration).

11 Disconnect any cable retainers along the length of the cable.

12 Pull the shift cable through the floor from the inside.

➡Note: The grommet is integral to the cable assembly.

13 Installation is the reverse of removal. Be certain to adjust the new cable after installation.

14 Refill and bleed the cooling system when you're done (see Chapter 1). Have the refrigerant recharged.

ADJUSTMENT

15 Set the parking brake, then disconnect the cable from the negative battery terminal (see Chapter 5).

16 If you are working on a 3.5L model, remove the air filter housing (see Chapter 4).

17 Place the shifter in Drive.

4.9 On models without a spring clip, pry the cable end from the ballstud on the shift control lever

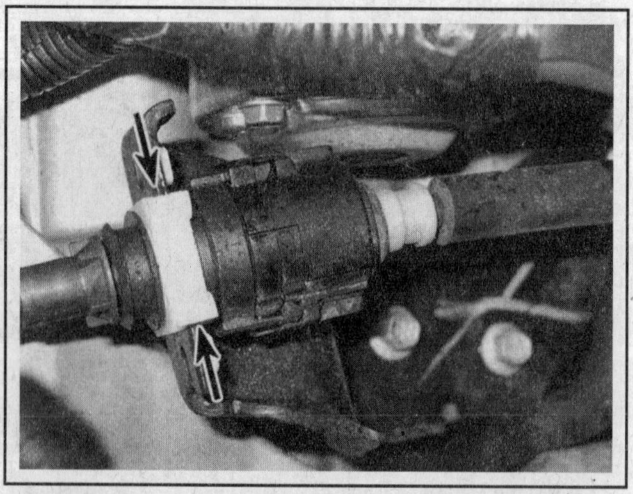

4.10 Squeeze the tabs to remove the cable from the bracket on the transmission

18 Remove the cable eye from the control arm on the transaxle.

19 Manually move the shift arm at the transaxle to Drive, then to the Park position.

20 Move the shift arm at the transaxle three clicks clockwise for five-speed transaxles, or three clicks counterclockwise for six-speed transaxles. The shift arm should now be in the Drive position.

21 The transmission end of the shift cable is equipped with an adjuster mechanism. Pull out on the two adjuster locking tabs, then move the lock Up from the cable end.

22 Attach the cable end to the stud on the control arm on the transaxle and push down. The adjuster should snap firmly onto the control arm.

23 After installing any remaining components, apply the parking brake, and operate the vehicle in each range to verify the adjustment is correct.

5 Automatic transaxle - removal and installation

➡Note: This is a difficult procedure, requiring the use of a vehicle hoist, an engine support fixture, and a transmission jack.

REMOVAL

➧ Refer to illustrations 5.7 and 5.26

1 Disconnect the cables from the battery and remove the battery and battery tray (see Chapter 5).

2 Remove the air filter housing and duct (see Chapter 4).

3 Disconnect the TCM harness electrical connector at the transmission range sensor. Also disconnect the ground straps and remove the bolts holding the electrical harness to the transaxle.

4 Disconnect the shift cable from the transaxle shift control arm (see Section 4). Remove the two bolts and one nut securing the transaxle cable mount.

5 Remove the transaxle front and rear wire harness brackets from the transaxle.

6 Disconnect the electrical connectors for the vehicle speed sensor and at the Transaxle control module (see Chapter 6).

7 Attach an engine support fixture to the lifting hook at the transaxle end of the engine (see illustration). On V6 engines, the upper intake manifold must be removed (see Chapter 2B). If no hook is provided, use a bolt of the proper size and thread pitch to attach the support fixture chain to a hole at the end of the cylinder head.

➡Note: Engine support fixtures can be obtained at most equipment rental yards and some auto parts stores.

8 Remove the four (three on some models) upper engine-to-transmission mounting bolts.

9 Loosen the driveaxle/hub nuts and the wheel lug nuts, raise the front of the vehicle and support it securely on jackstands or a lift. Remove the wheels.

10 Disconnect the shift cable from the transaxle, and remove the bolts securing the shift cable brackets.

11 Remove the EGR valve (see Chapter 6).

12 Unbolt the power steering hose bracket.

13 Disconnect the flexible exhaust pipe sections and the Y-pipe. Remove the right-side exhaust heat shield and remove the catalytic converter (see Chapter 4).

14 Remove the heat shield over the roll restrictor, then unbolt the roll restrictor.

15 Remove the driveaxles (see Chapter 8).

16 Remove the splash aprons from the left and right fenderwells.

17 Place a block of wood above the lower control arm to protect the outer CV joint on the left side. Remove the left steering knuckle (see Chapter 10).

18 Remove the starter (see Chapter 5).

19 On AWD models, remove the rear driveshaft and wire it aside.

20 Drain the transaxle lubricant (see Chapter 1). Disconnect and plug the transmission fluid hoses.

21 Remove the bolts securing the transaxle support insulator brackets, then remove the brackets.

22 If you're working on an AWD model, remove the transfer case (see Chapter 7, Part C).

23 Remove the front suspension subframe (see Chapter 2C, Section 7).

24 Support the transaxle with a jack - preferably a transmission jack made for this purpose (available at most tool rental yards). Safety chains will help steady the transaxle on the jack.

5.7 Use an overhead support fixture to secure the engine while the transmission and subframe are removed - note the chain locations

5.26 Mark the relationship of the torque converter to the driveplate

25 Disconnect the oxygen sensors (see Chapter 6).

26 Remove the torque converter cover and mark the relationship of the torque converter to the driveplate (see illustration). Remove the converter mounting nuts.

27 Remove the remaining bolts securing the transaxle to the engine.

28 Move the transaxle away from the engine to disengage it from the engine block dowel pins. Carefully lower the transmission jack to the floor and remove the transaxle.

INSTALLATION

29 Installation of the transaxle is a reversal of the removal procedure, but note the following points:

a) *As the torque converter is reinstalled, ensure that the drive tangs at the center of the torque converter hub engage with the recesses in the automatic transaxle fluid pump inner gear. This can be confirmed by turning the torque converter while pushing it towards the transaxle. If it isn't fully engaged, it will clunk into place.*
b) *When installing the transaxle, make sure the matchmarks you made on the torque converter and driveplate line up.*
c) *Install all of the driveplate-to-torque converter nuts before tightening any of them.*
d) *Tighten the driveplate-to-torque converter nuts to the specified torque.*
e) *Tighten the transaxle mounting bolts to the specified torque.*
f) *Tighten the suspension crossmember mounting bolts to the torque values listed in this Chapter's Specifications.*
g) *Tighten the driveaxle/hub nuts to the torque value listed in the Chapter 8 Specifications.*
h) *Tighten the wheel lug nuts to the torque listed in the Chapter 1 Specifications.*
i) *Fill the transaxle with the correct type and amount of automatic transmission fluid as described in Chapter 1.*
j) *On completion, adjust the shift cable as described in Section 4.*

6 Automatic transaxle overhaul - general information

In the event of a problem occurring, it will be necessary to establish whether the fault is electrical, mechanical or hydraulic in nature, before repair work can be contemplated. Diagnosis requires detailed knowledge of the transaxle's operation and construction, as well as access to specialized test equipment, and so is deemed to be beyond the scope of this manual. It is therefore essential that problems with the automatic transaxle are referred to a dealer service department or other qualified repair facility for assessment.

Note that a faulty transaxle should not be removed before the vehicle has been diagnosed by a knowledgeable technician equipped with the proper tools, as troubleshooting must be performed with the transaxle installed in the vehicle.

Specifications

General

Fluid type and capacity	See Chapter 1

Torque specifications	Ft-lbs (unless otherwise indicated)	Nm

➡Note: One foot-pound (ft-lb) of torque is equivalent to 12 inch-pounds (in-lbs) of torque. Torque values below approximately 15 foot-pounds are expressed in inch-pounds, because most foot-pound torque wrenches are not accurate at these smaller values.

Torque specifications	Ft-lbs (unless otherwise indicated)	Nm
Crossmember mounting bolts	35	47
Driveshaft bolts (AWD)	52	71
Fluid pan bolts	115 in-lbs	13
Torque converter-to-driveplate nuts	27	37
Transaxle-to-engine mounting bolts		
3.0L V6	30	40
Four-cylinder and 3.5L V6	35	47

7C

TRANSFER CASE

Section

1 General information

On the covered vehicles, models equipped with V6 engines are offered with optional All Wheel Drive (AWD). The transfer case sends power to the rear differential and rear driveaxles through a driveshaft that delivers the torque to a rear differential and two rear driveaxles. The AWD control module will shift into AWD when the PCM initiates the need due to differences in wheelslip speed between the front and rear wheels. The system requires no driver input to operate, thus there is no select button on the instrument panel.

Due to the complexity of the transfer case covered in this manual and the need for specialized equipment to perform most service operations, this Chapter contains only routine maintenance and removal and installation procedures.

If the transfer case requires major repair work, it must be replaced as a unit.

2 Transfer case rear output shaft oil seal - removal and installation

Refer to illustration 2.11

1 Raise the vehicle and support it securely on jackstands.

2 Drain the transfer case lubricant (see Chapter 1).

3 Remove the driveshaft (see Chapter 8).

4 Mark the relative positions of the pinion, nut and flange.

5 Use a beam- or dial-type inch-pound torque wrench to determine the torque required to rotate the pinion (vehicle in Neutral). Record it for use later.

6 Count the number of threads visible between the end of the nut and the end of the pinion shaft and record it for use later.

7 Remove the flange mounting nut using a two-pin spanner to hold the pinion flange while loosening the locknut.

8 Remove the companion flange, using a puller whose bolt-holes can be attached to two, three or all four of the flange's driveshaft bolt holes. Tighten the puller center bolt to press the flange off the shaft.

9 Pry out the seal with a screwdriver or a seal removal tool. Don't damage the seal bore.

10 Remove the seal deflector, then use a seal-puller to remove the pinion seal.

11 With the seal removed, remove the collapsible bearing spacer (see illustration).

12 Install a new collapsible spacer.

13 Lubricate the lips of the new seal with multi-purpose grease and tap it evenly into position with a seal installation tool or a large socket. Make sure it enters the housing squarely and is tapped in to its full depth.

14 Align the mating marks made before disassembly and install the companion flange. If necessary, tighten the pinion nut to draw the flange into place.

15 Tighten the NEW nut carefully until the original number of threads are exposed and the marks are aligned.

16 Measure the torque required to rotate the pinion and tighten the nut in small increments until it matches the figure recorded in Step 5.

CAUTION:

If you exceed the original torque reading by more than three in-lbs, the assembly will need to be taken apart again to install a new collapsible spacer.

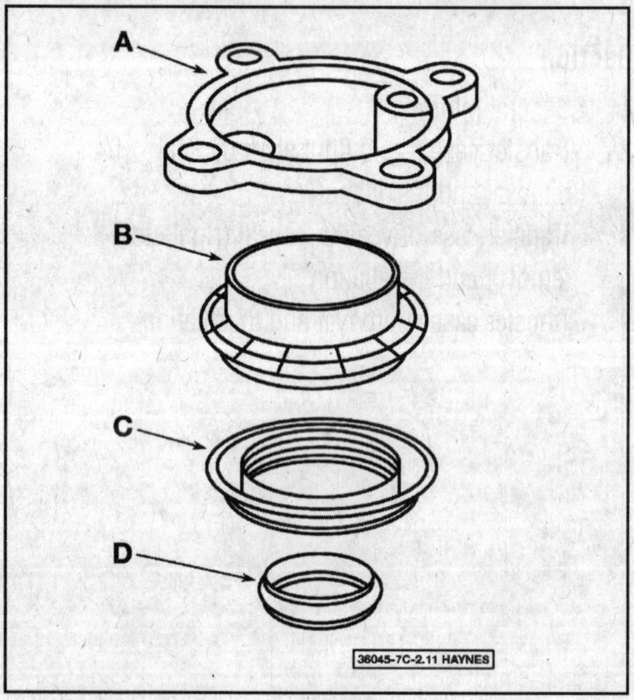

2.11 Rear output shaft seal details

A Collapsible bearing spacer
B Output shaft seal
C Seal deflector
D Driveshaft companion flange

17 Connect the driveshaft (see Chapter 8), add the specified lubricant to the transfer case (see Chapter 1) and lower the vehicle.

CAUTION:

All driveshaft flange and support bearing bolts must be replaced with New fasteners.

3 Transfer case driveaxle oil seal (right side) - removal and installation

1 Remove the wheel cover or hub cap on the right side. Break the hub nut loose with a socket and large breaker bar.

2 Loosen the wheel lug nuts, raise the vehicle and support it securely on jackstands. Remove the right wheel and the splash panel from the right fenderwell.

3 Remove the right driveaxle and intermediate shaft (see Chapter 8).

4 Remove the three bolts securing the heat shield and remove the heat shield.

5 Remove the dust shield.

6 Carefully remove the seal (there is a non-serviceable bearing behind it). There are several types of seal removal tools. The manufacturer recommends using a slide-hammer tool with an internal-expanding type of seal-puller. Using a long, threaded extension on the slide-hammer allows the seal to be removed without removing the exhaust system.

7 Using a seal installer or a large deep socket as a drift, install the new oil seal. Drive it into the bore squarely and make sure it's completely seated.

8 Lubricate the lip of the new seal with multi-purpose grease, then install a new dust shield.

9 Install the intermediate shaft and driveaxle (see Chapter 8).

10 The remainder of installation is the reverse of removal. Check the transfer case lubricant level and add some, if necessary, to bring it to the appropriate level (see Chapter 1).

4 Transfer case - removal and installation

1 Models equipped with V6 engines are offered with optional All Wheel Drive (AWD). The transfer case sends power to the rear differential and rear driveaxles.

2 Remove the wheel cover or hub cap. Break the hub nut loose with a socket and large breaker bar. Loosen the wheel lug nuts.

3 Raise the front of the vehicle and support it securely on jackstands. Remove the right wheel.

4 Unbolt the front portion of the driveshaft (see Chapter 8) and suspend it from a piece of wire (don't let it hang from the center support bearing).

5 Remove the right driveaxle and intermediate shaft (see Chapter 8). Remove the right-side catalytic converter (see Chapter 6).

6 Remove the two bolts securing the transfer case to the support bracket.

7 Remove the three bolts securing the transfer case support bracket to the engine.

8 Support the transfer case with a suitable jack.

9 Working on the right side of the transfer case, remove the three transfer case-to-transaxle mounting bolts.

10 Working on the left side, remove the final two mounting bolts (bellhousing-to-transfer case).

11 To remove the transfer case from the vehicle, rock the transfer case until it comes free of the transaxle.

12 Installation is the reverse of removal, noting the following points:

- *a) Install a new compression seal to the case.*
- *b) Tighten the exhaust system fasteners to the torque listed in the Chapter 4 Specifications.*
- *c) Tighten the NEW driveshaft fasteners to the torque listed in the Chapter 8 Specifications.*
- *d) Tighten the transfer case fasteners to the torque listed in this Chapter's Specifications.*
- *e) Refill the transfer case with the proper type and amount of fluid (see Chapter 1).*
- *f) Tighten the wheel lug nuts to the torque listed in the Chapter 1 Specifications.*

Specifications

Transfer case fluid type	See Chapter 1

Torque specifications	Ft-lbs	Nm
Transfer case-to-transaxle bolts	66	89
Transfer case support bracket-to-engine block mounting bolts		
2009 and earlier models	52	71
2010 models	35	47
Transfer case support bracket-to-transfer case mounting bolts		
2009 and earlier models	52	71
2010 models	35	47

8

CLUTCH AND DRIVELINE

Section

Reference to other Chapters

Differential lubricant level check (AWD models) - See Chapter 1

1 General information

The information in this Chapter deals with the components from the rear of the engine to the drive wheels, except for the transaxle, which is dealt with in the previous Chapter.

Since nearly all the procedures covered in this Chapter involve working under the vehicle, make sure it's securely supported on sturdy jackstands or on a hoist where the vehicle can be easily raised and lowered.

2 Clutch - description and check

1 All vehicles with a manual transaxle have a single dry plate, diaphragm spring-type clutch. The clutch disc has a splined hub which allows it to slide along the splines of the transaxle input shaft. The clutch and pressure plate are held in contact by spring pressure exerted by the diaphragm in the pressure plate.

2 The clutch release system is operated by hydraulic pressure. The hydraulic release system consists of the clutch pedal, a master cylinder and a shared common reservoir with the brake master cylinder, a release (or slave) cylinder and the hydraulic line connecting the two components.

3 When the clutch pedal is depressed, a pushrod pushes against brake fluid inside the master cylinder, applying hydraulic pressure to the release cylinder, which pushes the release bearing against the diaphragm fingers of the clutch pressure plate.

4 Terminology can be a problem when discussing the clutch components because common names are in some cases different from those used by the manufacturer. For example, the driven plate is also called the clutch plate or disc, the clutch release bearing is sometimes called a throwout bearing, the release cylinder is sometimes called the slave cylinder.

5 Unless you're replacing components with obvious damage, perform these preliminary checks to diagnose clutch problems:

a) The first check should be of the fluid level in the clutch master cylinder. If the fluid level is low, add fluid as necessary and inspect the hydraulic system for leaks. If the master cylinder reservoir is dry, bleed the system as described in Section 5 and recheck the clutch operation.

b) To check clutch spin-down time, run the engine at normal idle speed with the transaxle in Neutral (clutch pedal up - engaged). Disengage the clutch (pedal down), wait several seconds and shift the transaxle into Reverse. No grinding noise should be heard. A grinding noise would most likely indicate a bad pressure plate or clutch disc.

c) To check for complete clutch release, run the engine (with the parking brake applied to prevent vehicle movement) and hold the clutch pedal approximately 1/2-inch from the floor. Shift the transaxle between 1st gear and Reverse several times. If the shift is rough, component failure is indicated.

d) Visually inspect the pivot bushing at the top of the clutch pedal to make sure there's no binding or excessive play.

3 Clutch master cylinder - removal and installation

REMOVAL

1 Working under the dashboard, disconnect the clutch master cylinder pushrod from the clutch pedal.

2 Clamp a pair of locking pliers onto the clutch fluid feed hose, a couple of inches downstream of the brake fluid reservoir (the clutch master cylinder is supplied with fluid from the brake fluid reservoir). The pliers should be just tight enough to prevent fluid flow when the hose is disconnected. Disconnect the reservoir hose from the clutch master cylinder.

3 Using a flare-nut wrench, disconnect the hydraulic line fitting at the cylinder. Have rags handy, as some fluid will be lost as the line is removed. Cap or plug the ends of the line to prevent fluid leakage and the entry of contaminants.

4 Remove the battery tray and battery (see Chapter 5).

5 Disconnect and remove the PCM and its mounting bracket from under the instrument panel (see Chapter 6).

6 On 2010 models, remove the large nut securing the clutch master cylinder to the driver's side of the firewall. It's just above where the clutch rod comes through the firewall.

7 Remove the two nuts (one nut on 2010 models) on the engine side that secure the clutch master cylinder to the power brake booster.

8 Detach the cylinder from the firewall.

⁂ CAUTION:

Don't allow brake fluid to come into contact with the paint, as it will damage the finish.

INSTALLATION

9 Place the master cylinder in position on the firewall and install the interior mounting nut (2010 models) finger tight.

10 Connect the hydraulic line fitting to the clutch master cylinder and tighten it finger tight (since the cylinder is still a bit loose, it'll be easier to start the threads into the cylinder).

11 Tighten the engine-side mounting nuts (one nut on 2010 models) to the torque listed in this Chapter's Specifications, then tighten the hydraulic line fitting securely.

12 Attach the fluid feed hose from the reservoir to the clutch master cylinder and tighten the hose clamp. Remove the locking pliers.

13 Working under the dash, install the remaining mounting nut and connect the pushrod to the clutch pedal. Reinstall the PCM (see Chapter 6).

14 Fill the reservoir with brake fluid conforming to DOT 3 specifications and bleed the clutch system as outlined in Section 5.

4 Clutch release cylinder - removal and installation

REMOVAL

1 Disconnect the hydraulic line at the release cylinder using a flare-nut wrench. Have a small can and rags handy, as some fluid will be spilled as the line is removed. Plug the line to prevent excessive fluid loss and contamination.

2 Remove the release cylinder mounting bolts.

3 Remove the release cylinder.

INSTALLATION

4 Connect the hydraulic line fitting to the release cylinder, using your fingers only at this time (since the cylinder is still a bit loose, it'll be easier to start the threads into the cylinder).

5 Tighten the mounting bolts to the torque listed in this Chapter's Specifications.

6 Tighten the hydraulic fitting securely, using a flare-nut wrench.

7 Check the fluid level in the brake fluid reservoir, adding brake fluid conforming to DOT 3 specifications until the level is correct.

8 Bleed the system as described in Section 5, then recheck the brake fluid level.

5 Clutch hydraulic system - bleeding

1 Bleed the hydraulic system whenever any part of the system has been removed or the fluid level has fallen so low that air has been drawn into the master cylinder. The bleeding procedure is very similar to bleeding a brake system.

2 Fill the brake master cylinder reservoir with new brake fluid conforming to DOT 3 specifications.

**** CAUTION:**

Do not re-use any of the fluid coming from the system during the bleeding operation or use fluid which has been inside an open container for an extended period of time.

3 Have an assistant depress the clutch pedal and hold it. Open the bleeder valve on the release cylinder, allowing fluid and any air to escape. Close the bleeder valve when the flow of fluid (and bubbles) ceases. Once closed, have your assistant release the pedal.

4 Continue this process until all air is evacuated from the system, indicated by a solid stream of fluid being ejected from the bleeder valve each time with no air bubbles. Keep a close watch on the fluid level inside the brake master cylinder reservoir - if the level drops too far, air will get into the system and you'll have to start all over again.

➡**Note: Wash the area with water to remove any excess brake fluid.**

5 Check the brake fluid level again, and add some, if necessary, to bring it to the appropriate level. Check carefully for proper operation before placing the vehicle into normal service.

6 Clutch components - removal, inspection and installation

**** WARNING:**

Dust produced by clutch wear is hazardous to your health. DO NOT blow it out with compressed air and DO NOT inhale it. DO NOT use gasoline or petroleum-based solvents to remove the dust. Brake system cleaner should be used to flush the dust into a drain pan. After the clutch components are wiped clean with a rag, dispose of the contaminated rags and cleaner in a covered, marked container.

REMOVAL

▸ Refer to illustration 6.5

1 Access to the clutch components is normally accomplished by removing the transaxle, leaving the engine in the vehicle. If the engine is being removed for major overhaul, check the clutch for wear and replace worn components as necessary. However, the relatively low cost of the clutch components compared to the time and trouble spent gaining access to them warrants their replacement anytime the engine or transaxle is removed, unless they are new or in near-perfect condition. The following procedures are based on the assumption the engine will stay in place.

2 Remove the transaxle from the vehicle (see Chapter 7, Part A). Support the engine while the transaxle is out. An engine support fixture or a hoist should be used to support it from above.

3 The clutch fork and release bearing can remain attached to the transaxle housing for the time being.

4 To support the clutch disc during removal, install a clutch alignment tool through the clutch disc hub.

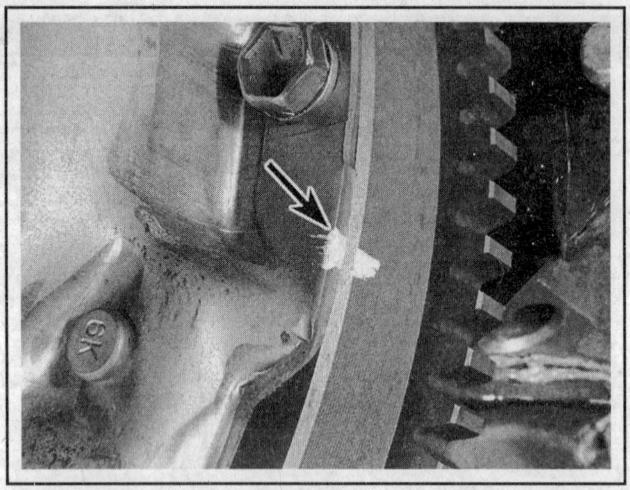

6.5 Mark the relationship of the pressure plate to the flywheel (if you're planning to re-use the old pressure plate)

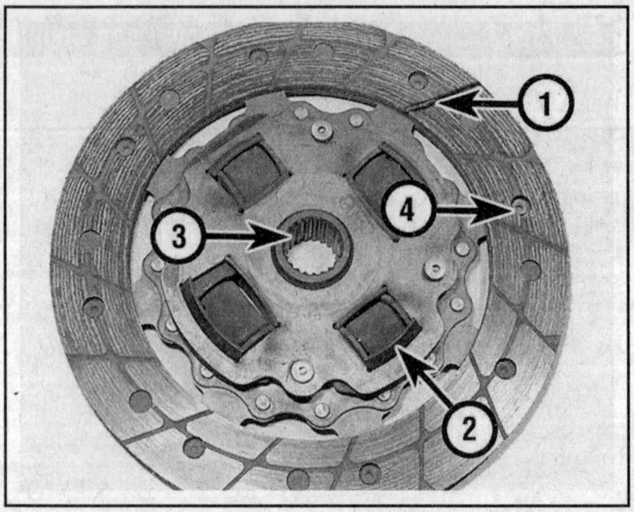

6.9 The clutch disc

1 ***Lining*** *- this will wear down in use*
2 ***Springs or dampers*** *- check for cracking and deformation*
3 ***Splined hub*** *- the splines must not be worn and should slide smoothly on the transaxle input shaft splines*
4 ***Rivets*** *- these secure the lining and will damage the flywheel or pressure plate if allowed to contact the surfaces*

5 Carefully inspect the flywheel and pressure plate for indexing marks. The marks are usually an X, an O or a white letter. If they cannot be found, scribe or paint marks yourself so the pressure plate and the flywheel will be in the same alignment during installation (see illustration).

6 Turning each bolt a little at a time, loosen the pressure plate-to-flywheel bolts. Work in a criss-cross pattern until all spring pressure is relieved. Then hold the pressure plate securely and completely remove the bolts, followed by the pressure plate and clutch disc.

INSPECTION

➧ **Refer to illustrations 6.9, 6.11a and 6.11b**

7 Ordinarily, when a problem occurs in the clutch, it can be attributed to wear of the clutch driven plate assembly (clutch disc). However, all components should be inspected at this time.

8 Inspect the flywheel for cracks, heat checking, grooves and other obvious defects. If the imperfections are slight, a machine shop can machine the surface flat and smooth, which is highly recommended regardless of the surface appearance. Refer to Chapter 2 for the flywheel removal and installation procedure.

9 Inspect the lining on the clutch disc. There should be at least 1/16-inch of lining above the rivet heads. Check for loose rivets, distortion, cracks, broken springs and other obvious damage (see illustration). As mentioned above, ordinarily the clutch disc is routinely replaced, so if in doubt about the condition, replace it with a new one.

10 The release bearing should also be replaced along with the clutch disc (see Section 7).

11 Check the machined surfaces and the diaphragm spring fingers of the pressure plate (see illustrations). If the surface is grooved or otherwise damaged, replace the pressure plate. Also check for obvious damage, distortion, cracking, etc. Light glazing can be removed with emery cloth or sandpaper. If a new pressure plate is required, new and re-manufactured units are available.

12 Check the pilot bearing in the end of the crankshaft for excessive wear, scoring, dryness, roughness and any other obvious damage. If any of these conditions are noted, replace the bearing.

13 Removal can be accomplished with a slide hammer and puller attachment, which are available at most auto parts stores or tool rental yards. Refer to Chapter 2 for the flywheel removal procedure (it must be removed before the pilot bearing is removed).

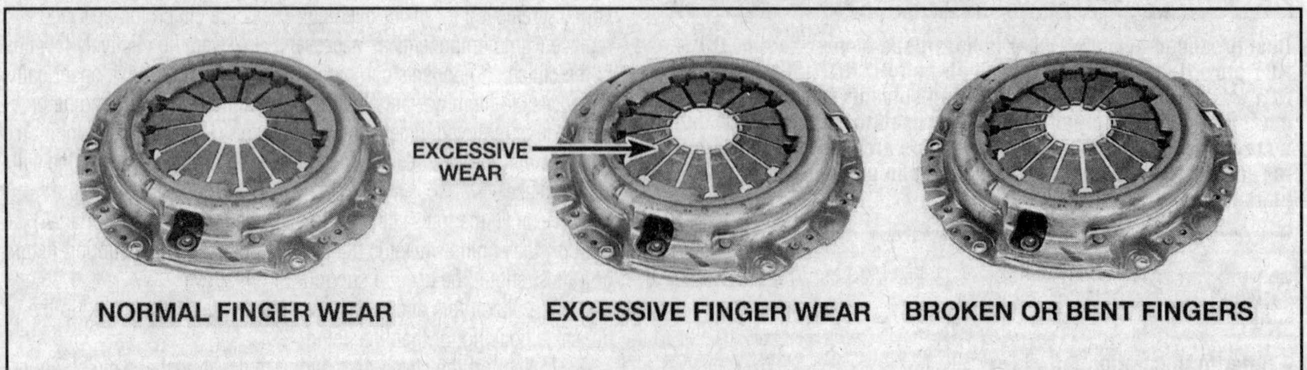

6.11a Replace the pressure plate if excessive wear or damage are noted

6.11b Inspect the pressure plate surface for excessive score marks, cracks and signs of overheating

6.16 Center the clutch disc in the pressure plate with a clutch alignment tool

INSTALLATION

➧ Refer to illustration 6.16

14 To install a new pilot bearing, lightly lubricate the outside surface with grease, then drive it into the recess with a bearing driver or a socket. Install the flywheel (see Chapter 2).

15 Before installation, clean the flywheel and pressure plate machined surfaces with brake cleaner, lacquer thinner or acetone. It's important that no oil or grease is on these surfaces or the lining of the clutch disc. Handle the parts only with clean hands.

16 Position the clutch disc and pressure plate against the flywheel with the clutch held in place with an alignment tool (see illustration). Make sure the disc is installed properly (most replacement clutch discs will be marked "flywheel side" or something similar - if not marked, install the clutch disc with the damper springs toward the transaxle).

17 Tighten the pressure plate-to-flywheel bolts only finger tight, working around the pressure plate.

18 Center the clutch disc by ensuring the alignment tool extends through the splined hub and into the pilot bearing in the crankshaft. Wiggle the tool up, down or side-to-side as needed to center the disc. Tighten the pressure plate-to-flywheel bolts a little at a time, working in a criss-cross pattern to prevent distorting the cover. After all of the bolts are snug, tighten them to the torque listed in this Chapter's Specifications. Remove the alignment tool.

19 Using high-temperature grease, lubricate the inner groove of the release bearing (see Section 7). Also place a small amount of grease on the release lever contact areas and the transaxle input shaft bearing retainer.

20 Install the clutch release bearing (see Section 7).

21 Install the transaxle and all components removed previously.

7 Clutch release bearing and lever - removal, inspection and installation

⁂ WARNING:

Dust produced by clutch wear is hazardous to your health. DO NOT blow it out with compressed air and DO NOT inhale it. DO NOT use gasoline or petroleum-based solvents to remove the dust. Brake system cleaner should be used to flush the dust into a drain pan. After the clutch components are wiped clean with a rag, dispose of the contaminated rags and cleaner in a covered, marked container.

REMOVAL

1 Remove the transaxle (see Chapter 7A).

2 Pull the clutch release fork off the ballstud and slide the release bearing off the input shaft along with the release fork.

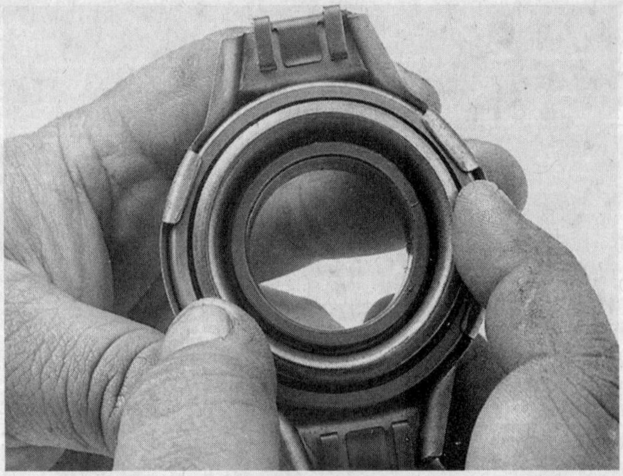

7.4 **To check the bearing, hold it by the outer race and rotate the inner race while applying pressure; if the bearing doesn't turn smoothly or if it is noisy, replace the bearing**

INSPECTION

Refer to illustration 7.4

3 Wipe off the bearing with a clean rag and inspect it for damage, wear and cracks. Don't immerse the bearing in solvent - it's sealed for life and immersion in solvent will ruin it.

4 Hold the center of the bearing and rotate the outer portion while applying pressure (see illustration). If the bearing doesn't turn smoothly or if it's noisy or rough, replace it.

Note: Considering the difficulty involved with replacing the release bearing, we recommend replacing the release bearing whenever the clutch components are replaced.

INSTALLATION

5 Lightly lubricate the friction surfaces of the release bearing, ballstud and the input shaft bearing retainer with high-temperature grease.

6 Install the release lever and bearing onto the input shaft.

7 The remainder of installation is the reverse of removal.

8 Driveaxles - removal and installation

WARNING:

Wait until the engine is completely cool before beginning this procedure.

FRONT

Removal

Refer to illustrations 8.1 and 8.12

1 Remove the wheel cover or hub cap. Break the driveaxle/hub nut loose with a socket and large breaker bar (see illustration).

2 Loosen the wheel lug nuts, raise the vehicle and support it securely on jackstands. Remove the wheel. Remove the pushpins securing the splash apron in the fenderwell.

3 Separate the upper control arm from the steering knuckle (see Chapter 10).

4 Remove the brake caliper and wire it aside, so that the flexible brake hose is not under tension (see Chapter 9).

5 Disconnect the brake hose tab that secures the brake hose to the steering knuckle.

6 Remove the driveaxle/hub nut from the axle and discard it. Remove the wheel speed sensor and set it aside.

7 Separate the upper balljoint from the steering knuckle (see Chapter 10).

8 Remove the bolts and flag-nuts securing the damper fork to the lower control arm (see Chapter 10).

9 Use a tool such as a hub driver to push the outboard end of the driveaxle from the steering knuckle.

10 Swing the knuckle/hub assembly out (away from the vehicle) until the end of the driveaxle is free of the hub.

8.1 Loosen the driveaxle/hub nut with a long breaker bar

Note: If the driveaxle splines stick in the hub, tap on the inner end of the driveaxle with a brass or plastic hammer.

Support the outer end of the driveaxle with a piece of wire to avoid unnecessary strain on the inner CV joint.

11 If you're removing the right driveaxle, carefully pry the inner CV joint off the intermediate shaft using a large screwdriver or prybar positioned between the CV joint housing and the intermediate shaft bearing support.

12 If you're removing the left driveaxle, pry the inner CV joint out of the transaxle using a large screwdriver or prybar positioned between the transaxle and the CV joint housing (see illustration). Be careful not to damage the differential seal.

13 Support the CV joints and carefully remove the driveaxle from the vehicle.

8.12 Carefully pry the inner end of the driveaxle from the transaxle

8.27 Remove the bolts securing the intermediate shaft bearing support

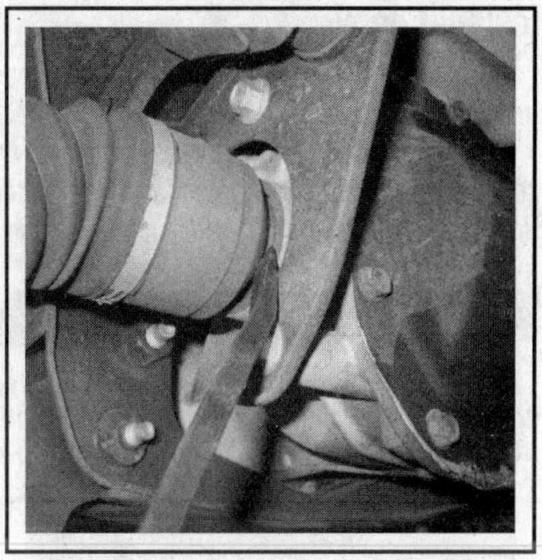

8.38 Carefully pry the inner end of the driveaxle from the differential

Installation

14 Pry the old spring clip from the inner end of the driveaxle (left side) or outer end of the intermediate shaft (right side) and install a new one. Lubricate the differential or intermediate shaft seal with multi-purpose grease and raise the driveaxle into position while supporting the CV joints.

➡Note: Position the spring clip with the opening facing down; this will ease insertion of the driveaxle and prevent damage to the clip.

15 Push the splined end of the inner CV joint into the differential side gear (left side) or onto the intermediate shaft (right side) and make sure the spring clip locks in its groove.

➡Note: The inner driveaxle end must go through the damper fork before the inner driveaxle end goes into the transaxle.

16 Apply a light coat of multi-purpose grease to the outer CV joint splines, pull out on the steering knuckle assembly and install the stub axle into the hub.

17 Insert the upper balljoint stud into the steering knuckle and tighten the pinch bolt to the torque listed in the Chapter 10 Specifications.

18 Reinstall the bottom of the damper fork to the lower control arm and use New bolts and flag nuts.

19 Install a new driveaxle/hub nut. Tighten the hub nut securely, but don't try to tighten it to the actual torque specification until you've lowered the vehicle to the ground.

20 Grasp the inner CV joint housing (not the driveaxle) and pull out to make sure the driveaxle has seated securely in the transaxle or on the intermediate shaft.

21 Install the wheel and lug nuts, then lower the vehicle. Tighten the lug nuts to the torque listed in the Chapter 1 Specifications.

22 Tighten the driveaxle/hub nut to the torque listed in this Chapter's Specifications. Install the hub cap or wheel cover.

INTERMEDIATE SHAFT

Removal

➧ Refer to illustration 8.27

➡Note: On AWD models, the intermediate shaft bearing support is bolted to the right-side of the transfer case with two bolts.

23 Remove the right side wheel cover or hub cap. Break the hub nut loose with a socket and large breaker bar.

24 Loosen the wheel lug nuts, raise the vehicle and support it securely on jackstands. Remove the wheel.

25 Follow the Steps at the beginning of this Section and remove the right driveaxle.

26 Remove the bolts and nuts securing the catalytic converter support bracket.

27 Remove the bearing-support mounting bolts (see illustration) and slide the intermediate shaft out of the transaxle. Be careful not to damage the differential seal when pulling the shaft out.

28 Check the support bearing for smooth operation by turning the shaft while holding the bearing. If you feel any roughness, take the intermediate shaft to an automotive machine shop or other qualified repair facility to have a new bearing installed.

Installation

29 Lubricate the lips of the transaxle seal with multi-purpose grease. Carefully guide the intermediate shaft into the transaxle side gear, then install the mounting nuts for the bearing support. Tighten the nuts to the torque listed in this Chapter's Specifications.

30 The remainder of installation is the reverse of removal.

REAR (AWD MODELS)

Removal

➧ Refer to illustration 8.38

31 Remove the wheel cover or hub cap. Break the driveaxle/hub nut loose with a socket and large breaker bar (see illustration 8.1).

32 Block the front wheels to prevent the vehicle from rolling. Loosen the wheel lug nuts, raise the rear of the vehicle and support it securely on jackstands. Remove the wheel.

33 Remove the driveaxle/hub nut and discard it.

34 Disconnect the ABS hose nut.

35 While supporting the lower control arm with a jack, unbolt the upper arm from the steering knuckle and the shock absorber lower bolt.

36 Remove the four mounting nuts that secure the tie-rod bracket.

37 Follow Steps 9 through 11 to remove the rear driveaxle.

38 Pry the inner end of the driveaxle out of the differential and remove it from the vehicle (see illustration).

Installation

39 Pry the old spring clip from the inner end of the driveaxle and install a new one.

40 Apply a light film of grease to the area on the inner CV joint stub shaft where the seal rides, then insert the splined end of the inner CV joint into the differential. Make sure the spring clip locks in its groove.

CAUTION:

Take care not to damage the differential seal with the driveaxle splines. It is recommended to use a plastic seal protector (Manufacturer tool #205-816).

41 Apply a light film of grease to the outer CV joint splines, pry the trailing arm outward and insert the outer end of the driveaxle into the hub.

42 The remainder of installation is the reverse of removal.

43 Install a new driveaxle/hub nut. Tighten the hub nut securely, but don't try to tighten it to the actual torque specification until you've lowered the vehicle to the ground.

44 Install the wheel and lug nuts, then lower the vehicle. Tighten the lug nuts to the torque listed in the Chapter 1 Specifications.

45 Tighten the driveaxle/hub nut to the torque listed in this Chapter's Specifications. Install the wheel cover or hub cap.

9 Driveaxle boot - replacement

Note: If the CV joints are worn, indicating the need for an overhaul (usually due to torn boots), explore all options before beginning the job. Complete rebuilt driveaxles are available on an exchange basis, which eliminates much time and work.

Note: Some auto parts stores carry split type replacement boots, which can be installed without removing the driveaxle from the vehicle. This is a convenient alternative; however, the driveaxle should be removed and the CV joint disassembled and cleaned to ensure the joint is free from contaminants such as moisture and dirt which will accelerate CV joint wear.

Note: Models equipped with ABS are equipped with ABS sensor rings on the outer CV joints. Be sure to inspect the sensor rings for chipped or missing teeth. Replace the sensor ring if necessary.

1 Remove the driveaxle from the vehicle (see Section 8).

2 Mount the driveaxle in a vise. The jaws of the vise should be lined with wood or rags to prevent damage to the driveaxle.

9.3 Cut off the boot clamps and discard them

FRONT

Inner CV joint and boot

Removal

Refer to illustrations 9.3, 9.4, 9.5, 9.6a, 9.6b and 9.7

3 Remove the boot clamps (see illustration).

4 Pull the boot back from the inner CV joint and slide the joint housing off. Be sure to mark the relationship of the tri-pod to the outer race (see illustration).

5 Use a center punch to mark the tri-pod and axleshaft to ensure that they are reassembled properly (see illustration).

9.4 Mark the relationship of the tri-pod assembly to the outer race

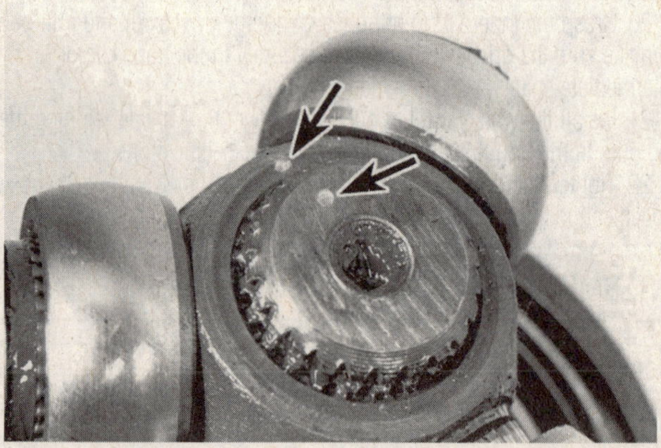

9.5 Use a center punch to ...

9.6a Spread the ends of the stop-ring apart and slide it towards the center of the shaft . . .

9.6b . . . then slide the tri-pod assembly back and remove the retainer clip

9.7 Drive the tri-pod joint from the axleshaft with a brass punch and hammer - make sure you don't damage the bearing surfaces or the splines on the shaft

6 Spread the ends of the stop-ring apart, slide it towards the center of the shaft, then remove the retainer clip from the end of the axleshaft (see illustrations).

7 Use a hammer and a brass punch to drive the tri-pod joint from the driveaxle (see illustration).

8 Remove the stop-ring from the axleshaft and discard it.

Inspection

9 Clean the old grease from the outer race and the tri-pod bearing assembly. Carefully disassemble each section of the tri-pod assembly, one at a time so as not to mix up the parts. Clean the needle bearings with solvent.

10 Inspect the rollers, tri-pod, bearings and outer race for scoring, pitting or other signs of abnormal wear, which will warrant the replacement of the inner CV joint.

Reassembly

➧ Refer to illustrations 9.11, 9.14, 9.16, 9.17a, 9.17b, 9.17c, 9.17d and 9.17e

11 Slide the clamps and boot onto the axleshaft. It's a good idea to wrap the axleshaft splines with tape to prevent damaging the boot (see illustration).

12 Install a new stop-ring on the axleshaft, but don't seat it in its groove; position it on the shaft past the groove.

13 Place the tri-pod on the shaft (making sure the marks are aligned) and install a new bearing retainer clip. Now slide the tri-pod up against the retainer clip and seat the stop-ring in its groove.

14 Apply CV joint grease to the tri-pod assembly, the inside of the joint housing and the inside of the boot (see illustration).

15 Slide the boot into place.

16 Position the CV joint mid-way through its travel, then equalize the pressure in the boot (see illustration).

9.11 Wrap the splined area of the axleshaft with tape to prevent damage to the boot(s) when installing it

9.14 Pack the outer race with CV joint grease and slide it over the tri-pod assembly - make sure the match marks on the CV joint housing and tri-pod line up

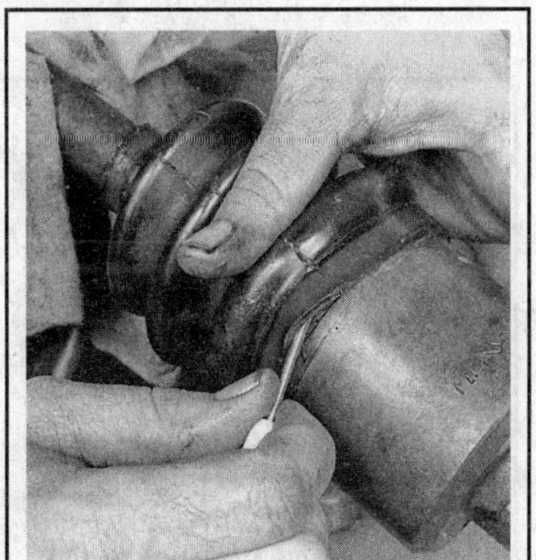

9.16 Equalize the pressure inside the boot by inserting a small, dull screwdriver between the boot and the outer race

9.17a To install new fold-over type clamps, bend the tang down . . .

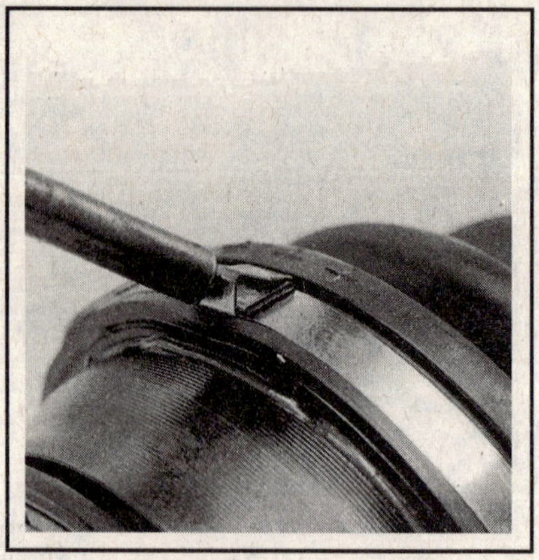

9.17b . . . and flatten the tabs to hold it in place

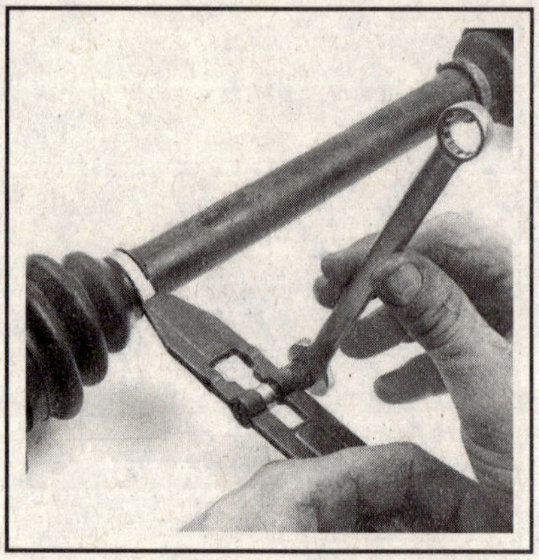

9.17c To install band-type clamps you'll need a special tool; install the band with its end pointing in the direction of axle rotation and tighten it securely, then pivot the tool up 90-degrees and tap the center of the clip with a center punch . . .

17 Tighten the boot clamps (see illustrations).
18 Install the driveaxle assembly (see Section 8).

Outer CV joint and boot

Removal

➧ Refer to illustration 9.20

19 Remove the boot clamps (see illustration 9.3).
20 Strike the edge of the CV joint housing sharply with a soft-face hammer to dislodge the outer CV joint from the axleshaft (see illustration). Remove and discard the bearing retainer clip from the axleshaft.
21 Slide the outer CV joint boot off the axleshaft.

Inspection

22 Thoroughly clean all components with solvent until the old CV grease is completely removed. Inspect the bearing surfaces of the inner tri-pods and housings for cracks, pitting, scoring, and other signs of wear. If any part of the outer CV joint is worn, you must replace the entire driveaxle assembly (inner CV joint, axleshaft and outer CV joint).

Reassembly

➧ Refer to illustrations 9.25a, 9.25b and 9.25c

23 Slide a new sealing boot clamp and sealing boot onto the axleshaft. It's a good idea to wrap the axleshaft splines with tape to prevent damaging the boot (see illustration 9.11).
24 Place a new bearing retainer clip onto the axleshaft.
25 Place half the grease provided in the sealing boot kit into the outer CV joint assembly housing (see illustration). Put the remaining grease into the sealing boot (see illustrations).
26 Align the splines on the axleshaft with the splines on the outer CV joint assembly and, using a soft-faced hammer, gently drive the CV joint onto the axleshaft until the CV joint is seated to the axleshaft.

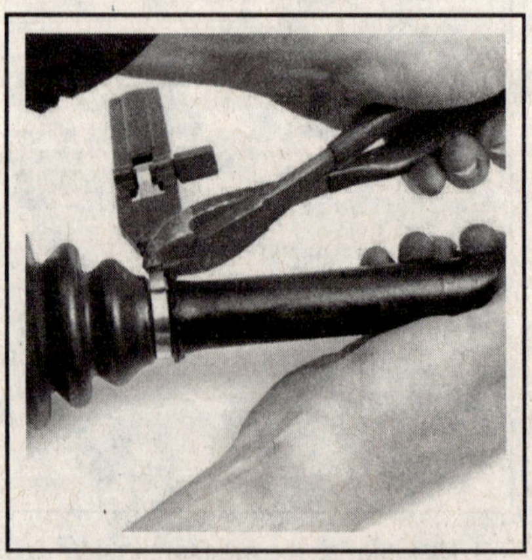

9.17d . . . then bend the end of the clamp back over the clip and cut off the excess

9.17e If you're installing crimp-type boot clamps, you'll need a pair of special crimping pliers (available at most auto parts stores)

9.20 Strike the edge of the CV joint housing sharply with a soft-faced hammer to dislodge the CV joint from the shaft

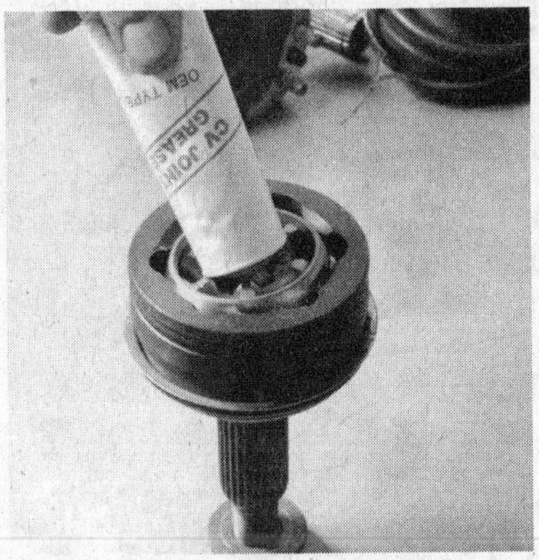

9.25a **Pack the outer CV joint assembly with CV grease . . .**

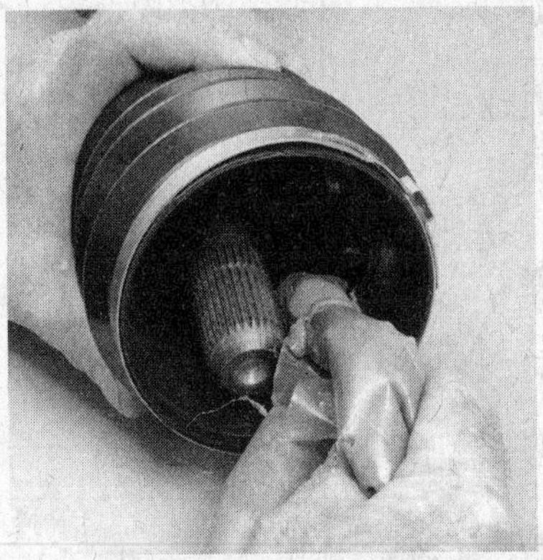

9.25b **. . . then apply grease to the inside of the boot . . .**

9.25c **. . . until the level is up to the end of the axle**

27 Position the CV joint mid-way through its travel, then equalize the pressure in the boot (see illustration 9.16).

28 Tighten the boot clamps (see illustrations 9.17a through 9.17e).

29 Install the driveaxle as outlined in Section 8.

REAR (AWD MODELS)

➡Note: This procedure applies to both the inner and outer CV joint boots.

Removal

30 Remove the driveaxle from the vehicle (see Section 8).

31 Mount the driveaxle in a vise. The jaws of the vise should be lined with wood or rags to prevent damage to the driveaxle.

32 Remove the boot clamps (see illustration 9.3).

33 Strike the edge of the CV joint housing sharply with a soft-face hammer to dislodge the outer CV joint from the axleshaft (see illustration 9.20).

34 Remove and discard the bearing retainer clip and snap-ring from the axleshaft.

35 Slide the CV joint boot off the axleshaft.

Inspection

36 Thoroughly clean all components with solvent until the old grease is completely removed. Inspect the bearing surfaces of the inner tripods and housings for cracks, pitting, scoring, and other signs of wear. If any part of the CV joint is worn, you must replace the entire driveaxle assembly (inner CV joint, axleshaft and outer CV joint).

Reassembly

37 Slide a new sealing boot clamp and sealing boot onto the axleshaft.

38 Install a new snap-ring and bearing retainer clip onto the axleshaft.

39 Place half the grease provided in the sealing boot kit into the outer CV joint assembly housing. Put the remaining grease into the sealing boot (see illustrations 9.25a through 9.25c).

40 Align the splines on the axleshaft with the splines on the CV joint assembly and, using a soft-faced hammer, gently drive the CV joint onto the axleshaft until the CV joint is seated to the axleshaft.

41 Position the CV joint mid-way through its travel, then equalize the pressure in the boot (see illustration 9.16).

42 Tighten the boot clamps (see illustrations 9.17a through 9.17e).

43 Install the driveaxle as outlined in Section 8.

10 Driveshaft (AWD models) - removal and installation

➧ Refer to illustrations 10.2 and 10.6

➡Note: The manufacturer recommends replacing driveshaft fasteners with new ones when installing the driveshaft.

1 Raise the vehicle and support it securely on jackstands. Place the selector lever in Neutral.

2 Remove the bolt securing the ground strap, if equipped (see illustration). Remove the exhaust Y-pipe (see Chapter 4).

3 Use chalk or a scribe to mark the relationship of the driveshaft to the differential pinion yoke. This ensures correct alignment when the driveshaft is reinstalled.

4 Remove the bolts securing the universal joint flange to the differential pinion yoke.

5 Working at the front of the driveshaft, remove the bolts securing the driveshaft to the transaxle/transfer case.

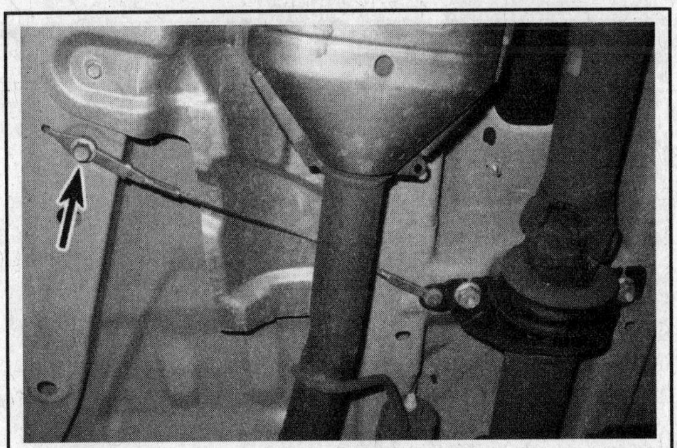

10.2 **Remove the ground strap mounting bolt**

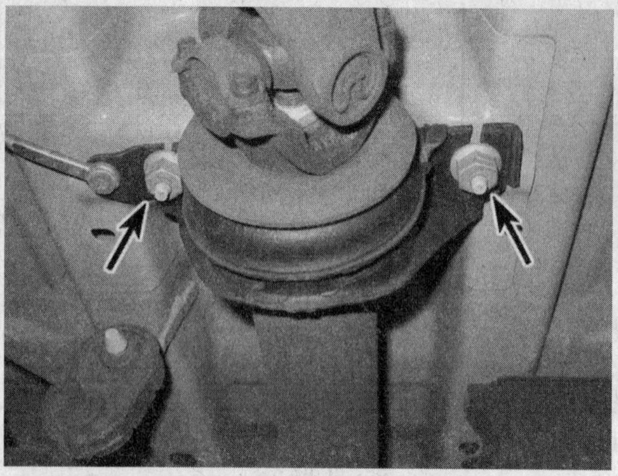

10.6 Remove the nuts securing the center support bearing (typical)

6 Remove the nuts securing the two center support bearings (see illustration).

7 With help from an assistant, carefully remove the driveshaft from the vehicle.

8 Installation is the reverse of removal. Make sure the universal joint caps are properly placed in the flange seat. Tighten the fasteners to the torque listed in this Chapter's Specifications.

11 Rear driveaxle oil seals (AWD models) - replacement

1 Raise the rear of the vehicle and support it securely on jackstands. Place the transaxle in Neutral with the parking brake off. Block the front wheels to prevent the vehicle from rolling.

2 Remove the driveaxle(s) (see Section 8).

3 Carefully pry out the driveaxle oil seal with a seal removal tool or a large screwdriver. Be careful not to damage or scratch the seal bore.

4 Using a seal installer or a large deep socket as a drift, install the new oil seal. Drive it into the bore squarely and make sure it's completely seated.

5 Lubricate the lip of the new seal with multi-purpose grease, then install the driveaxle. Be careful not to damage the lip of the new seal.

6 Check the differential lubricant level and add some, if necessary, to bring it to the appropriate level (see Chapter 1).

12 Differential (AWD models) - removal and installation

1 Raise the rear of the vehicle and support it securely on jackstands. Block the front wheels to prevent the vehicle from rolling.

2 Remove the driveshaft (see Section 10).

3 Remove the driveaxles (see Section 8).

4 There are four rear differential mounting brackets securing the differential to the subframe, one at either side at the top-front of the assembly and two at the top-rear. Remove the two bolts on each front bracket.

5 Support the rear of the differential with a floor jack. Remove the three bolts securing the differential to the rear mounting brackets.

6 Lower the differential with the floor jack

7 Installation is the reverse of removal. Tighten all fasteners to the torque listed in this Chapter's Specifications.

13 Differential pinion oil seal - replacement

1 Loosen the wheel lug nuts. Raise the rear of the vehicle and support it securely on jackstands. Block the opposite set of wheels to keep the vehicle from rolling off the stands. Remove the wheels.

2 Disconnect the driveshaft from the differential companion flange and fasten it out of the way (see Section 10).

3 Mark the relationship of the pinion flange to the shaft, then count and write down the number of exposed threads on the shaft.

4 A flange holding tool will be required to keep the companion flange from moving while the self-locking pinion nut is loosened. A chain wrench will also work.

5 Remove the pinion nut.

6 Withdraw the flange. It may be necessary to use a two-jaw puller engaged behind the flange to draw it off. Do not attempt to pry or hammer behind the flange or hammer on the end of the pinion shaft.

7 Pry out the old seal and discard it.

8 Lubricate the lips of the new seal and fill the space between the seal lips with wheel bearing grease, then tap it evenly into position with a seal installation tool or a large socket. Make sure it enters the housing squarely and is tapped in to its full depth.

9 Install the pinion flange, lining up the marks made in Step 3. If necessary, tighten the pinion nut to draw the flange into place. Do not try to hammer the flange into position.

10 Install a new pinion nut, then tighten it to the torque listed in this Chapter's Specifications.

11 The remainder of installation is the reverse of removal.

Specifications

Clutch fluid type	See Chapter 1

Torque specifications

➡Note: One foot-pound (ft-lb) of torque is equivalent to 12 inch-pounds (in-lbs) of torque. Torque values below approximately 15 foot-pounds are expressed in inch-pounds, because most foot-pound torque wrenches are not accurate at these smaller values.

Torque specifications	Ft-lbs (unless otherwise indicated)	Nm
Clutch		
Clutch master cylinder mounting nuts	15	20
Clutch pressure plate-to-flywheel bolts	21	28
Clutch release cylinder mounting bolts	168 in-lbs	19
Rear differential (AWD models)		
Differential-to-insulator bracket bolts	66	89
Differential side insulator bracket bolts	66	89
Filler plug	21	28
Differential pinion nut	180	244
Driveaxles		
Brake hose-to-knuckle bolt	17	23
Driveaxle/hub nut		
Front driveaxle	185	251
Rear driveaxle (AWD models)	188	255
Intermediate shaft bearing support bracket bolts	30	40
Driveshafts (AWD)		
Driveshaft flange bolts at transfer case	52	71
Driveshaft center support bearing nuts	41	56
Driveshaft-to-transfer case bolts	27	37
Rear driveshaft-to-differential pinion flange bolts	52	71

Notes

9 BRAKES

Section

Reference to other Chapters

Brake check - See Chapter 1

Brake fluid level check - See Chapter 1

1 General information

The vehicles covered by this manual are equipped with hydraulically operated front and rear brake systems. The front and rear brakes are disc type. Both the front and rear brakes are self adjusting. The disc brakes automatically compensate for pad wear.

HYDRAULIC SYSTEM

The hydraulic system consists of two separate circuits. The master cylinder has separate reservoirs for the two circuits, and, in the event of a leak or failure in one hydraulic circuit, the other circuit will remain operative. A dual proportioning valve on the firewall provides brake balance between the front and rear brakes.

POWER BRAKE BOOSTER

The power brake booster, utilizing engine manifold vacuum and atmospheric pressure to provide assistance to the hydraulically operated brakes, is mounted on the firewall in the engine compartment.

PARKING BRAKE

The parking brake operates the rear brakes only, through cable actuation. It's activated by a lever mounted in the center console.

SERVICE

After completing any operation involving disassembly of any part of the brake system, always test drive the vehicle to check for proper braking performance before resuming normal driving. When testing the brakes, perform the tests on a clean, dry, flat surface. Conditions other than these can lead to inaccurate test results.

Test the brakes at various speeds with both light and heavy pedal pressure. The vehicle should stop evenly without pulling to one side or the other. Avoid locking the brakes, because this slides the tires and diminishes braking efficiency and control of the vehicle.

Tires, vehicle load and wheel alignment are factors which also affect braking performance.

PRECAUTIONS

There are some general cautions and warnings involving the brake system on this vehicle:

a) *Use only brake fluid conforming to DOT 3 specifications.*
b) *The brake pads contain fibers which are hazardous to your health if inhaled. Whenever you work on brake system components, clean all parts with brake system cleaner. Do not allow the fine dust to become airborne. Also, wear an approved filtering mask.*
c) *Safety should be paramount whenever any servicing of the brake components is performed. Do not use parts or fasteners which are not in perfect condition, and be sure that all clearances and torque specifications are adhered to. If you are at all unsure about a certain procedure, seek professional advice. Upon completion of any brake system work, test the brakes carefully in a controlled area before putting the vehicle into normal service. If a problem is suspected in the brake system, don't drive the vehicle until it's fixed.*

2 Troubleshooting

PROBABLE CAUSE	CORRECTIVE ACTION
No brakes - pedal travels to floor	
1 Low fluid level 2 Air in system	1 and 2 Low fluid level and air in the system are symptoms of another problem - a leak somewhere in the hydraulic system. Locate and repair the leak
3 Defective seals in master cylinder	3 Replace master cylinder
4 Fluid overheated and vaporized due to heavy braking	4 Bleed hydraulic system (temporary fix). Replace brake fluid (proper fix)
Brake pedal slowly travels to floor under braking or at a stop	
1 Defective seals in master cylinder	1 Replace master cylinder
2 Leak in a hose, line, caliper or wheel cylinder	2 Locate and repair leak
3 Air in hydraulic system	3 Bleed the system, inspect system for a leak
Brake pedal feels spongy when depressed	
1 Air in hydraulic system	1 Bleed the system, inspect system for a leak
2 Master cylinder or power booster loose	2 Tighten fasteners
3 Brake fluid overheated (beginning to boil)	3 Bleed the system (temporary fix). Replace the brake fluid (proper fix)
4 Deteriorated brake hoses (ballooning under pressure)	4 Inspect hoses, replace as necessary (it's a good idea to replace all of them if one hose shows signs of deterioration)

PROBABLE CAUSE	CORRECTIVE ACTION
Brake pedal feels hard when depressed and/or excessive effort required to stop vehicle	
1 Power booster faulty	1 Replace booster
2 Engine not producing sufficient vacuum, or hose to booster clogged, collapsed or cracked	2 Check vacuum to booster with a vacuum gauge. Replace hose if cracked or clogged, repair engine if vacuum is extremely low
3 Brake linings contaminated by grease or brake fluid	3 Locate and repair source of contamination, replace brake pads or shoes
4 Brake linings glazed	4 Replace brake pads or shoes, check discs and drums for glazing, service as necessary
5 Caliper piston(s) or wheel cylinder(s) binding or frozen	5 Replace calipers or wheel cylinders
6 Brakes wet	6 Apply pedal to boil-off water (this should only be a momentary problem)
7 Kinked, clogged or internally split brake hose or line	7 Inspect lines and hoses, replace as necessary
Excessive brake pedal travel (but will pump up)	
1 Drum brakes out of adjustment	1 Adjust brakes
2 Air in hydraulic system	2 Bleed system, inspect system for a leak
Excessive brake pedal travel (but will not pump up)	
1 Master cylinder pushrod misadjusted	1 Adjust pushrod
2 Master cylinder seals defective	2 Replace master cylinder
3 Brake linings worn out	3 Inspect brakes, replace pads and/or shoes
4 Hydraulic system leak	4 Locate and repair leak
Brake pedal doesn't return	
1 Brake pedal binding	1 Inspect pivot bushing and pushrod, repair or lubricate
2 Defective master cylinder	2 Replace master cylinder
Brake pedal pulsates during brake application	
1 Brake drums out-of-round	1 Have drums machined by an automotive machine shop
2 Excessive brake disc runout or disc surfaces out-of-parallel	2 Have discs machined by an automotive machine shop
3 Loose or worn wheel bearings	3 Adjust or replace wheel bearings
4 Loose lug nuts	4 Tighten lug nuts
Brakes slow to release	
1 Malfunctioning power booster	1 Replace booster
2 Pedal linkage binding	2 Inspect pedal pivot bushing and pushrod, repair/lubricate
3 Malfunctioning proportioning valve	3 Replace proportioning valve
4 Sticking caliper or wheel cylinder	4 Repair or replace calipers or wheel cylinders
5 Kinked or internally split brake hose	5 Locate and replace faulty brake hose
Brakes grab (one or more wheels)	
1 Grease or brake fluid on brake lining	1 Locate and repair cause of contamination, replace lining
2 Brake lining glazed	2 Replace lining, deglaze disc or drum

Troubleshooting (continued)

PROBABLE CAUSE	CORRECTIVE ACTION
Vehicle pulls to one side during braking	
1 Grease or brake fluid on brake lining	1 Locate and repair cause of contamination, replace lining
2 Brake lining glazed	2 Deglaze or replace lining, deglaze disc or drum
3 Restricted brake line or hose	3 Repair line or replace hose
4 Tire pressures incorrect	4 Adjust tire pressures
5 Caliper or wheel cylinder sticking	5 Repair or replace calipers or wheel cylinders
6 Wheels out of alignment	6 Have wheels aligned
7 Weak suspension spring	7 Replace springs
8 Weak or broken shock absorber	8 Replace shock absorbers
Brakes drag (indicated by sluggish engine performance or wheels being very hot after driving)	
1 Brake pedal pushrod incorrectly adjusted	1 Adjust pushrod
2 Master cylinder pushrod (between booster and master cylinder)	2 Adjust pushrodincorrectly adjusted
3 Obstructed compensating port in master cylinder	3 Replace master cylinder
4 Master cylinder piston seized in bore	4 Replace master cylinder
5 Contaminated fluid causing swollen seals throughout system	5 Flush system, replace all hydraulic components
6 Clogged brake lines or internally split brake hose(s)	6 Flush hydraulic system, replace defective hose(s)
7 Sticking caliper(s) or wheel cylinder(s)	7 Replace calipers or wheel cylinders
8 Parking brake not releasing	8 Inspect parking brake linkage and parking brake mechanism, repair as required
9 Improper shoe-to-drum clearance	9 Adjust brake shoes
10 Faulty proportioning valve	10 Replace proportioning valve
Brakes fade (due to excessive heat)	
1 Brake linings excessively worn or glazed	1 Deglaze or replace brake pads and/or shoes
2 Excessive use of brakes	2 Downshift into a lower gear, maintain a constant slower speed (going down hills)
3 Vehicle overloaded	3 Reduce load
4 Brake drums or discs worn too thin	4 Measure drum diameter and disc thickness, replace drums or discs as required
5 Contaminated brake fluid	5 Flush system, replace fluid
6 Brakes drag	6 Repair cause of dragging brakes
7 Driver resting left foot on brake pedal	7 Don't ride the brakes
Brakes noisy (high-pitched squeal)	
1 Glazed lining	1 Deglaze or replace lining
2 Contaminated lining (brake fluid, grease, etc.)	2 Repair source of contamination, replace linings
3 Weak or broken brake shoe hold-down or return spring	3 Replace springs
4 Rivets securing lining to shoe or backing plate loose	4 Replace shoes or pads
5 Excessive dust buildup on brake linings	5 Wash brakes off with brake system cleaner
6 Brake drums worn too thin	6 Measure diameter of drums, replace if necessary
7 Wear indicator on disc brake pads contacting disc	7 Replace brake pads
8 Anti-squeal shims missing or installed improperly	8 Install shims correctly

➡Note: Other remedies for quieting squealing brakes include the application of an anti-squeal compound to the backing plates of the brake pads, and lightly chamfering the edges of the brake pads with a file. The latter method should only be performed with the brake pads thoroughly wetted with brake system cleaner, so as not to allow any brake dust to become airborne.

PROBABLE CAUSE	CORRECTIVE ACTION

Brakes noisy (scraping sound)

PROBABLE CAUSE	CORRECTIVE ACTION
1 Brake pads or shoes worn out; rivets, backing plate or brake shoe metal contacting disc or drum	1 Replace linings, have discs and/or drums machined (or replace)

Brakes chatter

PROBABLE CAUSE	CORRECTIVE ACTION
1 Worn brake lining	1 Inspect brakes, replace shoes or pads as necessary
2 Glazed or scored discs or drums	2 Deglaze discs or drums with sandpaper (if glazing is severe, machining will be required)
3 Drums or discs heat checked	3 Check discs and/or drums for hard spots, heat checking, etc. Have discs/drums machined or replace them
4 Disc runout or drum out-of-round excessive	4 Measure disc runout and/or drum out-of-round, have discs or drums machined or replace them
5 Loose or worn wheel bearings	5 Adjust or replace wheel bearings
6 Loose or bent brake backing plate (drum brakes)	6 Tighten or replace backing plate
7 Grooves worn in discs or drums	7 Have discs or drums machined, if within limits (if not, replace them)
8 Brake linings contaminated (brake fluid, grease, etc.)	8 Locate and repair source of contamination, replace pads or shoes
9 Excessive dust buildup on linings	9 Wash brakes with brake system cleaner
10 Surface finish on discs or drums too rough after machining especially on vehicles with sliding calipers)	10 Have discs or drums properly machined
11 Brake pads or shoes glazed	11 Deglaze or replace brake pads or shoes

Brake pads or shoes click

PROBABLE CAUSE	CORRECTIVE ACTION
1 Shoe support pads on brake backing plate grooved or	1 Replace brake backing plateexcessively worn
2 Brake pads loose in caliper	2 Loose pad retainers or anti-rattle clips
3 Also see items listed under Brakes chatter	

Brakes make groaning noise at end of stop

PROBABLE CAUSE	CORRECTIVE ACTION
1 Brake pads and/or shoes worn out	1 Replace pads and/or shoes
2 Brake linings contaminated (brake fluid, grease, etc.)	2 Locate and repair cause of contamination, replace brake pads or shoes
3 Brake linings glazed	3 Deglaze or replace brake pads or shoes
4 Excessive dust buildup on linings	4 Wash brakes with brake system cleaner
5 Scored or heat-checked discs or drums	5 Inspect discs/drums, have machined if within limits (if not, replace discs or drums)
6 Broken or missing brake shoe attaching hardware	6 Inspect drum brakes, replace missing hardware

Rear brakes lock up under light brake application

PROBABLE CAUSE	CORRECTIVE ACTION
1 Tire pressures too high	1 Adjust tire pressures
2 Tires excessively worn	2 Replace tires
3 Defective proportioning valve	3 Replace proportioning valve

Brake warning light on instrument panel comes on (or stays on)

PROBABLE CAUSE	CORRECTIVE ACTION
1 Low fluid level in master cylinder reservoir (reservoirs with fluid level sensor)	1 Add fluid, inspect system for leak, check the thickness of the brake pads and shoes
2 Failure in one half of the hydraulic system	2 Inspect hydraulic system for a leak
3 Piston in pressure differential warning valve not centered	3 Center piston by bleeding one circuit or the other (close bleeder valve as soon as the light goes out)
4 Defective pressure differential valve or warning switch	4 Replace valve or switch

Troubleshooting (continued)

PROBABLE CAUSE	CORRECTIVE ACTION
Brake warning light on instrument panel comes on (or stays on) (continued)	
5 Air in the hydraulic system	5 Bleed the system, check for leaks
6 Brake pads worn out (vehicles with electric wear sensors - small probes that fit into the brake pads and ground out on the disc when the pads get thin)	6 Replace brake pads (and sensors)
Brakes do not self adjust	
Disc brakes	
1 Defective caliper piston seals	1 Replace calipers. Also, possible contaminated fluid causing soft or swollen seals (flush system and fill with new fluid if in doubt)
2 Corroded caliper piston(s)	2 Same as above
Drum brakes	
1 Adjuster screw frozen	1 Remove adjuster, disassemble, clean and lubricate with high-temperature grease
2 Adjuster lever does not contact star wheel or is binding	2 Inspect drum brakes, assemble correctly or clean or replace parts as required
3 Adjusters mixed up (installed on wrong wheels after brake job)	3 Reassemble correctly
4 Adjuster cable broken or installed incorrectly (cable-type adjusters)	4 Install new cable or assemble correctly
Rapid brake lining wear	
1 Driver resting left foot on brake pedal	1 Don't ride the brakes
2 Surface finish on discs or drums too rough	2 Have discs or drums properly machined
3 Also see Brakes drag	

3 Anti-lock Brake System (ABS) - general information

GENERAL INFORMATION

1 The anti-lock brake system is designed to maintain vehicle steerability, directional stability and optimum deceleration under severe braking conditions on most road surfaces. It does so by monitoring the rotational speed of each wheel and controlling the brake line pressure to each wheel during braking. This prevents the wheels from locking up.

2 The ABS system has three main components - the wheel speed sensors, the electronic control unit (ECU) and the hydraulic unit. Four wheel-speed sensors - one at each wheel - send a variable voltage signal to the control unit, which monitors these signals, compares them to its program and determines whether a wheel is about to lock up. When a wheel is about to lock up, the control unit signals the hydraulic unit to reduce hydraulic pressure (or not increase it further) at that wheel's brake caliper. Pressure modulation is handled by electrically-operated solenoid valves.

3 If a problem develops within the system, an "ABS" warning light will glow on the dashboard. Sometimes, a visual inspection of the ABS system can help you locate the problem. Carefully inspect the ABS wiring harness. Pay particularly close attention to the harness and connections near each wheel. Look for signs of chafing and other damage caused by incorrectly routed wires. If a wheel sensor harness is damaged, the sensor must be replaced.

WARNING:

Do NOT try to repair an ABS wiring harness. The ABS system is sensitive to even the smallest changes in resistance. Repairing the harness could alter resistance values and cause the system to malfunction. If the ABS wiring harness is damaged in any way, it must be replaced.

CAUTION:

Make sure the ignition is turned off before unplugging or reattaching any electrical connections.

DIAGNOSIS AND REPAIR

4 If a dashboard warning light comes on and stays on while the vehicle is in operation, the ABS system requires attention. Although

special electronic ABS diagnostic testing tools are necessary to properly diagnose the system, you can perform a few preliminary checks before taking the vehicle to a dealer service department.

a) *Check the brake fluid level in the reservoir.*
b) *Verify that the computer electrical connectors are securely connected.*
c) *Check the electrical connectors at the hydraulic control unit.*
d) *Check the fuses.*
e) *Follow the wiring harness to each wheel and verify that all connections are secure and that the wiring is undamaged.*

5 If the above preliminary checks do not rectify the problem, the vehicle should be diagnosed by a dealer service department or other qualified repair shop. Due to the complex nature of this system, all actual repair work must be done by a qualified automotive technician.

WHEEL SPEED SENSOR - REMOVAL AND INSTALLATION

6 Loosen the wheel lug nuts, raise the vehicle and support it securely on jackstands. Remove the wheel.

7 Make sure the ignition key is turned to the Off position.

8 Trace the wiring back from the sensor, detaching all brackets and clips while noting its correct routing, then disconnect the electrical connector.

9 Remove the mounting bolt and carefully pull the sensor out from the knuckle.

10 Installation is the reverse of the removal procedure. Tighten the mounting bolt securely.

11 Install the wheel and lug nuts, tightening them securely. Lower the vehicle and tighten the lug nuts to the torque listed in the Chapter 1 Specifications.

4 Disc brake pads - replacement

Refer to illustrations 4.5, 4.6a through 4.6m and 4.7a through 4.7k

WARNING:

Disc brake pads must be replaced on both front or both rear wheels at the same time - never replace the pads on only one wheel. Also, the dust created by the brake system is harmful to your health. Never blow it out with compressed air and don't inhale any of it. An approved filtering mask should be worn when working on the brakes. Do not, under any circumstances, use petroleum-based solvents to clean brake parts. Use brake system cleaner only!

1 Remove the cap from the brake fluid reservoir.

2 Loosen the wheel lug nuts, raise the vehicle and support it securely on jackstands. Block the wheels at the opposite end.

3 Remove the wheels. Work on one brake assembly at a time, using the assembled brake for reference if necessary.

4 Inspect the brake disc carefully as outlined in Section 6. If machining is necessary, follow the information in that Section to remove the disc, at which time the pads can be removed as well.

5 Before disassembling the brake, wash it thoroughly with brake system cleaner and allow it to dry (see illustration). Position a drain pan under the brake to catch the residue - DO NOT use compressed air to blow off the brake dust.

6 Follow the accompanying photos (illustrations 4.6a through 4.6m) for the actual pad replacement procedure. Be sure to stay in order and read the caption under each illustration.

4.5 Always wash the brakes with brake cleaner before disassembling anything

4.6a Depress the piston into the bottom of its bore in the caliper with a large C-clamp to make room for the new pads - make sure the fluid in the master cylinder reservoir doesn't overflow

4.6b Using two wrenches, hold the guide pin (A) while loosening the caliper mounting bolt (B)

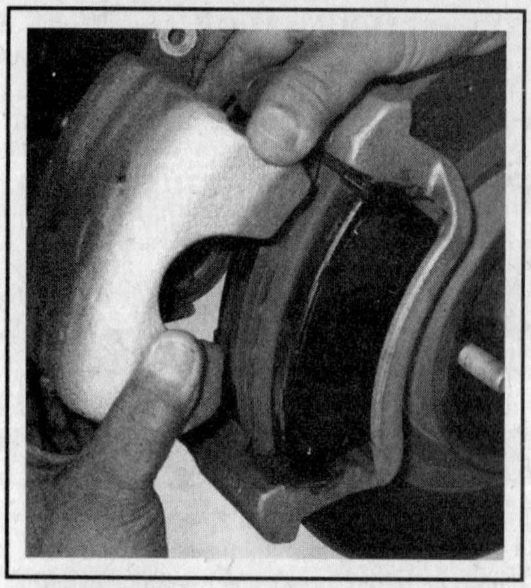

4.6c Pull the caliper from the caliper mounting bracket

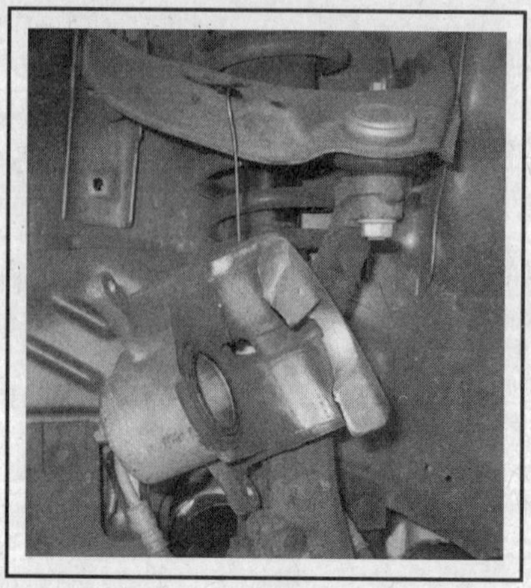

4.6d Secure the caliper to the suspension with a length of stiff wire

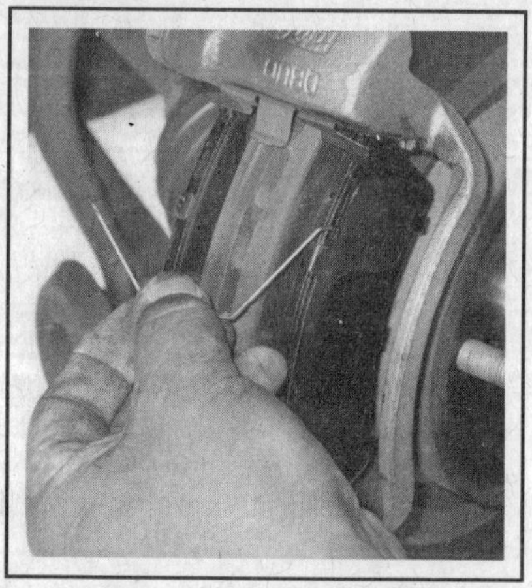

4.6e Remove the brake pad retraction springs from the pads

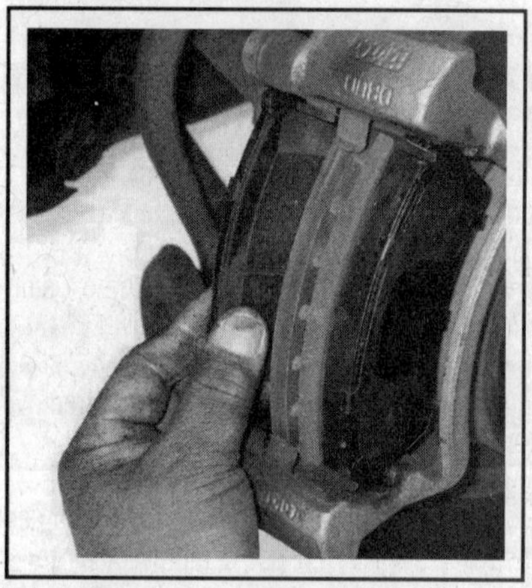

4.6f Remove the inner brake pad

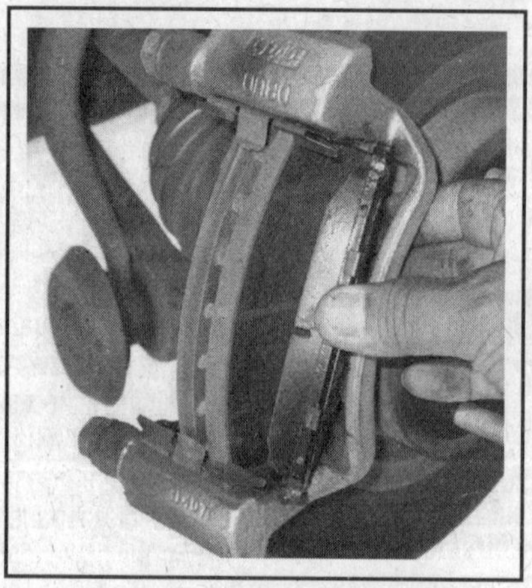

4.6g Remove the outer brake pad

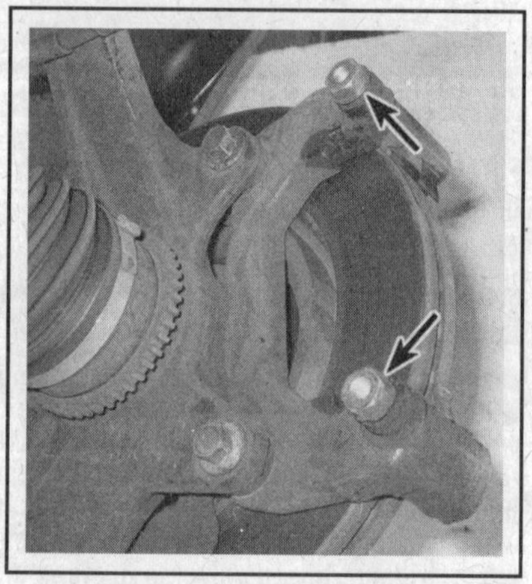

4.6h Remove the two caliper guide pins

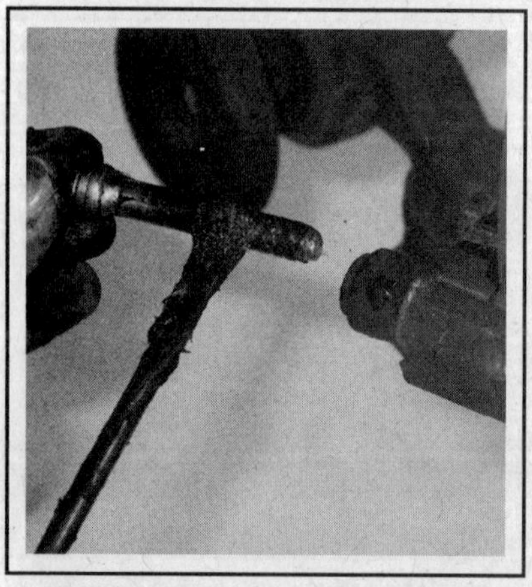

4.6i Pull out the caliper guide pins and clean them, then apply a coat of high-temperature grease to the pins and reinstall the pins in the caliper bracket

4.6j Remove the pad slide clips, clean them and lubricate the wear points with high-temp brake grease, then reinstall on the caliper mounting bracket

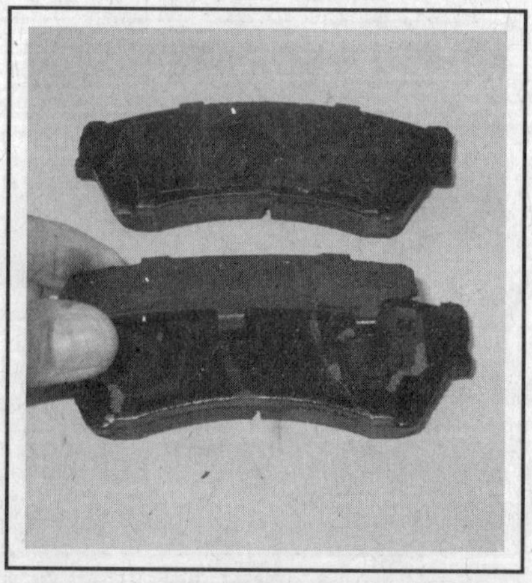

4.6k Snap the two stainless-steel shims to the back of each pad, then apply anti-squeal compound to the outboard side of the shims

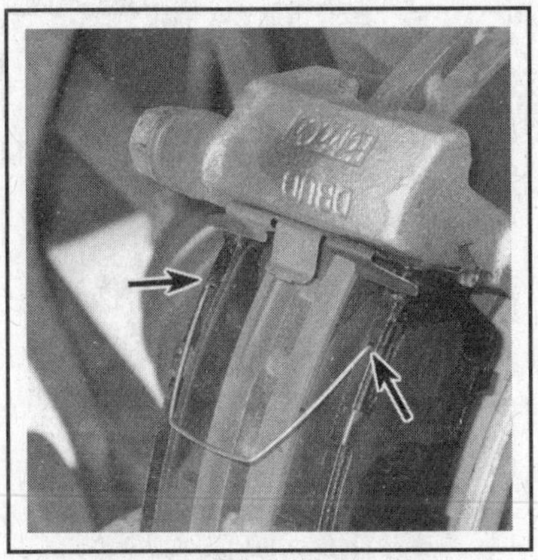

4.6l Place the pads in the caliper mounting bracket and install the upper and lower pad retraction springs

4.6m Install the caliper and tighten the caliper mounting bolts to the torque listed in this Chapter's Specifications

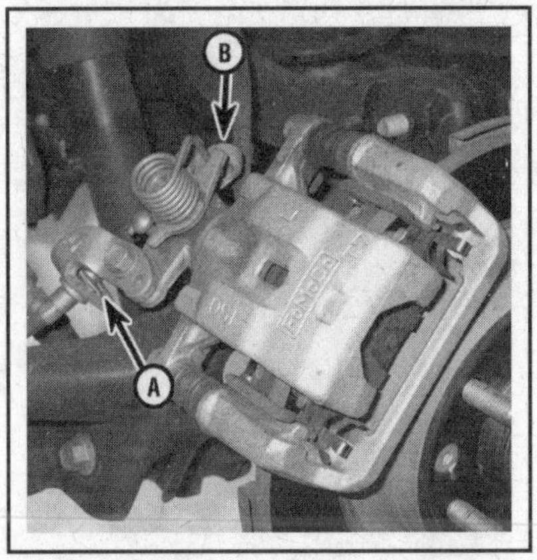

4.7a Rear pads - pull the clip (A) on the parking brake cable, then detach the cable from the lever (B)

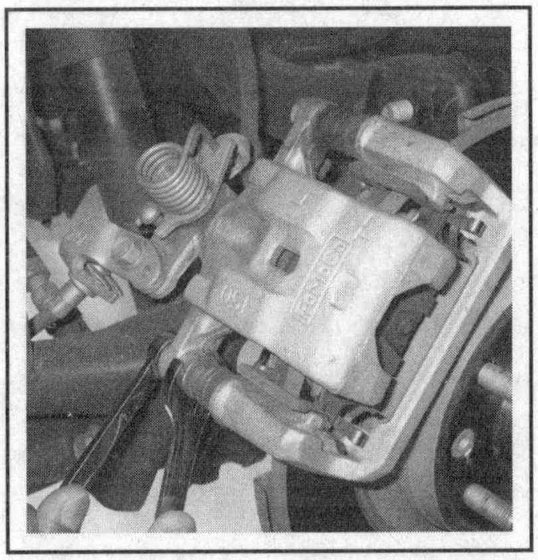

4.7b Hold the caliper guide pins with one wrench while loosening the caliper mounting bolts

4.7c Remove the caliper and use needle-nose pliers to rotate the piston clockwise while pushing it back in the caliper - make sure the fluid in the master cylinder reservoir doesn't overflow

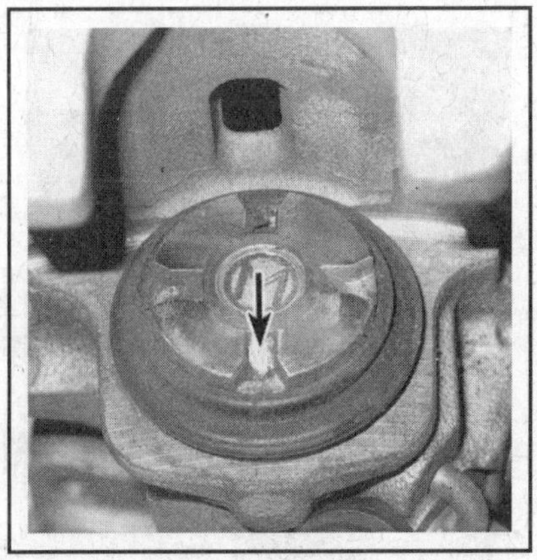

4.7d One of the notches must be at the bottom position to align with the pin on the inner pad

7 For the rear brake pad replacement sequence, follow Steps 1 through 5 and see illustrations 4.7a through 4.7k.

8 When reinstalling the caliper, be sure to tighten the mounting bolts to the torque listed in this Chapter's Specifications. After the job has been completed, firmly depress the brake pedal a few times to bring the pads into contact with the disc. Check the level of the brake fluid, adding some if necessary. Check the operation of the brakes carefully before placing the vehicle into normal service.

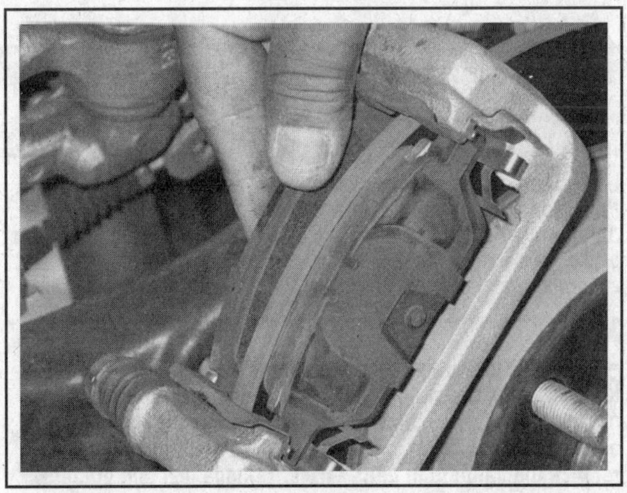

4.7e Remove the inner brake pad

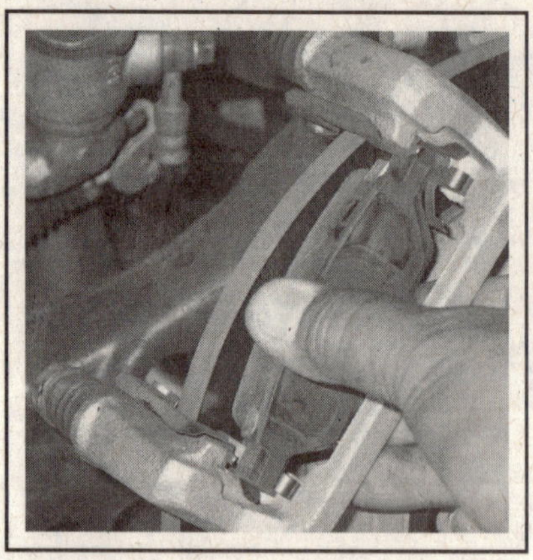

4.7f Remove the outer brake pad

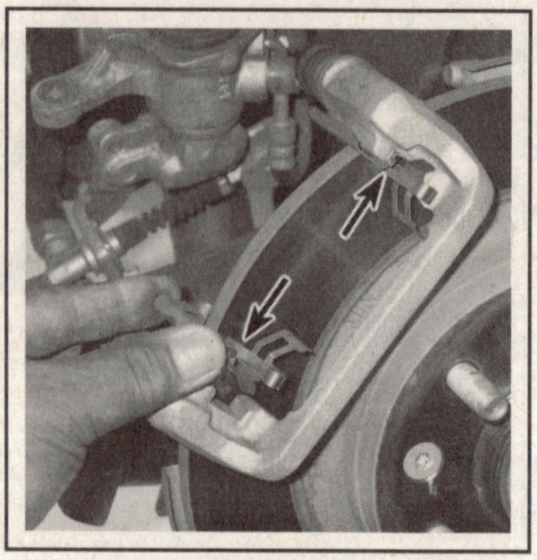

4.7g Remove the slide clips, clean them and lubricate the pad contact areas with high-temp brake grease

4.7h Attach the shims to the outside of each pad - the longer shim goes on the outer pad - then apply anti-squeal compound to the backs of the shims

4.7i Pull out the caliper guide pins and clean them, then apply a coat of high-temperature grease to the pins and reinstall the pins in the caliper bracket

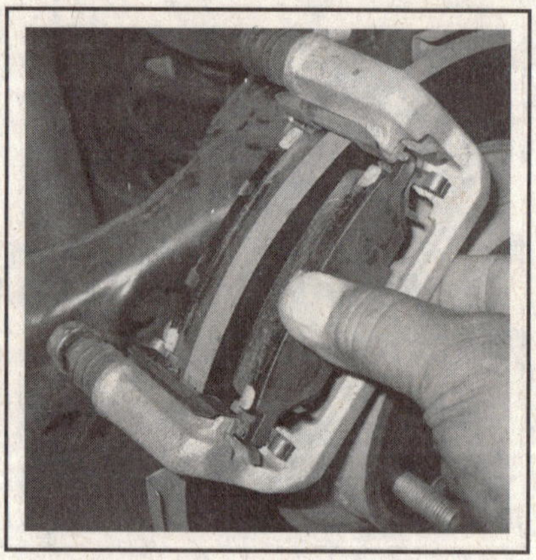

4.7j install the pads

4.7k Install the caliper, tighten the caliper mounting bolts and reattach the parking brake cable. Check the operation of the parking brake, adjusting it if necessary (see Section 11)

5 Disc brake caliper - removal and installation

WARNING:

Dust created by the brake system is harmful to your health. Never blow it out with compressed air and don't inhale any of it. An approved filtering mask should be worn when working on the brakes. Do not, under any circumstances, use petroleum-based solvents to clean brake parts. Use brake system cleaner only.

Note: If replacement is indicated (usually because of fluid leakage), it is recommended that the calipers be replaced, not overhauled. New and factory rebuilt units are available on an exchange basis, which makes this job quite easy. Always replace the calipers in pairs - never replace just one of them.

REMOVAL

Refer to illustration 5.2

1 Loosen the wheel lug nuts, raise the vehicle (front or rear) and place it securely on jackstands. Remove the wheels.

2 Remove the banjo fitting bolt and disconnect the brake hose from the caliper (see illustration). Discard the sealing washers from each side of the hose fitting. Plug the brake hose to keep contaminants out of the brake system and to prevent losing any more brake fluid than is necessary.

Note: If the caliper is being removed for access to another component, don't disconnect the hose.

3 Refer to illustrations 4.6b (front) or 4.7b (rear) for the caliper removal procedure. If the caliper is being removed just to access another component, use a piece of wire to securely hang it out of the way (see illustration 4.6d).

⁂ CAUTION:

Do not let the caliper hang by the brake hose.

4 If you are replacing a rear caliper, disconnect the parking brake cable from the caliper by removing the retaining clip (see illustration 4.7a).

INSTALLATION

5 Install the caliper by reversing the removal procedure, tightening the mounting bolts to the torque listed in this Chapter's Specifications. Be sure to use new sealing washers and tighten the banjo fitting bolt to the torque listed in this Chapter's Specifications.

6 Bleed the brake circuit according to the procedure in Section 9. Make sure there are no leaks from the hose connections. Test the brakes carefully before returning the vehicle to normal service.

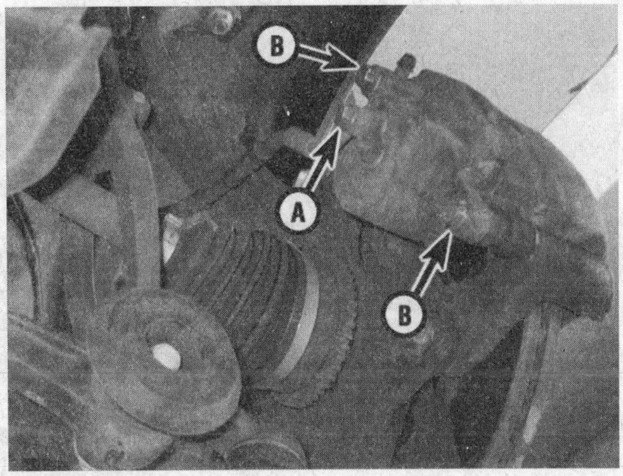

5.2 Remove the brake line banjo bolt (A), then remove the caliper mounting bolts (B)

7 If you removed/replaced a rear caliper, check and, if necessary, adjust the parking brake (see Section 11).

6 Brake disc - inspection, removal and installation

INSPECTION

➧ Refer to illustrations 6.3, 6.4a, 6.4b, 6.5a and 6.5b

1 Loosen the wheel lug nuts, raise the vehicle and support it securely on jackstands.

2 Remove the brake caliper as outlined in Section 5. It isn't necessary to disconnect the brake hose. After removing the caliper bolts, suspend the caliper out of the way with a piece of wire (see illustration 4.6d).

3 Visually inspect the disc surface for score marks and other damage. Light scratches and shallow grooves are normal after use and may not always be detrimental to brake operation, but deep scoring requires disc removal and refinishing by an automotive machine shop. Be sure to check both sides of the disc (see illustration). If pulsating has been noticed during application of the brakes, suspect disc runout.

6.3 The brake pads on this vehicle were obviously neglected, as they wore down completely and cut deep grooves into the disc - wear this severe means the disc must be replaced

6.4a To check disc runout, mount a dial indicator as shown and rotate the disc

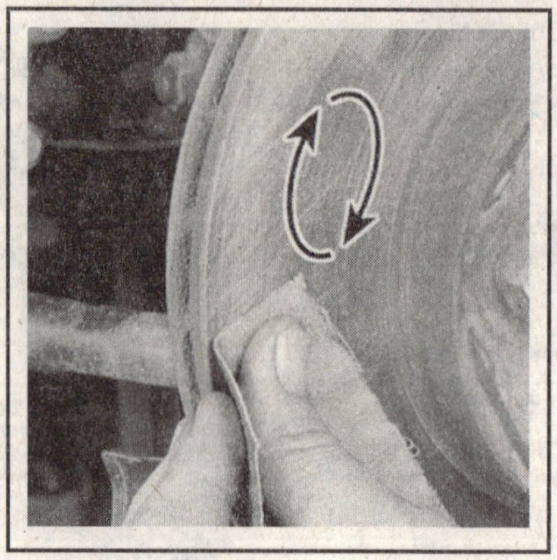

6.4b Using a swirling motion, remove the glaze from the disc surface with sandpaper or emery cloth

6.5a The minimum thickness dimension is cast into the front or back side of the disc

6.5b Use a micrometer to measure disc thickness

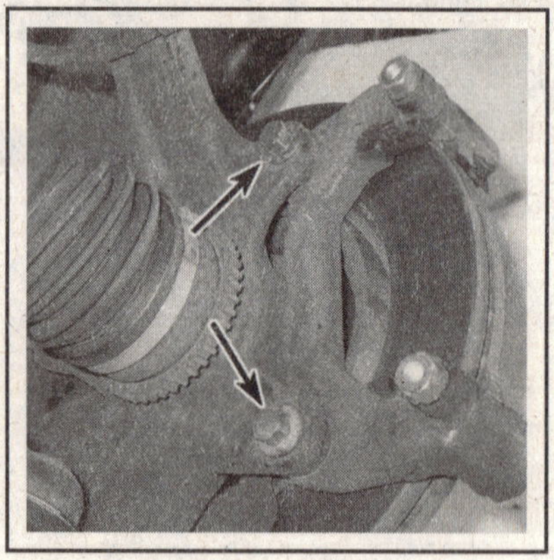

6.6a Caliper mounting bracket-to-knuckle bolts

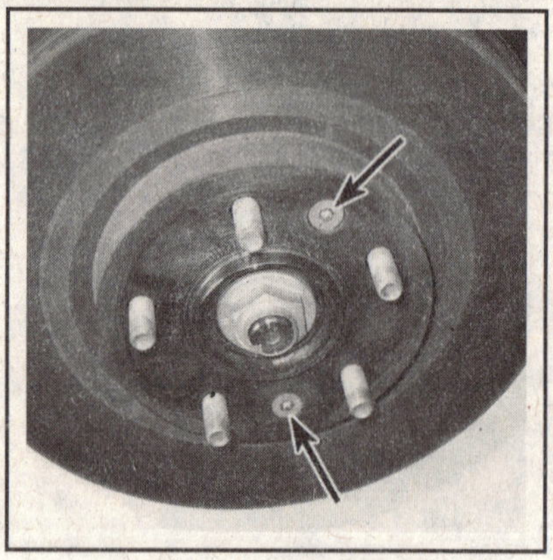

6.6b Two screws secure the disc to the hub

4 To check disc runout, reinstall the lug nuts (inverted) and place a dial indicator at a point about 1/2-inch from the outer edge of the disc (see illustration). Set the indicator to zero and turn the disc. The indicator reading should not exceed the specified allowable runout limit. If it does, the disc should be refinished by an automotive machine shop.

➡Note: The discs should be resurfaced regardless of the dial indicator reading, as this will impart a smooth finish and ensure a perfectly flat surface, eliminating any brake pedal pulsation or other undesirable symptoms related to questionable discs. At the very least, if you elect not to have the discs resurfaced, remove the glaze from the surface with emery cloth or sandpaper, using a swirling motion (see illustration).

5 It's absolutely critical that the disc not be machined to a thickness under the specified minimum thickness. The minimum (or discard) thickness is cast or stamped into the inside of the disc (see illustration). The disc thickness can be checked with a micrometer (see illustration).

REMOVAL

➧ Refer to illustrations 6.6a and 6.6b

6 Remove the caliper mounting bracket (see illustration). Also remove the lug nuts, if they were reinstalled for the runout check. Remove the two screws that secure the disc to the hub, then remove the disc (see illustration).

INSTALLATION

7 While the disc is off, wire-brush the backside of the center portion that contacts the wheel hub. Also clean off any rust or dirt on the hub face.

8 Apply small dots of high-temperature anti-seize around the circumference of the hub, and around the raised center portion.

9 Place the disc in position over the threaded studs. Install the disc retaining screws, tightening them securely.

10 Install the caliper mounting bracket and caliper, tightening the bolts to the torque values listed in this Chapter's Specifications.

11 Install the wheel, then lower the vehicle to the ground. Tighten the lug nuts to the torque listed in the Chapter 1 Specifications. Depress the brake pedal a few times to bring the brake pads into contact with the disc. Bleeding won't be necessary unless the brake hose was disconnected from the caliper. Check the operation of the brakes carefully before driving the vehicle.

12 If new or resurfaced rear discs are being installed, check the operation of the parking brake and adjust it if necessary (see Section 11).

13 Check the operation of the brakes carefully before driving the vehicle.

7 Master cylinder - removal and installation

REMOVAL

Refer to illustrations 7.5 and 7.7

1 The master cylinder is located in the engine compartment, mounted to the power brake booster.

2 Remove as much fluid as you can from the reservoir with a syringe, such as an old turkey baster.

WARNING:

If a baster is used, never again use it for the preparation of food.

Note: On 2010 models with a 3.5L engine, the brake fluid reservoir is mounted remotely from the master cylinder.

3 Place rags under the fluid fittings and prepare caps or plastic bags to cover the ends of the lines once they are disconnected.

CAUTION:

Brake fluid will damage paint. Cover all body parts and be careful not to spill fluid during this procedure.

4 On manual transaxle models, disconnect the clutch master cylinder supply hose from the brake fluid reservoir and pinch it shut with a clamp.

5 Loosen the fittings at the ends of the brake lines where they enter the master cylinder (see illustration). To prevent rounding off the corners on these nuts, the use of a flare-nut wrench, which wraps around the nut, is preferred. Pull the brake lines slightly away from the master cylinder and plug the ends to prevent contamination.

6 Disconnect the electrical connector at the brake fluid level switch on the master cylinder reservoir, then remove the nuts attaching the master cylinder to the power booster. Pull the master cylinder off the studs and out of the engine compartment. Again, be careful not to spill the fluid as this is done.

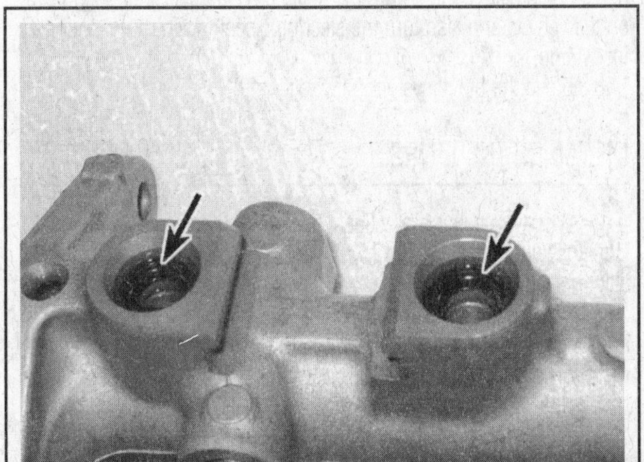

7.7 **After the reservoir has been removed, replace the O-rings with new ones**

7 If a new master cylinder is being installed, remove the reservoir from the old master cylinder and transfer it to the new master cylinder.

Note: Be sure to install new seals when transferring the reservoir (see illustration).

INSTALLATION

Refer to illustrations 7.9 and 7.14

8 Bench bleed the new master cylinder before installing it. Mount the master cylinder in a vise, with the jaws of the vise clamping on the mounting flange.

9 Attach a pair of master cylinder bleeder tubes to the outlet ports of the master cylinder (see illustration).

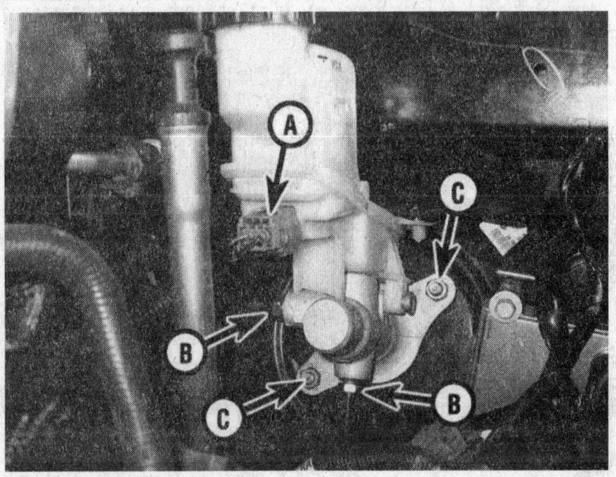

7.5 **Master cylinder mounting details**

A Fluid level warning switch connector
B Brake line fittings
C Mounting nuts

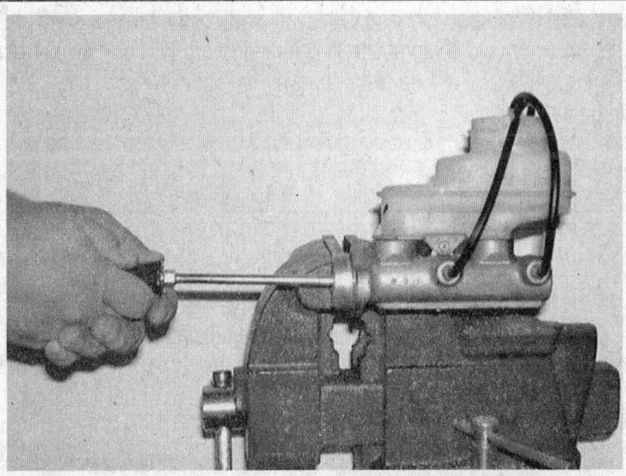

7.9 **The best way to bleed air from the master cylinder before installing it on the vehicle is with a pair of bleeder tubes that direct brake fluid into the reservoir during bleeding**

7.14 Install a new O-ring onto the master cylinder sleeve

10 Fill the reservoir with brake fluid of the recommended type (see Chapter 1).

11 Slowly push the pistons into the master cylinder (a large Phillips screwdriver can be used for this) - air will be expelled from the pressure chambers and into the reservoir. Because the tubes are submerged in fluid, air can't be drawn back into the master cylinder when you release the pistons.

12 Repeat the procedure until no more air bubbles are present.

13 Remove the bleed tubes, one at a time, and install plugs in the open ports to prevent fluid leakage and air from entering. Install the reservoir cap.

14 Install the master cylinder over the studs on the power brake booster and tighten the attaching nuts only finger tight at this time.

➡Note: Be sure to install a new O-ring into the sleeve of the master cylinder (see illustration).

15 Thread the brake line fittings into the master cylinder. Since the master cylinder is still a bit loose, it can be moved slightly in order for the fittings to thread in easily. Do not strip the threads as the fittings are tightened.

16 Tighten the mounting nuts to the torque listed in this Chapter's Specifications, then tighten the brake line fittings securely.

17 Fill the master cylinder reservoir with fluid, then bleed the master cylinder and the brake system as described in Section 9. To bleed the cylinder on the vehicle, have an assistant depress the brake pedal and hold the pedal to the floor. Loosen the fitting to allow air and fluid to escape. Repeat this procedure on both fittings until the fluid is clear of air bubbles.

***** CAUTION:**

Have plenty of rags on hand to catch the fluid - brake fluid will ruin painted surfaces. After the bleeding procedure is completed, rinse the area under the master cylinder with clean water.

18 Test the operation of the brake system carefully before placing the vehicle into normal service.

***** WARNING:**

Do not operate the vehicle if you are in doubt about the effectiveness of the brake system. It is possible for air to become trapped in the anti-lock brake system hydraulic control unit, so, if the pedal continues to feel spongy after repeated bleedings or the BRAKE or ANTI-LOCK light stays on, have the vehicle towed to a dealer service department or other qualified shop to be bled with the aid of a scan tool.

8 Brake hoses and lines - inspection and replacement

1 About every six months, with the vehicle raised and placed securely on jackstands, the flexible hoses which connect the steel brake lines with the front and rear brake assemblies should be inspected for cracks, chafing of the outer cover, leaks, blisters and other damage. These are important and vulnerable parts of the brake system and inspection should be complete. A light and mirror will be needed for a thorough check. If a hose exhibits any of the above defects, replace it with a new one.

FLEXIBLE HOSES

➧ Refer to illustrations 8.3a and 8.3b

2 Clean all dirt away from the ends of the hose.

3 To remove a brake hose, unscrew the tube nut with a flare-nut wrench, if available, to prevent rounding-off the corners of the nut, then remove the bolt(s) or clip(s) securing the hose to the body (and any suspension components) (see illustrations).

4 Disconnect the hose from the caliper, discarding the sealing washers on either side of the fitting.

5 Using new sealing washers, attach the new brake hose to the caliper. Tighten the banjo fitting bolt to the torque listed in this Chapter's Specifications.

6 Reverse the removal procedure to install the hose, making sure it isn't twisted.

7 Carefully check to make sure the suspension or steering components don't make contact with the hose. Have an assistant push down on the vehicle and also turn the steering wheel lock-to-lock during inspection.

8 Bleed the brake system (see Section 9).

METAL BRAKE LINES

9 When replacing brake lines, be sure to use the correct parts. Don't use copper tubing for any brake system components. Purchase steel brake lines from a dealer parts department or auto parts store.

10 Prefabricated brake line, with the tube ends already flared and fittings installed, is available at auto parts stores and dealer parts departments. These lines can be bent to the proper shapes using a tubing bender.

11 When installing the new line make sure it's well supported in the brackets and has plenty of clearance between moving or hot components.

12 After installation, check the master cylinder fluid level and add fluid as necessary. Bleed the brake system as outlined in Section 9 and test the brakes carefully before placing the vehicle into normal operation.

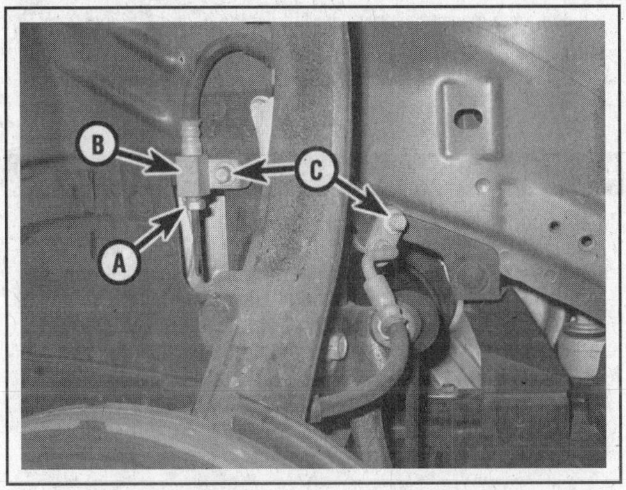

8.3a To remove a front brake hose, unscrew the brake line fitting (A) while holding the fitting block (B) with another wrench, remove the mounting bolts (C), then unscrew the banjo bolt (see illustration 5.2) and detach the hose from the caliper

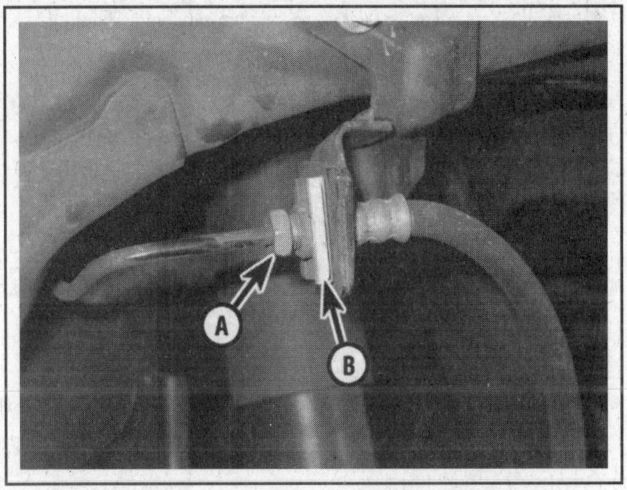

8.3b To remove a rear brake hose, unscrew the brake line fitting (A) while holding the bracket with a pair of pliers, remove the clip (B), then unscrew the banjo bolt and detach the hose from the caliper

9 Brake hydraulic system - bleeding

Refer to illustration 9.8

WARNING:

If air has found its way into the hydraulic control unit, the system must be bled with the use of a scan tool. If the brake pedal feels spongy even after bleeding the brakes, or the ABS light on the instrument panel does not go off, or if you have any doubts whatsoever about the effectiveness of the brake system, have the vehicle towed to a dealer service department or other repair shop equipped with the necessary tools for bleeding the system.

WARNING:

Wear eye protection when bleeding the brake system. If the fluid comes in contact with your eyes, immediately rinse them with water and seek medical attention.

Note: Bleeding the brake system is necessary to remove any air that's trapped in the system when it's opened during removal and installation of a hose, line, caliper, wheel cylinder or master cylinder.

1 It will probably be necessary to bleed the system at all four brakes if air has entered the system due to low fluid level, or if the brake lines have been disconnected at the master cylinder.

2 If a brake line was disconnected only at a wheel, then only that caliper or wheel cylinder must be bled.

3 If a brake line is disconnected at a fitting located between the master cylinder and any of the brakes, that part of the system served by the disconnected line must be bled.

4 Remove any residual vacuum (or hydraulic pressure) from the brake power booster by applying the brake several times with the engine off.

5 Remove the master [illegible] cap and fill the reservoir

Note: Check the fluid level often during the bleeding operation and add fluid as necessary to prevent the fluid level from falling low enough to allow air bubbles into the master cylinder.

6 Have an assistant on hand, as well as a supply of new brake fluid, an empty clear plastic container, a length of plastic, rubber or vinyl tubing to fit over the bleeder valve and a wrench to open and close the bleeder valve.

7 Beginning at the right rear wheel, loosen the bleeder screw slightly, then tighten it to a point where it's snug but can still be loosened quickly and easily.

8 Place one end of the tubing over the bleeder screw fitting and submerge the other end in brake fluid in the container (see illustration).

9.8 When bleeding the brakes, a hose is connected to the bleed screw at the caliper and submerged in brake fluid - air will be seen as bubbles in the tube [illegible] (all air

9 Have the assistant slowly depress the brake pedal and hold it in the depressed position.

10 While the pedal is held depressed, open the bleeder screw just enough to allow a flow of fluid to leave the valve. Watch for air bubbles to exit the submerged end of the tube. When the fluid flow slows after a couple of seconds, tighten the screw and have your assistant release the pedal.

11 Repeat Steps 9 and 10 until no more air is seen leaving the tube, then tighten the bleeder screw and proceed to the left rear wheel, the right front wheel and the left front wheel, in that order, and perform the same procedure. Be sure to check the fluid in the master cylinder reservoir frequently.

12 Never use old brake fluid. It contains moisture which can boil, rendering the brake system inoperative.

13 Refill the master cylinder with fluid at the end of the operation.

14 Check the operation of the brakes. The pedal should feel solid when depressed, with no sponginess. If necessary, repeat the entire process.

**** WARNING:**

Do not operate the vehicle if you are in doubt about the effectiveness of the brake system. It is possible for air to become trapped in the anti-lock brake system hydraulic control unit, so, if the pedal continues to feel spongy after repeated bleedings or the BRAKE or ANTI-LOCK light stays on, have the vehicle towed to a dealer service department or other qualified shop to be bled with the aid of a scan tool.

10 Power brake booster - check, removal and installation

OPERATING CHECK

1 Depress the brake pedal several times with the engine off and make sure that there is no change in the pedal reserve distance.

2 Depress the pedal and start the engine. If the pedal goes down slightly, operation is normal.

AIRTIGHTNESS CHECK

3 Start the engine and turn it off after one or two minutes. Depress the brake pedal several times slowly. If the pedal goes down farther the first time but gradually rises after the second or third depression, the booster is airtight.

4 Depress the brake pedal while the engine is running, then stop the engine with the pedal depressed. If there is no change in the pedal reserve travel after holding the pedal for 30 seconds, the booster is airtight.

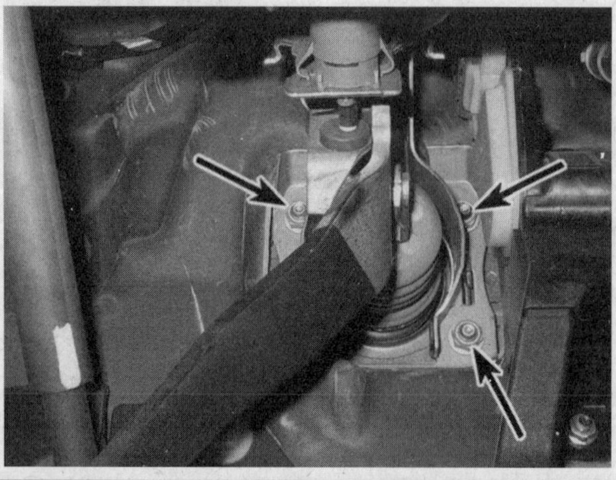

10.11 To detach the power brake booster from the firewall, remove the four nuts (one nut not visible here)

REMOVAL AND INSTALLATION

Refer to illustration 10.11

5 Disassembly of the power unit requires special tools and is not ordinarily performed by the home mechanic. If a problem develops, it's recommended that a new or factory rebuilt unit be installed.

6 In the engine compartment, remove the nuts attaching the master cylinder to the booster and carefully pull the master cylinder forward until it clears the mounting studs. Be careful not to bend or kink the brake lines. On 3.0L models, it may be necessary to disconnect the EVAP canister purge valve (see Chapter 6).

7 Disconnect the vacuum hose where it attaches to the power brake booster.

8 Disconnect both cables from the battery, then remove the battery tray (see Chapter 5).

9 Disconnect and remove the PCM (see Chapter 6), then remove the PCM bracket.

10 Under the instrument panel, remove the retaining pin and washer, then disconnect the pushrod from the top of the brake pedal.

11 Remove the nuts attaching the booster to the firewall (see illustration).

12 Carefully lift the booster unit away from the firewall and out of the engine compartment.

13 To install the booster, place it into position and tighten the retaining nuts to the torque listed in this Chapter's Specifications. Connect the pushrod to the brake pedal.

Note: If the booster-to-firewall gasket has been damaged, replace it with a new gasket.

14 Install the master cylinder. Reconnect the vacuum hose.

15 Carefully test the operation of the brakes before placing the vehicle in normal service.

11 Parking brake - adjustment

Refer to illustrations 11.2, 11.3

1 Release the parking brake lever.

2 Using a plastic trim tool, remove the rear access panel of the floor console, taking care not to damage the panel (see illustration).

3 Adjust the nut so that the exposed threads equal 0.59 inch/15 mm (see illustration). When the parking brake cables are old, they may have stretched and require more threads showing on the adjuster.

4 Verify the parking brake is actually holding the vehicle when applied. Raise and support the rear of the vehicle and block the front wheels. You can rotate the rear tires by hand to check for proper cable adjustment.

5 Pull the handle up two clicks. This should apply noticeable drag on the rear brakes. At five clicks, the rear brakes should be locked.

11.2 Pry the rear console cover off to access the park brake adjuster

11.3 Turn the adjusting nut until the exposed threads measure 0.59-inch (15mm)

12 Brake light switch - replacement

Refer to illustration 12.1

1 Disconnect the electrical connector at the switch, then rotate the switch 45-degrees clockwise and remove the switch (see illustration).

2 The brake light switch is self-adjusting.

Note: Do not press on the brake pedal during installation of the switch.

3 Connect the switch electrical connector.

12.1 Disconnect the electrical connector (A) then rotate the switch (B) 45-degrees clockwise to remove it

Specifications

General

Brake fluid type	See Chapter 1

Disc brakes

Minimum pad lining thickness	See Chapter 1
Disc lateral runout limit	0.004 inch (0.10 mm)
Disc minimum thickness	Cast into disc

Torque specifications

➡Note: One foot-pound (ft-lb) of torque is equivalent to 12 inch-pounds (in-lbs) of torque. Torque values below approximately 15 foot-pounds are expressed in inch-pounds, because most foot-pound torque wrenches are not accurate at these smaller values.

Torque specifications	Ft-lbs (unless otherwise indicated)	Nm
Brake line banjo bolt	18	25
Caliper mounting bracket bolts		
Front	66	89
Rear	52	71
Caliper mounting bolts	19	26
Master cylinder fluid reservoir pin bolts	53 in-lbs	6
Master cylinder mounting nuts	18	24
Power brake booster mounting nuts	17	23
Remote fluid reservoir mounting bolts (3.5L models)	62 in-lbs	7
Wheel lug nuts	See Chapter 1	

10
SUSPENSION AND STEERING SYSTEMS

Section

1 General information

Refer to illustrations 1.1 and 1.2

The front suspension is made up of two lower control arms and an upper control arm, a steering knuckle/hub assembly, coil-over shock absorbers and a stabilizer bar (see illustration).

The rear suspension employs a trailing arm, upper and lower control arms, a coil spring and shock absorber per side, and an adjustable toe-link that permits toe setting adjustment for each rear wheel (see illustration).

The rack-and-pinion steering gear is located behind the engine/transaxle assembly on the front suspension subframe and actuates the tie-rods, which are attached to the steering knuckles. The inner ends of the tie-rods are protected by rubber boots which should be inspected periodically for secure attachment, tears and leaking lubricant (which would indicate a failed rack seal).

The power assist system on most models consists of a belt-driven pump and associated lines and hoses. The fluid level in the power steering pump reservoir should be checked periodically (see Chapter 1). 2010 models equipped with a four-cylinder engine or a 3.0L V6 engine are equipped with an electronic power assist steering gear.

The steering wheel operates the steering shaft, which actuates the steering gear through universal joints. Looseness in the steering can be caused by wear in the steering shaft universal joints, the steering gear, the tie-rod ends and loose retaining bolts.

PRECAUTIONS

Frequently, when working on the suspension or steering system components, you may come across fasteners which seem impossible to loosen. These fasteners on the underside of the vehicle are continually subjected to water, road grime, mud, etc., and can become rusted or

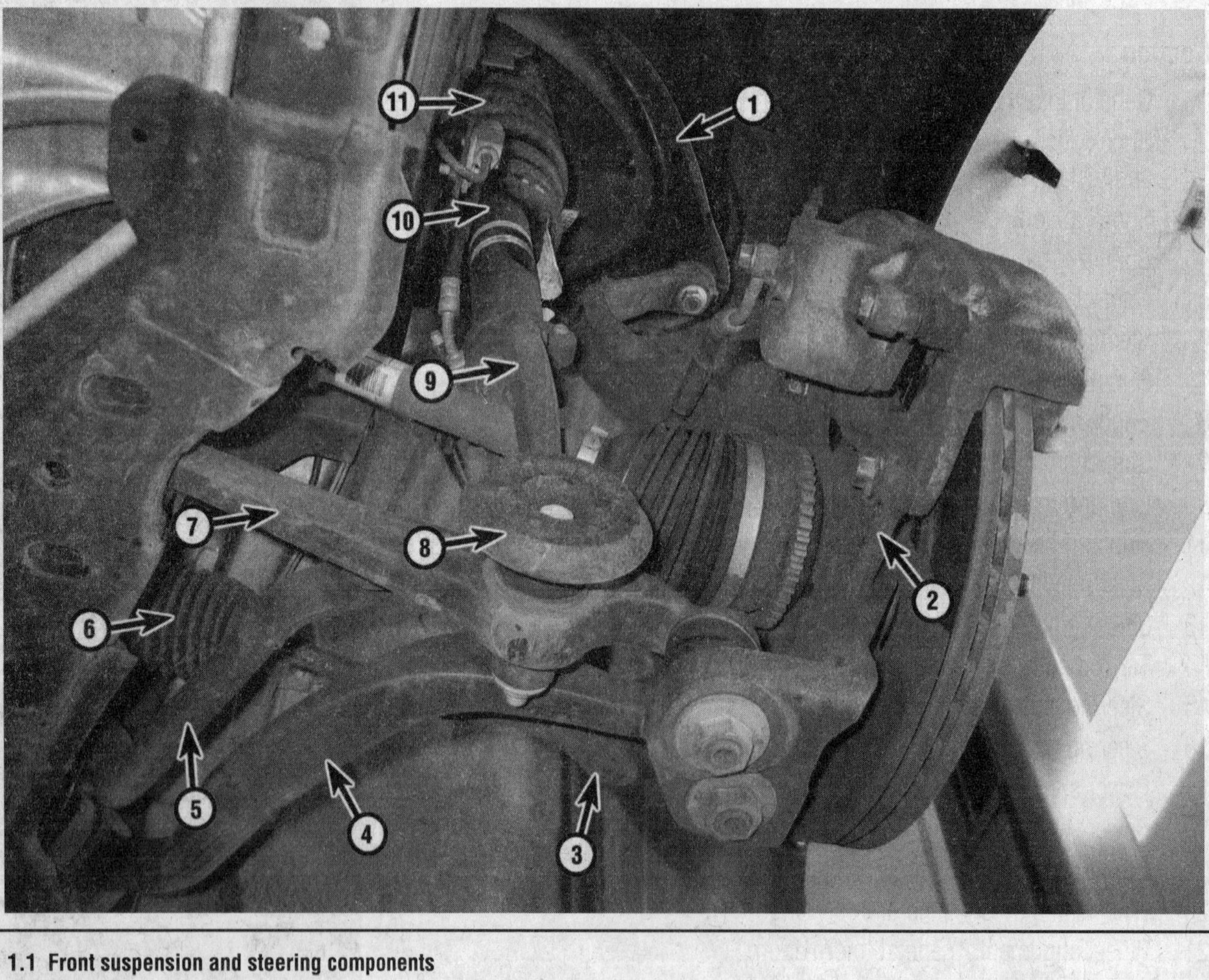

1.1 Front suspension and steering components

1 *Upper control arm*
2 *Steering knuckle*
3 *Tie-rod end*
4 *Lower control arm (rear)*
5 *Stabilizer bar*
6 *Steering gear boot*
7 *Lower control arm (front)*
8 *Damper weight*
9 *Damper fork*
10 *Shock absorber*
11 *Coil spring*

frozen, making them extremely difficult to remove. In order to unscrew these stubborn fasteners without damaging them (or other components), be sure to use lots of penetrating oil and allow it to soak in for a while. Using a wire brush to clean exposed threads will also ease removal of the nut or bolt and prevent damage to the threads. Sometimes a sharp blow with a hammer and punch will break the bond between a nut and bolt threads, but care must be taken to prevent the punch from slipping off the fastener and ruining the threads. Heating the stuck fastener and surrounding area with a torch sometimes helps too, but isn't recommended because of the obvious dangers associated with fire. Long breaker bars and extension, or cheater, pipes will increase leverage, but never use an extension pipe on a ratchet - the ratcheting mechanism could be damaged. Sometimes tightening the nut or bolt first will help to break it loose. Fasteners that require drastic measures to remove should always be replaced with new ones.

Since most of the procedures dealt with in this Chapter involve jacking up the vehicle and working underneath it, a good pair of jackstands will be needed. A hydraulic floor jack is the preferred type of jack to lift the vehicle, and it can also be used to support certain components during various operations.

⁂ WARNING:

Never, under any circumstances, rely on a jack to support the vehicle while working on it. Whenever any of the suspension or steering fasteners are loosened or removed they must be inspected and, if necessary, replaced with new ones of the same part number or of original equipment quality and design. Torque specifications must be followed for proper reassembly and component retention. Never attempt to heat or straighten any suspension or steering components. Instead, replace any bent or damaged part with a new one.

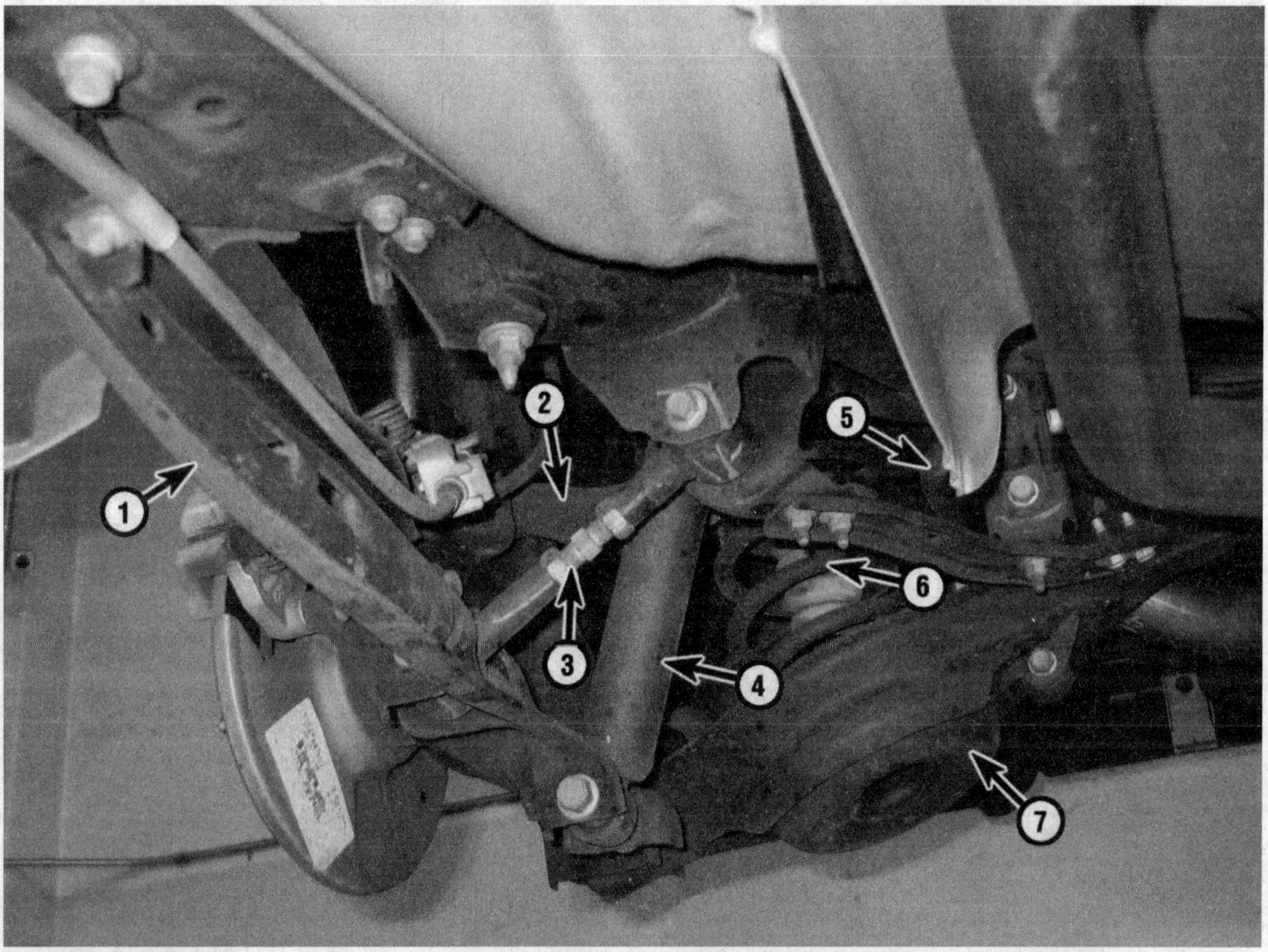

1.2 Typical rear suspension components

1 *Trailing arm*
2 *Upper suspension arm*
3 *Toe adjuster link*
4 *Shock absorber*
5 *Stabilizer bar*
6 *Coil spring*
7 *Lower suspension arm*

2 Shock absorber/coil spring assembly (front) - removal, inspection and installation

CAUTION:

The manufacturer recommends replacing all fasteners with new ones during installation.

REMOVAL

Refer to illustrations 2.3, 2.5, 2.6 and 2.7

1 Loosen the wheel lug nuts, raise the vehicle and support it securely on jackstands. Remove the wheel.

2 Unbolt the brake hose bracket from the shock absorber. Remove the ABS speed sensor and detach the wiring harness by removing the clamp bracket bolt.

3 Detach the stabilizer bar link from the damper fork (see illustration). If the ballstud spins, hold it with an Allen wrench placed in the center of the stud while loosening the nut.

4 Support the steering knuckle with a floor jack.

5 Remove the bolt and flag nut securing the damper fork to the lower control arm (see illustration).

6 Remove the pinch-bolt securing the damper fork to the bottom of the shock absorber (see illustration). Tap the fork with a hammer, if necessary, to remove it from the shock body.

7 In the engine compartment, mark the relationship of the outer mounting stud to the body. Support the shock absorber/coil spring assembly, then remove the three upper mounting nuts (see illustration).

8 Lower the knuckle to allow room to remove the shock absorber/coil spring assembly, but be careful not to overextend the inner CV joint.

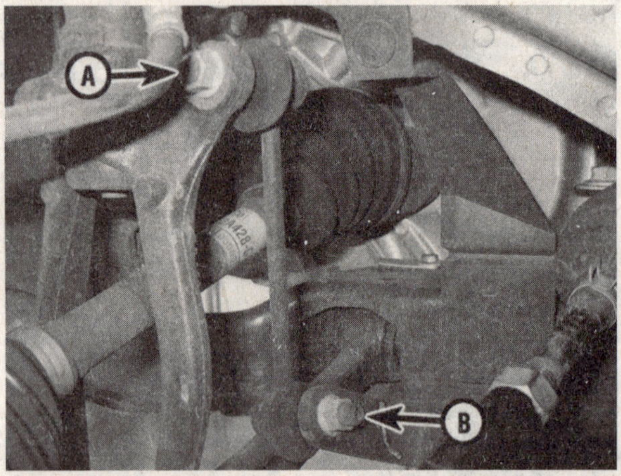

2.3 Disconnect the stabilizer bar link from the damper fork (A). If you're removing the stabilizer bar, disconnect the link from the bar (B)

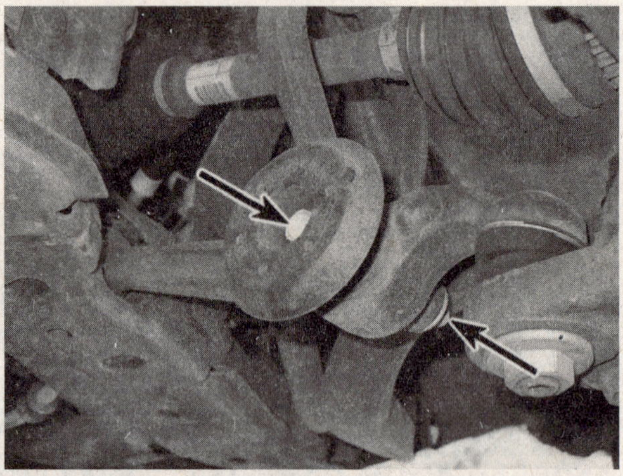

2.5 Remove the bolt and flag-nut securing the damper fork to the lower control arm

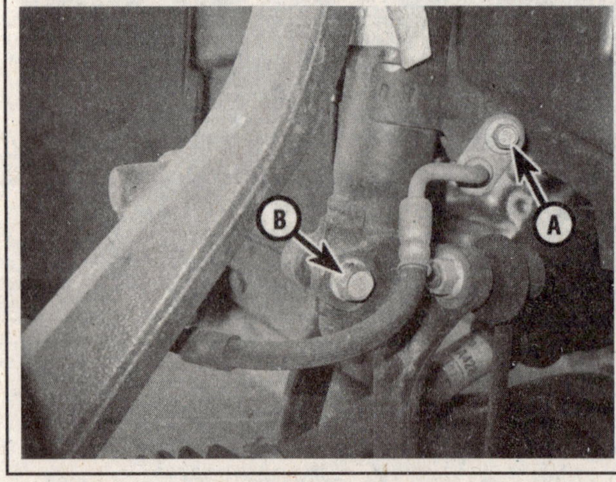

2.6 Remove the brake-hose mounting bolt (A), then the damper fork-to-shock absorber pinch bolt (B)

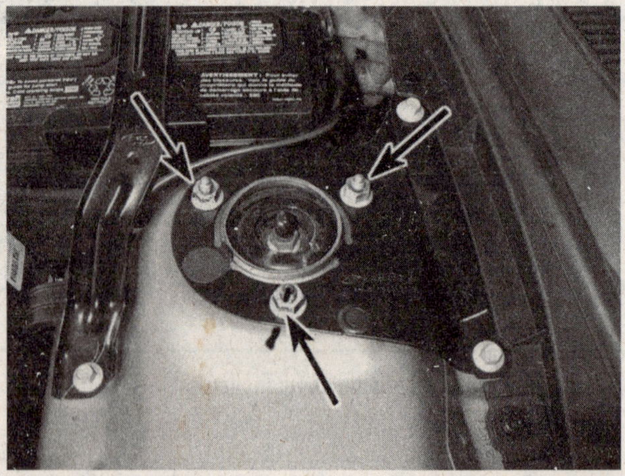

2.7 Mark the relationship of the outer mounting stud to the body, then remove the upper mounting nuts

INSPECTION

9 Check the shock body for leaking fluid, dents, cracks and other obvious damage which would warrant replacement.

10 Check the coil spring for chips or cracks in the spring coating (this will cause premature spring failure due to corrosion). Inspect the spring seat for cuts, hardness and general deterioration.

11 If any undesirable conditions exist, proceed to the shock absorber/coil spring disassembly procedure (see Section 3).

INSTALLATION

12 Guide the assembly up into the fenderwell, align the previously made matchmarks and insert the upper mounting studs through the holes in the body. Once the studs protrude, install the new nuts so the shock won't fall back through. This is most easily accomplished with the help of an assistant, as the strut is quite heavy and awkward.

13 Push the damper fork onto the bottom of the shock body. Install a new pinch-bolt but do not tighten it at this time.

14 Align the bottom of the damper fork such that the new bolt can be inserted to secure it to the lower control arm.

15 Use the jack to position the steering knuckle to approximate the normal ride height, then tighten the fork bolts.

16 Connect the stabilizer bar link to the damper fork. Tighten the nut to the torque listed in this Chapter's Specifications. The remainder of installation is the reverse of removal.

17 Install the wheel and lug nuts, then lower the vehicle and tighten the lug nuts to the torque listed in the Chapter 1 Specifications.

18 Tighten the upper mounting nuts to the torque listed in this Chapter's Specifications.

19 Drive the vehicle to an alignment shop to have the front end alignment checked, and if necessary, adjusted.

3 Shock absorber/coil spring assembly (front) - replacement

➧ Refer to illustrations 3.3, 3.4, 3.5a, 3.5b, 3.5c, 3.5d and 3.9

WARNING:

Before attempting to disassemble the shock absorber/coil spring assembly, a tool to hold the coil spring in compression must be obtained. Do not attempt to use makeshift methods. Uncontrolled release of the spring could cause damage and personal injury or even death. Use a high-quality spring compressor, and carefully follow the tool manufacturer's instructions provided with it. After removing the coil spring with the compressor still installed, place it in a safe, isolated area.

1 If the front suspension shock absorber/coil springs exhibit signs of wear (leaking fluid, loss of damping capability, sagging or cracked coil springs) then they should be disassembled and overhauled as necessary. The shock absorbers themselves cannot be serviced, and should be replaced if faulty; the springs and related components can be replaced individually. To maintain balanced characteristics on both sides of the vehicle, the components on both sides should be replaced at the same time.

2 With the assembly removed from the vehicle (see Section 2), clean away all external dirt, then mount it in a vise.

3 Install the coil spring compressor tools (ensuring that they are fully engaged), and compress the spring until all tension is relieved from the upper mount (see illustration).

4 Hold the shock absorber piston rod with an Allen key and unscrew the thrust bearing retaining nut with a box-end wrench (see illustration).

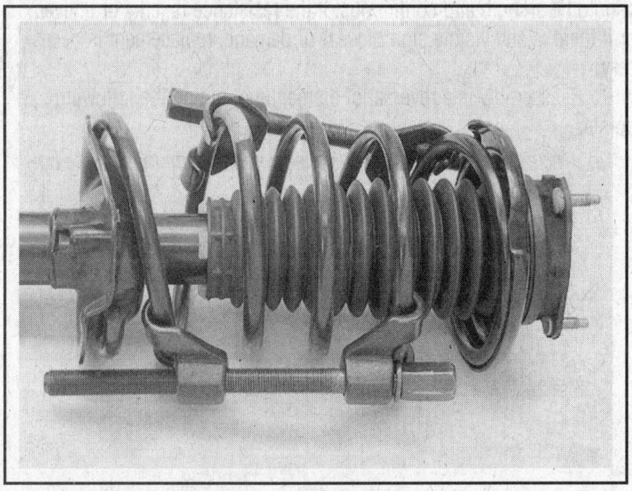

3.3 Make sure the spring compressor tool is on securely

3.4 Loosen and remove the piston rod nut

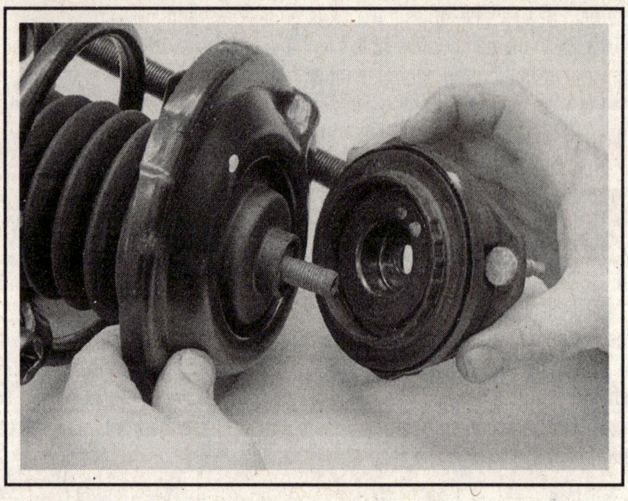

3.5a Remove the upper mount and spring seat . . .

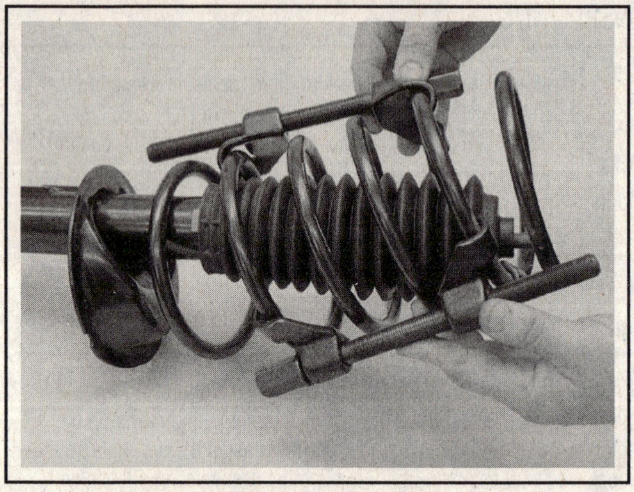

3.5b . . . then carefully remove the spring . . .

3.5c . . . followed by the boot . . .

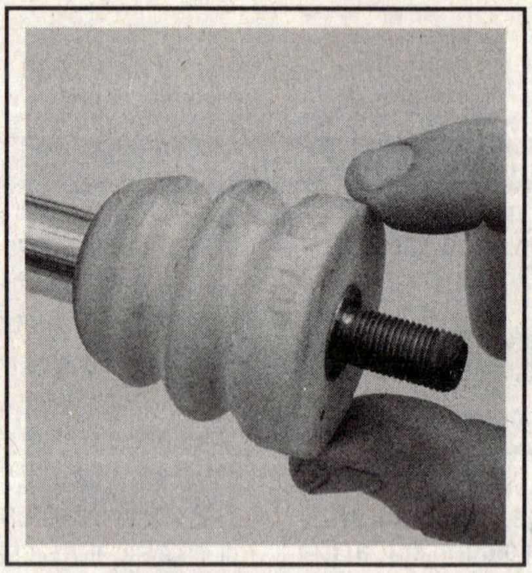

3.5d . . . and the bump stop

3.9 When installing the spring, make sure the ends fit into the recessed portion of the seats

5 Withdraw the top mount, upper spring seat and spring, followed by the boot and the bump stop (see illustrations).

6 If a new spring is to be installed, the original spring must now be carefully released from the compressor. If it is to be re-used, the spring can be left in compression.

7 With the strut assembly now completely disassembled, examine all the components for wear and damage, and check the bearing for smoothness of operation. Replace components as necessary.

8 Examine the shock for signs of fluid leakage. Check the piston rod for signs of pitting along its entire length, and check the shock body for signs of damage. Test the operation of the shock, while holding it in an upright position, by moving the piston through a full stroke, then through short strokes of 2 to 4 inches. In both cases, the resistance felt should be smooth and continuous. If the resistance is jerky or uneven, or if there is any visible sign of wear or damage, replacement is necessary.

9 Reassembly is a reversal of dismantling, noting the following points:

- *a) The coil springs must be installed with the paint mark at the bottom.*
- *b) Make sure that the coil spring ends are correctly located in the upper and lower seats before releasing the compressor (see illustration).*
- *c) Tighten the piston rod nut to the specified torque.*

4 Stabilizer bar and bushings (front) - removal and installation

REMOVAL

➧ Refer to illustration 4.8

1 Loosen the front wheel lug nuts. Raise the front of the vehicle and support it securely on jackstands. Apply the parking brake and block the rear wheels to keep the vehicle from rolling off the stands. Remove the front wheels.

2 Detach the stabilizer bar links from the bar (see illustration 2.3). If the ballstud turns with the nut, use an Allen wrench to hold the stud.

3 Disconnect the steering shaft from the steering gear (see Chapter 10).

⁂ CAUTION:

Don't allow the steering wheel to turn after the steering shaft is disconnected - the airbag clockspring could be damaged

4 Disconnect the tie-rod ends from the steering knuckles (see Section 14), then remove the steering gear mounting bolts (see Section 16).

5 Detach the exhaust pipe(s) from the exhaust manifold(s).

6 If you're working on an All-Wheel Drive model, detach the driveshaft from the transfer case.

7 Support the rear of the subframe with a floor jack. Loosen the front subframe mounting fasteners and remove the rear subframe fasteners, then lower the rear of the subframe with the jack.

8 Unbolt the stabilizer bar bushing clamps (see illustration). Guide the stabilizer bar out from between the subframe and the body.

9 While the stabilizer bar is off the vehicle, slide off the retainer bushings and inspect them. If they're cracked, worn or deteriorated, replace them.

10 Clean the bushing area of the stabilizer bar with a stiff wire brush to remove any rust or dirt.

4.8 Stabilizer bar bracket nuts

INSTALLATION

11 Lubricate the inside and outside of the new bushing with vegetable oil (used in cooking) to simplify reassembly.

⁂ CAUTION:

Don't use petroleum or mineral-based lubricants or brake fluid - they will lead to deterioration of the bushings. The slits of the bushings must face the rear of the vehicle.

12 Installation is the reverse of removal. Tighten the fasteners to the torque values listed in this Chapter's Specifications.

5 Control arms (front) - removal, inspection and installation

⁂ CAUTION:

All suspension bolts should be replaced with new fasteners during assembly.

REMOVAL

Lower arms

➧ Refer to illustrations 5.7 and 5.10

1 Loosen the wheel lug nuts on the side to be dismantled, raise the front of the vehicle, support it securely on jackstands and remove the wheel.

Rear lower arm

2 Disconnect the steering shaft from the steering gear (see Chapter 10).

⁂ CAUTION:

Don't allow the steering wheel to turn after the steering shaft is disconnected - the airbag clockspring could be damaged.

3 Disconnect the tie-rod ends from the steering knuckles (see Section 14), then remove the steering gear mounting bolts (see Section 16).

4 Detach the exhaust pipe(s) from the exhaust manifold(s).

5 If you're working on an All-Wheel Drive model, detach the driveshaft from the transfer case.

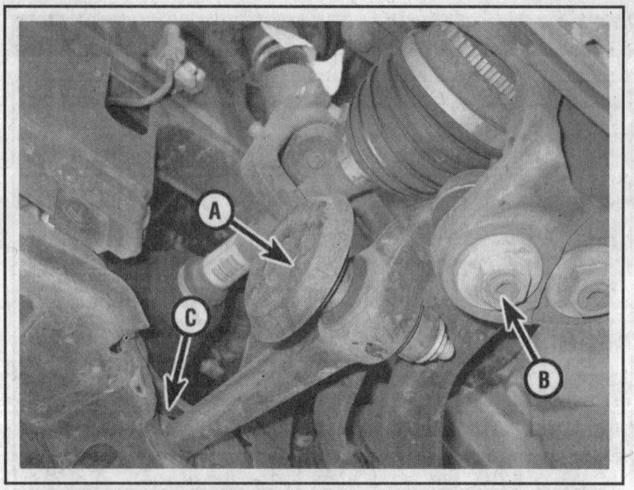

5.7 Front lower control arm details

A Damper fork bolt/nut
B Balljoint nut
C Pivot bolt

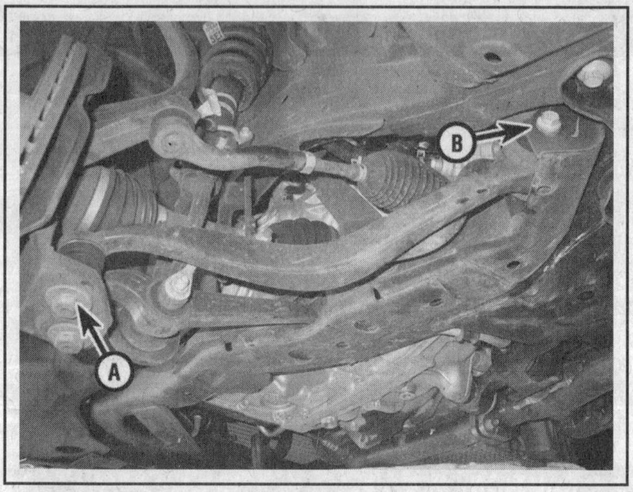

5.10 Rear lower control arm details

A Balljoint nut
B Pivot bolt

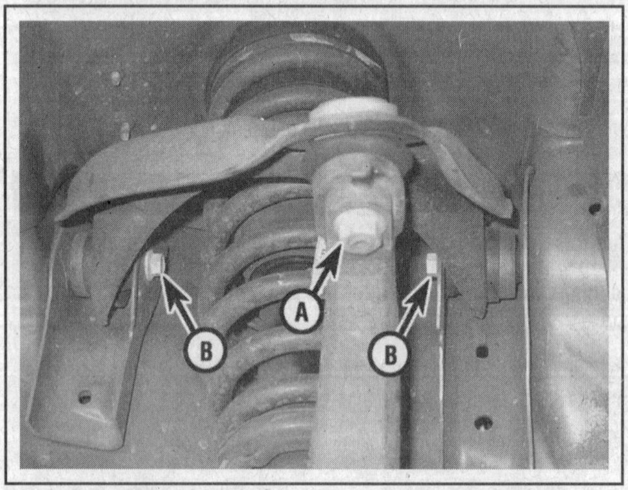

5.13 Remove the nut (A) and separate the balljoint, then remove the two pivot bolts (B)

6 Support the rear of the subframe with a floor jack. Loosen the front subframe mounting fasteners and remove the rear subframe fasteners, then lower the rear of the subframe with the jack.

Either lower arm

7 Loosen the lower arm-to-balljoint nut (see illustration). Position a block of wood under the outer CV joint of the driveaxle to prevent damage to the joint when the balljoint at the steering knuckle is disconnected. Using a balljoint removal tool, separate the balljoint.

8 If you're removing the front lower arm, remove the damper fork mounting bolt at the front lower control arm.

9 Remove the arm-to-subframe mounting bolt.

10 Remove the lower control arm (see illustration).

Upper arm

Refer to illustration 5.13

11 The upper control arm is attached to the top of the steering knuckle with a balljoint, and to two positions on the chassis with pivot bolts.

12 Unbolt the wheel speed sensor and the three upper strut-to-body nuts (see Section 2).

13 Disconnect the balljoint at the top of the steering knuckle, then remove the inner arm mounting bolts and the upper arm (see illustration).

INSPECTION

14 Check the control arm for distortion and the bushings for wear, replacing parts as necessary. Do not attempt to straighten a bent control arm.

INSTALLATION

15 Installation is the reverse of removal. Tighten all of the fasteners to the torque values listed in this Chapter's Specifications.

Note: Before tightening the control arm fasteners, raise the outer end of the control arm with a floor jack to simulate normal ride height. The center of the wheel hub should be 15.8-inches below the bottom edge of the fender. On upper control arms, install the pivot bolts loosely, then install a 0.25-inch drill bit through the two holes in the chassis just below the bushing. This will set the proper height for tightening of the pivot bolts.

16 Install the wheel and lug nuts, lower the vehicle and tighten the lug nuts to the torque listed in the Chapter 1 Specifications.

17 It's a good idea to have the front wheel alignment checked and, if necessary, adjusted after this job has been performed.

6 Steering knuckle and hub - removal and installation

WARNING:

Dust created by the brake system is harmful to your health. Never blow it out with compressed air and don't inhale any of it. Do not, under any circumstances, use petroleum-based solvents to clean brake parts. Use brake system cleaner only.

CAUTION:

All suspension bolts should be replaced with new fasteners during assembly.

REMOVAL

1 Remove the wheel cover and loosen, but don't remove, the driveaxle/hub nut. Loosen the wheel lug nuts, raise the vehicle and support it securely on jackstands, then remove the wheel.

2 Remove the brake caliper (don't disconnect the hose), the caliper mounting bracket and the brake disc (see Chapter 9). Disconnect the brake hose from the strut. Hang the caliper from the coil spring with a piece of wire - don't let it hang by the brake hose.

3 Remove the ABS wheel speed sensor and remove the harness bolt (see Chapter 9).

4 Separate the tie-rod end from the steering knuckle arm (see Section 14).

5 Place a block of wood above the lower control arm to prevent damage to the inner CV joint. Separate the two lower control arm balljoints from the steering knuckle (see Section 5).

6 Remove the driveaxle/hub nut and push the driveaxle from the hub as described in Chapter 8. Support the end of the driveaxle with a piece of wire.

7 Separate the upper control arm balljoint from the steering knuckle (see Section 5).

INSTALLATION

8 Guide the knuckle and hub assembly into position, inserting the driveaxle into the hub.

9 Connect the balljoints to the knuckle and tighten the nuts to the torque listed in this Chapter's Specifications.

CAUTION:

All suspension bolts should be replaced with new ones during assembly.

10 Attach the tie-rod end to the steering knuckle arm (see Section 14). Tighten the nut to the torque listed in this Chapter's Specifications.

➡Note: Before tightening the control arm fasteners, raise the outer end of the control arm with a floor jack to simulate normal ride height. The center of the wheel hub should be 15.8-inches below the center of the fender lip.

11 Place the brake disc on the hub, install the two disc-locating bolts, and install the caliper as outlined in Chapter 9.

12 Install the driveaxle/hub nut and tighten it securely, but not completely yet.

13 Install the wheel and lug nuts. Lower the vehicle and tighten the lug nuts to the torque listed in the Chapter 1 Specifications.

14 Tighten the driveaxle/hub nut to the torque listed in the Chapter 8 Specifications. Install the wheel cover.

15 Have the front-end alignment checked and, if necessary, adjusted.

7 Hub and bearing assembly (front) - removal and installation

Due to the special tools and expertise required to press the hub and bearing from the steering knuckle, this job should be left to a professional mechanic. However, the steering knuckle and hub may be removed and the assembly taken to an automotive machine shop or other qualified repair facility equipped with the necessary tools. See Section 6 for the steering knuckle and hub removal procedure.

8 Shock absorber (rear) - removal and installation

➧ Refer to illustrations 8.3 and 8.4

1 Loosen the wheel lug nuts, raise the vehicle and support it securely on jackstands. Block the front wheels to prevent the vehicle from rolling. Remove the wheel.

2 Support the rear lower control arm with a floor jack, then remove the upper control arm (see Section 9).

8.3 Remove the rear shock lower mounting nut and bolt

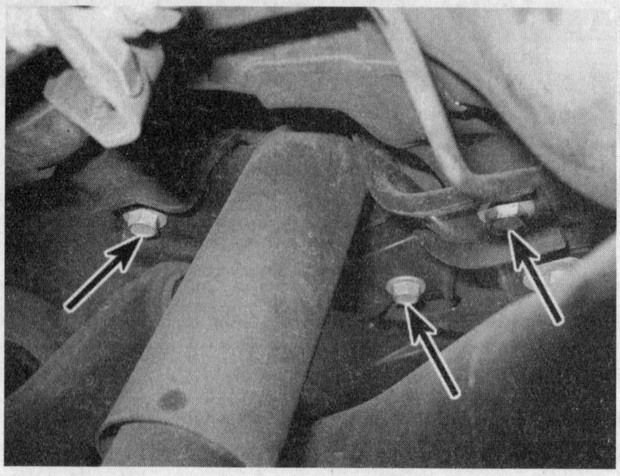

8.4 Remove the three shock mount-to-body bolts

3 Remove the lower shock mounting bolt (see illustration).

4 Remove the three bolts securing the upper shock mount to the body (see illustration).

5 Maneuver the shock out of the vehicle. If new shocks are to be installed, swap the bracket to the top of the new shock.

6 Installation is the reverse of the removal procedure.

⁂ CAUTION:

New shock absorbers are gas-filled and come compressed and retained with a fiberglass strap. Do NOT remove the strap until the shock is installed.

7 Tighten the mounting fasteners to the torque listed in this Chapter's Specifications.

➡Note: Any rear suspension fasteners should be replaced with new fasteners on assembly, and should only be tightened with the hub raised to a height of 15.5 inches from the hub center to the center of the fenderwell lip.

9 Suspension arms (rear) - removal and installation

➡Note: Any rear suspension fasteners should be replaced with new fasteners on assembly, and should only be tightened with the hub raised to a height of 15.5 inches from the hub center to the center of the fenderwell lip.

1 Loosen the wheel lug nuts, raise the vehicle and support it securely on jackstands. Block the front wheels to prevent the vehicle from rolling. Remove the wheel.

UPPER SUSPENSION ARM

➧ Refer to illustration 9.3

2 Support the rear lower control arm with a floor jack, then remove the lower shock absorber mounting bolt (see Section 8).

3 Raise the lower control arm with a floor jack. Remove the outboard bolt securing the upper arm to the trailing arm (see illustration).

4 Lower the jack to remove tension from the upper arm, and move the shock absorber as needed to remove the upper arm.

9.3 Rear upper control arm inner pivot bolt (A) and arm-to-trailing arm bolt (B)

5 Remove the pivot bolt from the inner end of the arm. Remove the arm from the vehicle.

6 Installation is the reverse of removal. Tighten the fasteners to the torque listed in this Chapter's Specifications.

LOWER SUSPENSION ARM

➧ Refer to illustration 9.8

7 Remove the rear coil spring (see Section 10).

8 Mark the position of the cam adjuster bolt to the subframe, then remove the cam adjuster bolt and nut (see illustration). Remove the arm from the vehicle.

9 Installation is the reverse of removal. When installing the cam adjuster bolt, align the matchmarks and install a new nut. Tighten the fasteners to the torque listed in this Chapter's Specifications.

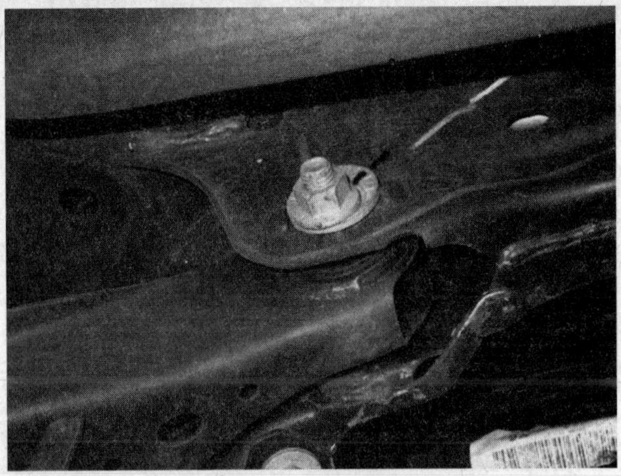

9.8 Mark the position of the cam to the subframe, then remove the lower control arm inner pivot bolt

TRAILING ARM

10 If a new arm is being installed, remove the caliper dust shield and the four bolts on the inboard side of the trailing arm and remove the wheel spindle. If the arm is to be reused, leave the wheel spindle bolted in place.

11 Unbolt the brake hose and brake line brackets from the trailing arm. Unbolt the parking brake cable brackets from the caliper and trailing arm (see Chapter 9).

12 Remove the ABS wheel speed sensor and unbolt the harness brackets from the trailing arm.

13 On AWD models, remove the driveaxle (see Chapter 8).

14 Support the lower control arm with a floor jack positioned underneath the coil spring pocket.

✲✲ WARNING:

The jack must remain in this position until the trailing arm is reinstalled.

15 Remove the lower shock absorber bolt (see Section 8).

16 Remove the outboard toe-link bolt and remove the trailing arm.

17 Remove the outboard bolt at the upper arm, and the outboard bolts at the lower arm.

18 Remove the two front trailing arm mounting bolts.

19 Inspect the trailing arm pivot bushing for signs of deterioration. If it is in need of replacement, take the trailing arm to an automotive machine shop to have the bushing replaced.

20 Installation is the reverse of removal, noting the following points:

a) *Use new fasteners during assembly.*
b) *Tighten all fasteners to the proper torque specifications.*
c) *It won't be necessary to bleed the brakes unless a hydraulic fitting was loosened.*
d) *Have the rear wheel alignment checked and, if necessary, adjusted.*

10 Coil spring (rear) - removal and installation

✲✲ WARNING:

Always replace the springs as a set - never replace just one of them.

➡Note: Any rear suspension fasteners should be replaced with new fasteners on assembly, and should only be tightened with the hub raised to a height of 15.5 inches from the hub center to the center of the fenderwell lip.

1 Loosen the wheel lug nuts, raise the vehicle and support it securely on jackstands. Block the front wheels to prevent the vehicle from rolling. Remove the wheel.

2 Support the lower control arm with a floor jack positioned underneath the coil spring pocket.

3 Support the trailing arm with another floor jack.

➡Note: If you don't have another floor jack, remove the caliper and hang it out of the way with a length of wire (see Chapter 9).

4 Disconnect the stabilizer bar link.

5 Remove the lower control arm outboard bolt.

6 Lower the trailing arm slowly with the floor jack until the coil spring is extended.

✲✲ WARNING:

The spring is under considerable pressure. Use a chain and bolts to secure the bottom of the spring to the lower arm until it can be safely removed.

7 Mark the position of the coil spring to the spring insulators.

8 Check the spring for cracks and chips, replacing the springs as a set if any defects are found. Also check the upper insulator for damage and deterioration, replacing it if necessary.

9 Installation is the reverse of removal. Be sure to position the lower end of the coil spring in the depressed area of the trailing arm. Use new fasteners and tighten all fasteners to the proper torque specifications.

11 Hub and bearing assembly (rear) - removal and installation

1 Raise and support the rear of the vehicle and remove the wheel speed sensor (see Chapter 9).

2 Unbolt and set aside the caliper and caliper mounting bracket. Do not let the caliper hang by the rubber brake hose; wire the caliper to the spring or shock absorber with mechanic's wire.

3 Remove the brake disc (see Chapter 9).

4 Pry off the grease cap with a screwdriver, tapping it with a small hammer if necessary.

5 Remove the hub nut and slide the hub and bearing assembly from the wheel spindle.

6 Installation is the reverse of removal. Tighten all fasteners to the proper torque specifications. Use a new hub nut.

12 Steering wheel - removal and installation

WARNING:

These models are equipped with a Supplemental Restraint System (SRS), more commonly known as airbags. Always disable the airbag system before working in the vicinity of any airbag system component to avoid the possibility of accidental deployment of the airbag(s), which could cause personal injury (see Chapter 12).

WARNING:

Do not use a memory saving device to preserve the PCM or radio memory when working on or near airbag system components.

REMOVAL

Refer to illustrations 12.3, 12.4, 12.6 and 12.8

1 Turn the ignition key to Off, then disconnect the cable from the negative terminal of the battery. Wait at least two minutes before proceeding.

2 Turn the steering wheel so the wheels are pointing straight ahead and remove the key.

3 Use a small screwdriver or a 3 mm Allen wrench through the holes in the backside of the steering wheel to release the airbag module clips (see illustration). Gently pull the airbag module away from the wheel on the side you have released, then repeat this Step on the other side of the wheel.

4 Pry UP the connector locks and disconnect the airbag module electrical connectors (see illustration).

5 Remove the airbag and set the airbag module in a safe, isolated area.

WARNING:

Carry the airbag module with the trim side facing away from you, and set the steering wheel/airbag module down with the trim side facing up. Don't place anything on top of the steering wheel/airbag module.

6 Make match marks on the wheel and the steering shaft, then remove the steering wheel mounting nut (see illustration). Rock the wheel lightly to remove it from the shaft.

7 Feed the wires and connectors through the steering wheel as you remove it.

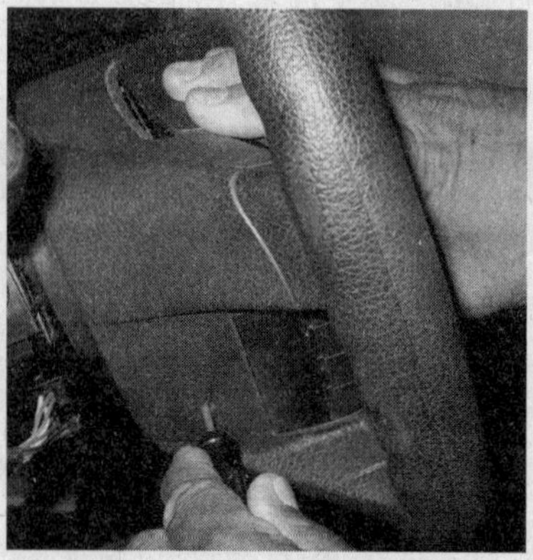

12.3 Depress the clips through the holes on each side of the steering wheel to release the airbag

12.4 Pry up the locking tabs, then disconnect the airbag connectors

12.6 Mark the position of the steering wheel to the shaft, then use a socket to loosen the steering wheel nut

8 Tape the clockspring so that it cannot rotate (see illustration).

✲✲ CAUTION:

Do not rotate the steering shaft at any time while the wheel and airbag are removed or the clockspring could be damaged.

9 If the clockspring is to be removed, remove the steering column covers (see Chapter 11), unplug its connectors and remove the mounting screws.

INSTALLATION

10 If the clockspring was removed, install it now, then center it (even if it was not removed, but if the inner rotor has turned, it must be centered).

a) Rotate the inner rotor of the clockspring counterclockwise until you feel resistance.

✲✲ CAUTION:

Don't apply too much force.

b) Turn the rotor clockwise approximately 2 to 2-1/4 turns, placing the electrical connector in the 12 o'clock position.

11 To install the wheel, feed the wiring and airbag connectors through the wheel and place the steering wheel on the steering shaft, aligning the match marks you made.

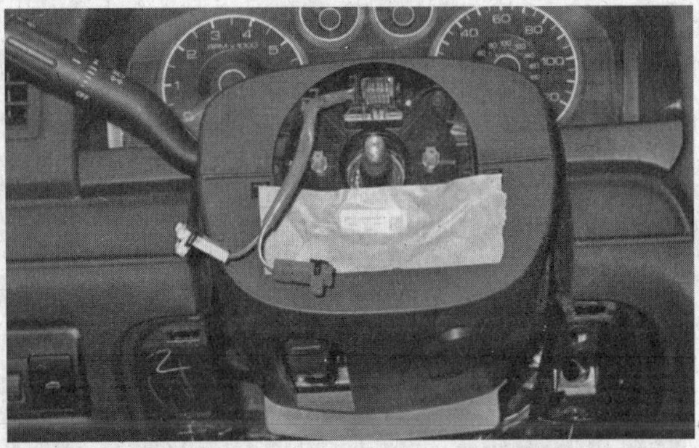

12.8 Apply a piece of tape to the clockspring to prevent it from rotating

12 Tighten the steering wheel nut to the torque listed in this Chapter's Specifications.

13 The remainder of installation is the reverse of removal.

✲✲ CAUTION:

Make sure the connectors fit correctly on the airbag module (with the safety tabs still UP). When connecting the two airbag connectors, follow the color-coding. The orange connector goes to the orange connection on the airbag. Do not push the connectors on if the clips are down. After the clips are secured, push the airbag module down toward the wheel until the retaining clips lock.

13 Steering column - removal and installation

✲✲ WARNING:

These models are equipped with a Supplemental Restraint System (SRS), more commonly known as airbags. Always disable the airbag system before working in the vicinity of any airbag system component to avoid the possibility of accidental deployment of the airbag(s), which could cause personal injury (see Chapter 12).

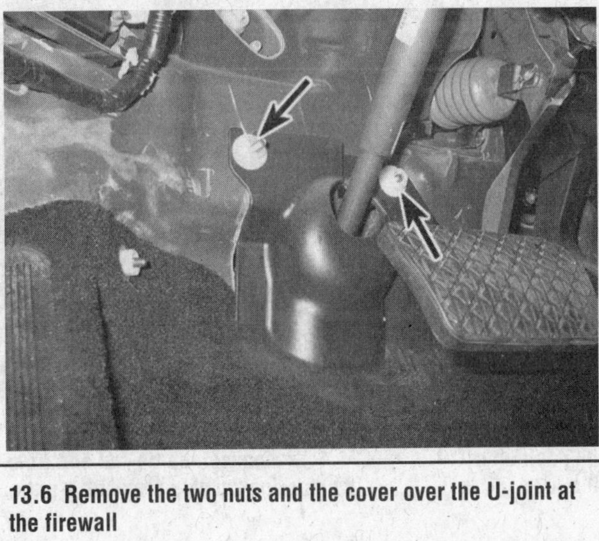

13.6 Remove the two nuts and the cover over the U-joint at the firewall

✲✲ WARNING:

Do not use a memory saving device to preserve the PCM or radio memory when working on or near airbag system components.

REMOVAL

➧ Refer to illustrations 13.6, 13.7 and 13.8

1 Park the vehicle with the wheels pointing straight ahead. Disconnect the cable from the negative terminal of the battery (see Chapter 5).

2 Remove the steering wheel (see Section 12)

3 Remove the steering column covers, then tape the airbag clockspring to prevent it from turning.

✲✲ CAUTION:

If this is not done, the airbag clockspring could be damaged.

Remove the steering column reinforcement panel (see Chapter 11).

4 Remove the clockspring (see Section 12).

5 Disconnect the electrical connectors for the multi-function switch (see Chapter 12).

6 Remove the fasteners securing the cover at the firewall (see illustration).

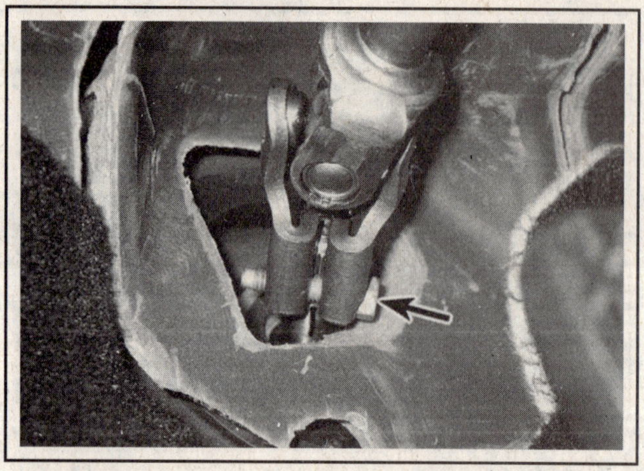

13.7 Mark the U-joint-to-intermediate shaft, then remove the pinch bolt

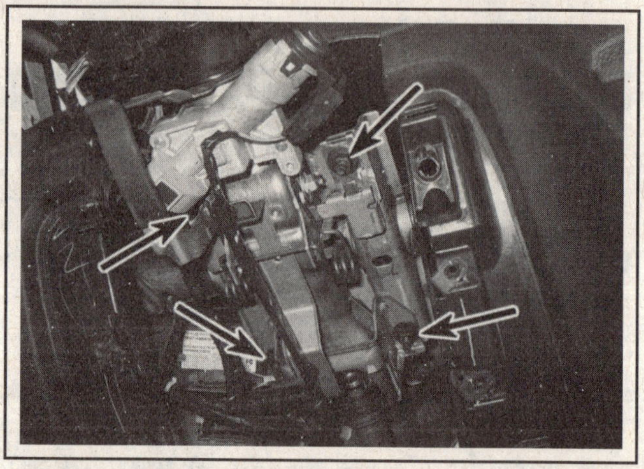

13.8 Remove the four nuts securing the steering column

7 Mark the relationship of the U-joint to the intermediate shaft, then remove and discard the pinch bolt (see illustration).

8 Remove the steering column mounting fasteners (see illustration). Lower the column and pull it to the rear, making sure nothing is still connected, then remove the column.

INSTALLATION

9 Guide the steering column into position, engaging the U-joint with the bottom of the steering shaft, then install the steering column mounting fasteners and tighten them to the torque listed in this Chapter's Specifications.

Note: An assistant will be very helpful in this procedure.

10 Connect the U-joint to the intermediate shaft. Install a New intermediate shaft pinch bolt, tightening it to the torque listed in this Chapter's Specifications.

11 The remainder of installation is the reverse of removal.

14 Tie-rod ends - removal and installation

REMOVAL

Refer to illustrations 14.2a, 14.2b and 14.4

1 Loosen the front wheel lug nuts. Apply the parking brake, raise the front of the vehicle and support it securely on jackstands. Remove the front wheel.

2 Hold the tie-rod with a pair of locking pliers or wrench and loosen the jam nut enough to mark the position of the tie-rod end in relation to the threads (see illustrations).

3 Remove the cotter pin and loosen (but don't remove) the nut on the tie-rod end stud.

4 Disconnect the tie-rod end from the steering knuckle arm with a puller (see illustration). Remove the nut and detach the tie-rod end.

5 Unscrew the tie-rod end from the tie-rod.

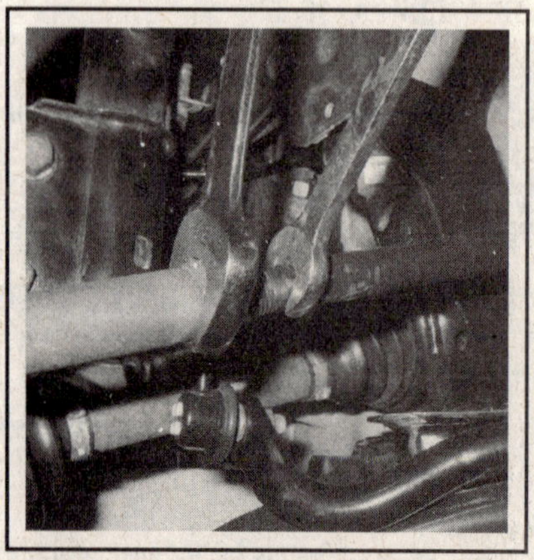

14.2a Loosen the jam nut . . .

14.2b . . . then mark the position of the tie-rod end in relation to the threads

14.4 Disconnect the tie-rod end from the steering knuckle arm with a puller

INSTALLATION

6 Thread the tie-rod end on to the marked position and insert the stud into the steering knuckle arm. Tighten the jam nut securely.

7 Install the nut on the stud and tighten it to the torque listed in this Chapter's Specifications. Install a new cotter pin.

8 Install the wheel and lug nuts. Lower the vehicle and tighten the lug nuts to the torque listed in the Chapter 1 Specifications.

9 Have the alignment checked and, if necessary, adjusted.

15 Steering gear boots - replacement

Refer to illustration 15.3

1 Loosen the lug nuts, raise the vehicle and support it securely on jackstands. Remove the wheel.

2 Remove the tie-rod end and jam nut (see Section 14).

3 Remove the outer steering gear boot clamp with a pair of pliers (see illustration). Cut off the inner boot clamp with a pair of diagonal cutters. Slide off the boot.

4 Before installing the new boot, wrap the threads and serrations on the end of the steering rod with a layer of tape so the small end of the new boot isn't damaged.

5 Slide the new boot into position on the steering gear until it seats in the groove in the steering rod and install new clamps.

6 Remove the tape and install the tie-rod end (see Section 14).

7 Install the wheel and lug nuts. Lower the vehicle and tighten the lug nuts to the torque listed in the Chapter 1 Specifications.

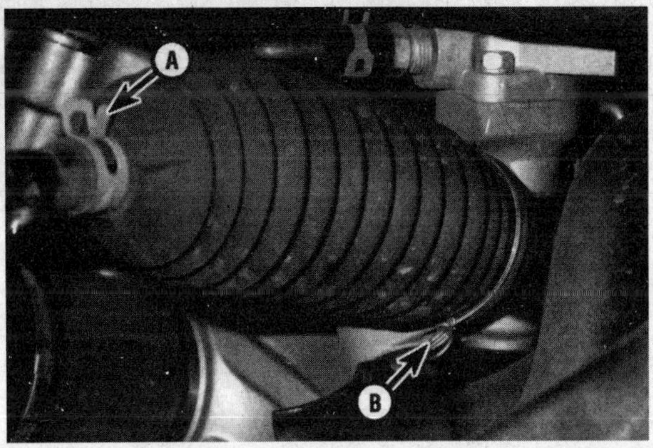

15.3 The outer ends of the steering gear boots are secured by band-type clamps (A); they're easily released with a pair of pliers. The inner ends of the steering gear boots are retained by boot clamps which must be cut off and discarded (B)

16 Steering gear - removal and installation

WARNING:

These models are equipped with airbags. Always disable the airbag system before working in the vicinity of airbag system components (see Chapter 12). Make sure the steering column shaft is not turned while the steering gear is removed or you could damage the airbag system clockspring. To prevent the shaft from turning, turn the ignition key to the lock position before beginning work, and run the seat belt through the steering wheel and clip it into its latch.

Note: Some models are equipped with electric power steering. On these models, ignore the steps which don't apply.

REMOVAL

Refer to illustrations 16.7 and 16.9

Note: On some vehicles equipped with the 3.0L V6 engine, it may be necessary to remove the EGR valve (see Chapter 6).

1 Disconnect the cable from the negative terminal of the battery (see Chapter 5).

2 From inside the vehicle under the instrument panel, remove and discard the intermediate shaft pinch bolt (see Section 13).

3 Loosen the front wheel lug nuts. Raise the vehicle and place it securely on jackstands. Remove both front wheels.

4 Detach the tie-rod ends from the steering knuckles (see Section 14).

5 If you're working on an All-Wheel Drive model, disconnect the driveshaft from the transfer case. Support the driveshaft - don't let it hang.

6 Remove the front portion of the exhaust system (see Chapter 4).

7 Place a drain pan under the steering gear and detach the power steering pressure and return lines (see illustration). Cap the ends to prevent excessive fluid loss and contamination.

Note: Some models have a sheetmetal shield (secured by two bolts) that must be removed for access to the fittings.

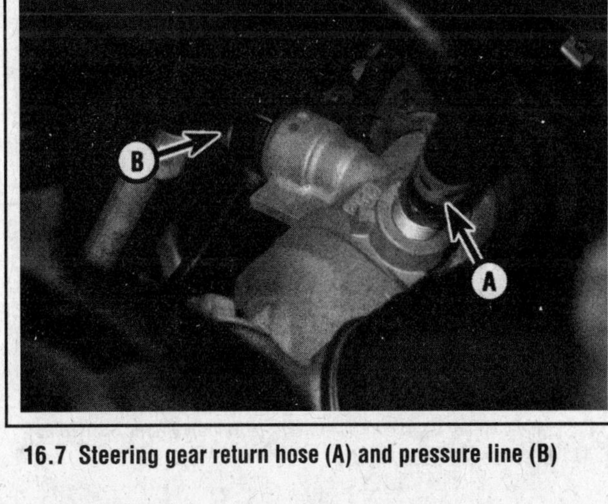

16.7 Steering gear return hose (A) and pressure line (B)

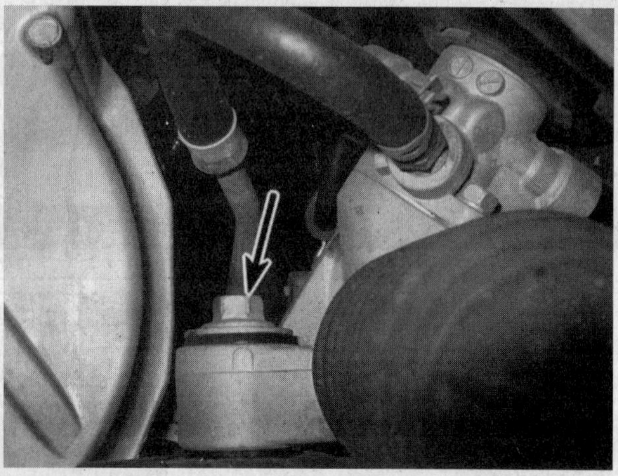

16.9 Left-side steering gear front mounting bolt

8 Support the rear of the subframe with a floor jack. Loosen the front subframe mounting fasteners and remove the rear subframe fasteners, then lower the rear of the subframe with the jack approximately 3 inches.

9 Remove the three steering gear mounting bolts (see illustration).

10 Remove the steering gear from the vehicle.

INSTALLATION

11 Installation is the reverse of removal, noting the following points:

a) *When connecting the steering gear input shaft to the intermediate shaft U-joint, be sure to align the matchmarks, and install a new pinch bolt.*
b) *Use new subframe mounting fasteners.*
c) *Use a new banjo bolt and sealing washers for the power steering pressure line.*
d) *Tighten all fasteners to the torque values listed in this Chapter's Specifications.*
e) *Tighten the lug nuts to the torque listed in the Chapter 1 Specifications.*
f) *Fill the power steering reservoir with the recommended fluid (see Chapter 1). Bleed the power steering hydraulic system as described in Section 18.*
g) *Have the front end alignment checked and, if necessary, adjusted.*

17 Power steering pump - removal and installation

REMOVAL

Refer to illustration 17.6

1 Disconnect the cable from the negative battery terminal (see Chapter 5).

2 Using a large syringe or suction gun, suck as much fluid out of the power steering fluid reservoir as possible. Place a drain pan under the vehicle to catch any fluid that spills out when the hoses are disconnected. On models with a remote fluid reservoir, remove the power steering fluid reservoir.

3 Remove the drivebelt (see Chapter 1).

4 Disconnect the electrical connector at the power steering pump.

5 Unscrew and remove the bolt securing the high pressure fluid line support bracket.

6 Disconnect the supply and pressure hoses from the power steering pump (see illustration).

7 Unscrew and remove the mounting bolts, and withdraw the power steering pump from the engine.

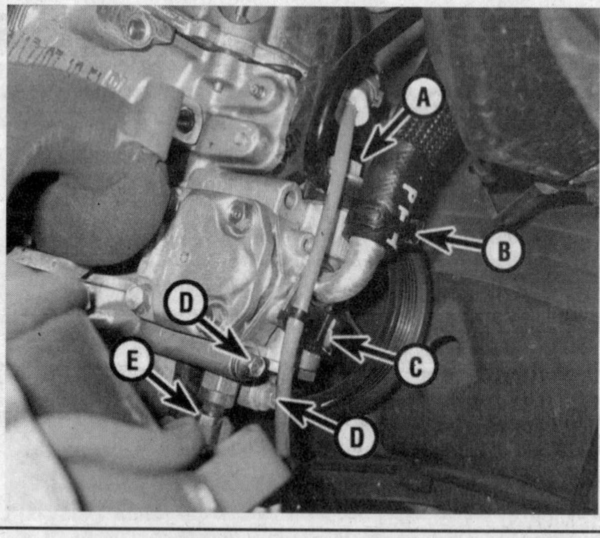

17.6 Typical power steering pump details (3.0L V6 engine)

A Pressure line banjo bolt
B Supply hose
C Oxygen sensor harness clip
D Mounting bolts (upper bolt not visible)
E Electrical connector

INSTALLATION

8 Installation is the reverse of removal, noting the following points:

a) *The banjo bolt and sealing washers on the high-pressure line should be replaced.*
b) *Tighten the mounting bolts and banjo bolt to the torque listed in this Chapter's Specifications.*
c) *Fill the power steering reservoir with the recommended fluid (see Chapter 1). Bleed the power steering hydraulic system as described in Section 18.*

18 Power steering system - bleeding

1 The power steering system must be bled whenever a line is disconnected. Bubbles can be seen in power steering fluid that has air in it and the fluid will often have a tan or milky appearance. Low fluid level can cause air to mix with the fluid, resulting in a noisy pump as well as foaming of the fluid.

2 Open the hood and check the fluid level in the reservoir, adding the specified fluid necessary to bring it up to the proper level (see Chapter 1).

3 Start the engine and slowly turn the steering wheel several times from left-to-right and back again. Do not turn the wheel completely from lock-to-lock. Check the fluid level, topping it up as necessary until it remains steady and no more bubbles are visible.

19 Power steering fluid cooler - removal and installation

The power steering fluid cooler is an integral part of the air conditioning condenser (see Chapter 3). The power steering fluid cooler can only be replaced as a unit with the condenser. If the power steering fluid should become contaminated for any reason, make sure to flush the power steering fluid cooler also, through the two hose connections at the top of the condenser.

20 Wheels and tires - general information

Refer to illustration 20.1

1 All vehicles covered by this manual are equipped with metric-sized fiberglass or steel belted radial tires (see illustration). Use of other size or type of tires may affect the ride and handling of the vehicle. Don't mix different types of tires, such as radials and bias belted, on the same vehicle as handling may be seriously affected. It's recommended that tires be replaced in pairs on the same axle, but if only one tire is being replaced, be sure it's the same size, structure and tread design as the other.

2 Because tire pressure has a substantial effect on handling and wear, the pressure on all tires should be checked at least once a month or before any extended trips (see Chapter 1).

3 Wheels must be replaced if they are bent, dented, leak air, have elongated bolt holes, are heavily rusted, out of vertical symmetry or if the lug nuts won't stay tight. Wheel repairs that use welding or peening are not recommended.

4 Tire and wheel balance is important in the overall handling, braking and performance of the vehicle. Unbalanced wheels can adversely affect handling and ride characteristics as well as tire life. Whenever a tire is installed on a wheel, the tire and wheel should be balanced by a shop with the proper equipment.

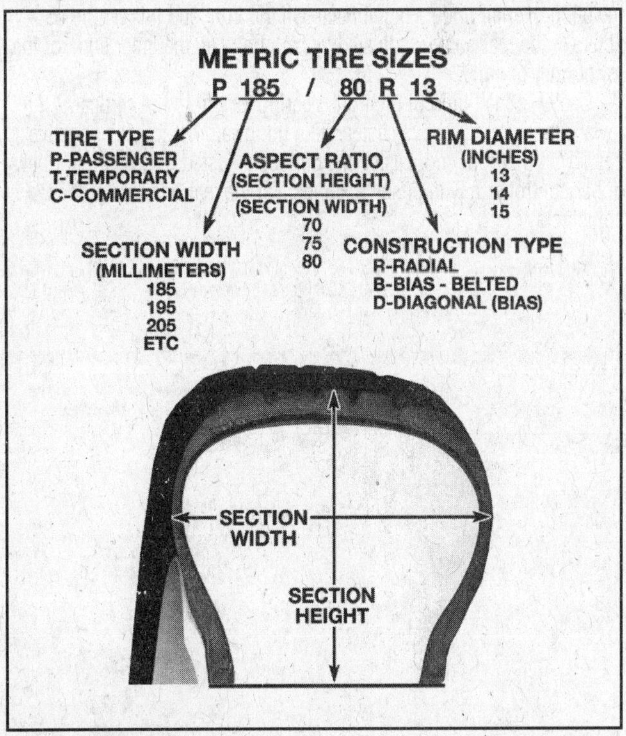

20.1 Metric tire size code

21 Wheel alignment - general information

Refer to illustration 21.1

A wheel alignment refers to the adjustments made to the wheels so they are in proper angular relationship to the suspension and the ground. Wheels that are out of proper alignment not only affect vehicle control, but also increase tire wear. The front end angles normally measured are camber, caster and toe-in (see illustration). Toe-in and camber are adjustable; if the caster is not correct, check for bent components. Rear toe-in is also adjustable.

Getting the proper wheel alignment is a very exacting process, one in which complicated and expensive machines are necessary to perform the job properly. Because of this, you should have a technician with the proper equipment perform these tasks. We will, however, use this space to give you a basic idea of what is involved with a wheel alignment so you can better understand the process and deal intelligently with the shop that does the work.

Toe-in is the turning in of the wheels. The purpose of a toe specification is to ensure parallel rolling of the wheels. In a vehicle with zero toe-in, the distance between the front edges of the wheels will be the same as the distance between the rear edges of the wheels. The actual amount of toe-in is normally only a fraction of an inch. On the front end, toe-in is controlled by the tie-rod end position on the tie-rod. On the rear end, it's controlled by a threaded toe-link. Incorrect toe-in will cause the tires to wear improperly by making them scrub against the road surface.

Camber is the tilting of the wheels from vertical when viewed from one end of the vehicle. When the wheels tilt out at the top, the camber is said to be positive (+). When the wheels tilt in at the top the camber is negative (-). The amount of tilt is measured in degrees from vertical and this measurement is called the camber angle. This angle affects the amount of tire tread which contacts the road and compensates for changes in the suspension geometry when the vehicle is cornering or traveling over an undulating surface. On the front end it is not adjustable. On the rear end it's adjusted by cam bolts on the inner ends of the lower control arms.

Caster is the tilting of the front steering axis from the vertical. A tilt toward the rear is positive caster and a tilt toward the front is negative caster. On the front end, caster can only be adjusted by installing a new upper control arm with offset bushings. On the rear end, caster isn't adjustable.

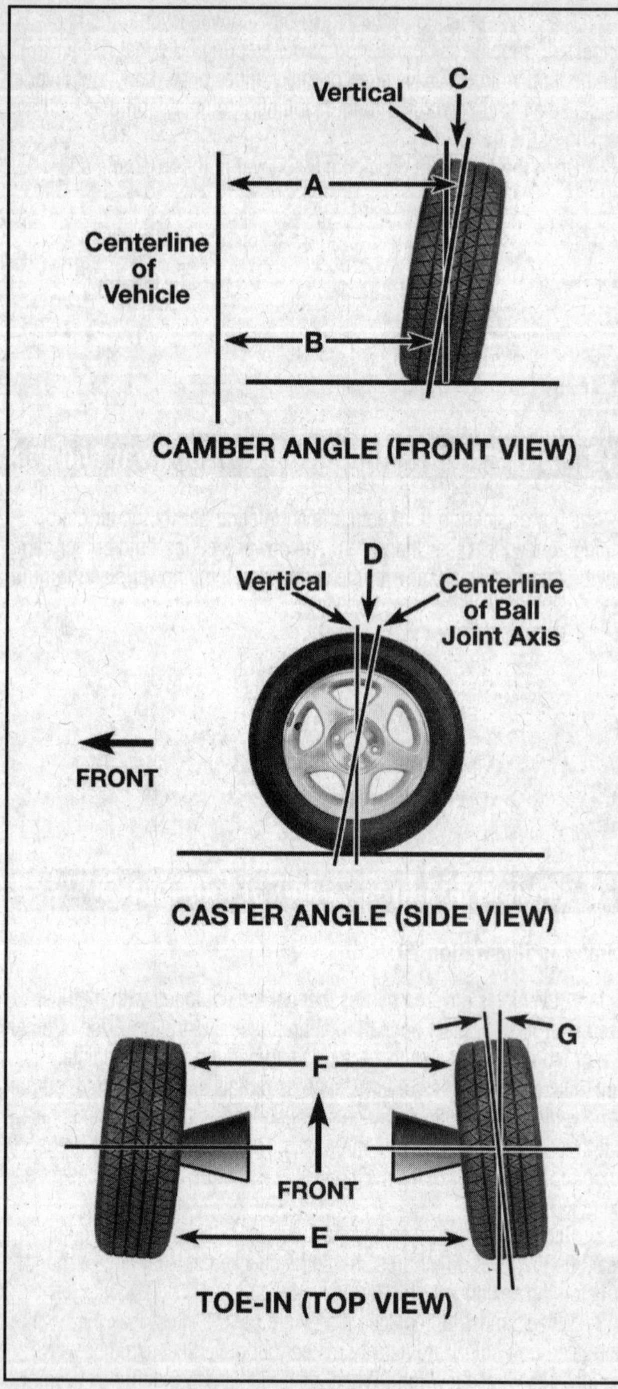

21.1 Camber, caster and toe-in angles

A minus B = C (degrees camber)
D = degrees caster
E minus F = toe-in (measured in inches)
G = toe-in (expressed in degrees)

Torque specifications	Ft-lbs (unless otherwise indicated)	Nm
➡Note: One foot-pound (ft-lb) of torque is equivalent to 12 inch-pounds (in-lbs) of torque. Torque values below approximately 15 foot-pounds are expressed in inch-pounds, because most foot-pound torque wrenches are not accurate at these smaller values.		
Front suspension		
Upper control arm		
Arm-to-chassis pivot bolts		
2006 and 2007 models	35	48
2008 and later models	41	55
Balljoint-to-knuckle nut	35	48
Lower control arms		
Balljoint-to-knuckle nut	148	200
Front lower arm-to-subframe bolt		
2006 models		
Step 1	48	65
Step 2	Tighten an additional 90-degrees	
2007 and later models		
Step 1	81	110
Step 2	Tighten an additional 90-degrees	
Rear lower arm-to-subframe bolt		
2006 models		
Step 1	48	65
Step 2	Tighten an additional 90-degrees	
2007 models		
Step 1	81	110
Step 2	Tighten an additional 90-degrees	
2008 and later models		
Step 1	48	65
Step 2	Tighten an additional 90-degrees	
Stabilizer bar		
Bracket bolts	35	48
Link nuts	31	42
Shock absorber/coil spring assembly		
Upper mounting nuts	22	30
Damper fork pinch bolt	35	47
Damper fork-to-front lower control arm bolt	76	103
Shock absorber piston rod-to-upper mount nut	30	40
Subframe		
Subframe mounting nuts	111	150
Subframe mounting bolts	76	103

Torque specifications (continued)	Ft-lbs (unless otherwise indicated)	Nm

➡Note: One foot-pound (ft-lb) of torque is equivalent to 12 inch-pounds (in-lbs) of torque. Torque values below approximately 15 foot-pounds are expressed in inch-pounds, because most foot-pound torque wrenches are not accurate at these smaller values.

Torque specifications (continued)	Ft-lbs (unless otherwise indicated)	Nm
Rear suspension		
Shock absorber		
Bracket-to-body bolts		
2006 models	35	48
2007 and later models	30	40
Upper mounting bolt/nut		
2006 and 2007 models	76	103
2008 and later models		
FWD models	76	103
AWD models	66	90
Lower mounting bolt		
2006 models	85	115
2007 models	66	90
2008 and later models		
FWD models	85	115
AWD models	66	90
Upper control arm		
Outer bolt/nut	81	110
Inner bolt		
2006 models	81	110
2007 and later models		
Step 1	74	100
Step 2	Tighten an additional 90-degrees	
Lower control arm		
Outer bolt		
2006 models	74	100
2007, 2008 and 2010 models	76	103
2009 models	81	110
Inner bolt (cam bolt)	74	100
Trailing arm-to-body bolts		
2006 models	98	133
2007 and later models	92	125
Toe link		
Outer bolt		
2006 through 2008 models	81	110
2009 and later models		
FWD models	81	110
AWD models	66	90

Torque specifications	Ft-lbs (unless otherwise indicated)	Nm

➡Note: One foot-pound (ft-lb) of torque is equivalent to 12 inch-pounds (in-lbs) of torque. Torque values below approximately 15 foot-pounds are expressed in inch-pounds, because most foot-pound torque wrenches are not accurate at these smaller values.

Torque specifications	Ft-lbs (unless otherwise indicated)	Nm
Steering		
Power steering pump mounting bolts	18	24
Power steering pressure line banjo bolts		
2006 models	26	35
2007 models		
To pump	35	48
To steering gear	41	55
Steering shaft-to-gear U-joint pinch bolt		
2009 and earlier models	18	24
2010 models		
2.5L and 3.0L models	177 in-lbs	20
3.5L models	18	24
Steering column mounting nuts	15	21
Steering wheel nut	26	35
Steering gear mounting bolts	79	107
Tie-rod end-to-steering knuckle nut	35	48

Notes

11 BODY

Section

1 General information

⁂ WARNING:

The models covered by this manual are equipped with Supplemental Restraint Systems (SRS), more commonly known as airbags. Always disable the airbag system before working in the vicinity of any airbag system components to avoid the possibility of accidental deployment of the airbags, which could cause personal injury (see Chapter 12).

Certain body components are particularly vulnerable to accident damage and can be unbolted and repaired or replaced. Among these parts are the hood, doors, tailgate, liftgate, bumpers and front fenders.

Only general body maintenance practices and body panel repair procedures within the scope of the do-it-yourselfer are included in this Chapter.

2 Repair minor paint scratches

No matter how hard you try to keep your vehicle looking like new, it will inevitably be scratched, chipped or dented at some point. If the metal is actually dented, seek the advice of a professional. But you can fix minor scratches and chips yourself. Buy a touch-up paint kit from a dealer service department or an auto parts store. To ensure that you get the right color, you'll need to have the specific make, model and year of your vehicle and, ideally, the paint code, which is located on a special metal plate under the hood or in the door jamb.

Make sure the damaged area is perfectly clean and rust free. If the touch-up kit has a wire brush, use it to clean the scratch or chip. Or use fine steel wool wrapped around the end of a pencil. Clean the scratched or chipped surface only, not the good paint surrounding it. Rinse the area with water and allow it to dry thoroughly

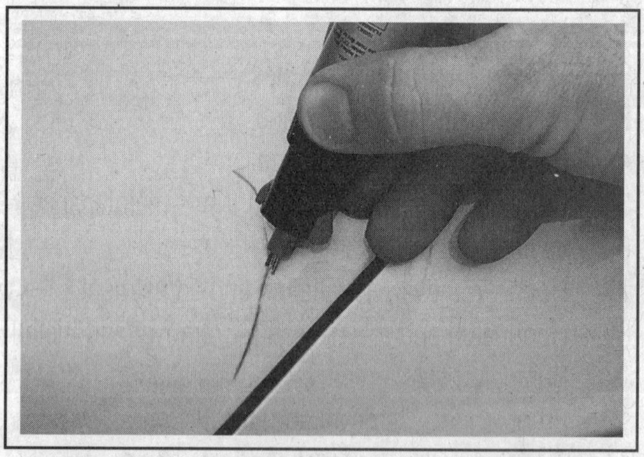

Thoroughly mix the paint, then apply a small amount with the touch-up kit brush or a very fine artist's brush. Brush in one direction as you fill the scratch area. Do not build up the paint higher than the surrounding paint

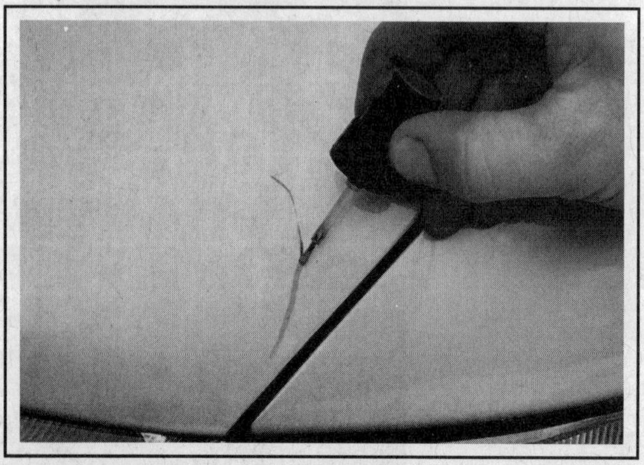

If the vehicle has a two-coat finish, apply the clear coat after the color coat has dried

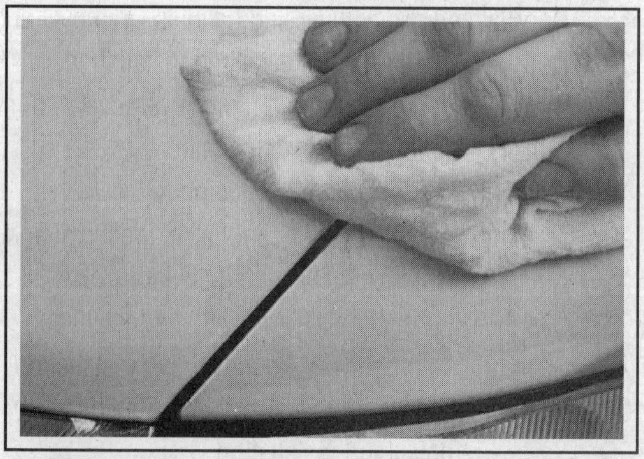

Wait a few days for the paint to dry thoroughly, then rub out the repainted area with a polishing compound to blend the new paint with the surrounding area. When you're happy with your work, wash and polish the area

3 Body repair - minor damage

PLASTIC BODY PANELS

The following repair procedures are for minor scratches and gouges. Repair of more serious damage should be left to a dealer service department or qualified auto body shop. Below is a list of the equipment and materials necessary to perform the following repair procedures on plastic body panels.

Wax, grease and silicone removing solvent
Cloth-backed body tape
Sanding discs
Drill motor with three-inch disc holder
Hand sanding block
Rubber squeegees
Sandpaper
Non-porous mixing palette
Wood paddle or putty knife
Curved-tooth body file
Flexible parts repair material

Flexible panels (bumper trim)

1 Remove the damaged panel, if necessary or desirable. In most cases, repairs can be carried out with the panel installed.

2 Clean the area(s) to be repaired with a wax, grease and silicone removing solvent applied with a water-dampened cloth.

3 If the damage is structural, that is, if it extends through the panel, clean the backside of the panel area to be repaired as well. Wipe dry.

4 Sand the rear surface about 1-1/2 inches beyond the break.

5 Cut two pieces of fiberglass cloth large enough to overlap the break by about 1-1/2 inches. Cut only to the required length.

6 Mix the adhesive from the repair kit according to the instructions included with the kit, and apply a layer of the mixture approximately 1/8-inch thick on the backside of the panel. Overlap the break by at least 1-1/2 inches.

7 Apply one piece of fiberglass cloth to the adhesive and cover the cloth with additional adhesive. Apply a second piece of fiberglass cloth to the adhesive and immediately cover the cloth with additional adhesive in sufficient quantity to fill the weave.

8 Allow the repair to cure for 20 to 30 minutes at 60-degrees to 80-degrees F.

9 If necessary, trim the excess repair material at the edge.

10 Remove all of the paint film over and around the area(s) to be repaired. The repair material should not overlap the painted surface.

11 With a drill motor and a sanding disc (or a rotary file), cut a "V" along the break line approximately 1/2-inch wide. Remove all dust and loose particles from the repair area.

12 Mix and apply the repair material. Apply a light coat first over the damaged area; then continue applying material until it reaches a level slightly higher than the surrounding finish.

13 Cure the mixture for 20 to 30 minutes at 60-degrees to 80-degrees F.

14 Roughly establish the contour of the area being repaired with a body file. If low areas or pits remain, mix and apply additional adhesive.

15 Block sand the damaged area with sandpaper to establish the actual contour of the surrounding surface.

16 If desired, the repaired area can be temporarily protected with several light coats of primer. Because of the special paints and techniques required for flexible body panels, it is recommended that the vehicle be taken to a paint shop for completion of the body repair.

STEEL BODY PANELS

➧ See photo sequence

Repair of dents

17 When repairing dents, the first job is to pull the dent out until the affected area is as close as possible to its original shape. There is no point in trying to restore the original shape completely as the metal in the damaged area will have stretched on impact and cannot be restored to its original contours. It is better to bring the level of the dent up to a point that is about 1/8-inch below the level of the surrounding metal. In cases where the dent is very shallow, it is not worth trying to pull it out at all.

18 If the backside of the dent is accessible, it can be hammered out gently from behind using a soft-face hammer. While doing this, hold a block of wood firmly against the opposite side of the metal to absorb the hammer blows and prevent the metal from being stretched.

19 If the dent is in a section of the body which has double layers, or some other factor makes it inaccessible from behind, a different technique is required. Drill several small holes through the metal inside the damaged area, particularly in the deeper sections. Screw long, self-tapping screws into the holes just enough for them to get a good grip in the metal. Now pulling on the protruding heads of the screws with locking pliers can pull out the dent.

20 The next stage of repair is the removal of paint from the damaged area and from an inch or so of the surrounding metal. This is easily done with a wire brush or sanding disk in a drill motor, although it can be done just as effectively by hand with sandpaper. To complete the preparation for filling, score the surface of the bare metal with a screwdriver or the tang of a file or drill small holes in the affected area. This will provide a good grip for the filler material. To complete the repair, see the Section on filling and painting.

Repair of rust holes or gashes

21 Remove all paint from the affected area and from an inch or so of the surrounding metal using a sanding disk or wire brush mounted in a drill motor. If these are not available, a few sheets of sandpaper will do the job just as effectively.

22 With the paint removed, you will be able to determine the severity of the corrosion and decide whether to replace the whole panel, if possible, or repair the affected area. New body panels are not as expensive as most people think and it is often quicker to install a new panel than to repair large areas of rust.

23 Remove all trim pieces from the affected area except those which will act as a guide to the original shape of the damaged body, such as headlight shells, etc. Using metal snips or a hacksaw blade, remove all loose metal and any other metal that is badly affected by rust. Hammer the edges of the hole in to create a slight depression for the filler material.

24 Wire-brush the affected area to remove the powdery rust from the surface of the metal. If the back of the rusted area is accessible, treat it with rust inhibiting paint.

25 Before filling is done, block the hole in some way. This can be done with sheet metal riveted or screwed into place, or by stuffing the hole with wire mesh.

26 Once the hole is blocked off, the affected area can be filled and painted. See the following subsection on filling and painting.

These photos illustrate a method of repairing simple dents. They are intended to supplement Body repair - minor damage in this Chapter and should not be used as the sole instructions for body repair on these vehicles.

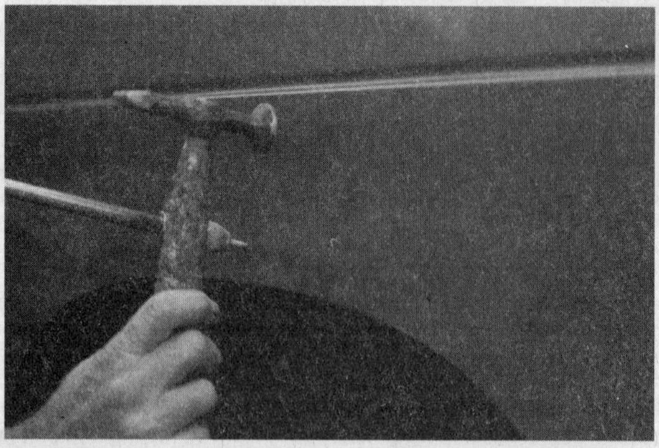

1 If you can't access the backside of the body panel to hammer out the dent, pull it out with a slide-hammer-type dent puller. Tap with a hammer near the edge of the dent to help 'pop' the metal back to its original shape, about 1/8-inch below the surface of the surrounding metal

2 Using coarse-grit sandpaper, remove the paint down to the bare metal. Clean the repair area with wax/silicone remover.

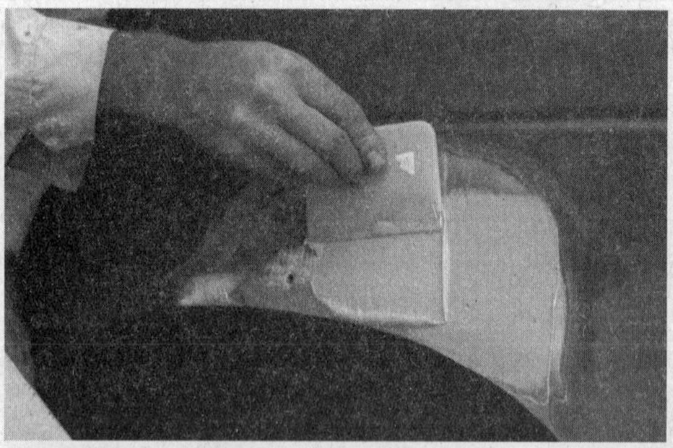

3 Following label instructions, mix up a batch of plastic filler and hardener, then quickly press it into the metal with a plastic applicator. Work the filler until it matches the original contour and is slightly above the surrounding metal

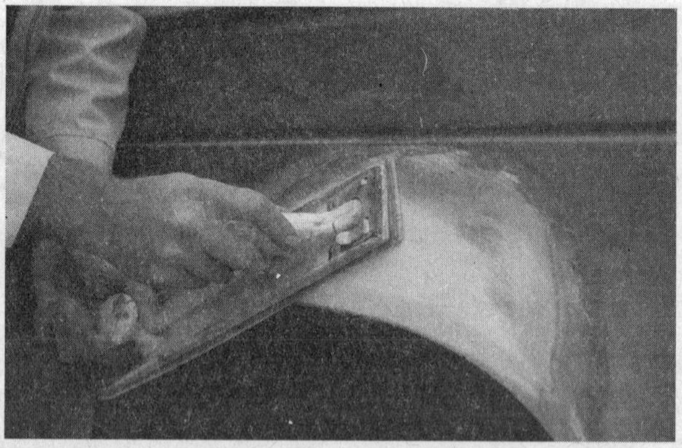

4 Let the filler harden until you can just dent it with your fingernail. File, then sand the filler down until it's smooth and even. Work down to finer grits of sandpaper - always using a board or block - ending up with 360 or 400 grit

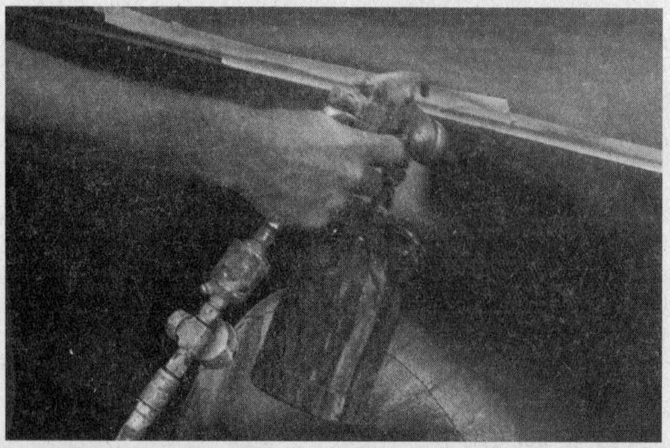

5 When the area is smooth to the touch, clean the area and mask around it. Apply several layers of primer to the area. A professional-type spray gun is being used here, but aerosol spray primer works fine

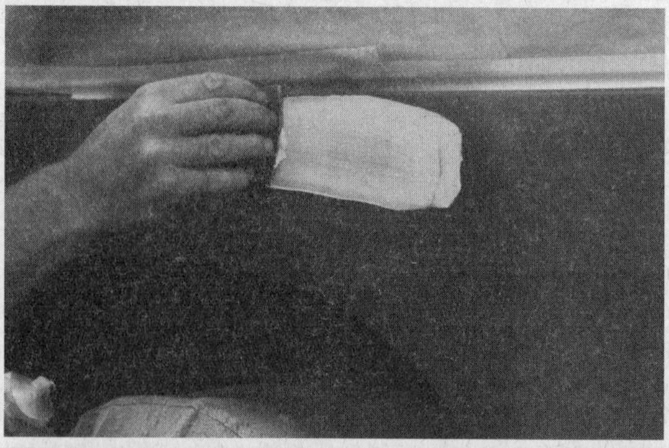

6 Fill imperfections or scratches with glazing compound. Sand with 360 or 400-grit and re-spray. Finish sand the primer with 600 grit, clean thoroughly, then apply the finish coat. Don't attempt to rub out or wax the repair area until the paint has dried completely (at least two weeks)

Filling and painting

27 Many types of body fillers are available, but generally speaking, body repair kits which contain filler paste and a tube of resin hardener are best for this type of repair work. A wide, flexible plastic or nylon applicator will be necessary for imparting a smooth and contoured finish to the surface of the filler material. Mix up a small amount of filler on a clean piece of wood or cardboard (use the hardener sparingly). Follow the manufacturer's instructions on the package, otherwise the filler will set incorrectly.

28 Using the applicator, apply the filler paste to the prepared area. Draw the applicator across the surface of the filler to achieve the desired contour and to level the filler surface. As soon as a contour that approximates the original one is achieved, stop working the paste. If you continue, the paste will begin to stick to the applicator. Continue to add thin layers of paste at 20-minute intervals until the level of the filler is just above the surrounding metal.

29 Once the filler has hardened, the excess can be removed with a body file. From then on, progressively finer grades of sandpaper should be used, starting with a 180 grit paper and finishing with 600-grit wet-or-dry paper. Always wrap the sandpaper around a flat rubber or wooden block, otherwise the surface of the filler will not be completely flat. During the sanding of the filler surface, the wet-or-dry paper should be periodically rinsed in water. This will ensure that a very smooth finish is produced in the final stage.

30 At this point, the repair area should be surrounded by a ring of bare metal, which in turn should be encircled by the finely feathered edge of good paint. Rinse the repair area with clean water until all of the dust produced by the sanding operation is gone.

31 Spray the entire area with a light coat of primer. This will reveal any imperfections in the surface of the filler. Repair the imperfections with fresh filler paste or glaze filler and once more smooth the surface with sandpaper. Repeat this spray-and-repair procedure until you are satisfied that the surface of the filler and the feathered edge of the paint are perfect. Rinse the area with clean water and allow it to dry completely.

32 The repair area is now ready for painting. Spray painting must be carried out in a warm, dry, windless and dust free atmosphere. These conditions can be created if you have access to a large indoor work area, but if you are forced to work in the open, you will have to pick the day very carefully. If you are working indoors, dousing the floor in the work area with water will help settle the dust that would otherwise be in the air. If the repair area is confined to one body panel, mask off the surrounding panels. This will help minimize the effects of a slight mismatch in paint color. Trim pieces such as chrome strips, door handles, etc., will also need to be masked off or removed. Use masking tape and several thickness of newspaper for the masking operations.

33 Before spraying, shake the paint can thoroughly, then spray a test area until the spray painting technique is mastered. Cover the repair area with a thick coat of primer. The thickness should be built up using several thin layers of primer rather than one thick one. Using 600-grit wet-or-dry sandpaper, rub down the surface of the primer until it is very smooth. While doing this, the work area should be thoroughly rinsed with water and the wet-or-dry sandpaper periodically rinsed as well. Allow the primer to dry before spraying additional coats.

34 Spray on the top coat, again building up the thickness by using several thin layers of paint. Begin spraying in the center of the repair area and then, using a circular motion, work out until the whole repair area and about two inches of the surrounding original paint is covered. Remove all masking material 10 to 15 minutes after spraying on the final coat of paint. Allow the new paint at least two weeks to harden, then use a very fine rubbing compound to blend the edges of the new paint into the existing paint. Finally, apply a coat of wax

4 Body repair - major damage

1 Major damage must be repaired by an auto body shop specifically equipped to perform body and frame repairs. These shops have the specialized equipment required to do the job properly.

2 If the damage is extensive, the frame must be checked for proper alignment or the vehicle's handling characteristics may be adversely affected and other components may wear at an accelerated rate.

3 Due to the fact that all of the major body components (hood, fenders, etc.) are separate and replaceable units, any seriously damaged components should be replaced rather than repaired. Sometimes the components can be found in a wrecking yard that specializes in used vehicle components, often at considerable savings over the cost of new parts.

5 Upholstery, carpets and vinyl trim - maintenance

UPHOLSTERY AND CARPETS

1 Every three months remove the floormats and clean the interior of the vehicle (more frequently if necessary). Use a stiff whiskbroom to brush the carpeting and loosen dirt and dust, then vacuum the upholstery and carpets thoroughly, especially along seams and crevices.

2 Dirt and stains can be removed from carpeting with basic household or automotive carpet shampoos available in spray cans. Follow the directions and vacuum again, then use a stiff brush to bring back the "nap" of the carpet.

3 Most interiors have cloth or vinyl upholstery, either of which can be cleaned and maintained with a number of material-specific cleaners or shampoos available in auto supply stores. Follow the directions on the product for usage, and always spot-test any upholstery cleaner on an inconspicuous area (bottom edge of a backseat cushion) to ensure that it doesn't cause a color shift in the material.

4 After cleaning, vinyl upholstery should be treated with a protectant.

➡**Note: Make sure the protectant container indicates the product can be used on seats - some products may make a seat too slippery.**

⁂ CAUTION:

Do not use protectant on vinyl-covered steering wheels.

5 Leather upholstery requires special care. It should be cleaned regularly with saddlesoap or leather cleaner. Never use alcohol, gasoline, nail polish remover or thinner to clean leather upholstery.

6 After cleaning, regularly treat leather upholstery with a leather conditioner, rubbed in with a soft cotton cloth. Never use car wax on leather upholstery.

7 In areas where the interior of the vehicle is subject to bright sunlight, cover leather seating areas of the seats with a sheet if the vehicle is to be left out for any length of time.

VINYL TRIM

8 Don't clean vinyl trim with detergents, caustic soap or petroleum-based cleaners. Plain soap and water works just fine, with a soft brush to clean dirt that may be ingrained. Wash the vinyl as frequently as the rest of the vehicle.

9 After cleaning, application of a high-quality rubber and vinyl protectant will help prevent oxidation and cracks. The protectant can also be applied to weather-stripping, vacuum lines and rubber hoses, which often fail as a result of chemical degradation, and to the tires.

6 Fastener and trim removal

➧ Refer to illustration 6.4

1 There is a variety of plastic fasteners used to hold trim panels, splash shields and other parts in place in addition to typical screws, nuts and bolts. Once you are familiar with them, they can usually be removed without too much difficulty.

2 The proper tools and approach can prevent added time and expense to a project by minimizing the number of broken fasteners and/or parts.

3 The following illustration shows various types of fasteners that are typically used on most vehicles and how to remove and install them (see illustration). Replacement fasteners are commonly found at most auto parts stores, if necessary.

Fasteners

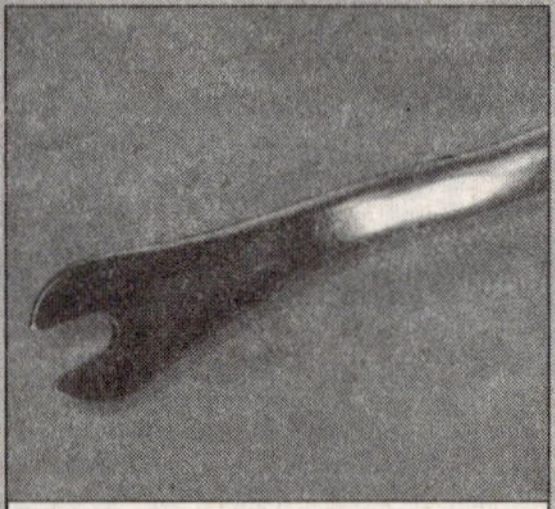

This tool is designed to remove special fasteners. A small pry tool used for removing nails will also work well in place of this tool

A Phillips head screwdriver can be used to release the center portion, but light pressure must be used because the plastic is easily damaged. Once the center is up, the fastener can easily be pried from its hole

Here is a view with the center portion fully released. Install the fastener as shown, then press the center in to set it

This fastener is used for exterior panels and shields. The center portion must be pried up to release the fastener. Install the fastener with the center up, then press the center in to set it

This type of fastener is used commonly for interior panels. Use a small blunt tool to press the small pin at the center in to release it . . .

. . . the pin will stay with the fastener in the released position

Reset the fastener for installation by moving the pin out. Install the fastener, then press the pin flush with the fastener to set it

This fastener is used for exterior and interior panels. It has no moving parts. Simply pry the fastener from its hole like the claw of a hammer removes a nail. Without a tool that can get under the top of the fastener, it can be very difficult to remove

4 Trim panels are typically made of plastic and their flexibility can help during removal. The key to their removal is to use a tool to pry the panel near its retainers to release it without damaging surrounding areas or breaking-off any retainers. The retainers will usually snap out of their designated slot or hole after force is applied to them. Stiff plastic tools designed for prying on trim panels are available at most auto parts stores (see illustration). Tools that are tapered and wrapped in protective tape, such as a screwdriver or small pry tool, are also very effective when used with care.

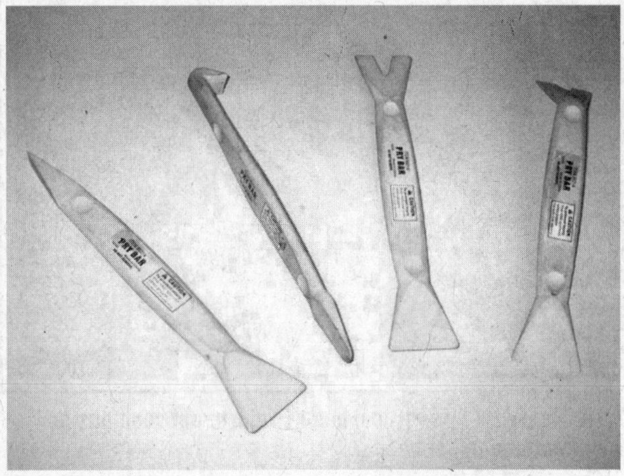

6.4 These small plastic pry tools are ideal for prying off trim panels

7 Hood - removal, installation and adjustment

➡Note: The hood is awkward to remove and install; at least two people should perform this procedure.

REMOVAL AND INSTALLATION

➧ Refer to illustrations 7.2 and 7.3

1 Open the hood, then place blankets or pads over the fenders and cowl area of the body. This will protect the body and paint as the hood is lifted off.

2 Make marks around the hood hinge to ensure proper alignment during installation (see illustration).

3 Have an assistant support one side of the hood. Grasp the lower corner of the hood and use your shoulder to brace the hood (see illustration). Take turns removing the hinge-to-hood bolts and lift off the hood.

4 Installation is the reverse of removal. Align the hinge bolts with the marks made in Step 2.

7.2 Draw alignment marks around the hood hinges to ensure proper alignment of the hood when it's reinstalled

7.3 Support the hood with your shoulder while removing the hood bolts

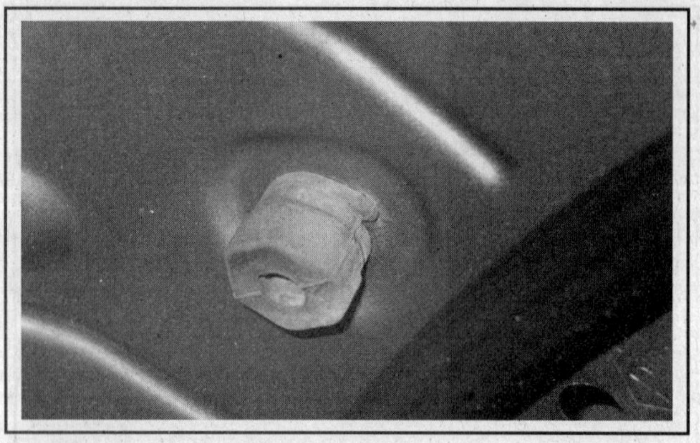

7.8a There are two vertical height adjustment cushions on the underside of the hood . . .

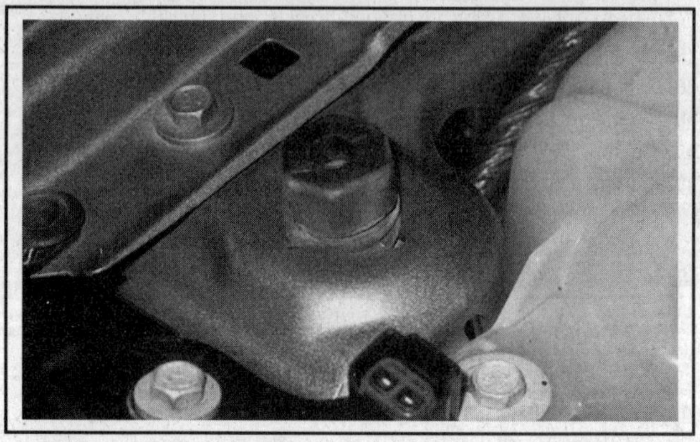

7.8b . . . and two on small brackets adjacent to the front fenders

ADJUSTMENT

Refer to illustrations 7.8a and 7.8b

5 Fore-and-aft and side-to-side adjustment of the hood is done by moving the hinges after loosening the hinge-to-body bolts.

6 Loosen the bolts and move the hood into correct alignment. Move it only a little at a time. Tighten the hinge bolts and carefully lower the hood to check the position.

7 The hood can also be adjusted vertically so that it's flush with the fenders.

8 Turn each cushion clockwise to lower the hood or counterclockwise to raise the hood (see illustrations).

9 The hood latch assembly, as well as the hinges, should be periodically lubricated with white, lithium-base grease to prevent binding and wear.

8 Hood latch and release cable - removal and installation

HOOD LATCH

Refer to illustrations 8.1 and 8.2

1 Open the hood and scribe a line around the latch to aid alignment when installing, then remove the retaining bolts securing the hood latch to the radiator support (see illustration). Remove the latch.

2 Squeeze the cable retainer to release the cable from the latch assembly, then disengage the cable end plug from the latch (see illustration).

3 Installation is the reverse of removal.

RELEASE CABLE

Refer to illustration 8.9

4 Working in the engine compartment, remove the hood latch and disconnect the hood release cable from the latch (see Steps 1 and 2).

5 Detach the two release cable clips from the radiator grille opening panel reinforcement.

6 Loosen the wheel lug nuts. Raise the vehicle and place it securely on jackstands. Remove the left front wheel. Remove the inner fender splash shield (see Section 10).

8.1 Hood latch assembly bolts

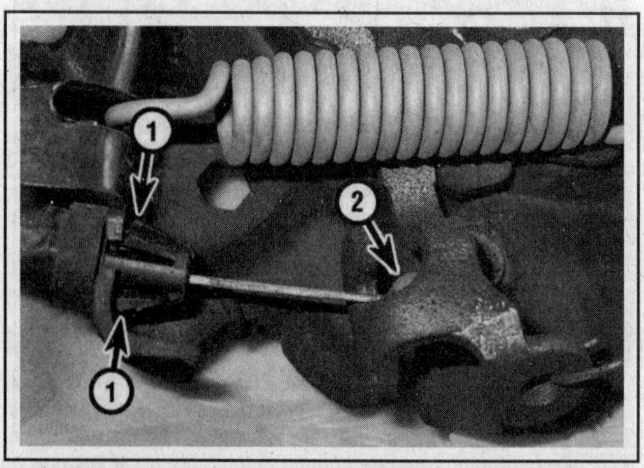

8.2 Hood release cable connection at latch assembly:

1 *Retainer fingers*
2 *Cable end plug*

7 Open the two release cable clips in the upper part of the fender opening and detach the release cable from the clips.

8 Disengage the release cable clip from the wiring harness. On 2010 models, remove the Smart Junction Box (see Chapter 12).

9 Remove the two hood release handle mounting bolts (see illustration), pull out the handle, then disengage the release cable from the release handle and pull the release cable through the firewall.

10 The remainder of the installation is the reverse of removal.

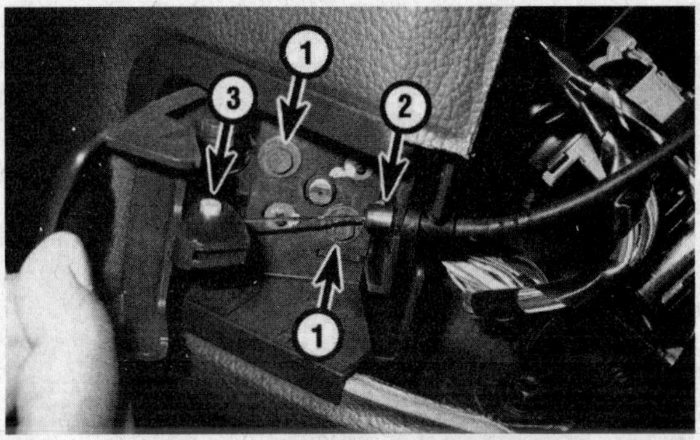

8.9 Hood release cable and release handle details:

1 Release handle mounting bolts
2 Release cable retainer
3 Release cable end plug

9 Bumper covers - removal and installation

➡Note: Refer to Section 6 for fastener and trim removal.

FRONT BUMPER COVER

➧ Refer to illustrations 9.1, 9.4, 9.5 and 9.6

1 Remove the upper fasteners from the radiator grille (see illustration).

2 Loosen the front wheel lug nuts, raise the vehicle and support it securely on jackstands. Remove the front wheels.

3 Disconnect the electrical connectors from the fog lamps, if equipped (see Chapter 12).

4 Remove the fasteners that secure the inner fender splash shields to the bumper cover (see illustration).

5 Remove the bumper cover lower fasteners (see illustration).

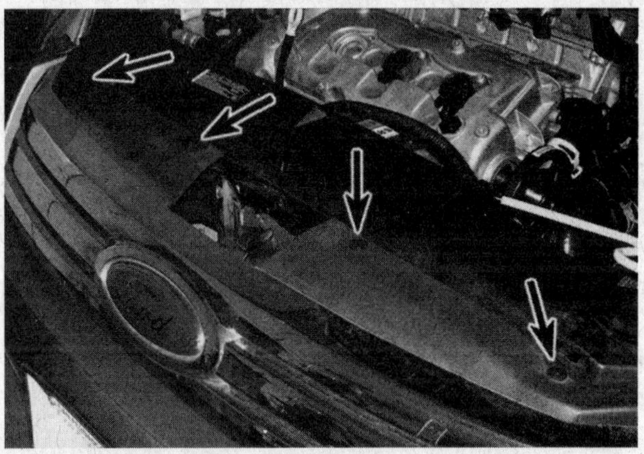

9.1 Radiator grille upper fasteners

9.4 Inner fender splash shield-to-bumper cover fasteners

9.5 Bumper cover lower fasteners

9.6 Pop loose the bumper cover mounting tabs along the upper rear edges of the bumper cover from their corresponding slots in the lower edge of the front fenders

9.12 Rear wheel well splash shield pin-type retainers to access rear bumper cover screws (left side shown)

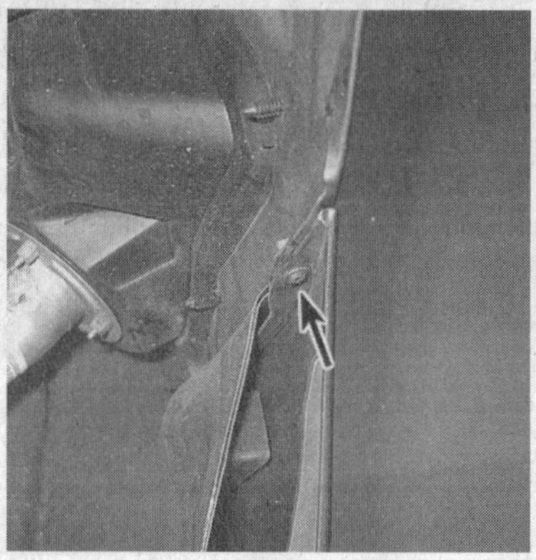

9.13 Rear bumper cover screw, upper front corner (left side shown)

6 Disengage the clips that secure the upper rear edges of the bumper cover to the fender (see illustration).

7 Using a flashlight, do a final inspection and verify that the bumper cover is completely detached, all electrical connectors are disconnected and all wiring harnesses are safely out of the way.

8 With an assistant's help, remove the front bumper cover.

9 Installation is the reverse of removal.

REAR BUMPER COVER

Refer to illustrations 9.12, 9.13, 9.14 and 9.15

10 Remove the taillight housing assemblies (see Chapter 12).

11 Loosen the rear wheel lug nuts, raise the vehicle and support it securely on jackstands. Remove the rear wheels.

12 To access the rear bumper cover screws, remove the pin-type retainers from the rear part of the wheel well splash shield (see illustration) and push the shields aside.

13 Remove the screw from the underside of each upper front corner of the bumper cover (see illustration).

14 Remove the pin-type fasteners from the underside of the rear bumper cover (see illustration).

15 In the taillight area, remove the pin-type fastener and bolt from each upper corner of the rear bumper cover (see illustration).

16 Using a flashlight, do a final inspection and verify that the bumper cover is completely detached, all electrical connectors are disconnected and all wiring harnesses are safely out of the way.

17 With an assistant's help, remove the rear bumper cover.

18 Installation is the reverse of removal. Again, get help when putting the bumper cover back into position.

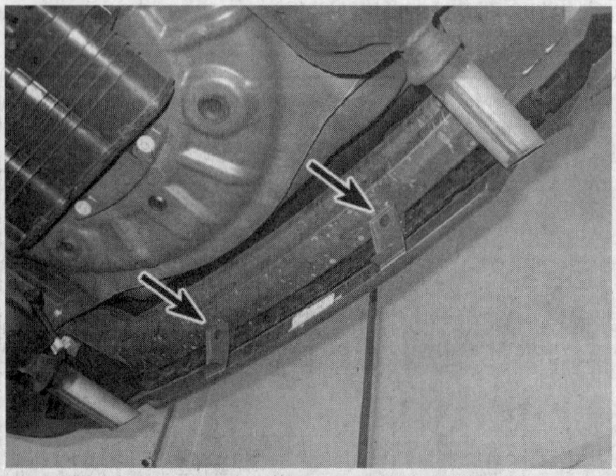

9.14 Rear bumper cover lower mounting fasteners

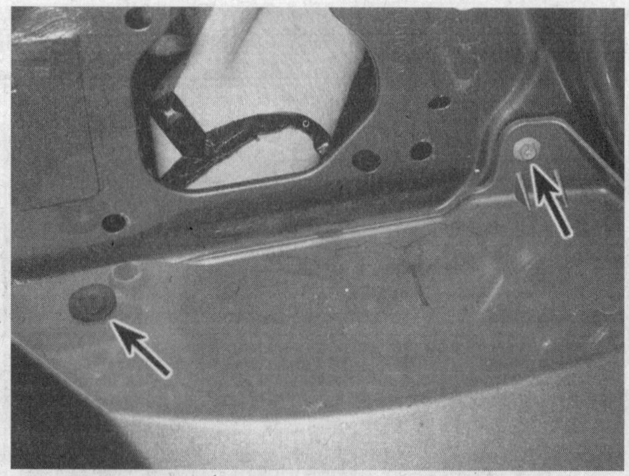

9.15 Rear bumper cover upper corner bolt and pin-type fastener (left corner shown)

10 Front fender - removal and installation

Refer to illustrations 10.3, 10.5a, 10.5b, 10.6, 10.7, 10.8, 10.9a and 10.9b

Note: Refer to Section 6 for fastener and trim removal.

1 Remove the headlight housing (see Chapter 12).

2 Loosen the front wheel lug nuts. Raise the vehicle, support it securely on jackstands and remove the front wheel.

3 Remove the fasteners that secure the inner fender splash shield (see illustration) and remove the splash shield.

4 Remove the front bumper cover (see Section 9).

5 Disconnect the electrical connector from the front sidemarker light, remove the bumper cover mounting bracket fasteners (see illustrations) and remove the bumper cover mounting bracket and sidemarker light assembly.

6 Remove the two lower fender bolts (see illustration).

7 Open the front door, then remove the upper rear fender bolt from inside the doorjamb (see illustration).

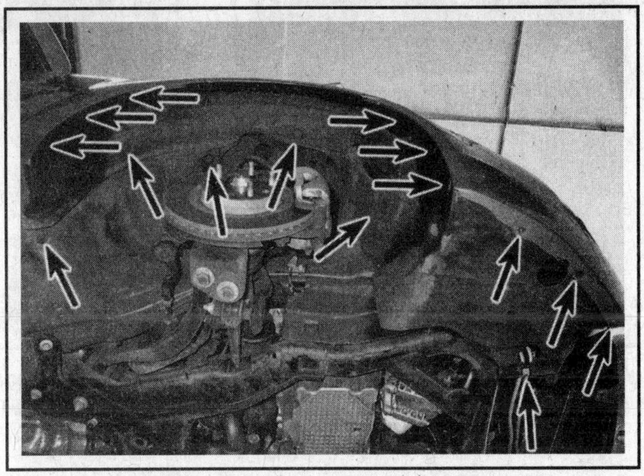

10.3 Inner fender splash shield pin-type fasteners

10.5a Rear mounting screw for the bumper cover mounting bracket

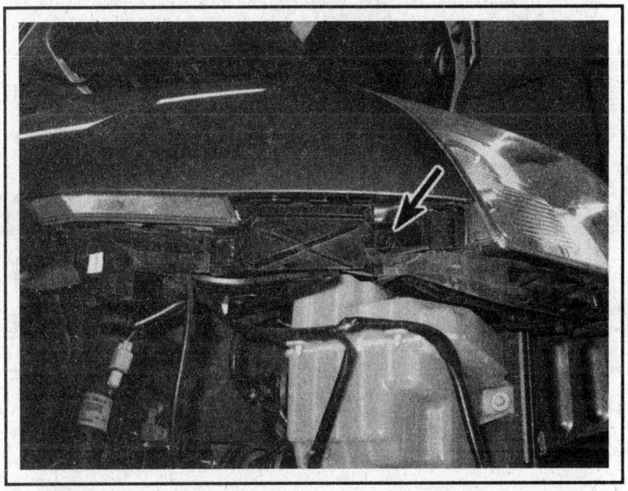

10.5b Front mounting bolt for the bumper cover mounting bracket

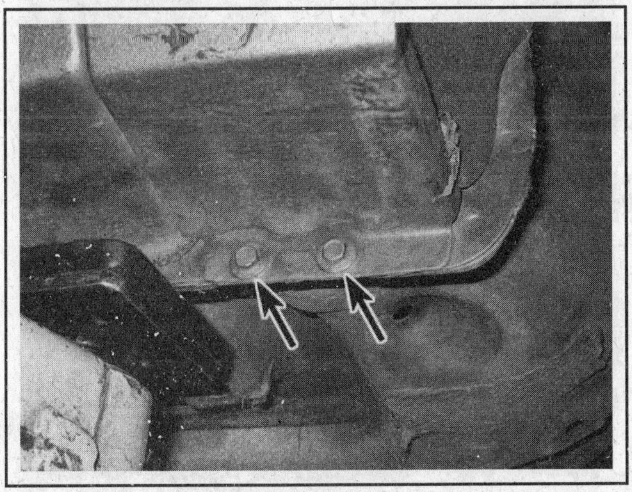

10.6 Front fender lower bolts

10.7 Upper rear fender bolt

10.8 Front fender mounting nut (inside rear part of the wheel well)

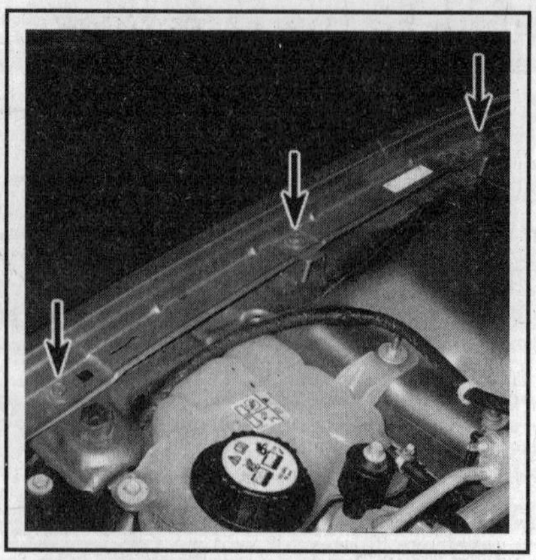

10.9a Front fender upper mounting bolts

10.9b Inner rear fender bolt

8 Remove the front fender mounting nut inside the back part of the front wheel well (see illustration).

9 Remove the fender upper bolts and the inner rear fender bolt (see illustrations), then lift off the fender. It's a good idea to have an assistant support the fender while it's being moved away from the vehicle to prevent damage to the surrounding body panels.

10 Installation is the reverse of removal. Check the alignment of the fender to the hood and front edge of the door before tightening the bolts.

11 Radiator grille - removal and installation

1 Remove the front bumper cover (see Section 9).

2006 THROUGH 2009 MODELS

Fusion

➧ Refer to illustration 11.2

2 To remove the manufacturer nameplate, simply remove the two nuts that secure it to the radiator grille (see illustration), then pull it off.

3 To remove just the upper and/or lower radiator grille, remove the grille mounting nuts. The lower radiator grille is also secured by a pair of locator pins; to disengage each locator pin, squeeze the legs together and push them out from the backside of the grille assembly.

4 To remove the radiator grille reinforcement, disengage the mounting tabs from the bumper cover.

5 Installation is the reverse of removal.

11.2 Radiator grille-to-bumper cover fasteners (2006 through 2009 Fusion models):

1. *Radiator grille upper mounting nuts (two center nuts also secure the manufacturer nameplate to the grille)*
2. *Radiator grille lower mounting nuts*
3. *Radiator grille lower locator pins*
4. *Radiator grille reinforcement mounting screws*
5. *Radiator grille reinforcement mounting tabs*

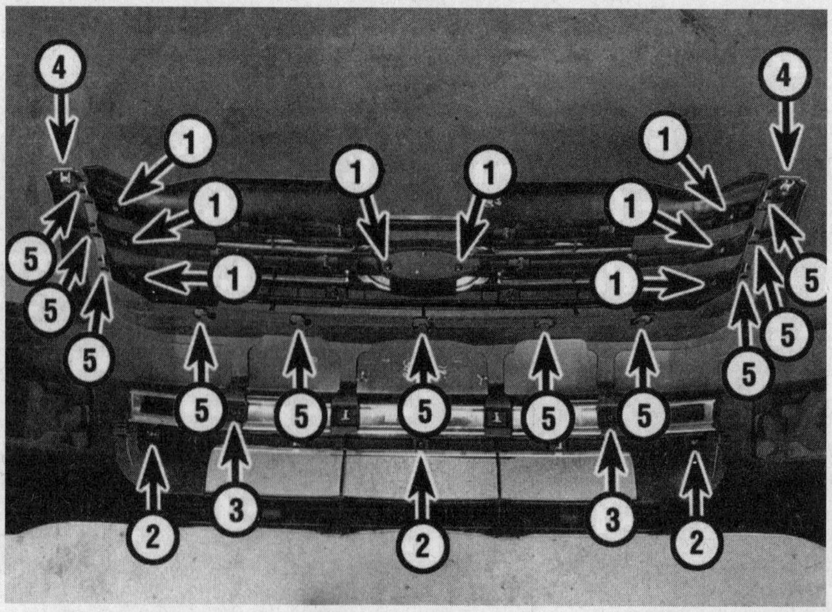

Milan

6 Detach the upper radiator grille from the clips on the bumper cover.

7 Detach the lower radiator grille trim outer trim cover from the clips on the bumper cover.

8 Remove the lower radiator grille from the clips on the bumper cover.

9 Installation is the reverse of removal.

2010 MODELS

Fusion

10 Remove the two upper radiator grille nuts and two center radiator grille nuts.

11 Remove the two badge nuts, then remove the badge.

12 Remove the upper radiator grille from the grille reinforcement.

13 Remove the center radiator grille from the grille reinforcement.

14 Remove the radiator grille reinforcement

15 Remove the nine lower radiator grille molding clips, then remove the lower radiator grille.

16 Remove the lower radiator grille molding.

17 Installation is the reverse of removal.

Milan

18 Remove the two upper radiator grille nuts.

19 Remove the upper radiator grille reinforcement.

20 Remove the upper radiator grille and badge.

21 Remove the front bumper cover valence screws, then remove valence cover.

22 Remove the lower radiator grille.

23 Installation is the reverse of removal.

12 Cowl panels - removal and installation

➡Note: Refer to Section 6 for fastener and trim removal techniques.

UPPER COWL PANEL

➧ Refer to illustrations 12.2 and 12.3

1 Remove the wiper arms (see "Windshield wiper motor - replacement" in Chapter 12).

2 Two small trim pieces fill the gap between the windshield and the front fenders. Both of them must be removed before you can remove the upper cowl panel. Remove the two screws (see illustration) from each trim piece and remove the trim.

3 Remove the screws, pin-type retainers and any retainer clips from the upper cowl panel (see illustration).

4 Remove the upper cowl panel.

5 Installation is the reverse of removal.

LOWER COWL PANEL

➧ Refer to illustrations 12.8 and 12.9

6 Remove the upper cowl panel (see Steps 1 through 4).

7 Remove the windshield wiper motor and linkage assembly (see "Windshield wiper motor - replacement" in Chapter 12).

12.2 Two small trim pieces - one at each end of the upper cowl trim panel - fill the gap between the windshield and the front fender (left trim piece shown). They also overlap the upper cowl trim panel, so they must be removed to remove the cowl trim (2006 through 2009 Fusion shown)

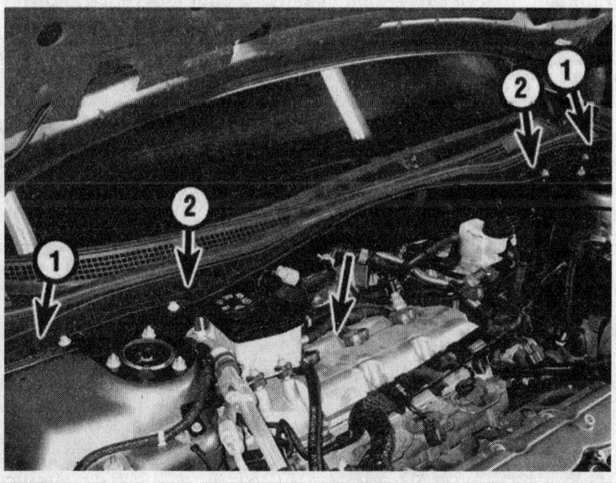

12.3 Upper cowl panel details (2006 through 2009 Fusion shown):

1 *Screws*
2 *Pin-type retainers*

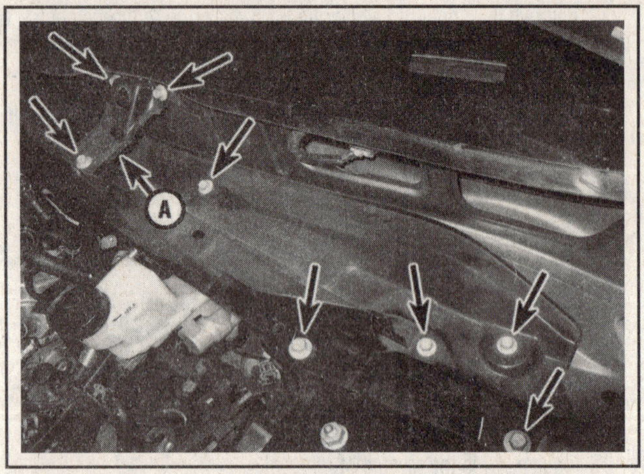

12.8 Remove the three bolts from the cowl panel support bracket (A), then remove the five bolts that secure the left end of the panel

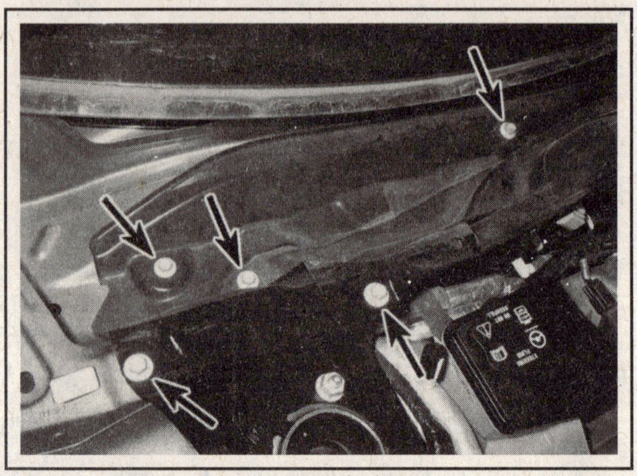

12.9 Lower cowl panel bolts (right side)

8 Remove the three bolts from the lower cowl panel support bracket (see illustration).

9 Remove the 10 lower cowl panel bolts (see illustration) and remove the lower cowl panel.

10 Installation is the reverse of removal.

13 Door trim panel - removal and installation

Refer to illustrations 13.2a, 13.2b, 13.3a, 13.3b, 13.4, 13.5 and 13.6

CAUTION:

Wear gloves when working inside the door openings to protect against sharp metal edges.

Note: This procedure applies to both front and rear door trim panels. The only difference is that rear door trim panels do not have a screw at the center of the lower edge of the panel.

Note: Refer to Section 6 for fastener and trim removal.

1 Disconnect the cable from the negative battery terminal (see Chapter 5).

2 Remove the trim cover from the inside door handle bezel (see illustration) and remove the screw from the bezel. Pull out the bezel and disconnect the electrical connector (see illustration).

3 Pry the trim cap from the small trim panel in the armrest, remove the screw that secures the trim panel to the armrest, carefully pry the back end of the trim panel loose, lift up the panel and disconnect the electrical connectors from the power window switch (see illustrations).

4 Remove the door trim panel screw from the upper end of the trail-

13.2a Remove the trim cover from the inside door handle and remove the screw

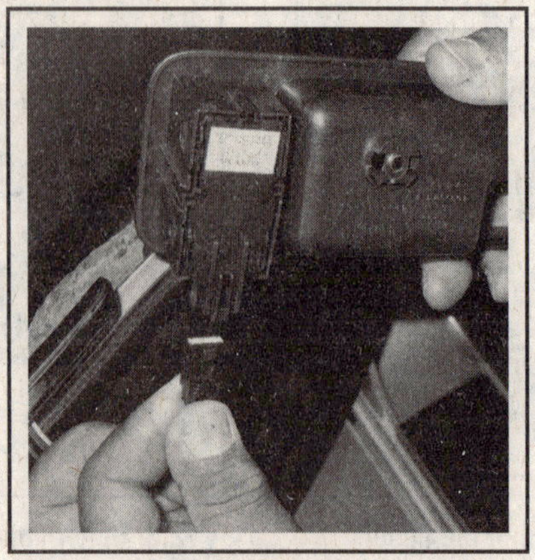

13.2b Pull out the inside door handle bezel and disconnect the electrical connector

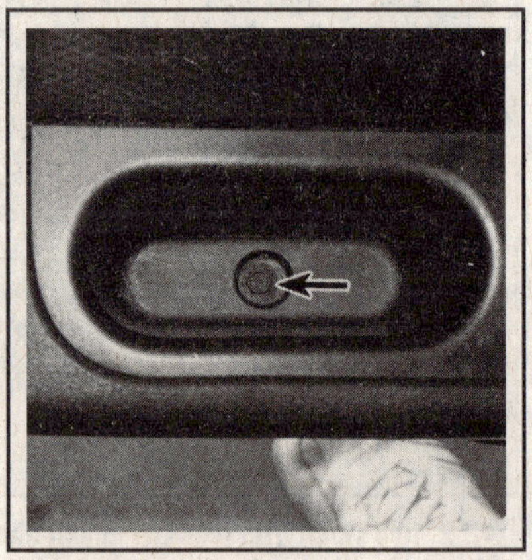

13.3a Armrest trim panel screw (trim cap removed)

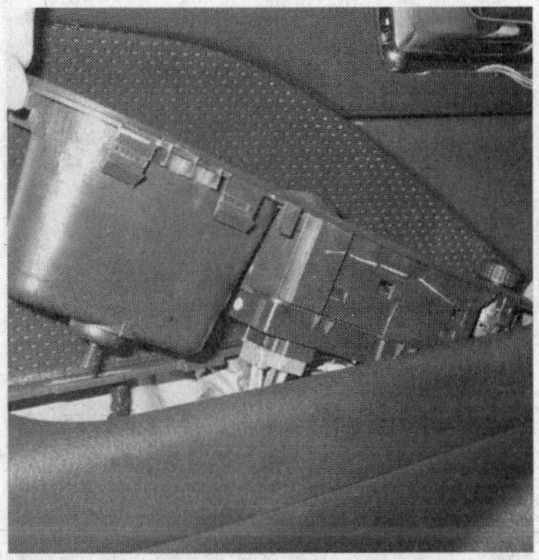

13.3b Pry the back end of the armrest trim panel loose first (the front end has a mounting clip that hooks under the armrest)

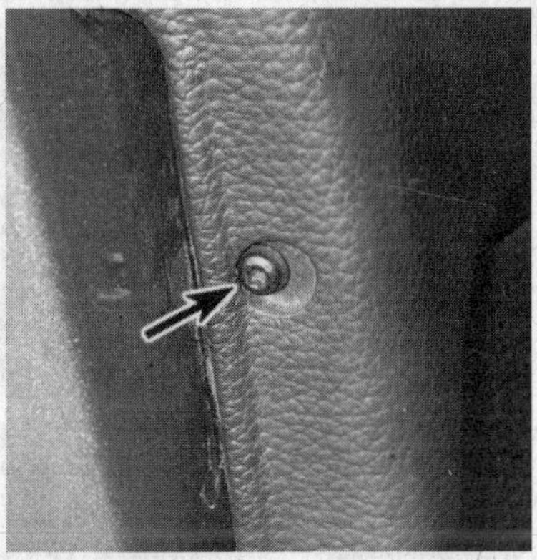

13.4 Upper door trim panel screw (upper rear trailing edge of the door)

13.5 Center lower trim panel screw (front doors only)

ing edge of the door (see illustration).

5 On front doors, remove the screw from the center of the lower edge of the trim panel (see illustration).

6 To detach the door trim panel from its mounting clips, work your way around the periphery of the trim panel, carefully prying loose the clips with a suitable door trim removal tool (see illustration), then pull off the panel and disconnect any electrical connectors.

7 Installation is the reverse of removal.

13.6 Carefully pry the door trim panel loose from its mounting clips

14 Door - removal, installation and adjustment

**** WARNING:**

The models covered by this manual are equipped with Supplemental Restraint Systems (SRS), more commonly known as airbags. Always disable the airbag system before working in the vicinity of any airbag system component to avoid the possibility of accidental deployment of the airbag, which could cause personal injury (see Chapter 12).

REMOVAL AND INSTALLATION

Refer to illustrations 14.4 and 14.5

Note: The door is heavy and somewhat awkward to remove - at least two people should perform this procedure.

Note: This procedure applies to front and rear doors.

1 Raise the window completely in the door.

2 Disconnect the cable from the negative battery terminal (see Chapter 5).

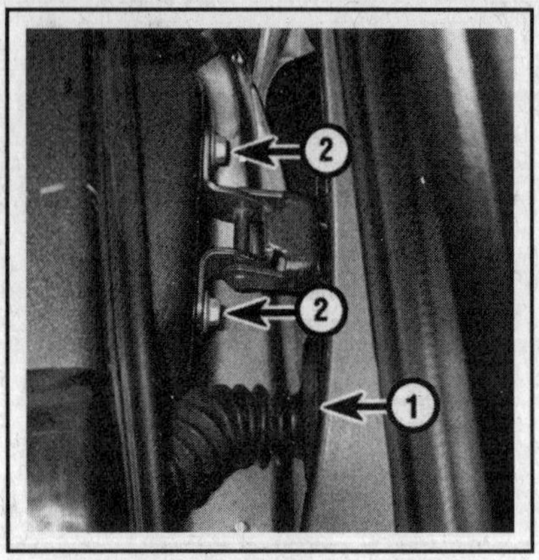

14.4 Door assembly details:

1. *Wiring harness rubber conduit*
2. *Door hinge mounting bolts*

14.5 Door stop strut bolt

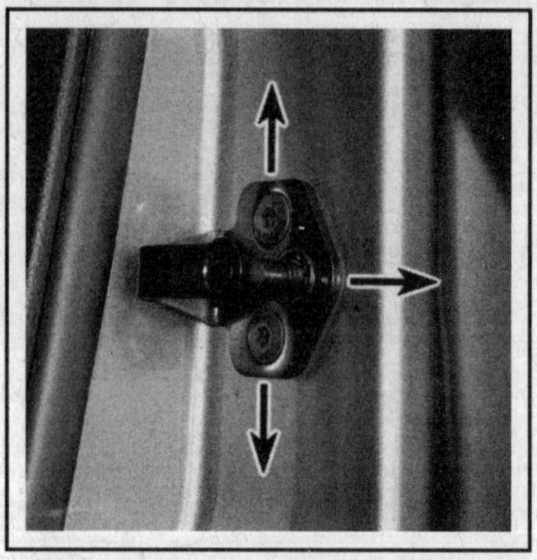

14.12 Adjust the door latch striker by loosening the mounting screws and gently tapping the striker in the desired direction

3 Open the door all the way and support it with a jack or blocks covered with rags to prevent damaging the outer surface.

4 Pull off the rubber conduit (see illustration) that protects the door's wiring harness, then disconnect the connector.

5 Remove the door check arm mounting bolt (see illustration).

6 Mark around the door hinges with a pen or a scribe to facilitate realignment during reassembly.

7 With an assistant holding the door to steady it, remove the hinge-to-door bolts and lift off the door.

8 Installation is the reverse of removal.

ADJUSTMENT

➧ **Refer to illustration 14.12**

9 Correct door-to-body alignment is a critical part of a well-functioning door assembly. First check the door hinge pins for excessive play. Fully open the door and lift up and down on the door without lifting the body. If a door has 1/16-inch or more excessive play, replace the hinges.

10 If you need to adjust or replace the hinges for a front door, remove the front fender (see Section 10).

11 Make door-to-body alignment adjustments by loosening the hinge-to-body bolts or hinge-to-door bolts and moving the door. When body alignment is correct, the top of each door is parallel with the roof section, the front door is flush with the fender, the rear door is flush with the rear quarter panel and the bottom of each door is aligned with the lower rocker panel. If you're unable to adjust the door correctly, you might be able to obtain body alignment shims that are inserted behind the hinges to correctly align the door.

12 To adjust the door-closed position, scribe a line or mark around the striker plate (see illustration) to provide a reference point, then verify that the door latch is contacting the center of the striker. If not, adjust the up and down position first. To move the striker, tap it gently with a small hammer.

13 Once the door latch is contacting the center of the striker, adjust the latch striker sideways position, so that the door panel is flush with the center pillar or rear quarter panel and provides positive engagement with the latch mechanism.

15 Door latch, lock cylinder and handles - removal and installation

OUTSIDE DOOR HANDLE LEVER

➧ **Refer to illustrations 15.1, 15.2 and 15.3**

➡**Note: This procedure only applies to the outside door handle lever. If you need to replace the outside door handle reinforcement (the actual mechanism for the outside door handle), you will need to remove it along with the door latch as a single assembly, then disconnect it from the latch (see Steps 10 through 15).**

1 Remove the trim cap for the outside handle retaining screw (see illustration). On 2006 through 2009 models, remove the screw. On 2010 models, loosen, but don't remove, the screw.

2 Remove the cover from the outside handle (see illustration).

3 To remove the outside door handle, pull it out of the door and to the rear to disengage it from the handle reinforcement inside the door (see illustration).

4 Remove and inspect the outside door handle seals. If the seals are cracked, torn or otherwise deteriorated, replace them.

5 Installation is the reverse of removal.

INSIDE DOOR HANDLE

➧ **Refer to illustration 15.7 and 15.8**

6 Remove the door trim panel (see Section 13).

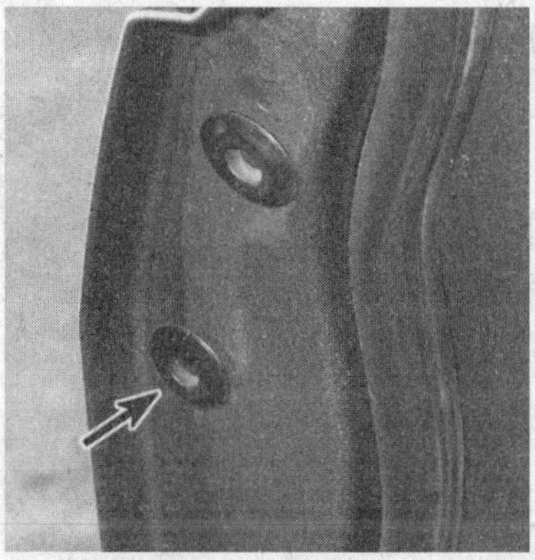

15.1 Trim cap for outside door handle cover retaining screw

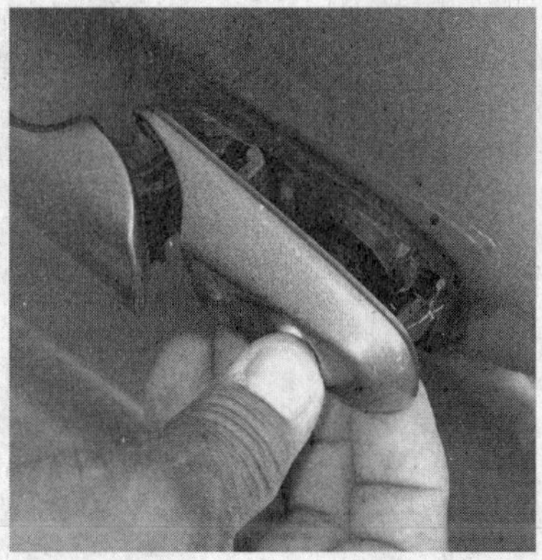

15.2 Remove the outside door handle cover

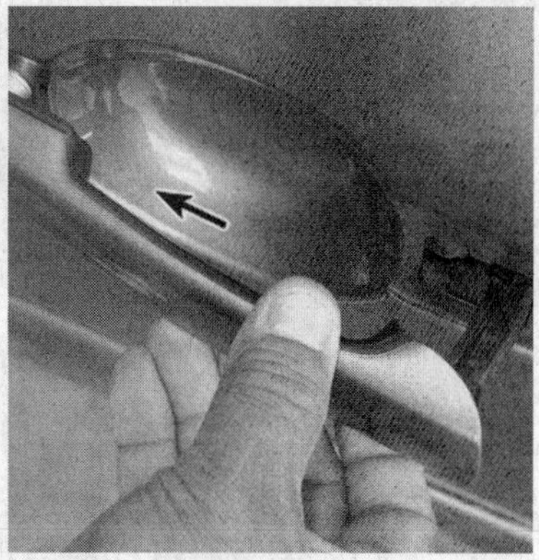

15.3 To disengage the outside door handle lever from the handle reinforcement inside the door, pull it out of the door and to the rear

15.7 Inside door handle retaining bolt

15.8 Pry out the bushing (A), then line up the cable with the slot in the handle lever (B) and pull out the cable end plug

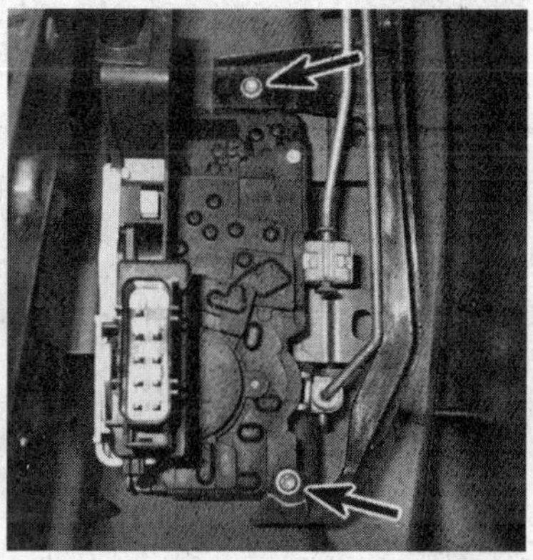

15.11a Lower anti-theft-guard bolts

7 Remove the inside door handle retaining bolt (see illustration) and detach the handle assembly from the door.

8 Disconnect the actuator cable from the inside door handle (see illustration), then remove the handle.

9 Installation is the reverse of removal.

DOOR LATCH OR OUTSIDE DOOR HANDLE REINFORCEMENT

➧ Refer to illustration 15.11a, 15.11b, 15.13, 15.15a and 15.15b

10 Remove the outside door handle lever (see Steps 1 through 3), then remove the door trim panel (see Section 13) and the power window regulator (see Section 17).

11 Remove the anti-theft-guard bolts (see illustrations) and remove the guard from the latch and the outside door handle reinforcement.

12 Remove the outside door handle reinforcement retaining bolt.

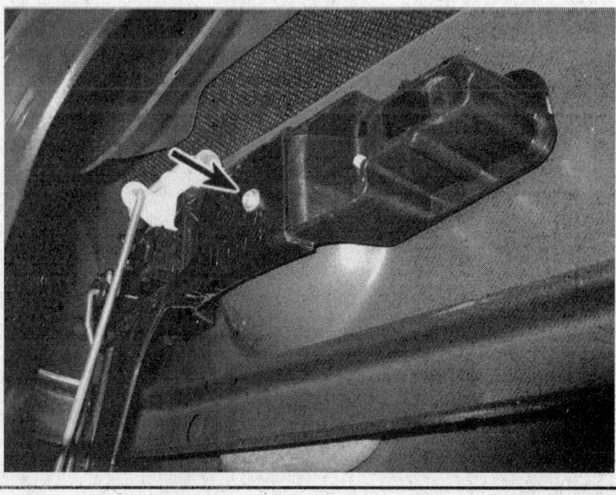

15.11b Upper anti-theft-guard bolt

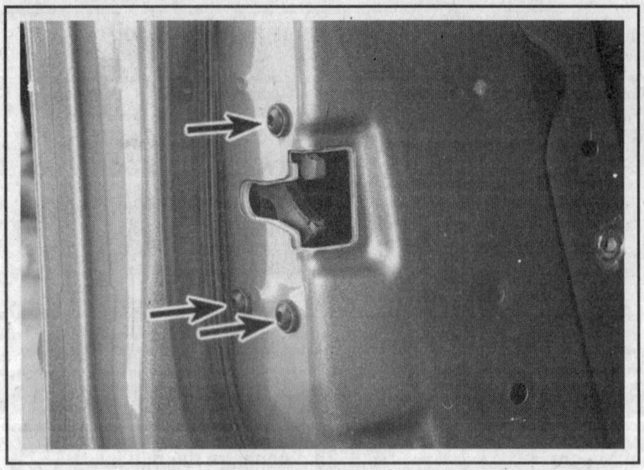

15.13 Door latch mounting fasteners

15.15a To disconnect the actuator rods from the latch mechanism, depress the lock tabs with a pair of needle nose pliers and pull out the rods

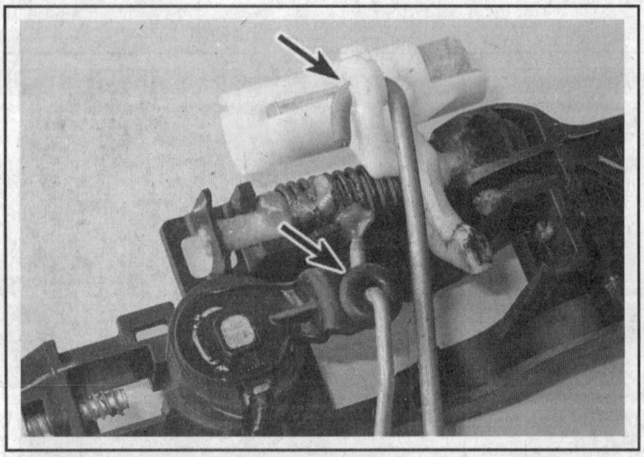

15.15b To disconnect the actuator rods from the outside door handle reinforcement, angle the reinforcement as necessary to disengage each rod

15.18 To remove the door lock cylinder from the outside door handle reinforcement, depress the release button with an awl or a small screwdriver and pull out the cylinder (2006 through 2009 models)

13 Remove the latch mounting fasteners (see illustration).

14 Pull out the latch and outside door handle reinforcement from the door as a single assembly, then disconnect the electrical connector from the latch if you haven't already done so, and disconnect the inside door handle actuator cable from the latch (for help, see illustration 15.8; it's the same setup at both ends of the cable).

15 Place the latch and outside door handle reinforcement on a clean workbench, then disconnect the outside handle and lock cylinder actuator rods from the latch (see illustration) or from the outside door handle reinforcement (see illustration).

16 Installation is the reverse of removal.

DOOR LOCK CYLINDER

2006 through 2009 models

➧ Refer to illustration 15.18

17 Remove the door latch and outside door handle reinforcement (see Steps 10 through 15).

18 Press the release button (see illustration) and remove the lock cylinder.

19 When installing the lock cylinder, push it all the way into the outside door handle reinforcement until it clicks into place.

20 Installation is otherwise the reverse of removal.

2010 models

➡Note: Before removing the door lock cylinder on these models, be aware that you cannot simply install a new door lock cylinder. Instead, you must discard the old cylinder and build a new unit with the appropriate lock repair package, which you can obtain from your dealer. The lock repair package includes instructions for how to build the new lock cylinder to the key code of the vehicle.

21 Remove the door trim panel (see Section 13), the power window regulator (see Section 17) and the outside door handle (see Steps 1 through 4).

22 Disengage the release tab and remove the lock cylinder.

23 When installing the rebuilt lock cylinder, align the D-slot in the lock cylinder with the D-slot in

16 Door window glass - removal and installation

Refer to illustrations 16.2 and 16.3

1 Remove the door trim panel (see Section 13).
2 Remove the wiring harness cover plate and access hole plug (see illustration).
3 Lower the window glass until the glass clamp bolts are accessible through the access holes (see illustration). Loosen (but don't remove) both glass clamp bolts, then secure the window in place with tape so that it won't go down.

Note: If the door window regulator motor is broken or disconnected, you'll have to remove it (see Section 17) and move the window glass manually.

4 Lower the window regulator, then guide the window up and tilt it outward to remove it through the window opening.
5 Installation is the reverse of removal. Be sure to perform the De-initialization/initialization procedures in the following order.

DE-INITIALIZATION PROCEDURE

6 Turn the ignition key to ON.
7 Activate the power window control switch in the one-touch up-mode and simultaneously remove power from the window motor while the window is moving, by one of the following methods:

a) Disconnect the battery negative cable while the window is moving.
b) Disconnect the power window motor electrical connector while the window is moving.
c) Remove the left or right front power window motor fuse while the window is moving.

8 The power window motor is now de-initialized and the motor is reset to its original factory settings.
9 Reconnect the battery negative cable, power window motor electrical connector or power window motor fuse before proceeding to the initialization procedure.

INITIALIZATION PROCEDURE

10 Turn the ignition key to ON.
11 Press and hold the window control switch until the window glass stalls for two seconds into the glass top run, then release the switch.
12 Pull and hold the power window control switch until the window glass stalls for two seconds at the bottom of its travel, then release the switch.
13 Test the operation of the power window by activating the power window switch in the one-touch up-mode. If the window doesn't operate correctly, repeat this procedure.

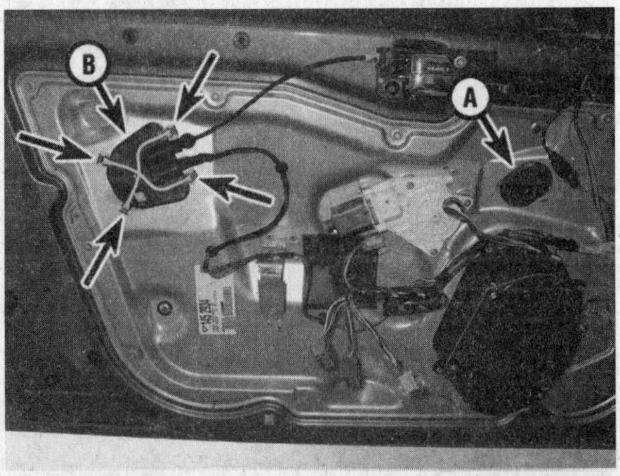

16.2 Front glass clamp bolt access cover (A) and rear clamp bolt access cover (B). The rear access cover is secured by four clips

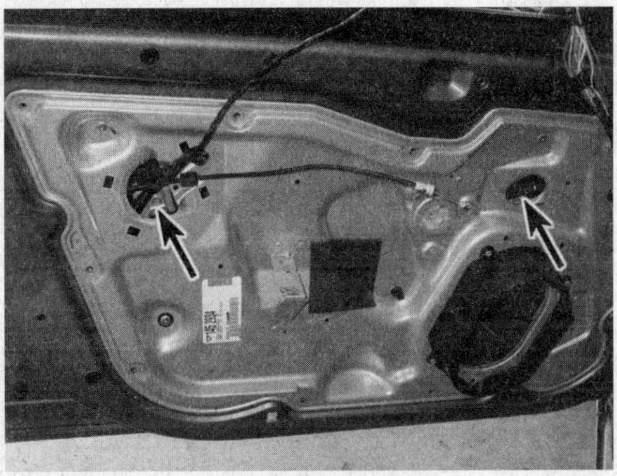

16.3 Front window glass clamp bolts

17 Door window regulator and motor - removal and installation

REGULATOR MOTOR

Refer to illustration 17.2

1 Remove the door trim panel (see Section 13).
2 Disconnect the electrical connector from the regulator motor (see illustration).
3 Secure the window in place with tape.
4 Remove the three regulator motor mounting screws, then remove the motor.
5 Installation is the reverse of removal. Be sure to perform the De-initialization/initialization procedures (see Section 16).

17.2 Power window regulator motor electrical connector (A) and mounting screws (B)

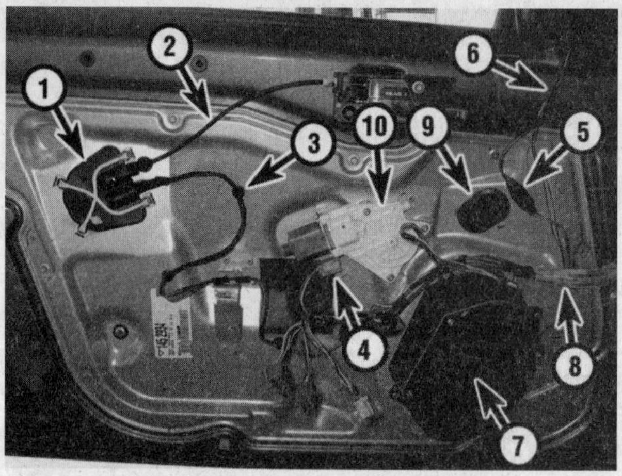

17.7 Typical door window regulator and motor assembly details:

1 *Rear glass clamp bolt access cover*
2 *Inside door handle actuator cable*
3 *Door latch and power door lock harness and clips*
4 *Power window regulator motor electrical connector*
5 *Door tweeter electrical connector*
6 *Power mirror harness*
7 *Door speaker assembly*
8 *Door assembly harness*
9 *Front glass clamp bolt access cover*
10 *Power window regulator motor*

REGULATOR ASSEMBLY

Refer to illustrations 17.7 and 17.12

6 Remove the door trim panel (see Section 13).

7 Disconnect all electrical wiring harness connectors and harness clips (see illustration), including the door latch electrical connector (see Section 15), the keyless entry keypad and door lock electrical connector and the power mirror electrical connector (see Section 18).

8 Remove the inside door handle and disconnect the actuator cable from the handle (see Section 15).

9 Remove the wiring harness cover plate and access hole plug, then lower the window glass until the glass clamp bolts are accessible through the access holes (see Section 16). Loosen (but don't remove) both glass clamp bolts, then secure the window in place with tape so that it won't go down.

Note: If the door window regulator motor is broken or disconnected, you'll have to remove it (see Steps 2 through 4) and move the window glass manually.

10 Lower the window regulator mechanism until it reaches stops at the bottom of the regulator tracks.

11 Remove the front door speaker (see "Radio and speakers - removal and installation" in Chapter 12).

12 Remove the regulator assembly mounting bolts (see illustration) and remove the regulator.

13 Installation is the reverse of removal. Be sure to perform the De-initialization/initialization procedures (see Section 16).

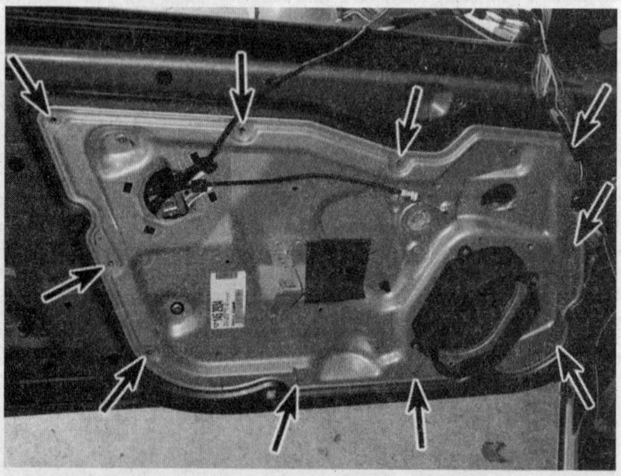

17.12 Regulator assembly mounting bolt locations

18 Mirrors - removal and installation

Refer to illustration 18.2

1 Remove the door trim panel (see Section 13).

2 Remove the front door mirror cover (see illustration). If the mirror cover is equipped with a speaker, disconnect the speaker electrical connector (see illustration 17.7).

3 Disconnect the electrical connector from the mirror.

4 Remove the mirror mounting nuts and remove the mirror.

5 Installation is the reverse of removal.

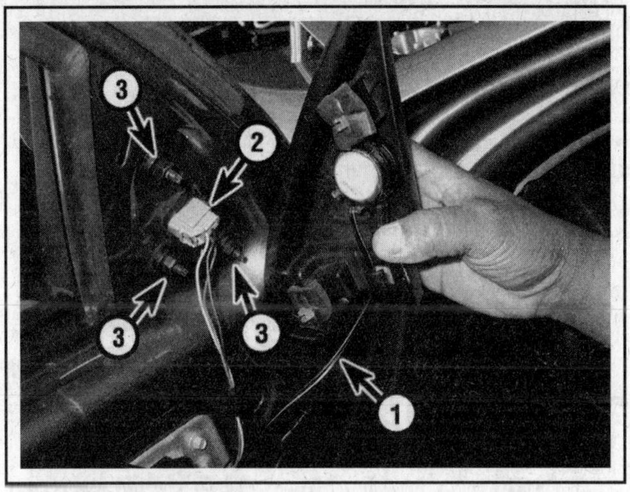

18.2 Mirror details:

1 Door tweeter electrical lead
2 Mirror electrical connector
3 Mirror mounting nuts

19 Trunk lid - removal and installation

Refer to illustrations 19.1 and 19.3

Note: The trunk lid is heavy and awkward to remove, so have a helper handy to assist you.

1 Remove the trunk lid trim panel (see illustration).

2 Disconnect the electrical connectors of all wiring between the vehicle body and the trunk lid. Disengage all wiring harness clips and set the harnesses aside.

3 With an assistant helping you to support the trunk lid, remove the nuts from the trunk lid hinges (see illustration) and remove the trunk lid.

4 Installation is the reverse of removal.

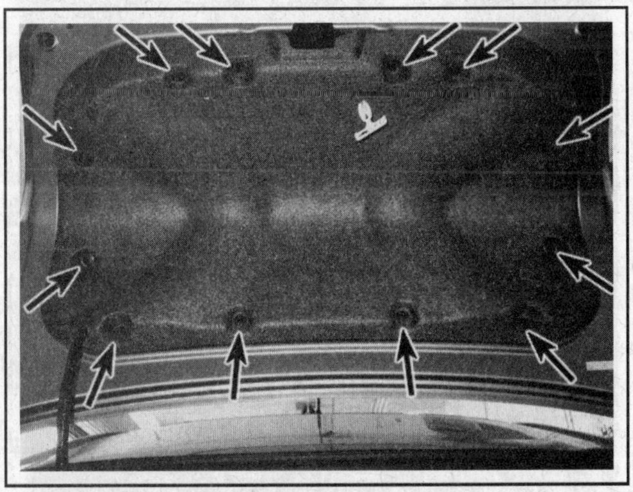

19.1 Trunk lid trim panel pin-type fasteners

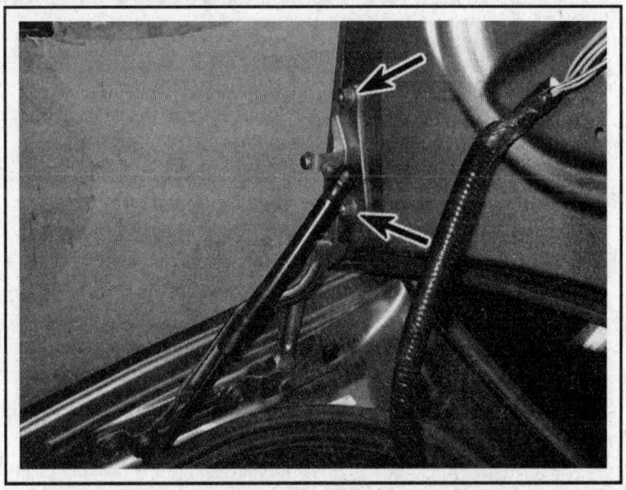

19.3 Trunk lid hinge nuts

20 Trunk lid key lock cylinder and latch - removal and installation

KEY LOCK CYLINDER

Refer to illustration 20.2

Note: A special rivet installation tool is required to install new rivets during key lock cylinder installation.

1 Remove the trunk lid trim panel (see illustration 19.1).
2 Disconnect the trunk lid actuator cable from the trunk lid key lock cylinder (see illustration).
3 Disconnect the electrical connector from the lock cylinder.
4 Drill out the two lock cylinder rivets and remove the lock cylinder.
5 Installation is the reverse of removal.

LATCH

Refer to illustration 20.8

6 Remove the trunk lid trim panel (see illustration 19.1).
7 Disconnect the actuator cable from the trunk lid lock cylinder (see illustration 20.2).
8 Disconnect the electrical connector from the trunk lid latch (see illustration).
9 Remove the latch mounting nuts and remove the latch.
10 Installation is the reverse of removal.

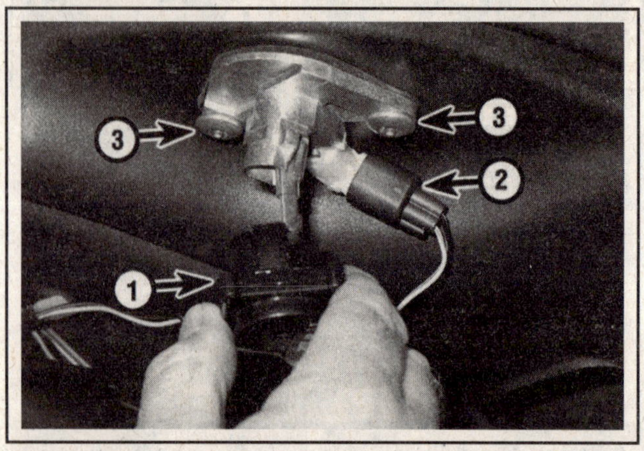

20.2 Trunk lid lock cylinder details:

1 *Trunk lid latch actuator cable*
2 *Lock cylinder electrical connector*
3 *Lock cylinder mounting rivets*

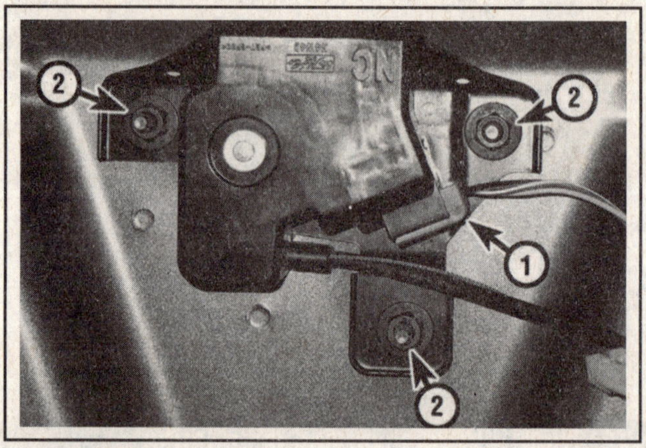

20.8 Trunk lid latch details:

1 *Latch electrical connector*
2 *Latch mounting nuts*

21 Center console - removal and installation

Refer to illustrations 21.1, 21.2, 21.3, 21.4a, 21.4b, 21.5, 21.6 and 21.7

1 Slide the front seats all the way forward, remove the two rear console bolts (see illustration), then slide the seats all the way rearward.
2 Using a trim removal tool, carefully pry off the shift lever trim ring from the console (see illustration).
3 Carefully pry loose the storage bin from the console (see illustration). Lift out the bin and disconnect the electrical connector.
4 Carefully pry loose the console finish panel and disengage it from the mounting clips (see illustrations).
5 Remove the bolt trim caps (see illustration) and remove the bolts from the upper forward corners of the console.
6 Remove the two bolts (2006 through 2009 models) (see illustration) or four bolts (2010 models) from inside the center console.
7 Remove the two screws from the forward end of the console (see illustration).
8 Lift up the console and disconnect all electrical connectors from the console.
9 Remove the center console.
10 Installation is the reverse of removal.

21.1 Center console rear bolt (right side shown, passenger seat removed for clarity)

21.2 Carefully pry off the shift lever trim ring

21.3 Pry loose the storage bin from the console and disconnect the electrical connector underneath

21.4a Pry loose the console finish panel . . .

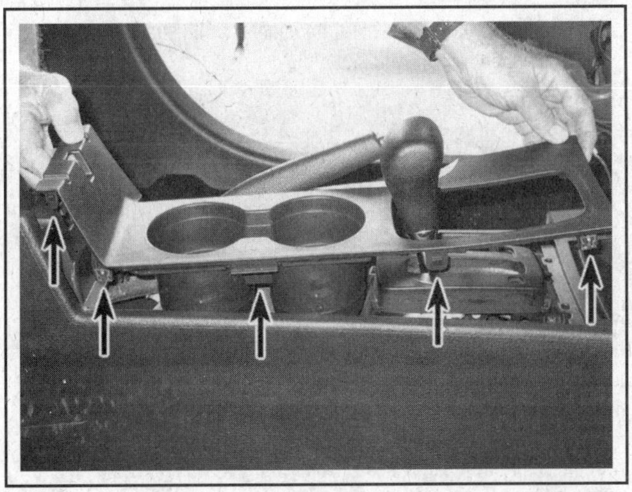

21.4b . . . and disengage it from the mounting clips along each side

21.5 Remove the bolt trim caps and remove the bolts from the upper forward corners of the console (right side bolt shown)

21.6 Center console inner bolts (2006 through 2009 model shown)

21.7 Center console forward mounting screws

22 Dashboard trim panels - removal and installation

WARNING:

Models covered by this manual are equipped with a Supplemental Restraint System (SRS), more commonly known as airbags. Always disable the airbag system before working in the vicinity of any airbag system component to avoid the possibility of accidental deployment of the airbag, which could cause personal injury (see Chapter 12).

Note: Refer to Section 6 for fastener and trim removal.

1 Removing various dashboard trim panels provides access to electrical/electronic components such as the instrument cluster, the audio unit, the heater and air conditioning control unit and various instrument panel-mounted switches. If you're going to remove the entire instrument panel, you'll need to remove all of the trim panels to access the instrument panel mounting bolts.

LEFT OR RIGHT DASHBOARD END TRIM PANELS

Refer to illustration 22.2

2 Carefully pry off the end trim panel (see illustration).
3 Installation is the reverse of removal.

INSTRUMENT CLUSTER TRIM PANEL

2006 through 2009 models

4 On these models, the cluster trim panel - a thin narrow trim piece that runs along the lower edge of the instrument cluster - though technically a separate trim piece, is permanently connected to the upper steering column cover (see Section 23).

2010 models

5 Remove the two retaining screws from the underside of the upper part of the cluster trim panel (above the instrument cluster).
6 Pull the cluster trim panel to the rear to disengage the two retaining clips located at the lower corners of the trim panel.

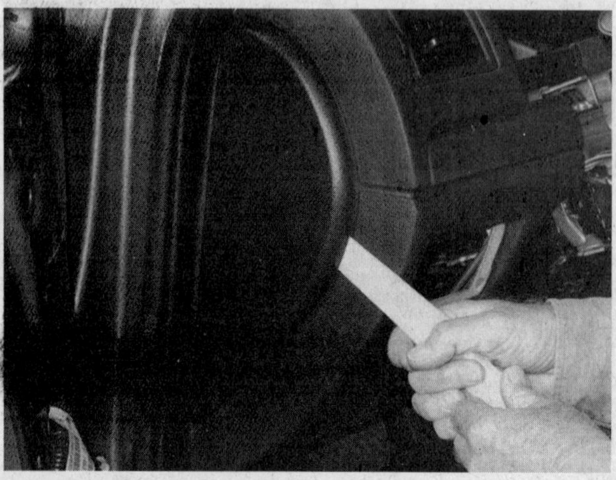

22.2 Pry off the end trim panel

7 Installation is the reverse of removal. Make sure that the two lower retaining clips snap into place before installing the two upper screws.

LEFT, CENTER AND RIGHT APPLIQUÉS (SOME 2006 THROUGH 2009 MODELS)

Note: These three appliqués are only used on upper trim levels.

8 Carefully pry off the left, center or right appliqué.
9 Installation is the reverse of removal.

CENTER TRIM PANEL

2006 through 2009 models

Refer to illustration 22.10

10 Carefully pry off the center trim panel (see illustration).
11 Installation is the reverse of removal.

2010 models

12 Remove the center console finish panel and storage bin from the center console (see Section 21).
13 Remove the upper storage bin (see Steps 21 through 24).
14 Remove the two retaining screws from the upper edge of the center trim panel.
15 Pull the center trim panel to the rear to disengage the six retaining clips. Disconnect the antenna cable from the radio and disconnect the electrical connectors from the radio and the heater and air conditioning control unit. Remove the center trim panel, radio and heater and air conditioning controls as a single assembly.
16 If you want to detach the air conditioning and control assembly from the center trim panel, see Chapter 3. If you want to detach the audio unit, see Chapter 12.
17 Installation is the reverse of removal.

UPPER STORAGE BIN

2006 through 2009 models

Refer to illustrations 22.19a and 22.19b

18 Remove the center trim panel (see Step 10).
19 Remove the two upper storage bin retaining screws, disengage the storage bin mounting clips and remove the upper storage bin (see illustrations).
20 Installation is the reverse of removal.

2010 models

21 Remove the lower steering column cover (see Section 23).
22 Remove the mounting nut from the lower left side of the upper storage bin.
23 Remove the mat from the upper storage bin, then remove the two storage bin mounting screws.
24 To remove the storage bin, grasp it firmly and pull it back to disengage it from the mounting clips, then pull it out far enough to access and disconnect the electrical connectors from the storage bin.
25 Installation is the reverse of removal.

22.10 Pry off the center trim panel (2006 through 2009 models)

22.19a Upper storage bin retaining screws (2006 through 2009 models)

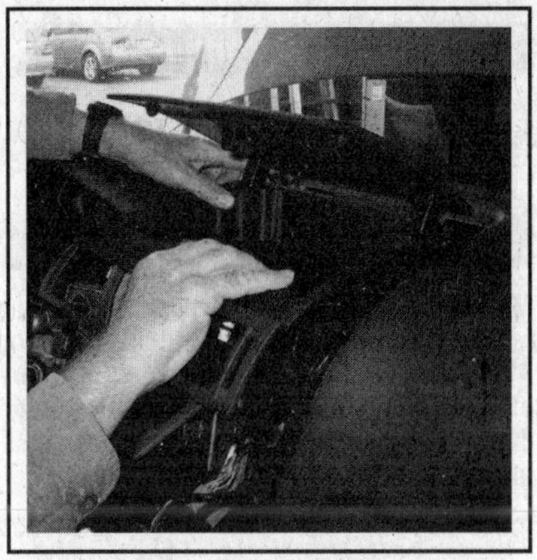

22.19b Grasp the storage bin firmly and pull it to the rear to disengage the mounting clips (2006 through 2009 models)

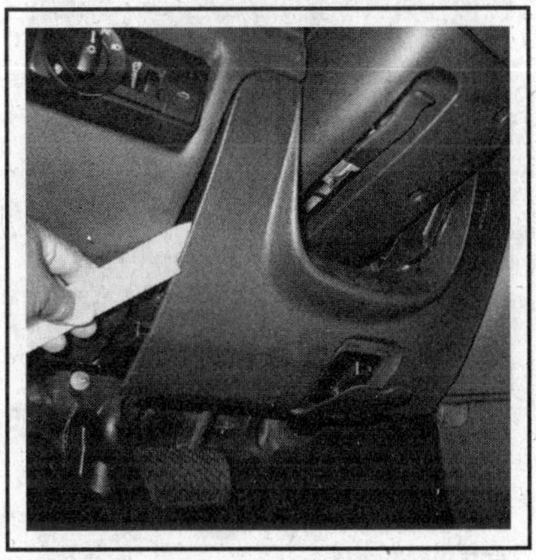

22.26 Pry off the knee bolster trim panel

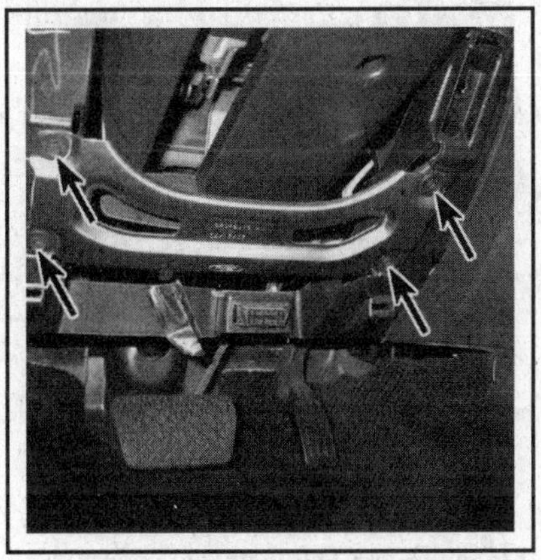

22.27 Knee bolster retaining bolts

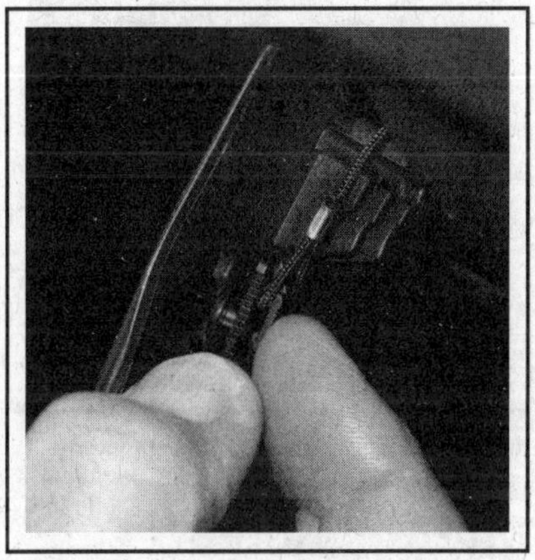

22.29 Disengage the damper clip from this slot on the right end of the glove box

KNEE BOLSTER TRIM PANEL AND KNEE BOLSTER

➧ Refer to illustrations 22.26 and 22.27

26 Carefully pry off the knee bolster trim panel (see illustration).

27 Remove the fasteners securing the knee bolster (see illustration) and remove the bolster.

28 Installation is the reverse of removal.

GLOVE BOX

➧ Refer to illustrations 22.29 and 22.30

29 Disengage the damper clip from the right end of the glove box (see illustration).

30 Firmly grasp the hinge areas at each end of the glove box, push in to disengage the hinge pins (see illustration) and remove the glove box.

31 Installation is the reverse of removal.

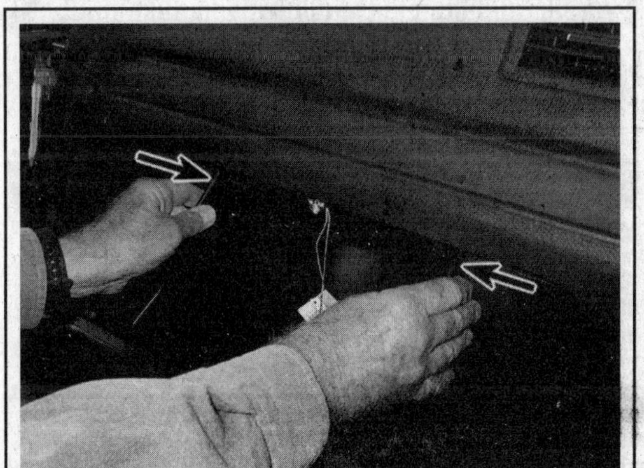

22.30 Push in the hinge pin areas to disengage the pins, then pull out the glove box

23 Steering column covers - removal and installation

➧ **Refer to illustrations 23.2, 23.3a, 23.3b and 23.4**

✲✲ WARNING:

Models covered by this manual are equipped with a Supplemental Restraint System (SRS), more commonly known as airbags. Always disable the airbag system before working in the vicinity of any airbag system component to avoid the possibility of accidental deployment of the airbag, which could cause personal injury (see Chapter 12).

1 Disconnect the cable from the negative terminal of the battery (see Chapter 5).

2 Remove the knee bolster retaining bolts and remove the knee bolster (see Section 22).

3 Remove the bolts from the lower steering column cover, then press in on the sides of the upper cover and separate the two covers (see illustrations).

4 To remove the upper column cover, use a trim removal tool to separate the instrument cluster trim panel (see illustration).

➡**Note: Technically, the instrument cluster trim panel is considered a separate part, but it's permanently connected to the upper steering column cover, so both of them must be removed together.**

5 Installation is the reverse of removal.

23.3a Lower steering column cover retaining bolts

23.3b To separate the upper and lower steering column covers, squeeze both sides (A) of the cover together and pull the covers apart

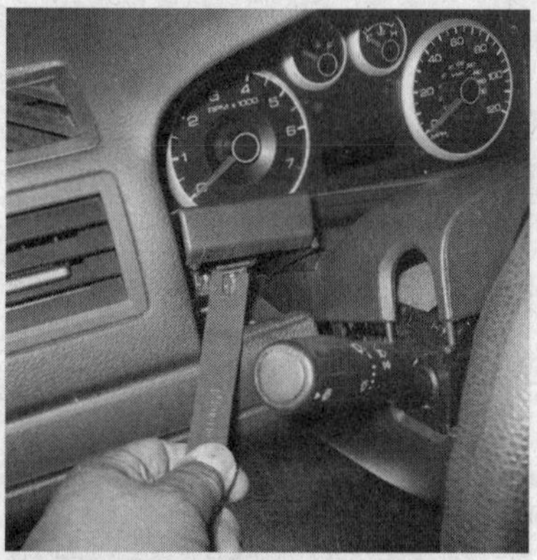

23.4 Carefully disengage the instrument cluster trim panel (left end of panel shown, right end identical)

24 Instrument panel - removal and installation

➧ **Refer to illustrations 24.2, 24.3, 24.12, 24.13, 24.14, 24.15, 24.18a, 24.18b, 24.18c and 24.18d**

✲✲ WARNING:

Models covered by this manual are equipped with a Supplemental Restraint System (SRS), more commonly known as airbags. Always disable the airbag system before working in the vicinity of any airbag system component to avoid the possibility of accidental deployment of the airbag, which could cause personal injury (see Chapter 12).

➡**Note: This is a difficult procedure for the home mechanic. There are many hidden fasteners, difficult angles to work in and many electrical connectors to tag and disconnect/connect. We recommend that this procedure be done only by an experienced do-it-yourselfer.**

➡**Note: During removal of the instrument panel, make careful notes of how each piece comes off, where it fits in relation to other pieces and what holds it in place. If you note how each part is installed before removing it, getting the instrument panel back together again will be much easier.**

1 Remove the following parts:

Steering wheel (see Chapter 10)
All the dashboard trim panels and the glove box (see Section 22)
Air conditioning and heater control assembly (see Chapter 3)
Instrument cluster and radio (see Chapter 12)
Right lower instrument panel insulator, if equipped (2010 models only)
Front seats (though not absolutely necessary, removing both front seats allows more room to work and eliminates the possibility of the occurrence of damage to the seats during this procedure)
Center console (see Section 21)

2 Carefully remove the left and right A-pillar (windshield pillar) trim panels (see illustration).

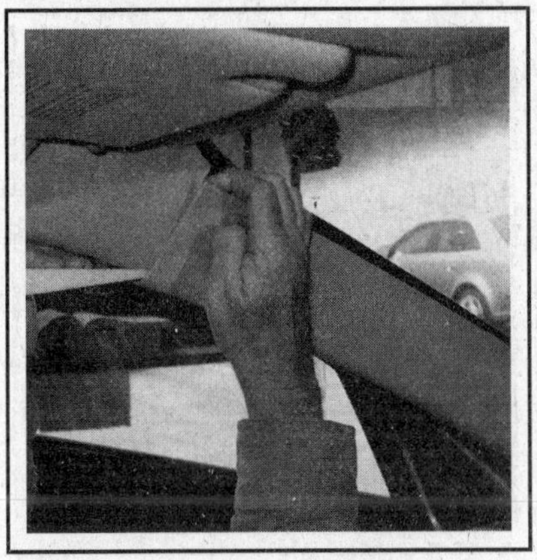

24.2 Carefully remove the A-pillar trim panels by prying them off

24.3 Remove each of the front door opening weather strip/sill panel/ kick panels

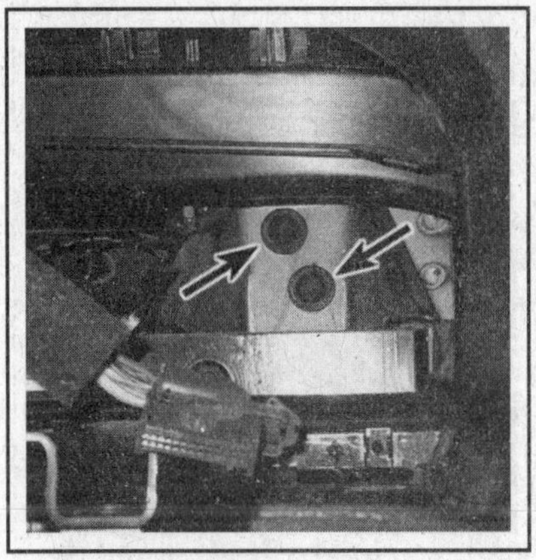

24.12 Instrument cluster opening bolts

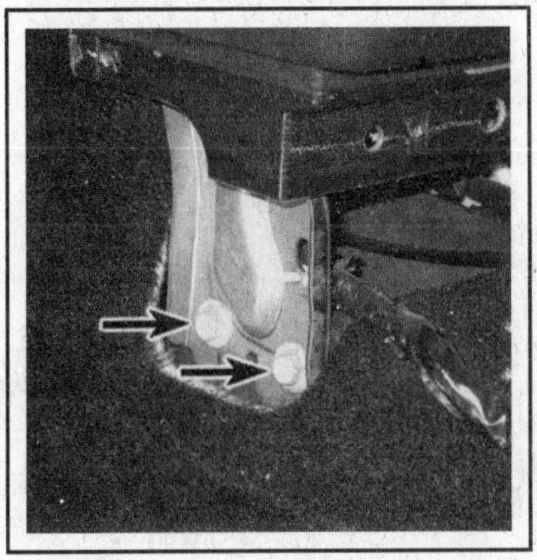

24.13 Instrument panel center brace bolts

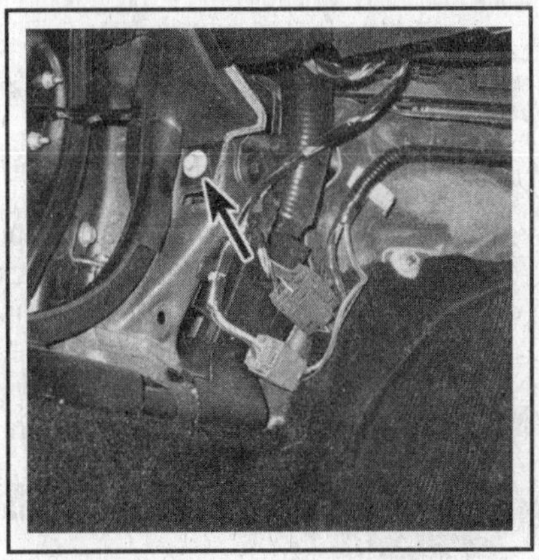

24.14 Left lower instrument panel bolt (right side similar)

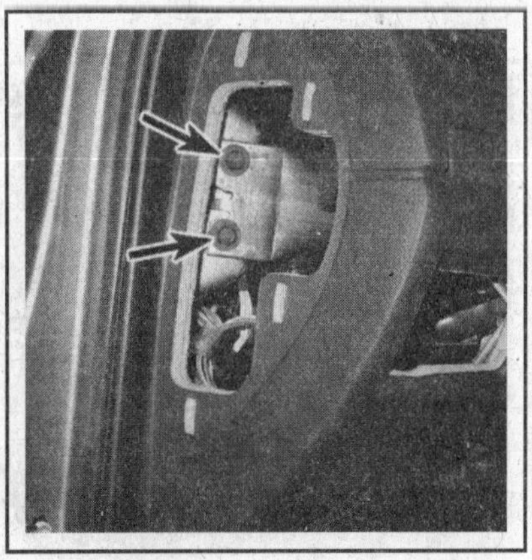

24.15 Left side instrument panel end bolts (right side similar)

3 Grasp each front door opening weather strip/sill panel/kick panels and pull it off (see illustration).

4 Disconnect the two electrical connectors in the left kick panel area and the bulkhead electrical connector and antenna cable in the right kick panel area. On 2010 models, disconnect the satellite antenna, if equipped.

5 On 2010 models, disconnect the small gray and black electrical connectors from the Smart Junction Box (SJB), which is located under the left end of the dash. For more information on the SJB, refer to Chapter 12.

6 In the glove box area, disconnect all air conditioning system electrical connectors.

7 Disconnect all electrical connectors and wiring harness clips located on the floor between the two front seats.

8 Disconnect any other connectors, not already specifically mentioned, that connect wiring between the vehicle and the instrument panel.

9 On 2010 models, remove the two nuts that secure the steering column pinch bolt cover and set the cover aside. On all models, mark the relationship of the upper steering column shaft to the lower shaft, remove the steering column pinch-bolt and separate the upper column shaft from the lower shaft. Discard the old pinch bolt and install a new one when you reassemble the steering column.

10 Remove the two hood release handle screws and set the handle aside (see Section 8).

11 Disconnect the in-vehicle temperature sensor aspirator hose from the heater core and evaporator core housing, if equipped, as follows: Separate the aspirator hose retaining clips from the heater core/evaporator core housing, then pull the hose away from the heater core/evaporator core housing.

12 Remove the two bolts in the instrument cluster opening (see illustration).

13 Remove the two bolts (2006 through 2009 models) or three bolts (2010 models) from the instrument panel center brace (see illustration).

14 Remove the bolts from the left and right lower corners of the instrument panel (see illustration).

15 Remove the three instrument panel end bolts (see illustration). There are two bolts at the left end and a single bolt at the right end.

CAUTION:

To avoid damage to the instrument panel when removing these last three bolts, have an assistant support the instrument panel. You'll also need an assistant's help when installing the instrument panel and these three bolts.

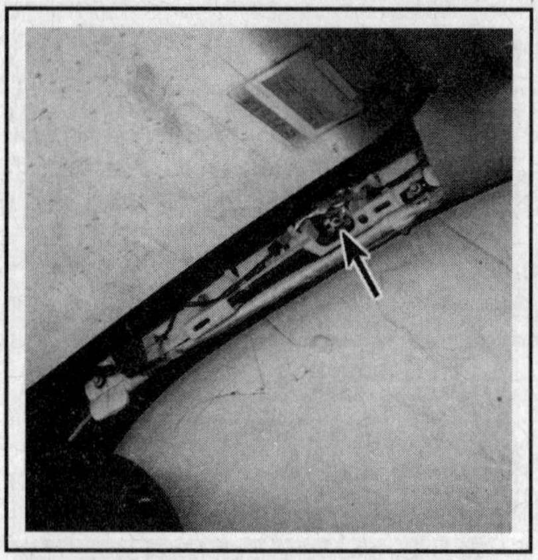

24.18a When the A-pillar trim panels are removed from the A-pillars, the trim panel clips remain stuck in the A-pillars

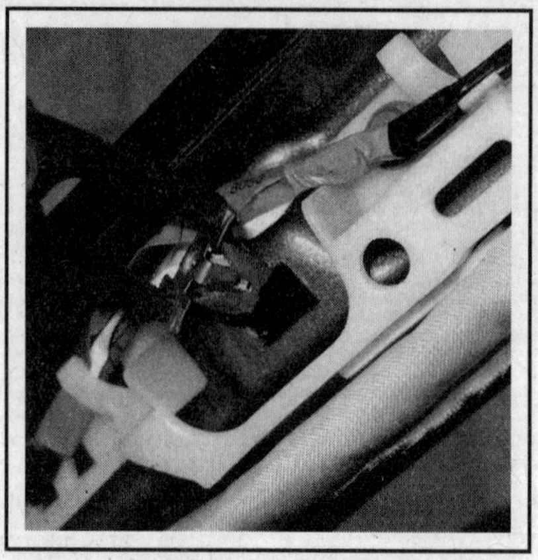

24.18b Remove each clip from the A-pillar . . .

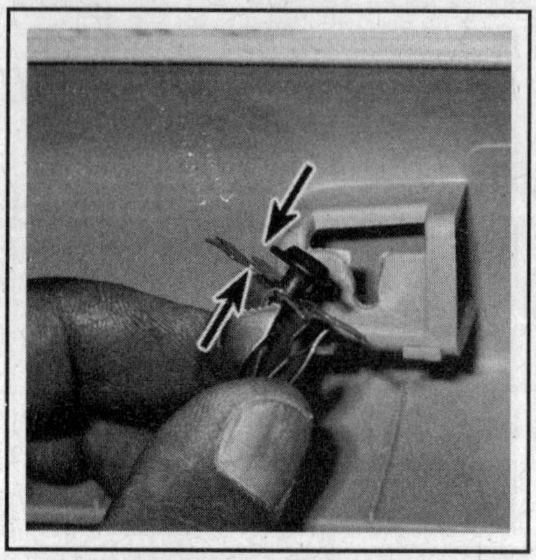

24.18c . . . and adjust the gap between each clip mounting screw and the clip . . .

24.18d . . . so that the clip fits tightly into its mounting bracket on the A-pillar trim panel

16 With an assistant helping you, remove the instrument panel from the vehicle.

17 Installation is the reverse of removal, except for the following item.

18 When the A-pillar trim panels were removed from the A-pillars in Step 2, the trim clips disengaged from the trim panels and remained stuck in the A-pillars (see illustration). Before installing the two A-pillar trim panels, remove the trim panel clips from the A-pillars, tighten the clip retaining screws and install the clips in their brackets on the undersides of the pillar trim panels (see illustrations).

➡**Note: The trim panels cannot be installed on the A-pillars without putting the clips back where they belong.**

25 Seats - removal and installation

FRONT SEATS

➧ **Refer to illustrations 25.1, 25.2a and 25.2b**

⁂ WARNING:

All models covered by this manual are equipped with a Supplemental Restraint System (SRS), more commonly known as airbags. Always disable the airbag system before working in the vicinity of any airbag system component to avoid the possibility of accidental deployment of the airbag, which could cause personal injury (see Chapter 12).

⁂ CAUTION:

The seats are heavy, so have an assistant handy to help you lift the seat from the vehicle.

➡**Note: This procedure applies to the driver and passenger seats.**

1 If you're removing the passenger seat, remove the cover from the seatbelt anchor, then remove the anchor bolt and disconnect the seatbelt from the seat (see illustration).

2 Remove the covers from the seat mounting bolts and remove the seat mounting bolts (see illustrations).

3 Tilt the seat forward and disconnect all electrical connectors underneath the seat.

4 Using a helper, carefully lift the seat out of the vehicle.

⁂ WARNING:

The seat is heavy, so trying to remove it by yourself could cause injury.

5 Installation is the reverse of removal.

25.1 Remove the cover from the seatbelt anchor, remove the anchor bolt and disconnect the seatbelt from the front passenger seat

25.2a Front seat mounting bolt covers and mounting bolts (front)

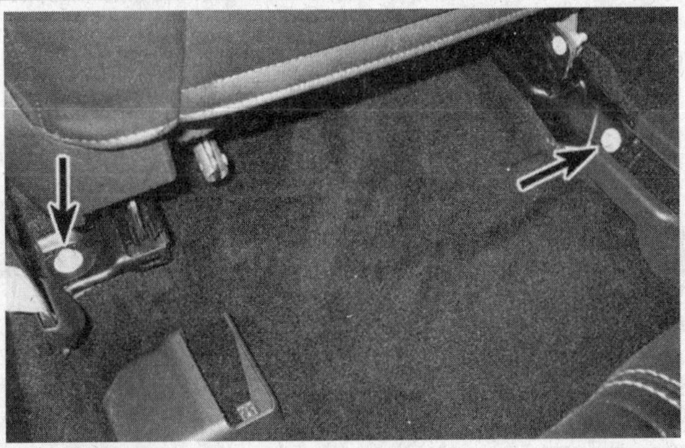

25.2b Front seat mounting bolt covers and mounting bolts (rear)

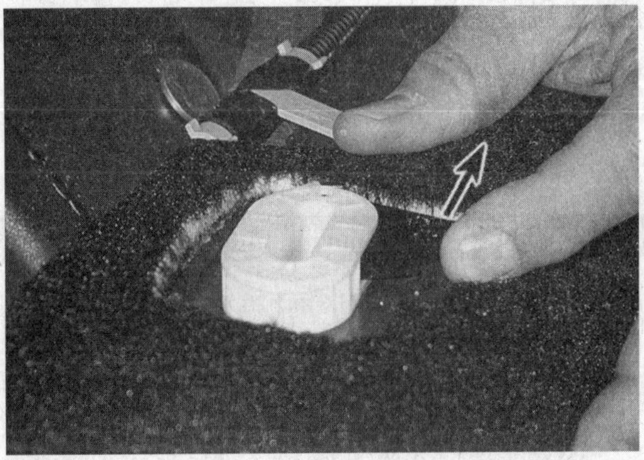

25.6 To disengage the rear seat cushion latches from the wire hoops on the underside of the cushion, pull this lever toward you (seat cushion already disengaged and raised, for clarity)

REAR SEAT CUSHION

➧ Refer to illustrations 25.6 and 25.7

6 Open the left rear door, insert your hand between the carpet and the lower edge of the rear seat cushion, then push your hand toward the other side of the vehicle. The release lever for the rear seat cushion latches is located about 18 inches from the left rear door. Pull the release lever toward you (see illustration) and pull up on the front edge of the cushion to disengage the two wire hoops on the underside of the cushion from the latches.

⁂ CAUTION:

Make sure that these two hoops are fully disengaged from the latches before proceeding, or you could damage the seat cushion.

7 Push the rear seat cushion firmly to the rear to disengage the wire hoops on the underside of the rear part of the cushion from their retainer hooks (see illustration).

8 Lift out the seat cushion. The cushion isn't that heavy, but get help if you need it, so that you don't hurt your back.

9 When installing the seat cushion, make SURE that the wire hoops

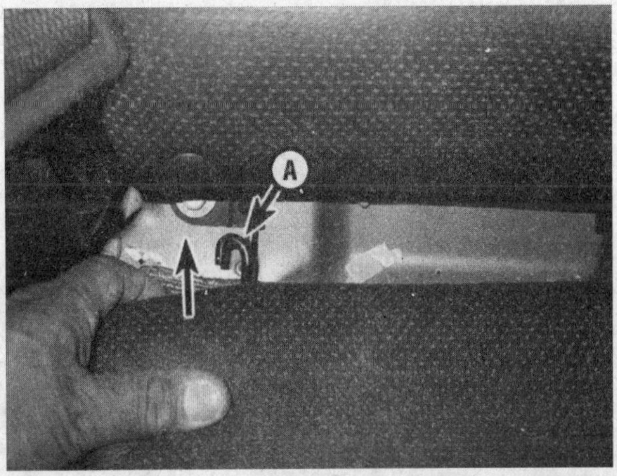

25.7 To disengage each of the two wire hoops (on the underside of the rear part of the cushion) from its corresponding retainer hook (A), push the cushion firmly to the rear (seat cushion already disengaged and pulled forward, for clarity)

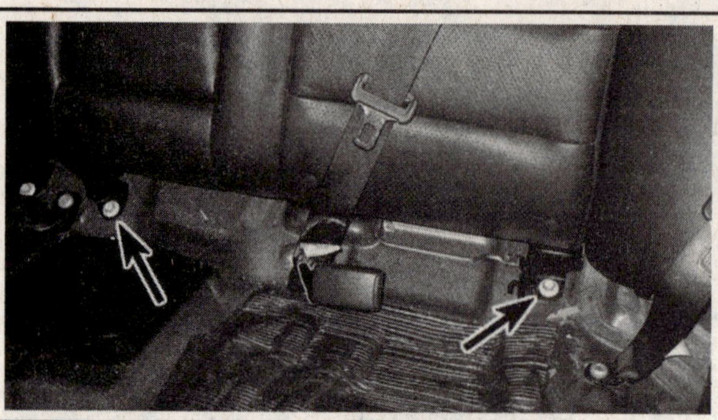

25.11a Left rear seat back lower mounting bolts

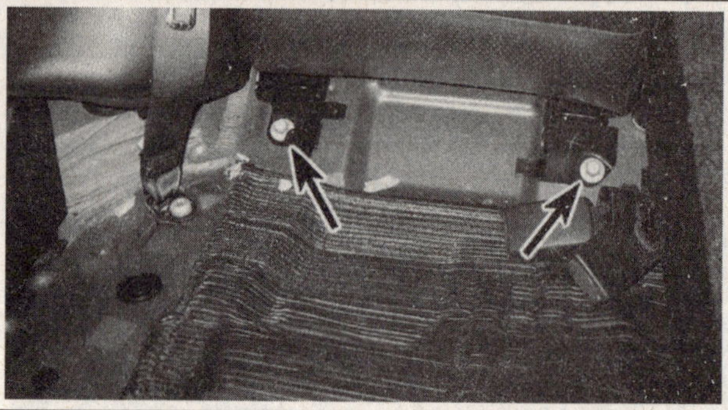

25.11b Right rear seat back lower mounting bolts

at the lower rear edge of the cushion engage the rear retainer hooks. And make sure that the two latches fully engage the lower front edge of the seat cushion.

REAR SEAT BACKS

➧ Refer to illustrations 25.11a and 25.11b

10 Remove the rear seat cushion (see Steps 6 through 8).

11 To detach the lower part of either rear seat back, remove the two mounting bolts at the bottom (see illustrations).

12 To detach the upper part of either rear seat back, open the trunk lid and pull the release handle inside the trunk. The release handle for the left seat back is located on the upper left edge of the trunk opening; the handle for the right seat back is located on the upper right edge of the trunk.

13 Installation is the reverse of removal.

26 Package tray - removal and installation

➧ Refer to illustrations 26.2, 26.3 and 26.4

1 Remove the rear seat cushion (see Section 25).

2 Remove the retaining bolt from each rear seat bolster (see illustration)

3 Release the rear seat backs (see your owner's manual, if necessary), fold them down, then carefully pry off both bolsters (see illustration).

4 Remove the trim cap and screw from the left and right C-pillar trim panels (see illustration).

5 Using a trim removal tool, carefully pry off both C-pillar trim panels.

6 Pull off the covers from the seat back latches.

7 Remove the four pushpins that secure the front of the package tray.

8 It is not necessary to disconnect any seatbelts to remove the package tray. Instead, pull the package tray forward slightly, then disengage the three seatbelts from the tray by threading each belt through the gap in the bottom of each plastic belt guide, then through the gap between the belt guide and the lower edge of the tray.

9 Remove the package tray.

⁂ WARNING:

Pay close attention to how the seatbelts are routed. They must be installed exactly the same way. Failure to do so could result in serious injury to someone secured by an incorrectly routed seatbelt in the event of an accident.

10 Installation is the reverse of removal.

26.2 Remove the rear seat bolster retaining bolt . . .

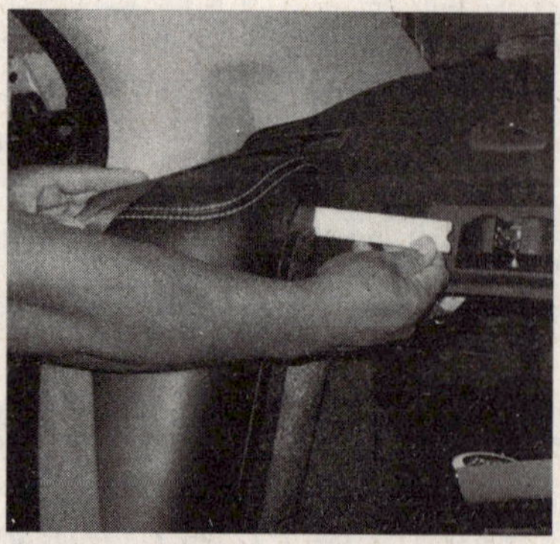

26.3 . . . then fold down the seat backs and carefully pry off the seat bolster (right bolster shown)

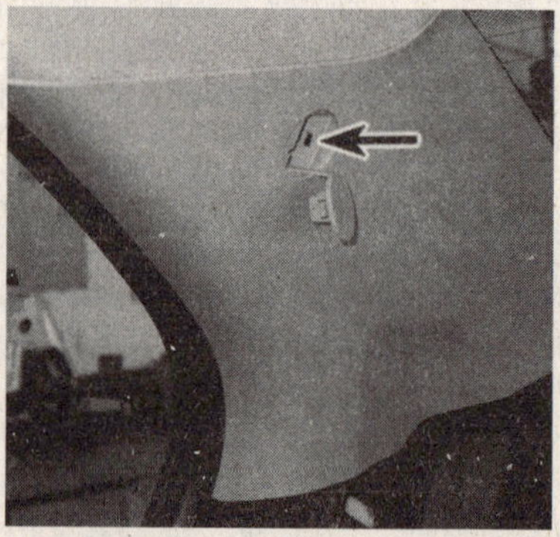

26.4 To remove a C-pillar trim panel, pry off the trim cap, remove the pillar retaining screw, then carefully pry off the panel with a trim removal tool

12 CHASSIS ELECTRICAL SYSTEM

Section

Reference to other Chapters

Turn signals and hazard flashers - See Section 7

1 General information

The electrical system is a 12-volt, negative ground type. Power for the lights and all electrical accessories is supplied by a lead/acid-type battery that is charged by the alternator.

This Chapter covers repair and service procedures for the various electrical components not associated with the engine. Information on the battery, alternator, ignition system and starter motor can be found in Chapter 5.

It should be noted that when portions of the electrical system are serviced, the negative cable should be disconnected from the battery to prevent electrical shorts and/or fires.

2 Electrical troubleshooting - general information

Refer to illustrations 2.5a, 2.5b, 2.6 and 2.9

A typical electrical circuit consists of an electrical component, any switches, relays, motors, fuses, fusible links or circuit breakers related to that component and the wiring and connectors that link the component to both the battery and the chassis. To help you pinpoint an electrical circuit problem, wiring diagrams are included at the end of this Chapter.

Before tackling any troublesome electrical circuit, first study the appropriate wiring diagrams to get a complete understanding of what makes up that individual circuit. Trouble spots, for instance, can often be narrowed down by noting if other components related to the circuit are operating properly. If several components or circuits fail at one time, chances are the problem is in a fuse or ground connection, because several circuits are often routed through the same fuse and ground connections.

Electrical problems usually stem from simple causes, such as loose or corroded connections, a blown fuse, a melted fusible link or a failed relay. Visually inspect the condition of all fuses, wires and connections in a problem circuit before troubleshooting the circuit.

If test equipment and instruments are going to be utilized, use the diagrams to plan ahead of time where you will make the necessary connections in order to accurately pinpoint the trouble spot.

The basic tools needed for electrical troubleshooting include a circuit tester or voltmeter (a 12-volt bulb with a set of test leads can also be used), a continuity tester, which includes a bulb, battery and set of test leads, and a jumper wire, preferably with a circuit breaker incorporated, which can be used to bypass electrical components (see illustrations). Before attempting to locate a problem with test instruments, use the wiring diagram(s) to decide where to make the connections.

VOLTAGE CHECKS

Voltage checks should be performed if a circuit is not functioning properly. Connect one lead of a circuit tester to either the negative battery terminal or a known good ground. Connect the other lead to a connector in the circuit being tested, preferably nearest to the battery or fuse (see illustration). If the bulb of the tester lights, voltage is present, which means that the part of the circuit between the connector and the battery is problem free. Continue checking the rest of the circuit in the same fashion. When you reach a point at which no voltage is present, the problem lies between that point and the last test point with voltage. Most of the time the problem can be traced to a loose connection.

➡Note: Keep in mind that some circuits receive voltage only when the ignition key is in the Accessory or Run position.

FINDING A SHORT

One method of finding shorts in a circuit is to remove the fuse and connect a test light or voltmeter in place of the fuse terminals. There should be no voltage present in the circuit. Move the wiring harness from side-to-side while watching the test light. If the bulb goes on,

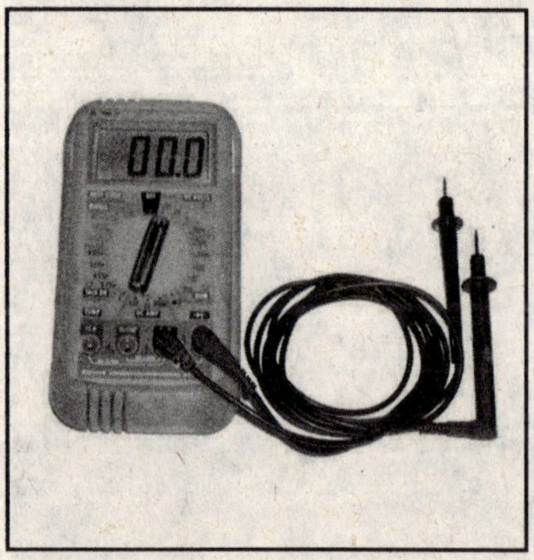

2.5a The most useful tool for electrical troubleshooting is a digital multimeter that can check volts, amps, and test continuity

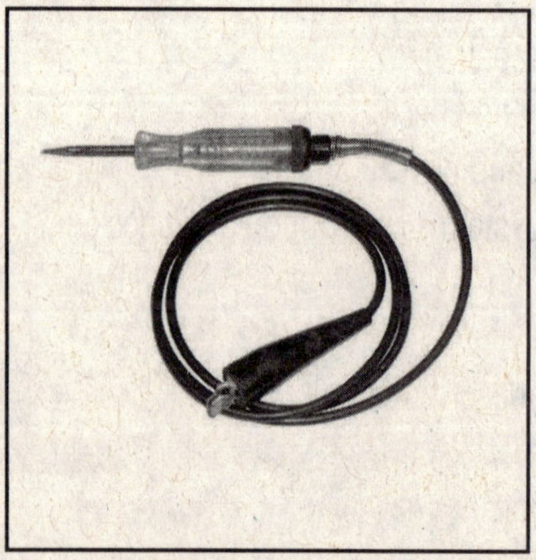

2.5b A test light is a very handy tool for checking voltage

2.6 In use, a basic test light's lead is clipped to a known good ground, then the pointed probe can test connectors, wires or electrical sockets - if the bulb lights, the part being tested has battery voltage

there is a short to ground somewhere in that area, probably where the insulation has rubbed through. The same test can be performed on each component in the circuit, even a switch.

GROUND CHECK

Perform a ground test to check whether a component is properly grounded. Disconnect the battery and connect one lead of a continuity tester or multimeter (set to the ohms scale), to a known good ground. Connect the other lead to the wire or ground connection being tested. If the resistance is low (less than 5 ohms), the ground is good. If the bulb on a self-powered test light does not go on, the ground is not good.

CONTINUITY CHECK

A continuity check is done to determine if there are any breaks in a circuit - if it is passing electricity properly. With the circuit off (no power in the circuit), a self-powered continuity tester or multimeter can be used to check the circuit. Connect the test leads to both ends of the circuit (or to the power end and a good ground), and if the test light comes on the circuit is passing current properly (see illustration). If the resistance is low (less than 5 ohms), there is continuity; if the reading is 10,000 ohms or higher, there is a break somewhere in the circuit. The same procedure can be used to test a switch, by connecting the continuity tester to the switch terminals. With the switch turned On, the test light should come on (or low resistance should be indicated on a meter).

FINDING AN OPEN CIRCUIT

When diagnosing for possible open circuits, it is often difficult to

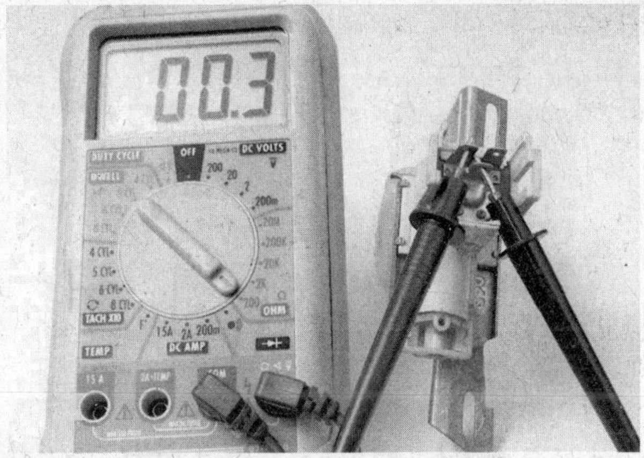

2.9 With a multimeter set to the ohms scale, resistance can be checked across two terminals - when checking for continuity, a low reading indicates continuity, a high reading indicates lack of continuity

locate them by sight because the connectors hide oxidation or terminal misalignment. Merely wiggling a connector on a sensor or in the wiring harness may correct the open circuit condition. Remember this when an open circuit is indicated when troubleshooting a circuit. Intermittent problems may also be caused by oxidized or loose connections.

Electrical troubleshooting is simple if you keep in mind that all electrical circuits are basically electricity running from the battery, through the wires, switches, relays, fuses and fusible links to each electrical component (light bulb, motor, etc.) and to ground, from which it is passed back to the battery. Any electrical problem is an interruption in the flow of electricity to and from the battery.

3 Fuses and fusible links - general information

FUSES

Refer to illustrations 3.1a, 3.1b and 3.3

The electrical circuits of the vehicle are protected by a combination of fuses, circuit breakers and fusible links. The main fuse/relay panel is in the engine compartment (see illustration), while the interior fuse/relay panel is located inside the passenger compartment (see illustration). Each of the fuses is designed to protect a specific circuit, and the various circuits are identified on the fuse panel itself.

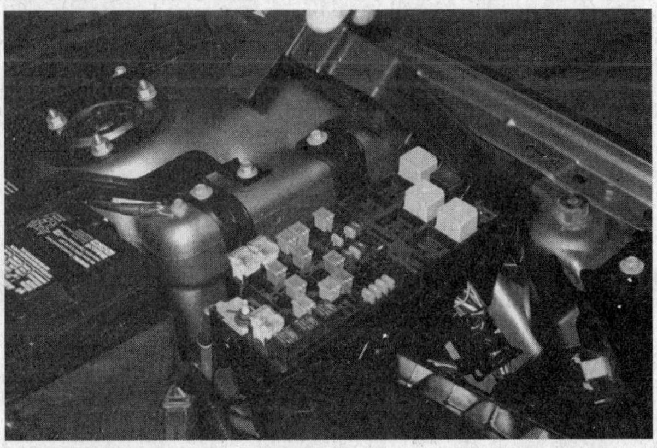

3.1a The engine compartment fuse and relay panel is located at the left side of the engine compartment

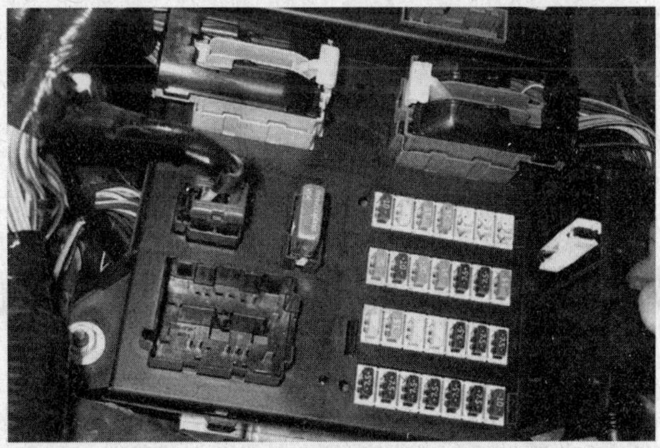

3.1b The passenger compartment fuse box is located on the Smart Junction Box (SJB), under the left end of the instrument panel

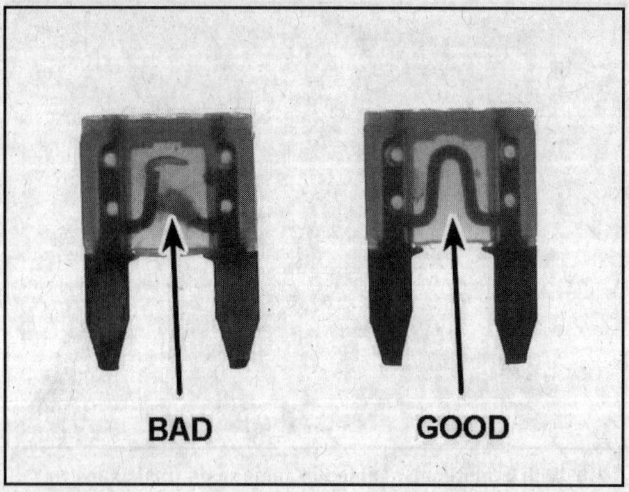

3.3 When a fuse blows, the element between the terminals melts

Several sizes of fuses are employed in the fuse blocks. There are small, medium and large sizes of the same design, all with the same blade terminal design. The medium and large fuses can be removed with your fingers, but the small fuses require the use of pliers or the small plastic fuse-puller tool found in most fuse boxes.

If an electrical component fails, always check the fuse first. The best way to check the fuses is with a test light. Check for power at the exposed terminal tips of each fuse. If power is present at one side of the fuse but not the other, the fuse is blown. A blown fuse can also be identified by visually inspecting it (see illustration).

Be sure to replace blown fuses with the correct type. Fuses (of the same physical size) of different ratings may be physically interchangeable, but only fuses of the proper rating should be used. Replacing a fuse with one of a higher or lower value than specified is not recommended. Each electrical circuit needs a specific amount of protection. The amperage value of each fuse is molded into the top of the fuse body.

If the replacement fuse immediately fails, don't replace it again until the cause of the problem is isolated and corrected. In most cases, this will be a short circuit in the wiring caused by a broken or deteriorated wire.

FUSIBLE LINKS

Some circuits are protected by fusible links. The links are used in circuits which are not ordinarily fused, or which carry high current, such as the circuit between the alternator and the battery. Fusible links, which are usually several wire gauges smaller in size than the circuit that they protect, are designed to melt if the circuit is subjected to more current than it was designed to carry. If you have to replace a blown fusible link, make sure that you replace it with one of the same specification. If the replacement fusible link blows in the same circuit, make sure that you troubleshoot the circuit in which the fusible link melted BEFORE installing another fusible link.

4 Circuit breakers - general information

Circuit breakers protect certain circuits, such as the power windows or heated seats. Depending on the vehicle's accessories, there may be one or two circuit breakers, located in the fuse/relay box in the engine compartment.

Because the circuit breakers reset automatically, an electrical overload in a circuit breaker-protected system will cause the circuit to fail momentarily, then come back on. If the circuit does not come back on, check it immediately.

For a basic check, pull the circuit breaker up out of its socket on the fuse panel, but just far enough to probe with a voltmeter. The breaker should still contact the sockets. With the voltmeter negative lead on a good chassis ground, touch each end prong of the circuit breaker with the positive meter probe. There should be battery voltage at each end. If there is battery voltage only at one end, the circuit breaker must be replaced.

Some circuit breakers must be reset manually.

5 Relays - general information

Several electrical accessories in the vehicle, such as the fuel injection system, horns, starter, and fog lamps use relays to transmit the electrical signal to the component. Relays use a low-current circuit (the control circuit) to open and close a high-current circuit (the power circuit). If the relay is defective, that component will not operate properly. Most relays are mounted in the engine compartment and interior fuse/relay boxes (see illustrations 3.1a and 3.1b).

6 Electrical connectors - general information

Most electrical connections on these vehicles are made with multiwire plastic connectors. The mating halves of many connectors are secured with locking clips molded into the plastic connector shells. The mating halves of some large connectors, such as some of those under the instrument panel, are held together by a bolt through the center of the connector.

To separate a connector with locking clips, use a small screwdriver to pry the clips apart carefully, then separate the connector halves. Pull only on the shell, never pull on the wiring harness, as you may damage the individual wires and terminals inside the connectors. Look at the connector closely before trying to separate the halves. Often the locking clips are engaged in a way that is not immediately clear. Additionally, many connectors have more than one set of clips.

Each pair of connector terminals has a male half and a female half. When you look at the end view of a connector in a diagram, be sure to understand whether the view shows the harness side or the component side of the connector. Connector halves are mirror images of each other, and a terminal shown on the right side end-view of one half will be on the left side end-view of the other half.

It is often necessary to take circuit voltage measurements with a connector connected. Whenever possible, carefully insert a small straight pin (not your meter probe) into the rear of the connector shell to contact the terminal inside, then clip your meter lead to the pin. This kind of connection is called "backprobing." When inserting a test probe into a terminal, be careful not to distort the terminal opening. Doing so can lead to a poor connection and corrosion at that terminal later. Using the small straight pin instead of a meter probe results in less chance of deforming the terminal connector.

Most electrical connectors have a single release tab that you depress to release the connector

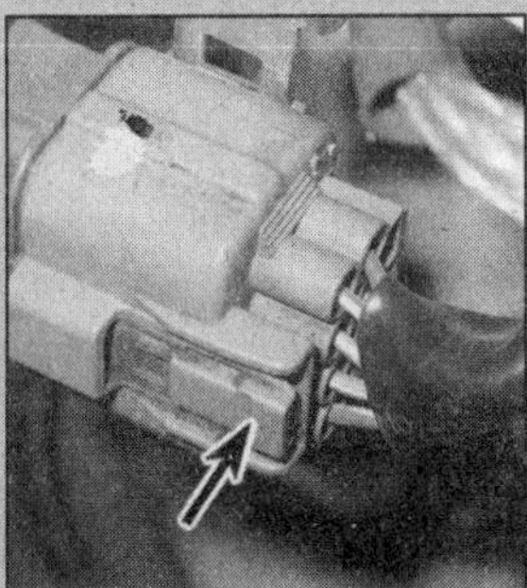

The single release tab might be on the side of the connector instead of on top (or on bottom!)

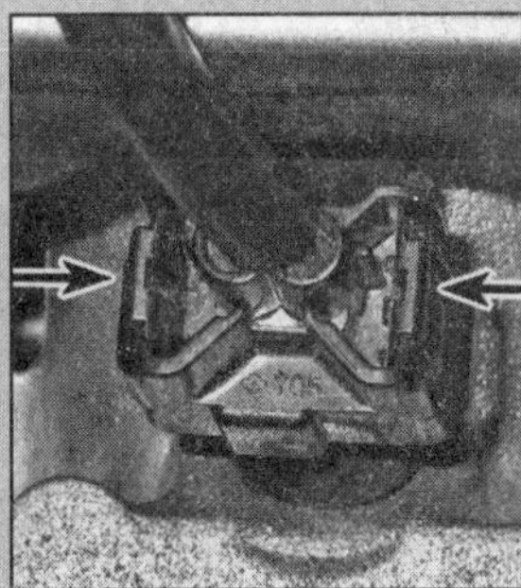

Some connectors have two release tabs that you must squeeze to release the connector

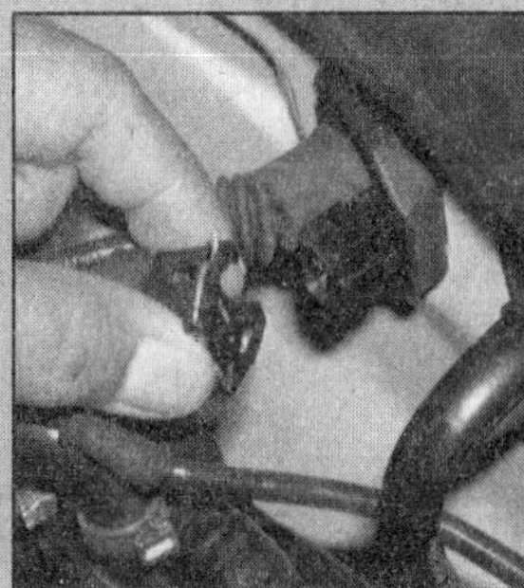

Some connectors use wire retainers that you squeeze to release the connector

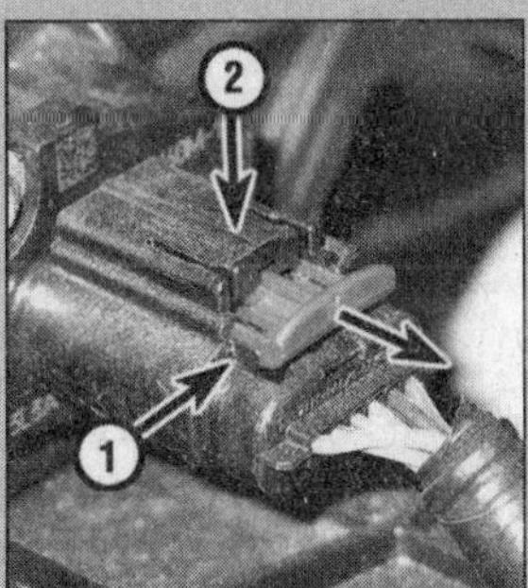

Critical connectors often employ a sliding lock (1) that you must pull out before you can depress the release tab (2)

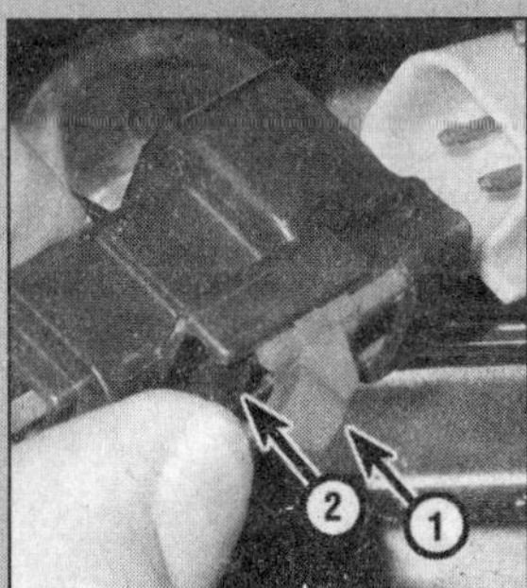

Here's another sliding-lock style connector, with the lock (1) and the release tab (2) on the side of the connector

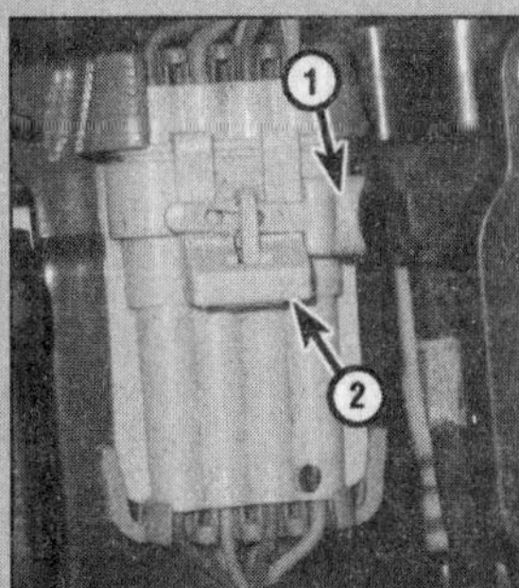

On some connectors the lock (1) must be pulled out to the side and removed before you can depress the release tab (2)

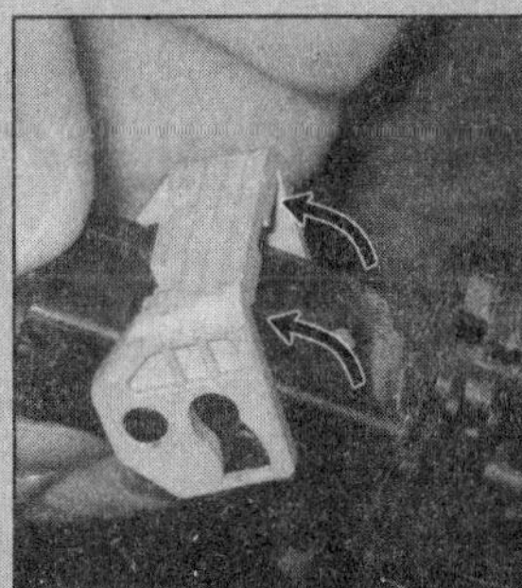

Some critical connectors, like the multi-pin connectors at the Powertrain Control Module employ pivoting locks that must be flipped open

7 Smart Junction Box (SJB) - general information

Refer to illustration 7.1

1 The SJB (see illustration), which is located under the left end of the instrument panel, is a multi-function module and interior power junction box that houses interior fuses, and provides power to the exterior and interior lights, the horn, the remote keyless entry system, the power door locks, the smart locks and the windshield wiper system. The SJB also functions as the flasher relay for the turn signal and hazard flasher lights and as the speed control relay for the wiper system. Because of its location, high up in the left corner of the firewall, the SJB is extremely difficult to access.

2 The module configuration information must be uploaded from the old SJB into the appropriate diagnostic equipment, then downloaded into the new SJB once it's installed, so replacement must be done by a dealer service department or other properly equipped repair facility.

7.1 The Smart Junction Box (SJB) is located under the instrument panel, on the upper left corner of the firewall (instrument panel removed for clarity)

8 Multi-function switch - replacement

Refer to illustration 8.2

✻✻ WARNING:

The models covered by this manual are equipped with Supplemental Restraint Systems (SRS), more commonly known as airbags. Always disable the airbag system before working in the vicinity of any airbag system components to avoid the possibility of accidental deployment of the airbags, which could cause personal injury (see Section 29).

1 Remove the knee bolster trim panel, the knee bolster and the steering column covers (see Chapter 11).

2 Disconnect the multi-function switch electrical connector (see illustration).

3 Remove the multi-function switch retaining screws and remove the switch.

4 Installation is the reverse of removal.

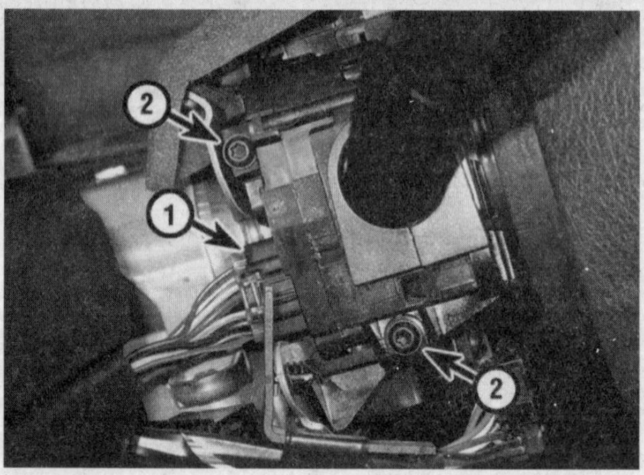

8.2 Multi-function switch details

1 Electrical connector *2 Switch retaining screws*

9 Ignition switch and key lock cylinder - replacement

✻✻ WARNING:

The models covered by this manual are equipped with Supplemental Restraint Systems (SRS), more commonly known as airbags. Always disable the airbag system before working in the vicinity of any airbag system components to avoid the possibility of accidental deployment of the airbags, which could cause personal injury (see Section 29).

1 Disconnect the cable from the negative terminal of the battery (see Chapter 5).

2 Remove the knee bolster trim panel, the knee bolster and the upper and lower steering column covers (see Chapter 11). Lower the steering column to its lowest position.

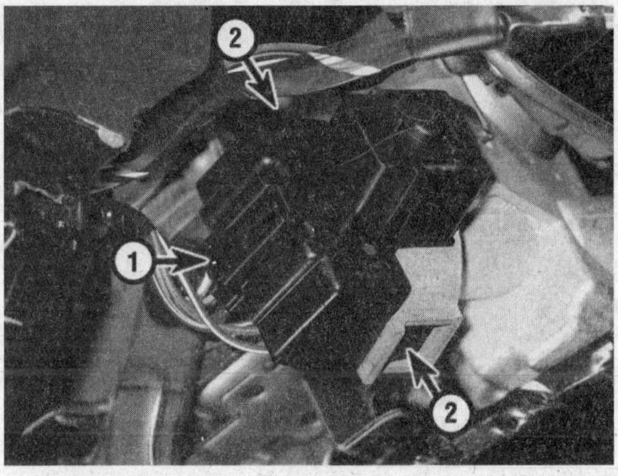

9.3 Ignition switch details

1 *Electrical connector*
2 *Release tabs (upper tab not visible in this photo)*

IGNITION SWITCH

➧ Refer to illustration 9.3

✻✻ CAUTION:

Do not remove the ignition switch and the key lock cylinder at the same time. According to the manufacturer, doing so could damage the steering column.

3 Disconnect the electrical connector from the ignition switch (see illustration).

4 Depress the release tabs to detach the ignition switch from the steering column.

5 When installing the switch, make sure that it snaps into place. Installation is otherwise the reverse of removal.

KEY LOCK CYLINDER

➧ Refer to illustration 9.7

✻✻ CAUTION:

Do not remove the ignition switch and the key lock cylinder at the same time. According to the manufacturer, doing so could damage the steering column.

6 On 2006 through 2009 models, turn the ignition key to the ON position; on 2010 models, turn the ignition key to the ACC position.

7 Using a suitable tool, depress the key lock cylinder release button (see illustration) and remove the key lock cylinder.

8 To install the key lock cylinder, insert it into the lock cylinder housing and push it in until it clicks into place.

9 Verify that the ignition switch operates correctly in the OFF, ACC, RUN and START positions.

9.7 Insert a suitable tool through this hole and push the release button to release the ignition key lock cylinder

9.11 Key lock cylinder illumination ring details

1 *Electrical connector*
2 *Lock tabs (upper lock tab not visible in this photo)*

10 Installation is otherwise the reverse of removal.

KEY LOCK CYLINDER ILLUMINATION RING

➧ Refer to illustration 9.11

➡Note: Removal of the lock cylinder illumination ring is not necessary for lock cylinder replacement.

11 Disconnect the electrical connector from the illumination ring (see illustration).

12 Disengage the lock tabs and remove the illumination ring.

13 Installation is the reverse of removal. Make sure that the ring snaps into place.

10 Instrument panel switches - replacement

WARNING:

The models covered by this manual are equipped with Supplemental Restraint Systems (SRS), more commonly known as airbags. Always disable the airbag system before working in the vicinity of any airbag system components to avoid the possibility of accidental deployment of the airbags, which could cause personal injury (see Section 29).

HEADLIGHT SWITCH/INSTRUMENT PANEL DIMMER SWITCH/TRUNK LID OPENER SWITCH ASSEMBLY

Refer to illustration 10.3

1 Disconnect the cable from the negative terminal of the battery (see Chapter 5).

2 Remove the left end trim panel from the instrument panel (see *Dashboard trim panels - removal and installation* in Chapter 11).

3 Reach through the opening in the end of the instrument panel and push on the back of the switch while simultaneously prying the switch out of the dash with a trim removal tool (see illustration). Disconnect the electrical connectors and remove the switch assembly.

4 No further disassembly is possible. If you're replacing the headlight switch, you must replace this assembly.

5 Pop a new instrument panel dimmer switch into the bezel and make sure that it snaps into place. Installation is otherwise the reverse of removal.

HAZARD FLASHER SWITCH

Refer to illustration 10.8

6 Disconnect the cable from the negative terminal of the battery (see Chapter 5).

7 On 2006 through 2009 models, remove the center trim panel; on 2010 models, remove the upper storage bin (see *Dashboard trim panels - removal and installation* in Chapter 11).

8 Spread the release tabs (see illustration) and remove the hazard flasher switch from the center trim panel or the upper storage bin.

9 Installation is the reverse of removal.

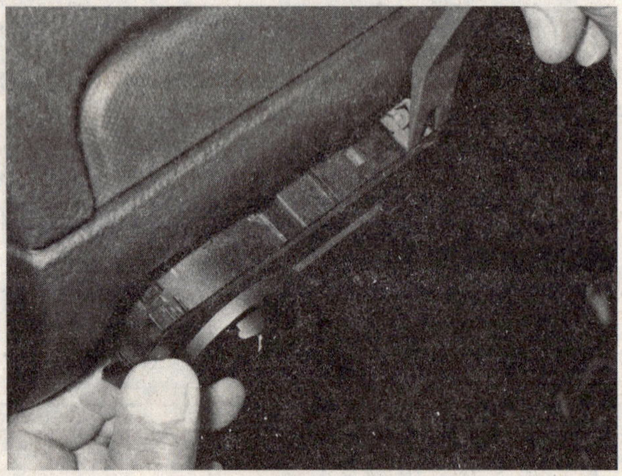

10.3 Use a trim removal tool to pry the headlight switch/instrument panel dimmer switch/trunk release switch assembly out of the instrument panel

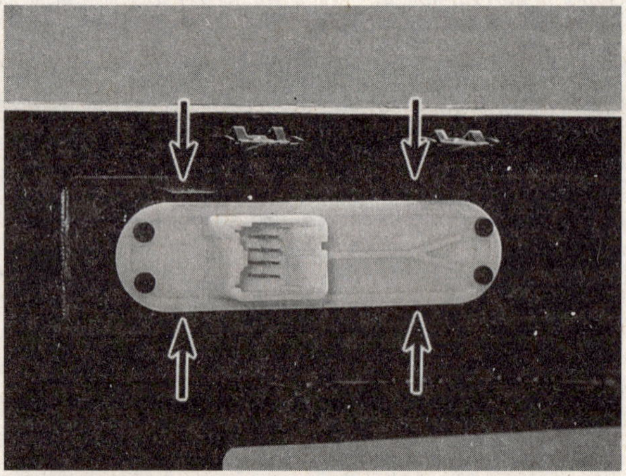

10.8 Release tabs for the hazard flasher switch (2006 through 2009 models)

11 Instrument cluster - removal and installation

Refer to illustration 11.4

WARNING:

The models covered by this manual are equipped with Supplemental Restraint Systems (SRS), more commonly known as airbags. Always disable the airbag system before working in the vicinity of any airbag system components to avoid the possibility of accidental deployment of the airbags, which could cause personal injury (see Section 29).

1 Disconnect the cable from the negative battery terminal (see Chapter 5).

2 Release the tilt wheel lever and lower the steering wheel to its lowest position.

3 Remove the instrument cluster trim panel (see *Dashboard trim panels - removal and installation* in Chapter 11).

4 Remove the instrument cluster mounting screws (see illustration). On 2006 through 2009 models there are two screws; on 2010 models there are three screws.

5 Carefully pull out the instrument cluster from the instrument panel and disconnect the electrical connectors.

6 Installation is the reverse of removal.

11.4 Instrument cluster mounting screws (2006 through 2009 models)

12 Radio and speakers - removal and installation

⁂ WARNING:

The models covered by this manual are equipped with Supplemental Restraint Systems (SRS), more commonly known as airbags. Always disable the airbag system before working in the vicinity of any airbag system components to avoid the possibility of accidental deployment of the airbags, which could cause personal injury (see Section 29).

RADIO

2006 through 2009 models

Refer to illustration 12.3

1 Disconnect the cable from the negative battery terminal (see Chapter 5).

2 Remove the center trim panel and the glove box (see *Dashboard trim panels - removal and installation* in Chapter 11).

3 Remove the radio mounting screws (see illustration). Do not try to pull out the radio yet; it cannot be removed until the large multi-pin electrical connector is disconnected from the backside of the radio, because the harness is too short to pull out the radio.

4 Reach through the glove box opening and disconnect the electrical connector from the back of the radio, then pull out the radio and disconnect the antenna cable from the back of the radio.

5 Installation is the reverse of removal.

2010 models

➡Note: The radio consists of the Front Controls Interface Module (FCIM) and the Audio Control Module (ACM). The FCIM (the controls) is what you see in the center trim panel; the ACM (the radio) is a separate component in the dash behind the FCIM. You can replace the FCIM at home, but not the ACM. You can instrument panel, but if the ACM must be replaced, it will have to be done by a dealer service department because module configuration must be programmed into the new ACM unit. Without the correct module configuration, the new ACM will not work.

6 Disconnect the cable from the negative battery terminal (see Chapter 5).

7 Remove the center trim panel (see *Dashboard trim panels - removal and installation* in Chapter 11).

8 On models with a navigation system, remove the four Front Display Interface Module (FDIM) screws and remove the FDIM.

9 If you're replacing the FCIM (the radio controls), or the center trim panel, remove the screws and detach the FCIM from the center trim panel.

10 If you're removing the ACM (the radio), remove the ACM mounting screws, then pull out the ACM and disconnect the antenna cable and all electrical connectors.

11 Installation is the reverse of removal.

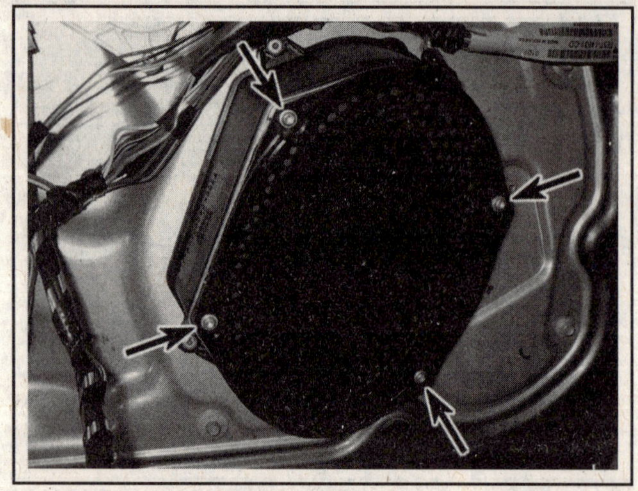

12.13 Door speaker mounting screws

12.17 Door tweeter details

1 *Electrical connector* 2 *Tweeter mounting screws*

SPEAKERS

Door speakers

Refer to illustration 12.13

Note: This procedure applies to front and rear door speakers.

12 Remove the door trim panel (see Chapter 11).
13 Remove the speaker mounting screws (see illustration).
14 Pull the speaker out of its enclosure and disconnect the speaker electrical connectors.
15 Installation is the reverse of removal.

Door tweeters

Refer to illustration 12.17

16 Remove the door trim panel and the sail panel (see Chapter 11).
17 Disconnect the tweeter electrical connector (see illustration).
18 Remove the tweeter mounting screws.
19 Disengage the tweeter harness from the clip on the back of the sail panel and remove the tweeter.
20 Installation is the reverse of removal.

Instrument panel speaker

21 Carefully pry off the instrument panel cover.
22 Remove the four speaker retaining screws.
23 Lift the speaker out of the instrument panel and disconnect the electrical connector.
24 Installation is the reverse of removal.

Rear speakers

Note: Depending on the year and model, there are various configurations of rear speakers and woofers located behind the back seat, underneath the package tray. This procedure applies to any of them.

25 Remove the package tray (see Chapter 11).
26 Remove the speaker mounting screws, then lift up the speaker and disconnect the electrical connector.
27 Installation is the reverse of removal.

13 Antenna, module and cables - removal and installation

ANTENNA

1 The antenna is an integral component of the rear window. It cannot be serviced separately from the rear window.

ANTENNA MODULE

2 Remove the C-pillar trim (see *Package tray - removal and installation* in Chapter 11).
3 Disconnect the electrical connectors from the antenna module.
4 Remove the module mounting bolts and remove the module.
5 Installation is the reverse of removal.

ANTENNA CABLES

6 The antenna cable consists of two cables: front and rear. The rear cable is routed down the right C-pillar, between the body and the left and right ends of the back seat, then along the rocker, under the front and rear door sill panels and carpeting, and ends at the right kick panel, where it connects to the front cable. The front cable is routed up behind the right kick panel, then turns left and goes across the glove box area and connects to the backside of the radio. The antenna cables are an integral part of the wiring harness under the carpeting. If one of these cables must be replaced, it's impractical to try to extricate it from the wiring harness. Instead, simply disconnect it at both ends and leave it in place, install a new cable and plug it in.

Rear antenna cable

7 To access the rear antenna cable, remove the following components (see Chapter 11):

Back seat cushion
Right C-pillar
Front and rear door sills
Front passenger seat
Carpeting
Right kick panel

8 Disconnect the antenna cable from the antenna module and from the front antenna cable, then install the new cable and plug it in.

Front antenna cable

9 To access the front antenna cable, remove the following components (see Chapter 11, unless otherwise noted):

Right kick panel
Glove box
Radio (see Section 12)

10 Disconnect the front antenna cable from the radio and from the rear antenna cable, then install the new cable and plug it in.

14 Headlight bulb - replacement

⁂ WARNING:

Halogen bulbs are gas-filled and under pressure and might shatter if the surface is scratched or the bulb is dropped. Wear eye protection and handle the bulbs carefully, grasping only the base whenever possible. Don't touch the surface of the bulb with your fingers because the oil from your skin could cause it to overheat and fail prematurely. If you do touch the bulb surface, clean it with rubbing alcohol.

2006 THROUGH 2009 MODELS

➧ Refer to illustration 14.2

➡Note: The low-beam bulbs are the upper bulbs; the high-beam bulbs are the lower bulbs.

1 To access either bulb on the left (driver's side) headlight housing, remove the air filter housing air inlet duct (see Chapter 4).

2 To access the high-beam bulb on the right (passenger's side) headlight housing, detach and set aside the windshield washer fluid filler tube (see Chapter 3). To access the low-beam bulb on the right headlight housing of a vehicle with ABS, remove the bulb access cover screw (see illustration) and remove the access cover from the fender splash shield.

2010 MODELS

➡Note: The low-beam bulbs are the outer bulbs and the high-beam bulbs are the inner bulbs.

3 To access the left (driver's side) high-beam or low-beam bulb on four-cylinder and 3.0L V6 models, remove the air filter housing (see Chapter 4).

4 To access the right (passenger's side) high-beam bulb on four-cylinder and 3.0L V6 models, detach the windshield washer fluid reservoir (don't disconnect any hoses) and set it aside.

5 To access the right (passenger's side) low-beam bulb on all models, turn the steering wheel all the way to the left, then remove the press pins from the inner fender splash shield.

6 To access the right (passenger's side) high-beam bulb on 3.5L V6 models, remove the headlight housing (see Section 15).

ALL MODELS

Low-beam bulbs

➧ Refer to illustrations 14.7, 14.9a, 14.9b and 14.10

7 Remove the rubber cover from the back of the headlight housing (see illustration).

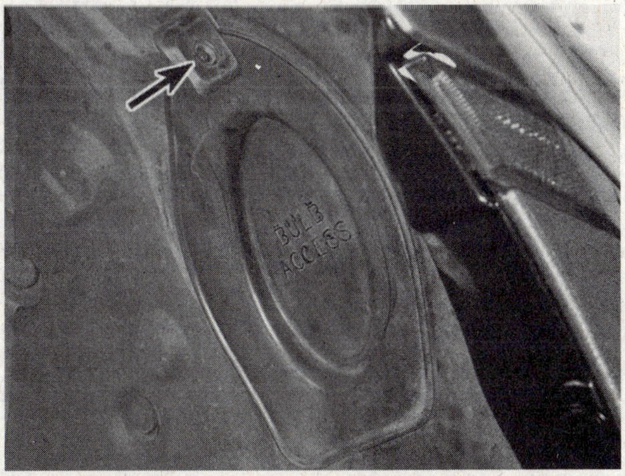

14.2 Fender splash shield access cover for the right low-beam headlight bulb (2006 through 2009 models)

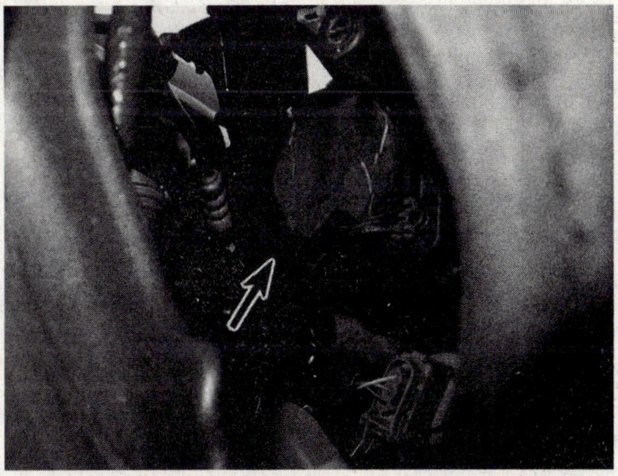

14.7 Typical protective rubber cover (2006 through 2009 model shown; 2010 models similar)

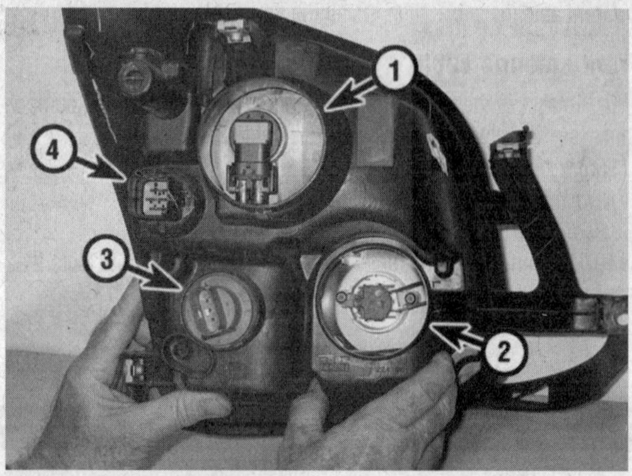

14.9a Headlight housing details, left housing shown (2006 through 2009 models):

1. *Low-beam bulb*
2. *High-beam bulb*
3. *Front turn signal/parking light bulb*
4. *Headlight housing electrical connector*

14.9b To remove the low-beam headlight bulb, rotate the bulb counterclockwise and pull it out of the housing, then spread the locking tabs apart and disconnect the electrical connector

14.10 To install a low-beam bulb, align the lugs on the bulb holder with the cutouts in the headlight housing

14.12 To remove the high-beam headlight bulb, turn it counterclockwise and pull it out

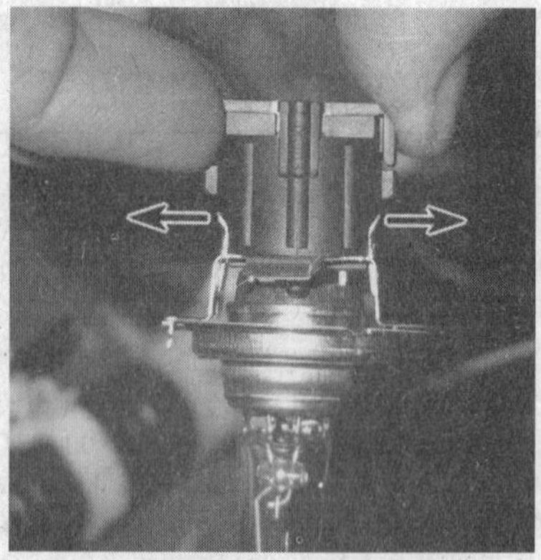

14.13 To disconnect the high-beam bulb from the electrical connector, spread these locking tabs apart and pull off the bulb

8 Turn the bulb counterclockwise and remove it from the headlight housing.

9 Disconnect the electrical connector from the bulb (see illustrations).

10 When installing the bulb, align the lugs on the bulb's locking flange with their corresponding cutouts in the headlight housing (see illustration), insert the bulb into the headlight housing and twist it clockwise to lock it into place. When installing the new bulb, make sure that you don't touch it with your fingers, because the oil from your hands will cause the bulb to overheat and fail prematurely. If you do touch the bulb, be sure to wipe it off with alcohol and a clean soft cloth. Installation is otherwise the reverse of removal.

High-beam bulbs

Refer to illustrations 14.12 and 14.13

Remove the protective cover (see illustration 14.7).

12 Rotate the bulb counterclockwise and pull it out (see illustration).

Note: The electrical connector cannot be disconnected from the bulb until the bulb is removed.

13 Disengage the bulb clips from the electrical connector (see illustration) and remove the bulb.

14 When installing the new bulb, make sure that you don't touch it with your fingers, because the oil from your hands will cause the bulb to fail. If you do touch the bulb, be sure to wipe it off with alcohol and a clean soft cloth.

15 When connecting the new bulb to the electrical connector, make sure that it snaps into place, then insert the bulb/connector into the headlight housing and turn it clockwise to lock it into place. Installation is otherwise the reverse of removal.

15 Headlight housing - removal and installation

Refer to illustration 15.2

1 Remove the front bumper cover (see Chapter 11).
2 Remove the pin-type retainer and the four headlight housing bolts (see illustration).
3 Pull out the headlight housing and disconnect the electrical connectors.
4 Installation is the reverse of removal.

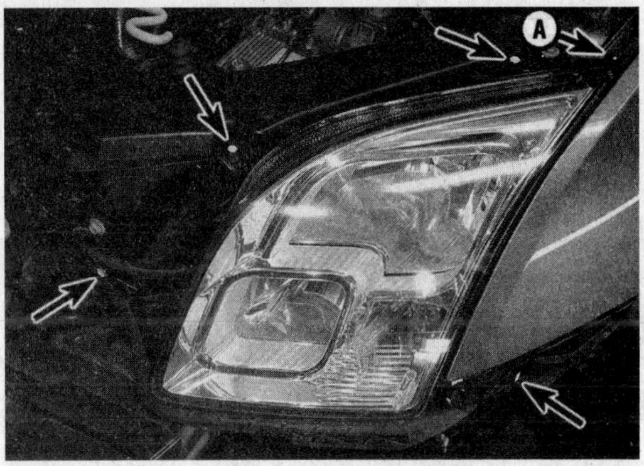

15.2 To remove the headlight housing, remove the pin-type retainer (A) and the four headlight housing bolts (2006 through 2009 model shown; 2010 models similar)

16 Headlights - adjustment

Refer to illustrations 16.1 and 16.2

WARNING:

The headlights must be aimed correctly. If adjusted incorrectly, they could temporarily blind the driver of an oncoming vehicle and cause an accident or seriously reduce your ability to see the road. The headlights should be checked for proper aim every 12 months and any time a new headlight is installed or front-end bodywork is performed. The following procedure is only an interim step to provide temporary adjustment until the headlights can be adjusted by a properly equipped shop.

1 The headlight adjustment screws (see illustration) control up-and-down movement. Left-and-right movement is not adjustable.
2 There are several methods of adjusting the headlights. The simplest method requires a blank wall 25 feet in front of the vehicle and a level floor (see illustration).
3 Position masking tape on the wall in reference to the vehicle centerline and the centerlines of both headlights.

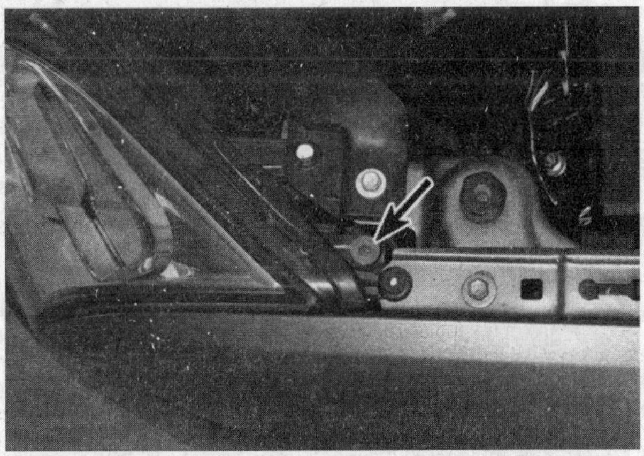

16.1 Vertical adjustment screw location (2006 through 2009 model shown, 2010 models similar)

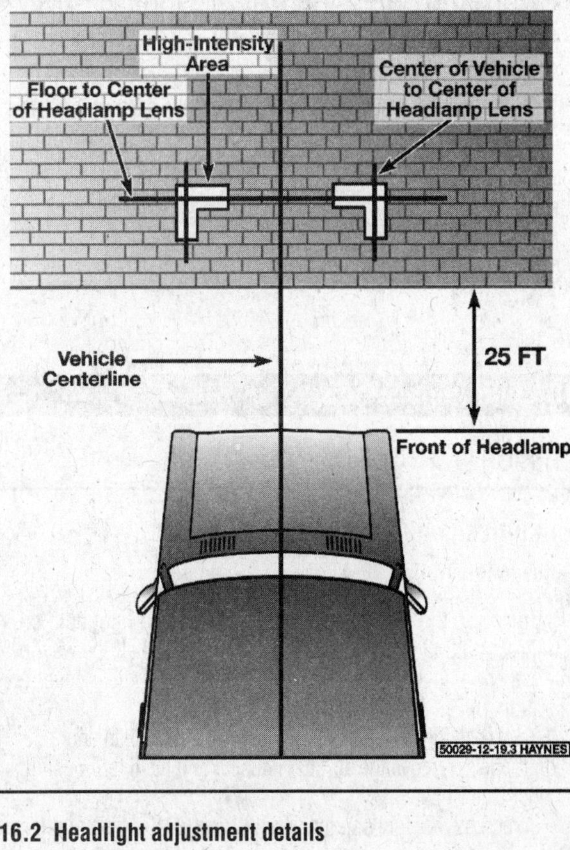

16.2 Headlight adjustment details

4 Measure the height of the headlight reference marks (in the centers of the headlight lenses) from the ground. Position a horizontal tape line on the wall at the same height as the headlight reference marks.

➡Note: It may be easier to position the tape on the wall with the vehicle parked only a few inches away.

5 Adjustment should be made with the vehicle sitting level, the gas tank half-full and no unusually heavy load in the vehicle.

6 Turn on the low beams. Turn the adjusting screw to position the high intensity zone so it is two inches below the horizontal line.

7 Have the headlights adjusted by a dealer service department at the earliest opportunity.

17 Taillight housing - removal and installation

TAILLIGHT HOUSING

➧ Refer to illustration 17.2

1 Fold back the trunk floor carpeting mat, then pull out and reposition the flexible trunk side trim panel that covers the taillight housing and the wheelhousing.

⁂ CAUTION:

Do not leave the trunk side panel bent or out of shape too long, or it will permanently deform it.

2 Disconnect the electrical connectors from the taillight housing (see illustration).

3 Remove the three taillight housing nuts and remove the taillight housing.

4 Installation is the reverse of removal.

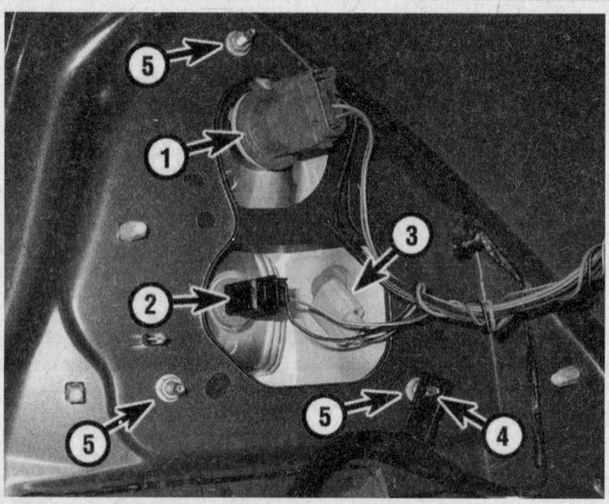

17.2 Taillight housing details

1 *Taillight/brake light/turn signal bulb electrical connector*
2 *Back-up light bulb electrical connector*
3 *Marker light bulb electrical connector*
4 *Wiring harness clip*
5 *Mounting nuts*

BACK-UP LIGHT HOUSING (MILAN MODELS ONLY)

5 Remove the trunk lid trim panel, if equipped.

6 Disconnect the electrical connector from the back-up light bulb holder.

7 Remove the three back-up light housing mounting nuts and remove the housing from the trunk lid.

8 Installation is the reverse of removal.

18 Bulb replacement

EXTERIOR LIGHT BULBS

Front turn signal/parking light bulbs

➧ Refer to illustration 18.4

1 To access the right (passenger's side) parking light bulb on 2006 through 2009 models, turn the steering wheel all the way to the left, then remove the bulb access cover screw and the cover (see illustration 14.2).

2 To access the left parking light bulb on 2010 Milan and 3.5L Fusion models, remove the air filter housing and the filter housing air inlet duct (see Chapter 4).

3 To access the right parking light bulb on 2010 Milan and Fusion models, remove the four pin-type retainers and push the fender splash shield aside.

4 Turn the bulb holder counterclockwise (see illustration) and remove it from the headlight housing. It's not necessary to disconnect the electrical connector to replace the bulb.

5 To remove the bulb, pull it straight out of the holder.

6 Installation is the reverse of removal.

Front sidemarker light bulbs

➧ Refer to illustration 18.8

7 On 2006 through 2009 models, raise the vehicle, then remove the bulb access cover screw and cover in the fender splash shield (see illustration 14.2).

Bulb removal

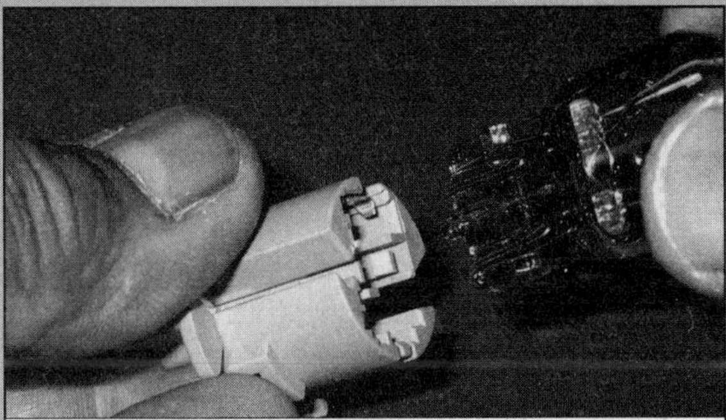

To remove many modern exterior bulbs from their holders, simply pull them out

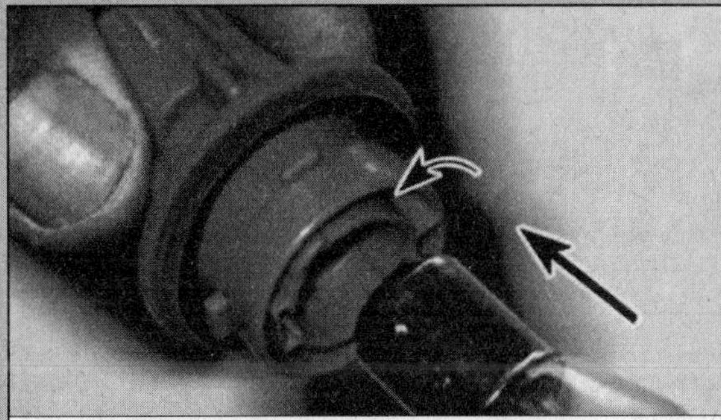

On bulbs with a cylindrical base ("bayonet" bulbs), the socket is spring-loaded; a pair of small posts on the side of the base hold the bulb in place against spring pressure. To remove this type of bulb, push it into the holder, rotate it 1/4-turn counterclockwise, then pull it out

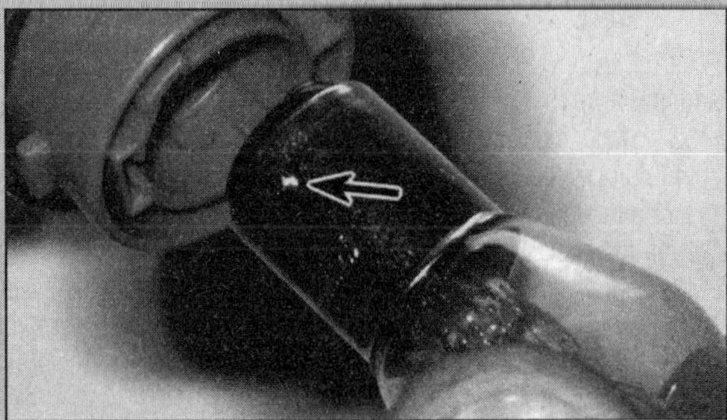

If a bayonet bulb has dual filaments, the posts are staggered, so the bulb can only be installed one way

To remove most overhead interior light bulbs, simply unclip them

18.4 To remove a front turn signal/parking light bulb, rotate the bulb holder counterclockwise and pull it out

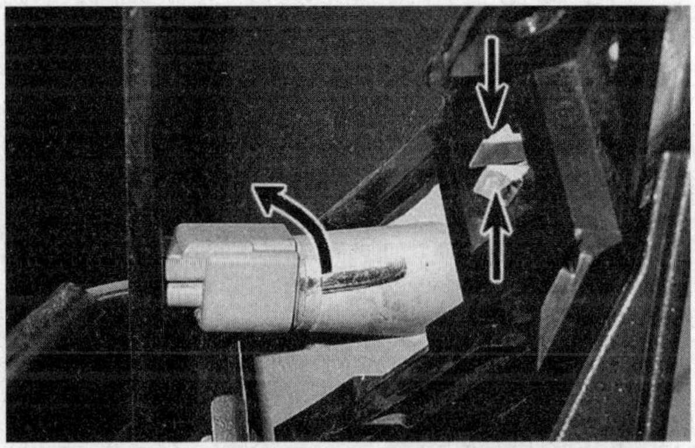

18.8 To release the sidemarker from the bumper cover on 2006 through 2009 models, squeeze these two tabs together, then rotate the bulb holder counterclockwise and pull it out of the sidemarker housing (inner fender splash shield removed for clarity)

8 On 2006 through 2009 models, the horizontal sidemarker housing is secured to the bumper cover by two tabs (see illustration). Squeeze the tabs together to release the sidemarker housing from the bumper cover.

9 On 2010 models, the vertical sidemarker housing is secured to the trailing edge of the bumper cover by a tab at the top and a locator pin and nut at the bottom. Remove the nut, then disengage the locator pin and the tab to remove the sidemarker housing from the bumper cover.

10 Rotate the bulb holder counterclockwise 1/4-turn and pull it out of the housing. It's not necessary to disconnect the electrical connector to replace the bulb.

18.15 To replace a fog lamp bulb, disconnect the electrical connector, then rotate the bulb counterclockwise 1/4-turn and pull it out of the fog lamp housing

18.27 Turn the bulb holder counterclockwise and pull it out of the center high-mount brake light housing (2006 through 2009 models)

11 To remove the bulb, pull it straight out of the bulb holder.
12 Installation is the reverse of removal.

Fog light bulbs

➧ **Refer to illustration 18.15**

⁂ WARNING:

Halogen bulbs are gas-filled and under pressure and might shatter if the surface is scratched or the bulb is dropped. Wear eye protection and handle the bulbs carefully, grasping only the base whenever possible. Don't touch the surface of the bulb with your fingers because the oil from your skin could cause it to overheat and fail prematurely. If you do touch the bulb surface, clean it with rubbing alcohol.

13 Raise the front of the vehicle and place it securely on jackstands.
14 Remove the four fasteners and pull back the front part of the inner fender splash shield below the fog lamp (see *Front fender - removal and installation* in Chapter 11).
15 Disconnect the fog light bulb electrical connector (see illustration).
16 Turn the fog light bulb counterclockwise and remove it from the fog light housing.
17 To install the new fog light bulb, insert it into the fog light housing and turn it clockwise to lock it into place.
18 Installation is otherwise the reverse of removal.

Puddle light bulbs

➡**Note: The puddle lights, which illuminate the ground below the front doors, are located in the outside mirrors.**

19 Using the power mirror switch, angle the mirror glass down as far as it will go, then firmly grasp the upper edge of mirror glass and pull it out and up to disengage the locking tabs from the motor. If the mirror is heated, disconnect the electrical connector.

⁂ WARNING:

Use gloves or a towel to protect your hands in the event that the mirror glass breaks.

20 Release the puddle light housing tab and remove the puddle light housing from the mirror housing.
21 Rotate the puddle light bulb socket (clockwise for the left mirror; counterclockwise for the right mirror) to release it from the housing.
22 Remove the puddle light bulb from its socket and install a new bulb in the socket.
23 To install the bulb socket in the puddle light housing, insert the socket into the housing and rotate it (counterclockwise for the left mirror; clockwise for the right mirror). You will hear an audible click when the socket is fully seated and locked into place.
24 Install the puddle light housing in the mirror. You will hear an audible click when the housing tab snaps into place.
25 If the mirror is heated, connect the electrical connector. To install the mirror glass, position it on the mirror motor and press the upper edge of the mirror glass into the upper mirror motor retainers.

Center high-mounted brake light bulb

Package tray-mounted (2006 through 2009 models)

➧ **Refer to illustration 18.27**

26 From inside the luggage compartment, disconnect the electrical connector.
27 Rotate the bulb holder counterclockwise and pull it out of the high-mounted brake light housing (see illustration).
28 To replace the bulb, pull it straight out of the bulb holder.
29 Installation is the reverse of removal.

Package tray-mounted (2010 models)

30 From inside the luggage compartment, disconnect the electrical connector.
31 Push the high-mounted brake light housing to the rear to disengage the front mounting tabs, then tilt it to the rear and pull it forward to disengage the rear mounting tabs and lift the housing up and out of its mounting hole in the package tray.
32 No further disassembly is possible. The high-mounted brake light LEDs are an integral part of the housing, and not separately serviceable.
33 Installation is the reverse of removal.

Spoiler-mounted (2010 models)

34 Remove the two rubber access covers, then remove the high-mounted brake light housing screws, pull down the housing and

18.44 License plate light lens screws

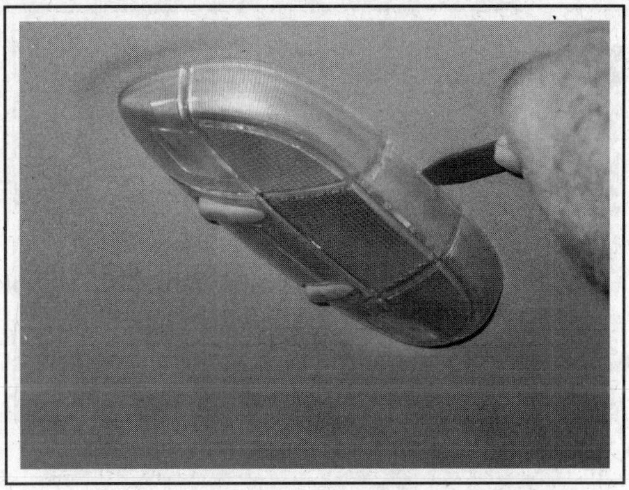

18.47 To remove an overhead light lens, carefully pry it off with a trim removal tool or screwdriver

disconnect the electrical connector. No further disassembly is possible. The light emitting diodes (LEDs) are an integral part of the housing; they're not separately serviceable.

35 Installation is the reverse of removal.

Trunk lid-mounted (2010 models)

36 Remove the four trunk lid trim panel nuts, then remove the trim panel from the trunk lid.

37 Remove the four mounting nuts, then remove the luggage compartment lid molding and disconnect the electrical connectors.

38 Remove the four mounting nuts, then remove the high-mounted brake light bracket.

39 Release the two tabs, remove the high-mounted brake light and disconnect the electrical connector. No further disassembly is possible. The light emitting diodes (LEDs) are an integral part of the housing, and not separately serviceable.

40 Installation is the reverse of removal.

Taillight bulbs

41 Fold back the trunk floor carpeting mat, then pull out and reposition the flexible trunk side trim panel that covers the taillight housing and the wheelhousing.

⁂ CAUTION:

Do not leave the trunk side panel bent or out of shape too long, or it will permanently deform it.

42 To remove a taillight bulb socket, rotate it counterclockwise and pull it out of the taillight housing. To remove the bulb from the socket, pull it straight out.

➡Note: If you're not sure about the location of the bulb you want to replace, see illustration 17.2.

43 Installation is the reverse of removal.

License plate light bulbs

➧ Refer to illustration 18.44

44 Remove the license plate light lens screws (see illustration) and remove the lens and bulb.

45 Remove the bulb from the terminals.

46 Installation is the reverse of removal.

INTERIOR FRONT OR REAR OVERHEAD LIGHT BULBS

➧ Refer to illustration 18.47

47 Carefully pry off the overhead lens (see illustration).

48 Pull the bulb straight out of its socket.

49 Installation is the reverse of removal.

19 Wiper motor - replacement

➧ Refer to illustrations 19.1, 19.3, 19.5, 19.6 and 19.8

1 Remove the wiper arm nuts and mark the relationship of the wiper arms to their shafts (see illustration). Remove both wiper arms.

2 Remove the plastic cowl cover (see Chapter 11).

3 Disconnect the electrical connector from the wiper motor (see illustration).

4 Remove the two wiper motor and link assembly mounting bolts and remove the wiper motor and link assembly.

5 Using a trim removal tool or a screwdriver, carefully separate the linkage from the motor's crank arm (see illustration).

6 Remove the nut that secures the crank arm to the motor shaft (see illustration).

7 Mark the relationship of the crank arm to the motor shaft and remove the crank arm from the shaft.

8 Remove the two motor mounting bolts (see illustration) and remove the motor from its mounting bracket.

9 Installation is the reverse of removal.

19.1 Remove the wiper arm trim cap and the wiper arm nut

19.3 Wiper motor assembly details

1 *Electrical connector*
2 *Wiper motor assembly mounting bolts*

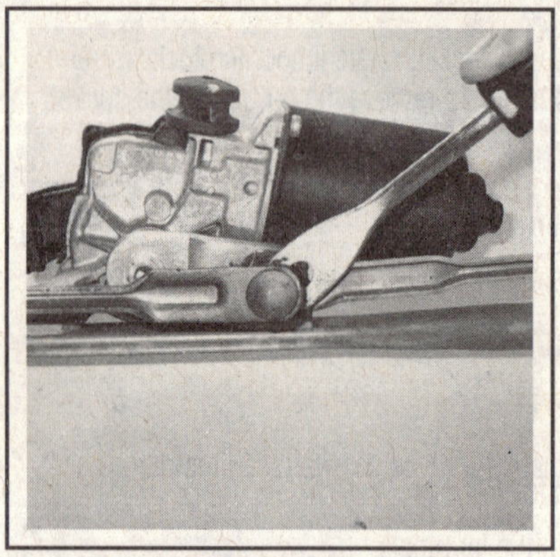

19.5 Separate the linkage from the crank arm with a trim removal tool or screwdriver

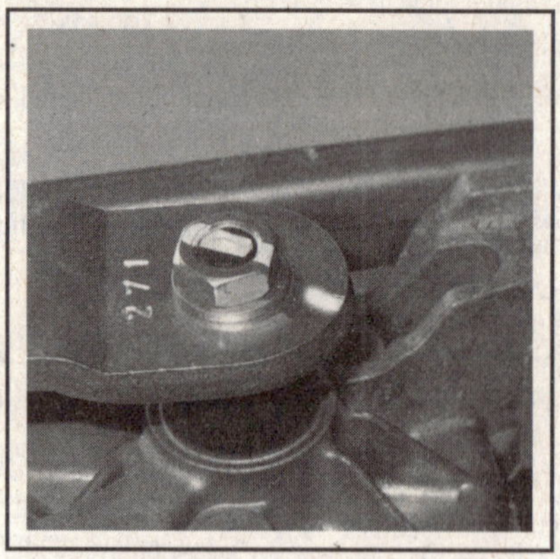

19.6 Remove the nut that secures the crank arm to the motor shaft

19.8 Wiper motor mounting bolts

20 Horn - replacement

Refer to illustration 20.3

Note: The horn is located at the lower right corner of the vehicle, in the void ahead of the right front wheel well.

1 Raise the vehicle and place it securely on jackstands.
2 To access the horn, remove the four right front fender splash shield screws and pull down the splash shield (see "Front fender - removal and installation" in Chapter 11).
3 Disconnect the horn electrical connector (see illustration).
4 Remove the horn mounting bolt, then remove the horn.
5 Installation is the reverse of removal.

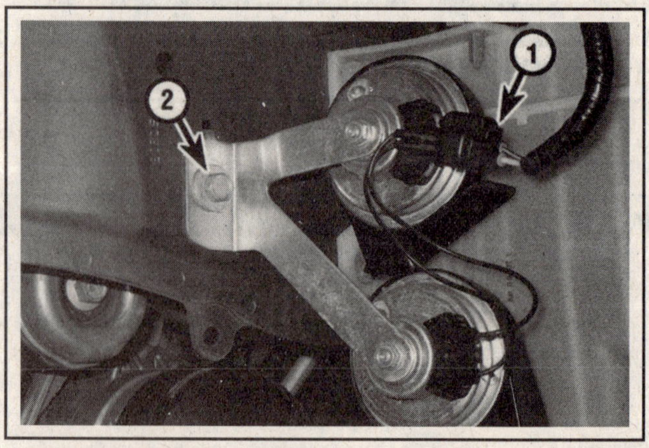

20.3 Horn assembly details

1 *Electrical connector* 2 *Mounting bolt*

21 Daytime Running Lights (DRL) - general information

The Daytime Running Lights (DRL) system used on all models illuminates the low beam headlights at reduced intensity when the engine is running. The only exception is with the engine running and the shift lever in Park. Once the parking brake is released or the shift lever is moved, the lights will remain on as long as the ignition switch is on.

22 Rear window defogger - check and repair

1 The rear window defogger consists of a number of horizontal elements baked onto the glass surface.

2 Small breaks in the element can be repaired without removing the rear window.

CHECK

Refer to illustrations 22.4, 22.5 and 22.7

3 Turn the ignition switch and defogger system switches to the ON position. Using a voltmeter, place the positive probe against the defogger grid positive terminal and the negative probe against the ground terminal. If battery voltage is not indicated, check the fuse, defogger switch and related wiring. If voltage is indicated, but all or part of the defogger doesn't heat, proceed with the following tests.

4 When measuring voltage during the next two tests, wrap a piece of aluminum foil around the tip of the voltmeter positive probe and press the foil against the heating element with your finger (see illustration). Place the negative probe on the defogger grid ground terminal.

5 Check the voltage at the center of each heating element (see illustration). If the voltage is 5 or 6-volts, the element is okay (there is no break). If the voltage is zero, the element is broken between the center of the element and the positive end. If the voltage is 10 to 12-volts, the element is broken between the center of the element and ground. Check each heating element.

6 Connect the negative lead to a good body ground. The reading should stay the same. If it doesn't, the ground connection is bad.

7 To find the break, place the voltmeter negative probe against the defogger ground terminal. Place the voltmeter positive probe with the foil strip against the heating element at the positive terminal end and slide it toward the negative terminal end. The point at which the voltmeter deflects from several volts to zero is the point at which the heating element is broken (see illustration).

REPAIR

Refer to illustration 22.13

8 Repair the break in the element using a repair kit specifically recommended for this purpose, available at most auto parts stores. Included in this kit is plastic conductive epoxy.

9 Prior to repairing a break, turn off the system and allow it to cool off for a few minutes.

22.4 When measuring the voltage at the rear window defogger grid, wrap a piece of aluminum foil around the positive probe of the voltmeter and press the foil against the wire with your finger

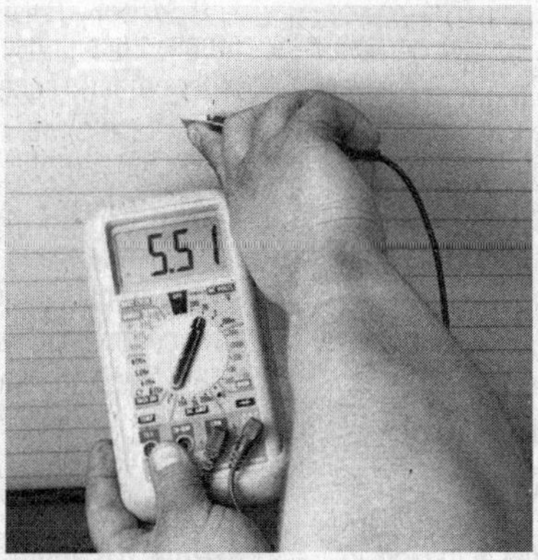

22.5 To determine if a heating element has broken, check the voltage at the center of each element; if the voltage is 5 or 6 volts, the element is unbroken, but if the voltage is 10 or 12 volts, the element is broken between the center and the ground side. If there is no voltage, the element is broken between the center and the positive side

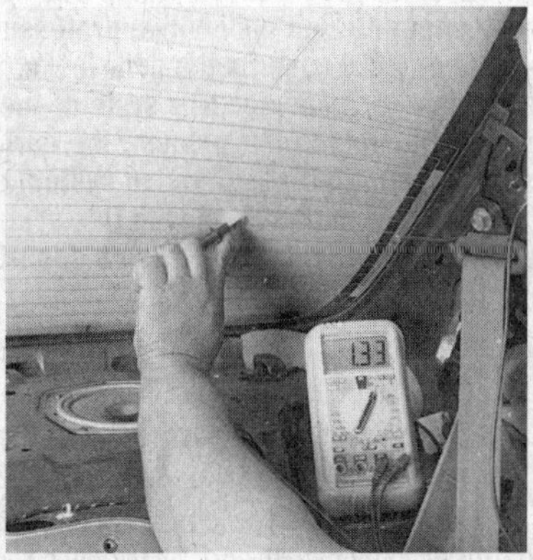

22.7 To find the break, place the voltmeter negative lead against the defogger ground terminal, place the voltmeter positive lead with the foil strip against the heating element at the positive terminal end and slide it toward the negative terminal end. The point at which the voltmeter reading changes abruptly is the point at which the element is broken

10 Lightly buff the element area with fine steel wool, then clean it thoroughly with rubbing alcohol.

11 Use masking tape to mask off the area being repaired.

12 Thoroughly mix the epoxy, following the instructions provided with the repair kit.

13 Apply the epoxy material to the slit in the masking tape, overlapping the undamaged area about 3/4-inch on either end (see illustration).

14 Allow the repair to cure for 24 hours before removing the tape and using the system.

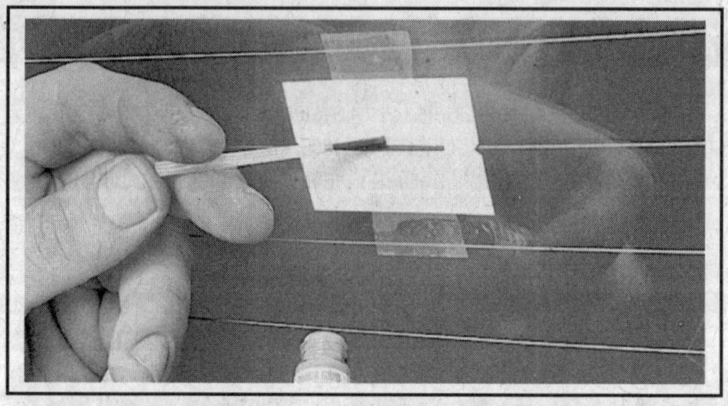

22.13 To use a defogger repair kit, apply masking tape to the inside of the window at the damaged area, then brush on the special conductive coating

23 Cruise control system - description and check

1 The cruise control system maintains vehicle speed with the Powertrain Control Module (PCM), throttle actuator control motor, brake switch, control switches and associated wiring. There is no mechanical connection, such as a vacuum servo or cable. Some features of the system require special testers and diagnostic procedures that are beyond the scope of the home mechanic. Listed below are some general procedures that may be used to locate common problems.

2 Check the fuses (see Section 3).

3 The Brake Pedal Position (BPP) switch (or brake light switch) deactivates the cruise control system. Have an assistant press the brake pedal while you check the brake light operation.

4 If the brake lights do not operate properly, correct the problem and retest the cruise control.

5 Check the wiring between the PCM and throttle actuator motor for opens or shorts and repair as necessary.

6 The cruise control system uses information from the PCM, including the Vehicle Speed Sensor (VSS), which is located in the transmission or transfer case. Refer to Chapter 6 for more information on the VSS.

7 Test drive the vehicle to determine if the cruise control is now working. If it isn't, take it to a dealer service department or other qualified repair shop for further diagnosis.

24 Power window system - description and check

➡Note: These models are equipped with a Smart Junction Box (SJB) (manufacturer terminology), otherwise known as a Body Control Module (BCM). Several systems are linked to this centralized control module, which allows simple and accurate troubleshooting, but only with a professional-grade scan tool. The SJB or BCM governs the door locks, the power windows, the ignition lock and security system, the interior lights, the Daytime Running Lights system, the horn, the windshield wipers, the heating/air conditioning system and the power mirrors. In the event of malfunction with this system, have the vehicle diagnosed by a dealership service department or other qualified automotive repair facility.

1 The power window system operates electric motors, mounted in the doors, which lower and raise the windows. The system consists of the control switches, the motors, regulators, glass mechanisms, the Smart Junction Box (SJB) and associated wiring.

2 The power windows can be lowered and raised from the master control switch by the driver or by remote switches located at the individual windows. Each window has a separate motor that is reversible. The position of the control switch determines the polarity and therefore the direction of operation.

3 The circuit is protected by a fuse and a circuit breaker. Each motor is also equipped with an internal circuit breaker; this prevents one stuck window from disabling the whole system.

4 The power window system will only operate when the ignition switch is ON, and for a period of time after the ignition key has been turned Off (unless one of the doors is opened). In addition, many models have a window lockout switch at the master control switch that, when activated, disables the switches at the rear windows and, sometimes, the switch at the passenger's window also. Always check these items before troubleshooting a window problem.

5 These procedures are general in nature, so if you can't find the problem using them, take the vehicle to a dealer service department or other properly equipped repair facility.

6 If the power windows won't operate, always check the fuse and circuit breaker first.

7 If only the rear windows are inoperative, or if the windows only operate from the master control switch, check the rear window lockout switch for continuity in the unlocked position. Replace it if it doesn't have continuity.

8 Check the wiring between the switches and fuse panel for continuity. Repair the wiring, if necessary.

9 If only one window is inoperative from the master control switch, try the other control switch at the window.

➡Note: This doesn't apply to the driver's door window.

10 If the same window works from one switch, but not the other, check the switch for continuity.

11 If the switch tests OK, check for a short or open in the circuit between the affected switch and the window motor.

12 If one window is inoperative from both switches, remove the switch panel from the affected door. Check for voltage at the switch and at the motor (refer to Chapter 11 for door panel removal) while the switch is operated.

while checking for binding and damage. Also check for binding and damage to the regulator. If the regulator is not damaged and the window moves up and down smoothly, replace the motor. If there's binding or damage, lubricate, repair or replace parts, as necessary.

14 If voltage isn't reaching the motor, check the wiring in the circuit for continuity between the switches and the body control module, and between the body control module and the motors. You'll need to consult the wiring diagram at the end of this Chapter. If the circuit is equipped with a relay, check that the relay is grounded properly and receiving voltage.

15 Test the windows after you are done to confirm proper repairs.

25 Power door lock and keyless entry system - description and check

➡Note: These models are equipped with a Smart Junction Box (SJB) (manufacturer terminology), otherwise known as a Body Control Module (BCM). Several systems are linked to this centralized control module, which allows simple and accurate troubleshooting, but only with a professional-grade scan tool. The SJB or BCM governs the door locks, the power windows, the ignition lock and security system, the interior lights, the Daytime Running Lights system, the horn, the windshield wipers, the heating/air conditioning system and the power mirrors. In the event of malfunction with this system, have the vehicle diagnosed by a dealership service department or other qualified automotive repair facility.

1 The power door lock system operates the door lock actuators mounted in each door. The system consists of the switches, actuators, Smart Junction Box (SJB) and associated wiring. Diagnosis can usually be limited to simple checks of the wiring connections and actuators for minor faults that can be easily repaired.

2 Power door lock systems are operated by bi-directional solenoids located in the doors. The lock switches have two operating positions: Lock and Unlock. These switches send a signal to the SJB, which in turn sends a signal to the door lock solenoids.

3 If you are unable to locate the trouble using the following general steps, consult your dealer service department.

4 Always check the circuit protection first. Some vehicles use a combination of circuit breakers and fuses. Refer to the wiring diagrams at the end of this Chapter.

5 Check for voltage at the switches. If no voltage is present, check the wiring between the fuse panel and the switches for shorts and opens.

6 If voltage is present, test the switch for continuity. Replace it if there's not continuity in both switch positions. To remove the switch, use a flat-bladed trim tool to pry out the door/window switch assembly (see Chapter 11).

7 If the switch has continuity, check the wiring between the switch and door lock solenoid.

8 If all but one lock solenoids operate, remove the trim panel from the affected door (see Chapter 11) and check for voltage at the solenoid while the lock switch is operated. One of the wires should have voltage in the Lock position; the other should have voltage in the Unlock position.

9 If the inoperative solenoid is receiving voltage, replace the solenoid.

10 If the inoperative solenoid isn't receiving voltage, check for an open or short in the wire between the lock solenoid and the relay.

11 On the models covered by this manual, power door lock system communication goes through the Smart Junction Box. If the above tests do not pinpoint a problem, take the vehicle to a dealer or qualified shop with the proper scan tool to retrieve trouble codes from the SJB.

KEYLESS ENTRY SYSTEM

12 The keyless entry system consists of a remote control transmitter that sends a coded infrared signal to a receiver, which then operates the door lock system.

13 Replace the battery when the transmitter doesn't operate the locks at a distance of ten feet. Normal range should be about 30 feet.

KEY REMOTE CONTROL BATTERY REPLACEMENT

➧ Refer to illustrations 25.14 and 25.15

14 Use a coin to carefully separate the case halves (see illustration).
15 Replace the battery (see illustration).
16 Snap the case halves together.

TRANSMITTER PROGRAMMING

17 Programming replacement transmitters requires the use of a specialized scan tool. Take the vehicle and the transmitter(s) to a dealer service department or other qualified repair shop equipped with the necessary tool to have the transmitter(s) programmed to the vehicle.

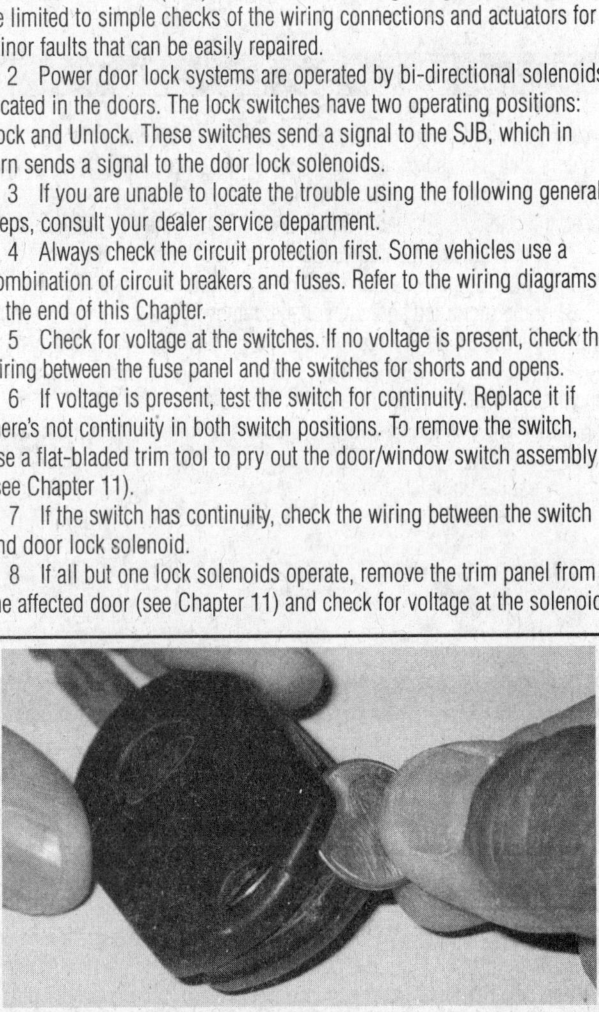

25.14 Using a coin, carefully pry the halves of the transmitter apart

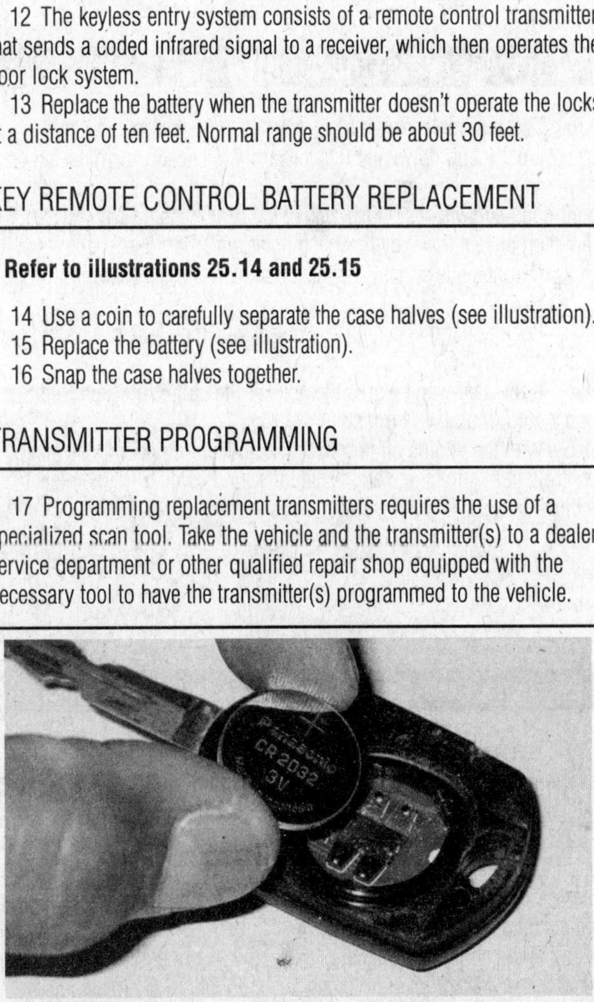

25.15 Carefully pry out the old battery

26 Electric side view mirrors - description

➡Note: These models are equipped with a Smart Junction Box (SJB) (manufacturer terminology), otherwise known as a Body Control Module (BCM). Several systems are linked to this centralized control module, which allows simple and accurate troubleshooting, but only with a professional-grade scan tool. The SJB or BCM governs the door locks, the power windows, the ignition lock and security system, the interior lights, the Daytime Running Lights system, the horn, the windshield wipers, the heating/air conditioning system and the power mirrors. In the event of malfunction with this system, have the vehicle diagnosed by a dealership service department or other qualified automotive repair facility.

1 The electric rear view mirrors use two motors to move the glass; one for up and down adjustments and one for left-right adjustments.

2 The control switch has a selector portion which sends voltage to the left or right side mirror. With the ignition in the ACC position and the engine OFF, roll down the windows and operate the mirror control switch through all functions (left-right and up-down) for both the left and right side mirrors.

3 Listen carefully for the sound of the electric motors running in the mirrors.

4 If the motors can be heard but the mirror glass doesn't move, there's probably a problem with the drive mechanism inside the mirror. Power mirrors have no user-serviceable parts inside - a defective mirror must be replaced as a unit (see Chapter 11).

5 If the mirrors don't operate and no sound comes from the mirrors, check the fuses (see Section 3).

6 If the fuses are OK, remove the mirror control switch. Have the switch continuity checked by a dealer service department or other qualified shop.

7 Check the ground connections.

8 If the mirror still doesn't work, remove the mirror and check the wires at the mirror for voltage.

9 If there's not voltage in each switch position, check the circuit between the mirror and control switch for opens and shorts.

10 If there's voltage, remove the mirror and test it off the vehicle with jumper wires. Replace the mirror if it fails this test.

27 Power seats - description

1 These models feature a six-way seat that goes forward and backward, up and down and tilts forward and backward. The seats are powered by three reversible motors, mounted in one housing, that are controlled by switches on the side of the seat. Each switch changes the direction of seat travel by reversing polarity to the drive motor.

2 Diagnosis is usually a simple matter, using the following procedures.

3 Look under the seat for any object which may be preventing the seat from moving.

4 If the seat won't work at all, check the circuit breaker. See Section 4 for circuit breaker testing.

5 With the engine off to reduce the noise level, operate the seat controls in all directions and listen for sound coming from the seat motors.

6 If the motors make noise or don't work, check for voltage at the motors while an assistant operates the switch. With the door open, try the seat switch again. If the dome light dims while trying to operate the seat, this indicates something may be jammed in the seat tracks.

7 If the motor is getting voltage but doesn't run, test it off the vehicle with jumper wires. If it still doesn't work, replace it.

8 If the motor isn't getting voltage, remove the switch and check for voltage. If there's no voltage to the switch, check the wiring between the fuse block and the switch. If there's battery voltage at the switch, check the other terminals for voltage while moving the switch around. If the switch is OK, check for a short or open in the wiring between the switch and motor.

9 Test the completed repairs.

28 Data Link Communication system - description

1 The vehicles covered by this manual have a complex electrical system, encompassing many power accessories, and a number of separate electronic modules.

2 The Powertrain Control Module (PCM) is mainly responsible for engine and transaxle control, but also communicates with other modules around the vehicle through a Data Link Communication system, which sends serial port data very quickly between the various modules. Many of the computer functions involved in the operation of body systems are routed through the Smart Junction Box (SJB) (manufacturer terminology), otherwise known as a Body Control Module (BCM), which communicates with the PCM.

3 Among the modules in the Data Link system besides the BCM and PCM are the Sensing Diagnostic Module (airbag system), the Electronic Brake Control Module and the instrument panel cluster. The BCM further communicates with various body subsystems.

4 All of the modules in the vehicle have associated trouble codes. When other troubleshooting procedures fail to pinpoint the problem, check the wiring diagrams at the end of this Chapter to see if the BCM or PCM are involved in the circuit. If so, take your vehicle to a dealer service department or other qualified repair shop with the proper diagnostic tools to extract the trouble codes.

29 Airbag system - general information

All models are equipped with a Supplemental Restraint System (SRS), more commonly known as the airbag system. The airbag system is designed to protect the driver and the front seat passenger from serious injury in the event of a head-on or frontal collision. It consists of the impact sensors, a driver's airbag module in the center of the steering wheel, a passenger's airbag module in the glove box area of the instrument panel and a sensing/diagnostic module mounted under the center console. Some models are also equipped with side-curtain airbags and seat belt pre-tensioners.

AIRBAG MODULES

Driver's airbag

The airbag inflator module contains a housing incorporating the cushion (airbag) and inflator unit, mounted in the center of the steering wheel. The inflator assembly is mounted on the back of the housing over a hole through which gas is expelled, inflating the bag almost instantaneously when an electrical signal is sent from the system. A spiral cable (or clockspring) assembly on the steering column under the steering wheel carries this signal to the module. This clockspring can transmit an electrical signal regardless of steering wheel position.

Passenger's airbag

The airbag is mounted inside the right side of the instrument panel, in the area above the glove box. It's similar in design to the driver's airbag, except that it's larger than the steering wheel unit. The trim cover (on the side of the instrument panel that faces toward the passenger) is textured and colored to match the instrument panel and has a molded seam that splits open when the bag inflates.

Side curtain airbags

In addition to the side-impact airbags, extra side-impact protection is also provided by side-curtain airbags on some models. These are long airbags that, in the event of a side impact, come out of the headliner at each side of the car and come down between the side windows and the seats. They are designed to protect the heads of both front seat and rear seat passengers.

SENSING AND DIAGNOSTIC MODULE

The sensing and diagnostic module supplies the current to the airbag system in the event of a collision, even if battery power is cut off. It checks this system every time the vehicle is started, causing the "AIR BAG" light to go on then off, if the system is operating properly. If there is a fault in the system, the light will go on and stay on, flash, or the dash will make a beeping sound. If this happens, the vehicle should be taken to your dealer immediately for service. This module is mounted under the center console. There is also a roll-over sensor located directly behind it on later models.

SEAT BELT PRE-TENSIONERS

Some models are equipped with pyrotechnic (explosive) units in the front seat belt retracting mechanisms. During an impact that would trigger the airbag system, the airbag control unit also triggers the seat belt retractors. When the pyrotechnic charges go off, they accelerate the retractors to instantly take up any slack in the seat belt system to more fully prepare the driver and front seat passenger for impact.

The airbag system should be disabled any time work is done to or around the seats.

⁂ WARNING:

Never strike the pillars or floorpan with a hammer or use an impact-driver tool in these areas unless the system is disabled.

DISARMING THE SYSTEM AND OTHER PRECAUTIONS

➧ Refer to illustration 29.8

⁂ WARNING:

Failure to follow these precautions could result in accidental deployment of the airbag and personal injury.

Whenever working in the vicinity of the steering wheel, steering column or any of the other SRS system components, the system must be disarmed.

To disarm the airbag system:

a) *Point the wheels straight ahead and turn the key to the Lock position.*
b) *Remove the Restraints Control Module (RCM) fuse from the under-dash fuse panel (see illustration). On 2009 and earlier models, it's fuse no. 25; on 2010 models, it's fuse no. 32.*
c) *Turn the ignition key to the On position and look at the AIR BAG light on the instrument panel for at least 30 seconds. If you removed the correct fuse, the light will remain lit continuously (not flash). If the light doesn't remain lit continuously, remove the proper fuse.*
d) *Turn the ignition key to the Off position.*
e) *Disconnect the cable from the negative battery terminal (see Chapter 5).*
f) *Wait at least two minutes for the back-up power supply to be depleted.*

29.8 The RCM fuse is fuse no. 25 in the under-dash fuse box on 2009 and earlier models (shown). On 2010 models, it's fuse no. 32 (be sure to refer to the fuse box cover)

To re-arm the airbag system:

a) *Turn the ignition key to the On position, then reinstall the RCM fuse.*
b) *Make sure there is nobody inside the vehicle and that there are no objects near any of the airbag modules, then reconnect the cable to the negative terminal of the battery.*
c) *Turn the ignition switch to the Off position, wait ten seconds, then turn it to the On position. The AIR BAG light on the instrument panel should come on continuously for about six seconds, then turn off.*

➡Note: The light might take up to 30 seconds to come on after the key is turned to the On position (during this time the Restraints Control Module is performing a self-check of the system). If the light fails to come on, or if it flashes, or if a chime sounds in patterns of five sets of five beeps, have the vehicle diagnosed by a dealer service department or other qualified repair shop.

Whenever handling an airbag module:

Always keep the airbag opening (the trim side) pointed away from your body. Never place the airbag module on a bench or other surface with the airbag opening facing the surface. Always place the airbag module in a safe location with the airbag opening facing up.

Never measure the resistance of any SRS component. An ohmmeter has a built-in battery supply that could accidentally deploy the airbag.

Never use electrical welding equipment on a vehicle equipped with an airbag without first disconnecting the electrical connector for each airbag.

Never dispose of a live airbag module. Return it to a dealer service department or other qualified repair shop for safe deployment and disposal.

COMPONENT REMOVAL AND INSTALLATION

Driver's side airbag module and spiral cable

Refer to Chapter 10, *Steering wheel - removal and installation*, for the driver's side airbag module and clockspring removal and installation procedures.

Passenger's airbag module and other airbag modules

Even if you ever have to remove the instrument panel, it's not necessary to remove the passenger airbag module to do so; it can simply remain installed in the instrument panel. We don't recommend removing any of the other airbag modules either. These jobs are best left to a professional.

30 Wiring diagrams - general information

Since it isn't possible to include all wiring diagrams for every year and model covered by this manual, the following diagrams are those that are typical and most commonly needed.

Prior to troubleshooting any circuits, check the fuse and circuit breakers (if equipped) to make sure they're in good condition. Make sure the battery is properly charged and check the cable connections (see Chapter 1).

When checking a circuit, make sure that all connectors are clean, with no broken or loose terminals. When disconnecting a connector, do not pull on the wiring; pull only on the connector.

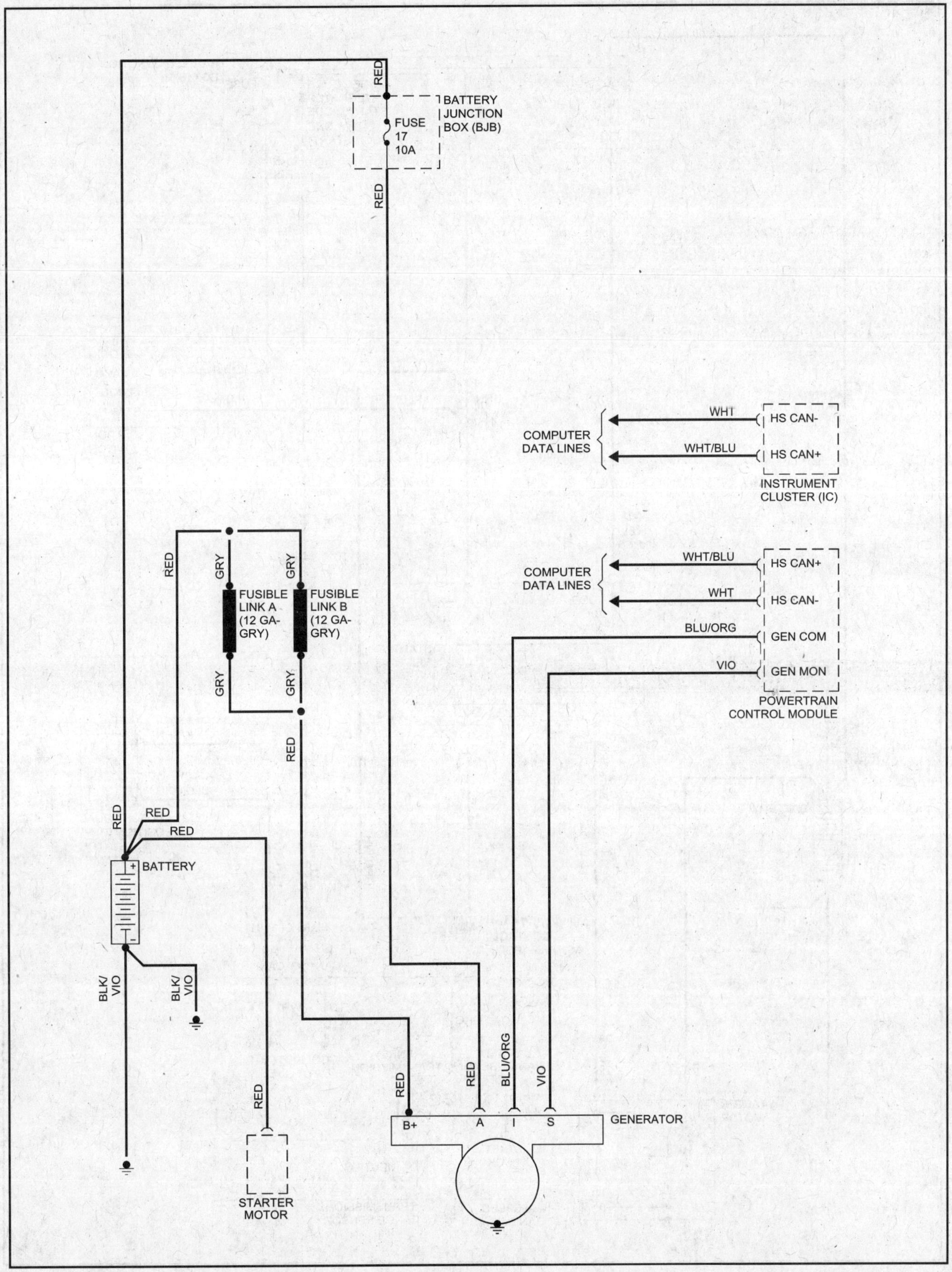

Charging system - 2006 through 2009 models

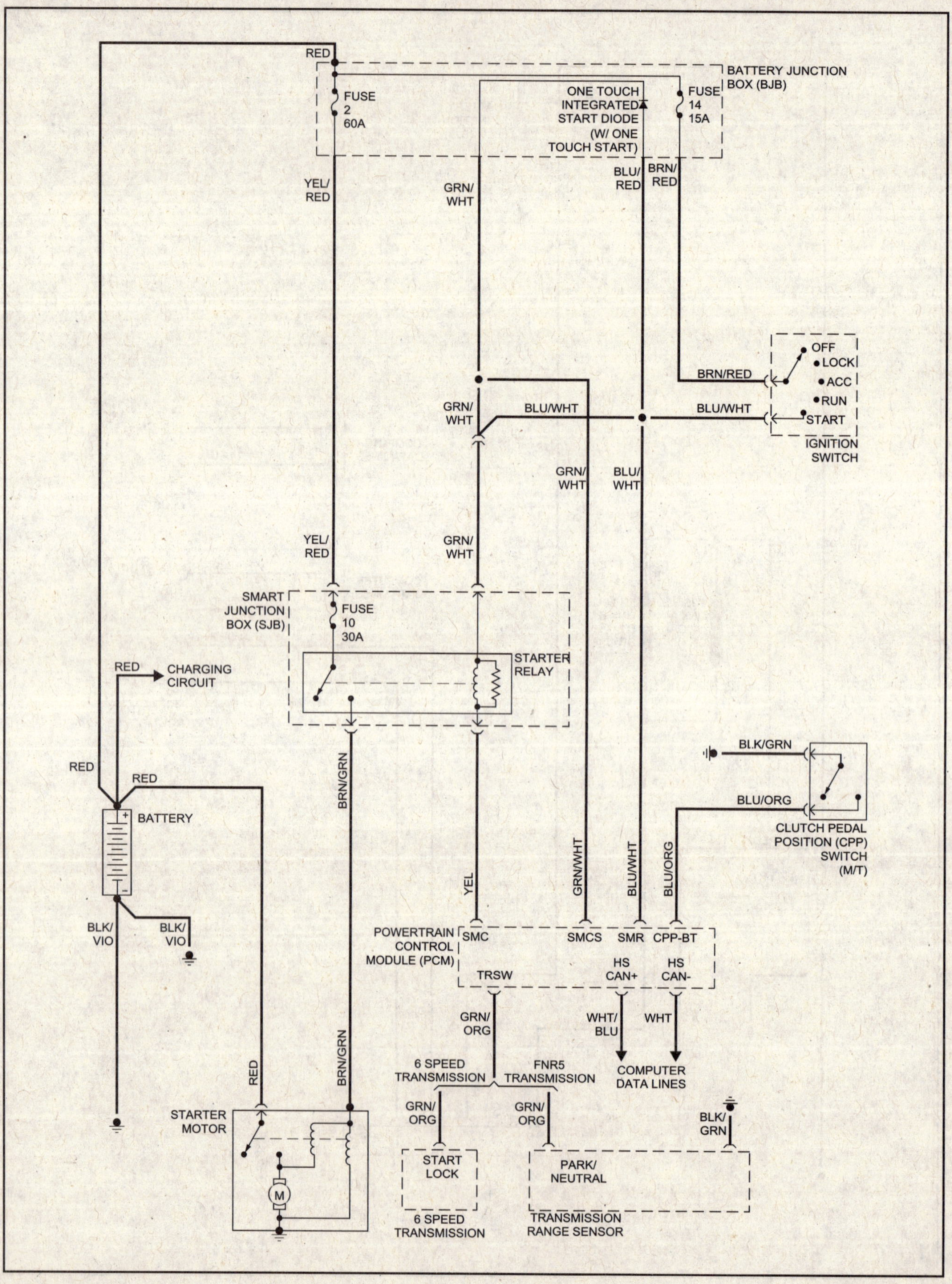

Starting system - 2006 through 2009 models

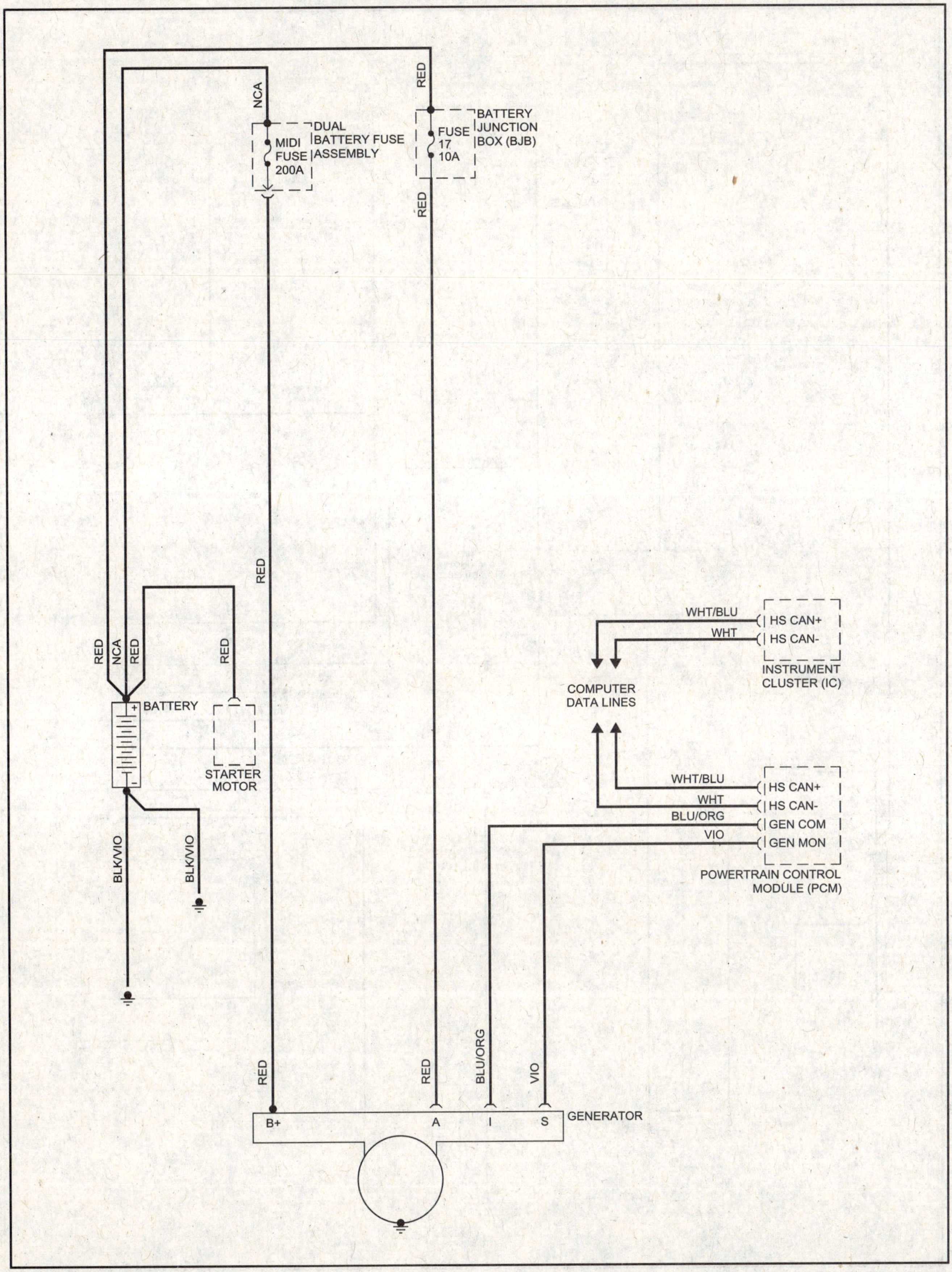

Charging system - 2010 models

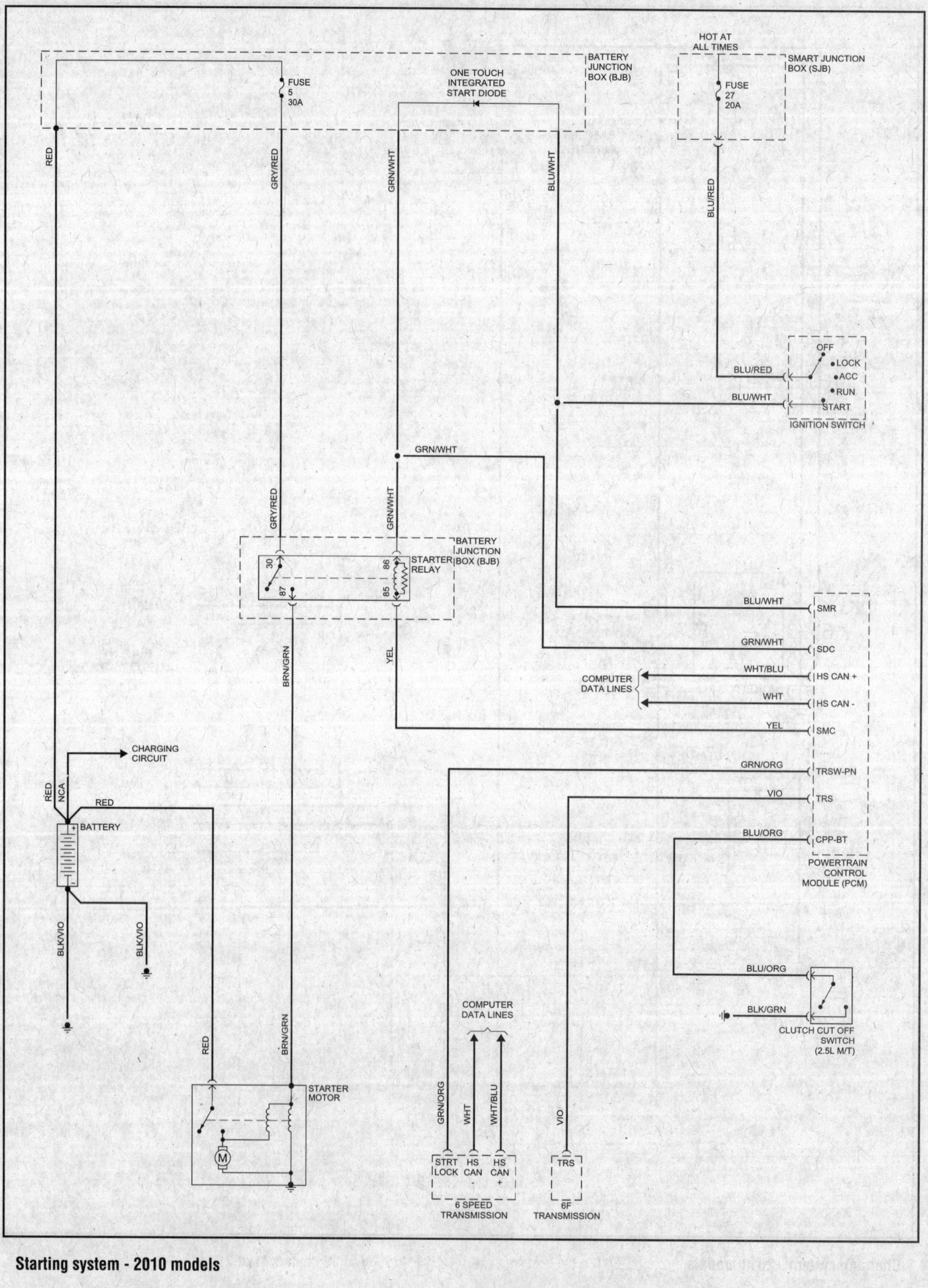

Starting system - 2010 models

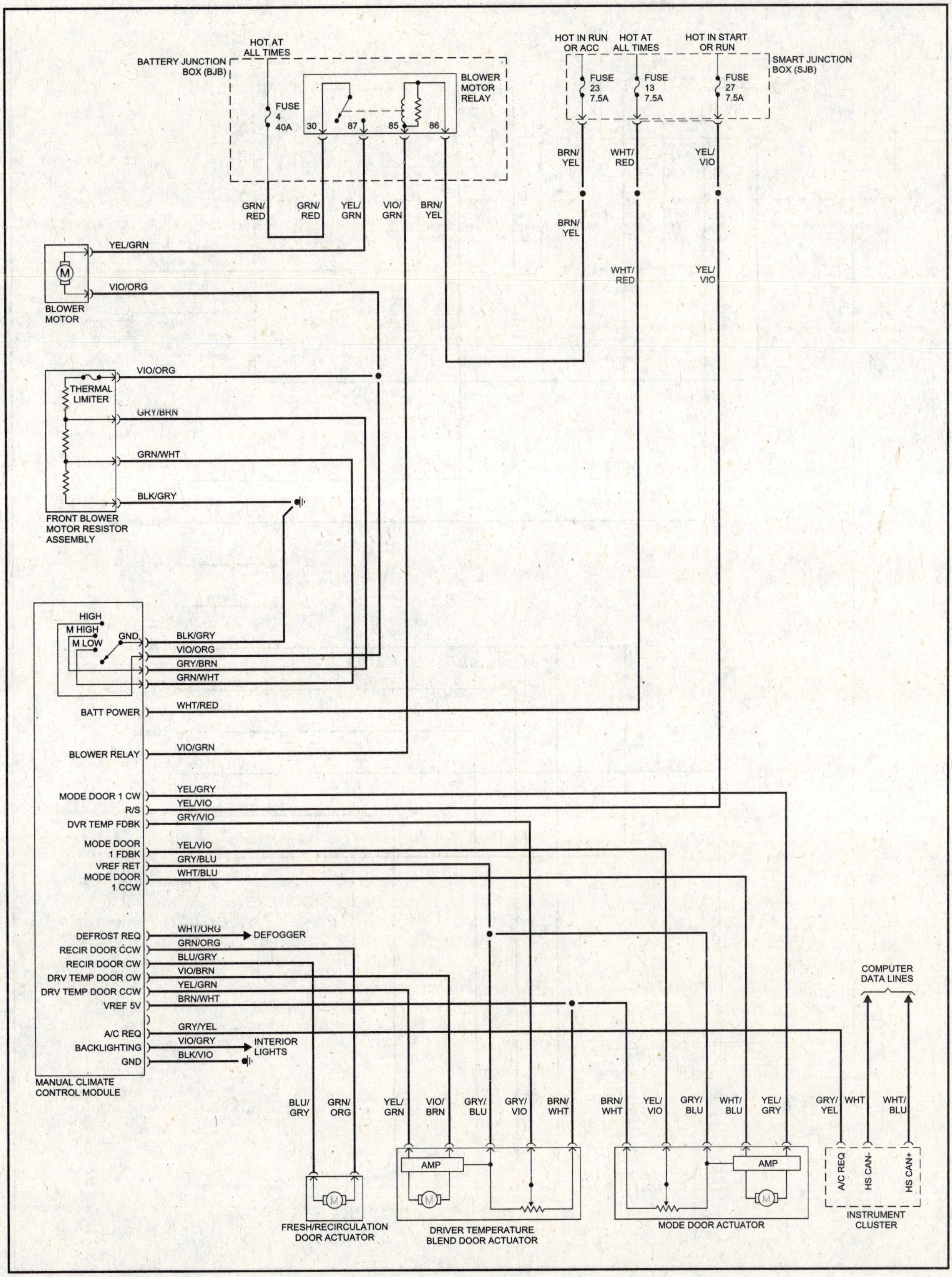

Air conditioning, heating and engine cooling fan system (manual) - 2006 through 2009 models (1 of 2)

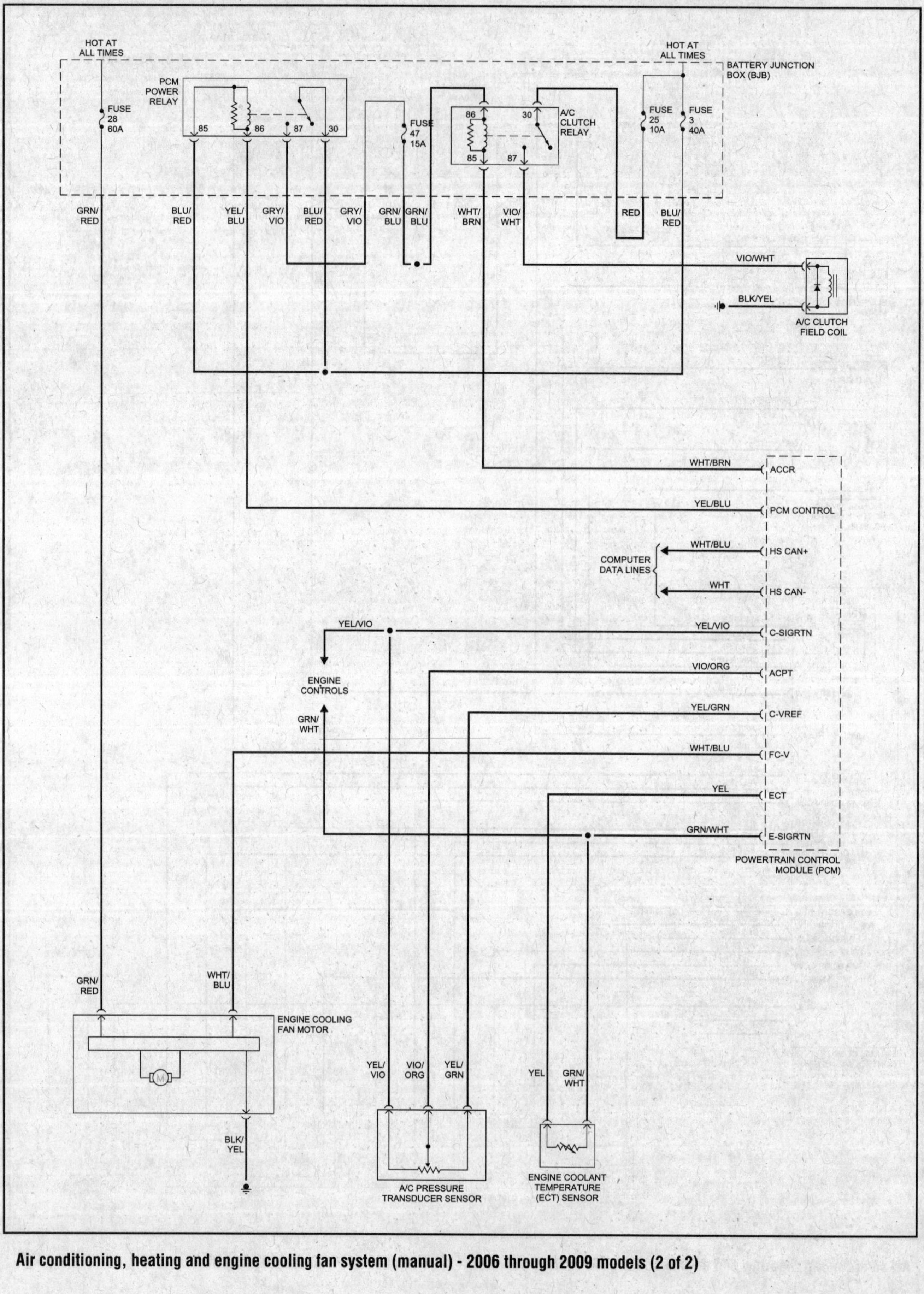

Air conditioning, heating and engine cooling fan system (manual) - 2006 through 2009 models (2 of 2)

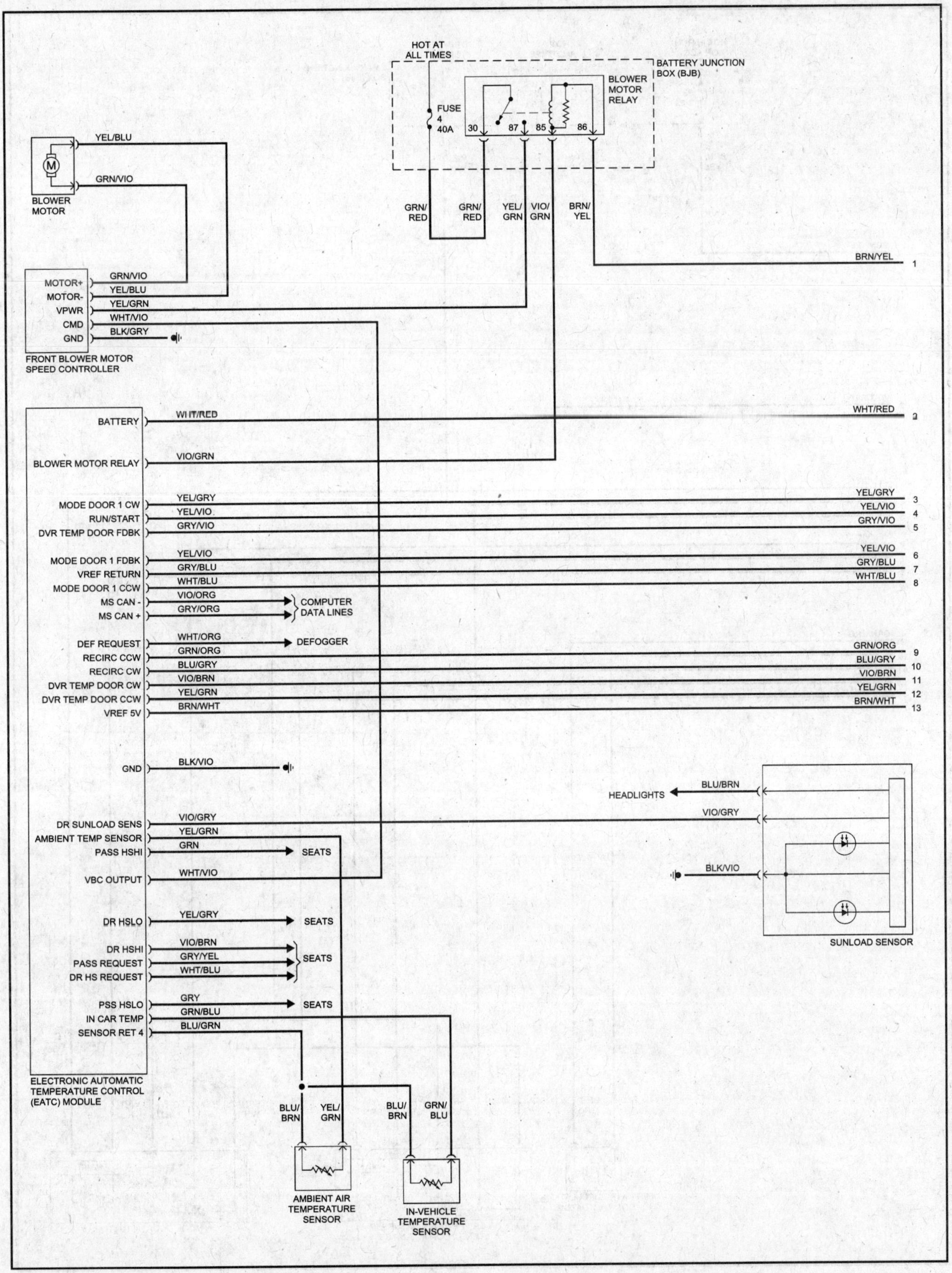

Air conditioning, heating and engine cooling fan system (automatic) - 2006 through 2009 models (1 of 3)

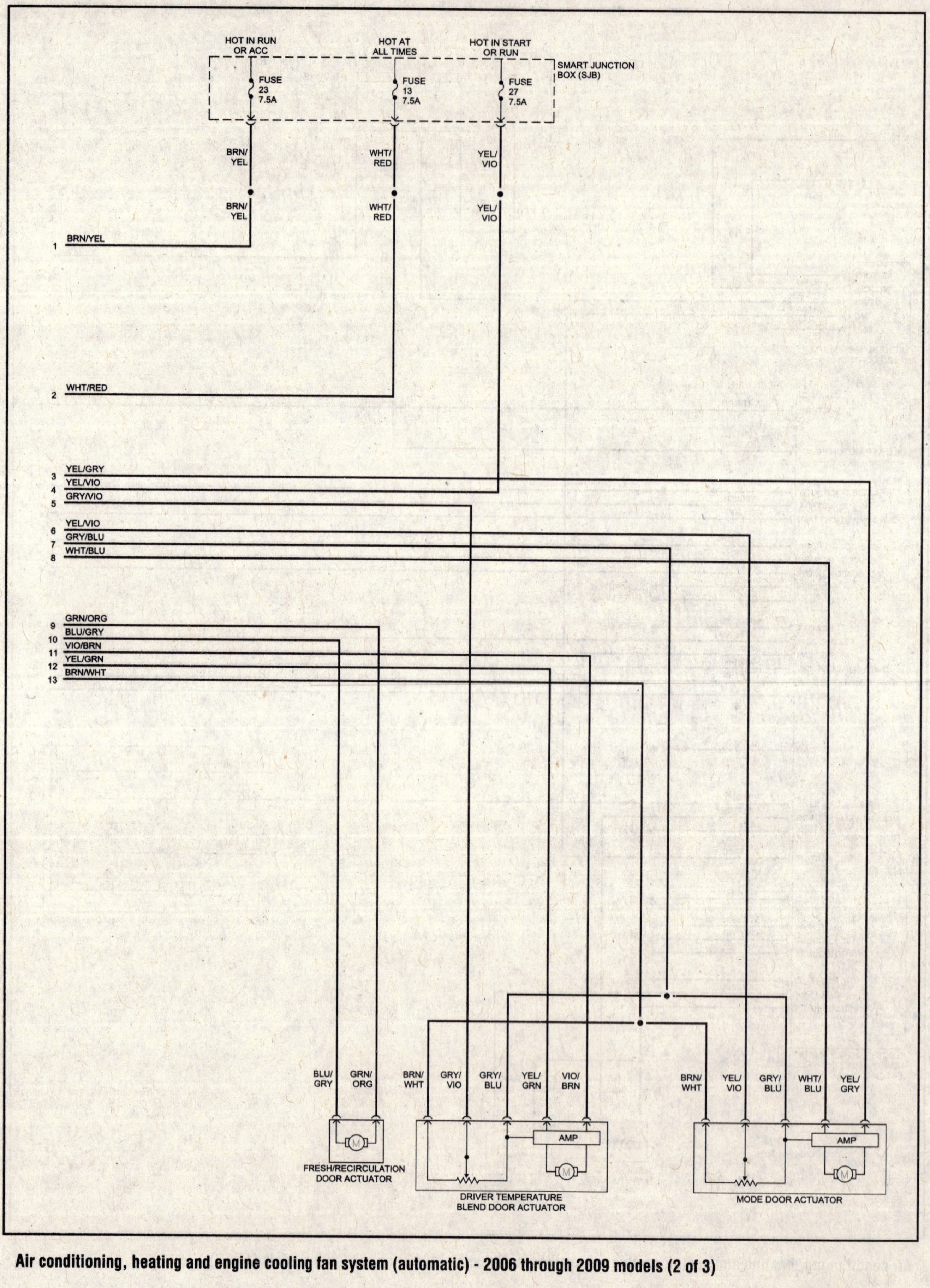

Air conditioning, heating and engine cooling fan system (automatic) - 2006 through 2009 models (2 of 3)

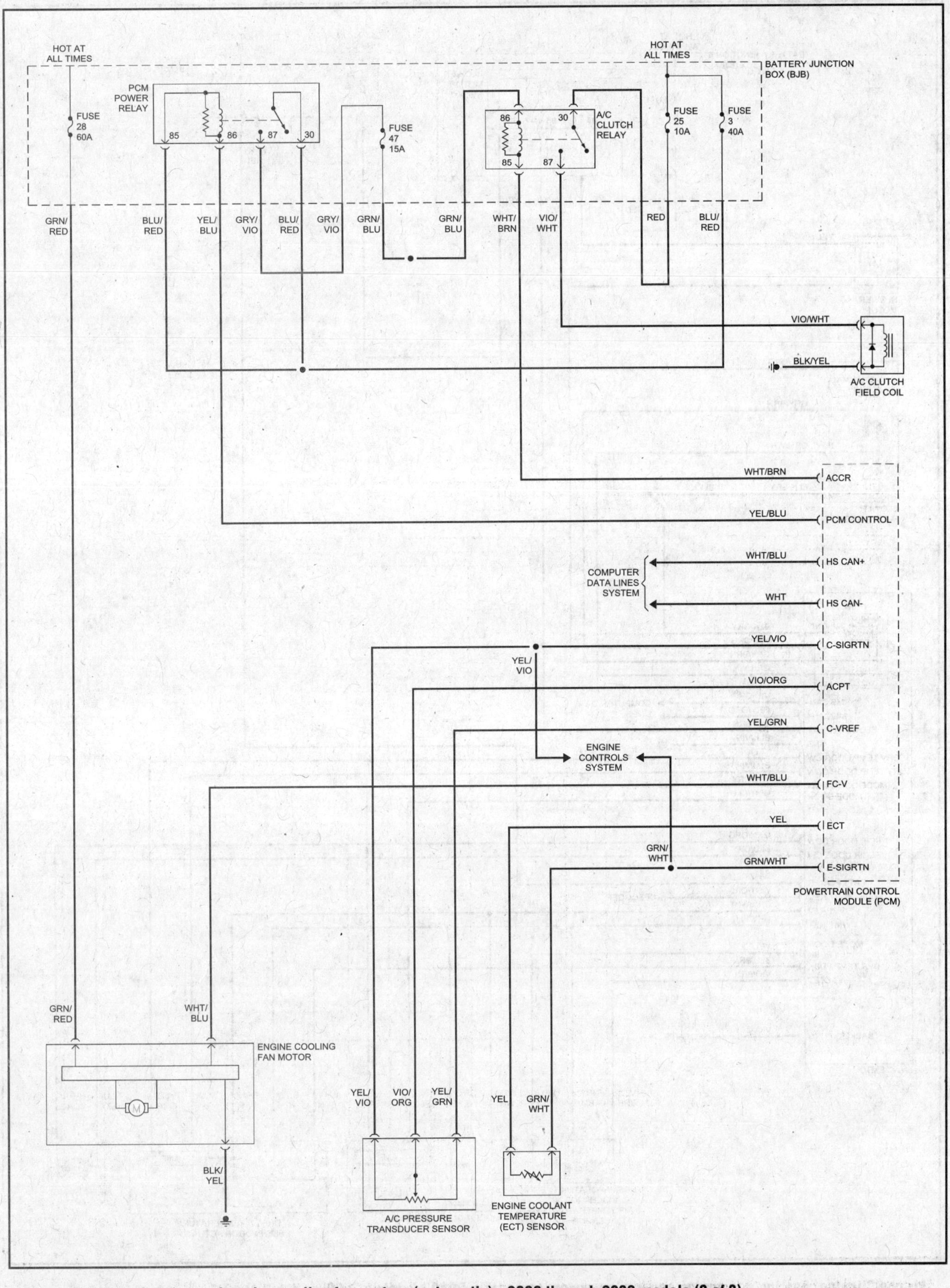

Air conditioning, heating and engine cooling fan system (automatic) - 2006 through 2009 models (3 of 3)

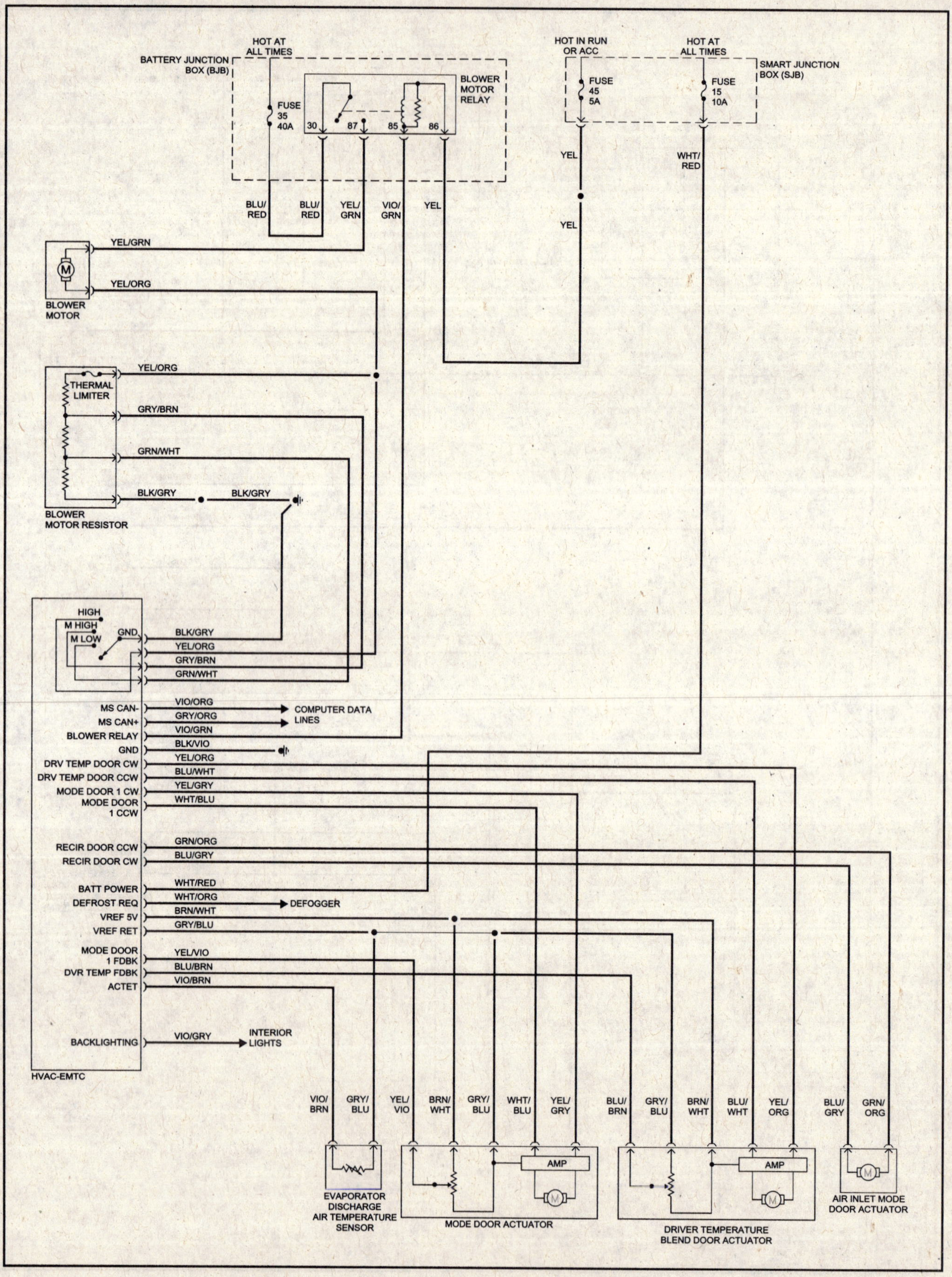

Air conditioning, heating and engine cooling fan system (manual) - 2010 models (1 of 2)

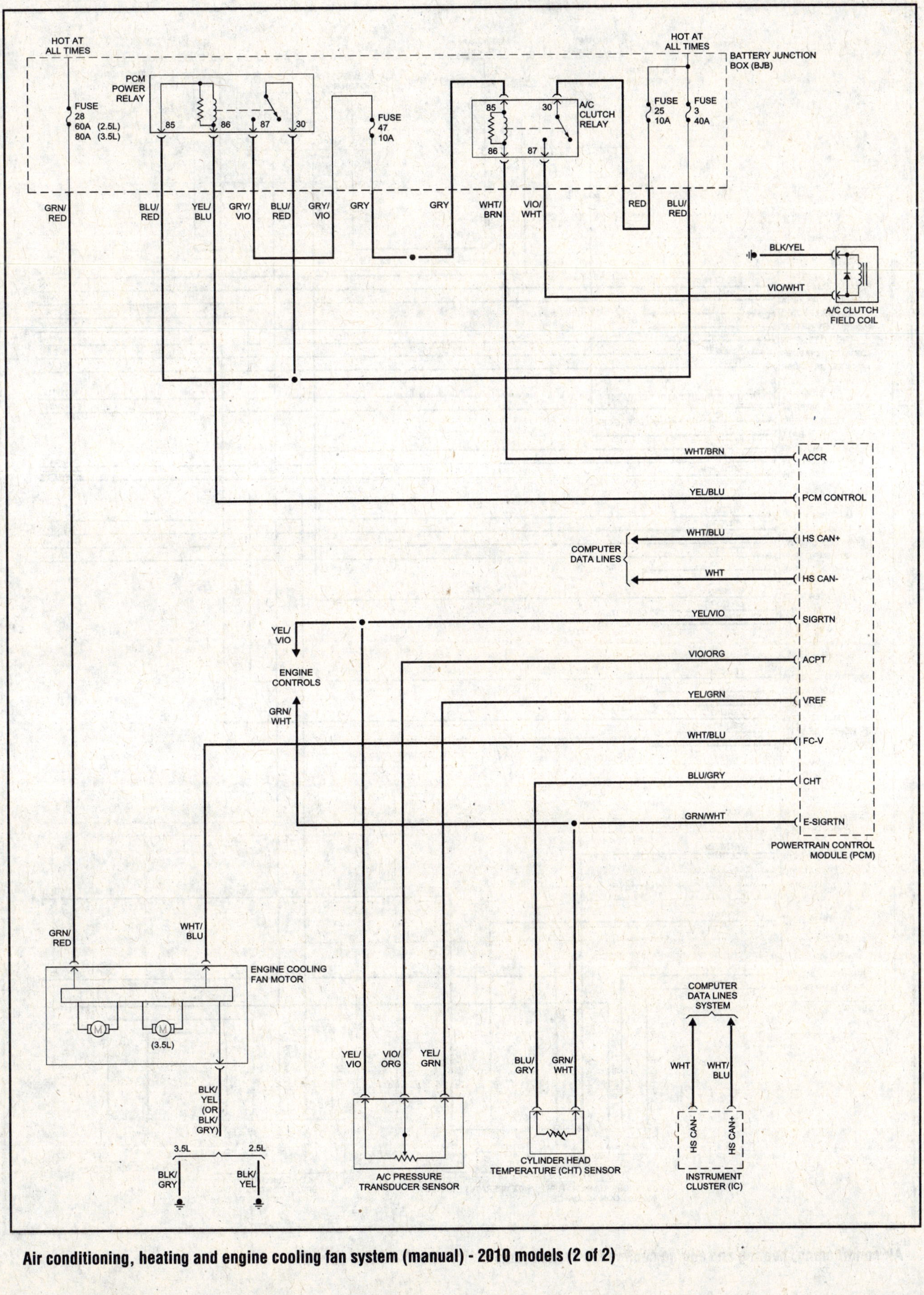

Air conditioning, heating and engine cooling fan system (manual) - 2010 models (2 of 2)

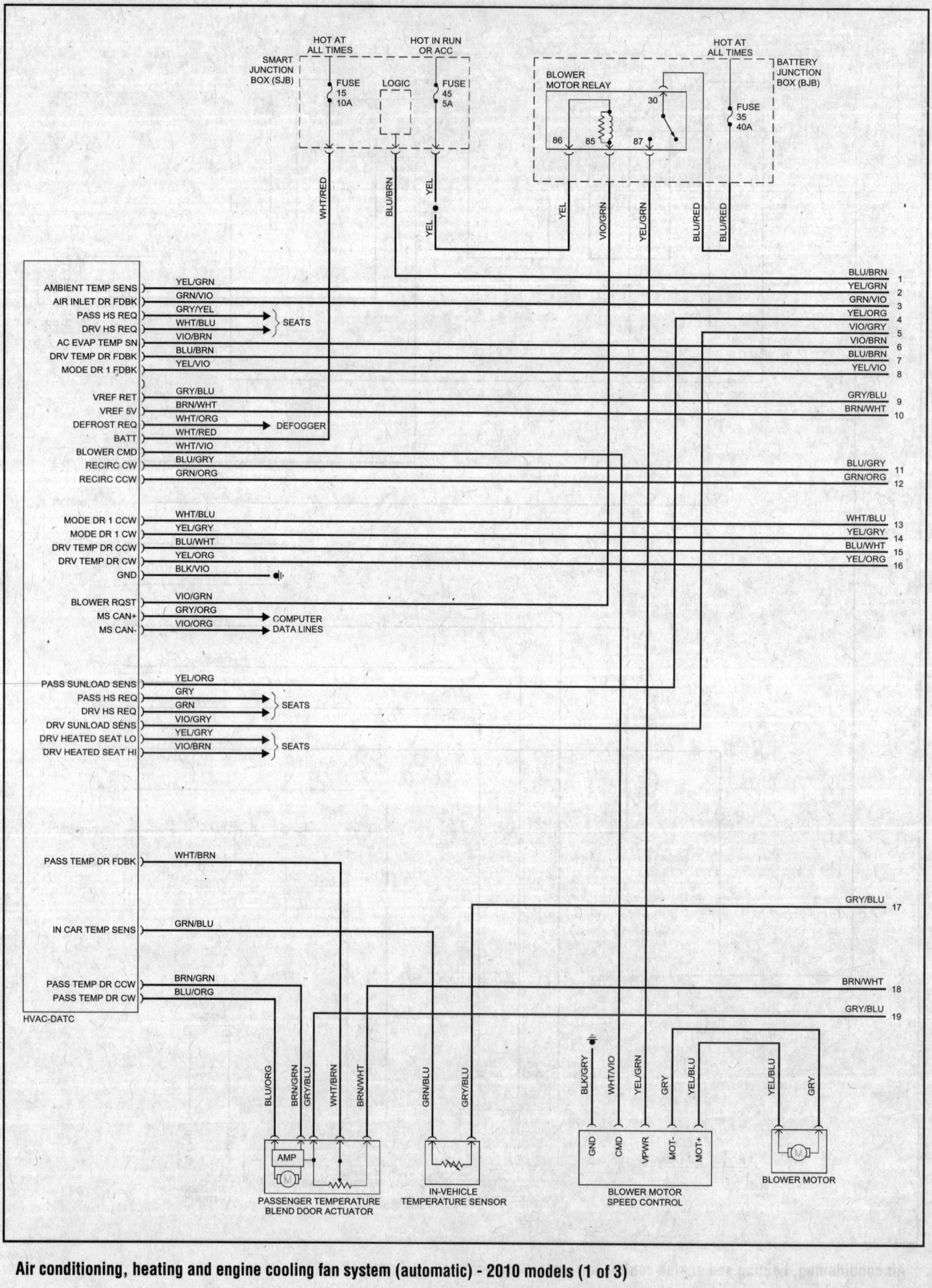

Air conditioning, heating and engine cooling fan system (automatic) - 2010 models (1 of 3)

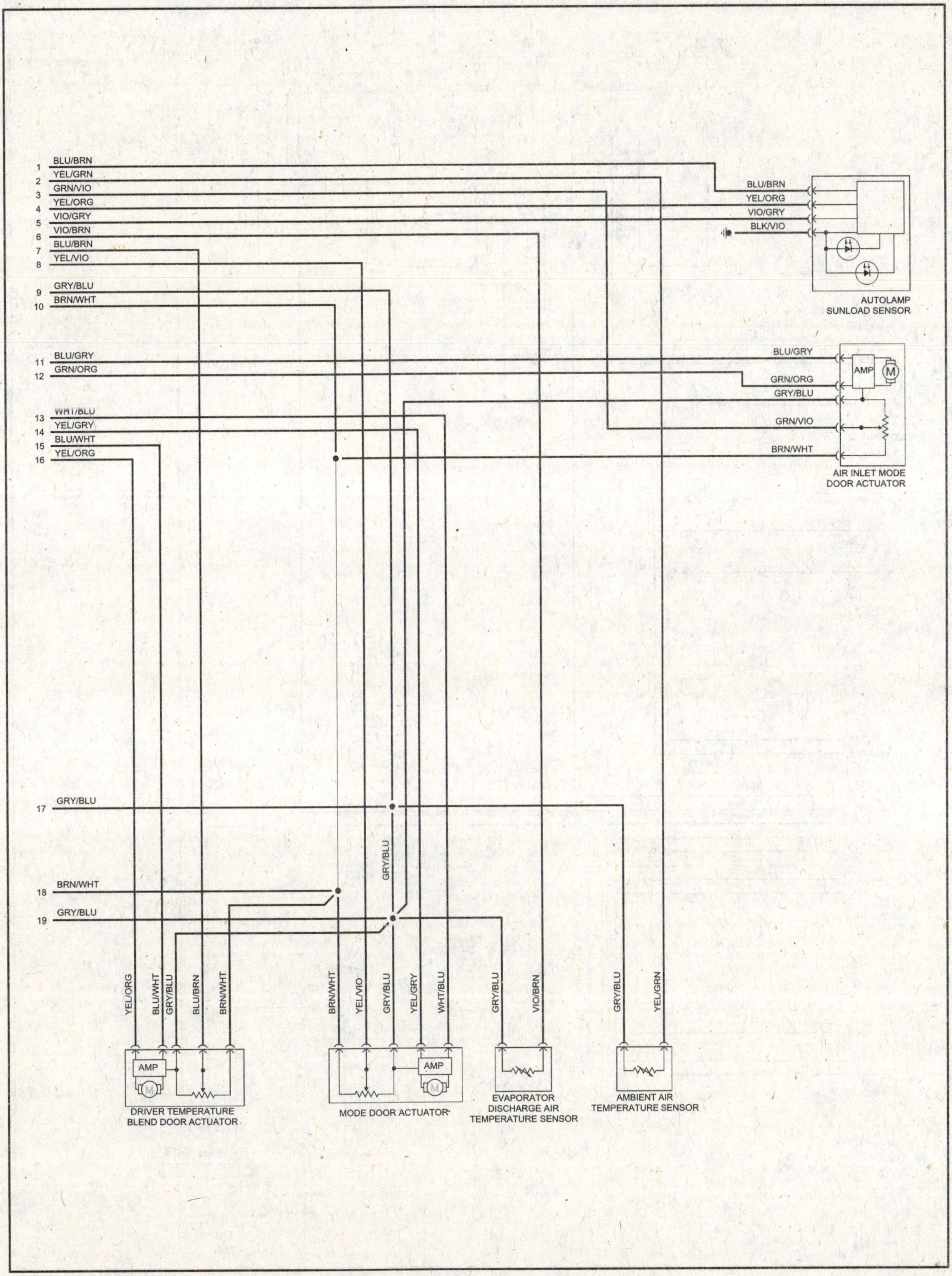

Air conditioning, heating and engine cooling fan system (automatic) - 2010 models (2 of 3)

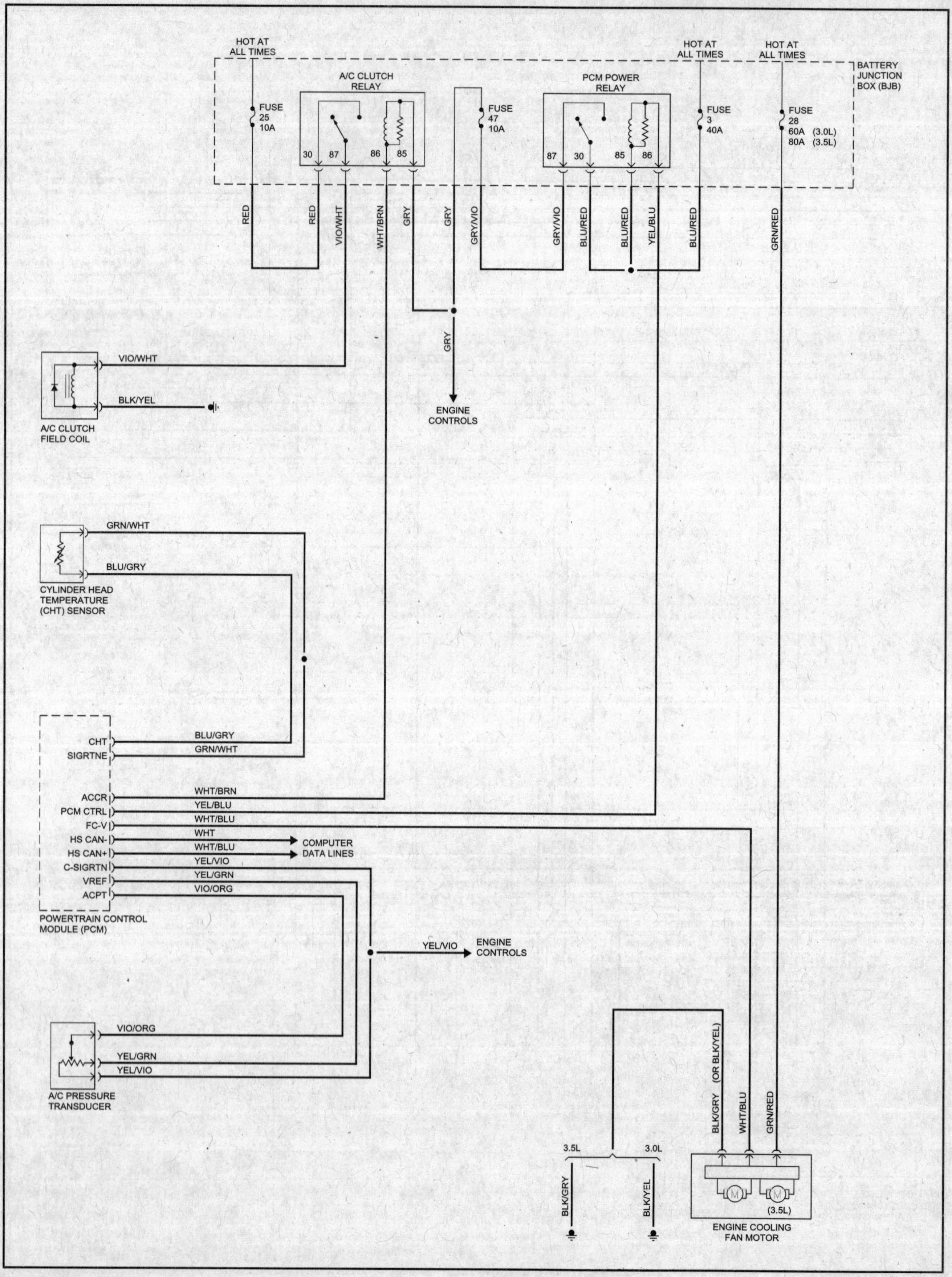

Air conditioning, heating and engine cooling fan system (automatic) - 2010 models (3 of 3)

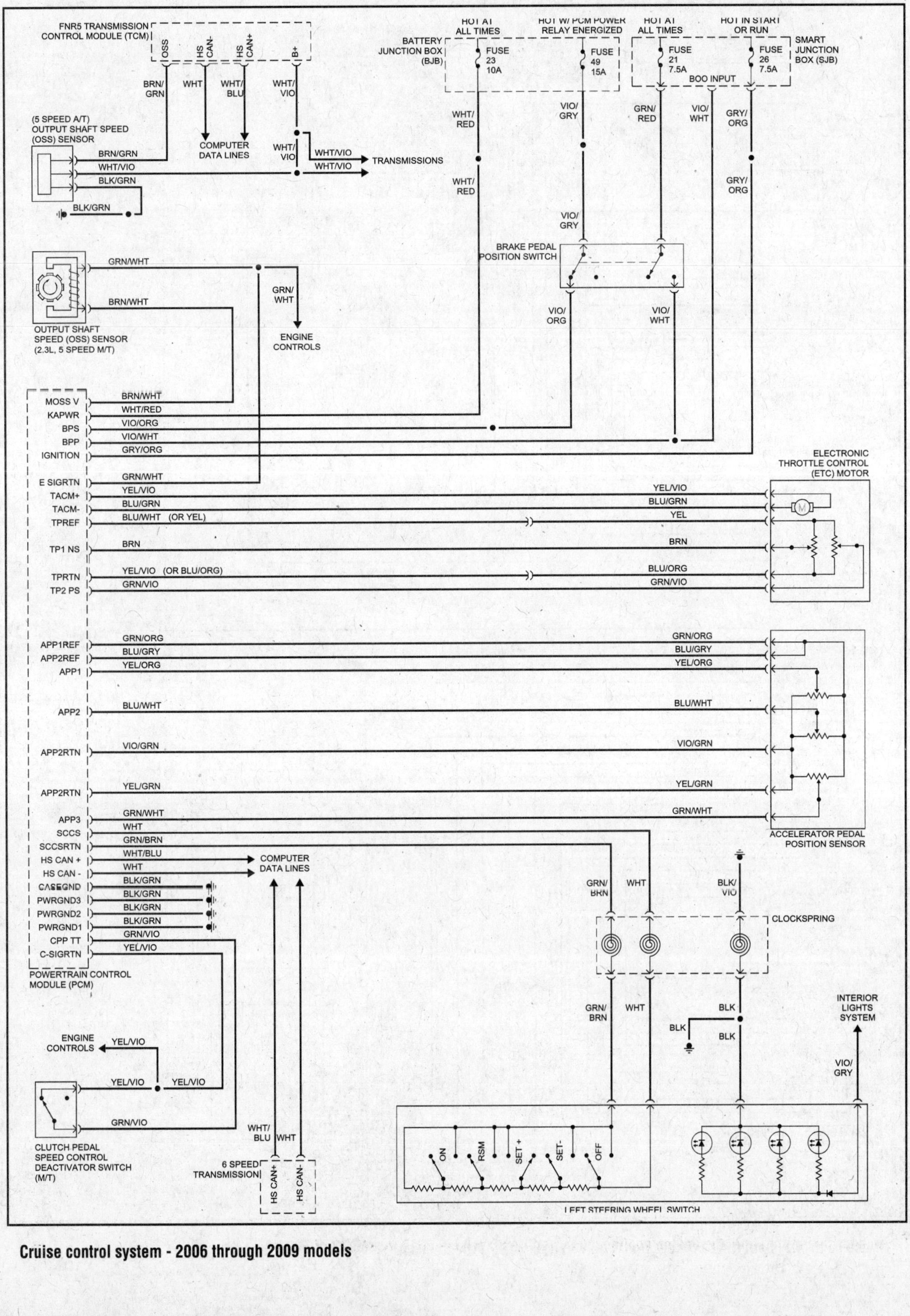

Cruise control system - 2006 through 2009 models

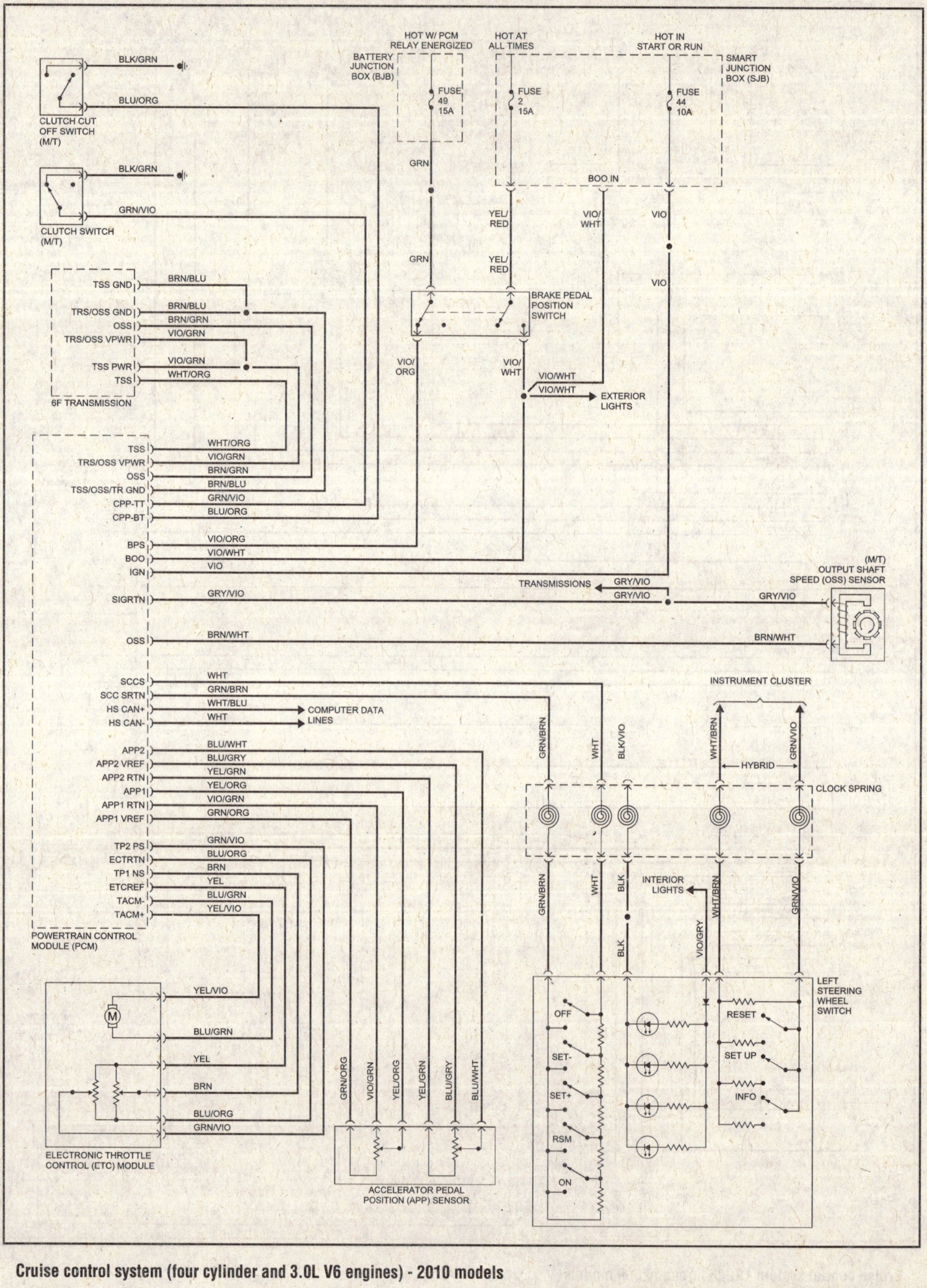

Cruise control system (four cylinder and 3.0L V6 engines) - 2010 models

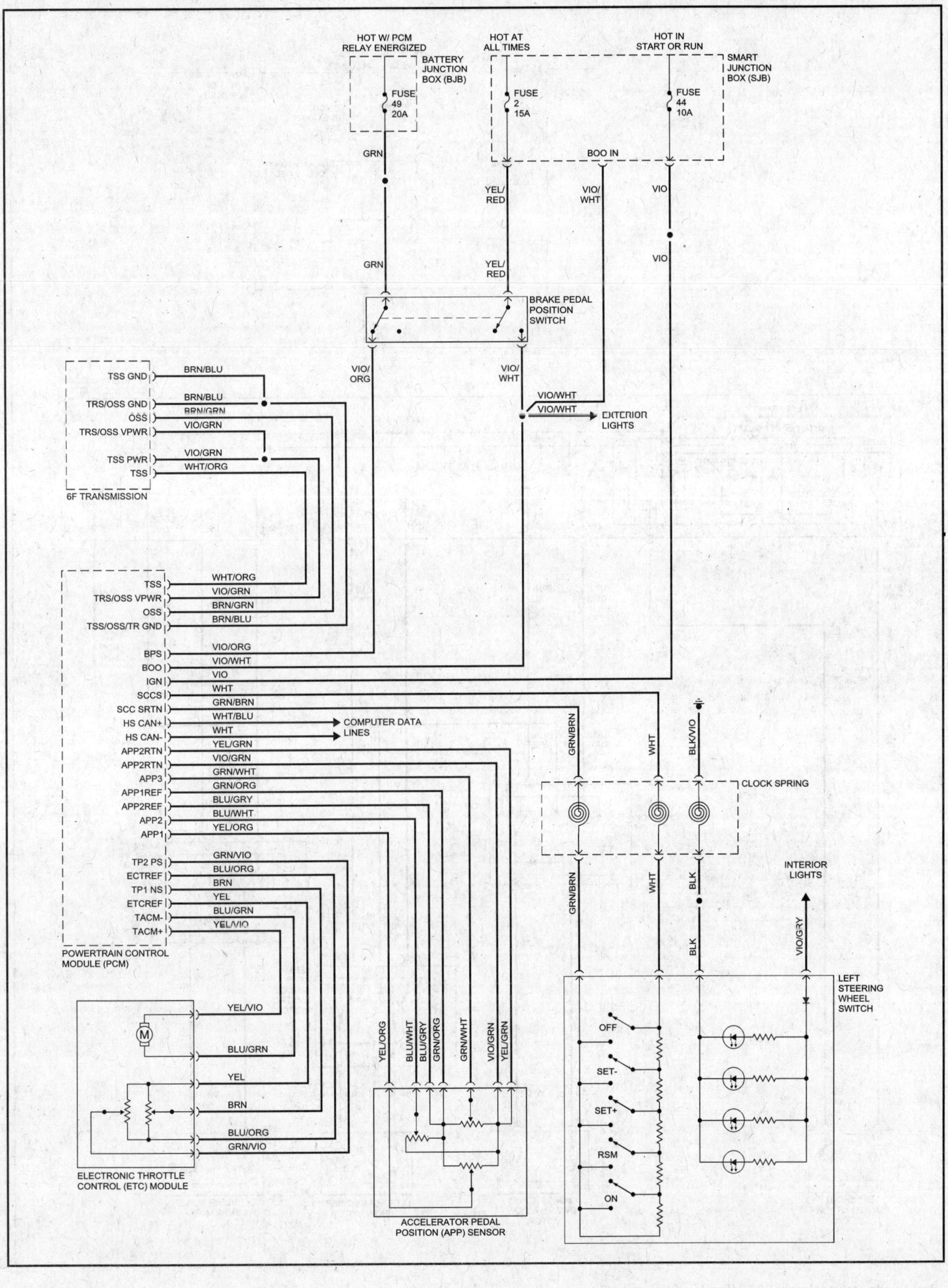
HOT W/ PCM RELAY ENERGIZED
BATTERY JUNCTION BOX (BJB)
FUSE 49 20A
HOT AT ALL TIMES
FUSE 2 15A
HOT IN START OR RUN
SMART JUNCTION BOX (SJB)
FUSE 44 10A
BOO IN
BRAKE PEDAL POSITION SWITCH
EXTERIOR LIGHTS
TSS GND
TRS/OSS GND
OSS
TRS/OSS VPWR
TSS PWR
TSS
6F TRANSMISSION
TSS
TRS/OSS VPWR
OSS
TSS/OSS/TR GND
BPS
BOO
IGN
SCCS
SCC SRTN
HS CAN+
HS CAN-
APP2RTN
APP2RTN
APP3
APP1REF
APP2REF
APP2
APP1
TP2 PS
ETCREF
TP1 NS
ETCREF
TACM-
TACM+
POWERTRAIN CONTROL MODULE (PCM)
COMPUTER DATA LINES
CLOCK SPRING
INTERIOR LIGHTS
LEFT STEERING WHEEL SWITCH
OFF
SET-
SET+
RSM
ON
ELECTRONIC THROTTLE CONTROL (ETC) MODULE
ACCELERATOR PEDAL POSITION (APP) SENSOR

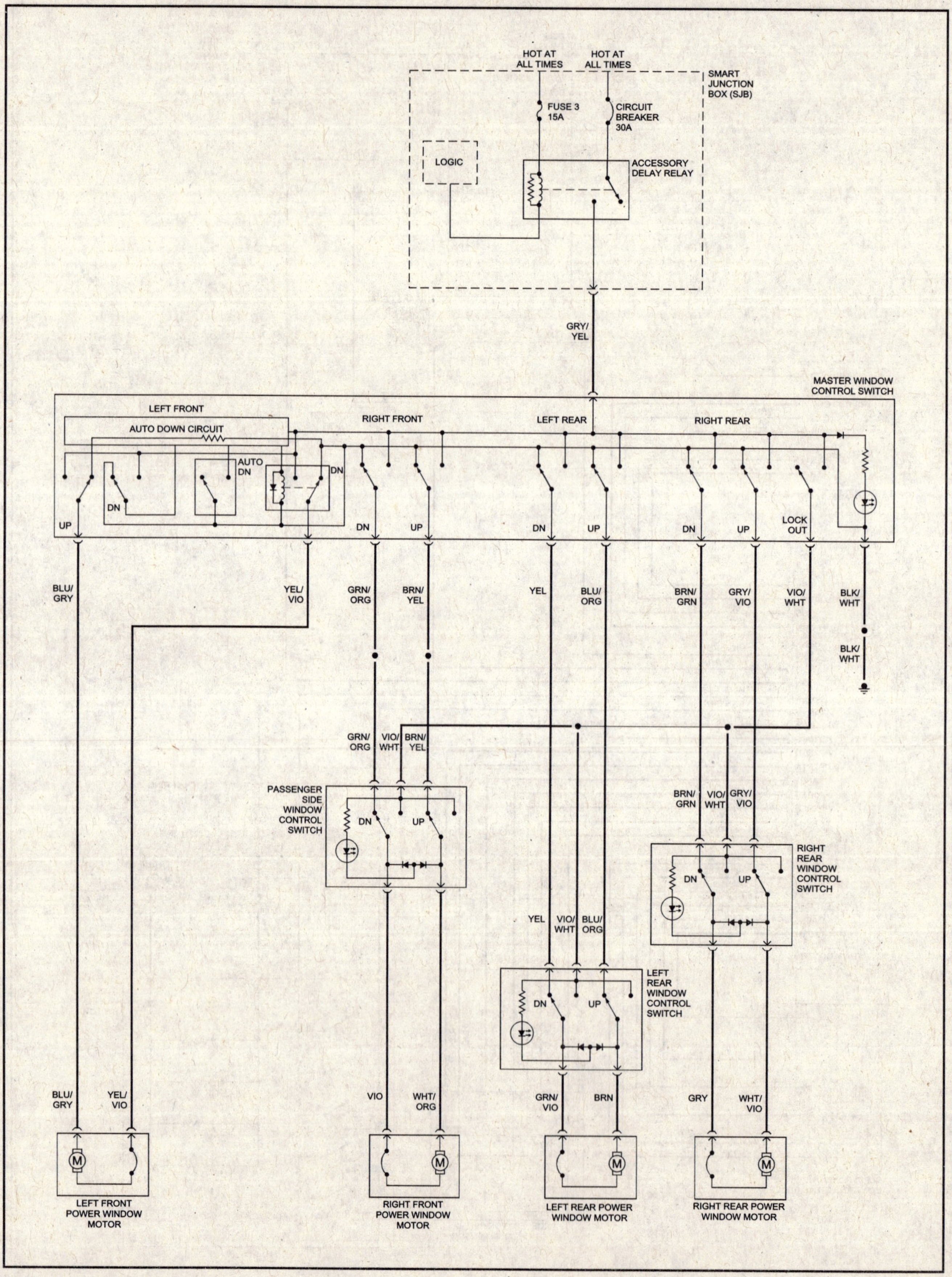

Power window system - 2006 through 2009 models

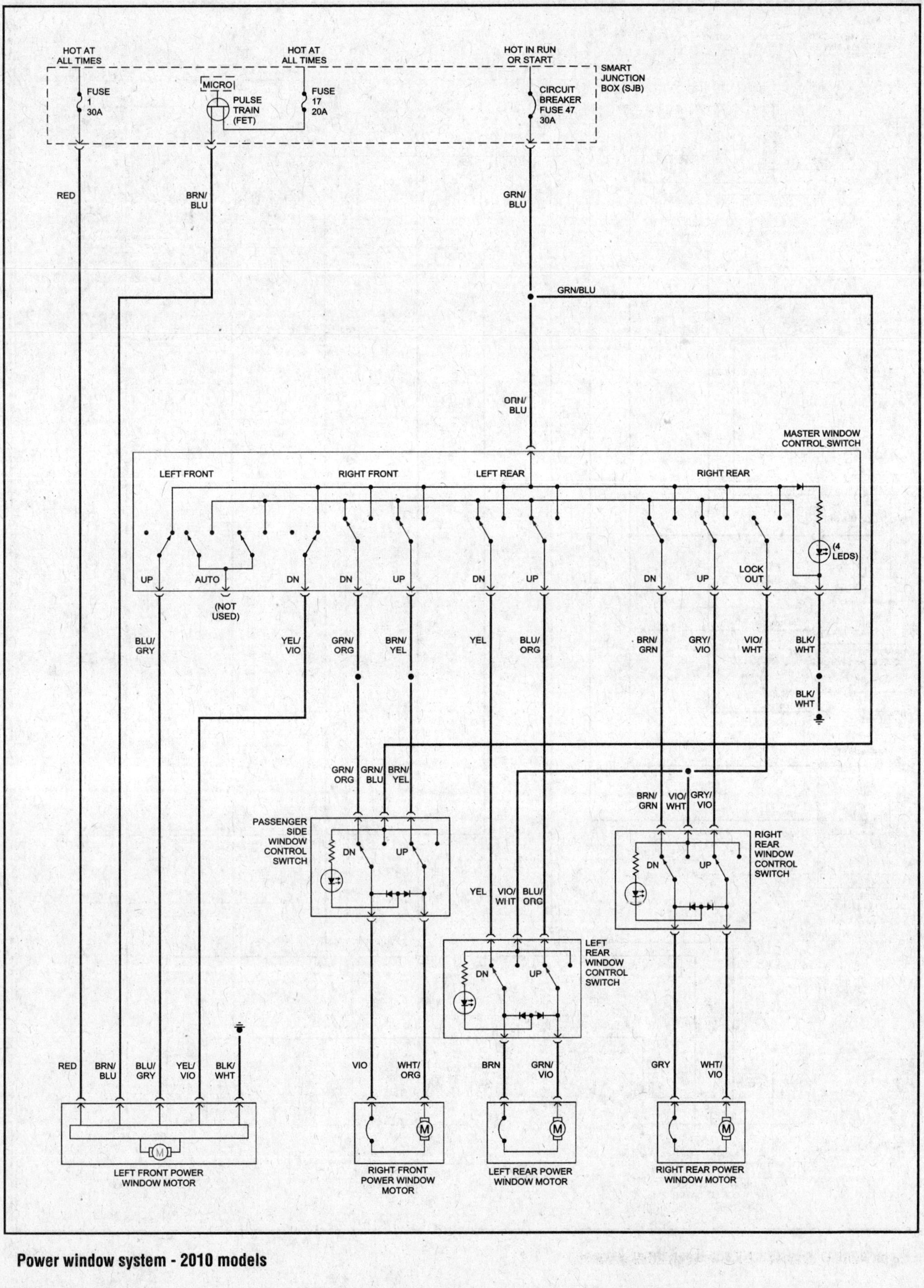

Power window system - 2010 models

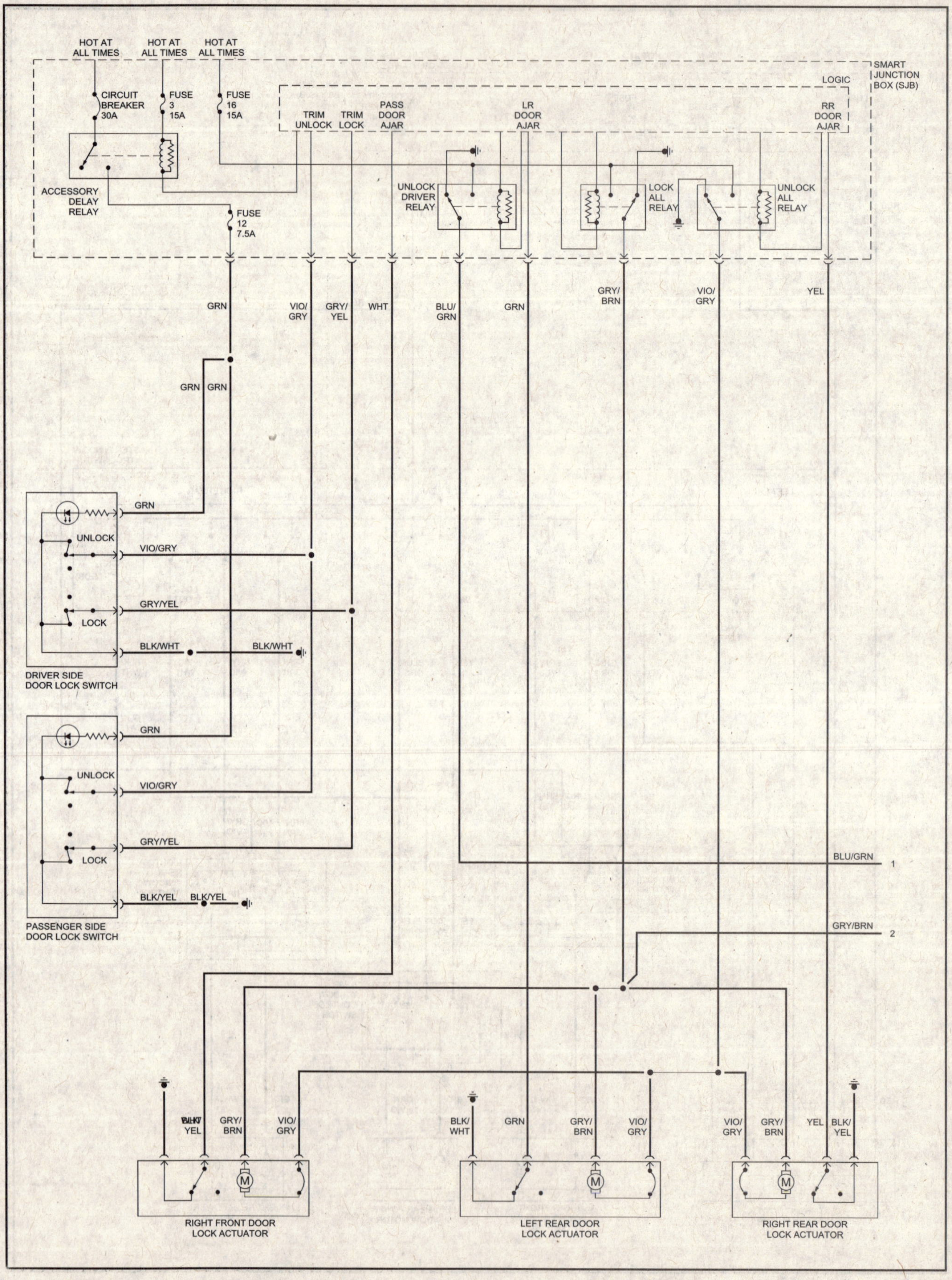

...er door lock system - 2006 through 2009 models (1 of 2)

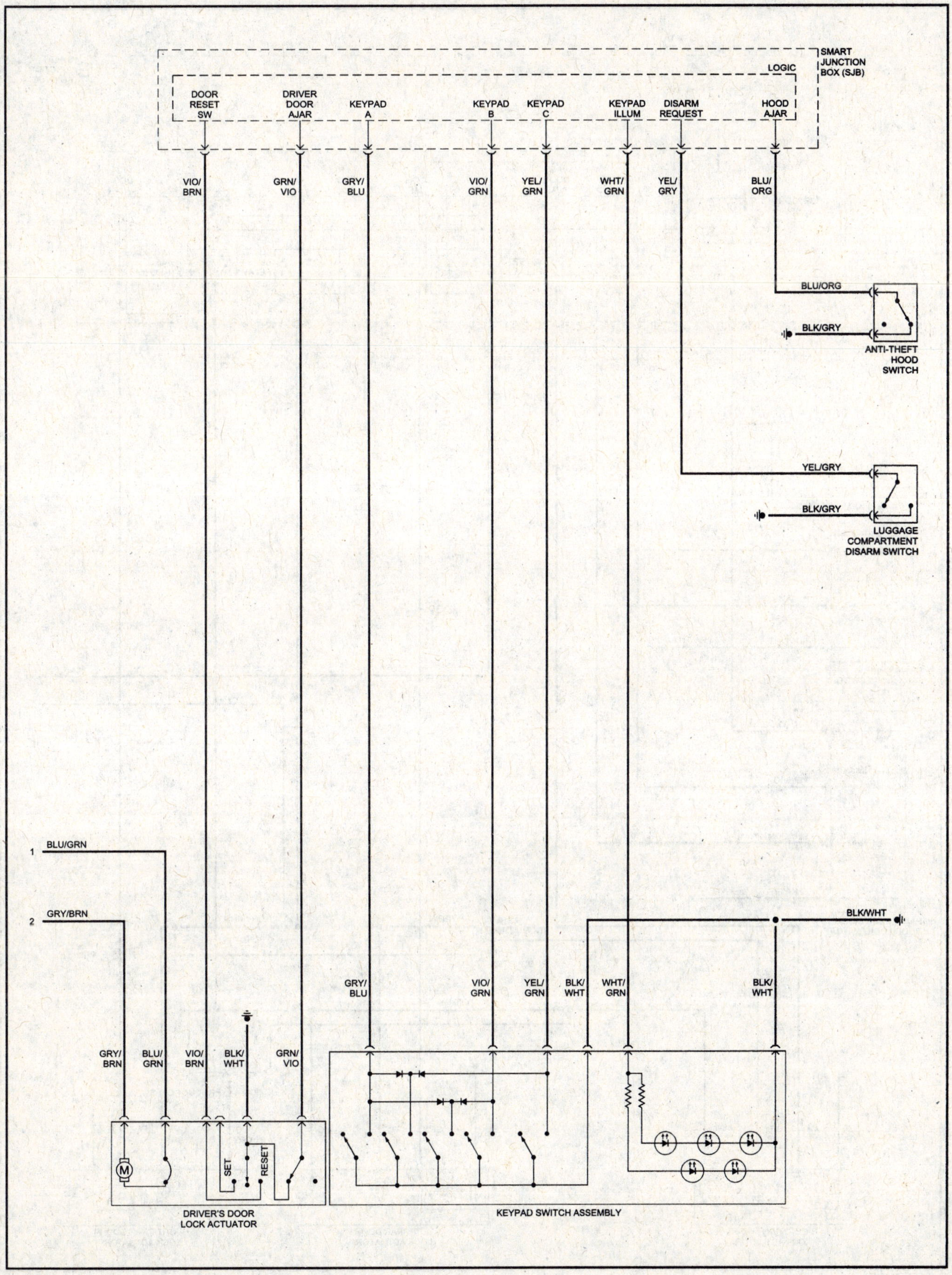

Power door lock system - 2006 through 2009 models (2 of 2)

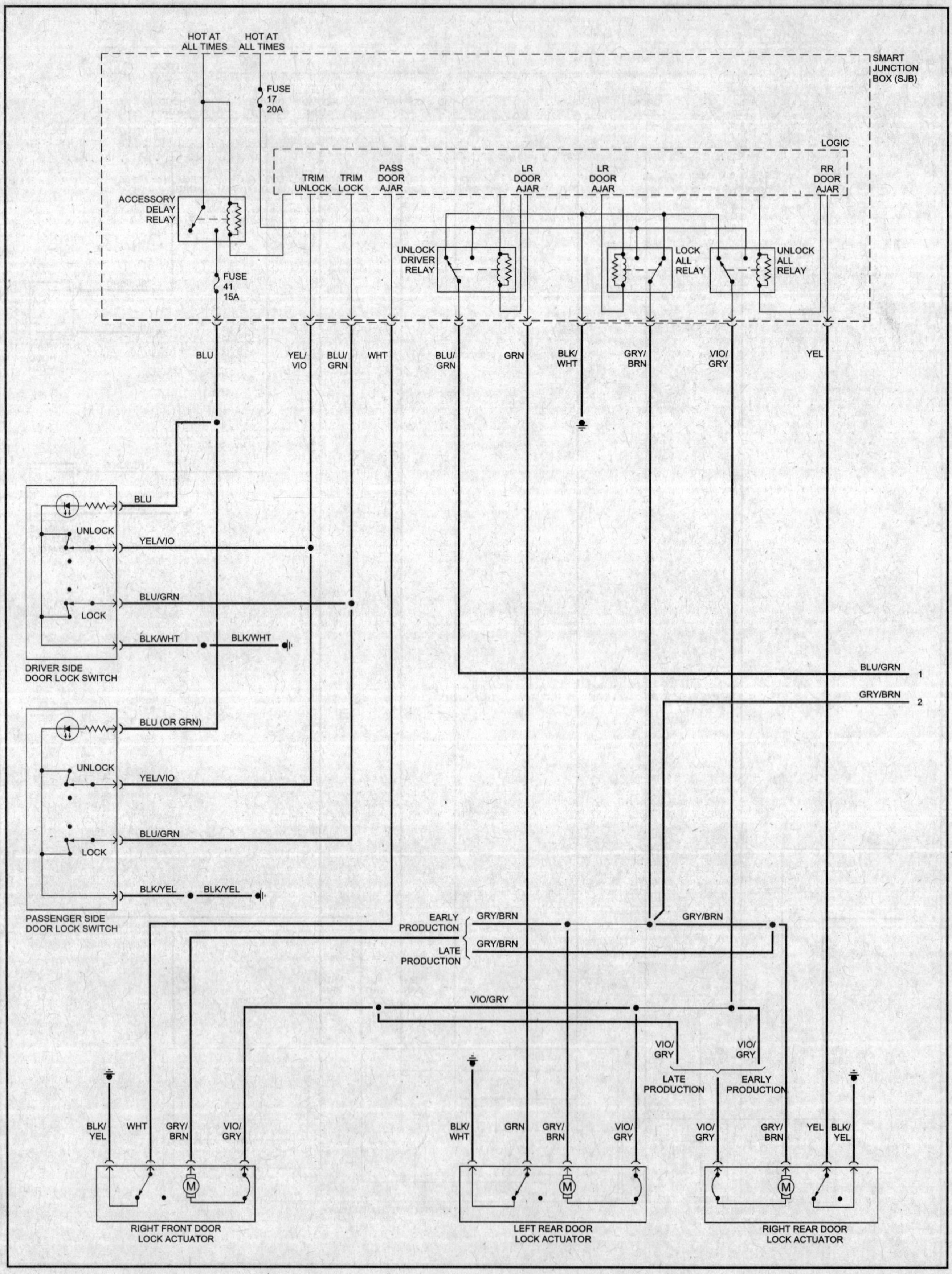

Power door lock system - 2010 models (1 of 2)

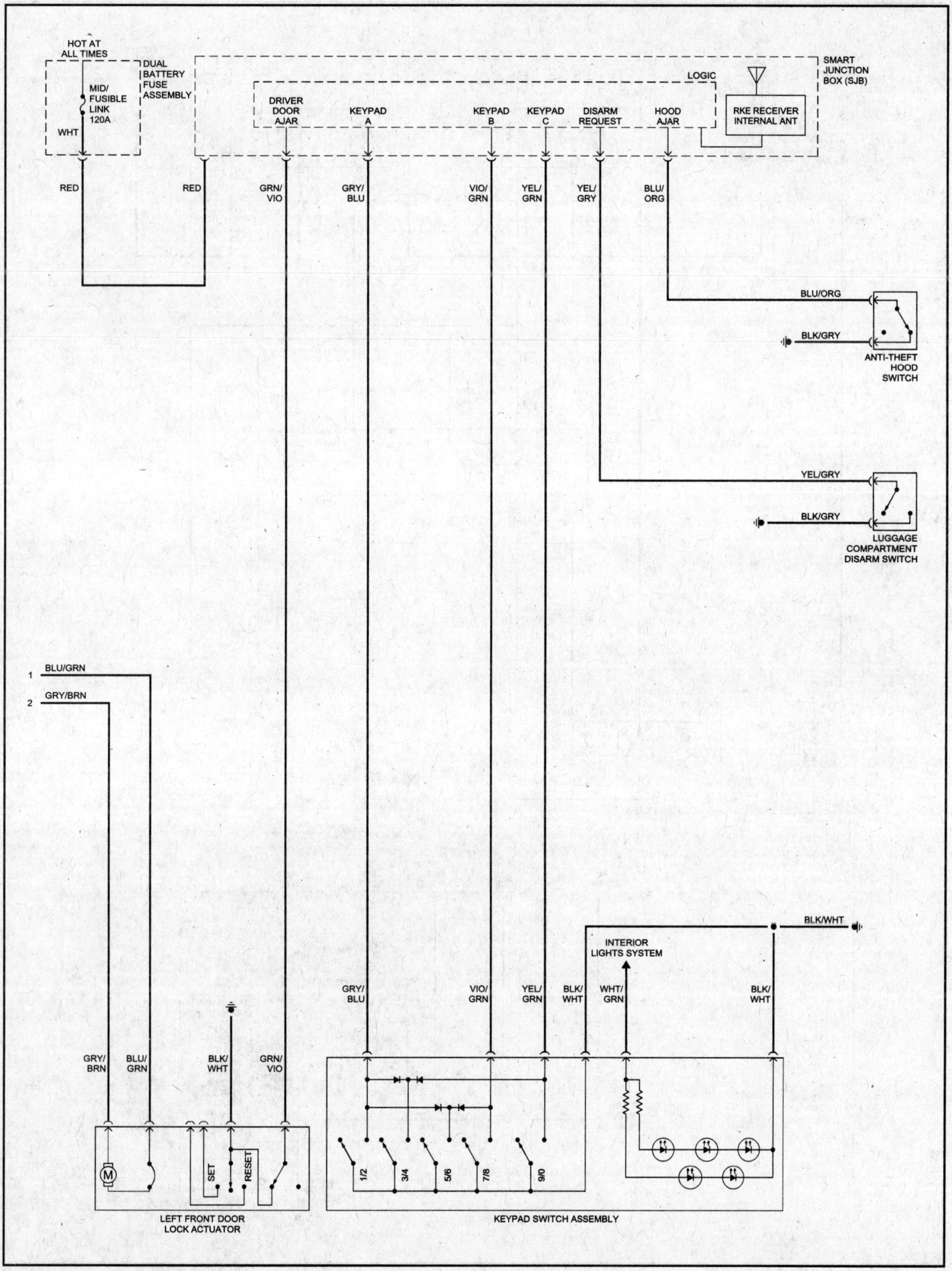

Power door lock system - 2010 models (2 of 2)

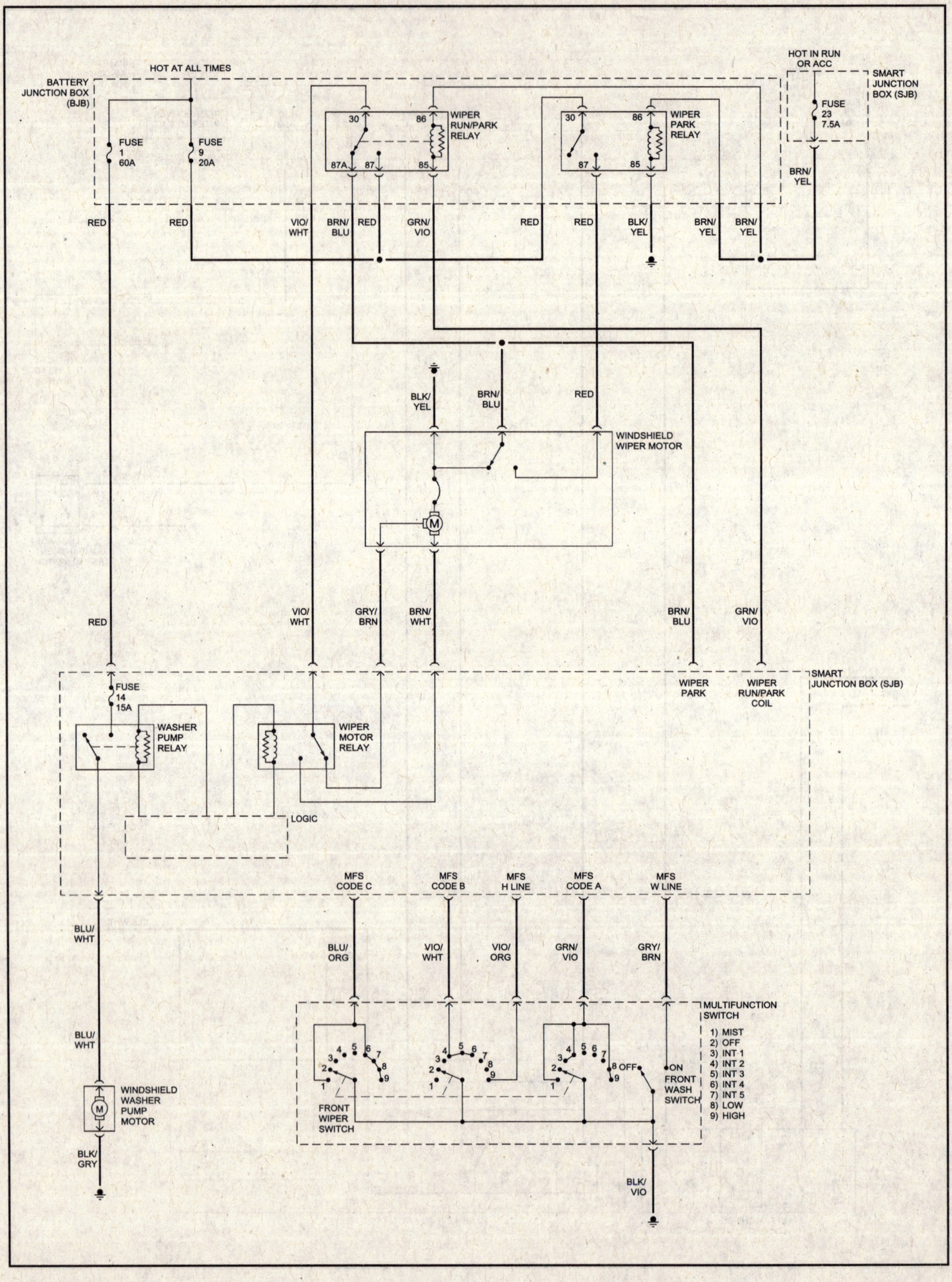

Windshield wiper/washer system - 2006 through 2009 models

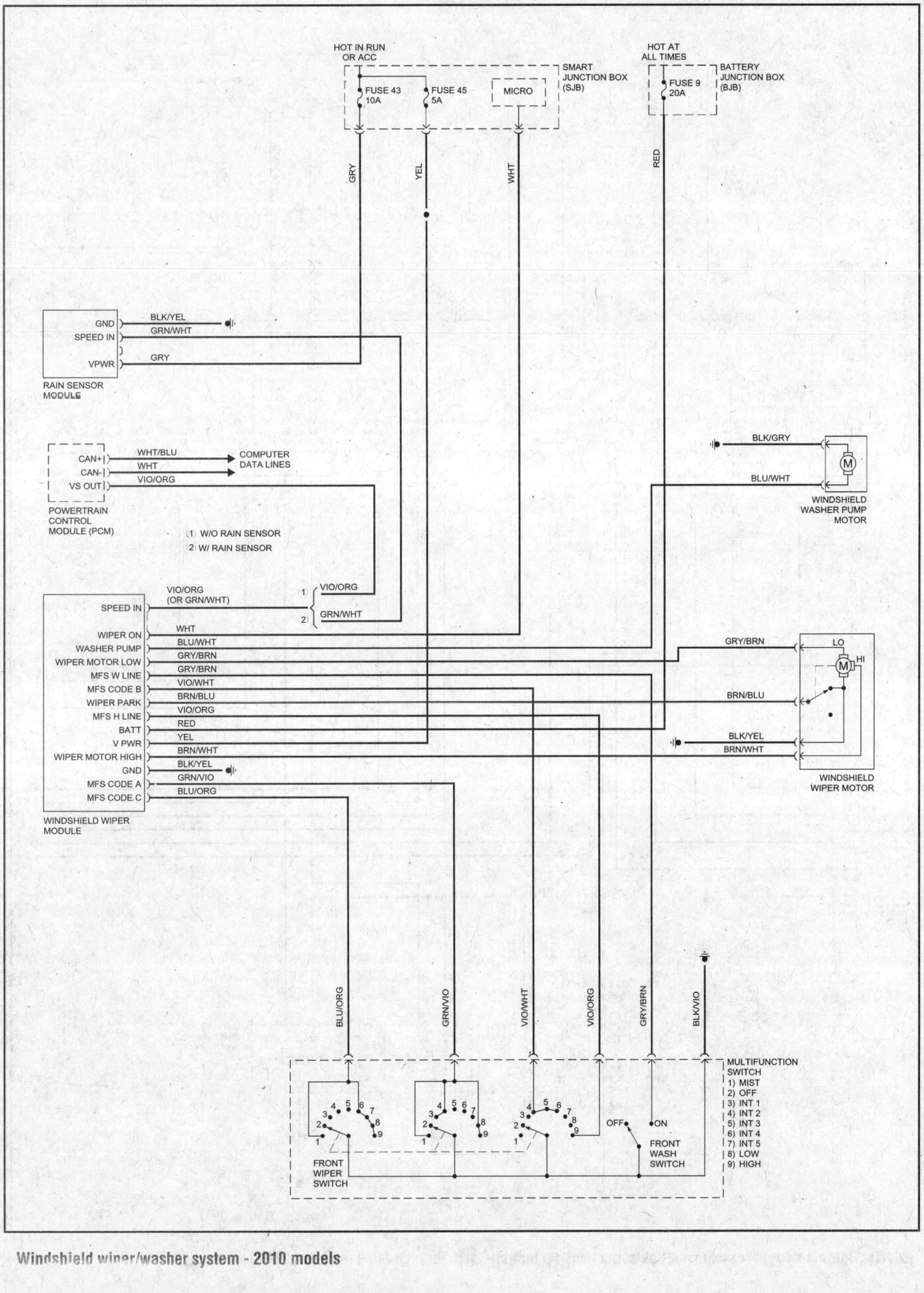

Windshield wiper/washer system - 2010 models

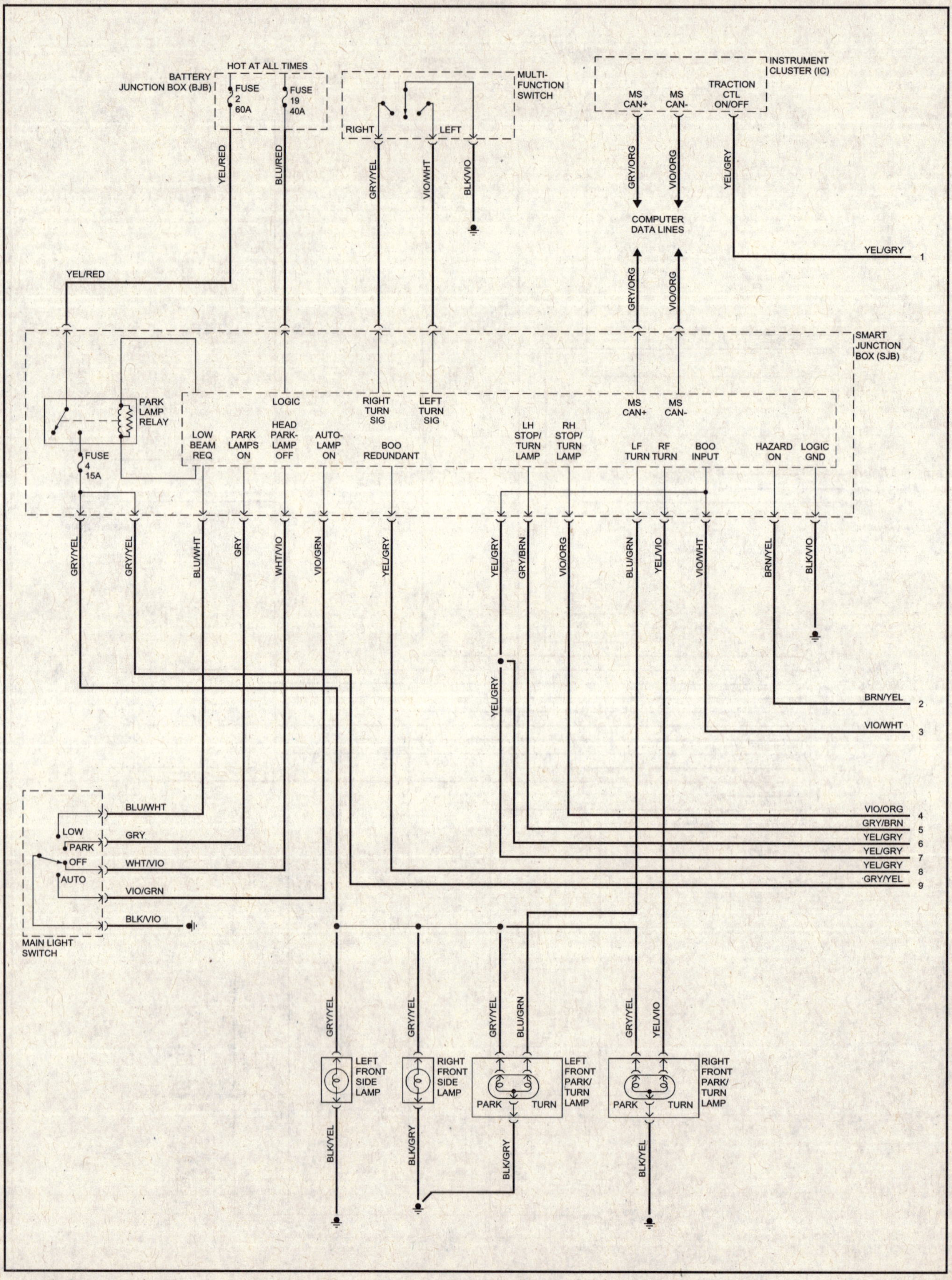

Exterior lighting system (except headlights and back-up lights) - 2006 through 2009 models (1 of 2)

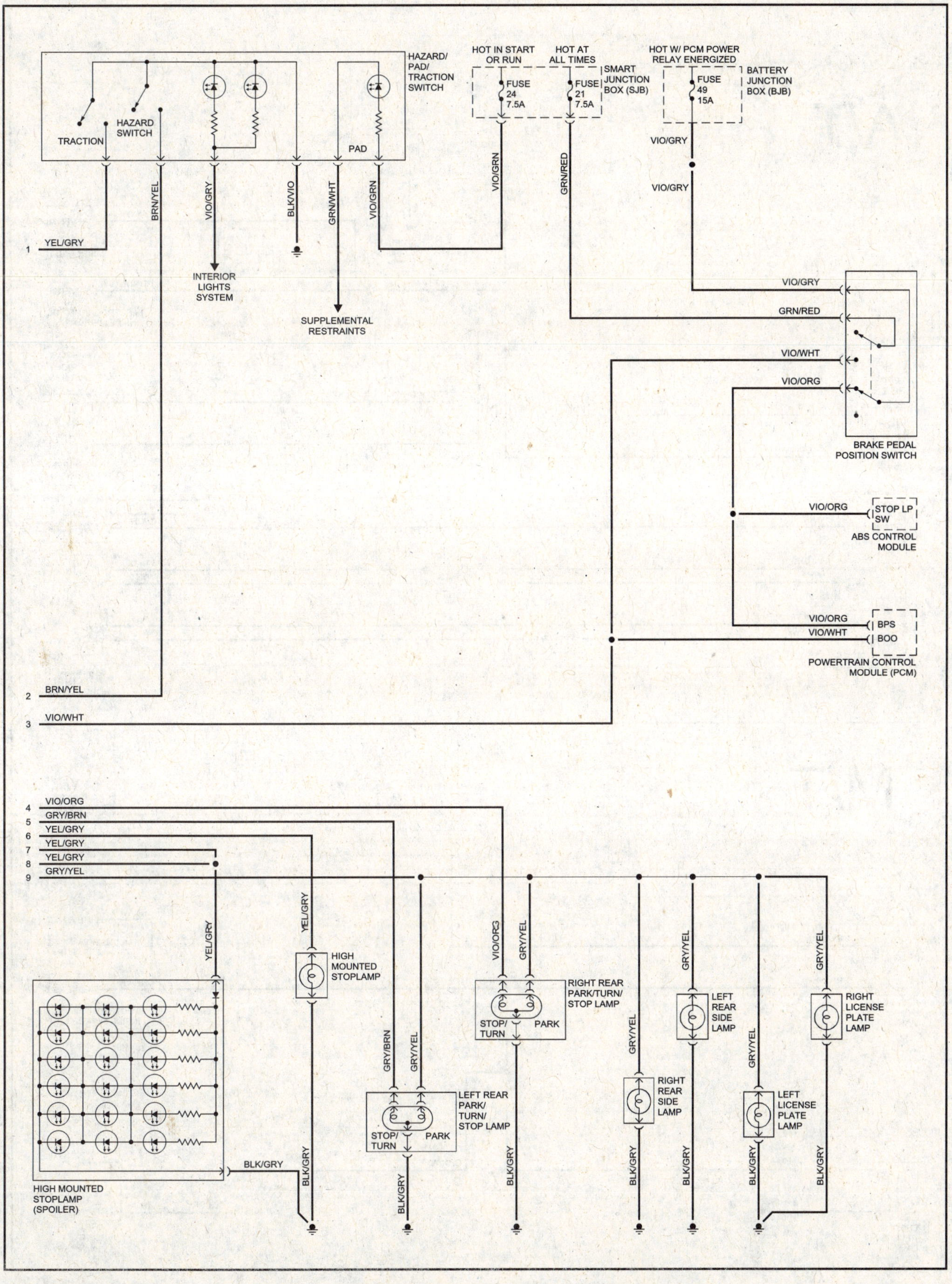

Exterior lighting system (except headlights and back-up lights) - 2006 through 2009 models (2 of 2)

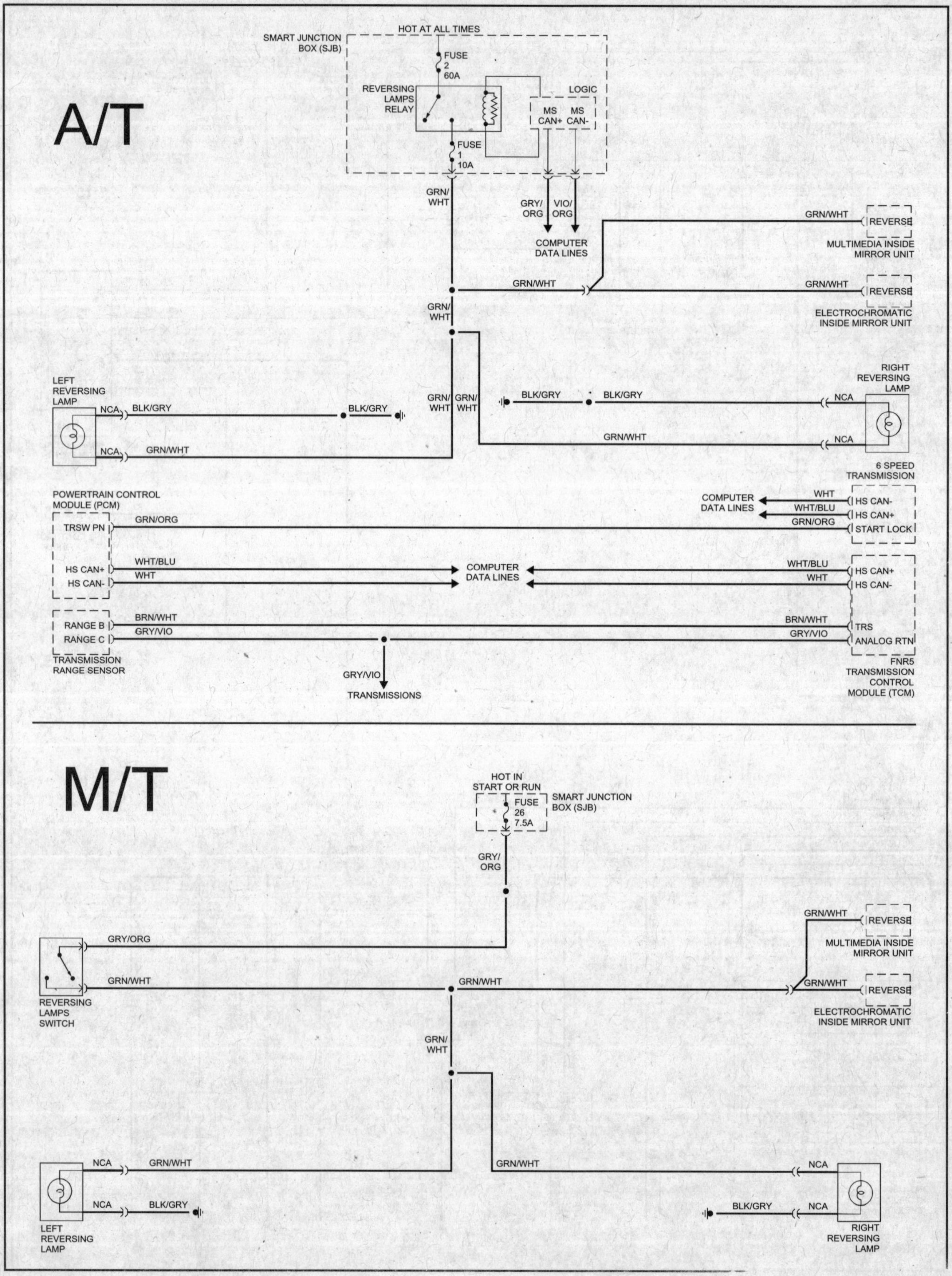

Back-up light system - 2006 th[illegible]

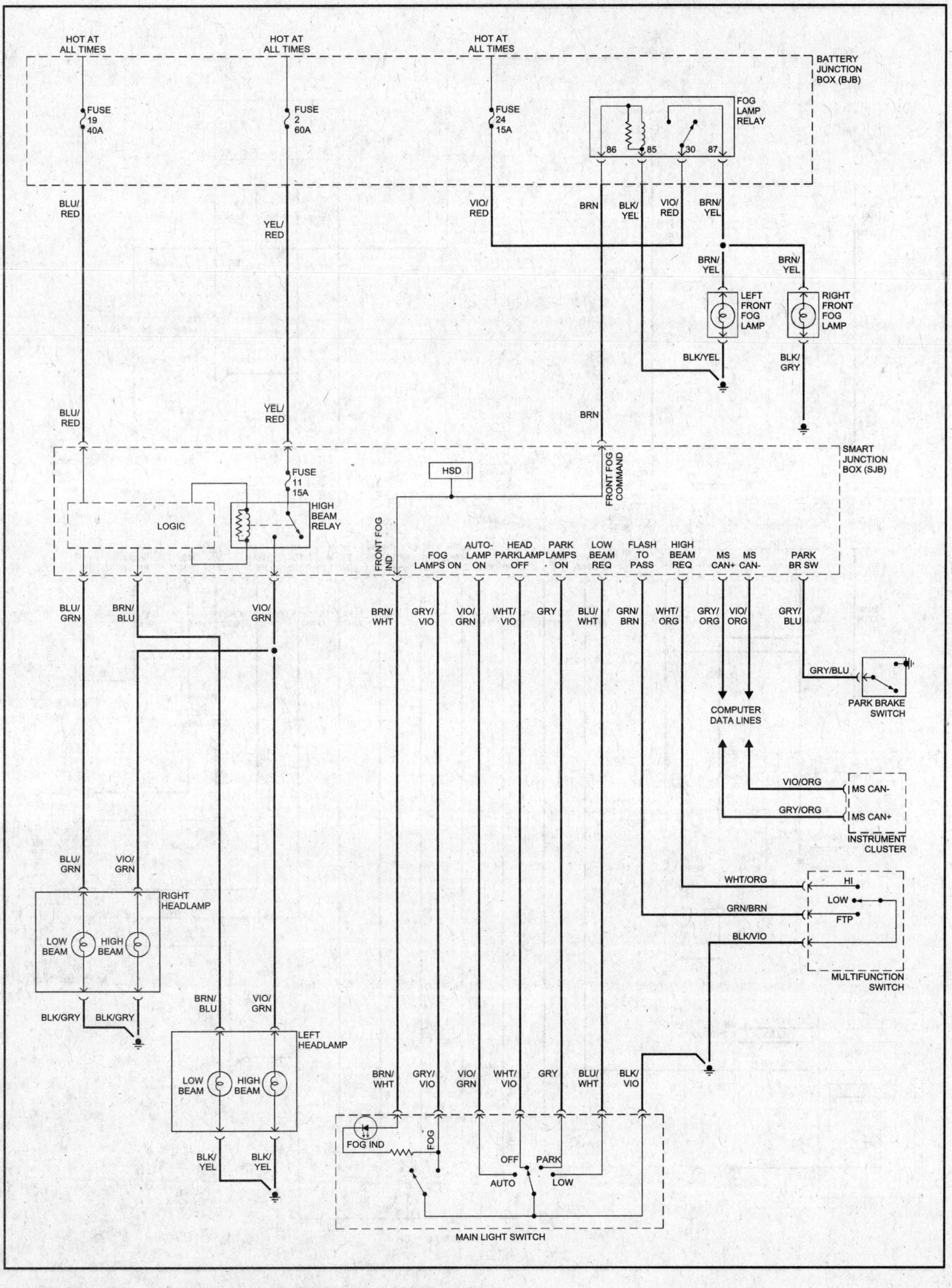

Headlight system (without Autolamps) - 2006 through 2009 models

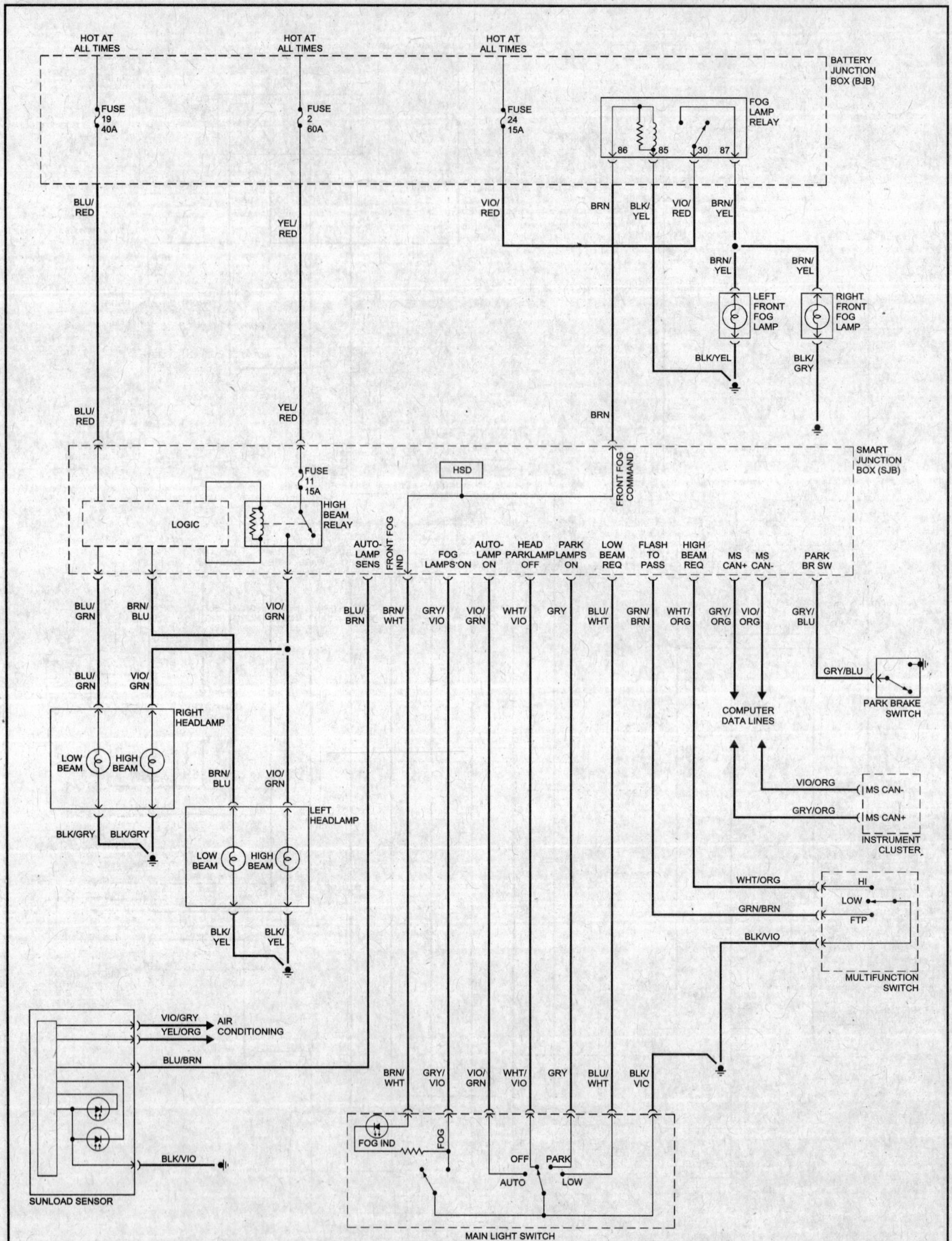

Headlight system (with Autolamps) - 2006 through 2009 models

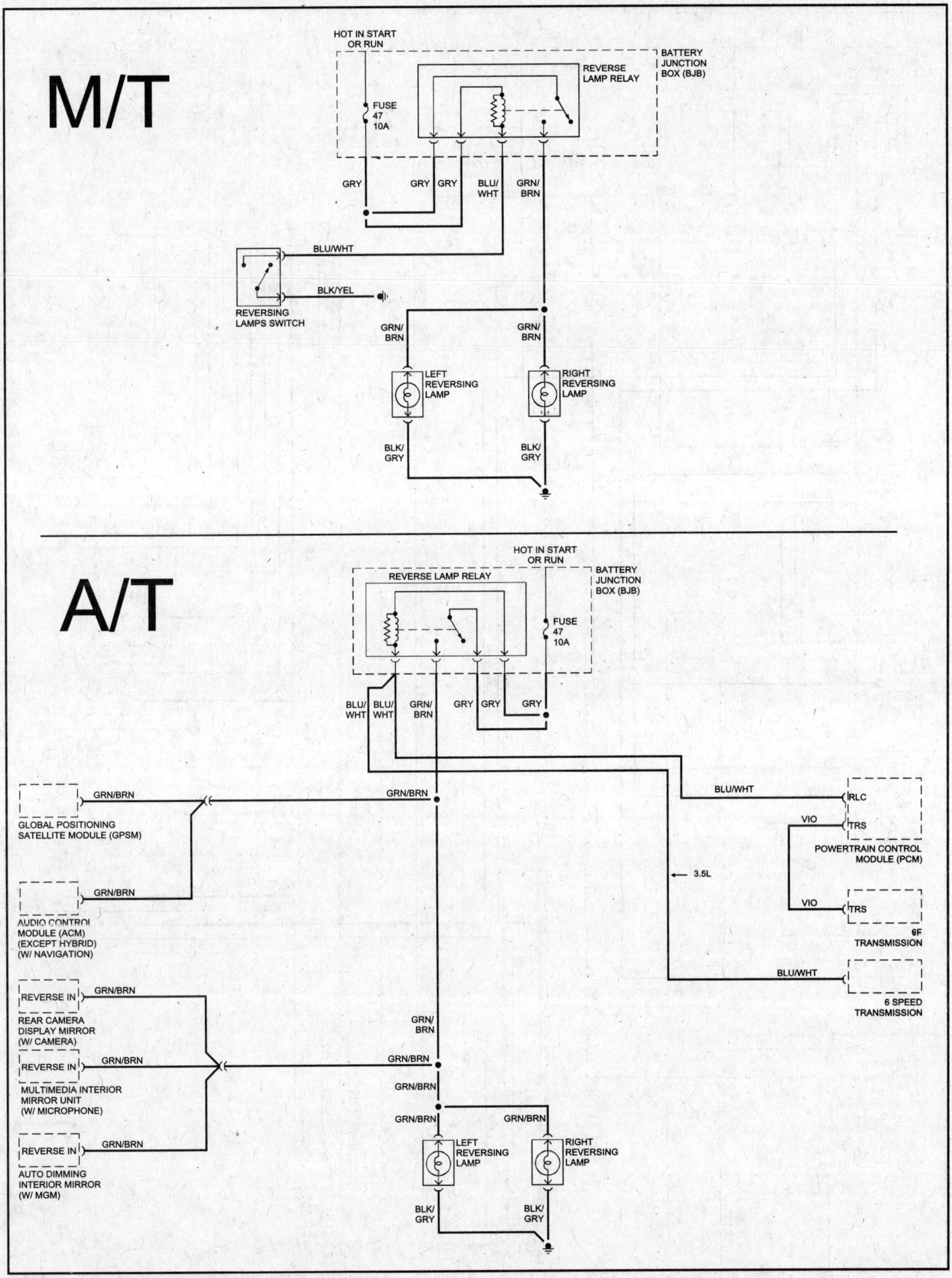

Back-up light system - 2010 models

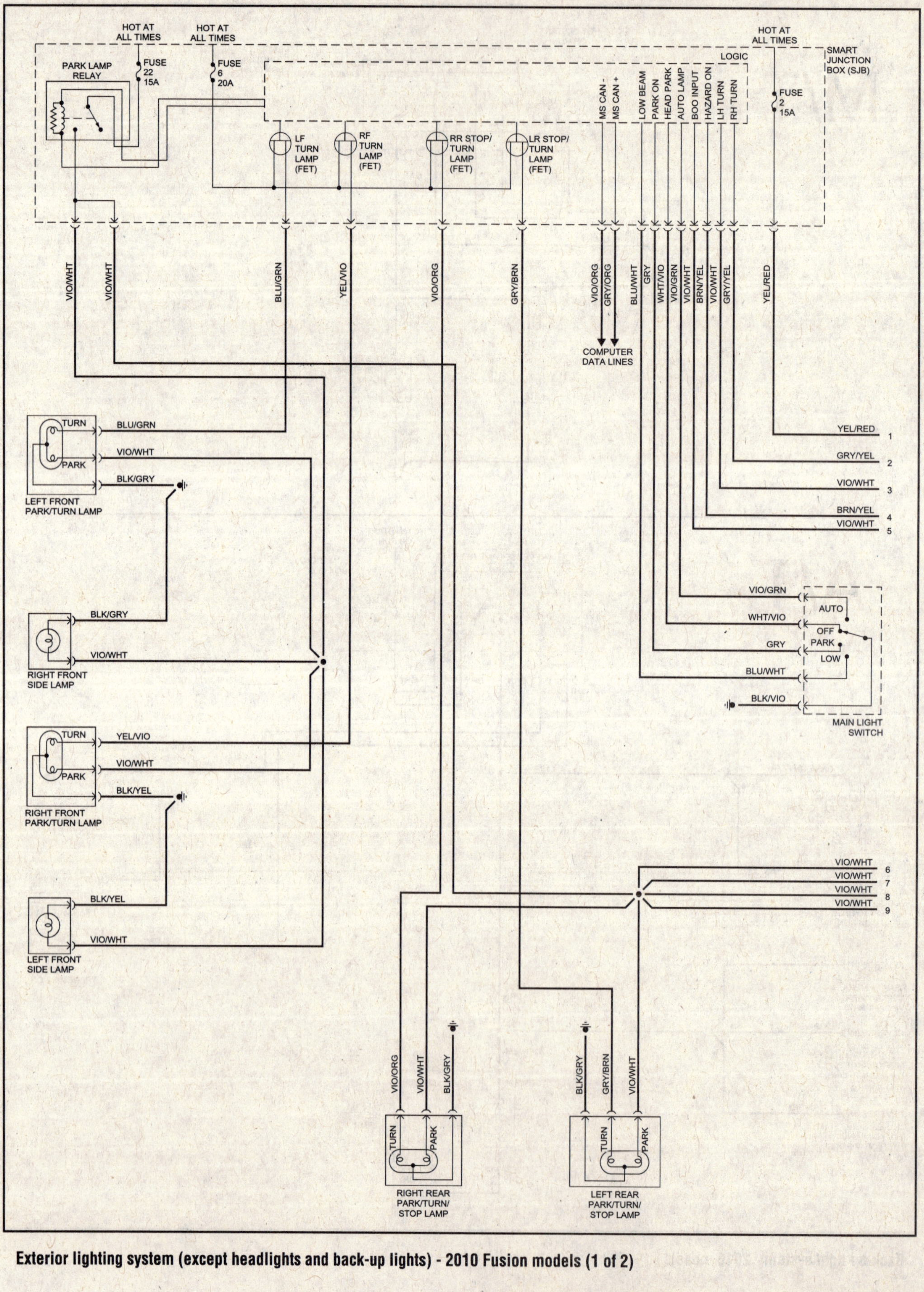

Exterior lighting system (except headlights and back-up lights) - 2010 Fusion models (1 of 2)

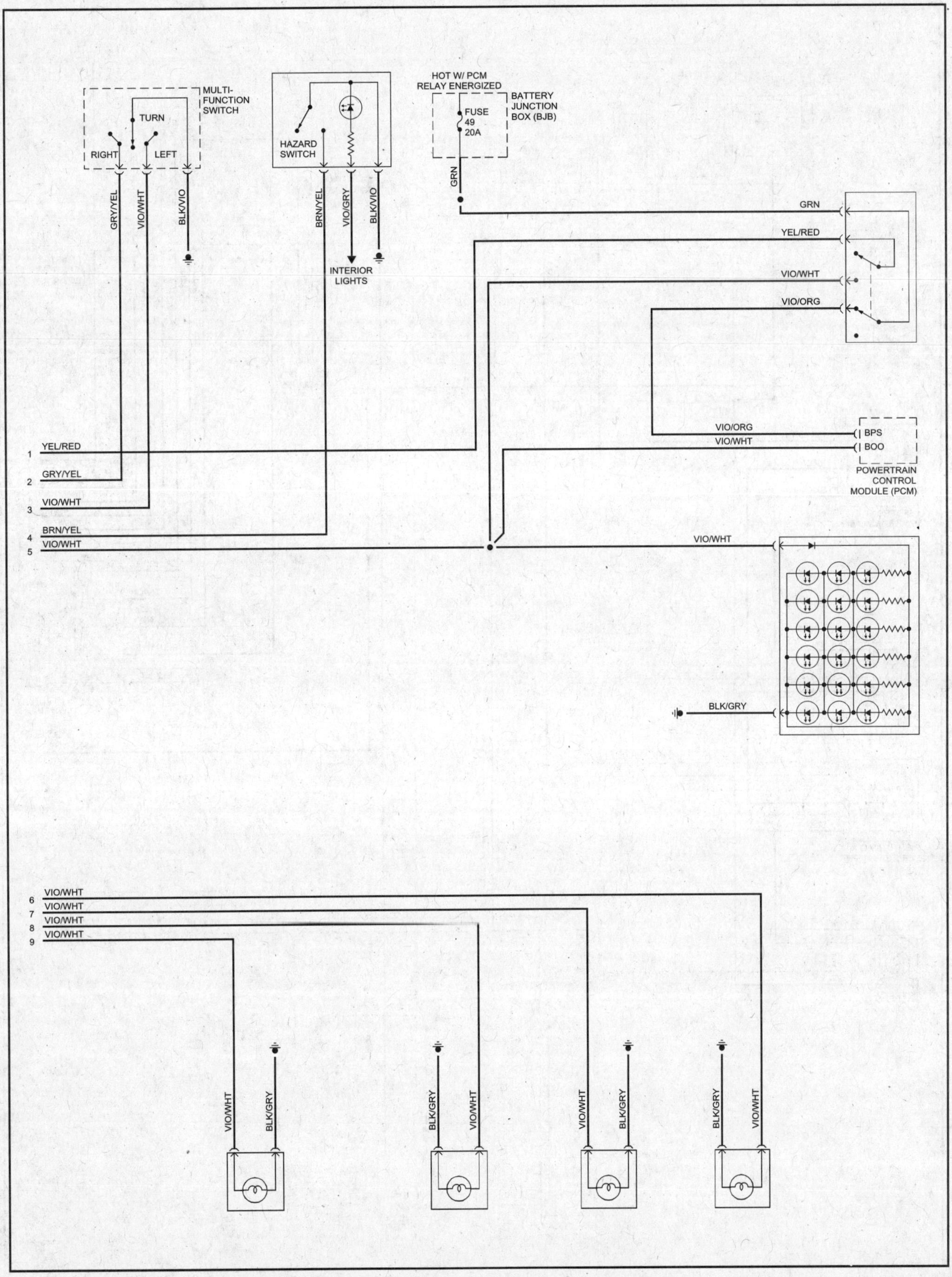

Exterior lighting system (except headlights and back-up lights) - 2010 Fusion models (2 of 2)

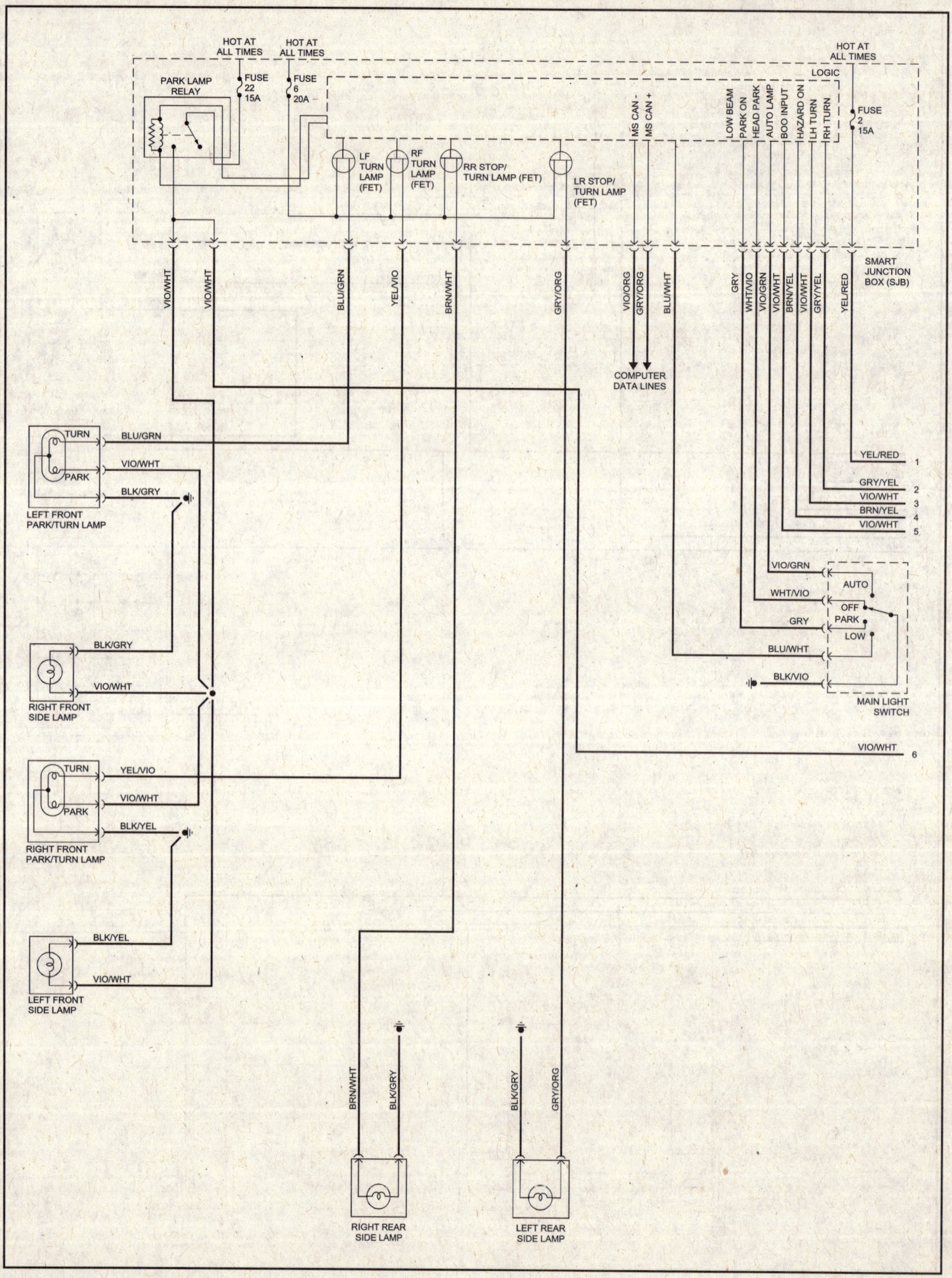

Exterior lighting system (except headlights and back-up lights) - 2010 Milan models (1 of 2)

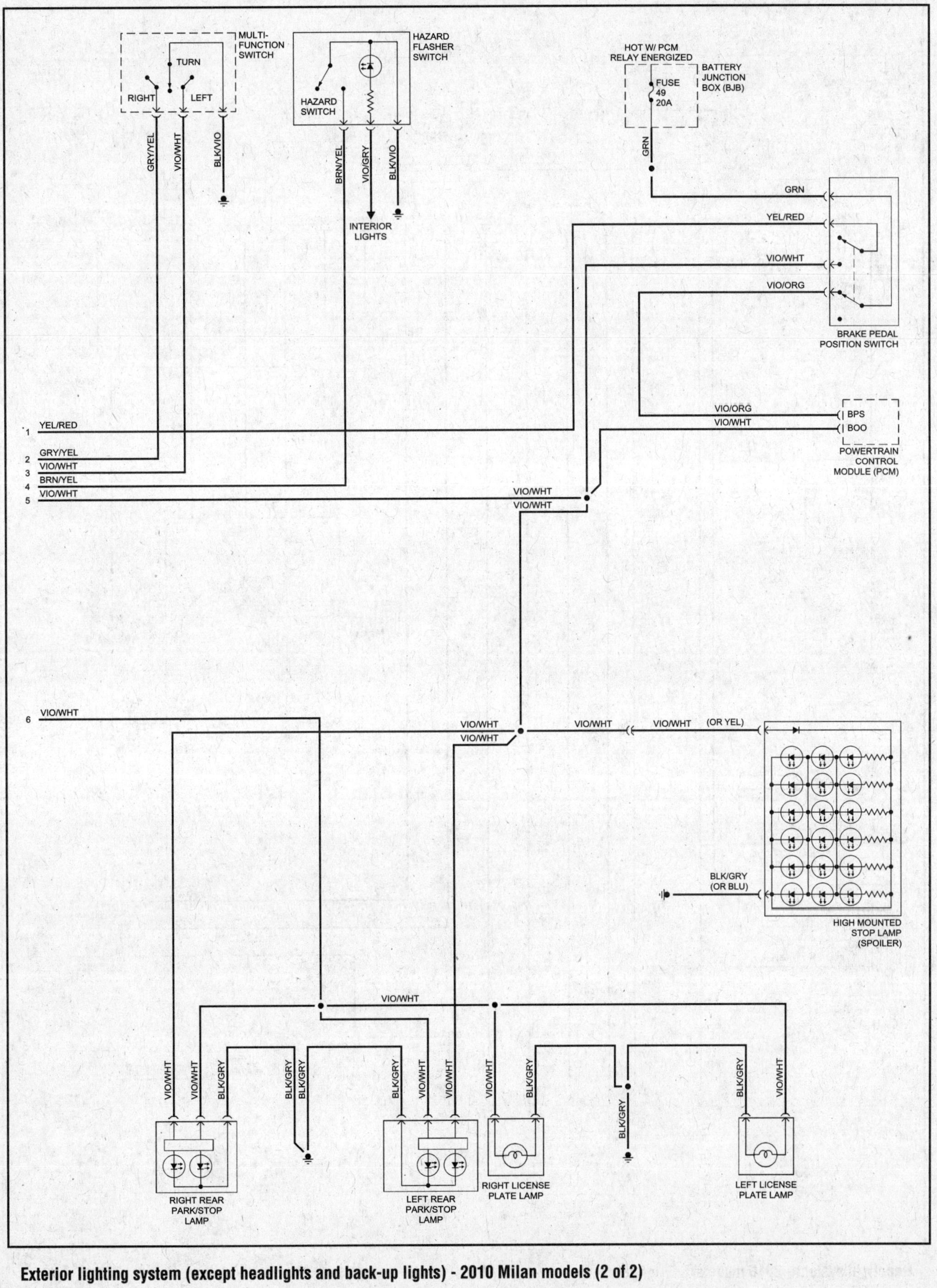

Exterior lighting system (except headlights and back-up lights) - 2010 Milan models (2 of 2)

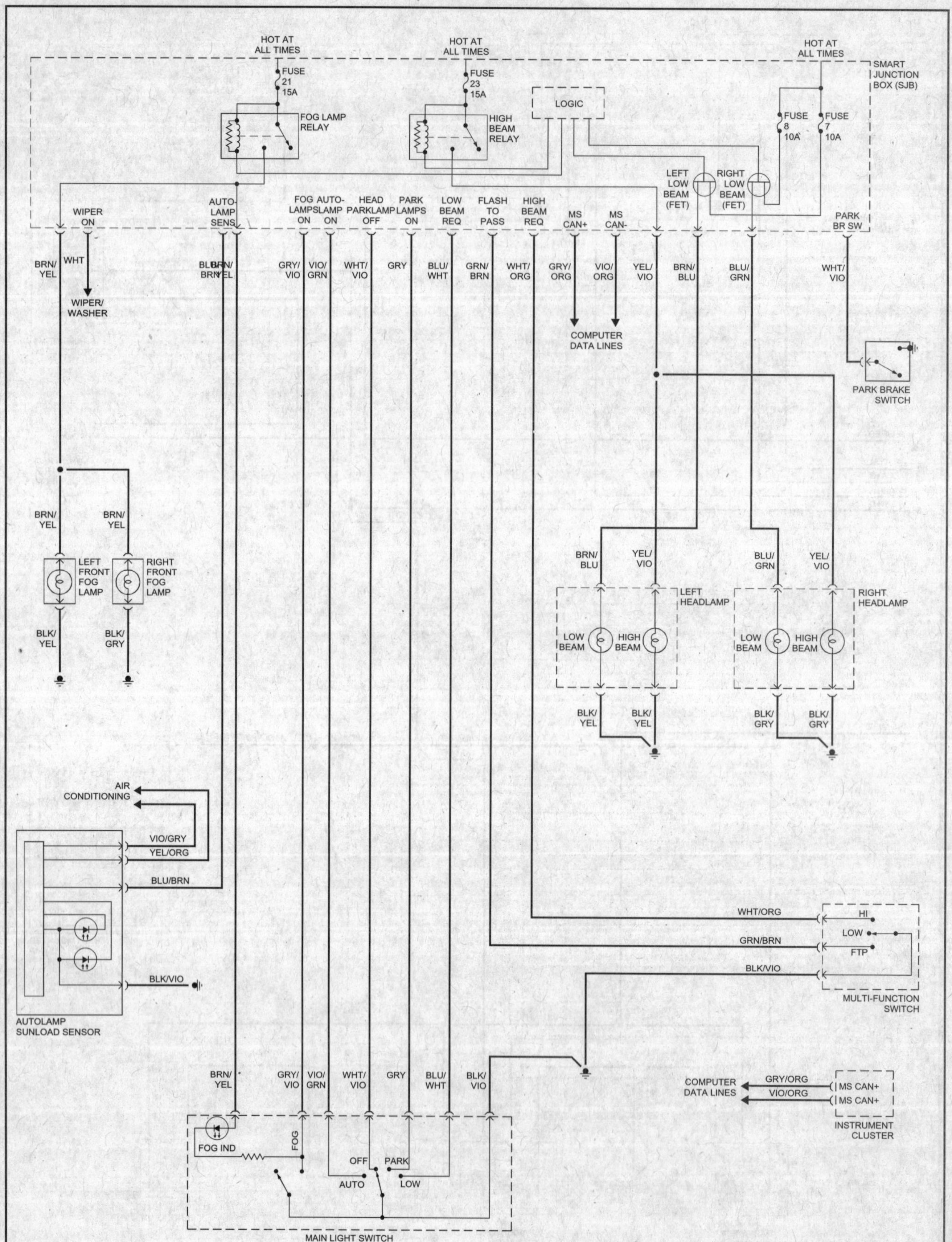

Headlight system - 2010 models

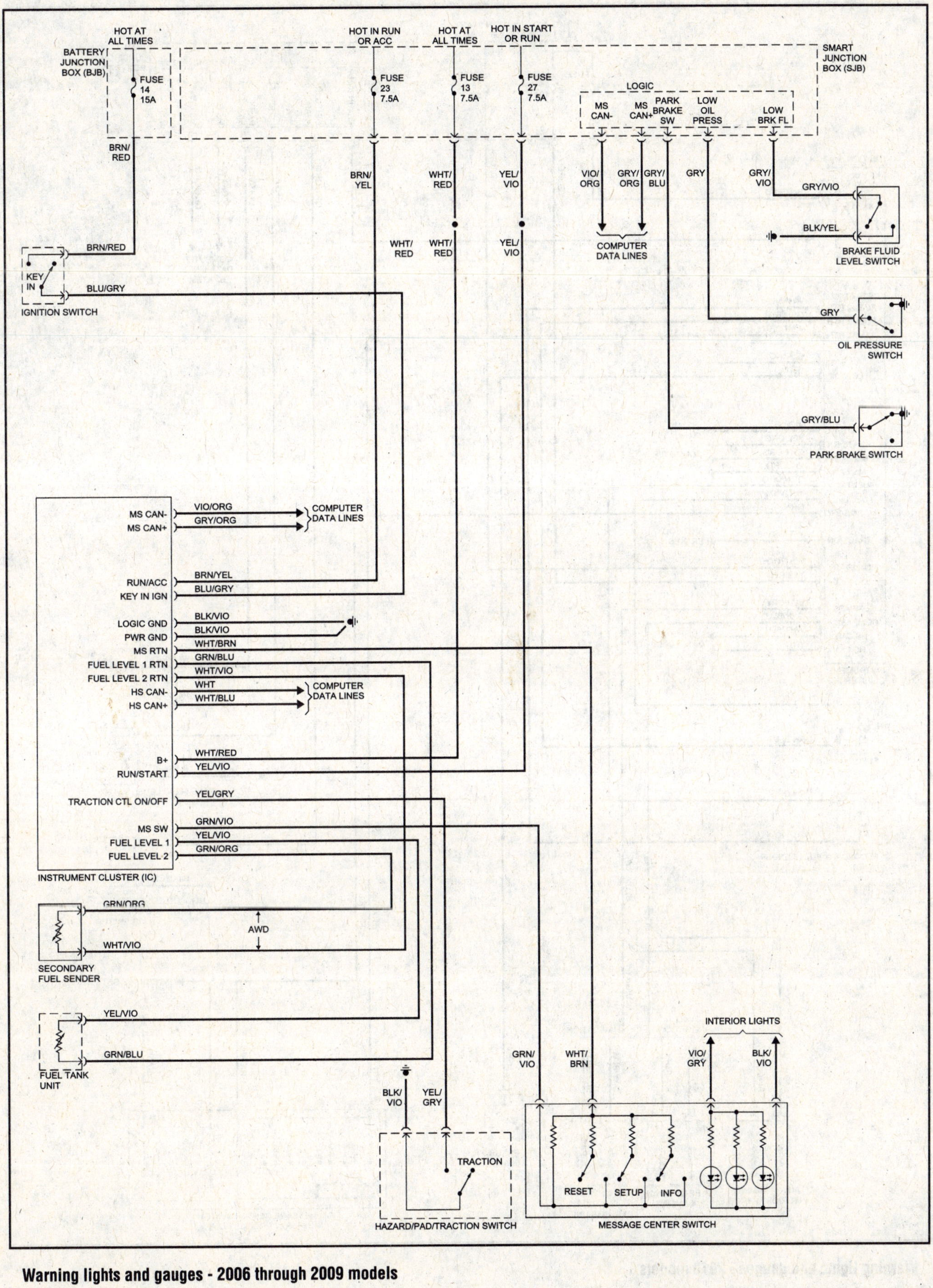

Warning lights and gauges - 2006 through 2009 models

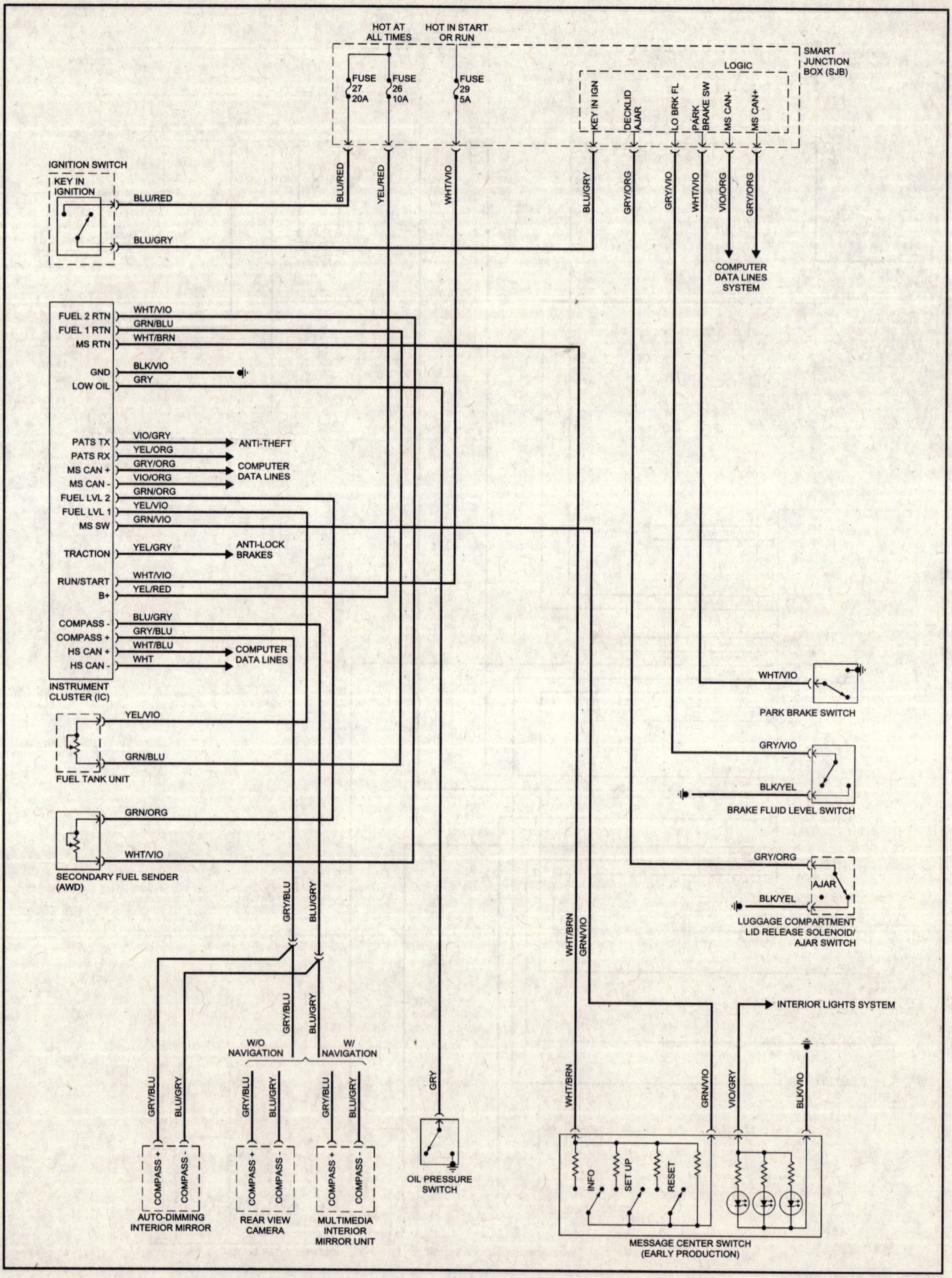

Warning lights and gauges - 2010 models

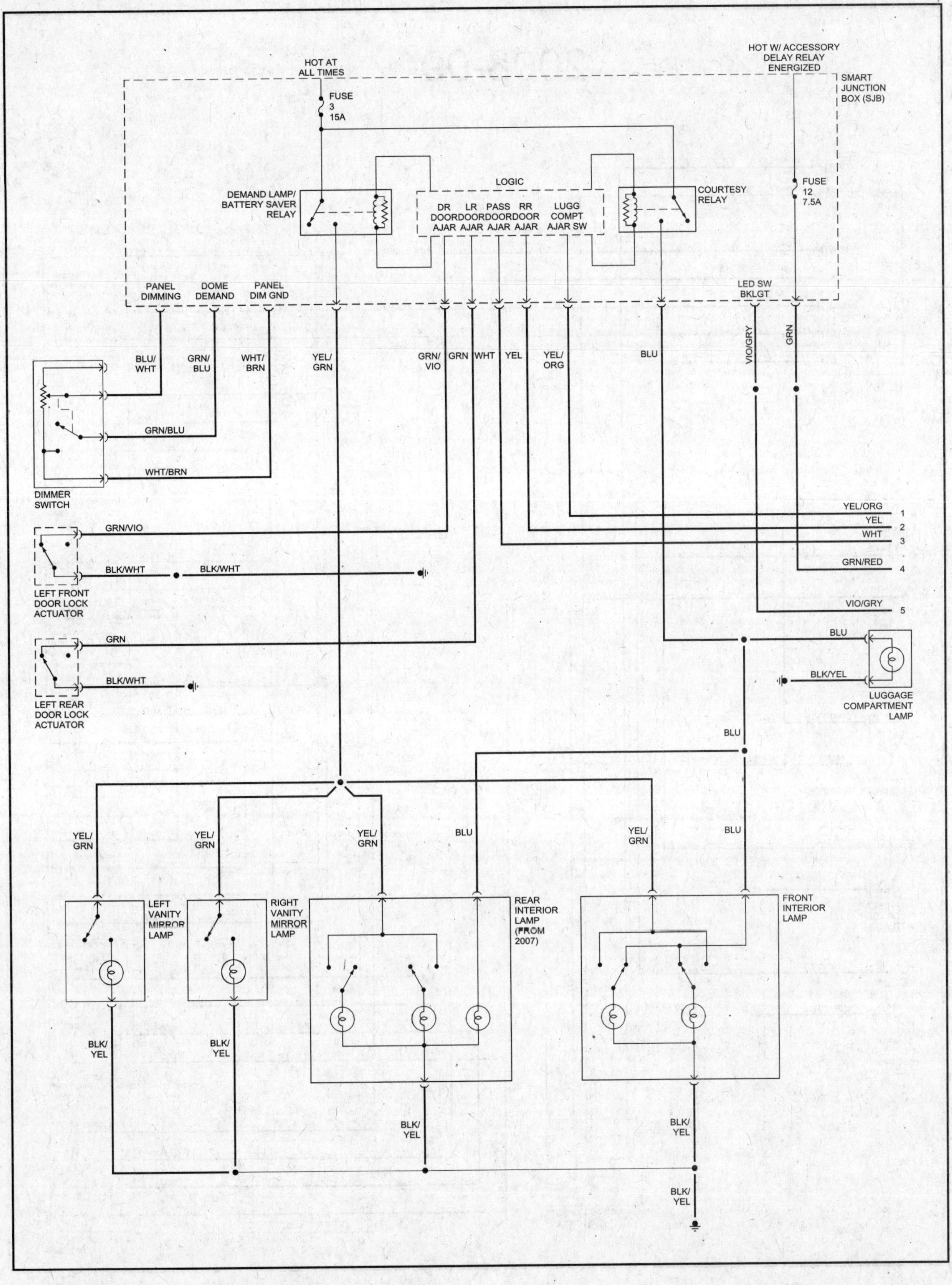

Interior lighting system - 2006 through 2009 models (1 of 2)

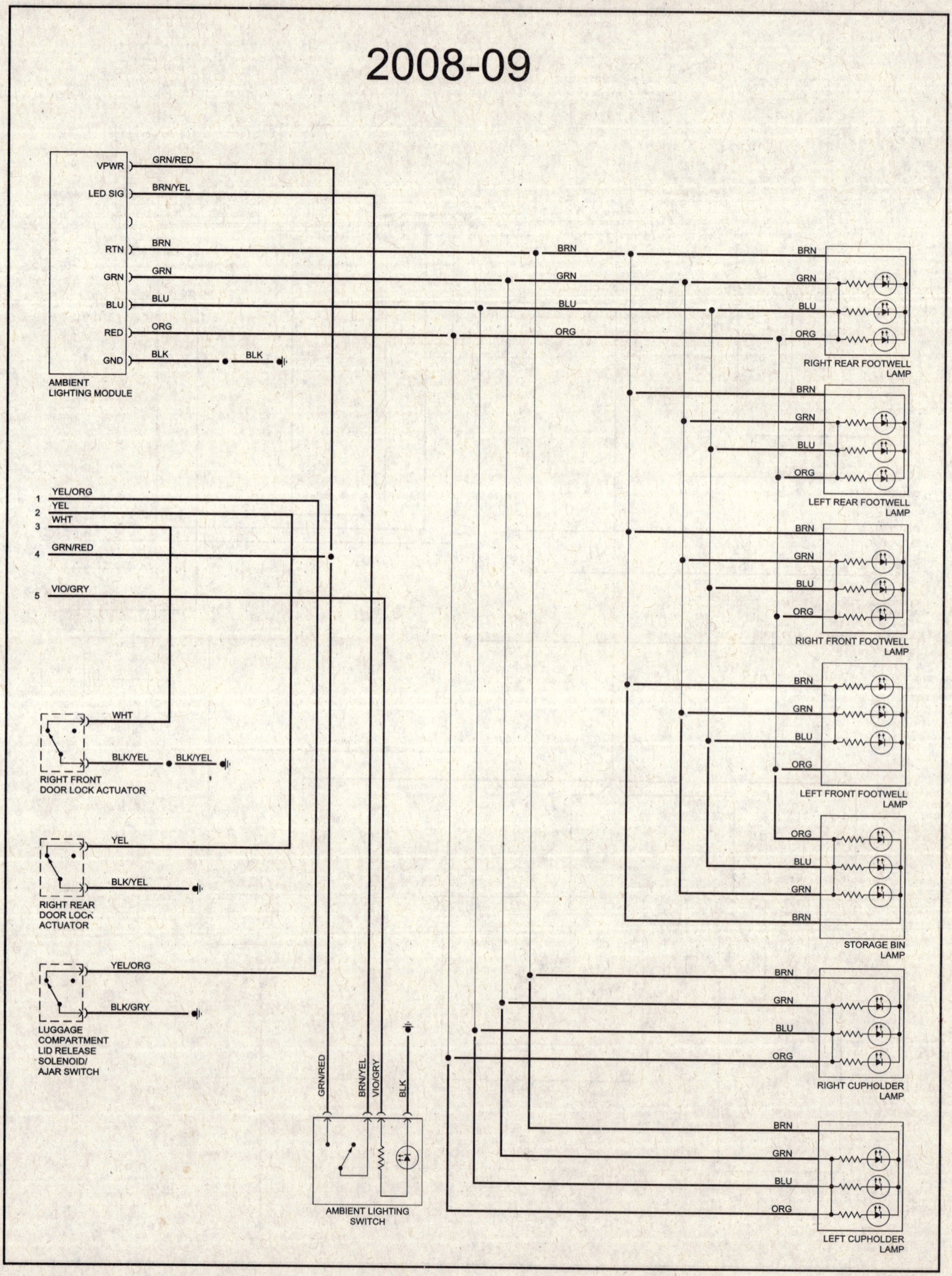

Interior lighting system - 2006 through 2009 models (2 of 2)

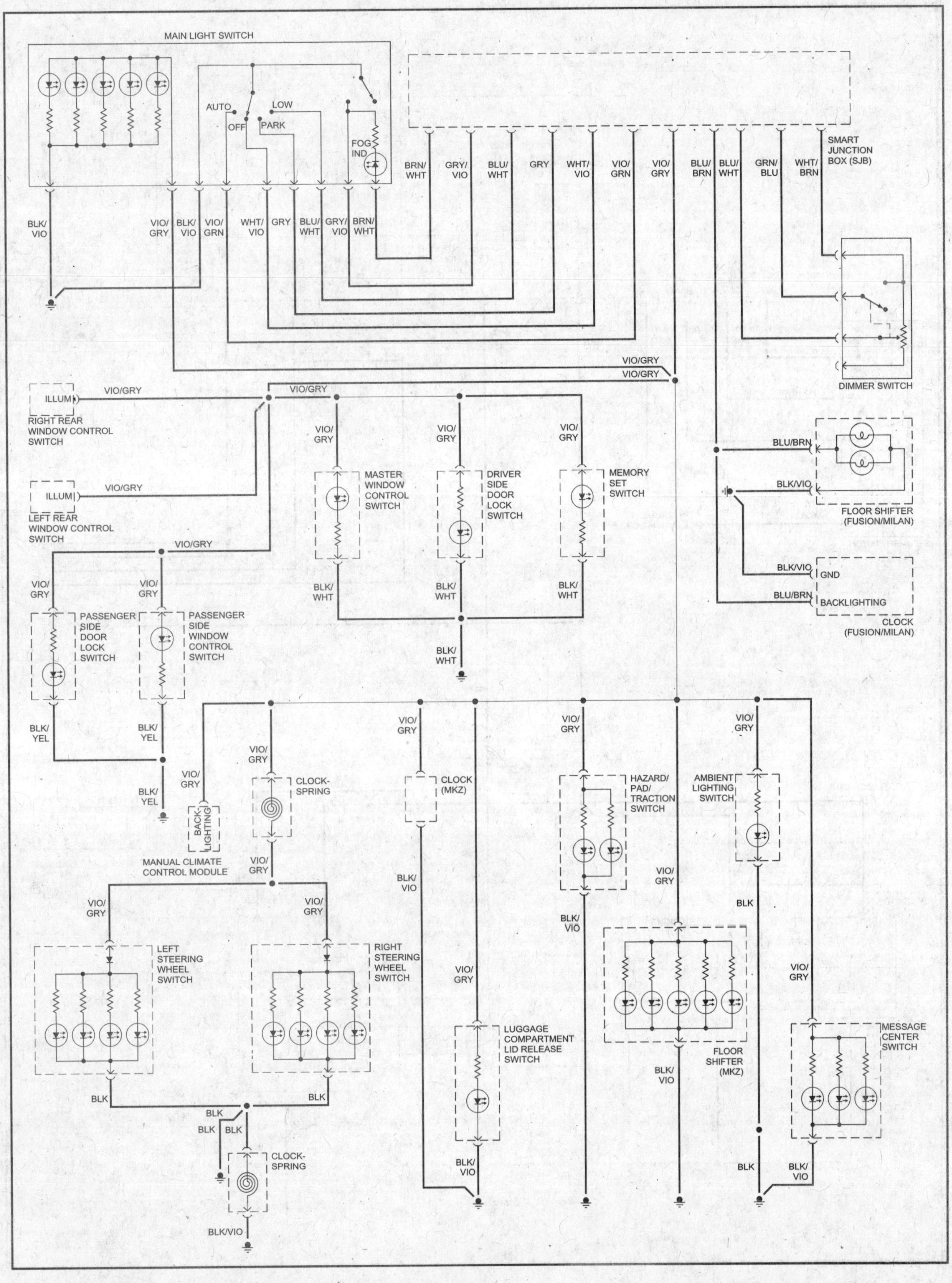

Instrument panel and switch illumination - 2006 through 2009 models

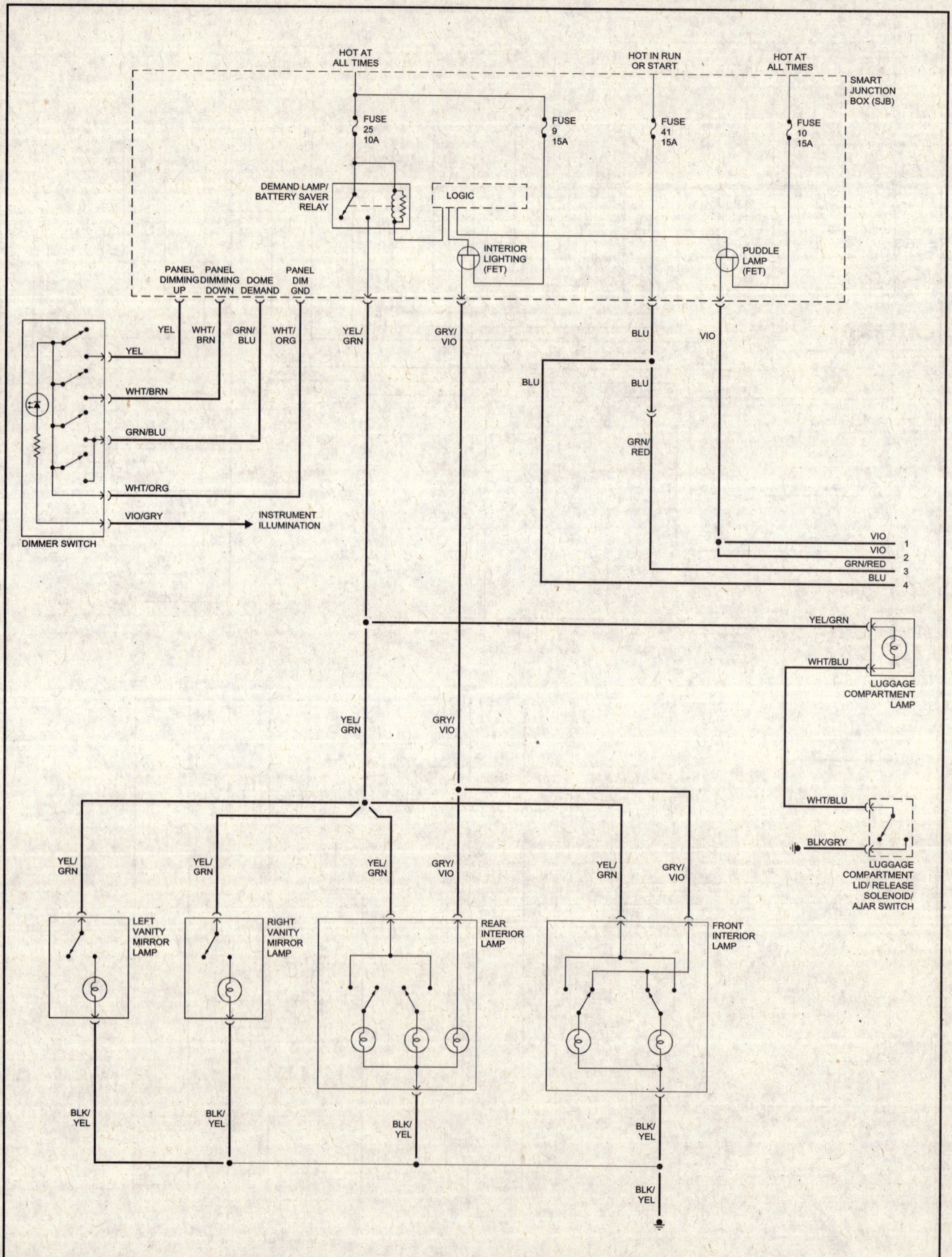

Interior lighting system - 2010 models (1 of 2)

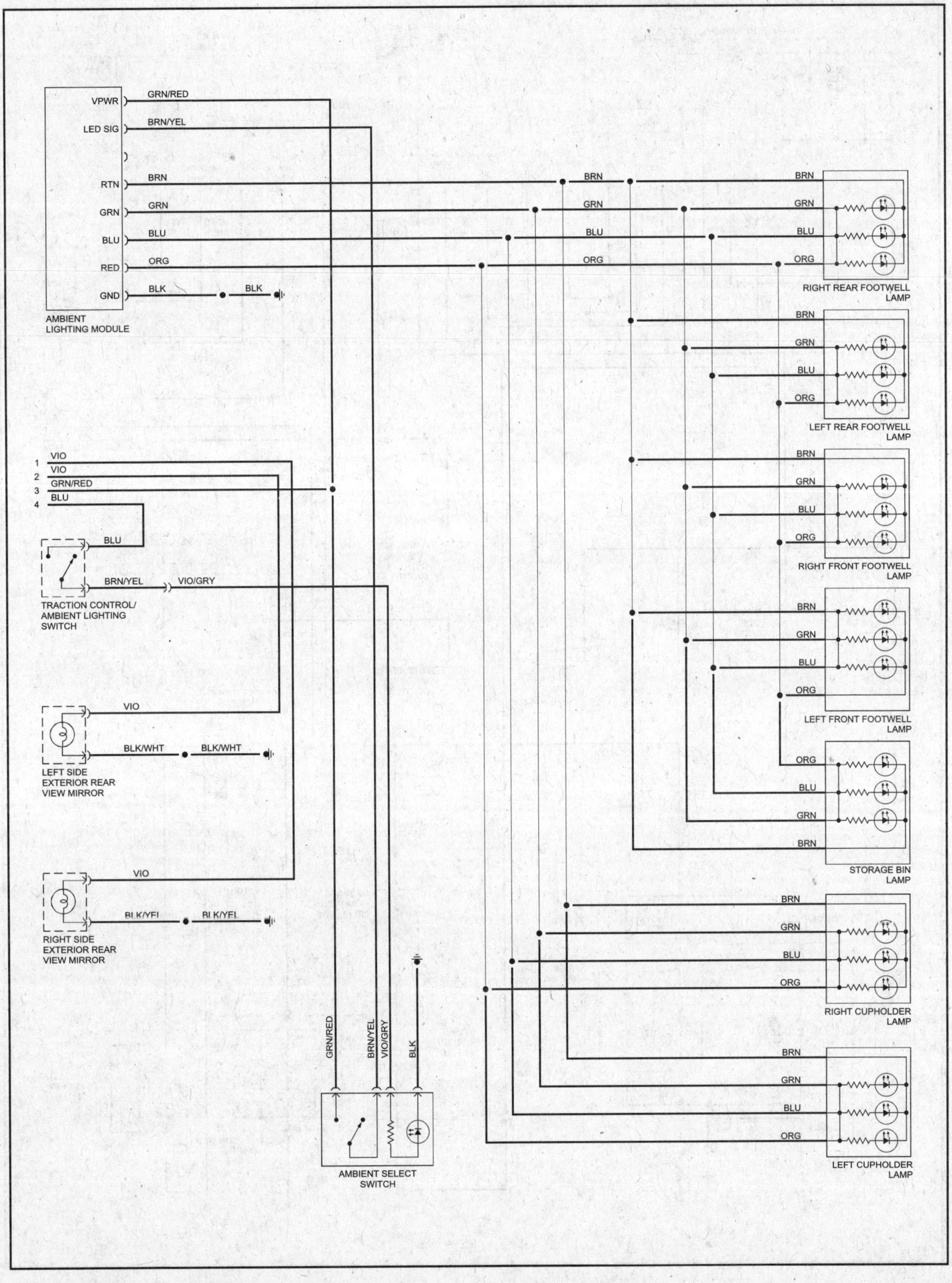

Interior lighting system - 2010 models (2 of 2)

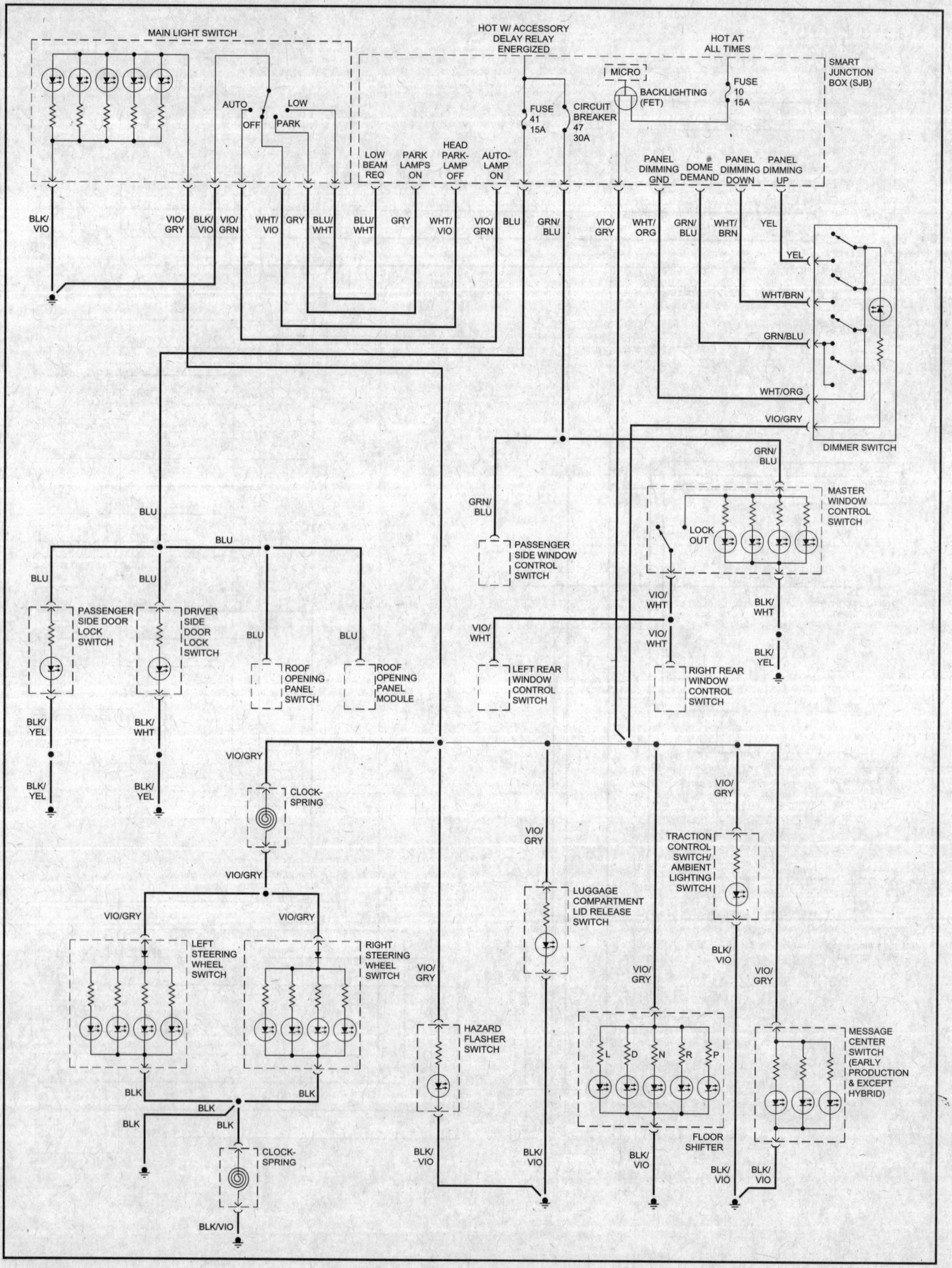

Instrument panel and switch illumination - 2010 models

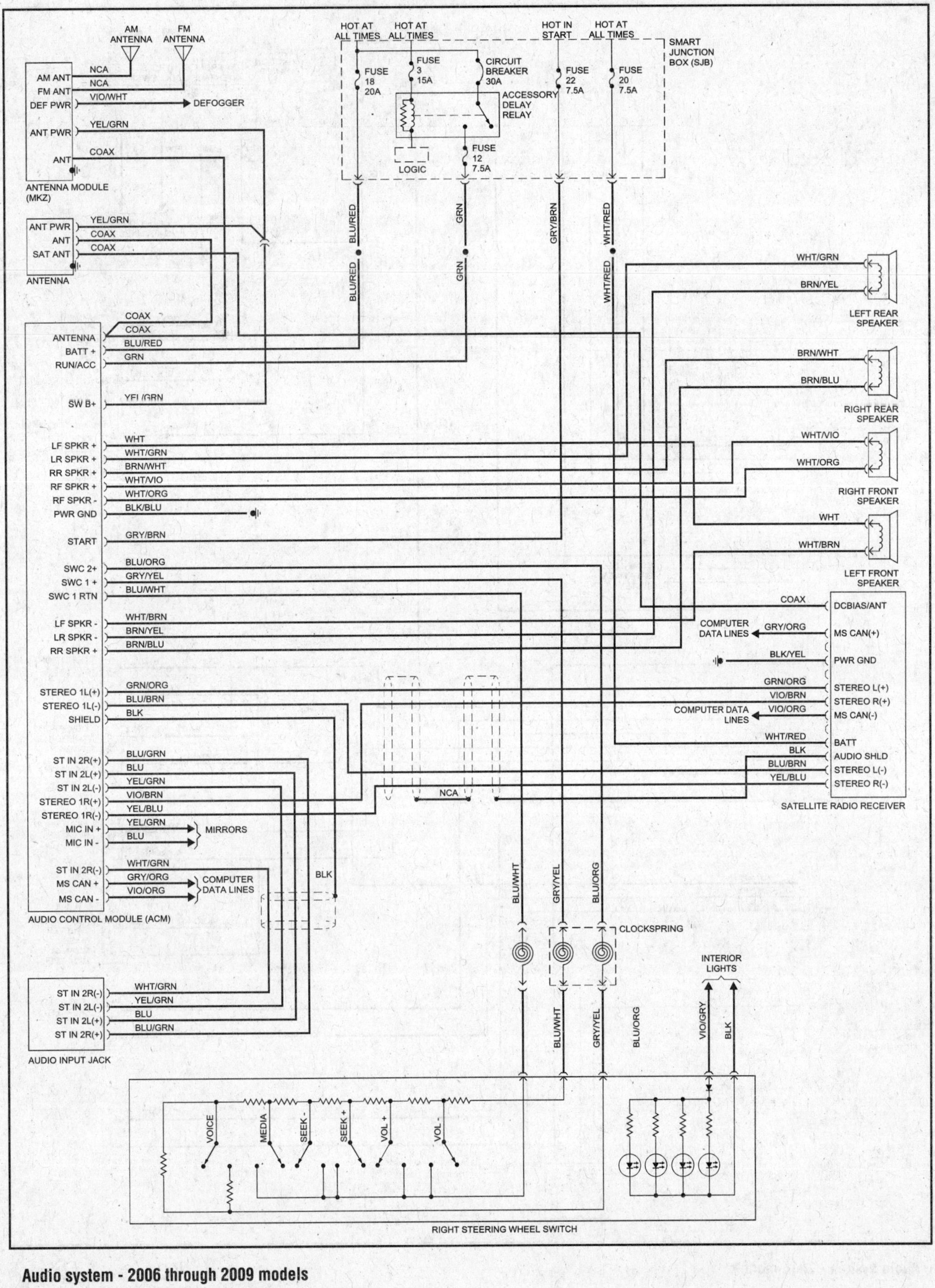

Audio system - 2006 through 2009 models

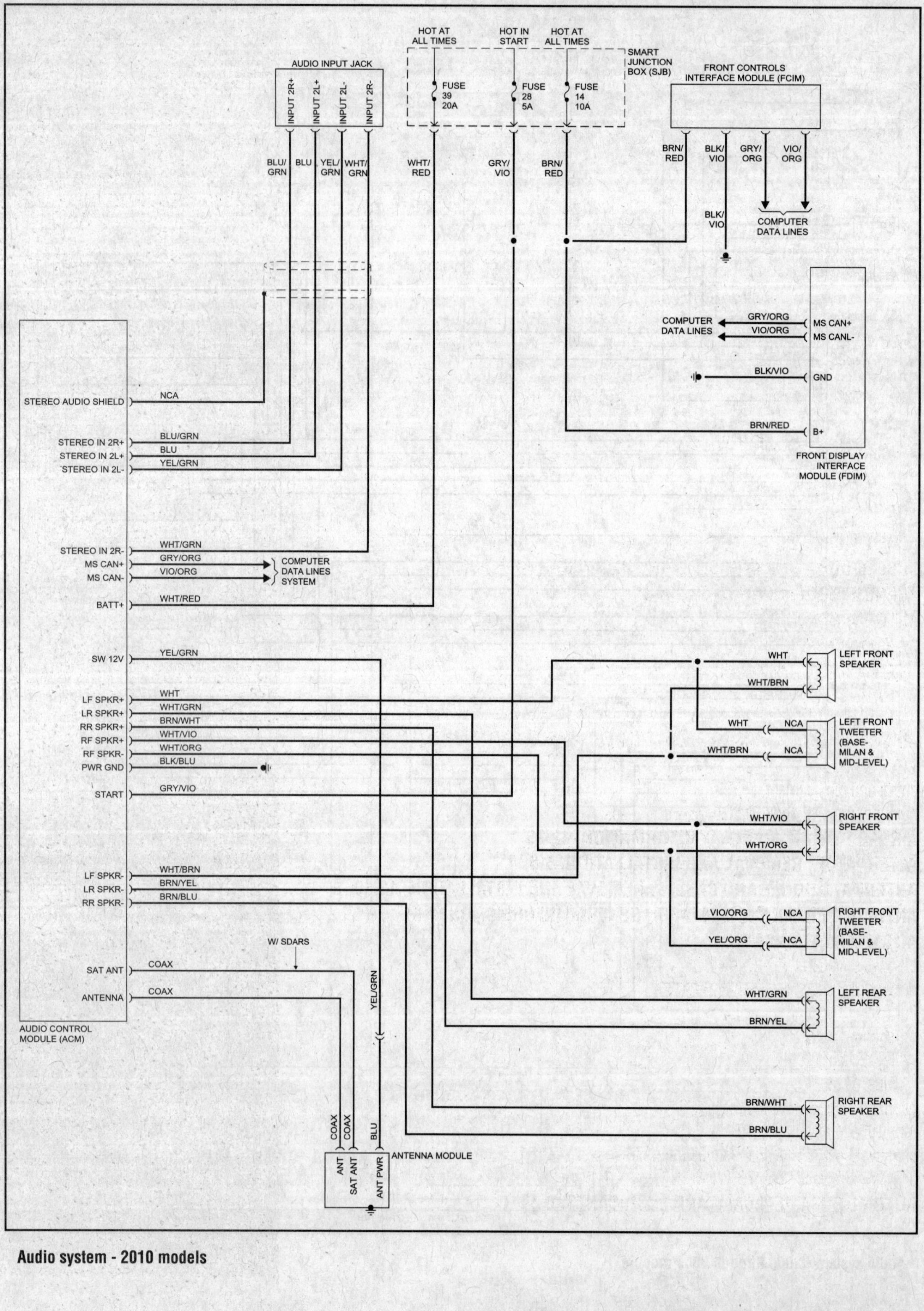

Audio system - 2010 models

MASTER INDEX

A

B

C

F

G

H

I

J

K

L

M

O

P

R

U

V

W